THE TRUTH

NEW TESTAMENT

COLIN URQUHART

Published by Integrity Media Europe
Unit 1, Hargreaves Business Park, Hargreaves Road,
Eastbourne, East Sussex BN23 6QW

Cover design: Jon Smethurst, Ezekiel Design
Set in Palatino 10pt
ISBN 978 190708 001 2

Printed in the UK by CPI William Clowes Beccles NR34 7TL

CONTENTS

INTRODUCTION

The task of producing another English version of the New Testament is not something I would have undertaken without a keen sense from the Holy Spirit that this was what God wanted me to do. Certainly, I have never had any personal desire for such a task.

It has proved to be a very rewarding experience for me personally. Having been a preacher and teacher of God's Word for over 45 years, I have a great love for the scriptures. I have been devoted to bringing understanding of its significance for modern living to people in over 40 nations, where I have had the privilege of ministering in the name of Jesus Christ.

As someone who has been interpreted into several languages I am familiar with the process of translating the meaning of the truth from one language to another. I have been blessed with many wonderful interpreters over the years. They have impressed on me that the best interpreters do not necessarily translate what I say literally, but express what I say in a way that will be understood clearly in their own language.

As the principal of a Bible College, among several other aspects of ministry, I have always been deeply concerned that any version of the New Testament should be accurate. But I have also been acutely aware that people will only translate God's Word into action in their lives if they clearly understand its meaning and implications for them personally.

I mention these things so that you can understand the principles behind this particular version, 'The Truth'. Any translation inevitably involves a certain amount of interpretation.

There are two types of translation available today. Some are strict word by word or phrase by phrase translations. These are accurate translations of the original Greek text, but do not necessarily draw out the meaning of the text. On the other extreme are modern paraphrases which are certainly edifying but often seem to depart from the original. I believe that God wanted me to chart a middle course between these two extremes.

I sought to do this by first translating the text literally, and then asking the questions, 'What does this mean? How would you express this in today's world, with the modern mindset that people have?'

It seemed an awesome task to maintain accuracy with the Greek text and yet have the freedom to expand the translation where necessary so that it can be readily understood. This I have done by sometimes giving the literal translation of the Greek followed by another phrase that puts the same truth in another way that can be readily appreciated by the reader.

I sensed the Lord encouraging me in this by reminding me frequently that this is exactly what a good preacher does. He reads the Word *and* explains it. Yet this had to be done without turning this edition into either a commentary or a study Bible! The text needed to be easily readable and readily understood.

The public reading of scripture is of great importance. This is enhanced when people can readily understand what is being read. It is my intention to produce an audio version of 'The Truth'.

Of course, the books of the New Testament were not originally written in chapters and verses. Although these are useful for reference, they have had the unfortunate effect of breaking up the text in an unreal way, often destroying the flow of the argument or the presentation of the original writers. Nevertheless I have included them for the ease of finding particular references, and headings have been inserted for ease in finding passages. They do not form part of the original Greek text and can be ignored when reading through this version.

I have used capitals when referring to the various names by which God is known and where pronouns refer to Him as Father, Son and Holy Spirit.

I trust that those who use this version will discover the benefit of reading whole books, or sizeable sections of the longer books, at a single sitting; that they will be gripped by the unfolding revelation of the text.

This has been an awesome task and one that has been approached with an overwhelming sense of humility and responsibility. I have been handling what is holy and has the capacity to transform the lives of those who read it.

If you are a Christian of long standing with an appreciable knowledge of the scriptures, please do not compare this with your favourite version. Use 'The Truth' to gain fresh insight into and revelation of the New Testament and then use your favoured version with new understanding.

If, on the other hand, you are not familiar with the scriptures, this version will help you to understand what God is saying to you through His Word which is 'The Truth.'

However, I pray that all readers, experienced or inexperienced in the things of God, will know the Spirit of Truth guiding them into the truth of the Word with fresh understanding, so that the Word will then be translated into action in their lives. For we are all called, not only to read God's Word, but to live it!

THE GOSPEL ACCORDING TO

MATTHEW

The Ancestry of Christ (1:1-17)

1 This is a record of the ancestry of Jesus Christ, the descendant
of David and Abraham. 2-6 In total, there were fourteen generations
from Abraham until the time of David: Abraham, Isaac, Jacob,
Judah and his brothers Perez and Zerah whose mother was Tamar,
Hezron, Ram, Amminadab, Nahshon, Salmon, Boaz whose mother
was Rahab, Obed – Ruth's son, and Jesse the father of king David.

7-11 There were a further fourteen generations between the time of
David until the exile in Babylon: David, Solomon whose mother
was Bathsheba, Rehoboam, Abijah, Asa, Jehoshaphat, Jehoram,
Uzziah, Jotham, Ahaz, Hezekiah, Manasseh, Amon the father of
Jeconiah and his brothers during the Babylonian exile.

12-17 And there were a further fourteen generations from the exile
to the coming of the Christ, the Messiah, God's Son: Jeconiah, Shealtiel,
Zerubbabel, Abiud, Eliakim, Azor, Zadok, Akim, Eliud, Eleazar,
Matthan, Jacob the father of Joseph who was the husband of Mary,
to whom Jesus the Christ was born.

Joseph's dream (1:18-25)

18 Now this is how the birth of Jesus took place: His mother Mary
was engaged to Joseph, but before they married they had no sexual
union; Mary became pregnant through the activity of the Holy Spirit.
19 Being a righteous man, Joseph did not want Mary to be disgraced
publicly, so he thought about releasing her quietly from her commit-
ment to him.

20 After thinking about this Joseph had a dream in which an angel
from the Lord appeared to him and said: "Joseph, son of David,
there is nothing for you to fear. Take Mary home as your wife
because she has conceived through the power of the Holy Spirit.
21 She will have a Son, whom you are to call Jesus, because He will
save the people from their sins."

22-23 All this happened to fulfil what the Lord had spoken prophetically: "The virgin will become pregnant and will bear a Son who
will be called Immanuel, meaning, 'God is with us.'"
24 When Joseph awoke he obeyed what the Lord's angel had told
him to do and took Mary home as his wife. 25 But he had no sexual
union with her before she gave birth to her Son. And Joseph named
Him Jesus.

Escape from Herod (2:1-23)

2 Jesus was born in Bethlehem in Judea during the time of King
Herod. Wise men came to Jerusalem from the east asking:
2 "Where has the King of the Jews been born? We followed a star
from the east and have come to worship Him."
3 This disturbed King Herod and those in authority in Jerusalem.
4 So Herod called together the chief priests and teachers of the law,
asking them where the Messiah, the Christ, was to be born. 5-6 "In
Bethlehem in Judea," they told him, "for the prophets predicted,
'You Bethlehem in the land of Judah are not the least in importance
among the places of Judah; for from you will come a ruler who will
shepherd My people Israel.'"
7 Then Herod contacted the wise men secretly to find out when
exactly the star had appeared to them. 8 He then sent them to
Bethlehem with these instructions: "Go and search carefully for the
child. When you find Him, report to me so that I also may come and
worship Him."
9 They went as the king ordered, following the star they had seen
in the east until it reached the place where the child lay. 10 They were
overjoyed to have the star to guide them.
11 When they entered the house they saw the Child with Mary, His
mother; and they bowed before Him in worship. Then they presented
the gifts they had brought – gold, incense and myrrh. 12 However,
they were warned in a dream not to return to Herod, and so they
made their way back to their own country by another route.
13 After their departure, one of the Lord's angels appeared in a
dream to Joseph, saying: "Go, escape immediately to Egypt taking
the Child and His mother with you. Stay there until I tell you it is
safe to return, for Herod will search for the Child with the intention
of killing Him."

1:22-23 Isaiah 7:14
2:5-6 Micah 5:2

[14] When he awoke, Joseph, the Child and Mary left for Egypt during
the night. [15] They stayed there until Herod's death, fulfilling what
was predicted by the prophet: "I called My Son out of Egypt."
[16] Herod was furious when he realised he had been outsmarted by
the wise men and ordered that all boys in and around Bethlehem
who were two years old or less were to be killed, estimating the
time from the information he received from the wise men.
[17-18] And so what the prophet Jeremiah wrote was fulfilled, 'In
Ramah a sound of weeping and great mourning is heard. Rachel is
weeping for her children and refuses to be comforted because they
have been taken from her.'
[19-20] After Herod's death, the Lord's angel appeared again in a
dream to Joseph, saying: "Go, take the Child and His mother and
return to the land of Israel, for those who wanted to take the Child's
life are themselves dead."
[21-22] So in obedience Joseph returned to Israel with Jesus and Mary.
But on hearing that Archelaus was now reigning in Judea in place
of his father Herod, he was afraid to go there, for he had again been
forewarned in a dream. [23] So they went instead to Galilee where they
set up home in a small town called Nazareth. This fulfilled another
prophecy: 'He will be called a Nazarene.'

John the Baptist (3:1-12)

3 Some years later, John the Baptist began to preach in the Judean
desert saying: [2] "Repent! Turn from your sins and return to
God, for the Kingdom of heaven is approaching." [3] John was the one
referred to by the prophet Isaiah: "A voice will be heard in the
desert calling, 'Make ready for the Lord's coming; make a straight
pathway for Him!'"
[4] John wore clothes of camel hair with a leather belt around his
waist, and he ate locusts and wild honey. [5] People came to him from
Jerusalem, all over Judea and from the whole region around the
river Jordan. [6] After confessing their sins, they were immersed by
John in the river.
[7] However, when John saw many of the Pharisees and Sadducees
arriving at the place where he was baptising, he addressed them by
saying: "You are a brood of poisonous snakes! Who warned you to
flee from the Lord's anger that is coming upon you? [8] You have to
produce fruit that proves you have genuinely repented. [9] It is no use

2:14 *Hosea 11:1*
2:17-18 *Jeremiah 31:15*
3:3 *Isaiah 40:3*

saying to yourselves, 'Abraham is our father, so we are safe!' I tell
you plainly that God is able to raise up children for Abraham out of
these stones. [10] The axe is ready to fell the trees, and every one who
does not produce good fruit will be cut down and thrown in the fire
of judgment.
[11] "I immerse in water those who have truly turned away from
their sins and surrendered to God. But after me someone more powerful than I is coming. I am not fit even to carry His sandals. He will
immerse people in the Holy Spirit and in God's purifying fire. [12] The
tools for gathering the harvest are in His hand. He will preside over
the spiritual threshing floor, gathering the good wheat into His
barn, but burning the useless chaff in unquenchable fire."

Jesus' baptism (3:13-17)

[13] One day Jesus came from Galilee to the Jordan to be baptised by
John. [14] But John was very reluctant to do this, saying to Jesus: "I
should be immersed by you, and yet you come to me!"
[15] Jesus replied: "This is how it should be for now; for in this way
it will be seen that we will fulfil everything necessary for righteousness." Then John agreed to do as Jesus wanted.
[16] After Jesus had been baptised He came out of the water. Then
the heavens were opened to Him, and the Spirit of God descended
upon Him as a dove and remained on Him. [17] And a voice from
heaven was heard, saying: "This is my Son whom I love; I am very
pleased with Him."

Jesus in the wilderness (4:1-11)

4 Then the Holy Spirit led Jesus into the desert where He had to
be subjected to temptation from the devil. [2] During a period of
forty days and nights He fasted, after which He was hungry. [3] The
tempter came to Jesus suggesting: "If you are really God's Son, you
could command these stones to become bread, and so satisfy your
hunger."
[4] Jesus replied: "It is written: 'Man is not to live only on bread, but
he is to feed on every word that comes from God's mouth.'"
[5] Then the devil took Him in a vision to the holy city, to stand on
the highest part of the temple. [6] "If You are really God's Son," the
devil suggested, "You could do something truly spectacular. For if
You jumped from here to the ground You know what is written:

4:4 Deuteronomy 8:3
4:6 Psalms 91:11-12

'God will command His angels on your behalf. They will catch hold
of you in their hands and prevent you from striking a single stone
with your foot.'"
7 Jesus replied: "It is also written: 'You are not to put the Lord
your God to the test!'"
8 In another vision, the devil took Jesus to the top of a very high
mountain and showed Him all the kingdoms of the world in their
splendour. 9 "All these I will give You," he lied, "if only You will bow
down before me in worship."
10 Jesus said to him: "Get away from me Satan! For it is written,
'You are to worship the Lord your God, and serve only Him.'"
11 Defeated, the devil then left Him and angels came to be with Jesus.

The calling of the first disciples (4:12-22)

12 Jesus returned to Galilee when He heard that John had been
imprisoned; but 13 He left His home in Nazareth and went to live in
Capernaum on the shore of the lake near Zebulun and Naphtali.
14-16 This fulfilled another prophecy spoken through Isaiah, 'In the
area of Zebulun and Naphtali along the Jordan by the way of the
sea, in the Galilee of the Gentiles, the people who formerly lived in
darkness have seen a great light. On those who lived in the shadow
of eternal death, a light has now dawned.'
17 This marked the beginning of Jesus' preaching. "Repent," He
proclaimed, "for now the Kingdom of heaven is within your reach."
18 When Jesus was walking by the Sea of Galilee He saw two
brothers, Simon known later as Peter and His brother Andrew. They
were fishermen and were casting their nets into the lake. 19 "Come
and follow Me," Jesus called to them, "and I will enable you to catch
men!" 20 Immediately they abandoned their nets and followed Jesus.
21-22 Further on Jesus saw two other brothers, James and John the
sons of Zebedee. They were with their father in a boat, preparing
their nets. Jesus called them and they immediately left their father
in the boat and followed Him.

Jesus teaches and heals (4:23-25)

23 Jesus then went throughout Galilee teaching in the synagogues
there, preaching the good news about God's Kingdom. He healed

4:7 Deuteronomy 6:16
4:10 Deuteronomy 6:13
4:14-16 Isaiah 9:1-2

people from every disease and sickness. 24 So the news of what He
was doing spread all over Syria as well. As a result, people were
brought to Him suffering from various diseases, often in severe
pain. Some were demon possessed, others suffered from seizures or
were paralysed. And He healed them all. 25 Large crowds came not
only from Galilee but from the Ten Towns on the far side of the lake,
from Jerusalem, Judea and the region across the Jordan. They followed
Him wherever He went.

Those who are blessed (5:1-12)

5 Because of the large crowds, Jesus went onto a hillside and sat
down. His disciples gathered around Him 2 and He began to
teach them, saying:

> 3 "The truly humble, those who are poor in spirit, are blessed, because the Kingdom of heaven is given to them.
>
> 4 Those who mourn are blessed, because they shall be comforted.
>
> 5 Those with gentle spirits, the meek, they also are blessed, because they will have the earth as their inheritance.
>
> 6 Those who long for righteousness are blessed, because they will be filled with God's life.
>
> 7 The merciful are blessed, for God will be merciful to them.
>
> 8 The pure in heart are blessed, because they will see God, the Holy One.
>
> 9 Those who make peace with God and with others are blessed, for they will be known as sons of God.
>
> 10 Even those who are persecuted for doing what is right are blessed, because the Kingdom of heaven is given to them.
>
> 11 "You are blessed when people insult you, persecute
> you or accuse you falsely of all forms of evil because of
> your allegiance to Me. 12 You should rejoice and be glad
> because a rich reward awaits you in heaven. The prophets
> who lived before you were persecuted in the same way.

Be salt and light (5:13-16)

13 "You are to be salt for the world. However, if salt is stale it loses its taste, and what can you do to restore its saltiness? Nothing! It may as well be thrown away and trampled underfoot!

[14] "You are to give light to the world. A city built on a hilltop cannot be hidden from sight. [15] Neither do people hide the light from a lamp under a basin. No, they place the lamp on a lamp-stand where it can give light to the whole house. [16] In the same way, your spiritual light is to be evident to all around you; so that they can see the good things you do and then praise your Father in heaven.

Jesus came to fulfil God's words (5:17-20)

[17] "Do not imagine that I have come to do away with God's law or with what the prophets have said. No, I have not come to abolish God's words, but to fulfil them. [18] I tell you the truth, until this present heaven and earth disappear, not one word of what God has said or written will be removed from the law; everything God has said will be fulfilled. [19] So anyone who breaks even the least of these commandments and encourages others to do the same will be numbered among the least in the Kingdom of heaven. But whoever obeys God's commands and teaches others to do likewise will be called great in God's Kingdom.

[20] "So I tell you clearly, your righteousness must surpass that of the Pharisees and teachers of the law; otherwise it is certain that you will not be part of the Kingdom of heaven!

Attitudes of the heart (5:21-32)

[21] "You have heard that long ago people were told, 'Do not murder, for anyone guilty of murder will be judged accordingly.' [22] However, I tell you that simply to be angry with your brother is enough to bring you under judgment.

"It is also acknowledged that anybody who treats another with contempt is to be answerable to the Council. But I tell you that anyone who condemns his brother as a fool will be in danger of being condemned himself, to the fire of hell!

[23-24] "This being the case, when you come to the altar to offer a gift, if you realise that a brother holds something against you, leave your gift before the altar while you go first to be reconciled with that brother; then you can come and offer your gift!

[25] "If your adversary takes you to court, settle matters with him quickly before your case is called; or you could find your destiny in the hands of the judge, who would then hand you over to the official who would throw you into prison. [26] I tell you the truth, if that is the case you will not be released until you have served your sentence in full and have paid back whatever you owe.

27 "You have heard that it has been said, 'Do not commit adultery!'
28 But I tell you clearly that just to look at a woman in a lustful way
means that you have already committed adultery with her in your
heart. 29 If you sin because of the way you use your eyes, it would be
better to gouge one out and throw it away. For it is better for you to
be without one part of your body than for your whole body to be
thrown into hell. 30 Similarly, if you sin because of the way you use
your hands, it would be better to have one cut off and thrown away,
if by losing one part of your body you avoid your whole body going
to hell.

31 "It has been said that if anyone decides to divorce his wife, he
has only to give her a certificate of divorce. 32 But I make it clear to
you that the only grounds on which to divorce your wife is marital
unfaithfulness. Under any other circumstances she would become
an adulteress and the one who marries her an adulterer!

Do not break your word (5:33-37)

33 "You are also aware that long in the past people were told, 'Do not
break your word, but keep the promises you have made to the
Lord!' 34 I tell you clearly, do not swear to keep your word by calling
on heaven as your witness, for this is God's throne. 35 Nor swear
with the earth as your witness, for that is His footstool. Do not
swear by Jerusalem, for this is the city of the great King. 36 Do not
swear by your own head, for you cannot make even one of your
hairs white or black naturally. 37 It is enough for your 'Yes' to mean
'Yes' and your 'No' to mean 'No'; only the evil one will tempt you
to go beyond this.

Love your neighbour (5:38-48)

38 "You are also aware of the saying, 'An eye for an eye and a tooth
for a tooth!' 39 But I tell you not to retaliate when attacked by an evil
person. So if someone slaps you on one cheek, offer him the other to
hit. 40 If someone wants to sue you and take the shirt off your back,
let him have whatever he wants and more besides. 41 If you are forced
to carry a soldier's burden for one mile, do the totally unexpected
and offer to go with him for two miles!

42 "This is the principle by which to live: Give to anyone who asks
you and do not refuse someone who wants to borrow from you.

43 "You have heard the saying, 'Love your neighbour, but hate
your enemy'. 44-45 What I tell you is different: Love even your enemies
and pray for those who persecute and oppose you and do good to

those who hate you, for this is the right way for the sons of your
heavenly Father to act! He allows the sun He created to rise on the
evil and the good alike. He sends rain on everyone, whether they
are good or bad.
46 "If you love only those who love you, what reward would you
expect for that? Even the tax collectors who swindle people do that,
don't they? 47 And if you associate only with your fellow believers,
what are you doing out of the ordinary? Even pagans act like that!
48 "So be perfect as your heavenly Father is perfect!

Give secretly (6:1-4)

6 "When you do what is right, make sure that you do not show
off before others. If you simply want applause from men, you
will have no reward from your Father in heaven. 2 So when you give
to those in need, do not trumpet what you are doing. Only hypocrites
do that kind of thing because, whether they give in a meeting or on
the streets, they want to be honoured by others. I tell you the truth,
such people have already received the only reward they will get!
3 "No, when you give to those in need, it should be as if your left
hand doesn't know what your right hand is doing. 4 In other words,
you will give secretly, without any flourish. Then your Father who
sees what you do secretly will reward you.

Teaching on prayer (6:5-15)

5 "And do not imitate the hypocrites when you pray. Again, they
want to be seen and applauded by others, whether they stand in the
meeting or on street corners in public. I tell you most emphatically,
they also have already received the only reward they will ever get!
6 Rather, when you pray, go in your private room, shut the door and
pray unseen by others to your Father, who is also unseen. Your
Father sees and rewards what you do secretly.
7 "And when you pray, do not keep babbling on like the pagans
do, thinking that the more words they use, the more effective their
prayers will be. 8 No, do not be like them, for your Father is well
aware of what you need even before you ask Him.
"This is the kind of outline you should use when praying:

9 "Our heavenly Father, let your Holy Name be praised.
10 May your Kingdom come and your will be done on earth
as is already the case in heaven. 11 Give us today everything we need. 12 Forgive us when we sin against you, just

as we forgive those who sin against us. 13 And do not lead
us into temptation but deliver us from all the power and
influence of the evil one.

14 "You can be sure that your heavenly Father will forgive you if you
forgive others when they sin against you. 15 But if you do not forgive
others their sins, there is no point in expecting your Father to forgive
your sins!

Fasting (6:16-18)

16 "Do not act like the hypocrites when you fast. They make it clear
to everyone that they are fasting. I tell you the truth, the praise they
seek from others is the only reward they will ever receive. 17-18 No,
when you fast, do not look drab and dreary, but do your hair nicely
and wash your face so that it will not be obvious to anyone that you
are fasting; only your Heavenly Father will know. Although you
cannot see Him, He sees you and knows what you do secretly, and
will reward you accordingly.

Store up heavenly riches (6:19-24)

19 "There is no point in storing up for yourselves money and earthly
possessions. Here moths and rust destroy things and thieves can
break in and steal what you have. 20 It is far better to store up heavenly riches, for such riches cannot be destroyed by either moths or
rust; and in heaven there are no thieves to break in and steal what
is yours.

21 "Here is the spiritual principle: wherever you put your money
shows where your heart is also.

22 "Your eye gives light to your body. So if your eyes are good,
your whole body will be filled with light. 23 But if your eyes are bad,
your entire body will be filled with darkness. If instead of light you
are filled with darkness, how deep that darkness will be!

24 "It is not possible for anyone to serve two different masters. For
he will hate one and love the other, or he will be truly devoted to
one and treat the other with contempt. You cannot serve both God
and money!

Do not worry (6:25-34)

25 "So I tell you clearly, do not worry about any aspect of your life,
what you should eat or drink or what you should wear on your
body. There are far more important things in life than food and

there are many more important things about you than what clothes
you wear!

26 "Think of the birds you see flying around. They neither sow nor
reap, nor do they store food away in barns; and yet your heavenly
Father supplies food for them. Do you not consider yourself more
valuable than the birds? 27 And who can add anything positive to his
life through worrying?

28 "So why worry about your clothes? Look how beautiful the
lilies in the field are! They neither work nor weave to make themselves appear so good. 29 And yet I tell you clearly that even Solomon
in his most glorious apparel could not match these lilies for beauty.
30 So if this is the way in which God dresses what grows naturally in
the fields, things that are here today and tomorrow are thrown
away and burned, will He not make sure that you are well clothed?
How weak your faith is!

31 "Therefore, do not worry by saying, 'What shall we eat?' or
'What have we to drink?' or 'What can we wear?' 32 The pagans are
concerned about such things, but your heavenly Father is well
aware of everything you need. 33 Let the Kingdom of heaven and living
in a right relationship with God be your priorities; then everything
else you need will be given to you as well. 34 So do not worry about
what will happen tomorrow. Let tomorrow worry about itself! You
have enough to think about today, and that is true for every day!

Do not judge (7:1-5)

7 "Do not judge others, or you will also be judged. 2 Yes, you will
be judged in the same way that you judge others. The way you
treat others will be the way you yourselves will be treated.

3 "Why do you search for the tiny speck of sawdust in your brother's
eye, while ignoring the plank of wood in your own eye? 4 What
justification would you have in saying to your brother, 'Allow me to
remove the speck from your eye,' when at the same time there is a
whole plank in your own eye? 5 What a hypocrite you would be.
First, remove the plank from your own eye and then you will see
clearly to take the speck from your brother's eye!

Value what is holy (7:6)

6 "Do not give what is holy to those who act like dogs. Do not throw
precious pearls of truth to those who live like pigs. If you do they
will only treat these holy things with contempt, trampling them underfoot like animals. They could even turn on you to tear you to pieces!

Ask, seek and knock (7:7-14)

7 "Continue to ask, and what you pray for will be given you. Go on
seeking and you will find what you are looking for. Keep knocking
and the door will be opened for you.

8 "For everyone who continues to ask receives. He who goes on
seeking finds. The door will be opened to the one who keeps knocking.

9 "If your son asks you for some bread, who among you would
give him a stone instead? 10 Or if he was to ask you for a fish, would
you give him a snake? 11 If you, then, who are by no means sinless,
know how to give good gifts to your children, how much more will
your perfect heavenly Father give good gifts to those who ask Him!

12 "This is a spiritual principle of both the law and the Prophets:
In everything do to others what you want them to do to you!

13 "Enter into life through the narrow gate. There is a wide gate
that leads to a wide road, but that leads to destruction and many go
that way. 14 But the gate to the narrow road that leads to life is small,
and only a few find it.

Good and bad fruit (7:15-23)

15 "Be on the watch for false prophets. They come appearing to be
one of My sheep, whereas they are really ferocious wolves. 16 You
will be able to discern who they are by the fruit they produce. Is it
possible for people to pick grapes from thorn bushes, or do they
gather figs from thistles? 17 You can see that a good tree will produce
good fruit, but a rotten tree will only produce rotten fruit. 18 A good
tree cannot bear rotten fruit; neither can a rotten tree produce good
fruit. 19 If a tree is rotten and cannot bear good fruit, it is cut down
and thrown into the fire. 20 So you can recognise whether a prophet
is true or false by the fruit you see in his life.

21 "Because someone says to Me, 'Lord, Lord,' does not mean he
or she will necessarily enter the Kingdom of heaven; that is reserved
for those who do the will of My Father who is in heaven. 22 Many
will say to Me on the Day of Judgment, 'Lord, Lord, did we not
prophesy in your name, cast out demons in your name and perform
many miracles?' 23 But I will tell them bluntly, 'Go away from Me,
you evil people. I never knew you!'

The wise man (7:24-29)

24 "Therefore, whoever hears what I say and puts my words into
practice is like a wise man who decided to build his house on solid

rock. 25 The storm rains fell, the streams rose, the gale winds buffeted it; yet it stood firm because it was built on solid rock.

26 "But whoever hears what I say and fails to act upon My words is like a foolish man who decided to build his house on shifting sand. 27 The storm rains fell, the streams rose, the gale winds buffeted the house and it came crashing down!"

28-29 After Jesus had said these things, the crowd that had gathered was amazed by such teaching because He spoke with great authority, not at all like the teachers of the law they were accustomed to hearing!

A leper healed (8:1-4)

8 When Jesus came down from the mountainside, large crowds still followed Him wherever He went. 2 A leper came, knelt before Him and said: "Lord, You can cleanse me and heal me, if You want to." 3 Jesus reached out His hand, touched him and said: "Of course I want to. Be cleansed!" At once he was healed of his leprosy. 4 Jesus then told him: "Be sure that you don't tell anyone immediately, but go and show yourself to the priest who will verify you have been healed. Then offer the gift that Moses commanded, for this will be a testimony recognised as valid by everyone."

The Centurion understands authority (8:5-13)

5 When Jesus had arrived at Capernaum, a Roman centurion approached Him seeking help. 6 He said to Jesus: "Lord, my servant lies paralysed at my home and is suffering terribly."

7 "I will go and heal him," Jesus offered. 8 But the centurion replied: "Lord I am not worthy enough to have You in my house. You only have to issue the command and my servant will be healed. 9 As a soldier I am myself under authority, with soldiers under my authority. If I say to one, 'Go,' he goes, or to another, 'Come,' he comes; I only have to say, 'Do this,' to my servant and he does it."

10 Jesus was astonished at what the centurion said and told those who were following Him: "I tell you the truth, nowhere among all the people of Israel have I found anyone with such faith as this Roman soldier. 11 I tell you clearly that many will come from the east and west and will be welcome to take their places at the feast alongside Abraham, Isaac and Jacob in the Kingdom of heaven. 12 Yet those who you would think would automatically be considered as belonging to that Kingdom will be excluded and thrown into outer darkness, where there will be deep mourning and cries of despair."

[13] Turning to the centurion, Jesus said: "Go! The healing will take place in precisely the way you believed it would happen." The soldier's servant was healed at exactly the time Jesus said this!

Jesus heals and delivers many (8:14-22)

[14] When Jesus arrived at Peter's house He found Peter's mother-in-law in bed, sick with a fever. [15] He touched her hand and the fever left immediately. She was able to get up and prepare a meal for them.

[16] In the evening many people possessed by demonic powers were brought to Jesus. He needed to speak only a word of command and the evil spirits were cast out of them, and He healed all who were sick. [17] This fulfilled what God spoke through the prophet Isaiah: 'He took our infirmities and diseases upon Himself.'

[18] Because of the great crowds that pressed around Him, Jesus told the disciples that they would cross to the other side of the lake. [19] But first a teacher of the religious law came to Him, saying: "Teacher, I am ready to follow You wherever You go."

[20] Jesus told him: "Foxes have holes to live in and the birds that fly around have their nests, but the Son of Man has no place of His own in which to rest."

[21] Another disciple said: "Lord, I want to follow You, but first I have to go and bury my father." [22] But Jesus told him: "Follow me now and leave the dead to bury their own dead."

Jesus stills the storm (8:23-27)

[23] Then Jesus boarded the boat together with His disciples. [24] As they were crossing the lake a sudden furious storm arose, causing waves to sweep over the sides of the boat. Jesus was sleeping peacefully through all this. [25] In desperation the disciples awoke Him. "Lord save us! We are about to drown!" they cried out in alarm.

[26] "What little faith you have," Jesus replied. "Why be so afraid?" Then He stood up and spoke with authority to the winds and waves, and it became completely calm.

[27] They were amazed at this and asked among themselves: "What kind of man can He be? Even the winds and the waves do whatever He says!"

Two demon possessed men delivered (8:28-34)

[28] When He arrived at the other side of the lake in the region of the Gadarenes, two demon-possessed men who lived among the tombs

8:17 Isaiah 53:4

approached Jesus. They were so violent that no one dared go near
them or the place where they lived. 29 They shouted to Jesus: "What
business do You have with us, Son of God? Have You come here to
torture us before our appointed time?"

30 Some way off a large herd of pigs was feeding. 31 The demons in
the men pleaded with Jesus: "If You drive us out, send us into the
herd of pigs."

32 Jesus spoke just one word: "Go!" The demons immediately
came out of the men and entered the pigs. The whole herd rushed
down the steep bank into the lake where they were all drowned.
33 Those who had been minding the pigs ran into the town and told
everyone all that had happened, including the way the demon-
possessed men had been set free. 34 The whole town came to see
Jesus; but instead of welcoming Him, they pleaded with Him to
leave their region.

A paralytic is healed (9:1-8)

9 So Jesus again boarded a boat and crossed back over the lake
to His own town. 2 There some men brought to Him a paralysed
man lying on a mattress. Jesus discerned the faith that had motivated
them and said to the paralysed man: "Be encouraged, son; all your
sins are forgiven."

3 "That is blasphemy!" some of the teachers of the law said among
themselves. 4 But Jesus knew what they were thinking and asked:
"Why do you have such evil thoughts in your hearts? 5 Is it easier to
say, 'Your sins are forgiven,' or to say, 'Get up and walk?' 6 But to
prove that the Son of man has authority on this earth to forgive
sins," Jesus turned to the paralytic and said: "Stand up, take your
mattress and go home!" 7 The man stood up and walked home. 8 The
crowd was filled with awe when they saw this and praised God for
giving such authority to men.

Jesus calls Matthew (9:9-13)

9 As Jesus continued on His way, He saw a man called Matthew sitting
where he collected the taxes. "Follow Me," Jesus said to him, and
Matthew obeyed and followed Him.

10 Jesus then went to Matthew's house for dinner. Many other tax
gatherers and those regarded as sinners came to eat with Jesus and
His disciples. 11 This scandalised the Pharisees, who asked His disciples:
"Why does your teacher eat with such people as these tax collectors
and sinners?"

12 Jesus overheard this and said to them: "Healthy people don't
need a doctor, but those who are sick. 13 Go and learn what this
scripture means when God says, 'I delight in mercy, not sacrifice!'
You see, I have not come to save people who think they are righteous,
but those who acknowledge they are sinners!"

Jesus questioned about fasting (9:14-17)

14 Some of John's disciples came to Jesus and asked Him: "Why is it
that we fast like the Pharisees do, but Your disciples don't fast?"

15 Jesus replied: "How can you expect the bridegroom's guests to
mourn while he is with them? When the bridegroom is taken away
from them, that will be the time for them to fast.

16 "No one would think of sewing a patch of unshrunk cloth on an
old garment. When the garment was washed, the patch would
shrink and only make the tear worse.

17 "Nor would men pour new wine into old, hardened wineskins.
If they were to do this, the skins would burst and both the wine and
the wineskins would be ruined. No, they pour new wine into new
flexible wineskins and then both are preserved."

A woman healed and a girl raised to life (9:18-26)

18 While He was speaking, a ruler of the synagogue came and knelt
before Jesus. "My daughter has just died," he said, "but if You come
and place Your hand on her, she will live again." 19 So Jesus stood
and went with him, accompanied by His disciples.

20-21 On the way a woman came up behind Jesus and touched the
border of His robe. She had suffered from constant bleeding for
twelve years and had said to herself: "If I only touch His robe, I
shall be healed."

22 Jesus looked round and said to her: "Be encouraged, daughter,
your faith has healed you." And the woman was healed instantly.

23 When Jesus arrived at the ruler's house, the flute players and a
noisy crowd of mourners had already gathered. 24 "Out of the house,"
He commanded them, "the girl is only sleeping; she is not dead."
But they laughed at Him. 25 Once the crowd was outside, Jesus went
in to where the girl lay, took hold of her hand and she stood up!
26 News of such an event spread rapidly through the whole region.

Two blind men healed (9:27-34)

27 As Jesus continued on His journey, two blind men followed Him
on the road, calling out to Him: "Son of David, be merciful to us."

[28] The blind men entered the house where Jesus was going. So He
asked them: "Do you believe I am able to restore your sight?"
"Yes, Lord," they replied.
[29] "Then Jesus reached out His hand, touched their eyes and said:
"It will now be done to you exactly as you have believed." [30] And
their sight was restored immediately. Then Jesus spoke strictly to
them: "Be sure that no-one knows about this." [31] But instead they left
the house and told people all over that region about Jesus and the
wonderful thing He had done for them.
[32] While they were leaving the house, a demon-possessed man
who was dumb was brought to Jesus. [33] As soon as He had cast out
the demon the man began to speak. This amazed the crowd.
"Nothing like this has ever been seen anywhere in Israel," they said.
[34] However, the Pharisees said: "He drives out demons through
the power of the prince of demons."

Jesus has compassion on the people (9:35-38)

[35] Jesus travelled through every town and village teaching in the
synagogues, preaching the good news of the Kingdom of heaven
and healing people from every disease and sickness. [36] Whenever He
saw the crowds that gathered He had compassion on them. They
seemed to be helpless to deal with the things that afflicted them.
They were like sheep who had no one to shepherd them and care
for them.
[37] He said to His disciples: "There is a plentiful harvest waiting to
be reaped, but so few workers. [38] So pray to the Lord of the harvest
and ask Him to send more workers into His harvest field."

The disciples sent out (10:1-23)

10 Jesus drew His twelve disciples around Him and gave them
the authority to drive out the evil spirits that afflicted people
and to heal all their diseases and sicknesses.
[2-4] The names of the twelve apostles are: first, Simon (known as
Peter) and his brother Andrew; James and his brother John, the sons
of Zebedee; Philip and Bartholomew; Thomas and Matthew the tax
collector; James the son of Alphaeus, and Thaddaeus; Simon the
Zealot and Judas Iscariot, who later betrayed Him.
[5] Jesus sent these twelve out with clear instructions: "You are not
to go among the non-Jews or into Samaritan towns. [6-7] Instead you
are to go to the lost sheep of Israel, with this message: 'The
Kingdom of heaven is fast approaching and is within your reach.'

8 Heal those who are sick, raise the dead, cleanse the lepers, drive out demonic powers. You have received the authority to do these things freely, so give to others freely. 9 Do not take any money with you, no gold, silver or even copper. 10 You will not need to take any luggage or extra clothing, no sandals nor a staff for your protection. Because the worker is worthy of his keep, everything you need will be provided for you.

11 "Whenever you enter a town or village, look for some responsible person and stay in his house until you leave that place. 12 When you enter his home, speak a blessing over it. 13 If deserving people live there, the blessing of peace will rest upon that place. But if you are not welcomed, that blessing of peace will come upon you instead. 14 If no one welcomes you or listens to what you say, shake the dust of that place off your feet when you leave. 15 I tell you the truth, on the Day of Judgment Sodom and Gomorrah will fare better than that town. 16 Yes, I am sending you out as sheep among wolves. So you will need to be as wise as snakes but as innocent as doves.

17 "Be wary of men, for they will hand you over to the local councils and you will even be flogged in their synagogues. 18 You will be brought before governors and kings because of your allegiance to Me. So you are witnesses to them and to the nations. 19 You will not have to be concerned about what to say or how to respond when you are arrested. At such times the Holy Spirit will give you the right words to say. 20 So it will not really be you speaking, but the Spirit of your heavenly Father speaking through you.

21 "One brother will betray another, even if it means he will die as a result. The same will happen with a father and his child. Children will rebel against their believing parents and be responsible for them being put to death. 22 It will seem that all men hate you because of your faith in Me. But he who remains faithful to the end will be saved.

23 "When they persecute you in one place, go somewhere else. I tell you the truth, the Son of Man will return before all the cities in Israel are reached with the gospel.

Further teaching (10:24-42)

24 "A student is not more important than his teacher, nor is a servant of greater significance than his master. 25 It is sufficient for the student to aim to be like his teacher and for the servant to imitate his master.

25 "If they call the head of the house the devil, it is likely that they will accuse the members of his household of also belonging to the devil! 26 But do not be afraid of those who oppose you. There is nothing

hidden that will not be openly revealed and made known publicly. 27 So what I tell you secretly, you can then speak openly. Whatever I whisper in your ear, you can shout in the open air. 28 Do not fear those who can kill the body but have no power over your soul. It is better to live in fear and awe of God who has the power to destroy both soul and body in hell!

29 "Two sparrows are sold for an insignificant amount. And yet your heavenly Father knows whenever one of them falls to the ground dead. 30 He even knows the number of hairs on your head, so great is His concern for you. 31 So there is nothing to fear; to Him you are worth far more than many sparrows.

32 "Anyone who honours Me before men I will honour before My Father in heaven. 33 But he who disowns Me before others, I shall disown before My Father in heaven.

34 "You should not think that I have come to bring peace to the earth. On the contrary, I have come with a sword, the Word of truth, and not to create a false peace by hiding the truth. 35 The result of My coming will turn a man against his father, a daughter against her mother, a daughter-in-law against her mother-in-law. 36 Sadly, a man's enemies will be the members of his own family!

37 "So anyone whose love for his father or mother is greater than his love for Me is not worthy of belonging to Me. Neither is anyone who has more love for his son or daughter than he has for Me. 38 Anyone who is not prepared to face whatever sacrifices are necessary to follow Me is not worthy of belonging to Me. 39 Whoever tries to hold onto his life for himself will lose it; but whoever is ready to lose his life for My sake will find the real life that only I can give.

40 "Anyone who receives you receives Me, and he who receives Me receives the One who sent Me. 41 If a person receives a prophet graciously because he is a prophet, that person will receive the same reward as a prophet. In like manner, anyone who treats a righteous person with honour because he is righteous, will receive the same reward as a righteous person. 42 A person will even be rewarded for giving a drink of water to one of My little ones simply because he is My disciple!"

The Kingdom of heaven is advancing (11:1-19)

11 Having given these instructions to His twelve disciples, Jesus moved on to teach and preach in other Galilean towns.

2-3 In prison John heard what Christ was doing and sent his disciples to ask Him: "Are you the long-expected Messiah, or should we await someone else?"

4-5 Jesus answered: "Return to John and tell him what you hear and see: the blind are receiving their sight, the lame are walking, those with leprosy are being healed, the deaf are able to hear, even the dead are being restored to life; and the good news is being preached to the poor. 6 The man who does not depart from his faith in Me is truly blessed."

7 As John's disciples were departing, Jesus spoke to the crowd about John. "When you went to see him in the desert, what did you expect to see? A reed swaying about in the wind? 8 No? Then what did you expect to see? A man dressed in fine clothes? No, such people are in king's palaces. 9 Then why go to see him? Because he is a prophet? I tell you, he is even greater than a prophet. 10 John is the one of whom it is written, 'I will send My messenger ahead of you to prepare the way before you!'

11 "I tell you the truth, of all those born of women, no one has been greater than John the Baptist. And yet even the least person in the Kingdom of heaven is greater than he. 12 From the time John the Baptist began to preach until now, the Kingdom of heaven has been advancing on earth by power, and forceful people are laying hold of it. 13 Before John you had the prophetic words written in the law and by all the Prophets. 14 If you only realise and believe it, John is the Elijah who was to come before the Christ. 15 He who has spiritual understanding, let him hear what I say.

16-17 "How would you describe this present generation? They are like children who sit in the marketplaces shouting to others, 'We played the flute for you but you refused to dance. When we sang a funeral song, you refused to mourn.' 18 For John did not come eating and drinking and they accused him of having a demon. 19 Then the Son of Man came both eating and drinking and they say, 'He is a glutton and a drunkard, who befriends the tax collectors and sinners.' True wisdom is demonstrated by the fruit that results from it!"

Unrepentant cities are cursed (11:20-24)

20 Because they had not repented, Jesus then began to speak against the cities in which most of His miracles had been performed. 21 "Korazin, you are cursed; Bethsaida, you also are cursed! If the miracles that took place among you had been performed in Tyre and Sidon, they would have repented in sackcloth and ashes long ago. 22 But I tell you plainly, on the Day of Judgment Tyre and Sidon will fare better than you! 23 And what about you Capernaum? Will

11:10 Malachi 3:1

you be exalted at that time? No, you will be cast down into the
depths. If the miracles you witnessed had been performed in
Sodom, it would still exist today. 24 So I make it clear to you that on
the Day of Judgment Sodom will fare better than you!"
25 Then Jesus worshipped: "I praise you Father, Lord of heaven
and earth, because you have hidden these things from those who
consider themselves wise and learned, and have revealed them to
those who regard themselves as your little children. 26 Yes, Father,
this is what it pleased you to do."

Rest in Jesus (11:25-30)

27 Then Jesus explained: "The Father has entrusted everything to Me.
Only He really knows the Son, and no-one truly knows the Father
except the Son and those to whom the Son chooses to make Him
known.
28 "Everyone who feels tired and oppressed, come to Me and I will
give you rest! 29 Be united with Me and learn from Me, for I have a
humble and gentle heart; then you will find peace for your souls.
30 When you are united with Me I make light of your burdens."

The Sabbath (12:1-14)

12 Around this time, Jesus was walking through some fields of
grain on the Sabbath. Because they were hungry, His disciples
picked some seeds and ate them. 2 Some Pharisees saw what they
did and challenged Jesus: "Look at what Your disciples are doing!
That is unlawful on the Sabbath."
3 Jesus replied: "Have you never read about what David did
when he and those with him were hungry? 4 He entered God's
house and together with his companions ate the consecrated bread
which only the priests are permitted to eat. 5 Or have you not read
what it says in the law, that on the Sabbath the priests are allowed
to work in the temple, and yet are regarded as innocent of any
offence against God? 6 I tell you clearly, One is here among you who
is greater than the temple. 7 Clearly you do not understand what
these words mean, 'I prefer mercy to sacrifice.' 8 If you had understood, you would not have condemned those who are innocent. For
the Son of Man is Lord of the Sabbath."
9 Moving on, Jesus went into their synagogue. 10 A man with a
shrivelled hand was present and because they wanted to find some
reason to accuse Jesus, the Pharisees asked Him: "Is it right, according to the law, to heal on the Sabbath?"

11 Jesus replied: "If one of you has a sheep that falls into a pit on
the Sabbath, will you not do whatever is needed to rescue it? 12 A
man is far more valuable than a sheep! So of course it is right,
according to God's law, to do good on the Sabbath."

13 Then He said to the man: "Stretch out your hand." When he did
so it was completely healed and was just as strong as the other
hand. 14 But this angered the Pharisees so much that they left the
synagogue and plotted how they could kill Jesus.

Prophecy fulfilled (12:15-21)

15-16 Aware of their plans, Jesus withdrew from there. But many followed
Him and He healed all the sick among them, warning them not to
say who He was. 17 This fulfilled what was spoken through the
prophet Isaiah:

> 18 "This is My chosen servant, the one I love and in whom
> I delight. My Spirit will be upon Him and He will proclaim
> justice to the nations. 19 He will not fight nor will He make
> His voice heard in the streets. 20 He will not snap a bruised
> reed, nor will He extinguish a smouldering wick, until
> He has first led those who love justice to victory. 21 In His
> Name, the nations will place their hope."

Address to the Pharisees (12:22-37)

22 Later, a demon-possessed man who was blind and mute was
brought to Him. Jesus healed him and he was able both to talk and
see. 23 Everyone was astonished. "Could this be the Christ, the Son
of David?" they asked.

24 However, when the Pharisees heard this they said: "This man
drives out demons by the devil, the prince of demons."

25 Knowing their thoughts, Jesus said to them: "Every kingdom
that fights against itself will be ruined. Every divided city or household
will not last. 26 So if Satan was to drive Satan out of people's lives, he
would be divided against himself. How could his kingdom last if
that was the case?

27 "And if it was true to say that I cast out demons by the devil
himself, by whom do your people drive them out? Even they will
judge you for what you have said. 28 However, if I drive out demons
through God's Spirit, then His Kingdom has come upon you.

12:21 Isaiah 42:1-4

[29] "Think again! Is it possible for anyone to enter the house of a
strong man and take away his possessions unless he first binds up
the strong man? Only then can he rob his house.
[30] "He who is not on My side is opposed to Me, and the one who
does not join with Me in gathering, scatters instead. [31] So I tell you
clearly, every sin and blasphemy men commit will be forgiven. [32] But
those who curse the Holy Spirit will not be forgiven. It is possible
for anyone who speaks against the Son of Man to be forgiven; but
anyone speaking against the Holy Spirit will not be forgiven, neither
in this present time nor in the eternal age that is to come.
[33] "If you have a good tree its fruit will be good. If you have a rotten
tree its fruit will be rotten, for each tree is evaluated by the fruit it
bears. [34] You collection of snakes, you are so evil; how can you recognise
what is good?
[34] "A person speaks from the overflow of his heart. [35] So the good
man expresses good things that flow out of the good stored up in
him. The evil person expresses evil things that flow from the evil
stored up in him. [36] So I tell you clearly that every man will have to
give account on Judgment Day for every careless word he has spoken.
[37] For by your words you will be declared innocent, and by the
words you have spoken you will be condemned."

A wicked and adulterous generation (12:38-45)

[38] Next some Pharisees and teachers of the religious law said to
Jesus: "Teacher, we want to see a miraculous sign that proves who
You are."
[39] He replied: "Only a wicked and adulterous generation would
ask for such a miraculous sign. No sign will be given it except the
sign of Jonah the prophet. [40] He was in the belly of a large fish for
three days and nights. In the same way, the Son of Man will be in
the heart of the earth for three days and nights. [41] At the judgment,
the men of Nineveh will stand in judgment on this generation and
will condemn it, for they repented when Jonah preached to them.
Now One who is far greater than Jonah is here among you.
[42] "The Queen of Sheba will speak in judgment on this generation
and will condemn it. She came from far away to hear Solomon's
wisdom, and now one far greater than Solomon is here among you!
[43] "What happens to an evil spirit when it comes out of a man? It
travels through desert places looking for rest, but is unable to find
it. [44] Then it decides, 'I will return to the place I inhabited before.'
When it arrives it discovers the house is vacant, clean and with
everything in order. [45] So it goes and gathers seven other spirits even

more wicked than itself. Together they enter to live there, so the man's final state is far worse than it was at first. This is exactly as it will be with this evil generation."

Jesus' true family (12:46-50)

46 While Jesus was still addressing the crowd, His mother and brothers came and stood outside wanting to speak to Him. 47 Someone gave Jesus the message: "Your mother and brothers are waiting outside, wishing to speak with You."

48 He replied: "Who is My mother, and who are truly My brothers?" 49 Then He pointed to His disciples and said: "Here is My family, My mother and brothers. 50 For anyone who obeys the will of My Father in heaven is My brother and sister and mother!"

The parable of the sower (13:1-23)

13 Later that same day Jesus left the house and went to sit by the lake. 2 Such large crowds gathered around Him that He had to sit in a boat, while the people remained on the shore. 3 Then He explained many things to them in parables.

"A farmer began to sow his seed. 4 As he scattered it around him, some fell on the pathway and the birds came and ate it. 5-6 Some fell in rocky places, where there was no depth to the soil. At first it grew quickly, but because the soil was so shallow the plants were soon scorched by the sun and withered because they did not have deep roots. 7 Some of the seed fell among thorns, which also grew and choked the plants. 8 But some of the other seed fell on good soil, where it produced a good crop. These seeds multiplied, producing a hundred, sixty or thirty times the amount that was sown. 9 He who has ears open to My Word let him hear and understand what I say."

10 The disciples came and asked Him: "Why do you speak to the people in parables?"

11 He replied: "The revelation of the secret things of the Kingdom of heaven has been given to you, but not to everybody. 12 Whoever has what I give will be given more until he has an abundance. But anyone who does not have what I offer will lose even what he does have. Everything will be taken from him. 13 I spoke in parables because it is written, 'Though they have eyes they do not see; though they have ears, they do not hear nor understand.' 14 So the prophecy of Isaiah is fulfilled in them:

13:13 Jeremiah 5:21

> 'You will keep hearing what is said, but never understand.
> You will keep looking but never receive the revelation
> placed before you. 15 For a hard skin covers the hearts of
> this people. They can hardly hear anything with their
> ears and they have closed their eyes to the truth. If this
> was not the case, they would see with their eyes, hear
> with their ears and understand with their hearts. Then
> they would turn to me and I would heal them.'

16 "But your eyes are blessed because you do see, and your ears are
blessed because you do listen. 17 For I tell you the truth, many
prophets and righteous men of the past longed to see what you now
see, but they never saw it. They longed to hear what you now hear,
but never heard it!

18 "Listen and I will explain what the parable of the sower means.
19 The seed on the path represents anyone who hears the gospel of
God's Kingdom, but does not understand it. The evil one is able to
come and steal the seed of truth that was sown in his hard heart.

20 "The person whose life is like the rocky soil receives with joy
the seed, the Word of truth, when he first hears the gospel. 21 But
because the Word is not deeply rooted in his shallow heart, his
response is short lived. As soon as difficulties arise or he has to face
persecution because of his faith in the Word, he rapidly deserts the
truth.

22 "The thorny soil represents the kind of person who hears and
knows the Word of truth, but he allows himself to be overcome
through other things in his life that cause him to worry, or because
he places his trust in his worldly possessions instead of in My
words. So, the truth cannot be fruitful in his life because he has a
divided heart.

23 However, the seed that falls on good soil signifies those who
receive the Word with faith. When they hear it they understand and
apply it to their lives; so they produce a harvest. They have good
hearts and the seed of truth is reproduced and multiplied in others,
a hundred, sixty or thirty times!"

The parable of the weeds (13:24-29)

24 Then Jesus told the people another parable: "The Kingdom of
heaven is like a man who sowed good seed in his field. 25 But under
cover of dark when all were asleep, his enemy came and sowed

13:15 Isaiah 6:9-10

weeds among the wheat, the good seed, and then quietly crept
away. 26 As the wheat grew and developed, so the weeds also
became obvious.

27 "The servants of the field's owner asked him, 'Sir, you sowed
good seed in your field, didn't you? So how is it that there are all
these weeds among the wheat?' 28 'An enemy must have done this,'
the owner replied.

28 "'Do you want us to pull the weeds up?' the servants asked.
29 'No,' he replied, 'because in the process you may also pull up the
wheat accidentally. 30 So let both the wheat and weeds grow together
until it is time to harvest the crop. Then I will give these instructions
to the reapers, 'First you are to collect the weeds, tie them in bundles
and burn them. Then you can gather the wheat and store it in my
barn.'''

The mustard seed and the yeast (13:31-35)

31 Jesus told them a further parable: "The Kingdom of heaven can be
likened to a mustard seed which a man planted in his field.
32 Although this is such a tiny seed, it becomes a large plant and then
a tree big enough for the birds to come and perch in its branches."

33 In yet another parable Jesus said: "The Kingdom of heaven is
like the yeast that a woman mixed into a large amount of flour. The
yeast permeated the whole lump of dough."

34 Jesus never spoke to the crowd without using such parables as
these. 35 In this way He fulfilled the prophetic words, 'I will speak
openly in parables. I will reveal things that have remained hidden
since the world was created.'

Jesus explains the parable of the weeds (13:36-43)

36 When Jesus left the people and entered the house, the disciples
said to Him: "Please explain to us the meaning of the parable of the
weeds in the field."

37 Jesus replied: "The Son of Man sowed the good seed, the Word
of truth. 38-39 The field represents the world and the good seeds stand
for those who believe, the sons of the Kingdom. The weeds are the
children of the evil one because they believe the lies sown by the
devil. Harvest time will be at the end of this age when the angels
will be sent to gather the harvest.

40 "At that time the weeds, the devil's children, will be uprooted
and thrown into the fire. 41 The Son of Man will send His angels to

13:35 Psalms 78:2

weed out of His Kingdom all who do evil and everything that causes
sin. 42 They will be thrown into the furnace of fire, where they will
mourn their foolishness and suffer eternally. 43 By contrast, the righteous ones will shine as brightly as the sun in the Kingdom of their
Father. Let the one with spiritual perception hear what I am saying.

More parables about the Kingdom (13:44-52)

44 "The Kingdom of heaven is like treasure that a man found hidden
in a field. He was so overjoyed that he concealed it again, then went
and sold everything he had so he could buy the field and own the
treasure.

45 "Similarly, the Kingdom of heaven is like a merchant who
sought the finest pearls. 46 He discovered one of such great value,
that he went and sold everything he had to enable him to buy that
one pearl.

47 "Again, you can liken the Kingdom of heaven to a net in which
all kinds of fish were caught when it was cast into the sea. 48 The
fishermen pulled it to shore when it was full and then sat and sorted
out the catch. The good fish they put in baskets, but the bad they
threw away. 49 This is what will happen at the time of judgment at
the end of this present age. The angels will come and separate the
wicked from the righteous. 50 They will throw the wicked into the
furnace of fire where they will mourn their foolishness and suffer
eternally."

51 Jesus asked His disciples: "Do you understand these things?"

"Yes," they replied.

52 So He then told them: "This being the case, every teacher of the
religious law who has himself been taught about the Kingdom of
heaven is like the house-owner who brings out of his storehouse
these new treasures, as well as the truth he already knew."

Jesus rejected in Nazareth (13:53-58)

53 It was time for Jesus to move on when He had finished telling
these parables. 54 He came to His hometown of Nazareth and began
teaching the people in their synagogue. They were astonished at
what they heard. They asked: "Where could this man have received
all this wisdom and the power to work such miracles? 55 This is the
carpenter's son, isn't it? We know Mary His mother and His brothers
James, Joseph, Simon and Judas. 56 And all His sisters lived here
among us, didn't they? So from where did this man receive all these
things He now teaches and does?" 57 They were offended by Him.

So Jesus said to them, "A prophet is honoured everywhere except in his own town and among his own family." [58]Because of this they failed to believe in Him, and so Jesus did not perform many miracles there.

Account of John the Baptist's death (14:1-12)

14 About that time Herod, the district ruler, heard reports about Jesus [2]and said to his staff: "This must be John the Baptist risen from the dead. This is why such miraculous powers are working through Him."

[3-4]John had been arrested and imprisoned by Herod through the influence of Herodias, his brother Philip's wife, for John had openly declared: "It is unlawful for you to have her as your wife." [5]Herod had wanted to kill John, but was afraid to do so because the people regarded him as a prophet.

[6-7]However, Herodias' daughter danced for the guests on Herod's birthday and this pleased him so much he swore on oath that he would give her anything she asked. [8]Her mother prompted her to say: "Give me the head of John the Baptist on a plate." [9]This concerned the king, but because he had given his oath before his dinner guests, he commanded that her desire should be fulfilled. [10-11]So John was beheaded in the prison and his head was carried on a plate and given to the girl, who in turn presented it to her mother. [12]Meanwhile John's disciples came and took his body for burial before going to tell Jesus what had happened.

Five loaves and two fish (14:13-21)

[13]On hearing this news, Jesus went away privately by boat, wanting to be alone. Aware of His departure, crowds of people from the surrounding towns went on foot around the lake and were waiting for Him when He landed. [14]When He saw such a vast crowd, His heart went out to them with compassion and He healed the sick among them.

[15]When evening approached, His disciples came and said: "It is getting late and this is such a remote place that you had better send the crowds away so they can go and buy food in the villages."

[16]"There is no need for them to leave," Jesus replied. "You provide food for them." [17]But they answered: "All we have between us is five loaves of bread and two fish."

[18]"Well, bring them to me," Jesus said. [19]After telling the people to sit on the grass, He took the five loaves and two fish, looked up to heaven and gave thanks to God. He then broke the loaves into

pieces and gave them to the disciples to distribute among the people.
20-21 They all ate as much as they wanted and when the disciples
collected what remained, they filled twelve baskets; yet about five
thousand men, plus women and children, had eaten.

Peter comes to Jesus on the lake (14:22-36)

22 Immediately after this, Jesus ordered the disciples to board the
boat and go on ahead of Him to the other side of the lake, while He
sent the crowds home. 23 Having done this, He went up on the side
of a mountain alone to pray. He was still there by Himself as it grew
dark. 24 The boat was by now some way from the land, but was
being buffeted by strong head winds.

25 About three o'clock in the morning, Jesus walked towards them
on the surface of the lake. 26 When the disciples saw Him walking on
top of the water, they were scared. "It must be a ghost," they said
and cried out in alarm.

27 Immediately Jesus called out to them: "Have faith! It is I. Don't
be afraid."

28 Peter said: "Lord, if it really is you, command me to come to you
walking on the water."

29 "Come," said Jesus.

Peter climbed out of the boat and began to walk on the water
towards Jesus. 30 However, he became conscious of the force of the
wind and began to fear. Immediately he began to sink and cried out:
"Save me, Lord!"

31 Jesus reached out His hand and caught hold of Peter. He said to
him: "Why did you doubt? Is your faith so weak?"

32 As soon as they had climbed together into the boat, the wind
died down. 33 The others in the boat worshipped Him, saying: "You
really are God's Son."

34 Having crossed the lake, they landed at Gennesaret. 35-36 The
local residents recognised Jesus and sent word around the surrounding district. People brought all the sick to Him, pleading with Him
to let them merely touch the edge of His robe. And everyone who
touched Him was healed!

The clean and the unclean (15:1-20)

15 Then some Pharisees and teachers of the law came from
Jerusalem and said to Jesus: 2 "Why do you allow your
disciples to break the traditions of the elders? For example, they do
not perform the ritual of washing their hands before a meal."

[3] Jesus replied: "Why do you break God's commands in order to keep your traditions? [4] God said, 'Honour your father and mother' and 'Anyone who curses his father or mother should be put to death.' [5-6] But you say that if a man tells his father or mother, 'What you could have received from me to help you has been given to God instead,' he is not to honour his father with that gift. So you disregard God's Word for the sake of your traditions. [7-8] What hypocrites you are! Isaiah was justified in prophesying about you, 'These people honour me by what they say, but their hearts are far from Me. [9] Their worship of Me is empty and their teaching is only rules that they have devised themselves.'"

[10] Then Jesus gathered the crowd around Him and said: "Listen to Me and understand what I say. [11] Nothing that enters a man's mouth can make him unclean. It is what comes out of his mouth, from his heart, which defiles him."

[12] Later the disciples asked Jesus: "Are you aware that the Pharisees were greatly offended by what you said?"

[13] To this Jesus replied: "Whatever is not planted by My heavenly Father will be uprooted. [14] Take no notice of these men; they are guides who are blind themselves. And if someone who is blind leads another who is blind, both will fall into a ditch."

[15] Peter said: "Explain clearly what you mean."

[16] "Do you still not understand?" Jesus asked them. [17] "Can you not see that whatever enters a man's mouth goes into his stomach before passing out of his body? [18] But whatever comes out of the mouth originated in his heart and such utterances make a man unclean. [19] For evil thoughts, murder, adultery, sexual immorality, theft, false testimony and slander all originate in the heart. [20] Such things prove a man is unclean. But acting without ritually washing your hands does not make you guilty of such things."

Canaanite girl set free (15:21-28)

[21] Jesus then left that place and journeyed to the region of Tyre and Sidon. [22] A local woman, who was a Canaanite, came to Him in distress: "Lord, Son of David, please have mercy on me! My daughter is demon-possessed and suffers terribly."

[23] At first Jesus did not answer her. His disciples urged Him: "Send her away, for she keeps on and on and won't leave us alone."

15:4 Exodus 21:17
15:4 Exodus 20:12
15:9 Isaiah 29:13

24 Jesus answered them: "My mission is to the lost sheep of Israel.
That is why I was sent."
25 The woman came, knelt before Him and pleaded: "Lord, please,
please help me!"
26 "It is not right to take the bread intended for the children and
throw it to the dogs instead," Jesus replied.
27 "True, Lord," she said, "but even the dogs are allowed to eat the
crumbs that fall from the master's table."
28 "Woman, your faith is great," Jesus answered. "What you ask
for is done." And her daughter was set free at that very moment.

Many healed by Jesus (15:29-31)

29 When Jesus left that area He returned to the Sea of Galilee. He
climbed the side of a mountain and sat down. 30 Great crowds came
to Him, bringing the lame, the blind and the crippled, the dumb and
many others in distress, who they laid at His feet. And He healed
them. 31 The people were awestruck when they witnessed those who
had been dumb now able to speak, the crippled completely restored
and those formerly blind able to see clearly. So they praised the God
of Israel.

Jesus feeds four thousand (15:32-39)

32 Jesus gathered the disciples around Him and said: "I feel such
compassion for these people. They have already been here with Me
for three days with nothing to eat. I don't want to send them away
hungry in case they collapse on their way home."
33 But His disciples responded: "Where in such a remote place can
we buy enough bread to feed so many people?"
34 "How many loaves do you have?" Jesus asked them.
"Seven, and a few small fish," they replied.
35 Jesus then told the crowd to sit on the ground. 36 Taking the
seven loaves and the fish, He first gave thanks for them, and then
broke them in pieces, giving them to the disciples to distribute
among the people. 37 They all ate as much as they wanted, and the
disciples filled seven baskets with the remaining pieces. 38 Four
thousand men plus the women and children had eaten. 39 Then Jesus
sent them all home before going by boat to the area near Magadan.

Warning against wrong influences (16:1-12)

16 The Pharisees and Sadducees came to test Jesus, wanting
Him to show them a sign from heaven. 2 He told them:

"When you see a red sky in the evening you say, 'Tomorrow the
weather will be good.' 3 But if you see a red and overcast sky in the
morning you say, 'It will be stormy today.' You can interpret the
way the sky appears, but you are unable to interpret the signs of
these present times. 4 Only a wicked, adulterous generation would
ask for a sign; and none shall be given to it, except what happened
to Jonah." With that Jesus turned away from them and left.

5 He went across the lake with his disciples, who had forgotten to
take any bread with them. 6 Jesus told them: "Be on your guard. Be
careful not to be influenced by the yeast of the Pharisees and
Sadducees."

7 They discussed among themselves what He meant by this and
concluded: "He is referring to the fact that we didn't bring any
bread with us." 8 Aware of what they were saying, Jesus asked them:
"Why do you talk about forgetting to bring bread? Is your faith still
so weak? 9 Do you still not understand what I mean? Surely you
remember how five thousand men were fed from five loaves, and
how many baskets were filled with the remaining pieces! 10 What
about the four thousand who were fed with seven loaves! How
many basketfuls did you gather on that occasion? 11 Why don't you
understand that I was not referring to bread at all? I repeat, be sure
that you do not allow the yeast of the Pharisees and Sadducees to
influence you in any way."

12 Then they realised that Jesus had not been referring to the yeast
used in making bread, but they were to be wary of what the
Pharisees and Sadducees taught.

Peter's revelation of Christ (16:13-20)

13 When they arrived in the area of Caesarea Philippi, Jesus asked
His disciples: "What do the people say about the Son of Man? Who
do they understand Him to be?"

14 They answered: "Some say He is John the Baptist, others Elijah
and others think He is Jeremiah or one of the other prophets."

15 "Well, what do you think?" Jesus asked. "Who do you say I
am?"

16 "You are the Christ, the Messiah, God's Son," Simon Peter
answered.

17 "Simon, son of Jonah, you are blessed," Jesus said. "This could
not have been revealed to you by any man, but only by My Father
in heaven. 18 And I tell you clearly that you are Peter, a rock, and I
will build My church on the bedrock on which you are placed. And

the very gates of hell shall not overcome My church. 19 I give you the
key truths that unlock the way into the Kingdom of heaven. So you
have the authority to restrict or prevent on earth what is not
allowed in heaven. And you have my permission to liberate on
earth whatever is liberated in heaven."

20 Then He forbade His disciples to tell anyone that He was the
Christ, the Messiah.

The cost of following Jesus (16:21-28)

21 Now they knew for certain who He was, Jesus began to explain to
His disciples that it was necessary for Him to go to Jerusalem,
where He would suffer greatly at the hands of the elders, chief
priests and teachers of the religious law. He must even be killed, but
He would be raised back to life on the third day after His death.

22 When he heard this, Peter took Jesus to one side and began to
rebuke Him. "God forbid that this should ever happen to You!" he
said.

23 Jesus turned and said directly to Peter's face: "Get out of My
way Satan! You only want to hinder Me, because you do not understand the things of God; you think only as men think."

24 Then Jesus said to all the disciples: "If anyone makes the decision
to be My follower, he will have to deny what he wants for himself.
He must be prepared to suffer willingly any cross of sacrifice asked
of him; then he can follow Me. 25 For whoever is intent only on his
own welfare will lose his life eternally. But whoever is prepared to
lose his life for Me will find eternal life.

26 "What good would it do a man if he were to have everything he
wanted in this world, yet lose his soul in the process? What could
be more valuable to anyone than the eternal destiny of his soul?
27 You see, the Son of Man will come again in His Father's glory
together with His angels. Then He will give each person the appropriate reward, according to what he or she has done. 28 So I tell you
the truth, some of you here with Me will not die before you see that
I, the Son of Man, reveal the glory of My Kingdom."

The Transfiguration (17:1-13)

17 Six days later Jesus took Peter, James and his brother John,
up a high mountain. 2 There He was transfigured before
their eyes. His face was radiant, shining like the brilliance of the
sun; His clothes shone with glorious light. 3 Moses and Elijah appeared
to them also, talking with Jesus.

4 "Lord, it is so good for us to be here to see this," Peter said to Jesus. "Would you like me to erect three canopies for you, one for You and one each for Moses and Elijah?"

5 While he was saying this, a bright cloud enveloped them all and they heard a voice speak from the cloud: "This is My beloved Son; I am very pleased with Him. So listen to what He says."

6 On hearing this voice the disciples were scared and fell to the ground on their faces. 7 Jesus came and touched each of them saying: "Stand up; there is no need to be afraid." 8 When they looked again, only Jesus was there with them.

9 While making their way down the mountain Jesus commanded them: "Do not tell anyone about what you have just seen until after the Son of Man has been raised from the dead."

10 The disciples wanted to know: "Why do the teachers of the law say that Elijah must appear before the Messiah comes?" 11 Jesus told them: "It is true, Elijah comes to restore everything that was lost.
12 But I tell you clearly, Elijah has come already but they did not recognise him. Instead they treated him exactly as they wished. And in similar fashion they will also cause the Son of Man to suffer."
13 The disciples then realised He was referring to John the Baptist.

A demon possessed boy is healed (17:14-23)

14 When they rejoined the crowd a man came and knelt before Jesus.
15 "Have mercy on my son, Lord," he said. "He suffers greatly from seizures that often throw him into fire or water. 16 I brought him to Your disciples but they were unable to heal him."

17 "What a generation of unbelief and perversion this is," Jesus said. "For how much longer must I remain among you? How much longer do I have to put up with you? Bring your son to me." 18 As soon as Jesus rebuked the demon in the boy, it came out of him and he was completely healed.

19 Later the disciples asked Jesus privately: "Why were we unable to cast that demon out of the boy?"

20 "Because your faith is so weak," Jesus answered. "Most emphatically I tell you this truth, if you had true faith that was even the size of a minute mustard seed, you would be able to say to this mountain, 'Move from here to there,' and it would move. Nothing would be impossible for you! 21 This kind of deliverance takes place when you pray with faith!"

22-23 When they were together in Galilee, Jesus told the disciples: "The Son of Man will be betrayed. Men will lay hands on Him and

kill Him; yet on the third day after His death, He will be raised back
to life." On hearing this, the disciples were grief-stricken.

Temple tax (17:24-27)

24 When Jesus and His disciples arrived at Capernaum, those responsible for collecting the tax for the temple asked Peter: "Doesn't your
teacher pay the temple tax?"

25 "Yes, He does," Peter replied.

When Peter entered the house, Jesus spoke first and asked:
"From whom do earthly kings collect the customs and taxes, from
their only sons or from others? What do you think Simon?"

26 "From others," he answered.

"This means the sons are exempt from paying taxes," Jesus said
to him. 27 "However, so that we may not offend them, go to the lake
and throw your line into the water. Open the mouth of the first fish
you catch and you will find a coin sufficient to pay the tax for both
of us. Take it and give it to those responsible."

The greatest in the Kingdom (18:1-9)

18 "Who is the greatest in the Kingdom of heaven?" the disciples
asked Jesus. 2 He called a little child over and had him stand
in their midst. 3 "I tell you the truth," He said, "you will never enter
the Kingdom of heaven unless you are converted and become like
little children. 4 So whoever humbles himself and becomes childlike
is the greatest in the Kingdom of heaven.

5 "What is more, anyone welcoming a little child like this in My
Name, also welcomes Me. 6 But if anyone causes one of My little
ones to sin, it would be better for him to be drowned in the sea with
a large millstone hung round his neck!

7 "The world is under a curse for the way it causes people to sin!
Such things inevitably happen, but the one through whom they
happen is cursed! 8 If you sin because of what you do with your
hand or foot, cut it off and throw it away. For it is better to enter
eternal life maimed or crippled than to have all your limbs and be
cast into eternal fire. 9 And if you sin by the wrong use of your eye,
gouge it out and throw it away. For it is better to enter eternal life
with one eye than to have both and be cast into the fire of hell.

The parable of the lost sheep (18:10-14)

10 "So be sure that you do not look down on one of my little children.
For I tell you clearly that in heaven their angels look continually on

the face of My Father." [11] The Son of Man came to save those who are
lost.

[12] "What do you think about this? Suppose a man owns a hundred
sheep and one of them strays, will he not leave the ninety-nine grazing
on the hills and go in search of the stray? [13] I tell you most emphatically, he is happier over that one sheep when he finds it than over
the rest which did not stray. [14] In the same way your Father in heaven
does not want even one of His little children to be lost.

Forgive your brother (18:15-20)

[15] "When a brother sins against you, go to him and between the two
of you show him how he has wronged you. If he listens, both of you
will be reconciled. [16] If he refuses to listen, then take one or two others
with you to confront him with his wrong. This fulfils what is written,
that the testimony of two or three witnesses is needed to determine
a dispute! [17] If he still refuses to acknowledge his guilt, then the
whole church needs to be told of the matter. If he still thinks he is in
the right, despite what the whole church says, then he is to be treated
in the same way as you would a pagan or a crooked tax collector.

[18] "I tell you this truth most emphatically, you have authority to
prevent on earth what heaven does not allow, and you can liberate
on earth what has been liberated in heaven.

[19] "I also tell you clearly that when two of you agree in faith about
the outcome of any matter about which you pray, it will be done for
you by My Father in heaven. [20] You see, whenever two or three of
you gather together with faith in the authority of My Name, I am
there with you."

The parable of the unmerciful servant (18:21-35)

[21] Peter then asked Jesus: "Well, Lord, how many times do you
expect me to forgive my brother when he wrongs me? Would seven
times be enough?"

[22] "No, not seven times," Jesus answered, "I tell you to forgive
seventy times seven.

[23] "Therefore the Kingdom of heaven is like a king who needed to
settle accounts with those indebted to him. [24] One man brought
before him owed him millions. [25] Because he was unable to settle the
debt, the master ordered that he, his wife, children and everything
he possessed should be sold in repayment.

[26] "At this the servant fell on his knees before him. 'Be patient
with me,' he pleaded, 'and I promise to pay back everything I owe.'

27 In compassion for him the servant's master cancelled the debt and
released him.

28 "As soon as the servant had left his master's presence, he went
in search of one of his fellow servants who owed him a pittance by
comparison. He took hold of him and began to throttle him. 'Pay me
what you owe me,' he demanded.

29 "His fellow servant fell on his knees and pleaded with him,
'Give me more time, and I will repay all I owe you.'

30 "But he refused to listen. Instead he had the man thrown into
prison, where he was to be kept until the debt was repaid fully.

31 "When the other servants realised what had happened, they
were so upset that they went and told their master everything that
had taken place.

32 "Then the master recalled the servant and said to him, 'You
wicked servant. I cancelled that enormous debt because you pleaded
with me to do so. 33 Should you not have been just as merciful to
your fellow servant?' 34 His master was so angry that he put him in
the hands of the jailers to be tortured until the debt that was previously cancelled was fully repaid."

35 Then Jesus warned: "This is how My heavenly Father will deal
with you unless you are merciful and forgive your brother from
your heart."

Divorce and marriage (19:1-12)

19 After teaching these things Jesus left Galilee and went to the
region of Judea on the far side of the Jordan. 2 As usual, large
crowds followed Him and He healed the sick among them.

3 Some Pharisees came to Him with another trick question. "Are
there any circumstances in which under the law a man is allowed to
divorce his wife?" they asked.

4-5 Jesus replied: "Surely you have read that in the beginning the
Creator made both male and female and said: 'Because of this, a
man is to leave his father and mother and become one with his wife;
the two then become one flesh.' 6 This being the case, they are no
longer two separate individuals. But by their union they have become
one. Therefore because God has joined them together and made
them one, no one should dare to separate them!"

7 The Pharisees then asked: "If this is the case, why did Moses
legislate that a man could give his wife a certificate of divorce and
separate from her?"

19:4-5 Genesis 2:24

8 Jesus answered: "It was only because of the hardness of your
hearts that Moses permitted you to divorce your wives. But from
the beginning this was never God's intention. 9 And I tell you clearly
that whoever divorces his wife, and then marries another woman,
is guilty of adultery in God's eyes, unless the wife has been unfaithful
sexually"

10 The disciples said to Jesus: "It would be better not to marry at
all, if that bond between a husband and wife is so great."

11 To this Jesus replied: "Not everybody is prepared to accept this
word of truth. It is for those to whom such grace is given. 12 Some are
born eunuchs, others are castrated, but there are those who have
renounced marriage so they can devote themselves to the work of
the Kingdom of heaven. But that is for those who can accept such a
sacrifice."

Children (19:13-15)

13 Some small children were brought to Jesus so that He could lay
His hands on them and pray for them. The disciples rebuked those
who bothered Jesus in this way. 14 But He told them: "Allow these little
ones to come to Me. Don't hinder them. Remember, the Kingdom of
heaven belongs to those who know they are God's little children."
15 Having prayed for them, Jesus then moved on.

A wealthy man talks to Jesus (19:16-30)

16 A man came to Him and asked: "Teacher, what good deed can I do
to ensure I receive eternal life?"

17 Jesus replied: "Why do you question me about doing good?
God is the only one who is good. So if you want to enter into His
life, obey His commandments."

18-19 "But which of them?" the man asked.

Jesus answered: "Do not murder, do not commit adultery, do not
steal, do not give false testimony, honour your father and mother
and love your neighbour as you love yourself."

20 "I have kept all these commandments; what else do I still need
to do?" the young man asked.

21 Jesus told him: "In your case, if you really want to be perfect,
you need to go and sell all your possessions and give to the poor.
Then you will have treasure in heaven and you can come and follow
Me."

22 He went away sad when he heard this, for he was very wealthy.
23 Jesus then said to His disciples: "I tell you this truth, it is difficult

for a wealthy person to enter into the Kingdom of heaven. 24 I tell
you clearly that it is easier for a camel to pass through the eye of a
needle than for a wealthy person to enter God's Kingdom."

25 The disciples were really amazed when they heard Jesus say
this and asked Him: "Who can possibly be saved then?"

26 Jesus looked straight at them and said: "It is impossible for man
to save anyone; but all things are possible for God!"

27 Then Peter said: "We have sacrificed everything to follow you!
What will our reward be?"

28 Jesus told them: "I tell you the truth, that at the fulfilment of all
things, when the Son of Man sits on His glorious throne, you who
have followed Me faithfully will also sit on thrones to judge the
twelve tribes of Israel. 29 Everyone who has left behind homes,
brothers, sisters, father, mother, children or possessions on My
behalf will receive a hundred times as much as he has sacrificed,
and will also inherit eternal life. 30 Many who in this world seem to
have everything will then have nothing, and many who appear to
have nothing will have everything!"

The parable of the vineyard (20:1-16)

20 "The Kingdom of heaven is like the owner of an estate who
early in the morning went to hire workers for his vineyard.
2 He agreed their pay for the day and set them to work.

3 "He went out again around nine o'clock and saw others standing
idly in the market place. 4 He said to them, 'Go and work in my vineyard, and I will pay you the right amount at the end of the day.' So
they also accepted his offer.

5 "The owner of the estate went out again about noon and at three
in the afternoon and hired others on the same understanding. 6 Even
at five o'clock he found others doing nothing and so asked them,
'Why have you been standing around all day with nothing to do?'

7 "They answered, 'Because no one hired us.' He replied: 'Well, go
and work in my vineyard.'

8 "At the end of the working day, the owner of the estate told his
foremen, 'Call the workers together and pay them, beginning with
those I hired last and working up to those I hired first.'

9 "Those employed around five o'clock came and each received a
full day's wage. 10 So when those who were hired at the beginning
of the day came forward, they expected to be paid more. But each
was given only the full day's wage. 11-12 At this they began to complain
about the owner, saying, 'Those who were hired to work for only

one hour have received the same amount as us, and we have been working all day long in the scorching heat.'

13-14 "The owner answered, 'My friends, I am not being unjust to you. You agreed to work for the amount I have paid you, didn't you? And I have paid you accordingly; so go on your way. It was my decision to pay those I hired last the same as you. 15 Surely I have the right to use my money as I choose? Are you jealous because I am so generous?'"

16 Then Jesus concluded: "So those who think they are last, the bottom of the pile, will become the first. And those who think they deserve the top positions will find themselves at the bottom of the pile."

Jesus predicts His death (20:17-19)

17-19 As Jesus was going up to Jerusalem with His twelve disciples, He said privately to them: "We are going up to Jerusalem and there the Son of Man will be betrayed to the chief priests and teachers of the religious law. They will condemn Him to death and will hand Him over to the Roman authorities to be ridiculed, flogged and crucified. But on the third day after His death, He will be raised back to life!"

The importance of serving (20:20-28)

20 Later, the mother of James and John came to Jesus with her two sons and knelt before Him to ask a favour of Him. "What do you want?" He asked.

21 She replied: "Please give my two sons the places of highest honour in your Kingdom, one immediately on your right and the other on your left."

22 Jesus told all three: "You don't appreciate the significance of what you are requesting. Are you able to drink the same cup of suffering that I will have to drink?"

"Yes, we can," James and John both answered.

23 Jesus replied: "You will surely have to drink from this cup, but it is not for Me to decide who should sit at My right and left. My Father has reserved these places for those He has chosen to fill them."

24 The other ten disciples were indignant with the two brothers when they heard about the request. 25 So Jesus called them all together and said: "You are aware that kings love to lord it over those beneath them, and their secular officials enjoy exercising their authority over them. 26-27 But this is not the way for you to behave. Those among you who want to become great must have servant

hearts and whoever wants a higher position must be prepared to
serve as if he were your slave. 28 For this is the example given you by
the Son of Man who came to serve others, not to be served by them!
He came to sacrifice His life as a ransom to save many!"

Two blind men healed (20:29-34)

29 A large crowd followed Jesus as He and His disciples left Jericho.
30 Sitting on the roadside were two blind men who shouted out as
Jesus passed: "Lord, Son of David, have mercy on us."

31 Those around them rebuked them, telling them to be quiet. But
this made them even more determined; so they shouted more loudly:
"Lord, Son of David, have mercy on us!"

32 Hearing them, Jesus stopped and called them forward. "What
is it that you want Me to do for you?" He asked them.

33 "Lord, we want our sight to be restored," they answered.

34 With compassion Jesus touched their eyes, and immediately
they received their sight and then followed Him.

Jesus enters Jerusalem (21:1-11)

21 Jesus and His disciples arrived at Bethphage on the Mount
of Olives, near Jerusalem. Jesus told two of the disciples:
2 "Go into the village ahead of us and there you will see a donkey
with her year-old colt tethered. Untie them and bring them here to
Me. 3 If anyone wonders what you are doing, simply tell him that
the Lord has need of them, and he will immediately agree that you
should take them."

4-5 This happened to fulfil the prophetic words: "Tell the daughter
of Zion, My people Israel, 'Look, your King comes humbly to you
riding on the colt of a donkey.'"

6 The disciples went and did what Jesus had said. 7 They returned
with the donkey and her colt. When they had placed their cloaks on
its back, Jesus sat on the colt. 8 As they made their way to Jerusalem,
a very large crowd laid their cloaks on the road. Others cut branches
from the trees and spread them in His path. 9 Both those ahead of
Him and those who followed shouted out: "Praise to the Saviour,
the Son of David." "Blessed is He who comes in the Lord's Name."
"Glory be to the One who saves."

10 The entire city was impacted as Jesus entered Jerusalem and
people asked: "Who is this creating such a stir?" 11 Those in the
crowd answered: "This is Jesus, the prophet from Nazareth in Galilee."

21:4-5 Zechariah 9:9

Jesus cleanses the temple (21:12-17)

12 When He entered the temple courts, Jesus began driving out all
who were buying and selling there. He overturned the tables of the
money changers and the seats of those selling doves. 13 He said: "It
is written, 'My house will be called a house of prayer,' but you have
made it into a den of thieves."

14 The blind and crippled came to Jesus in the temple and He healed
them. 15 When the chief priests and teachers of the religious law saw
these wonderful miracles and the children shouting in the temple
courts, 'Praise to the Saviour, the Son of David,' they were outraged.
16 They challenged Jesus: "Do you hear what these children are
shouting?"

"Of course," Jesus replied. "But have you never read the scripture,
'You have determined that children and infants will declare My
praises!'?"

17 Then Jesus left and went to spend the night at Bethany.

Faith in prayer (21:18-22)

18 As He was returning to the city on the next morning, He was hungry.
19 He noticed a fig tree on the roadside, but when He looked closely
at it there was no fruit, only leaves. So He said to the tree: "You will
never bear fruit again." Immediately the tree withered. 20 This amazed
the disciples who asked: "How could the fig tree wither so quickly?"

21 Jesus replied: "I tell you this truth most emphatically, if you
have faith and do not doubt the outcome, you can not only do similar
things to this, but you can also command this mountain, 'Go, throw
yourself into the sea,' and it will be moved. 22 You see, no matter
what you ask in prayer, you will receive if you truly believe."

Jesus' authority is questioned (21:23-27)

23 Jesus entered the temple courts. While He was teaching the people
there, the chief priests and elders challenged Him: "On whose
authority are You doing these things? Who gave You such authority?"

24 Jesus answered: "I will ask you a question as well. Answer Me
and then I will tell you on whose authority I do these things. What
about John's baptism? Was it inspired by heaven or only the work
of man?"

25 They discussed this among themselves. "If we say it was
inspired by heaven," they said, "He will ask, 'In that case why did

21:16 Psalms 8:2

you not believe John?' [26] But if we dare to say that it was only the work of man, we fear the reaction of the people; for they believe John to be a prophet."

[27] So they told Jesus: "We don't know the answer to your question."

"Then neither will I answer your question," Jesus said. "I will not tell you on whose authority I do these things.

The parable of the two sons (21:28-32)

[28] "What do you say to this? A man had two sons. He told one, 'Son, go and work today in the vineyard.' [29] 'No, I will not,' he answered; but he changed his mind later and went and did as his father had said.

[30] "Then the father gave the same order to his other son. He answered, 'Certainly sir, I will go,' but he never went.

[31] "Now which of the two sons obeyed his father?"

"The first," they answered.

So Jesus said to them: "I tell you this truth most emphatically, crooked tax collectors and prostitutes are entering God's Kingdom ahead of you self-righteous leaders. [32] John came to show you the way of true righteousness, but you refused to believe what he said; but the tax collectors and the prostitutes who recognised their need of forgiveness, did believe him. Even though you saw what was happening, still you refused to repent and believe the message he brought from God.

The parable of the tenants (21:33-46)

[33] "Listen to this parable: A landowner planted a vineyard, put a wall around it, dug a winepress and built a watchtower. Then he leased the vineyard to tenants while he went on a prolonged journey. [34] When it was nearing harvest time, the owner sent servants to the tenants to collect his share of the fruit.

[35] "But they seized the servants. They beat one, killed one and stoned another. [36] So the owner sent a greater number of servants to them, but the tenants treated them in a similar way. [37] Finally, he sent his own son saying, 'Surely they will respect my son.'

[38] "However, knowing him to be the heir, the tenants said to each other, 'We can take his inheritance if we kill him. Come on, let us do it.' [39] So they took hold of him, threw him out of the vineyard and then killed him.

[40] "So what will the owner do to those tenants when he returns?"

[41] The religious leaders answered: "He will be certain to send such terrible men to a horrific death. Then he will find responsible tenants for the vineyard, who will give him his rightful share of the harvest."

[42] Jesus then said to them: "Have you not read the scriptures that say: 'The builders rejected the stone that became the keystone. This was the Lord's purpose, and we now see how wonderful it is.'

[43] "Therefore I warn you that God's Kingdom will be taken from you and will be given to those who will reproduce its fruit.
[44] Anyone who falls on this Stone will be shattered and he on whom it falls will be crushed."

[45] The chief priests and the Pharisees realised that Jesus was referring to them in these parables. [46] So they wanted to find a way to arrest Him, but they were afraid of the reactions of the crowd because they held Jesus in such high regard.

The parable of the wedding feast (22:1-14)

22 Then Jesus taught them another parable: [2] "The Kingdom of heaven is like a king who prepared a wedding feast for his son. [3] He sent his servants to those already invited, telling them it was time to come to the feast; but they all refused to come.

[4] "So the king sent more servants with these instructions: 'Tell the invited guests that I have prepared the feast. The cattle have been slaughtered and the meat is cooked and ready. So come to the wedding feast immediately.'

[5] "But the guests ignored the pleas of the king and went about their daily business as usual, one to his farm, another to his office.
[6] Some took hold of the king's servants, abused them and then killed them. [7] This so angered the king that he sent his soldiers to kill the murderers and destroy their city by fire.

[8] "Then he instructed other servants, 'The wedding feast is ready, but those I invited did not deserve the honour of sitting at my table.
[9] So go now into the streets and invite anyone you find to come to the feast.' [10] The servants obeyed and gathered all those they found, whether good or bad characters; and so the place where the wedding feast was held was filled with guests.

[11] "When the king himself entered, he noticed among the guests one man who was not wearing wedding clothes. [12] He asked him, 'Friend how were you admitted without the right wedding clothes?' But the man had nothing to say in response.

21:42 Psalms 118:22

13 "So the king told his assistants, 'Bind his hands and feet and
throw him out into the spiritual darkness where people will weep
for their foolishness and suffer eternal affliction.'"

14 Then Jesus said: "I invite many to my heavenly wedding feast,
but only a few are chosen!"

Paying taxes to Caesar (22:15-22)

15 On hearing this the Pharisees left and planned how they could
trap Jesus by His own words, giving them opportunity to accuse
Him. 16 They sent some of their disciples along with some members
of Herod's political party, and said: "Teacher, we know that it is
clear You are a man of integrity who teaches God's ways according
to the truth of His Word. You will not be influenced by the opinions
of men, caring nothing for their rational ideas. 17 So tell us what to
think about this. Should we pay taxes to Caesar, or not?"

18 Jesus perceived the malice behind their question and replied:
"You are hypocrites, all of you. Why do you want to trap Me like
this? 19-20 Bring me a coin used to pay taxes." When they gave Him
the coin, he asked them, "Whose portrait is this? And to whom does
this inscription refer?"

21 "Caesar," they answered.

Then Jesus told them: "Give to Caesar what you owe Caesar, but
give to God what you owe God."

22 They were speechless when they heard this and could only go
away silent.

Marriage at the resurrection (22:23-33)

23 Later on that same day, the Sadducees tried to trick Jesus with
another question. Now the Sadducees do not believe there is any
resurrection after death. 24 So they said: "Teacher, Moses decreed
that the brother of a man who dies childless must marry his widow
so she can bear children. 25 Now imagine there were seven brothers.
The first married, died childless and left the widow for his brother.
26 But he also died childless, as did a third brother, and so on until all
seven had married her in turn. 27 Then the woman also died. 28 So in
the resurrection, since all seven were married to her, whose wife
will she be?"

29 Jesus answered: "You know neither the scriptures nor God's
power, so you have no understanding. 30 There will be no marriage
at the resurrection, for everyone in heaven will be like the angels.

31-32 "Now concerning whether the dead are raised or not, have
you not read the words of God Himself: 'I am the God of Abraham,

the God of Isaac, and the God of Jacob'? So He is not God of the
dead but of the living!"
33 When the crowds heard what He said they were amazed at how
Jesus silenced His critics by teaching the truth.

The most important commandment (22:34-40)

34-36 Seeing how Jesus had dealt with the Sadducees, one of the
Pharisees who was an expert in the religious law, asked Him another
test question: "Teacher, which is the most important commandment
God has given in the law?"
37 Jesus answered: 'You are to love the Lord your God with all
your heart and with all your soul life, every aspect of your person-
ality, and with all your mind.' 38 This is the greatest and most important of God's commands. 39 The second is similar: 'You are to love
your neighbour in the same way that you already care about yourself and your own welfare.' 40 Everything that is taught in God's law
and by the Prophets is based on these two commandments to love."

Christ, Messiah, Lord (22:41-46)

41 Then Jesus put a question to the group of Pharisees who were
present. 42 "What do you believe about the Christ, the Messiah?
Whose Son is He?"
They replied: "He is the Son of David."
43-44 So Jesus asked them: "If that is the case, how could David,
speaking under the inspiration of the Holy Spirit, call Him 'Lord'?
For David says, 'The Lord said to My Lord, 'Sit down at My right
hand while I bring all Your enemies into subjection until they are all
under Your feet."
45 "If David calls the Messiah 'Lord', how could He be his son?"
46 Again there was silence; no one had any answer to His question.
In fact from that day no one else dared to put any more trick questions
to Jesus.

Jesus instructs His followers (23:1-12)

23 Then Jesus addressed both the crowds and His disciples:
2 "The teachers of the law and the Pharisees are to interpret
the scriptures correctly. 3 When they do so, you are to obey whatever
they teach you. But do not follow the example they set by the way
they live, for they do not put into practice themselves what they

22:37 Deuteronomy 6:5
22:39 Leviticus 19:18

tell others to do. 4 They place heavy burdens of legalistic religious
traditions onto people, and do nothing to help them be free of their
real burdens.

5 "Instead, they act in ways they think will impress others as to
how religious they are. They wear large boxes containing scripture
verses on their arms and their robes have long tassels, for they think
this will prove what great authority they have. 6 They are mere
show-offs who want the places of honour at public events and the
most prominent seats in the synagogues. 7 They feel so proud when
others acknowledge them in the market places and treat them with
deference calling them 'Master!'

8 "But you, My followers, are not to be called 'master,' for you are
all brothers who have only one Master. 9 Neither are you to call anyone here on earth your spiritual 'father', for you have only one
Father spiritually, and He is in heaven. 10 Neither are you to be
addressed as 'teacher', for you have only one Teacher, the Christ.

11 "The greatest ones among you will be those who are happy to
serve others. 12 For whoever tries to place himself in a position of
prominence will be humbled, but whoever is humble before God
and others will be placed in a position of prominence before God.

Jesus rebukes the Pharisees (23:13-39)

13 "You teachers of the law and you Pharisees are hypocrites and are
cursed. Not only do you fail to enter the Kingdom of heaven yourselves, but you prevent others from doing so. You shut the door to
the Kingdom in their faces, even though they want to enter. 14 You
teachers of the law and you Pharisees are hypocrites and are cursed
for you take advantage of widows and pray long pretentious
prayers for effect. Your punishment will be more severe as a result.

15 "You teachers of the law and you Pharisees are cursed because
of your hypocrisy. You will travel great distances by land or sea to
win a single person over to your own ways; but if he becomes one
of you, then you have only succeeded in making him twice as much
a son of hell as you are yourselves.

16 "You are cursed, you blind guides! You teach, 'It means nothing
if someone swears by the temple when he makes an oath. But if
someone swears by the gold of the temple then his oath is valid and
must be kept.' 17 What blind fools you are! Really, which is greater,
the gold or the temple itself that is sacred to God?

18 "You also have a saying, 'It means nothing if someone swears
by the altar; but if anyone swears by the gift laid on the altar, he is

bound by the oath he has taken.' 19 How blind you are! Which is greater? The gift or the altar that makes the gift sacred? 20 Because this is the case, if you swear by the altar you swear by all that has been laid on it. 21 Also he who swears by the temple swears by God who reveals His presence in the temple. 22 And if anyone should swear by heaven, he swears by God's throne and by the One who sits in Majesty upon it.

23 "You hypocritical teachers of the law and Pharisees are cursed. You are so particular about tithing all you receive, that you even give a tenth of your spices. Yet at the same time you fail to observe the more important aspects of God's law: justice, mercy and forgiveness. These are the things you should practise, while still giving the first tenth of all you receive. 24 You blind guides! You are so concerned not to swallow a fly, but end up swallowing a camel instead!

25 "You teachers of the law and you Pharisees are cursed. You are hypocrites. You are meticulous about cleansing the external things, such as the cups and dishes you use. 26 But inside, in your own hearts, you are full of greed and self-indulgence. Blind Pharisees! If you first clean the inside of the cup and dish, your own heart, then the external things will also be clean!

27 "You are cursed, you teachers of the law and you Pharisees. You are hypocrites! You are like tombs whitewashed on the outside to look good, but inside you are full of the bones of the dead and everything that is foul and unclean. You are just like that. 28 Outwardly you give the impression of being so righteous, but inwardly you are full of hypocrisy and evil.

29 "You are cursed, you teachers of the law and you Pharisees. What hypocrites you are! You build ornate tombs for the prophets you say you honour, and you decorate the graves of the righteous who you say you revere. 30 You even say, 'If we had lived in their times, we would not have treated them as our ancestors did. We would never have shed the blood of the prophets.' 31 Actually, you are testifying against yourselves, for you are the descendants of the very ones who murdered the prophets. 32 You may as well finish what they started!

33 "You are snakes, the sons of vipers! How can you escape being condemned and thrown into hell? 34 I will send you prophets, those who are truly wise, who speak and live according to the truth. And what will you do to them? Some you will kill and have crucified. Others you will flog in your synagogues and still others you will persecute in every town. 35 And so you will be guilty of joining the long line of those who have murdered the truly righteous, from the

murder of Abel through to the killing of Zechariah, the son of
Berekiah, who was even murdered in the temple between the altar
and the holy place.
36 "I tell you the truth; this judgment will come on you in this
present generation.
37 "O Jerusalem, Jerusalem, you have killed the prophets and
stoned those God sent to you. Yet often I have longed to gather your
children together as a hen gathers her chicks under her wings to
protect them; but you would not allow Me to do so. 38 Look now, you
have inherited a house that has become desolate. 39 For I tell you
clearly, you will not see Me again until you say, 'We bless Him who
comes in the Lord's name.' "

Jesus foretells the demolition of the temple (24:1-3)

24 As Jesus was walking away from the temple, His disciples
drew His attention to the magnificence of the building. 2 He
said to them: "All these buildings you see will be demolished. I tell
you the truth, not one stone will be left on another; everything will
be destroyed."
3 Later, when He was sitting on the Mount of Olives, the disciples
approached Him privately and said: "Please tell us when these
things will take place. And what signs shall we look for that will
indicate You are about to come again and this age is about to end?"

Signs of the times (24:4-36)

4 Jesus replied: "Be very careful that you allow no one to deceive
you. 5 Many will claim to come in My name saying, 'I am the Christ,'
and they will deceive many.
6 "You will hear news about wars and potential wars, but be sure
not to be alarmed. It is inevitable that such events will take place,
but this does not mean the end of time has come. 7 Nations will
make war on other nations, kingdoms will oppose other kingdoms.
There will be times of famine, and earthquakes will cause destruction
in several places. 8 Yet all such events are only the very beginning of
the terrible things that will take place.
9 "Then My followers will be persecuted, killed and hated simply
because they believe in Me. 10 During the testing times ahead many
will deny their faith in Me and will betray those they formerly
regarded as brothers. Their love will turn to hatred. 11 And many
false prophets will appear and deceive many people. 12-13 Wickedness

will increase to such an extent that the love of many will grow cold; but he who stands firm in his faith to the very end will be assured of salvation.

14 "Despite all this, the gospel of the Kingdom will be preached throughout the world, so that all nations may hear the truth; only when that has happened will the end come.

15 "Pay particular notice of this: the prophet Daniel spoke of the
ungodly object that desecrates the Holy Place. 16 When you see that
this has taken place then you will know it is time for those who live
in Judea to flee to the mountains. 17-18 There will be no time for anyone on the roof of his house to gather his belongings together; neither
will those caught out in the open have time to go home for their
clothes. 19 At that time it will be terrible for those who are pregnant
or have young babies.

20 "Pray that you will not have to flee during the winter or on the
Sabbath. 21 But there has never been such a time of distress to match
what will happen then, nor will such an event be equalled in the
future. 22 Unless God intervenes to cut short this time, no one would
be able to survive. However He will ensure that these days will be
restricted for the sake of those He has chosen.

23 "Should anyone say to you then, 'See, here is the Christ!' or 'He
is over there!' do not believe him. 24 False Christs and false prophets
will appear and will even perform great demonic signs and miracles
that will deceive some who believe in Me. That hardly seems possible,
but it will happen. 25 And then you will remember this warning that
I gave you beforehand.

26 "If someone tells you the Christ is out in the desert, do not go
there to search for Him. If they say, 'He is concealed here', do not
believe what they say. 27 For the Son of Man will come as swiftly as
a flash of lighting that can be seen everywhere from east to west.

28 "You can tell where there is a dead carcass by the vultures that gather in that place. So you will see the evidence that demonstrates that the end is near.

29 "During the aftermath of these terrible events, 'the sun will be darkened, the moon will give no light, the stars will fall from the skies and the heavens will be shaken.'

30 "Then the sign of the Son of Man will be seen in the sky, and
every nation on earth will mourn. They will behold the Son of Man
coming among the clouds in the sky, with power and great glory.
31 And with the loud sound of the trumpet He will send His angels

24:29 Isaiah 13:10, 34:4

to gather all those He has chosen from every direction of the earth and every part of heaven.

32 "Now learn an important lesson from the fig tree. As soon as its branches come into bud, you know that summer approaches. 33 In the same way, when you see the events I am describing you know that the time is near, as if it was knocking on your door.

34 "I tell you the truth, all these things will have taken place before the end of this generation.

35 "The heavens and the earth will end, but My words are eternal and will remain forever. 36 No one knows the exact timing of the end of all things, not the angels in heaven, not even the Son. This is known only to the Father.

The second coming of the Son of Man (24:37-51)

37 "The second coming of the Son of Man will be as it was in Noah's time. 38 Before the flood, people were living their normal lives, eating, drinking, getting married. It was like this right up to the day when Noah entered the ark. 39 They had no idea of what was about to happen. Then suddenly the flood came and they were all destroyed. This is what it will be like when the Son of Man comes again. 40 Two men will be working in a field; one will be taken, the other left. 41 Two women will be grinding the grain; one will be taken and the other left behind.

42 "So be on the alert because you do not know when your Lord will come for you.

43 "However you can understand this analogy: If the owner of the house had known when the thief intended to come and rob him, he would have been ready and waiting for him and would not have allowed the break-in to take place. 44 In the same way, you must be ready and waiting because the Son of Man will come at a time when you least expect Him.

45 "Who, then, will be considered to be a faithful and wise servant whom the master can trust to be in charge of the other servants in his household, to ensure they are provided for in the right way and are ready? 46 That servant will be well rewarded if his master finds him fulfilling his duties diligently when he returns. 47 I tell you most emphatically, his master will put him in charge of all he possesses.

48-49 "But what if that servant is evil and says to himself, 'My master has been away a long time,' so he begins to mistreat his fellow servants and indulges in drugs and drink? 50 His master will come when that servant is totally unprepared and has no expectation of his arrival.

51 And the master will deal savagely with him and condemn him to
be eternally with the other hypocrites, in the place where there will
be continual mourning and eternal suffering.

The parable of the ten bridesmaids (25:1-13)

25 "This future revelation of the Kingdom of heaven can be
likened to ten bridesmaids who took their lamps and went
to meet the bridegroom. 2 Five were foolish and five were wise.
3 Although the foolish ones took their lamps they did not take any
spare oil with them. 4 However, the wise took jars of oil as well as
their lamps.

5 "Now because the bridegroom was such a long time in coming,
they all became tired and fell asleep. 6 Then at midnight they heard
a shout, 'Here comes the bridegroom! Come and meet him.'

7 "All the bridesmaids awoke and prepared their lamps. 8 But the
foolish ones said to the wise, 'Our lamps are going out. Give us
some of your oil.'

9 "But the wise ones replied, 'No, there is not enough for all of us.
You must go and buy some oil for yourselves.' 10 But while on their
way to the store, the bridegroom arrived. The wise bridesmaids
were ready and followed him into the wedding feast. Then the
doors were shut.

11 "Later the foolish ones arrived. 'Sir! Sir!' they pleaded, 'Open
the door so we can come in.' 12 But the bridegroom responded: 'I tell
you the truth, I do not know you!'

13 "So be on the alert because you do not know the day or the time
when the Bridegroom will come for you!

The parable of the faithful servants (25:14-30)

14 "You can also compare the Kingdom of heaven to a man who,
because he was going to be away on a long journey, called his servants
together and gave them various sums of money to put to use. 15 To
one he gave five thousand, to another two thousand and to a third
one thousand, knowing they had different abilities.

16 "The man who had been entrusted with five thousand used the
money well and doubled the amount, making a further five thousand.
17 The servant who had been given two thousand also doubled the
amount and made a further two thousand profit.

18 "However, the man with the one thousand merely found a safe
place and hid his master's money.

19 "The master returned after a long time and called the servants to account for how they had used the money. 20 The man who had received five thousand brought the further five thousand profit he had made, saying, 'Master, I have doubled the five thousand you entrusted to me.'

21 "His master replied, 'You have done well. You are a good and faithful servant! You have proved your faithfulness in a small way; now I will give you much more responsibility. Come and share in your master's joy!'

22 "Then the man who had been given two thousand came forward and said, 'Master, I have doubled the two thousand you gave me to use.'

23 "His master replied, 'You also have done well and are a good and faithful servant. You have proved your faithfulness so now I can promote you. Come and share in my delight!'

24 "Then the man who had been entrusted with one thousand came forward and said, 'Master, I regarded you as a hard man, expecting to gather a harvest where you have not sown the seed yourself. 25 So in fear I went and put your money in a safe place. So here it is. I return what belongs to you.'

26-27 "His master replied, 'You are a wretched lazy servant! If you knew that I expected to gather a harvest where I have not sown personally, then you should at least have deposited my money in the bank, where it would have gained some interest by the time I returned.'

28 "Then he ordered, 'Take the thousand from him and give it to the one who now has ten thousand. 29 For everyone who is faithful in using what he has received will be given more, so much more that he will have an abundance. But those who are unfruitful in the way they use the little they have will end up with nothing; everything will be taken from them. 30 Throw this useless servant out into the spiritual darkness, where there will be continual mourning and eternal suffering.'

The sheep and the goats (25:31-46)

31 "When the Son of Man returns He will come in glory attended by angels; and He will sit on His throne in heavenly glory. 32 All the nations will be gathered before Him and as a shepherd separates the sheep from the goats, so He will divide the people into two groups. 33 Those who are His sheep He will place on His right; the goats will be on His left.

34 "The King will say to the sheep on His right, 'You are blessed by
My Father. So come and claim your inheritance, the Kingdom He
prepared for you since creation began. 35 For you fed Me when I was
hungry and you satisfied My thirst. When I came to you in the form
of a stranger, you invited Me in to stay. 36 When I needed clothing
you gave Me clothes. When I was sick you cared for Me. And when
I was in prison you came and visited Me.'

37 "Then the righteous, the sheep, will answer, 'Lord, when did we
see You hungry and feed You or when did we satisfy Your thirst?
38 When did we invite You in as a stranger or clothe You? 39 When did
we see You sick or in prison and visit You?'

40 "The King will then reply, 'I tell you the truth, whatever you did
for another person who I regard as My brother, you actually did for
Me.'

41 "But then the King will say to the goats on His left, 'Go away
from Me into the eternal fire made ready for the devil and his
angels, for you are cursed. 42 I was hungry but you gave Me nothing,
I was thirsty and you did not care. 43 I was a stranger and you
ignored Me. I was cold and you gave Me nothing to wear. I was sick
and in prison and you avoided Me.'

44 "Then the goats will answer, 'Lord when did we see You hungry
or thirsty or as a stranger or cold, sick or in prison, and did nothing
to help You?'

45 "The King will reply, 'I tell you the truth, when you failed to do
any of these things for other people who I regard as My brothers,
you refused to do them for Me.'

46 "Then the goats will suffer eternal punishment, but the righteous
sheep will enjoy eternal life."

The plot to arrest Jesus (26:1-5)

26 When Jesus had finished speaking these things publicly, He
said to His disciples in private: 2 "You know that it is only two
days to Passover when the Son of Man will be betrayed and crucified."

3-4 The high priest, Caiaphas, called together a meeting of the chief
priests and elders of the people to plan how they could have Jesus
arrested secretly and then killed. 5 "This must not happen during the
Feast or the people could riot," they concluded.

A woman anoints Jesus (26:6-13)

6 Meanwhile, Jesus was at Bethany in the house of Simon who had
been healed of leprosy. 7 A woman carrying an alabaster jar of very

expensive perfume approached Him while at the table, and poured
the perfume over His head. 8 The disciples were indignant at this.
"What a waste," they said. 9 "This perfume is so valuable it could
have been sold and the money given to the poor."

10 Jesus was aware of their concern and asked them: "Why are you
worried about what this woman has done? She has blessed Me in a
beautiful way. 11 You will always have the poor with you, but I will
not always be with you. 12 When this dear woman anointed My
body with the perfume, she was preparing it for My burial. 13 I tell
you the truth, what she has done for Me today will be told throughout the world in her memory, wherever the gospel is preached."

Judas betrays Jesus (26:14-16)

14-15 At this point Judas Iscariot, one of the twelve disciples, went to
the chief priests and asked them: "What will you give me if I betray
Jesus to you?" They agreed to give him thirty silver coins that they
counted out there and then. 16 So from that moment Judas looked for
a suitable opportunity to betray Jesus.

The Last Supper (26:17-29)

17 On the first day of the feast of Unleavened Bread, the disciples
came and asked Jesus: "Where do You want us to prepare the
Passover meal?"

18 He told them: "Go to a certain man in the city and tell him, 'The
Teacher says, 'My appointed time has arrived. I intend to celebrate
the Passover with My disciples in your house.'" 19 They went and
did as Jesus had ordered and prepared for the Passover.

20-21 While eating the evening meal with the twelve, Jesus said: "I
tell you the truth, one of you is about to betray Me."

22 This grieved them and one after another they asked Him:
"Surely, it could not be me, Lord?"

23 Jesus replied: "One of you who shares this meal with Me now
will surely betray Me. 24 The Son of Man will die in precisely the way
that has been written prophetically about Him. But the one who
betrays the Son of Man will be cursed! He will wish he had never
been born!"

25 Then Judas, the guilty one, said: "Surely you don't refer to me,
Master?"

Jesus replied: "Yes, you are the betrayer."

26 During the meal Jesus took some bread into His hands, gave
thanks to the Father, broke it and then gave it to His disciples saying:
"Take this and eat it; for this is My body."

27 Then He took a cup in His hands, gave thanks and passed it to His disciples saying: "Drink this, all of you. 28 The new covenant is being established in My blood that is poured out for many, so their sins might be completely forgiven. 29 I tell you clearly, that I will not drink wine again from now until I drink the heavenly wine with you in My Father's Kingdom."

Jesus predicts His disciples will disown Him (26:30-35)

30 When they had sung praises to God, they left for the Mount of Olives. 31 Jesus warned them: "Tonight all of you are going to desert Me because of what happens to Me, for it is written, 'God will strike the shepherd, and the sheep of His flock will be scattered.' 32 But when I have risen after My death, I will go ahead of you to Galilee where you shall see Me again."

33 Peter reacted: "Even if everyone else leaves You because of what happens to You, I will never do so."

34 Jesus told Him: "I tell you the truth, three times before the cock crows at dawn you will disown the fact that you even know Me."

35 But Peter insisted: "Even if it means I have to die with You, I will never disown You." And all the other disciples gave the same undertaking.

Gethsemane (26:36-46)

36 Jesus then went to a place called Gethsemane. He said to His disciples who went with Him: "Sit here while I go and pray by Myself." 37 He took only Peter , James and John with Him, and was obviously troubled and full of sorrow. 38 He told them: "I feel that I could die of grief, so great is My sorrow. Stop here and keep praying for Me."

39 Jesus went a little further by Himself, fell to the ground on His face and prayed: "My Father, please take this cup of suffering away from Me if this is at all possible. Yet I want your will above any desires of My own."

40 When He returned to the three disciples, He found them asleep. "Could you not pray for Me even for one hour?" He asked Peter. 41 "Wake up and pray that you will not be overcome by temptation. Your spirit is willing, but your body is so weak."

42 Jesus again went by Himself and prayed: "My Father, if it is not possible for this cup of suffering to be taken away, I simply resign Myself to Your will. I am ready to drink from this cup."

26:31 Zechariah 13:7

[43] When He returned to the disciples, He discovered they had fallen
asleep again; they had been unable to stay awake. [44] So He left them
and went to pray for a third time, submitting Himself again to His
Father's will!
[45] Then He returned to them and said: "Are you still sleeping and
resting? Wake up! The time has come for the Son of Man to be
betrayed into the hands of sinners. [46] Come on, let us go! Here comes
My betrayer!"

Jesus' arrest (26:47-56)

[47] Even as He was speaking, Judas, who was one of the twelve disciples,
arrived with a large crowd armed with swords and clubs. They had
been sent by the chief priests and the other religious leaders. [48] Judas
had arranged to give them a signal, 'The man you are to arrest is the
one I kiss.' [49] He went straight up to Jesus and said: "It is good to see
You, Master!" Then Judas kissed Him.
[50] Jesus said to him: "My friend, what have you come here to do?"
But the other men immediately grabbed hold of Jesus and arrested
Him. [51] One of those with Jesus drew his sword and struck out at the
high priest's servant, cutting off his ear.
[52] "Put your sword away," Jesus commanded Him. "All who
depend on the sword will die by the sword! [53] Surely you realise that
if I chose to do so I could call on My Father to help Me, and immediately He would put thousands of angels at My disposal! [54] But if I
was to do that, how could the scriptures be fulfilled that predict that
all this must happen?"
[55] Then Jesus addressed the crowd: "Do you think I am the leader
of a rebellion? Why have you come with swords and clubs to capture
Me? I sat teaching in the temple courts every day, yet you did not
arrest Me then. [56] However, what the prophets wrote has to be fulfilled."
At this point all the disciples left Him and fled.

Jesus before the chief priests (26:57-68)

[57] The crowd that had arrested Jesus took Him to the house of the
high priest, Caiaphas, where the teachers of the law and other religious
leaders had gathered together. [58] Peter followed at a safe distance
and even entered the courtyard of the high priest's house, where he
sat with the guards to see what would happen to Jesus.
[59] The chief priests and the whole Jewish Council were trying to
find witnesses to testify falsely against Jesus so they could justify
putting Him to death. [60] But although many false witnesses came
forward, none of them agreed with each other.

Finally, they found two that did agree. 61 "We heard this man say,
'I can destroy God's temple and rebuild it in three days.' "
62 Then the chief priest stood and addressed Jesus: "Do you have
no answer to this charge? Can you refute the testimony these witnesses bring against you?" 63 But Jesus said nothing.

So the high priest said to Him: "I charge you in the Name of the living God, tell us plainly: Are You the Christ, the Messiah, God's Son?"

64 "Yes, what you have said is the truth," Jesus replied. "And I tell all of you that the time will come when you will see Me as the Son of Man, sitting at the right hand of the Mighty One in heaven and coming on the clouds of glory!"

65 Then the high priest tore his clothes as a sign of his disgust and
said: "This is blasphemy! We do not need to look for any further
witnesses, do we? You have all heard for yourselves the blasphemy
He has spoken. 66 What is your judgment?"

"He deserves the death penalty," they answered.

67-68 Then they spit in Jesus' face and punched Him. Others struck Him saying: "Prophesy to us now, O Christ. Who hit You?"

Peter denies knowing Christ (26:69-75)

69 As Peter was sitting in the courtyard, one of the servant girls challenged him: "You were with this Jesus of Galilee, weren't you?"

70 He denied this in front of everyone. "I have no idea what you are talking about," he said.

71 He went to the entrance, but there another servant girl looked at him and said to the others: "This man was with Jesus of Nazareth."

72 Again Peter denied this: "I swear I do not know the Man!"

73 A little while later, the others approached Peter and said: "You must be one of His followers. Your accent gives you away."

74 Then Peter began to curse and swear: "I do not even know this Man!" No sooner had he spoken, than he heard the cock crow and immediately remembered what Jesus had said: "Before you hear the cock crow, you will declare three times that you do not even know Me."

75 And Peter went out and wept bitter tears of remorse.

Judas hangs himself (27:1-10)

27 In the early hours of the morning, the chief priests and other religious leaders passed judgment on Jesus and condemned

Him to death. 2 They had Him bound and handed Him over to
Pilate, the Roman governor.
3-4 When Judas, the betrayer, saw how Jesus had been condemned,
he was so filled with remorse that he wanted to return the thirty silver
coins to the chief priests and religious leaders, saying: "I have
sinned greatly in betraying One who was innocent."
5 "Why should that concern us?" they replied. "You are responsible
for your own actions." So Judas threw the money down on the floor
of the temple. He then went and hanged himself.
6 The chief priests picked up the money but said: "It would be
unlawful for us to put this into the temple treasury because it has
the mark of death on it." 7 So they decided to use it to buy the potters
place to bury foreigners. 8 It has been called the Field of Blood ever
since. 9-10 This fulfilled what was said by the prophet, Jeremiah:
'They took the thirty pieces of silver, the amount He was valued at
by the people of Israel, and used them to buy the potter's field, as
the Lord had determined.'

On trial before Pilate (27:11-14)

11 As Jesus stood before the governor, Pilate asked Him: "Are You
really the King of the Jews?"
"Yes, it is as you say," Jesus answered.
12 But when the chief priests and religious leaders brought their
accusations against Him, Jesus made no response. 13 So Pilate asked
Him: "Surely You hear these charges that are being brought against
You?" 14 But Jesus still remained silent, refusing to answer any of
these false accusations, much to the governor's astonishment.

Barabbas released (27:15-25)

15 Now it was the Roman custom to release a prisoner of the people's
choice at the time of the Feast. 16 A notorious criminal called
Barabbas was in prison at that time. 17 So when the people were
assembled, Pilate asked them: "Who do you want me to release,
Barabbas or Jesus, the Christ?" 18 He was well aware that the religious
leaders had only handed Jesus over to him out of jealousy, not
because He was guilty of any crime.
19 While he was sitting on the judgment seat, Pilate's wife sent
him a message, 'Don't become involved because I have had a terrible
dream on account of this Man. He is innocent!'
20 But the chief priests and religious leaders stirred up the crowd
to shout for Barabbas to be released and for Jesus to be executed.

21 So when Pilate put the question, 'Which of the two do you want me to release?' they shouted: "Barabbas!"

22 "Then what do you want Me to do with Jesus, the Christ?" Pilate asked. They all shouted: "Crucify Him!"

23 "Why?" Pilate asked. "What crime is He guilty of?"

But they only shouted more loudly: "Crucify Him!"

24 Pilate saw that reason was of no avail and he was fearful of a riot breaking out. So he called for a bowl of water to be brought and publicly washed his hands before the crowd saying: "I am innocent of the blood of this Man. This is your responsibility!"

25 All the people responded: "Let the responsibility for His death be on us and on our children!"

The Crucifixion (27:26-44)

26 So Pilate released Barabbas as they wished. Then he had Jesus flogged before handing Him over to the soldiers for crucifixion. 27 First they took Him to their barracks and gathered all the soldiers around Jesus. 28 They stripped Him and put a scarlet robe on Him. 29 They made a crown out of thorns twisted together and placed this on His head. Instead of a sceptre, they put a wooden stick in His hand and then knelt before Him in mock homage. "All hail, King of the Jews!" they said. 30 They spat on Him and struck Him on the head again and again with the stick they had given Him.

31 When they had finished mocking Him, they took the robe off Him and replaced His own clothes, before leading Him to the place of crucifixion.

32 On the way, they forced a man from Cyrene called Simon to carry the cross. 33-34 When they reached the spot known as the Place of the Skull, they offered Jesus a drink of wine mixed with bitter gall. On tasting it, Jesus refused to drink.

35 Then they crucified Him. While He hung on the cross, the soldiers divided His clothes among them by casting lots. The prophetic word had to be fulfilled, 'They divided My apparel among them and cast lots for My clothing.' 36 Then they sat down to keep watch while Jesus died.

37 They had placed the charge brought against Him above His head. It read: 'This is Jesus, the King of the Jews.' 38 Two thieves were crucified, one on either side of Him. 39-40 People passing by ridiculed Him. They shook their heads and shouted abuse: "You said You were going to destroy the temple and rebuild it in three days. Come

27:35 Psalm 22:18

on, then, save Yourself. If You really are God's Son, come down
from the cross!"
41 The chief priests and religious leaders joined in this mockery.
42 They said: "He was able to save others, but look at Him now. He
cannot even save Himself! Yet He says He is Israel's King! Well, if
He comes down from the cross now, we will believe Him. 43 He says
He trusts in God. Let God rescue Him then, if He truly belongs to
Him. After all, He claimed to be God's Son!" 44 The thieves, who
were crucified with Him, ridiculed Him in similar fashion and
heaped insults on Him.

Jesus' death (27:45-56)

45 Darkness fell across the whole land and lasted from noon until
three in the afternoon. 46 At about three o'clock Jesus cried loudly:
"My God, My God, why have you forsaken Me?"
47 "He is calling for Elijah," some of those around said when they
heard this. 48 One of them immediately filled a sponge with wine
vinegar, put it on a stick and lifted it to Jesus' lips. 49 The others said:
"Leave Him alone. We will see if Elijah comes to save Him!"
50 When Jesus had given a loud cry, He then gave up His spirit.
51 At that very moment the curtain concealing the Holy of holies
in the temple was torn apart from top to bottom. 52 The earth shook,
rocks were split apart, tombs were opened and many holy people
were raised from the dead. 53 They came out of the tombs and
appeared to many people in the holy city of Jerusalem after Jesus'
resurrection.
54 The earthquake and these other phenomena terrified the centurion
and soldiers guarding Jesus' body. "Truly, this was God's Son," they
said.
55-56 Present at His death were many women who had followed
Jesus from Galilee to care for Him. They watched from a distance
and among them were Mary Magdalene, Mary the mother of James
and Joseph, and the mother of James and John.

The Burial of Jesus (27:57-66)

57-58 Towards evening a wealthy man from Arimathea, called Joseph,
went to Pilate to ask for Jesus' body; and Pilate released the body to
him. 59-60 Joseph took the body, wrapped it in a clean linen cloth and
laid it in his own new tomb that had been carved out of the rock. He

27:46 Psalm 22:1

rolled a large stone over the tomb's entrance and left. [61] Mary Magdalene and the other Mary watched all this.

[62] The next day was the one that followed the Day of Preparation. The chief priests and Pharisees went to see Pilate [63] and told him: "Sir, we remember that before He died that deceiver said, 'I will rise again after three days.' [64] Please order that the tomb should be guarded and kept secure until after the third day, or His disciples may come and steal the body and then claim to everyone that He has been raised from the dead. This would be an even greater deception."

[65] Pilate told them: "Go and set guards at the tomb to make it as secure as possible." So they went and sealed the tomb and posted guards.

The Resurrection (28:1-15)

28 As dawn broke on the Sunday morning, Mary Magdalene and the other Mary went to the tomb. [2] Suddenly the earth shook violently and an angel of the Lord came from heaven, rolled back the stone that covered the tomb entrance and sat on it. [3] He appeared radiant with clothes that were brilliantly white. [4] The guards were so terrified that they shook with fear and then fell to the ground as if dead.

[5] The angel spoke to the women: "There is no need to fear, for I know that you have come looking for Jesus who was crucified. [6] He is no longer here; He has risen from the dead, as He promised He would. Come and you can see the place where His body lay. [7] Then go at once and give His disciples this message: 'Jesus has risen from the dead and is going ahead of you to Galilee where He will meet with you.'" The angel added: "I came to give you this message."

[8] So the women ran from the tomb, afraid and yet filled with joy, to relay the message to Jesus' disciples. [9] Suddenly Jesus was there before them. "Rejoice!" He said to them. They fell before Him, took hold of His feet and worshipped Him. [10] Then Jesus told them: "Do not be afraid. Go and tell My brothers to go to Galilee, where they shall see Me."

[11] Meanwhile, some of the guards went to the city to report to the chief priests about all that had happened. [12] The chief priests then met with the other religious leaders to devise a plan. They bribed the soldiers with a large sum of money [13] and told them: "You are to say that during the night His disciples came and stole His body while we were sleeping. [14] If the governor hears about this, we will speak to him on your behalf so that you are not punished." [15] The

soldiers accepted the money and said what they were told to say. As a result this fabrication has been spread widely among the Jews, even to this present day.

The disciples commissioned to go (28:16-20)

[16]The eleven disciples went to the mountain in Galilee were Jesus
had instructed them to go. [17]When they saw him they worshipped
Him, but some still had doubts. [18]Jesus told them: "All heavenly
and earthly authority has been given to Me. [19]So now I tell you to go
and make disciples in every nation. Baptise them in the Name of the
Father, the Son and the Holy Spirit. [20]Teach them to obey all that I
have taught and commanded you. And be assured of this: I am
always present with you, even to the end of this age."

THE GOSPEL ACCORDING TO

MARK

A messenger sent ahead (1:1-8)

1 This is the beginning of my account of the good news about
Jesus Christ, the Son of God.
[2]In the prophecy of Isaiah, God says: "I will first send my messenger
ahead of You to prepare the way for You.' [3]In the desert his voice
will be heard, proclaiming: 'Prepare for the Lord's coming; make
the way ready for Him.'"
[4]In fulfilment of these prophetic words, John baptised people in
a desert region. He preached a baptism, a complete cleansing from
sin, when people turned away from a life of sin and sought God's
forgiveness instead.
[5]His ministry had such impact that people from all over the country
districts of Judea, as well as the city of Jerusalem, made the pilgrim-
age to the place where he was baptising. They confessed their sins
before being baptised by him in the river Jordan.
[6]John's clothes were made of coarse camel's hair and he wore a
leather belt around his waist. He ate a diet of locusts and wild honey.
[7]His message was straightforward: "Someone far more powerful
than I am is coming after me. I am not worthy to do the work of a slave
for Him, to even untie the thongs of His sandals. [8]For I immerse you
in water, but He will immerse you in God's Holy Spirit."

The beginning of Jesus' ministry (1:9-15)

[9]During this period, Jesus came from Nazareth in Galilee to be baptised
by John in the Jordan. [10]As Jesus came out of the water, John saw the
heavens above Him open and the Holy Spirit of God come upon
Him like a dove. [11]A voice from heaven spoke, saying: "You are my
Son, whom I love; I am very pleased with You."
[12-13]The first thing the Holy Spirit did was to send Jesus into the
desert where He remained for forty days. During this time He was

1:3 Malachi 3:1, Isaiah 40:3

subjected to temptations from Satan. But angels protected Him from the danger of wild animals.

[14]When John had been put into prison, Jesus returned to Galilee and began to preach openly the good news God had sent Him to proclaim. [15]"It is time", He said, "God's Kingdom is now within your reach. Turn away from your lives of sin and believe the good news that you can have a new and better life!"

Disciples called to be 'fishers of men' (1:16-20)

[16]One day Jesus was walking on the shore of the Sea of Galilee when He saw Simon and his brother Andrew throwing their nets into the water, for they were fishermen. [17]Jesus called to them: "Come and follow Me and I will make you fishermen of a different kind; you will catch men!" [18]Without hesitating, they abandoned their nets and followed Him.

[19]A little further along the shore He saw James and his brother John, the sons of Zebedee, preparing their nets. [20]He called them in the same way and they, too, did not hesitate to leave their father Zebedee, together with the hired men, and follow Jesus.

Authority of Jesus demonstrated (1:21-39)

[21]Together they all went to Capernaum where, on the Sabbath day, Jesus went to the synagogue and began to teach. [22]People were amazed at the authority with which He taught them, an authority the teachers of the religious law did not possess.

[23-24]While He was speaking, a man who belonged to the synagogue and who was in the grip of an evil spirit shouted out: "What do You want with us, Jesus of Nazareth? Is it Your intention to destroy us? I know who You are. You are the Holy One God has sent!"

[25]Jesus addressed him sternly: "Quiet! Come out of him!" [26]The evil spirit caused the man to have convulsions and came out of him with a great shriek. [27]All the people were astounded at this and began to question among themselves: "What are we to make of this? First we hear a new teaching with a greater authority than anything we have heard before. Then He issues commands to evil spirits and they obey Him!" [28]It was no wonder that the news about Jesus spread rapidly throughout the whole region of Galilee.

[29-30]From the synagogue they went directly with James and John to the home of Simon and Andrew, who told Jesus that Simon's mother-in-law was in bed, sick with a fever. [31]So Jesus went to her and took her by the hand, helping her to her feet. Immediately the fever went and she was able to prepare a meal for them all.

[32]That evening when the sun was set, people came from all over the town, bringing the sick and demon possessed to Jesus. [33]It seemed the whole town was at the door. [34]Jesus healed many from a whole variety of diseases. He also freed many who were in bondage to demonic powers. However, He would not permit the demons to speak because they knew He was God's Son.

[35]It was very early on the next morning and still dark when Jesus got up and, leaving the house, went to an isolated spot where He could pray without being disturbed. [36]But Simon and the others went looking for Him. [37]When they found Jesus, they said: "Everyone is searching for You!"

[38]Jesus replied, "We will go to the other villages in this area so I can preach there as well. This is the reason why I have come." [39]So He journeyed throughout Galilee, preaching in the synagogues and setting people free from demonic powers.

Leper healed by Jesus (1:40-45)

[40]On one occasion, a leper came to Him, fell to his knees and pleaded with Jesus: "If You want to, You can make me clean."

[41]Jesus was immediately filled with compassion for the man. He reached out His hand, touched him and said: "Of course I want to heal you. Be cleansed." [42]Immediately the man was completely healed of the leprosy; no trace of it was left.

[43-44]Jesus dismissed him but first warned him strictly: "Make sure you do not tell anyone what I have done for you. Instead, go and show yourself to the priest to have your healing verified. Then go and make a sacrificial thank-offering as Moses commanded, as a public testimony." [45]But instead the man went and told everyone he met of the wonderful healing he had received. Consequently Jesus could not venture openly into any town; He would have been mobbed! Instead He remained outside the populated areas, but still people came to Him from everywhere.

Jesus heals and forgives a paralytic (2:1-12)

2 [1-2]Jesus returned to Capernaum a few days later. This became known and people gathered where He was staying; they were both inside and outside the house. No more could be packed in; and Jesus preached the gospel of the Kingdom to them. [3]Four men arrived carrying a paralysed man. [4]They could find no way of getting him close to Jesus, so they climbed onto the roof and made a hole in it, through which they lowered the paralysed man as he lay on his

mat. [5]Jesus perceived that this was an act of true faith, so He said to the man: "My son, all your sins are forgiven."

[6-7]Some teachers of the law were present and started muttering among themselves, questioning why Jesus should dare to say such a thing. To them this was blasphemy, for only God can forgive sins!

[8]Jesus was so spiritually sensitive that He knew precisely what they were thinking in their hearts and asked them: "Why do you think such things? [9]Would it be easier to say to this paralysed man, 'All your sins are forgiven', or would you say, 'Stand, pick up your mat and walk?' [10-11]However, to prove to you that the Son of Man has the authority on earth to forgive sins," Jesus then addressed the paralysed man, "I tell you now, stand, pick up your mat and go home." [12]The man immediately stood, picked up his mat and walked out of the meeting before their eyes. Everyone was amazed and praised God saying: "Never have we seen anything like this!"

Matthew called to follow Jesus (2:13-17)

[13]Later, Jesus was beside the lake and again a large crowd gathered around Him; so He taught them. [14]Afterwards, as He was walking along, He saw Levi, son of Alphaeus (otherwise known as Matthew), sitting at the place where he collected taxes from the people. Jesus simply said to him: "Follow me," and immediately Levi obeyed; he left his tax collecting and followed Jesus.

[15]Many other tax collectors and notorious sinners were present later when Jesus had dinner at Levi's house. Because such people were drawn by His teaching, they ate together with Jesus and His disciples. [16]This outraged the Pharisees and the teachers of the religious law. When they saw Jesus eating with such people they asked His disciples: "Why does your Master eat with tax gatherers and sinners?"

[17]Overhearing what they said, Jesus answered: "It is the sick who need a doctor, not the healthy. I have come to call sinners to turn away from their sin. The truly righteous people have already done that!"

Jesus questioned about fasting (2:18-22)

[18]A time of fasting was being observed by John's disciples and the Pharisees, but not by Jesus' followers. So some people asked Jesus: "Why is it that the disciples who follow John and the Pharisees observe this fast, but Your disciples do not?"

[19]Jesus replied: "Would you expect the guests at a wedding feast to fast while the bridegroom was with them? They would not

dream of doing so! [20]However, after the Bridegroom has been taken
away from them, then My disciples will fast.
[21]"You would not sew a piece of unshrunk cloth on an old piece
of clothing. If you did, the new piece would shrink when washed
and pull away from the older cloth, and you would end up with a
worse tear than you had when you started. [22]Likewise, you would
not pour new wine into old wineskins. No-one would think of
doing such a thing because he knows that when it ferments, the new
wine would cause the old hardened skin to burst, and then both the
wine and the wineskin would be useless. No, you know well enough
that you always pour new wine into new wine skins."

Jesus' authority greater than Sabbath rules (2:23-3:6)

[23]While Jesus was walking through a wheat field with His disciples
one Sabbath, they picked some of the grains of wheat. [24]This upset
the Pharisees. "Look at them", they said to Jesus. "Why do they do
what is unlawful on the Sabbath?" For they regarded this as work!
[25]Jesus answered them: "What did David and his followers do
when they were hungry and in need of food? Surely you have read
these scriptures! [26]When Abiathar was the high priest, David went
into God's house and dared to eat the consecrated bread that only
the priests are allowed to eat. And he gave some of this bread to his
men also."
[27]Then Jesus taught them this principle: "God made the Sabbath
for men's benefit; He did not make man to be in bondage to the
Sabbath. [28]The Son of Man is Lord over the Sabbath. His authority
is much greater than your Sabbath rules!"

3 On another occasion, a man with a shrivelled hand was present
when Jesus was in the synagogue. [2]His opponents were always
looking for some excuse to criticise Jesus, so they watched closely to
see if He would heal the man on the Sabbath.
[3]"Stand up here where everyone can see," Jesus said to the man
with the shrivelled hand. [4]Then Jesus turned to His detractors and
asked them: "Do you think it is right according to God's law to do
good or to do evil on the Sabbath? Would you save a life or take it
away?" They said nothing in reply.
[5]Their stubbornness angered and upset Jesus deeply. "Stretch out
your hand," He said to the man. When he obeyed, his hand was
healed completely. [6]The Pharisees were furious and went to the
supporters of Herod to plot with them how they could kill Jesus.

Demons recognise and submit to Jesus (3:7-12)

7 Together with His disciples, Jesus went to the lakeside, followed by a large crowd. 8 Because of the things He was doing, His reputation was spreading widely; many people came to Him from Judea, Jerusalem, Idumea and even as far as the area on the other side of the Jordan and the region around Tyre and Sidon.

9 To stop the people from crushing Him, Jesus told His disciples to position a small boat from which He could speak to everyone. 10 The problem was the direct result of all those He was healing, for others wanted to push through the crowd to touch Him personally.

11 When those demonised by evil spirits saw Jesus, they fell down before Him shouting: "You are God's Son." 12 So He commanded them with great firmness that they were to be quiet and not reveal who He was.

Twelve apostles appointed (3:13-19)

13 On another occasion, Jesus took His closest disciples onto the side of a mountain. 14-15 He then appointed twelve of them to be apostles, those who would be with Him consistently and who He could send out to preach the gospel of God's Kingdom, with the authority to free people from the demonic spirits that oppose that Kingdom.

16-17 The twelve He appointed were Simon, who also became known as Peter, James and his brother John, the sons of Zebedee, to whom Jesus gave the name 'sons of thunder'. 18-19 Also Andrew, Philip, Bartholomew, Matthew, Thomas, James the son of Alphaeus, Thaddaeus, Simon who belonged to the party of zealots and Judas Iscariot who betrayed Him.

Jesus accused of being possessed (3:20-30)

20 Later, when Jesus and His disciples went to a house for a meal, they could not eat because so many people crowded into the place. 21 Members of His family heard of this and came to intervene, saying: "This whole thing is getting out of hand. He must be out of His mind."

22 The teachers of the law, who had come to Galilee from Jerusalem, said far worse things: "He is possessed by the devil; this is why He can drive out demons, for they have to submit to the prince of demons."

23 So Jesus addressed the people directly, using analogies: "How can it be possible for Satan to drive himself out? 24 Any kingdom divided against itself cannot last. 25 The same is true of any group

of people; where there is division they cannot prevail. 26 So if Satan
is opposing himself, that is the end of him; his dominion cannot last.
27 "The truth is that it is not possible for anyone to enter the house
belonging to a strong man to rob him of his possessions unless he
first binds up the strong man. Only then can he rob his house. 28 I tell
you the truth, every sin and blasphemy that people have committed
will be forgiven when they repent. 29 However, anyone who curses
the Holy Spirit will never be forgiven; his sin is eternal and his guilt
will remain."
30 Jesus said this in response to their accusation that an evil spirit
was working through Him.

Jesus' true family (3:31-35)

31-32 At this point, Jesus' mother and brothers arrived at the scene.
Being outside because of the crowd, they had a message passed to
those who were close to Him: "Your mother and brothers are outside waiting for You."
33 "Who are My mother and brothers?" Jesus asked. 34 Then He
looked at those seated around Him and said: "These are My mother
and brothers. 35 Anyone who does God's will is My brother and sister
and mother!"

Parable of the sower (4:1-20)

4 Later, Jesus was again teaching by the lake and the usual large
crowd gathered around Him, so large that He had to sit in a
boat as He spoke while all the people listened on the lake-shore. 2 He
used many parables, vivid illustrations, to explain God's Kingdom
to them.
3 On this occasion He said: "Listen closely to Me! It was time for
a farmer to sow his seed. 4 As he scattered the seed, some of it fell on
the path where the birds quickly devoured it. 5 Other seed fell on
rocky ground where there was little soil. 6 At first it seemed to take
root, but the young shoots were quickly scorched by the sun's heat
and ruined, because the shallowness of the soil prevented the seed
from being deeply rooted.
7 "Other seed fell among thorns. Even though the good seed
began to grow, it was choked by the growth of the weeds, so that it
never survived for the harvest. 8 However, some of the seed the
sower scattered fell on good soil. The seed grew and ripened so that
it multiplied, producing a crop thirty, sixty, even a hundred times
what was sown."

9 Then Jesus added: "Let the one who has ears open to the truth
hear what I am saying."

10 Later, the twelve disciples and their friends came to Jesus when
He was alone and asked Him why He used such parables when He
spoke. 11-12 He told them: "The secret about God's Kingdom is given
to you because you believe in Me. But I always use parables because
those who do not believe in Me are as those described in the prophecy
which says, 'They are always looking, but never seeing the answer.
They listen but never understand what is said. If they were able to
receive the revelation given, they would turn to God and be forgiven!' "

13 Then Jesus challenged them: "Are you saying that you do not
understand the parable that I gave about the sowing of the seed? I
will explain it to you. 14 The seed the farmer sows is the Word about
God's Kingdom. 15 Some people are like the path where some of the
seed falls. They hear what is said, but Satan immediately steals the
Word so that it does not take root in their hearts. 16 Others are like
rocky soil. They hear the Word and their immediate response is a
joyful one. 17 But the joy is short-lived because the Word does not
take deep root in their hearts. So as things become difficult, or they
are persecuted, they give up. 18-19 The thorny soil where other seeds
fell represents those who seem to receive the Word of truth, but
there are other things that they allow to grow in their lives and these
choke the revelation of God's Kingdom, such things as anxiety,
trusting in material wealth and possessions and the natural sinful
desires to please self. So the revelation of the truth never ripens and
come to fruitfulness in their lives.

20 However, those represented by the good soil not only hear the
Word, they believe it and put it into practice; so they enjoy a harvest
in their lives. They are able to multiply what was sown in their
hearts, thirty, sixty, even a hundred times over!"

Analogy of a lamp (4:21-25)

21 Jesus also asked them: "Do you place a lamp under the bed or
somewhere hidden? Of course not; you put it in a prominent place
where it can give light. 22 Whatever is hidden is only waiting to be
discovered; something concealed will become revealed. 23 Let the
one who has ears open to the truth, hear what I am saying."

24 Jesus added: "Be very careful what you listen to. For here is
another spiritual principle: whatever you do, the same will be
measured back to you. 25 The one who has My life will be given still
more; but whoever does not have that life, whatever he does have
will be taken from him."

Parable of growing seed (4:26-29)

26-27 Jesus spoke further about God's Kingdom in this way: "God's Kingdom develops like this: When a man scatters seed on the ground, it sprouts and grows night and day whether he sleeps or is awake. 28 The natural growth process is taking place irrespective of what he does. First you see the stalk growing out of the soil, then the head develops and finally the full grain in the head. 29 When it is ripe it is time to harvest the crop."

Parable of a mustard seed (4:30-34)

30 Jesus used another illustration: "How can we describe God's Kingdom; what parable can we use? 31-32 God's reign can be likened to a mustard seed. Although it is only a tiny seed, when planted it grows into such a large plant that birds come and perch in its branches and shelter under it."

33 Jesus used many similar parables when He spoke to the people, describing how God's Kingdom could grow within and among them. 34 He always used these illustrations to help their limited understanding. To His disciples He explained everything clearly, but only when alone with them.

Calming of the storm (4:35-41)

35 On the evening of that same day, Jesus told His disciples that they would cross to the other side of the lake. 36 So leaving the crowd, they took Jesus with them in one of the boats. 37 A sudden storm arose and the waves began to break over the side of the boat, causing it almost to sink. 38 Jesus was sleeping on a cushion in the stern, but in panic the disciples woke Him: "We are drowning, teacher; don't You care?"

39 Jesus stood up and commanded the wind and waves: "Quiet! Be still!" Immediately the wind died down and the sea was completely calm.

40 "Why are you afraid?" He asked the disciples. "Is your faith still so weak?"

41 They were in such awe that all they could do was question among themselves: "Who can this be? He commands even the wind and the waves and they obey Him!"

Demons cast into herd of pigs (5:1-13)

5 They crossed the lake to the region of the Gerasenes. 2 A man in bondage to an evil spirit came from among the tombs, where he lived, to meet Jesus as soon as He landed. 3 Nobody could control

this man. Even if people bound him with chains he would tear them
off. 4 They had often chained his hands and feet, but to no avail; no
one was strong enough to control him. 5 He lived among the tombs
or in the hills by day and night, often crying out desperately and
cutting himself with stones.

6 Seeing Jesus in the distance, he ran to meet Him and threw himself down on his knees before Him. 7 Then he shouted with all his
might: "Jesus, Son of the Most High God, what are You going to do
to me? Swear to God that You will not torture me!"

8 He said this because Jesus was already addressing the evil spirit
in the man: "Come out of him, you foul spirit!"

9 Jesus asked the man his name. He replied: "My name is Legion,
for I am possessed by many demons." 10 He kept pleading with Jesus
not to send these evil spirits anywhere else. 11-12 Instead the demons
begged Jesus to send them into a large herd of pigs that was feeding
on a hillside nearby, and Jesus agreed to this. 13 The evil spirits came
out of the man and entered the pigs, who then rushed down the
hillside into the lake where they drowned. There were about two
thousand of them.

Delivered man testifies to many (5:14-24)

14 The swine-herds ran off and told people in the town and surrounding area what Jesus had done. Many went to see for themselves
what had happened. 15 When they arrived at the place, they saw
Jesus together with the man now liberated from the legion of
demons that had possessed him. He was sitting calmly in his right
mind and was now dressed properly. The people were awestruck.

16 Those who had witnessed what had taken place told them how
the demon-possessed man had been set free by Jesus, and how the
demons had entered the pigs instead. 17 Out of fear, the people
begged Him to leave the area.

18 As Jesus was boarding the boat, the man who had been set free
pleaded to be allowed to go with Him. 19 Jesus did not agree to this,
but told him: "Go home, and tell your family about all the Lord has
done to set you free because He had mercy on you." 20 The man did
as Jesus said and began to travel around the area of the Ten Towns
telling people about all Jesus had done for him. Everyone who
heard his testimony was amazed.

21 Jesus again crossed the lake by boat and, as usual, a large crowd
gathered as soon as He landed. 22-23 Among the people was one of the
synagogue leaders called Jairus. As soon as he saw Jesus he came

and fell at His feet and desperately pleaded with Him: "My little daughter is dying. Please come and lay Your hands on her, for then she will be healed and will live." So Jesus went with him.

Woman healed by touching his garment (5:25-34)

24 A large crowd followed and were pushing and shoving from all sides, out of a desire to be near Jesus. 25 Among them was a woman who had suffered from bleeding for twelve years. 26 She had spent all her money on doctors to try to alleviate her suffering, but all to no avail; the problem had only become worse. 27-28 Having heard about Jesus, she pushed her way through the crowd, came up behind Him and touched His clothing because she thought, 'To touch His clothes will be enough; I will then be healed.' 29 Sure enough, as soon as she touched Him the bleeding stopped and she knew that her body was healed and her suffering ended.

30 When she touched Him, Jesus knew that power had flowed out of Him. He turned around and asked those nearest Him in the crowd: "Who touched my clothes?"

31 His disciples said: "You can see how many are pushing and shoving to be near You. Why do You ask such a question, so many are trying to touch You?"

32 Jesus would not be deterred but kept looking round to see who had touched Him, not just physically but with faith. 33 The woman, knowing she had been healed, came forward and fell on her knees before Jesus, afraid that He would be displeased. She told Him truthfully what she had done and why.

34 Jesus was not angry or upset. Far from it, for He said to her: "My daughter, you are healed because you showed such faith. You can go in peace and remain free, for your days of suffering are over."

Jairus' daughter raised to life (5:35-43)

35 During this conversation, some members of Jairus' household arrived with the news that the synagogue leader's daughter had died. "There is no point in troubling the teacher any further," they said.

36 Ignoring this, Jesus said to Jairus: "There is no cause to be afraid; continue to believe."

37 Now Jesus would not allow any of the crowd to follow Him; He took only Peter, James and John with Him. 38 By the time they arrived at Jairus' house there was already a great noise caused by people crying and mourning.

39 Jesus went into the house and asked them: "Why are you making
all this noise? The child is only asleep; she is not dead." But they
only laughed at Him for they knew the girl had certainly died.
40 He told them all to leave the house; then He took the child's
parents together with His three disciples into the child's room. 41 He
took her by the hand and said to her: "Little child, I say to you get
up!" 42 The girl stood up immediately and walked around, for she
was about twelve years old. 43 All present were amazed, but Jesus gave
strict instructions not to tell anyone about how this had happened.
He told them to give the girl something to eat.

A prophet without honour (6:1-6)

6 Jesus then left that place to return to His home town, Nazareth,
together with His disciples. 2 He taught in the synagogue on the
Sabbath and those who heard Him were amazed at what He said.
"Where did He learn all these things?" they asked. "He has been
given such great wisdom. And look at the miracles He performs!
3 But He is only the carpenter's son, isn't He? He is Mary's son and
we know His brothers James, Joseph, Judas and Simon, and His
sisters as well." So they chose to be offended by Him, instead of
believing in Him.
4 Jesus told them: "A prophet is not honoured in his own town or
by his relatives, even his own family." 5-6 Because they rejected Him,
Jesus was unable to perform many miraculous works there. A few
were healed because He laid hands on them, but Jesus was amazed
and saddened by the unbelief of the majority of the people.

Twelve sent out in pairs (6:7-13)

So Jesus then travelled from village to village teaching. 7 He sent out
the twelve disciples in pairs, having given them authority over the
evil spirits that put people into bondage. 8 He gave them these
instructions: "Take only the bare essentials for your journey. You
will not need to take food, baggage or money. 9 You will have the
clothes and sandals you stand up in, and they will prove sufficient.
10 Stay in the same house until you leave that place. 11 However, if
you come to a place where people will not welcome you and who
reject what you say, shake the dust of that place off your feet when
you leave, as a witness against them."
12 The twelve disciples went, preaching everywhere that people
should repent of their sins and turn to God. 13 They drove out
demons from many people and anointed the sick with oil, and they
were healed.

Account of John the Baptist's death (6:14-29)

14 King Herod heard of what was happening, for Jesus' reputation
was now widespread. Some suggested: "This must be John the
Baptist back from the dead; this is why He has such miraculous
powers working through Him."

15 Others thought that He was the prophet Elijah. And still others
said that He was a prophet like those who had lived centuries
before. 16 Herod himself said: "He must be John raised from the
dead, the man I beheaded."

17-18 It was on Herod's orders that John had been arrested, bound
and thrown into prison. Herod had married Herodias, who had been
his brother Philip's wife, an action that John denounced, telling
Herod: "It is not lawful for you to marry your brother's wife."

19 Herodias, seized with anger against John, wanted to kill him.
20 Herod would not agree to this because he was actually afraid of
John. He thought it better to protect him, for he recognised that he
was a righteous and holy man of God. He would listen to what John
said with interest, but without understanding.

21 To celebrate his birthday, Herod gave a banquet for the state
officials, military commanders and the leaders from Galilee. This
provided Herodias with the opportunity she had been longing for.
22 Her daughter danced for the assembled guests and this pleased
them and Herod so much that he said to her: "You can ask me for
anything you want and I promise to grant your wish. 23 Yes, I swear
to that. Even if you ask me for half my kingdom, I will give it to you."

24 The girl went and asked her mother: "What shall I ask for?"
Herodias answered: "The head of John the Baptist."

25 The girl quickly returned to Herod with her request: "I want
you to give me the head of John the Baptist on a dish – immediately!"

26 This caused the king great distress, but as he had made an oath
in front of the dinner guests, he could hardly refuse the girl's
request. 27-28 So he ordered that John be executed immediately and
his head brought on a dish. The executioner went and beheaded
John in the prison and returned with the head on a dish, as ordered.
He gave it to the girl who in turn gave it to her mother.

29 When they heard what had happened, John's disciples came for
his body and laid it in a tomb.

Jesus continues to teach (6:30-34)

30 When the apostles returned to Jesus, they told Him what they had
taught and the things they had done. 31 As usual, many people were

coming and going so that Jesus and the disciples did not have time
to eat. So Jesus said to them: "Come with me by yourselves. We will
go somewhere quiet together to rest."
32 So Jesus and the twelve went by boat and headed for a lonely
place. 33 However, many in the crowd saw them leave and ran
around the edge of the lake to arrive before they did. They came
from all the towns in the area.
34 When Jesus landed, there was already a large crowd awaiting
Him. Seeing them, His heart went out to them, for they were like
sheep without a shepherd to care for them. Moved with this compassion, He taught them many truths.

Feeding of the five thousand (6:35-44)

35 By now it was getting late, so His disciples came to Jesus and said:
"This is such a remote place and it is now very late. 36 Why not send
the people away so they can find something to eat in the villages in
the surrounding area."
37 "You give them something to eat yourselves," replied Jesus.
"That would require a vast amount of money, at least a man's
wages for many months," the disciples said. "Are you suggesting
that we should go and buy all that bread for them so they can eat?"
38 "Go and see how many loaves you have already," Jesus told
them.
After searching, they found that the total was only five loaves,
and two small fish.
39-40 So Jesus told the disciples to make all the people sit down on
the ground in groups of a hundred or fifty. 41 Then He took the five
loaves and the two fish, looked towards heaven and gave thanks to
God over them. He then broke the loaves in pieces and gave them
to the disciples to distribute among the people. He did the same
with the two fish.
42-43 Everyone ate as much as he or she wanted before the disciples
collected the remaining pieces of bread and fish, filling twelve baskets.
44 The number of men alone who had eaten was five thousand!

Jesus walks on the lake (6:45-52)

45 Then Jesus told the disciples to return to the boat at once and go
ahead of Him to Bethsaida, while He sent the crowd of people away.
46 When He had done so, Jesus then walked up the mountainside to
find a suitable place to pray alone.
47 By evening He was still on land while the disciples' boat was in
the middle of the lake. 48-49 He could see that they were struggling to

row against the strong headwind. In the early hours of the morning
Jesus walked on the lake in their direction. It seemed that He was
going to walk straight past them, but the disciples saw Him.
Thinking this must be a ghost, they cried out in fear.
[50]Jesus called to them immediately: "Have courage all of you. It
is I; don't be afraid!" [51]As soon as He climbed into the boat to be
with them, the wind died down. The disciples were awestruck.
[52]They had failed to understand from the multiplication of the
loaves that they were now experiencing the miraculous. They still
did not expect the supernatural, their minds were so conditioned by
natural thinking.

Many healed at Gennesaret (6:53-56)

[53]Having crossed the lake they landed at Gennesaret where they
anchored the boat. [54]No sooner had they landed than people recognised
Jesus. They ran throughout the area with the news. [55-56]So people
came from the entire region bringing the sick with them on mats to
whatever village, town or country area where Jesus happened to be.
They would place the sick in the market places, desperate that they
should be able to touch just the edge of His clothing. And all who
touched Him were healed!

What comes out of a man makes him unclean (7:1-23)

7 Some Pharisees and teachers of the law came from Jerusalem to
confront Jesus. [2]They noticed that some of His disciples ate
food without washing their hands in the ritual way; so they were
considered 'unclean'. [3]It should be explained that the Pharisees and
other Jews washed their hands in a ceremonial way before they ate,
as this is the tradition of their elders. [4]When they come in from
work, or even shopping, they never eat unless they wash first. (In
fact they keep many such traditions including the washing of cups,
jugs and kettles.)
[5]So these Pharisees and teachers of the law told Jesus: "Your disciples should live by the traditions of the elders, instead of eating
with unclean hands! Why don't they?"
[6]Jesus replied: "Isaiah prophesied correctly about you hypocrites
when he wrote: 'These people honour Me with what they say, but
there is no honour for Me in their hearts. [7]So their worship is futile
and their teachings only a load of rules made up by men.'

7:7 Isaiah 29:13

8 "Do you see where you have gone wrong? You have replaced God's commands with a series of your own traditions. 9 You are intent on keeping your own traditions instead of God's Word! 10 For example, Moses said, 'Honour your father and your mother;' he also said, 'Anyone who curses his father or mother must be put to death!' 11 But you have replaced these words with your own teaching. You suggest a person can say to his parents, 'What I might have given to help you, I have devoted to God instead!' 12 Consequently you say he has to do nothing to help his father or mother.

13 "This is typical of the way you cancel out God's Word by believing instead your own traditions, handed down through the generations. Yes, you do this in many ways."

14 Then Jesus called to the crowd to listen to what He said: "Listen to me all of you and understand what I say clearly to you. 15 A man cannot be made unclean by anything outside of him. No, it is what comes from within him that makes him unclean and causes him to sin."

17 After teaching the crowd, Jesus entered the house and His disciples asked Him about what He had just said. 18 "Are you so lacking in understanding?" Jesus said. "Isn't it obvious that nothing that enters a man from outside makes him unclean in God's eyes? 19 The food he eats goes into his stomach, not his heart. In due course it passes out of his body." (From this, it was obvious that Jesus declared all foods to be 'clean' and therefore permissible to eat.)

20-22 Jesus continued to explain: "It is what comes out of a man, from his own heart, that makes him unclean, such things as evil thoughts, sexual immorality, theft, murder, adultery, greed, malice, deception, lust, envy, slander, pride and foolishness. 23 These evils start in a person's heart and these are what make him unclean before God."

Gentile woman's faith honoured (7:24-30)

24 Jesus journeyed on to the area of Tyre and Sidon, where He could stay without this becoming public knowledge; but it was impossible to keep His presence secret. 25-26 There was a Greek woman born in Syrian Phoenicia whose small daughter was demonised. She discovered where Jesus was staying and came and fell at His feet, begging Jesus to set her daughter free from the demon within her.

27 Jesus replied: "First the children should eat what they want, for it is not right to throw the children's bread to the dogs."

7:10 Exodus 21:17

[28] "I agree, Lord," the woman replied, "but even the dogs under
the table are allowed to eat the children's crumbs."

[29] "For such a faith response, you may go," Jesus told her. "The
demon has now left your daughter."

[30] The woman returned home to find her child lying on the bed,
the demon gone.

Deaf and dumb man healed (7:31-37)

[31] Jesus then left the area of Tyre, travelled through Sidon to the Sea
of Galilee and then into the region of the Ten Towns. [32] While there,
a deaf man who was barely able to speak was brought to Him by
some people. They pleaded with Jesus to lay hands on the man to
heal him.

[33] Jesus took him to one side away from the crowd. First He put
His fingers into the man's ears. Next, He placed some of His spittle
on the man's tongue. [34] Then He looked toward heaven, sighed
deeply and said to the man: "Be opened." [35] Immediately the man's
ears were opened and he could hear; his tongue was released and
he could speak clearly.

[36-37] Jesus ordered the people not to tell anyone of this. But no matter
what He said, they kept telling everyone about such things that
Jesus did, causing great amazement among the people. They said of
Him: "Everything He does, He does well. He even enables the deaf
to hear and the dumb to speak!"

Jesus feeds 4000 (8:1-9)

8 During His time there, another large crowd gathered and had
nothing to eat. Jesus gathered His disciples around Him and
said: [2] "I feel great compassion for all these people; for three days
they have been here with Me without anything to eat. [3] If I send
them away now they will collapse on the way home for lack of
nourishment, for some have travelled far to be here."

[4] "But where in a remote place like this could we buy enough
bread to feed them?" His disciples asked.

[5] "How many loaves do you have? "Jesus asked them.

"Seven," they replied.

[6] Telling the people to sit on the ground, Jesus then took the seven
loaves and gave thanks to God over them. He broke them and gave
the pieces to the disciples to distribute among the people. [7] They
also had a few small fish. Jesus gave thanks for them and told the

disciples to share them out among the people. [8]Everyone ate as
much as he wanted. Then the disciples filled seven baskets with the
remaining pieces. [9]About four thousand men were present and had
been fed.

Yeast of the Pharisees and Herod (8:10-21)

[10]Then Jesus dismissed the crowd and went with His disciples by
boat to the region of Dalmanutha. [11]Again, Pharisees came to ask
Jesus testing questions. They wanted Him to perform some heavenly
sign to prove who He was. [12]Jesus sighed deeply and asked: "Why
does this generation want a miraculous sign? I tell you emphatically,
that no such sign will be given to it." [13]Then Jesus left them,
returned to the boat and crossed to the other side of the lake.

[14]The disciples had forgotten to bring food. They had only one
loaf with them in the boat. [15]Jesus warned them: "Be careful of the
yeast of the Pharisees and of Herod."

[16]They discussed among themselves what Jesus meant, concluding
that it must be something to do with their lack of bread. [17]Aware of
what they were saying, Jesus asked: "Why do you talk about your
lack of bread? Are you still unable to understand? Are your hearts
so hardened to the truth? [18]Are you guilty of having eyes yet you fail
to see, and ears yet you fail to hear? [19]Don't you remember what
happened when I fed the five thousand with five loaves? How
many baskets full of the remnants did you pick up then?"

"Twelve," they replied.

[20]"What about when I fed the four thousand with some loaves?
How many baskets did you fill then?"

"Seven," they replied.

[21]"Do you still not understand?" Jesus said to them.

Blind man healed (8:22-26)

[22]They arrived at Bethsaida where some people brought a blind
man, pleading with Jesus to heal him. [23]He took the man by the
hand and led him outside the village. He placed some of His spittle
on the man's eyes, laid His hands on him and asked: "Are you able
to see?"

[24]The man looked up and said: "I can see people, but they are
walking around looking like trees."

[25]Jesus again placed His hands over the man's eyes. When he
opened them, he could see perfectly; his sight was totally restored.
[26]Jesus told him to go straight home without going into the village.

Christ the Messiah, God's Son (8:27-30)

27 Jesus and His disciples continued on their way to the villages around Caesarea Philippi. There He asked them: "What are the people saying about Me? Who do they think I am?"

28 They replied: "Some say You are John the Baptist; others think You are Elijah and others say You must be one of the prophets."

29 "What about you; who do you say I am?" Jesus asked them.

"You are the Christ, the Messiah, God's Son," Peter answered.

30 Then Jesus warned them not to reveal His true identity to anyone else.

Jesus predicts His death (8:31)

31 Now they knew for certain who He was, Jesus began to teach them that the Son of Man would have to suffer many things. He would be rejected by the elders, chief priests and teachers of the law. It would even be necessary for Him to be killed, but He would rise again on the third day afterwards. What He said was very clear.

Jesus rebukes Peter (8:32-33)

32 But Peter took Him to one side and dared to rebuke Him; he could not believe such things would happen to Jesus.

33 Jesus turned towards the disciples and then rebuked Peter: "Get behind me Satan!" He said. "You have nothing to do with the truth of God, only with sinful men."

The cost of following Jesus (8:34-9:1)

34 Then Jesus addressed the crowd as well as the disciples, saying:
"Anyone who wants to be a follower of Mine will have to deny himself and be prepared to take up his own cross of sacrifice for the
gospel. Then, and only then, will he be able to follow Me. 35 For anyone who is intent on saving his own life will actually lose it. But
whoever is prepared to give his life wholeheartedly for Me and for
the gospel, he is the one who will enjoy salvation. 36 What is the use
of accumulating riches and all that this world offers, if in the
process you lose your own soul? 37 What can you possibly give in
exchange for your soul? 38 I tell you, this is an adulterous and sinful
generation; if anyone is ashamed to bear witness about Me and
what I say in this generation, the Son of Man will be ashamed of
him when He comes again in His Father's glory together with His
angels."

9 Then Jesus added: "I tell you the truth, some of you here today
will know that God's Kingdom has come into your lives with
power before you die."

The Transfiguration (9:2-10)

2 Six days later, Jesus took Peter, James and John up a high mountain
where they could be alone together. Suddenly He was transfigured
before their eyes. 3 His clothes shone brilliantly, whiter and brighter
than any natural bleach could effect. 4 Elijah and Moses appeared
with Jesus and were talking with Him.

5 Hardly knowing what to say, Peter blurted out: "Rabbi, it is so
wonderful for us to be here. Let us erect three canopies – one for You
and one each for Moses and Elijah." 6 They felt really frightened.

7 Then a cloud fell and enfolded them, and a voice spoke from the
cloud: "This is my Son, who I love greatly. Listen to what He says!"
8 Suddenly the cloud disappeared and only Jesus was standing
there alone. 9 As they came down from the mountain, Jesus warned
them not to tell anyone what they had seen until after the Son of
Man had risen from the dead. 10 So they told no one, but discussed
among themselves what 'rising from the dead' meant.

Disciples question Jesus about Elijah (9:11-13)

11 They asked Jesus: "Why do the teachers of the law say that Elijah
must come before the Messiah comes?"

12 Jesus replied: "This is right, Elijah does come first, so that everything might be restored, to call people back to God. 13 I tell you clearly that Elijah has already come and they did to him what they
wanted, as was predicted about him. Why then is it also written that
the Son of Man must suffer greatly and be rejected?"

Boy delivered from an evil spirit (9:14-29)

14 When they joined the other disciples, they saw that a large crowd
had gathered around them and the teachers of the law were arguing
with them. 15 When the people saw Jesus approaching they ran to
meet Him, overcome with joy.

16 "What is the argument about?" He asked. 17 A man in the crowd
answered, "Teacher, I brought my son to You. He is possessed by a
spirit that has struck him dumb. 18 At times he is thrown to the
ground by the seizures he has. He foams at the mouth, grinds his
teeth and his joints become rigid. As You were not here, I asked
Your disciples to drive the evil spirit out of the boy but they have
been unable to do so."

19 "What an unbelieving generation this is!" said Jesus. "How
much longer must I stay with you? How much longer do I have to
put up with your unbelief? Bring the boy here to Me."

20 They did so, but as soon as the spirit in the boy saw Jesus it
immediately threw him into a seizure. He fell to the ground and
rolled from side to side, foaming at the mouth. 21 "How long has he
suffered like this?" Jesus asked the boy's father.

22 "Since he was a small child," he answered. "This foul spirit has
tried to kill him by throwing him into the fire and drowning him in
water. But if You can do anything to help him, please have mercy on
us."

23 "If I can?" said Jesus. "When you believe, everything becomes
possible."

24 The boy's father replied straight away: "I do believe; help me to
overcome any unbelief I have!"

25 When Jesus saw all the attention this situation was attracting,
He rebuked the evil spirit: "You deaf and dumb spirit, I command
you to come out of him and never return."

26 The spirit in the boy shrieked, caused him to have a violent
seizure and then left him. At first the boy lay so still he appeared to
be dead. Some thought he had died. 27 But Jesus took him by the
hand and raised him to his feet and he stood up, completely free.

28 When Jesus had gone indoors where it was private, the disciples
asked him: "Why did we fail to drive the spirit out of the boy?"

29 Jesus replied: "This kind of spirit will only obey you when you
pray with faith."

Jesus spends time with His disciples (9:30-50)

30-31 They then left that place and journeyed through Galilee. Jesus
did not want others to know where they were because He needed
some time alone with the disciples in order to teach them. He told
them: "The Son of Man will be betrayed and handed over to those
who will kill Him; but on the third day He will rise back to life."
32 But they still did not understand what He meant by such words,
and were afraid to question Him further.

33 When they were in the house at Capernaum, Jesus asked His
disciples: "What were you arguing about on the way here?" 34 No
one wanted to answer Him, for they had been arguing about who
among them was the greatest.

35 Jesus sat down and gathered them around Him and said: "If
you want to be the first, then you must be prepared to be the last,
everyone else's servant." Then Jesus stood a young child among

them. [36]He took the child in His arms and told them: [37]"Whoever welcomes a little child in My Name welcomes Me; and whoever welcomes Me welcomes not only Me, but also the Father who sent Me."

[38]John said: "Teacher, we saw a man who was driving demons out of people in Your Name. As he was not one of us we told him to stop."

[39]"No, don't stop him," Jesus said. "Anyone who performs a miracle in My Name cannot immediately afterwards say anything bad about Me. [40]If someone is not against us, he is for us. [41]I tell you the truth, a person only has to give you a cup of water in My Name because you belong to Me, and he will certainly not lose the reward coming to him.

[42]"On the other hand, if anyone causes a little child who believes in Me to sin, it would be better for him to be thrown into the sea with a large millstone tied around his neck. [43]You may as well cut your hand off if it causes you to sin. For it would be better to enter eternal life maimed, than to go to hell with two hands. There the fire is never extinguished. [45]Similarly, if your foot is the problem leading you into sin, cut that off. It is better to enter eternal life as a cripple than to be thrown into hell with two feet. [47]And if your eye leads you to sin, it would be better to pluck it out and enter God's Kingdom with one eye, rather than be thrown into hell with two eyes. [48]It is written about hell that there the worms do not die, and the fire is never extinguished.

[49]"The refining fire is better than the fire of judgment! That refining fire is like salt. [50]Salt is useful, but if it loses its taste what good is it? You cannot restore its saltiness. So have the salt of God's refining within yourselves and live at peace, in unity with one another."

Pharisees question Jesus about divorce (10:1-12)

10 Jesus then went first to Judea and then across the Jordan River. As usual, crowds of people flocked to Him and He taught them the gospel. [2]Again, the Pharisees also came to try to catch Him out with tricky questions: "Is it right, according to God's law, for a man to divorce his wife?" they asked.

[3]"What command did Moses give you?" Jesus replied.

[4]"Moses allows a man to write a certificate of divorce and to send his wife away," they said.

[5]Jesus told them: "Moses only wrote that law because of the hardness of your hearts. [6]From the beginning God created male and

female. [7]This is why when a man leaves his father and mother he
becomes one with his wife. [8]They are no longer two, but have
become one because of their fleshly union. [9]So if God has joined
them together in such a way, no one had better separate them!"

[10]Later, when they were on their own with Jesus, the disciples
questioned Him further about this matter. [11]Jesus explained: "If anyone divorces his wife and marries another woman he commits
adultery against his wife. [12]Likewise, if the wife divorces her husband
and marries another man, she also commits adultery!"

Become like children to inherit the Kingdom (10:13-16)

[13]People brought small children to Jesus to be blessed by Him, but
the disciples tried to prevent them. [14]This annoyed Jesus and He
told them: "Allow these little ones to come to Me; don't try to stop
them, for God's Kingdom belongs to those who know they are little
children before God. [15]I tell you most emphatically, unless anyone
receives the gift of God's Kingdom like a little child, he will never
enter it at all."

[16]Then He took the children in His arms, laid His hands on them
and blessed them.

A rich man talks to Jesus (10:17-25)

[17]Just as Jesus was starting His journey, a man ran to Him and fell
on his knees before Him, saying: "Good teacher, please tell me what
I must do in order to receive eternal life."

[18]Jesus answered him: "Why do you call Me good? No one is
truly good apart from God Himself. [19]You know the commandments He has given: 'Do not murder, do not commit adultery, do
not steal, do not testify falsely, do not defraud others, honour your
father and mother.'"

[20]"Teacher, since boyhood I have kept all these commands," the
man said.

[21]Jesus looked at him with love; His heart went out to him.
Gently, He said: "You lack one thing. If you go and sell everything you
have and give generously to the poor, you will store up for yourself
treasure in heaven. Then you will be free to come and follow Me."

[22]The man looked crestfallen. He went away sad because he was
very wealthy. [23]Jesus turned and said to His disciples: "It is so hard
for the rich to enter God's Kingdom!"

[24]Jesus could see this stunned them, so He repeated: "Children,
this is true. It is very hard for the wealthy to enter God's Kingdom.

[25] In fact, it is easier for a camel to pass through the eye of a needle
than for a rich man to enter God's Kingdom!"

An eternal reward (10:26-31)

[26] This amazed the disciples even more and they began to question
among themselves: "If this is the case then who can be saved?"

[27] Jesus looked straight at them and said: "It is impossible for any
man to save himself, but it is not impossible for God; everything is
possible for Him!"

[28] "We have given up everything in order to follow You!" Peter
said to Jesus.

[29-30] He replied: "I tell you the truth, there is not a person who has
left his home or brother or sisters, mother or father, his children, his
land and possessions for Me and the gospel, who will not fail to
receive back a hundred times as much as he has given in this life –
homes, brothers, sisters, mothers, children, land and property. And
in the age that is to come he will also enjoy eternal life. [31] But many,
who in this life appear to have everything, will in the end have
nothing; and those who have given up everything shall possess
everything eternally!"

The cup of suffering (10:32-40)

[32-33] They continued on their way to Jerusalem. Jesus walked in front
and the disciples followed behind Him, still astounded at what He
was teaching. Some of His followers were really afraid of the implications of what He said.

Jesus took the twelve aside and warned them again of what had
to happen to Him: "We are now going to Jerusalem and there the
Son of Man will be betrayed into the hands of the chief priests and
teachers of the law. They will condemn Him to death and will hand
Him over to the Roman authorities. [34] They will mock Him, spit on
Him, flog Him and then kill Him. However, on the third day He
will rise back to life."

[35] Later James and John, the sons of Zebedee, came to Jesus with
a request: "Teacher, would You do for us whatever we ask of You?"

[36] "What do you want Me to do for you?" Jesus asked.

[37] "When You come into Your glory, let us sit on either side of
You," they replied.

[38] Jesus told them: "You don't understand the implications of
what you are asking. Are you able to drink the same cup of sacrifice
that I drink? Can you be immersed in the kind of rejection and suffering that will immerse me?"

39 "Yes, we can. We are willing to do that," they answered.
Jesus told them: "Yes, you will have to drink the cup I drink; you
will have to sacrifice yourselves for My sake. And even as I must
suffer so you will be immersed in suffering, the cost of your faithfulness. 40 However, it is not My prerogative to decide who should
sit either side of Me in the glory that is to come. Those places have
already been prepared for those to whom they are assigned."

Leaders to have servant hearts (10:41-45)

41 The other ten disciples were indignant with James and John when
they heard about their request. 42 So Jesus called them all together
and told them: "You know well that those who are thought of as
leaders among the nations rule with oppression. The leading officials
exalt themselves and suppress the people. 43-44 This is not how you
are to lead or rule; you belong to God's Kingdom. No, those of you
who want to become leaders must have servant hearts; those who
want the highest positions must live as devoted slaves of God. 45 For
even I, the Son of Man, did not come to be served by others, but to
serve them and to give My life for them in order that by My sacrifice
many would be able to belong to God eternally."

Blind Bartimaeus healed (10:46-52)

46 Jesus and His disciples visited Jericho. As they left the city, followed
by a large crowd, they came to a place where Bartimaeus, the son of
Timaeus, was begging by the side of the road. 47 When he heard that
Jesus of Nazareth was about to pass by he began shouting: "Jesus,
Son of David, have mercy on me!"

48 Those standing around rebuked him and told him to be quiet;
but he continued to shout at the top of his voice: "Son of David,
have mercy on me!"

49 Hearing him, Jesus stopped and ordered: "Tell him to come
here!" Then they called out to the blind man: "Take heart! Get on
your feet. The Master is calling you." 50 Bartimaeus then threw off
his cloak, jumped to his feet and came to Jesus.

51 Jesus asked him: "What is it you want? What can I do for you?"

"Rabbi, I want my sight restored," the blind man said.

52 "Go, because of your faith you are healed," Jesus said to him.
Immediately he could see and followed Jesus along with the crowd.

Jesus enters Jerusalem (11:1-14)

11 When Jesus and the disciples drew near to Jerusalem, they
came to Bethphage and Bethany, near the Mount of Olives.

2 Jesus told two of the disciples to go to the village ahead of them. "As you enter the village you will find a colt on which no-one has ridden. Untie it and bring it here to Me. 3 If anyone challenges you as to why you are taking the colt, tell him, 'The Lord needs it for now, but will see it is returned shortly.' "

4-5 The two disciples duly found the colt in the street tethered outside a doorway. As they untied it, some people who were standing nearby asked: "What are you doing? Who gave you permission to take that colt?" 6 The disciples answered in the manner Jesus had told them; so the people agreed to let them take the colt. 7 When they brought it to Jesus, they threw their cloaks on its back so He could sit on it.

8 As He journeyed into the city, many people spread their cloaks on the road in front of Him and others cut branches from trees in neighbouring fields and placed them on the road as well. Those ahead of Jesus and those who followed shouted out:

9 "The Lord save us! He who comes in the Lord's name be blessed!"

10 "The Kingdom of our father David is coming; God be praised."

"Our Saviour deserves the highest praise!"

11 Having entered Jerusalem, Jesus went to the temple. He looked at everything that was happening there; but as it was already late He took no action then. Instead He went with His disciples to stay at Bethany.

12 Jesus was hungry after they had left Bethany on the following day. 13 He noticed a little way off a fig tree that was in leaf, and so went to see if it was bearing any fruit. But He found nothing but leaves when He came to the tree; it was not the season for figs.

14 The disciples overheard Jesus say to the tree: "No one will ever eat fruit from you again."

Jesus clears the temple (11:15-18)

15 When they entered Jerusalem, Jesus went again to the temple area, where now He took action. He drove out those who were trading there. He then overturned the tables belonging to the money changers and the stalls of those selling doves for sacrifice. 16 He stopped everybody bringing merchandise into the temple courts. 17 He shouted out: "It is written in the scriptures, 'My house is to be called a house of prayer for all nations,' but look what you have done to it. It has become a den of robbers!"

18 When the chief priests and teachers of the law saw what Jesus was doing and heard what He said, they decided that they must

11:17 Isaiah 56:7, Jeremiah 7:11

find a way to kill Him. They were afraid of the influence He was having on all the people who were amazed at His teaching!

Faith in prayer (11:19-26)

19 In the evening, Jesus and His disciples left the city. 20 The following
morning, as they were returning to the city, they saw that the fig tree
Jesus had cursed had shrivelled from its roots. 21 Remembering what
Jesus had done, Peter said: "Rabbi, look! That fig tree you cursed –
it has withered!"

22 Jesus answered: "Have faith in God. 23 I tell you the truth, if anyone speaks to a mountain by saying, 'Go, throw yourself into the
sea,' the mountain will be moved for him so long as he does not
doubt in his heart, but truly believes that what he says must happen.
24 So I tell you, no matter what you ask in prayer, believe it is yours
already, and it will be yours!

25 "Whenever you pray, it is essential that you forgive anyone
against whom you hold anything; for then your heavenly Father
will also forgive you all your sins. 26 But if you do not forgive others
your heavenly father will not forgive your sins."

The authority of Jesus questioned (11:27-33)

27 When they arrived in Jerusalem, Jesus was again walking in the
temple courts when the chief priests, the teachers of the law and the
elders approached Him. 28 "By what authority are You doing these
things?" they demanded. "Who gave You the authority to act in
such a way?"

29 Jesus replied: "Let me ask you a question. If you answer Me
then I will answer your question, and I will tell you on whose
authority I do these things. 30 Tell Me, was John's baptism inspired
by heaven, or was it the work of man?"

31 They discussed this among themselves: "If we say that it was
from heaven, He will ask us why we did not believe John. 32 We dare
not say it was from man." (Because John was regarded as a prophet
by the people, they feared their reaction if they gave such an
answer.) 33 So they said to Jesus: "We don't know the answer to Your
question."

So Jesus replied: "In that case I will not tell you by whose authority I do these things."

The vineyard and the wicked tenants (12:1-12)

12 Jesus then began to teach using this illustration: "A man
planted a vineyard, surrounded it by a wall, dug a pit for

the winepress and built a watchtower. He then rented it to some
farmers while he was away on a journey. 2 He sent his servant to the
tenants at harvest time to collect his share of the fruit. 3 But the tenants
took hold of the man, beat him and sent him away with nothing. 4 So
the owner sent another servant, but they beat him about the head
and abused him also. 5 The next servant the owner sent they killed.
The owner continued to send other servants, but the tenants either
beat or killed them all.

6 "As a last resort he decided to send his own son whom he loved.
'They must respect my own son,' he said. 7 But the tenants said
among themselves: 'He is the heir. If we kill him we can take the
inheritance for ourselves.' 8 So they took hold of the son, killed him
and threw his body out of the vineyard."

9 Jesus then asked the people: "What do you think the owner of
the vineyard will do then? Obviously he will come himself, kill the
tenants and appoint others to take their place. 10 Have you not read
the scripture that says, 'the builders rejected the stone that has
become the key-stone? 11 This is the Lord's doing and it is wonderful
to behold.'"

12 The leaders realised Jesus had used this illustration against
them; so they were even more determined to arrest Him. However,
they were afraid of the way the crowd would react, so they did
nothing for the moment and went away instead.

Pay taxes to Caesar (12:13-17)

13 Later they sent some Pharisees and those of Herod's party to try
to trap Jesus in what He said. 14 So they put this question to Him:
"Teacher, we know that You are not swayed by the opinions of men,
but teach God's ways according to the truth, and do so with integrity.
You are not influenced by how important or otherwise a person is.
Tell us, is it right to pay the Roman taxes to Caesar, or not? 15 Should
we Jews pay such taxes, or not?"

Jesus immediately saw through their hypocrisy. "Why do you try
to trap Me with such a question? Bring Me a coin and then I can
show you." 16 When they handed Him the coin He asked them:
"Whose portrait is this on the coin, and who is the subject of this
inscription?"

"Caesar," they responded.

17 "Well then, give to Caesar what is rightly due to Caesar, and to
God what rightly belongs to Him," Jesus told them. Such an answer
both surprised and silenced them.

Questions about the resurrection (12:18-27)

[18]Then the Sadducees, who do not believe in resurrection, tried to
trap Him with another question. [19]"Teacher, Moses gave us all these
instructions. He wrote that when a man's brother dies and leaves
his wife childless, he is to marry the widow and so provide children
on behalf of his brother. [20]Now suppose there were seven brothers.
The first married but left no children when he died. [21]So the second
brother married the widow but also died leaving her childless. The
third did likewise. [22]In fact all seven brothers married the widow in
turn, but all of them died before she had children. Eventually the
woman also died. [23]Now, at the resurrection whose wife will she be?
After all, she had married all seven brothers!"

[24]Jesus replied: "You show by such senseless thinking that you
are ignorant of both the scriptures and God's power. [25]At the resurrection there will be no marriage, neither will people be given to
one another in marriage. Those who have been raised from the dead
will be as the angels in heaven.

[26]"Concerning the resurrection, have you not read what Moses
wrote about when God spoke to him from the bush? He said, 'I am
the God of Abraham, the God of Isaac and the God of Jacob.'

[27]"He is not God of the dead, but of successive generations of the
living! You are so wrong in what you believe!"

The greatest commandment (12:28-34)

[28]One of the teachers of the law listened to these debates and was
impressed by the good answers He gave. So he asked Jesus: "What
is the most important of all God's commandments?"

[29]Jesus answered: "The most important one is when God said:
'Listen, my people Israel, there is only one Lord, only one God.
[30]You are to love the Lord your God with all your heart and with all
your soul, with all your mind and with all your strength.' [31]The second
most important command is: 'Love your neighbour as much as you
already love yourself.' God has not given us commands greater
than these!"

[32]"That is a good answer, Master," replied the questioner. "You
are right when You say that there is but one God and no other
except for Him. [33]It is much more important to love Him with all
your heart, all your understanding and with all the strength you
have, and to love your neighbour as yourself, than to bring to God
a whole lot of burnt offerings and sacrifices."

[34]Jesus acknowledged this was a wise answer, so said to him:
"You are very near to receiving the gift of God's Kingdom." After
that, no one dared to try and trap Him with their questions.

Christ – David's Lord (12:35-40)

[35]While teaching in the temple courts, Jesus posed them a question:
"How can it be that the teachers of the law called the Christ David's
son? [36]For under the inspiration of the Holy Spirit, David himself
declared: 'The Lord said to my Lord, 'Sit now at My right hand
while I put Your enemies beneath Your feet.'"

[37]"If David calls Him 'Lord' how can the Christ, the Messiah, be
David's son?

The crowd listening to Him were delighted by the way He
silenced all the religious leaders. [38]Jesus warned them: "Beware of
the teachers of the law. They love to walk about in their long robes
and be acknowledged by everyone in the marketplaces. [39]They
enjoy the most prominent seats in the synagogues and the places of
honour at banquets. [40]They sponge off widows and try to impress
everyone with their long prayers. Little do they realise that those
who behave like this are only storing up severe punishment for
themselves."

The widow's offering (12:41-44)

[41]Jesus sat down directly opposite the place where people placed
their offerings. He watched them as they gave into the temple treasury.
Several of the wealthy threw in large amounts, often ostentatiously.
[42]However, a poor widow came along and put in two of the cheapest
copper coins, worth far less than a penny.

[43]Jesus drew the attention of His disciples to this: "I tell you the
truth, this poor widow has really put more into the treasury than
any of the others. [44]They gave out of their ample resources; but
despite her poverty, this widow put in everything she had to live
on!"

Signs of the end of the times (13:1-8)

13 As Jesus was leaving the temple, one of His disciples
remarked: "Teacher, look at those massive stones! What
magnificent buildings there are here!"

[2]Jesus replied: "You see all these great buildings? Not one stone
will be left on another. They will all be thrown down."

12:36 Psalm 110:1

3-4 When Jesus was sitting away from the others on the Mount of
Olives, across the valley from the temple, Peter, James, John and
Andrew approached Him and asked Him quietly: "Please tell us
when these things will take place? What sign should we be looking
for that will indicate that Your words are about to be fulfilled?"
5 Jesus told them: "Be very careful that you do not allow anyone
to deceive you. 6 Many will claim to have come in My Name. They
will say, 'I am the one!' And many will be deceived by them.
7 "You will hear about wars and fears of war breaking out, but do
not be afraid. There are bound to be many such conflicts, but this
does not indicate the end of time. 8 One nation will rise up in war
against other nations. One kingdom will oppose another kingdom.
There will be natural disasters such as earthquakes in some areas,
famine in other places. But these are only the birth pangs of what is
to come.

Stand firm in faith (13:9-13)

9 "So you need to be on your guard. You will be handed over to the
local authorities. You will be opposed in the synagogues and
flogged for preaching the gospel. Yes, because of your faithfulness
to Me, you will be brought before governors and kings, but these
will be opportunities to witness to them. 10 For the good news must
be preached to all people everywhere.
11 "When you are arrested and tried for your faith, you will not
need to worry about what to say. For when the time comes the Holy
Spirit will give you the right words to speak. It will seem that He is
the one doing the talking, not you.
12 "One brother will betray another brother, even causing his
death. A father will turn against his child. Children will rebel
against their parents and have them executed. 13 It will seem that
everyone hates you and is against you, simply because you believe
who I am. But anyone who stands firm in his faith to the end will be
saved eternally.

Warning of destruction and deception (13:14-37)

14 "When you see that which is an abomination to God and which
brings desolation to men, standing where it has no right to be, then
understand that those who live in Judea will need to escape to the
mountains. 15 At that terrible time anyone on the roof of his house
must not go into the house for any of his possessions. 16 There will
be no time for anyone in the open to fetch his coat. 17 Imagine how

awful it will be then for those who are pregnant or those who are
nursing young infants. 18-19 Pray that this calamity does not occur in
winter, for never will there have been days of such total desolation,
not since God created the world; and such devastation will never be
known again. 20 No-one would be able to survive, but for the fact
that God will cause this time of devastation to be ended. He will do
this for the sake of His children, those He has chosen for Himself.
For their sakes He will end these days of terrible suffering.

21 "Some will say at that time: 'The Messiah has come. He is over
here,' or 'Look, He is over there.' Do not believe such nonsense.
22 There will be false messiahs and false prophets who will perform
signs and miracles that will deceive even those who have been chosen
to know the truth. That seems hardly possible, but it will happen.
23 So be careful. I have given you warning that all these things shall
surely take place.

24 "In those distressing days even worse things will occur to fulfil
the prophetic words that have been written: 'It will seem that the
sun has been put out and the moon can give no light. 25 The stars will
fall from their appointed places in the sky and even the heavens will
be shaken.'

26 "This is the time when men will see Me, the Son of Man, coming
again, but then in clouds of glory and with great power. 27 Then I
will send My angels to gather My chosen ones from every direction,
from the farthest limits of both earth and the heavens.

28 "You can learn an important lesson from the fig tree to help you
understand what I am saying. When the branches of the tree
become tender you know that its leaves will sprout and the summer
is fast approaching. 29 In like manner, when you see the things I have
described happening, then as My followers you will know that
what I promise is about to happen; it is truly imminent.

30 "I tell you the truth, these things will all herald the end of this
age. 31 Heaven and earth as you know it will pass away, but My
words are eternal, they will never pass away.

32 "I tell you clearly, no-one knows the day or the precise time
when these things will happen. Not even the angels in heaven
know. I do not even know Myself; only the Father knows. So you
certainly do not know when that time is to come. 33 This is why I tell
you to be on your guard and to be ready. 34 You have to be like servants
left in charge of the master's house while he is away. Each has his
appointed task, and someone is always on guard duty, keeping watch.

13:25 Isaiah 13:10, 34:4

[35]"So be alert and ready because you do not know when the
owner of the house will return. It may be in the evening, or at midnight, before dawn breaks or when it does break. [36]Do not let him
find you asleep because he comes suddenly when you are unprepared.
[37]So I say to you again; be alert all the time! And I want everyone to
hear and to heed this warning."

Woman anoints Jesus (14:1-9)

14 It was just two days before the Passover and the Feast of the
Unleavened Bread. The chief priests and teachers of the law
were scheming how they could arrest Jesus without causing a public
outcry; they were determined to kill Him. [2]"We cannot do this during
the feast, for there will be a riot among the people if we do," they said.
[3]Meanwhile Jesus was staying at Bethany, a short distance from
Jerusalem. He was having a meal in Simon the Leper's house when
a woman entered the room and broke a flask of very expensive
perfume made of pure nard, and poured it over His head. [4-5]This
was so costly that some present were indignant: "What a waste,"
they said, "this perfume is worth more than a man earns in a year;
it would have been more useful to sell the perfume and give the
money to the poor." So they criticised the woman sharply.
[6]Jesus intervened: "Stop that; leave her alone. Why do you criticise
her? She has just done something very beautiful for Me. [7]You will
always have the poor with you and you can help them whenever
you choose. But I will not always be with you. [8]She has blessed Me
in the only way she could. By pouring this perfume on My body,
she has prepared it for burial. [9]I tell you the truth, in the future
when the gospel is preached anywhere in the world, what she has
just done for Me will be spoken about. Because of this loving action
she will have her place in history!"

Judas betrays Jesus (14:10-11)

[10]This was too much for one of the twelve, Judas Iscariot. He went
to the chief priests and offered to betray Jesus into their hands.
[11]They were overjoyed by this and offered Judas money in exchange
for his betrayal. So from that time he sought a suitable opportunity
to deliver Jesus into their hands.

The Last Supper (14:12-25)

[12]It was the custom to sacrifice the Passover Lamb on the first day of
the feast of Unleavened Bread. So the disciples asked Jesus: "Where
should we go to prepare for You to eat the Passover meal?"

[13-14]He sent two of the disciples into the city telling them: "You
will be met by a man carrying a jar of water," normally a task done
by women. "Follow him and say to the owner of the house he
enters, 'Take us to the guest room, where the Teacher will eat the
Passover with His disciples.' [15]He will take you to a large room
upstairs, furnished and suitable. Prepare for us to eat there together."

[16]The disciples went into the city and everything happened exactly
as Jesus had said. So they made preparations for the Passover.

[17]Jesus arrived with the twelve in the evening. [18]During the meal,
while they were reclining at the table, Jesus said: "I tell you truly,
one of you who is eating with Me now is going to betray Me."

[19]Such a thing seemed unthinkable and they were all shocked.
One by one they asked Him: "Surely I would never do that. It isn't
me, is it?"

[20]Jesus repeated: "It is one of you twelve who have been close to
Me, one who dips bread in the bowl with Me now. [21]The Son of Man
will leave you in the way that has been prophesied. It is already
written. But the man who betrays the Son of Man will be cursed
eternally. It would have been better for him if he had never been born."

[22]During the meal Jesus took some bread, gave thanks to God and
then broke it, giving a piece to each disciple saying: "Take this, for
this is My body." [23]Then He took a cup, gave thanks over it and
passed it round for all of them to drink. [24]As they did so, He said:
"This is My blood that is to be poured out for many, the blood of the
new covenant between God and man. [25]I tell you most emphatically
that I will not drink of the vine's fruit again until the day I drink the
new wine in God's heavenly Kingdom."

Jesus predicts Peter's denial (14:26-31)

[26]They sang a hymn of praise to God before leaving to go to the
Mount of Olives. [27]Jesus told them: "All of you will fail Me, for it has
been written, 'I will strike the shepherd and then the sheep will be
scattered.' [28]However, after I have risen, I will see you again in Galilee."

[29]"Even if everyone else fails You, I will never do that," declared
Peter. [30]Jesus told him: "I tell you, there is no doubt that tonight
even you will have denied three times that you know Me before you
hear the rooster crow for the second time."

[31]Peter was most insistent: "I am ready to die with you if necessary. I would certainly never deny that I knew You!" The attitude of
all the others was similar.

14:27 Zechariah 13:7

Gethsemane (14:32-42)

32 When they came to the place known as Gethsemane, Jesus said to
His disciples: "I am going to pray; sit here and wait for Me." 33 He
then took Peter, James and John with Him, but it was clear that He
was now very troubled and was in deep distress. 34 He told them: "I
am so overcome with such sadness that I feel I could die. Stay here
and pray for Me."

35 He went further ahead by Himself, fell to the ground on His
face and prayed that, if possible, He might not have to suffer what
lay ahead. 36 "Father, Father," He kept saying, "everything is possible
for You. Please take this cup of suffering from Me, but only if this is
Your will, not Mine."

37 When He returned to where He left the three disciples, He
found them asleep. "Are you sleeping, Simon?" He asked Peter.
"Was it too much to ask you to pray for Me for just one hour? 38 Be
on the watch and pray that you will not yield to temptation. Your
spirit may be willing, but your body is weak."

39 He went away on His own again and prayed in a similar manner
as before. 40 When He returned, He again found them asleep; they
were too tired to keep awake. Embarrassed, they did not know
what to say to Him.

41 After praying a third time, Jesus returned again: "Are you still
sleeping? All you can do is rest! Enough of this! My time has now
come. Look, the Son of Man is about to be betrayed into the hands
of sinners. 42 Get up! Let us go and meet My betrayer!"

Jesus' arrest (14:43-65)

43 Even as He was speaking, Judas, who had been one of the twelve
disciples, approached together with a crowd sent by the chief
priests, the teachers of the law and the elders. They were armed
with swords and clubs. 44 Judas had given them a signal, 'The one I
kiss is the man you want; arrest Him and take Him away; but guard
Him carefully.' 45 So he went directly to Jesus and greeted Him.
"Rabbi," he said, and kissed Him. 46 Immediately the crowd grabbed
hold of Him.

47 Then one of the disciples drew his sword and struck the high
priest's servant, cutting off his ear. 48 "Why have you come with
swords and clubs to seize Me?" Jesus asked them. "I am not leading
a rebellion. 49 Every day I taught you openly in the temple courts,
but you did not dare to take Me then. However, the scriptures have
to be fulfilled." 50 Then all Jesus' friends fled for their lives and left
Him alone.

51-52 A young man had been following Jesus. They tried to seize him but only grabbed the linen robe he was wearing; so he fled naked.

53 They took Jesus to a meeting that included the high priest, all the chief priests, elders and teachers of the law. 54 Peter followed at a safe distance, even entering into the courtyard of the high priest's house where the meeting was taking place. He sat together with the guards warming himself by the fire.

55-56 The chief priests and the entire Council wanted to find evidence against Jesus to justify putting Him to death. But they could not find anything against Him, even though many testified falsely. They could not accept their statements because they conflicted with one another.

57-58 Then some came forward with further false testimony against Jesus: "We heard Him say, 'I will destroy this temple made with the hands of men and in three days I will raise up another temple that has not been made by men.'" 59 Yet even then there were discrepancies in their testimony.

60 Then the high priest took over and demanded of Jesus: "Are You not going to answer these allegations? What do You say about these things the witnesses are charging You with?" 61 Jesus said nothing, refusing to answer.

So the high priest challenged Him directly: "Are You the Christ, the Messiah, the Son of the blessed One?"

62 "I AM," said Jesus. "And you will see Me sitting as the Son of Man at the right hand of the Mighty One, when I come again on the clouds of heaven."

63 At this the high priest tore his robe as a sign of disgust. "We do not need any further witnesses after such a blatant admission, do we?" he asked. 64 "You have heard the blasphemy for yourselves. How do you vote?"

They all condemned Him to death. 65 Some began to spit on Him. They blindfolded Him, punched Him and said: "Prophesy then! Tell us who hit You!" Then the guards took Him away and gave Him a further beating.

Peter denies association with Jesus (14:66-72)

66 While this was happening, Peter was still below in the courtyard where one of the high priest's servant girls saw Peter warming himself by the fire. 67 She looked closely at him and said: "You were one of those with that Nazarene, Jesus."

68 Peter denied it. "No, no, I don't know what you are talking
about," he said and then withdrew to the gateway; and a cock
crowed. 69 But the servant girl continued to look at him and said to
others standing about: "I am sure this man is one of them." 70 But
again Peter denied what she said.

A short time later, one of those standing near Peter said: "You
must be one of them, for you also come from Galilee." 71 Peter began
to curse and swear to them: "I do not even know this Man of whom
you speak."

72 No sooner were the words out of his mouth than the cock
crowed for the second time. Peter immediately remembered what
Jesus had said to Him: 'You will deny three times that you even
know Me before the rooster crows twice.' Peter felt heartbroken and
could not hold back his tears.

Jesus on trial before Pilate (15:1-5)

15 It was very early in the morning when the chief priests, elders,
teachers of the law and the whole Council reached their
decision. Jesus was bound, taken away and handed over to Pilate,
the Roman governor. 2 He asked Jesus: "Are you really the King of
the Jews?"

"Yes, what you have said is correct," Jesus answered.

3 Then the chief priest listed their accusations against Him. 4 "Will
you not answer all these allegations?" Pilate asked Jesus. 5 But, to
Pilate's astonishment, He made no reply.

Jesus condemned, mocked and beaten (15:6-19)

6 At the feast it was customary for the Roman occupying forces to
release one prisoner as a gesture to the people, and to them was
given the choice as to who should be released. 7 One prisoner was a
man called Barabbas who was guilty of murder in an uprising
against the Romans, and so was popular with many of the people.
8 They asked Pilate to fulfil the customary gesture.

9 "Shall I release the King of the Jews to you?" Pilate suggested.
10 He was well aware that the Pharisees had only accused Him out
of envy. 11 However, the chief priests had already put the word
around that they should ask Pilate to release Barabbas, not Jesus.

12 So Pilate asked: "What do you want me to do with the one you
call your King, the King of the Jews?"

13 "Crucify Him!" the crowd shouted.

[14]"Why? Of what crime is He guilty to deserve such a punishment?" Pilate asked.

They only shouted even louder: "Crucify Him!"

[15]To please the people, Pilate agreed to release Barabbas. Then he
had Jesus flogged and handed Him over to the military to crucify
Him.

[16-17]The soldiers took Jesus to the palace known as the Praetorium.
The whole company of soldiers gathered and put a purple robe on
Jesus to mock Him as a king. They even gave Him a crown of thorn
branches that had been twisted together, which they placed on His
head.

[18]"All hail, king of the Jews!" they mockingly cried out to Him.
[19]Repeatedly they hit Him around the head with a staff and then
spat on Him. Then they fell on their knees before Him as if to pay
Him homage, but they were only mocking Him further.

The Crucifixion (15:20-32)

[20]When they had finished toying with Him they removed the purple
robe and returned His own clothes, before taking Him to the place
of crucifixion.

[21]By now Jesus was very weak physically, so the soldiers forced a
man from Cyrene called Simon to carry the cross for Him. Simon,
the father of Alexander and Rufus, had come from the country for
the feast and just happened to be on hand.

[22]They led Jesus to Golgotha, which means the 'Place of the Skull.'
[23]When they offered Him the mixture of wine and myrrh to deaden
the pain, He refused to take it. [24]Then they nailed Him to the cross.
They decided to cast lots to see who should have His clothes.

[25]They crucified Jesus at nine o'clock in the morning. [26]They
nailed the charge against Him to the cross: THE KING OF THE
JEWS.

[27]Either side of Him they crucified two thieves. [28]In this way the
scripture was fulfilled that says He was counted among sinners.
[29]Those passing by shook their heads and shouted insults at Jesus:
"You said You would destroy the temple and rebuild it in three
days. So let us see You do it. [30]If You are really a saviour, come down
from the cross now and save Yourself!"

[31]The chief priests and teachers of the law mocked Him among
themselves in similar fashion saying: "He saved others but look at
Him now; He can't save Himself! [32]We will see and believe in You
as the Christ and the King of Israel if You come down now from the
cross." Even those crucified with Him also mocked Him.

Jesus' death (15:33-41)

[33-34]At noon it became completely dark over the entire land. The darkness lasted until around three o'clock when Jesus cried in a loud voice: "My God, My God, why have You forsaken Me?"

[35]Hearing this, some of the bystanders said: "Listen, He calls for Elijah." [36]One of them quickly filled a sponge with wine vinegar. Placing the sponge on a stick he lifted it to Jesus lips saying: "Leave Him alone. We will see if Elijah comes to rescue Him."

[37]Then with a loud cry, Jesus took His last breath and died.

[38]At that very moment the curtain in the temple that concealed the Holy of holies was torn apart from top to bottom. [39]The centurion who stood there before Jesus heard His cry and watched how He died. "This must really be the Son of God," he said.

[40-41]Some of the women, who had followed Jesus in Galilee to provide for His practical needs, watched from a distance. They included Mary Magdalene, Mary the Mother of James the younger and of Joses, and Salome. But there were many other women who had also followed Him to Jerusalem who were also present.

Jesus' burial (15:42-47)

[42-43]It was now the day before the Sabbath, known as the Day of Preparation. Towards evening a prominent member of the Council, Joseph of Arimathea, a man who longed for the coming of God's Kingdom, had the boldness to go to Pilate to ask Him to release Jesus' body to him for burial. [44]Pilate was surprised to learn that He had died already. He summoned the centurion to verify if this was indeed true. [45]When the centurion confirmed that Jesus had died, Pilate authorised Joseph to take His body.

[46]Joseph went and took His body down from the cross, wrapped it in a linen cloth he had brought with him and placed it in a tomb that had been cut out of the rock. Then he rolled a stone over the tomb's entrance. [47]Both Mary Magdalene and Mary the mother of Joses had watched where Jesus' body had been laid to rest.

The Resurrection (16:1-13)

16 When the Sabbath had ended, Mary Magdalene and the other Mary, together with Salome, went and bought spices with which to anoint Jesus' body. [2]They went to the tomb very early on the Sunday morning, just after sunrise. [3]However, they were concerned about who could roll the heavy stone away that covered the entrance to the tomb.

4 When they arrived at the place, to their surprise they discovered
that the large stone had been moved already. 5 So they entered the
tomb and to their astonishment found a young man sitting on the
right side, dressed in a white robe.

6 "Don't be afraid," he said, "You have come for Jesus the
Nazarene who was crucified. As you can see, He is not here. He has
risen from the dead. Look, there is the place where they laid Him.
7 Now go and give Peter and the other disciples this message, 'Jesus
is going ahead of you to Galilee and you will see Him there exactly
as He promised you!'"

8 Trembling with fear and utterly bewildered by what they had
seen, the women left the tomb and hurried away, too frightened to
say anything to anyone!

9 However, Jesus actually appeared later to Mary Magdalene,
from whom He had driven out seven demons. 10 She went and told
His friends who were gathered together, mourning and weeping
over His death. 11 But they could not believe her when she told them
that Jesus was not only alive, but that she had actually seen Him.

12 Later still, the risen Jesus appeared to two of them as they were
walking in the countryside, but they did not recognise at first that it
was indeed Jesus. 13 When they returned to Jerusalem and told the
others, they still did not believe.

Disciples commissioned (16:14-20)

14 So then Jesus appeared to the eleven disciples as they were eating
together. He reprimanded them for their lack of faith and stubborn
refusal to believe those who had reported seeing Him after He had
risen.

15 Jesus gave them this commission: "Go to every part of the
world and preach the good news everywhere. 16 Whoever believes
in Me and is then baptised will be saved and will be given eternal
life; but whoever does not believe will remain condemned. 17 Those
who believe will perform signs to verify the truth of what they
believe. They will drive out demons in My Name from those who
are in such bondage. They will speak in new languages given them
by the Holy Spirit. 18 Some will even pick up deadly snakes with
their hands without being harmed: others will be given deadly poison
to drink, but it will have no effect on them. They will lay their hands
on the sick and they will be healed."

19 When the Lord Jesus had finished speaking to them, they
watched as He was taken up into heaven, where He took His place
at God's right hand.

20 Then the disciples began to obey the commission Jesus had given them. Everywhere they went they preached the good news of all Jesus had said and done. The Lord Himself worked with them performing the miraculous signs that verified that what they preached was the truth!

Verses 9-19 only appear in later manuscripts and are widely regarded to have been added to the original at a later date.

THE GOSPEL ACCORDING TO

LUKE

Introduction (1:1-4)

1 [1-2]Most excellent Theophilus, many have written accounts of the events that took place among us, based on the eyewitness evidence of the first disciples who were taught the Word. [3-4]I myself have carefully investigated all these accounts of what took place from the very beginning; and it seemed right for me to produce this accurate account for you, so that you may know that what you have been taught is correct and true.

Birth of John the Baptist foretold (1:5-25)

[5]When Herod was king of Judea, there was a certain priest called Zechariah of the priestly order of Abijah, whose wife Elizabeth was also descended from the priestly line of Aaron. [6]Both lived righteous lives in God's eyes, carefully observing all the Lord's commandments and regulations. [7]However, they were unable to have children as Elizabeth was infertile, and by then both were very old.

[8-9]When Zechariah's priestly order was fulfilling its duty before God, he was chosen by lot, according to custom, to burn incense before the presence of the Lord in the temple. [10]While he was doing this the worshippers gathered together outside in prayer.

[11]While in the sanctuary Zechariah saw an angel of the Lord standing on the right side of the altar of incense. [12-13]He was both surprised and terrified, but the angel told him: "Don't be afraid, Zechariah, for God has heard your prayer. Your wife Elizabeth will bear you a son who you are to call John. [14]He will give you great joy and delight, and many others will be thankful because the Lord has a great purpose for him.

[15]"He is not to drink wine or any form of alcohol and he will be filled with the Holy Spirit from the time of his birth. [16]He will bring many people of Israel back to the Lord their God. He will prepare the way in the spirit and power of Elijah for the Lord's coming. [17]He will cause the hearts of fathers to be turned to their children and the

disobedient will repent of their sins, and instead will adopt the wisdom
of ways that please the Lord. This child is to prepare people for the
Lord's coming."

18 Zechariah asked the angel: "How can I be sure that all this will
happen? I am now old and my wife past the age of child-bearing."

19 The angel answered: "I am Gabriel. I stand in God's Presence
and He has sent me to give you this good news. 20 But because you
have disbelieved what I have said, you will now be dumb and
unable to speak until the birth of your son, which will surely take
place in due time."

21 While this was happening, the people waiting outside for
Zechariah wondered why he remained so long in the sanctuary. 22 So
when he finally came out and was unable to speak, but could only
make hand gestures, they realised that he must have received a
vision.

23 Zechariah returned home when he had completed his service.
24 Elizabeth duly became pregnant and remained in seclusion for
five months. "Only the Lord could have done this for me," she said.
25 "This is evidence that His favour is on me, for He has delivered me
from the disgrace of being childless."

Gabriel foretells Mary of Jesus' birth (1:26-38)

26 When Elizabeth had been pregnant for six months, God sent His
angel Gabriel to a town in Galilee called Nazareth. 27-28 There he
appeared to a virgin named Mary, who was to be married to a
descendant of David, called Joseph. "Greetings," he said to her.
"You are favoured by God and He is with you."

29 These words disturbed Mary greatly, for she could not understand what they meant. 30 But the angel assured her: "There is no
need to fear, Mary, for God is pleased with you. 31 You are to become
pregnant and will give birth to a Son who you are to call Jesus. 32 He
will be great and will become known as the Son of the Most High
God, who will place Him on the throne of His ancestor David. 33 His
reign over Israel will be eternal and His Kingdom will never end."

34 "How could such a thing happen?" Mary asked the angel. "I am
still a virgin."

35 He replied: "The Holy Spirit will come upon you and the power
of the Most High God will overshadow you. So the child you bear
will be Holy and called the Son of God. 36 Your relative Elizabeth is
already six months pregnant despite her age and her former inability
to bear children. 37 For nothing is impossible for God."

38 Mary answered: "I am the Lord's servant. So I submit willingly
to what you have said." Then the angel left her.

Mary visits Elizabeth (1:39-56)

39-40 Mary then went as soon as possible to the town in the hill country
of Judea where Zechariah lived. 41 When she greeted Elizabeth, the
baby leaped in her womb and she was filled with the Holy Spirit.
42 With joy she cried out: "Among all women you are the most
blessed and the child you bear is truly blessed. 43 But why should I
be treated with such favour, that the mother of my Lord should
come to visit me? 44 As soon as I heard your greeting, the child within
me leaped with joy. 45 You are blessed because you believed that
what the Lord said to you shall surely come to pass."

46-47 Then Mary said:

> "I glorify the Lord with all my soul, and my spirit rejoices
> in God, for He is my Saviour. 48-49 He knows that I am
> only His humble servant. Yet every future generation will
> consider me blessed, for the Mighty One has done such
> great things for me. And His name is Holy!
>
> 50 "He extends His mercy to those who fear Him in
> every generation. 51 For He has done mighty deeds through
> His power, and yet has scattered those whose hearts are
> proud. 52-53 He has dethroned rulers and has exalted the
> humble. He has supplied plentifully for the hungry, but
> the wealthy He has sent away with nothing.
>
> 54-55 "He has helped His people Israel, for He has continued
> to be merciful to Abraham and his descendants, just as
> He promised our forefathers."

56 Mary remained with Elizabeth for about three months before
returning home.

John is born (1:57-63)

57 In due time Elizabeth gave birth to a son. 58 When her neighbours
and relatives heard the news they shared her joy that the Lord had
shown her such great mercy.

59 On the eighth day after his birth, when it was time for him to be
circumcised, it was assumed that he would be named after his
father Zechariah. 60 But Elizabeth intervened: "No! He is to be called
John."

61 "But you have no relatives that bear that name," they objected.

62 So using signs they asked Zechariah what he should be called.
63 Asking for a writing tablet, to their astonishment he wrote: 'His name is John.'

Zechariah prophesies over John (1:64-80)

64 Immediately Zechariah was freed from his dumbness and began to speak by praising God. 65 Everyone was filled with such awe that soon they were talking about these events throughout the hill country of Judea. 66 And all who heard wondered, 'What is going to become of this child?' For clearly the hand of the Lord was upon him. 67 His father Zechariah, filled with the Holy Spirit, prophesied:

> 68 "May the Lord, the God of Israel, be praised! For He has come to His people and has redeemed them. 69-70 He has raised up a mighty Saviour in the line of His servant David, as He promised long ago through His holy prophets. 71 He has saved us from our enemies and from the power of all who hate us. 72-73 And so He has mercifully fulfilled what He promised to our forefathers, remembering to fulfil the holy covenant He made with the oath He swore to our Father Abraham. 74-75 This was His plan to rescue us from our enemies and so enable us to serve Him throughout our lives in holiness and righteousness, and without any need to be afraid.
>
> 76-79 "And you, my child, will be known as a prophet of the Most High God, for you are called to prepare the way for the Lord; to show God's people that they can be saved through the forgiveness of their sins because of God's tender mercy towards them. From heaven the sun will rise to shine on those living in darkness and the fear of death, and to guide us so that we can walk in peace with God."
>
> 80 And the child, John, became strong in his spirit as he grew, living in the desert until it was time to begin his public ministry to Israel.

Jesus born in Bethlehem (2:1-7)

2 Around that time, the emperor Caesar Augustus decreed that a census should be taken throughout the Roman Empire. 2 (This was the census to be taken when Quirinius was governor of Syria.)
3-4 Everyone had to go to his town of origin to register; so Joseph travelled from Nazareth in Galilee to Bethlehem, the town of David

his forefather. [5]There he registered, together with Mary who was
engaged to be married to him and was expecting the baby.
[6-7]While in Bethlehem, Mary gave birth to her firstborn, a Son,
who she wrapped in a cloth and laid in a manger, because no room
in any inn was available.

Angels appear to the shepherds (2:8-20)

[8-9]Nearby, some shepherds were in the fields watching over their
flocks during the night, when one of the Lord's angels appeared to
them. The Lord's glory shone all around them. [10]They felt scared but
the angel told them: "Don't be afraid. I have come to bring you
good news of tremendous joy for everyone. [11]Today a Saviour has
been born in Bethlehem, the Lord's Anointed One, the Christ, the
Messiah. [12]The sign by which you will know Him is this: He is the
baby you will find wrapped in a cloth lying in a manger."
[13-14]Then there appeared with the angels a great number of other
angels who were all praising God and saying: "Glory to the Most
High God in heaven and His peace to men on earth on whom His
favour rests."
[15]As soon as the angels had returned to heaven the shepherds
agreed: "Let us go to Bethlehem and see for ourselves this wonderful
event about which the Lord has told us." [16]They went as fast as possible and found Mary and Joseph with the baby lying in the manger.
[17-18]Having seen Him, they went and told everyone what they had
been told about this child, to the utter astonishment of all who heard
them. [19]But Mary treasured all these things in her heart, wondering
what they meant. [20]The shepherds returned to the fields, giving
glory and praise to God because of all they had seen and heard, for
everything had been exactly as had been revealed to them.

Jesus consecrated at the temple (2:21-40)

[21]When the child was circumcised on the eighth day He was named
Jesus, 'Saviour', the name given by the angel before He was conceived.
[22-23]As soon as the purification ceremony required under the law
of Moses was completed, Joseph and Mary took Jesus to Jerusalem
to offer Him to the Lord (for according to the law given by the Lord,
'Every firstborn son is to be consecrated to the Lord'. [24]They offered
the sacrifice stated in that law: 'a pair of doves or two young
pigeons.'

2:23 Exodus 13:2
2:24 Leviticus 12:8

25 A righteous and devout man named Simeon lived in Jerusalem.
He longed for the coming of the Messiah and the anointing of the
Holy Spirit was upon him. 26 The Holy Spirit had revealed to him
that before he died he would see the Messiah, God's Son. 27 He felt
led by the Holy Spirit to go to the temple courts at the very time
when Jesus' parents brought Him there to fulfil the requirements of
the law. 28 Simeon took Him in his arms and praised God saying:

> 29 "Sovereign Lord, now You have fulfilled Your promise,
> Your servant can die in peace. 30-31 For I have seen Your
> salvation that You have made available to all people. 32 He
> will reveal Your light to the Gentile nations and is the
> glory provided for Your people, Israel."

33 Mary and Joseph were amazed at these words. 34-35 Then Simeon
blessed them and said to Mary, His mother: "This child will cause
many in Israel to fall, for He will be rejected by them, exposing the
nature of their hearts. Others will rise to new spiritual heights
because of Him, but it will be then that a sword pierces your own
soul."

36-37 A prophetess, Anna, the daughter of Phanuel of the tribe of
Asher, was also present in the temple courts. She was eighty years
old, having been a widow after only seven years of marriage. She
never left the temple precincts, but remained there day and night
worshipping, fasting and praying.

38 She approached them at the same time and thanked God for the
Child before speaking about Him to all those present, who were
longing for the Messiah's coming to redeem His people in Jerusalem.

39 Having fulfilled all required of them by the law, Joseph and
Mary returned to their home town of Nazareth in Galilee. 40 As the
Child Jesus grew up, He became strong in spirit, filled with wisdom
and it was clear that God's grace was upon Him.

The young Jesus in the temple courts (2:41-52)

41 Jesus' parents went to Jerusalem every year for the Feast of the
Passover. 42 When He was twelve years old they went to the Feast as
usual. 43 After the Feast His parents set out on their journey home,
unaware that Jesus had remained in Jerusalem. 44 They travelled for
a whole day, assuming that He was with others in the group of
travellers. When they began looking for Him among their relatives
and friends, He was nowhere to be found. 45 So they returned to
Jerusalem to search for Him. 46 After three days they discovered Him

sitting with the teachers in the temple courts, both listening and
asking searching questions, to the amazement of all who heard
Him. 47 They were struck by His understanding and the way He
answered their questions.

48 Jesus' parents were also astounded. His mother said to Him:
"Son, why have You done this to us? Your father and I have been
worried about You and have been searching everywhere for You."

49 "Why did you have to search for Me?" Jesus asked. "Wasn't it
obvious that I would be in My Father's house?" 50 But they failed to
understand what He meant.

51 Then Jesus travelled to Nazareth with them, and His mother
kept all these matters in her heart. 52 As Jesus continued to grow, He
increased in wisdom and in the esteem both of God and all who
knew Him.

John prepares the way (3:1-6)

3 1-2 While he was living in the desert, God's Word came to John,
the son of Zechariah, during the fifteenth year of the reign of
the Emperor Tiberius, when Pontius Pilate was the governor of
Judea, Herod ruled in Galilee, his brother Philip was ruler of Iturea
and Traconitis and Lysanias ruled in Abilene. 2 This was during the
high priesthood of Annas and Caiaphas.

3 John travelled to the areas around the river Jordan, preaching a
baptism for the forgiveness of sins for those who turned to God in
repentance. He fulfilled the words written by the prophet Isaiah:

> 4 'He is a voice crying out in the desert, "Prepare the way
> for the Lord's coming; get ready to receive Him. 5 Every
> valley shall be filled and every mountain levelled. The
> crooked ways will be straightened and the rough ways
> made smooth. 6 Then everyone will see the Saviour sent
> by God."'

John preaches to the crowds (3:7-20)

7 John spoke to the crowds that came to be baptised by him: "You
brood of snakes! Who warned you to run from the impending judgment? 8 Produce the lifestyle that demonstrates you have truly
repented, that you have turned away from your sins and have turned
to God. It is no use saying to yourselves, 'We are safe because
Abraham is our father.' For I tell you that God is able to raise up

3:6 Isaiah 40:3-5

children for Abraham from among these stones. 9 His axe is poised,
ready to strike at the very roots of the trees that fail to produce good
fruit. They will be cut down and thrown into the fire."

10 "What are we to do then?" the people asked.

11 John replied: "He who has two sets of clothes should give to the
one who has nothing to wear, and the one who has plenty to eat
should give to the hungry."

12 Tax collectors, known for being corrupt, also came to be baptised
asking: "Teacher, what should we do?"

13 "Only collect what is due, nothing more," John replied.

14 Some soldiers asked him: "What is expected of us?"

John answered: "Don't use your authority to extort money from
people and don't bring false accusations against them. Be content
with your wages."

15 Because people were eager for the coming of the Messiah, they
wondered whether he might indeed be the one for whom they were
waiting. 16 But John made it clear: "I only baptise you with water.
But the One who will come after me is far more powerful than I am.
I am not even worthy to do the job of a slave for Him. He will baptise
you with the Holy Spirit and the fire of God. 17 He is ready to thresh
the wheat and gather the grains into His barn, but burn the chaff
with a fire that cannot be extinguished."

18 John often gave the people such warnings but also preached the
good news to them. 19 However John spoke against Herod Antipas
because he had married his brother's wife, Herodias, and was
guilty of many other evils. 20 So later Herod had John thrown into
prison, adding this to his many other sins.

John baptises Jesus (3:21-22)

21-22 When Jesus came to the place where the people were being
baptised, He also was baptised by John. Afterwards, while He was
praying, the heavens opened and the Holy Spirit came upon Jesus
in the form of a dove. A heavenly voice was heard saying: "You are
my Son whom I love; I am delighted with You."

Jesus' genealogy (3:23-38)

23 Jesus was about thirty years old when this happened, marking the
beginning of His ministry. He was considered to be the son of
Joseph, who was the son of Heli, 24 who was the son of Matthat, the
son of Levi, the son of Melki, the son of Jannai, the son of Joseph,
25 the son of Mattathias, the son of Amos, the son of Nahum, the son

of Esli, the son of Naggai, 26 the son of Maath, the son of Mattathias, the son of Semein, the son of Josech, the son of Joda, 27 the son of Joanan, the son of Rhesa, the son of Zerubbabel, the son of Shealtiel, the son of Neri, 28 the son of Melki, the son of Addi, the son of Cosam, the son of Elmadam, the son of Er, 29 the son of Joshua, the son of Eliezer, the son of Jorim, the son of Matthat, the son of Levi, 30 the son of Simeon, the son of Judah, the son of Joseph, the son of Jonam, the son of Eliakim, 31 the son of Melea, the son of Menna, the son of Mattatha, the son of Nathan, the son of David, 32 the son of Jesse, the son of Obed, the son of Boaz, the son of Salmon, the son of Nahshon, 33 the son of Amminadab, the son of Ram, the son of Hezron, the son of Perez, the son of Judah, 34 the son of Jacob, the son of Isaac, the son of Abraham, the son of Terah, the son of Nahor, 35 the son of Serug, the son of Reu, the son of Peleg, the son of Eber, the son of Shelah, 36 the son of Cainan, the son of Arphaxad, the son of Shem, the son of Noah, the son of Lamech, 37 the son of Methuselah, the son of Enoch, the son of Jared, the son of Mahalalel, the son of Kenan, 38 the son of Enosh, the son of Seth, the son of Adam, the son of God.

Jesus tempted by Satan (4:1-13)

4 Being full of the Holy Spirit, Jesus went from the Jordan and was led by the Spirit to go into the desert. 2 There He remained for forty days, being tempted by the devil. During that time He ate nothing and so was very hungry. 3 It was there that the devil said to Him: "If You really are God's Son, use Your power to command these stones to turn into bread."

4 Jesus replied: "It is written in God's Word, 'Man needs more than bread to live.'"

5-7 Then the devil gave Him an aerial view of all the nations of the world and said to Jesus: "I will give You authority over the whole earth and You can have the glory of these nations, if only You worship me. For all this has been given to me and I can put anyone I choose in charge of them."

8 But Jesus answered: "It is written in God's Word, 'You are to worship only the Lord your God and He is the only one you are to serve.'"

9-10 Then the devil took Jesus to the highest part of the temple in Jerusalem.

4:4 Deuteronomy 8:3
4:8 Deuteronomy 6:13

"If You really are God's Son," he said, "You can jump from here without harming Yourself, for the scripture says, 'God will order His angels to guard You and keep You safe. 11 They will keep hold of You so that You will not even strike Your foot against a stone.'"

12 Jesus replied: "The scriptures also say, 'You are not to test the Lord your God.'"

13 Having finished trying to tempt Jesus, the devil left Him to await another opportunity to try and destroy Him.

Jews react angrily to Jesus (4:14-30)

14 Jesus then returned to Galilee filled with the Holy Spirit's power. Soon news about what He said and did spread throughout the whole province. 15 Everyone praised Him for the teaching He gave in the synagogues.

16-17 When He came to His home town of Nazareth, He went as usual to the synagogue on the Sabbath. When He stood to read from the scriptures He was handed the scroll of the prophet Isaiah. He unrolled it to the place where it reads:

> 18-19 'The Lord's Spirit is on Me because He has anointed Me to preach good news to the poor. He has sent Me to tell the prisoners they can be set free and to tell the blind they will be able to see; to free people from the oppression that has crushed them and to announce that the year of God's favour has arrived.'

20-21 He then rolled up the scroll, returned it to the attendant and sat down (to indicate He was about to speak with authority). Everyone in the synagogue was watching Him closely and He began His address by saying: "This scripture is now being fulfilled in your presence."

22 Everyone spoke well of Jesus and people were astounded at the gracious words He spoke. "Isn't this the carpenter Joseph's son?" they asked.

23 Jesus said to them: "No doubt you will quote the proverb to Me, 'Doctor heal yourself.' Do here in Your home town similar miracles to those You did in Capernaum about which we have heard.

24 "I tell you truly, no prophet is accepted in his own town. 25 There were many widows in Israel in Elijah's time when no rain fell for three and a half years, causing a severe famine throughout the land.

4:11 *Psalms 91:12*
4:12 *Deuteronomy 6:16*
4:18-19 *Isaiah 61:1-2*

[26]Yet Elijah was not sent to any of them, but to a foreign widow in
Zarephath in Sidon.

[27]"In the time of the prophet Elisha, many in Israel suffered from
leprosy, yet none of them were cleansed; only Naaman the Syrian
was healed."

[28]When they heard this, all in the synagogue reacted angrily.
[29]They forcibly took Jesus out of the town to the edge of the cliff-face
on which the town was built, with the intention of throwing Him off
the cliff. [30]But He walked through the crowd unhindered and
unharmed.

Jesus ministers with authority (4:31-37)

[31]Jesus then returned to Capernaum, a town in Galilee, where He
taught the people on the Sabbath. [32]They were amazed because He
delivered His message with such authority.

[33-34]There was a man in the synagogue who was under the control
of a demonic spirit. He shouted at the top of his voice: "Why are
you disturbing us, Jesus of Nazareth? Have You come here to
destroy us? I know who You are – the Holy One of God."

[35]"Silence!" Jesus commanded the demon. "Come out of him!"
Immediately the demon threw the man to the ground in front of
everyone and then came out of him without harming him.

[36]Everyone was astonished and questioned among themselves,
'What is the authority and power behind this man's teaching. He
can give orders to evil spirits and they obey Him immediately. They
have to leave those they have afflicted!' [37]News of such events
spread rapidly throughout the entire region.

Jesus heals many sick people (4:38-41)

[38]On leaving the synagogue, Jesus went to Simon's house. His
mother-in-law had a high fever and they asked Jesus to heal her.
[39]So He leaned over her, rebuked the fever and it left her. She was
able to get up immediately and prepare a meal for them all.

[40]At sunset the people brought to Jesus all those suffering from a
variety of sicknesses. He laid hands on each one and healed them.
[41]Demons came out of many shouting, 'You are God's Son!' because
they knew He was the Christ. Jesus commanded them to be silent.

Jesus preaches throughout Judea (4:42-44)

[42]Early on the following morning Jesus went alone to a deserted
place. The people were looking for Him everywhere and when they
found Him they tried to persuade Him not to leave. [43]But He told

them: "I have to preach the good news of God's Kingdom to the
other towns and villages also. This is the reason that God sent Me."
44 So He kept travelling and preached in the synagogues throughout
Judea.

Simon Peter to fish for men (5:1-11)

5 On one occasion, Jesus was standing on the shore of the Sea of
Galilee and the people were pressing close to Him to hear
God's Word. 2 He noticed two boats left at the water's edge by the
fishermen who were cleaning their nets. 3 He boarded the boat
belonging to Simon and asked him to push away from the shore.
Then Jesus taught the people as He sat in the boat.
4 When He had finished speaking, He told Simon: "Row out into
deeper water and cast your nets for a catch."
5 "Master," Simon answered, "we have worked hard all night
without catching anything. But I will let down the nets again only
because You say so."
6 Having done so, the catch was so great that the nets were in danger
of tearing. 7 So they called to their partners in the other boat to come
to their aid. When they did, they filled both boats so full that they
began to sink.
8 Seeing this, Simon Peter fell to his knees before Jesus and said:
"Please forgive me, Lord; for I am such a sinner." 9-10 He and all his
crew were amazed at the size of the catch, as were his partners
James and John, the sons of Zebedee.
Then Jesus replied to Simon: "There is nothing to fear; in the
future you will be catching men!" 11 So they beached their boats, left
everything and followed Jesus.

A Leper is healed (5:12-16)

12 In one town a man approached Jesus in the advanced stages of
leprosy. He fell to the ground on His face before Jesus and pleaded
with Him: "Lord, You can make me clean if You want to."
13 Jesus reached out and laid His hand on the man and said: "Of
course I want to: Be healed!" And immediately he was cleansed
from his leprosy.
14 Then Jesus ordered him not to tell anyone what had happened,
but to go directly to show himself to the priest to have the healing
verified. "Make the sacrifice that Moses commanded for those
healed of leprosy as a witness to everyone." 15 Nevertheless, the
news of this event spread rapidly. As a result, crowds came to hear
Jesus preach and to be healed of their afflictions.

16 Whenever possible Jesus withdrew to lonely places in order to pray.

Pharisees accuse Jesus of blasphemy (5:17-26)

17 One day while Jesus was teaching, a number of Pharisees and teachers of the religious law were present. They had come from all over Galilee and from Judea and Jerusalem. The anointing of God's power was obviously present for Jesus to heal the sick. 18-19 Some men arrived carrying a paralytic on a stretcher. They wanted to bring him into the house where Jesus was speaking, to lay the man before Him; but there was no way through the throng of people. So they carried him onto the roof, removed some tiles and lowered him among the crowd directly in front of Jesus.

20 Seeing their faith, Jesus said: "Friend, your sins are forgiven."

21 The Pharisees and teachers of the religious law were thinking to themselves, 'Who does this man think He is? He speaks blasphemy! Only God can forgive sins!'

22 Jesus knew what they were thinking and so asked them: "Why do you have such attitudes in your hearts? 23 Is it easier to say, 'Your sins are forgiven,' or to say, 'Rise up and walk'? 24 But so that you may know that the Son of Man has the authority to forgive those who sin," He said to the paralysed man, "I command you to stand up, pick up your stretcher and go home." 25 Immediately the man stood up in front of everyone, took his stretcher and went out praising God. 26 Everyone present was amazed and joined in the praise. They were awestruck and said: "We have seen astonishing things today."

Calling of Levi (Matthew) (5:27-28)

27 As Jesus was leaving the town later He saw a tax collector named Levi sitting in his customary place. Jesus said to him: "Follow Me". 28 Levi rose and left everything to follow Jesus.

Jesus questioned about fasting (5:29-39)

29 Then he held a great banquet for Jesus at his house at which a large number of tax collectors and other undesirables sat down to eat with Jesus. 30 But the Pharisees and the teachers of the religious law complained to Jesus' disciples: "How can you eat and drink with tax-collectors and such sinners?"

31 To this Jesus replied: "The healthy don't need a doctor, but the sick do! 32 I have not come for those who consider themselves righteous: but to call to repentance those who recognise they are sinners."

33 They said to Jesus: "John's disciples often fast and pray, as do the disciples of the Pharisees, but your disciples carry on eating and drinking!"

34 Jesus replied: "Do you expect the bridegroom's guests to fast while he is still around? 35 The time will come when the Bridegroom will be taken from them. That will be the time to fast."

36 Then He told them this parable: "Nobody would think of tearing a patch from a new garment and sewing it onto an old one. If he did so, not only would he have ruined the new garment, but the patch would not match the old one.

37 "Neither would anyone pour new wine into old wineskins. If he were to do so, the fermenting process at work in the new wine would cause the hardened skins to burst, and both the wine and wineskin would be useless. 38 No, new wine must be poured into new, flexible wineskins.

39 "And no one who has drunk old wine wants to drink new wine, for he says, 'The old is better!'"

Lord of the Sabbath (6:1-11)

6 As Jesus was walking through some fields of grain on the Sabbath, His disciples picked some heads of wheat, rubbed them in their hands and ate the grains. 2 Some Pharisees asked: "Why are you doing this? It is unlawful to work by reaping grain on the Sabbath!"

3 Jesus replied: "What about David? You must have read what he did when he and his followers were hungry. 4 He went into God's house and ate the consecrated bread that only the priests are allowed to eat; and he gave some to his friends." 5 Then Jesus stated: "The Son of Man is Lord even over the Sabbath."

6 On another Sabbath day, Jesus was teaching in the synagogue when a man with a withered right hand was present. 7 The Pharisees and teachers of the religious law were seeking an opportunity to accuse Jesus; so they were watching Him closely to see if He would heal on the Sabbath. 8 Jesus, of course, knew what they were thinking and said to the man with the withered hand: "Come and stand here where everyone can see you." So the man came forward and stood in front of everybody.

9 Jesus then put this question to them: "I ask you, according to the religious law, on the Sabbath should you do what is good or what is sinful; should you save life or destroy it?"

10 He looked around at each one and then said to the man: "Stretch out your hand." When he did so, it was completely healed.

11 But the religious leaders were furious and began to discuss among themselves what they could do to Jesus.

The twelve apostles (6:12-16)

12 About this time, Jesus spent a whole night alone on a mountainside praying to God. 13-16 The following morning He called His disciples together and chose twelve to be apostles: Simon (to whom He had given the name Peter), his brother Andrew, James and John, Philip, Bartholomew, Matthew, Thomas, James the son of Alphaeus, Simon the zealot, Judas son of James and Judas Iscariot, who later betrayed Him.

Jesus demonstrates God's power (6:17-19)

17 When Jesus came down from the hillside with them, He stood on a level area to address a crowd of His disciples and a large number of people who had come from all over Judea, including Jerusalem, and from the coastal region of Tyre and Sidon. 18 They went to hear Him preach and to be healed from their various diseases. Those who had been afflicted by evil spirits were set free and healed. 19 Everyone wanted to touch Him because God's power flowed out of Him and healed them all.

Those who are blessed (6:20-26)

20 Turning to His disciples Jesus said: "Those of you who are poor are blessed; God's Kingdom is given to you. 21 Those of you who hunger now are blessed, for your needs will be met. Those of you who weep now are blessed, for the time is coming when you will laugh with joy. 22 You are even blessed when men hate you, throw you out of the synagogue, insult you in other ways and regard you as evil because you believe in Me, the Son of Man. 23 That will be the time to rejoice and leap for joy, because it signifies that your reward in heaven will be great. This is precisely how the prophets of old were treated by your forefathers.

24 "But those of you who are rich are in danger of being cursed, because you already have all you want. 25 Those of you who gorge yourselves with food are also in danger, for you will be spiritually hungry for all eternity. Those who simply live for their own enjoyment are also in danger of being eternally cursed, for then you will cry with continual grief. 26 You are even in danger of curse if you live to be popular now, for that is how your forefathers regarded the false prophets.

Love your enemies (6:27-36)

27 "So listen, those of you who take heed to what I say: Love even
your enemies and seek to bless those who hate you. 28 Yes, bless those
who curse you and pray for those who mistreat you. 29 If someone
slaps you on one cheek, offer the other to him as well. If someone
takes your coat, offer him your shirt also. 30 Give to anyone who asks
you for something, and if someone takes what is yours, do not insist
that it is returned to you.

31 "This is the spiritual principle by which to live: Treat others in
precisely the same way you would like them to treat you.

32 "What credit is it to you to love only those who love you? Even
sinners love those who love them. 33 And what do you gain by doing
good to those who are good to you? Even sinners behave like that.
34 Are you any different if you expect repayment when you lend to
others? Sinners expect repayment when they lend to fellow sinners.

35 "But you are to love your enemies and seek to do them good.
Lend to others without expecting repayment. Then your reward
will be great, for you will be acting as sons of the Most High God.
You see, He is kind even to the wicked and those who take Him for
granted.

36 "So act with mercy and compassion just as your heavenly
Father does, for He is full of mercy.

Do not judge others (6:37-42)

37 "If you do not judge others, you will not be judged yourselves. If
you do not condemn others, you will not be condemned. Forgive
and you will be forgiven. 38 Give and see what is given to you: a full
measure, pressed down, shaken together and running over! The
measure you receive is determined by the measure you use when
you give!"

39 Jesus also told them this parable: "Is it possible for a blind person
to lead others who are blind? If he tries, they will all fall into the
ditch! 40 You see, a student does not consider himself more important
than his teacher; he wants to be trained to be like his teacher.

41 "Why do you want to take the speck of dust out of your brother's
eye, while you ignore the log that is in your own eye? 42 How can
you say to him, 'Brother, allow me to take the speck of dust out of
your eye,' when your vision is distorted by the log in your own eye?
What a hypocrite you would be! First, take the log out of your own
eye, and then you will be able to see clearly when you remove the
speck from your brother's eye.

The nature of the heart (6:43-45)

43 "A good tree does not bear rotten fruit; neither does a rotten tree produce good fruit. 44 The health of each tree is recognised by the nature of the fruit it bears. People cannot pick figs from thorn bushes, nor can they gather grapes from bramble bushes!

45 "The good man does good deeds because he has a good heart; the evil man does evil things because of the evil in his heart. What a man says is the product of the nature of his heart!

Put Jesus' words into practice (6:46-49)

46 "Why do you say to Me, 'Lord, Lord,' and yet you do not put what I say into practice? 47-48 The one who comes to Me, hears My words and puts them into practice, is like a man who, when building a house, dug deeply into the ground and laid its foundations on the bedrock. During a flood the stream of water could not shake that house because it was built on the rock.

49 "But the person who hears what I say but fails to put My words into practice is like someone who built a house without proper foundations. As soon as the floodwaters struck that house it collapsed and everything was lost."

The centurion's faith (7:1-10)

7 After saying all these things to the crowd, Jesus went to Capernaum. 2-3 There, a centurion's servant was ill and on the point of death. He was highly thought of by his master, who had heard of Jesus and so sent some of the Jewish elders to Him, asking Him to come and heal his servant. 4-5 They approached Jesus to plead his case strongly: "This soldier loves our nation and built our synagogue; so he deserves this of You." Jesus agreed to go with them.

6 However, He was nearing the house when friends of the centurion gave Jesus this message: "Lord, there is no need for You to take the trouble of coming to my home; I am not worthy of such an honour. 7 I did not think myself worthy enough to approach You personally. You only have to issue the word of command and my servant will be healed. 8 For I myself know what it is to be under authority and so be given authority over the soldiers under me. I command this one, 'Go,' and he does. I tell this one, 'Come,' and he comes. I only have to say to my servant, 'Do this,' and he does it."

9 Jesus was amazed at the centurion's message. Turning to the crowd following He said: "I tell you clearly, nowhere in the whole

of Israel have I found such great faith." 10 When the messengers returned to the centurion's house, they found his servant fit and well!

Widow's son brought to life (7:11-17)

11 Soon after this, Jesus visited Nain, together with His disciples and the large crowd that followed Him. 12 The funeral procession of a widow's only son was passing through the town gate as Jesus approached. 13 When the Lord saw the woman, His heart was filled with compassion for her and He said to her: "Don't cry."

14 Then He went to the coffin and touched it. Shocked, those carrying it stood still. "Young man," Jesus said, "I command you to rise up!" 15 Immediately the dead man sat up and began speaking. Then Jesus restored him to his mother.

16 Everyone was filled with wonder and praised God saying, 'Surely this is a great prophet whom God has sent among us to come to the help of His people.' 17 The news of what Jesus had done spread throughout Judea and the whole of the surrounding districts.

John the Baptist's question (7:18-35)

18-19 When some of John the Baptist's disciples told him about these events, he sent two of them to the Lord asking: "Are you the One sent by God, or should we expect someone else?"

20 When they approached Jesus they said: "John the Baptist has sent us to ask you: 'Are You the One whom God has sent, or should we expect someone else?' "

21 At that time Jesus had cured many of a variety of diseases and sicknesses; He had freed them from evil spirits and restored sight to many who had been blind. 22 So He answered the messengers by saying: "Return to John and repeat what you have just seen and heard: The blind are receiving sight, the lame are now walking, those who had leprosy are healed, the deaf can hear, even the dead are restored to life; and the good news is being preached to the poor. 23 Any man who is not offended by what I do is blessed!"

24 When John's messengers had departed, Jesus spoke to the crowd about John: "When you went to him in the desert what did you expect to see? A reed easily swayed by the wind? 25 Obviously not! So what did you see? A man wearing fine clothes? No, those who wear expensive clothes and who indulge themselves in luxury live in palaces, not the wilderness. 26 So what did you see when you went to him? A prophet? Certainly, but I tell you clearly John was

more than just a prophet. He is the one referred to in scripture where it is written:

> 27 "I, the Lord, will send My messenger ahead of You. He will prepare the way for Your coming."

28 "I tell you clearly, among all those who have ever lived there is no one greater than John. Even so, the most insignificant person in God's Kingdom is greater than he."

29 Everyone, including the tax collectors who had been baptised by John, agreed with what Jesus said about John, recognising that this was God's plan. 30 But the Pharisees and the experts in the religious law had rejected this as God's purpose for them and so had not been baptised by John.

31 "To what can I compare the people of this present age?" Jesus asked. "What are they like? 32 They are like the children who sit around the market place, shouting to one another: 'We played the flute for you but you refused to dance. When we sang mournfully you refused to grieve.'

33 "John the Baptist neither ate bread nor did he drink wine and you accused him of having a demon. 34 The Son of Man came both eating and drinking and you say, 'He is a glutton and a drunkard. He is a friend of tax collectors and sinners.' 35 But those who live by wisdom demonstrate that to be the right way to live!"

Woman with alabaster jar anoints Jesus (7:36-50)

36 A Pharisee invited Jesus to his home for dinner. 37 While reclining at the table, a woman with a sinful past from that town, who had heard where Jesus was eating, entered the house carrying an alabaster jar of expensive perfume. 38 She stood behind Jesus and then knelt weeping at His feet. When her tears fell on His feet, she wiped them with her hair, then kissed them and poured the perfume on them.

39 When the host Pharisee saw this he thought, 'If this man was really a prophet, He would know what kind of a sinful woman this is that is touching Him.'

40 Jesus said to him: "Simon, I have a personal word for you."

"What is it, teacher?" he asked.

41 "Two men owed money to a particular money lender. One owed him five hundred, the other fifty. 42 But neither was able to repay him. So he cancelled both their debts. Now which of the two will have the greater love for him?"

7:27 Malachi 3:1

43 Simon answered: "I suppose the one with the larger debt that was cancelled."

44 "You have answered correctly," Jesus said. Then He turned towards the woman and said to Simon, the Pharisee: "Do you see this woman? When I came into your house you failed to give Me any water to wash My feet. Yet this woman has washed My feet with her tears and dried them with her hair. 45 You didn't greet Me with a welcoming embrace, but from the time I arrived this woman has not stopped kissing My feet. 46 You didn't anoint My head with fragrant oil, but she has poured expensive perfume on My feet. 47 So I tell you clearly, the many sins of which she was guilty have all been forgiven, for she has shown such great love for Me. But the one who has only been forgiven superficially will only love superficially."

48-50 Then Jesus said to the woman: "Your sins are forgiven. Your faith has saved you. Go in peace."

But the other guests murmured: "Who does He think He is to forgive sins?"

The women who supported Jesus (8:1-3)

8 1-3 Then Jesus travelled around proclaiming the good news of God's Kingdom in every town and village. He was accompanied by the twelve disciples and a group of women who had been healed and set free from demonic spirits. This group included Mary Magdalene, who had been delivered from seven demons, Joanna wife of Chuza, who managed Herod's household, Susanna and many others. These women used their personal resources to help support them.

The parable of the sower (8:4-15)

4 Large crowds from every town gathered around Jesus and He taught them this parable:

5 "A farmer went out to plant some seed. As he scattered the seed, some of it fell on the path where it was trodden upon and where the birds came and ate it. 6 Some seed fell on rocky soil. It began to grow but soon withered because it lacked sufficient moisture. 7 Some seed fell among thorns which continued to grow and choked the plants that developed from the seed.

8 But some of the seed fell on good soil and this grew and produced a good crop, a hundred times as much as was sown."

Then Jesus said clearly: "Anyone with ears to hear, let him hear
and understand what I say."

9-10 When His disciples asked Him to explain this parable, Jesus
said: "You have been given revelation about the secrets of God's
Kingdom, but I speak to others in parables to fulfil what was written,
'Though they have sight, they do not see; though they hear, they do
not understand.'

11 "This is what the parable means: The seed is God's Word. 12 The
path represents those who hear, but then the devil comes and steals
the Word from their hearts to prevent them from believing and so
being saved.

13 "The rock signifies those who at first receive the Word with joy,
but there is no depth to their faith. They believe until their faith is
tested, and then they fall away.

14 "The thorns stand for those who hear the Word, but the life
within them is choked because they worry and focus on their material
possessions and the pleasures the world offers. So they never
mature in their faith.

15 "However, the good soil consists of those with good sound
hearts. They not only hear the Word but maintain their trust in it
and, because they persevere in their faith, they produce a good harvest.

Let your light shine (8:16-18)

16 "It makes no sense to light a lamp and then hide it out of sight
under a bed. No, you would put it in a prominent place so people
can gain maximum benefit from the light.

17 "Everything that is hidden will in time be exposed, and everything that people can conceal will be revealed and brought out into
the open. 18 So it is important that you listen carefully to the truth.
For the one who has received what I say will be given further revelation. But whoever does not listen will find that even what he
imagines he has will be taken from him."

Jesus' mother and brothers (8:19-21)

19 Jesus' mother and brothers came looking for Him, but were unable
to get near Him because of the density of the crowd. 20 Someone told
Jesus: "Your mother and brothers are outside waiting for You."

21 To this Jesus replied: "My mother and brothers are those who
not only hear God's Word, but also put it into practice."

8:10 Isaiah 6:9

Jesus calms the storm (8:22-25)

22 One day Jesus said to His disciples: "Let us cross to the other side
of the lake." So they boarded a boat and set sail. 23 During the crossing
Jesus fell asleep. But a sudden storm hit the lake, causing the boat
to be swamped and placing them in great danger. 24 The disciples
woke Jesus saying: "Master, Master, we are going to drown!"

So Jesus rebuked the wind and the turbulent water and the storm
immediately subsided. All was calm. 25 "So where is your faith?" He
asked the disciples.

Full of awe and amazement they questioned among themselves: "Who is this? He is able to command the winds and the waves, and they obey Him!"

Demoniac delivered (8:26-39)

26 They landed in the region of the Gerasenes on the far side of the
lake from Galilee. 27 As soon as Jesus stepped ashore He was
approached by a demon-possessed man. With no home or clothes,
he had lived naked among the tombs. 28 On seeing Jesus, he fell at
His feet and screamed: "What have I to do with you Jesus, Son of the Most High God? Please don't torture me!"

29 Jesus had already commanded the evil spirit to leave the man. This spirit had often taken control of him, so that even though he was shackled with chains and kept under guard, he had broken the chains and was then driven into remote areas by the demon.

30 Jesus asked the man for his name. "Legion," he replied, because
he had many demons living in him. 31 And these kept pleading with
Jesus not to command them to be sent to the Abyss, the Bottomless Pit.

32 A large heard of pigs was feeding on the hillside nearby. So the
demons begged Jesus to allow them to enter the pigs. 33 When Jesus
gave them permission they came out of the man, entered the pigs and the whole herd rushed down the steep hillside into the lake and were drowned.

34 When those who cared for the pigs saw what had happened, they ran and spread the news in neighbouring towns and the surrounding countryside. 35 People came to see for themselves what
had happened. When they arrived at the place they found the man completely set free from the demons, sitting and listening to Jesus. He was now clothed and in his right mind, yet the people felt afraid.

36 Those who had witnessed the miracle explained how the demon-
possessed man had been completely liberated. 37 Then the people

from the local area of the Gerasenes asked Jesus to leave the area,
because they feared what He might do next. So He boarded the boat
and left them.
38-39 The man who had been delivered begged to go with Him, but
Jesus refused, saying: "Go to your home and tell of the wonderful
thing that God has done for you." The man obeyed and spread the
news all over the town, telling everything that Jesus had done for
him.

Woman healed from haemorrhage (8:40-48)

40 When Jesus returned to the Galilean side of the lake, a crowd who
had anticipated His arrival welcomed Him. 41-42 A man named Jairus,
who was a leader in the synagogue, came and fell at Jesus' feet, begging
Him to come to his house where his only daughter was dying. She
was twelve years old.

Jesus was being jostled by a crowd of people as He made His way
to the house. 43 Among them was a woman who had suffered from a
haemorrhage for twelve years. Even though she had spent all her
money on doctors, no one had been able to heal her. 44 She came up
behind Jesus to touch the fringe of His robe and her bleeding
stopped immediately.

45 "Who touched Me?" Jesus asked.

Everyone denied being responsible and Peter pointed out:
"Master, so many in the crowd are pushing to get near You."

46 But Jesus insisted: "I know that someone touched Me deliberately because power has flowed out of Me."

47 The woman realised that she could not continue to be undetected
and, trembling with fear, she came and fell at His feet. She publicly
admitted why she had touched Him and told how she had been
healed immediately.

48 Then Jesus said to her: "My daughter, it is because of your faith
that you have been healed. Now go in peace."

Jairus' daughter healed (8:49-56)

49 While Jesus was speaking, a messenger from Jairus' house arrived.
"You needn't trouble the teacher any further; your daughter has
died," he said.

50 When Jesus heard this He said to Jairus: "Don't be afraid; simply
go on believing and she will be healed." 51 On arriving at Jairus'
house, Jesus would not allow anyone to go in with Him except for
Peter, John, James and the child's parents. 52 He told all those who

were wailing and mourning: "Stop crying; she is not dead but is only sleeping."

[53]They knew for certain that she had died, so they laughed at Him. [54]But Jesus went to the girl, took her hand and said: "My child, rise up!" [55-56]Her spirit returned to her body and she stood up. Jesus told her astonished parents to give her some food; but He told them not to broadcast what had happened.

The Twelve sent out (9:1-6)

9 On one occasion, Jesus called together the twelve and gave them the power and authority to drive out every demon and to heal people from their diseases. [2-3]He sent them out to preach the gospel of God's Kingdom and to heal the sick, telling them: "Do not take a lot of baggage with you. You will not need a staff, nor bread, nor money, nor extra clothing. [4]In each place stay in only one house. [5]If you are not welcome, shake the dust off your feet when you leave as a sign against the people who have rejected you."

[6]So the twelve went from one village to another, preaching the gospel and healing the sick wherever they went.

Herod hears about Jesus (9:7-9)

[7-8]News of these exploits reached Herod Antipas. He was confused because some claimed that these things were happening because John the Baptist had been raised from the dead, while others said that Elijah had appeared or that one of the prophets from the past had been restored to life. [9]"I beheaded John," said Herod, "so who is this that I keep hearing about?" He wanted to meet personally whoever was responsible.

Feeding of the five thousand (9:10-17)

[10]When the apostles returned to Jesus, they told Him of the things they had done. Then Jesus took them away quietly towards the town of Bethsaida; [11]but news of this spread and crowds followed Him. He welcomed them and preached about God's Kingdom to them and healed all who were sick.

[12]In late afternoon, the Twelve came to Jesus and said: "Dismiss the crowd so they can find food and shelter in the surrounding villages and countryside, because there is nothing for them here in this remote place."

[13]To this Jesus replied: "In that case, you give them something to eat!"

They answered: "All we have is five small loaves of bread and two fish, unless we go and buy food for this entire crowd." 14About five thousand men were present.

But Jesus instructed the disciples to tell the people to be seated in groups of about fifty. 15-16This they did and then Jesus took the five loaves and two fish in His hands, looked up to heaven and gave thanks to God. He then broke them and gave each disciple a portion to set before the people.

17Everyone ate as much as he wanted and the disciples filled twelve baskets with the remaining pieces!

Peter acknowledges Jesus as the Christ (9:18-20)

18On another occasion, although His disciples were with Him, Jesus had been praying privately. He then asked them: "Who do the crowds of people think I am?"

19They replied: "Some say You are John the Baptist restored to life. Others think You are Elijah or one of the great prophets of the past who has returned."

20"But what do you believe?" Jesus asked them. "Who do you say I am?"

It was Peter who answered: "You are the Christ, God's anointed Son."

Jesus predicts His death (9:21-22)

21Jesus then gave them strict orders that they were not to make this known to anyone yet. 22He told them: "The Son of Man is going to undergo suffering. He will be rejected by the spiritual leaders, the chief priests and teachers of the religious law. He has to be killed, but will be raised back to life on the third day after His death."

Followers of Christ must take up their cross (9:23-27)

23Jesus then told them all: "If any of you wants to be My follower, he will have to deny doing with his life what he wants. He will have to take up his cross of sacrifice every day in order to follow Me. 24For whoever wants to live his life for himself will lose everything: but whoever is prepared to sacrifice his life for Me will find true salvation.

25"How would it benefit a person if he were to gain everything he wants in the world, but he lost or forfeited his own soul in the process?

26 "Anyone who is ashamed of Me and of what I teach will find that I, the Son of Man, will be ashamed of him when I return in My Father's glory together with the holy angels. 27 I tell you the truth, some of you with Me here will witness the presence of God's Kingdom before they die!"

Jesus is transfigured (9:28-36)

28 About eight days later Jesus took Peter, James and John with Him onto a mountain to pray. 29 As He was praying, Jesus' face was transformed and His clothes shone as brightly as a flash of lightning. 30-31 Moses and Elijah stood talking to Him and they, too, looked glorious. They were speaking about how Jesus would fulfil what He had said about His death in Jerusalem.

32 A deep sleepiness came over Peter and the other two disciples. When they awoke they saw Jesus still there in His glory with Moses and Elijah. 33 As these two were leaving Jesus, Peter said to Him: "Master, it is so good for us to be here. But how can we preserve this moment? Shall we erect three shelters, one for You and one each for Moses and Elijah?" Clearly Peter did not understand the significance of what was taking place.

34 While He was speaking, a cloud enveloped them causing them to feel afraid as to what would happen next. 35 Then a voice spoke from the cloud, saying: "This is My Son, who I have chosen; listen carefully to Him."

36 After hearing this, the cloud disappeared and they found that Jesus was now alone. The disciples kept this to themselves, telling nobody at that time about what they had witnessed.

A boy delivered from an evil spirit (9:37-45)

37 When they came down from the mountain on the following day, they were met by a large crowd. 38-39 A man called out to Jesus: "Teacher, please come and help my son, for he is my only child and an evil spirit takes hold of him. This spirit makes him scream and throws him into convulsions, causing him to foam at the mouth. It hardly ever leaves him alone and is slowly killing him. 40 I have already asked Your disciples to drive the spirit out of him, but they have been unable to do so."

41 "What an unbelieving and disobedient generation this is!" Jesus replied. "How much longer do I have to put up with you? Bring your son here to Me."

42 While the boy was being brought forward, the demon threw him to the ground in a convulsion. Jesus immediately commanded

the spirit to leave him. He healed the boy and returned him to his
father. 43-44 And everyone was amazed at this display of God's greatness.
While the people were still awestruck at all that Jesus was doing,
He said to His disciples: "Listen very carefully to what I am about
to tell you: The Son of Man will be betrayed and placed in the control
of sinful men." 45 But they could not understand what He meant by
this. Its significance was hidden from them and they were afraid to
ask Him to explain it to them.

The greatest is the most humble (9:46-50)

46 Later the disciples began to argue with one another as to who
among them was the most important. 47 Jesus knew well what they
were thinking and so brought forward a small child to stand beside
Him. 48 Then He said to the disciples: "Anyone who receives a little
child in My Name receives Me, and whoever receives Me receives
the One who sent Me. For the most humble is truly the greatest
among you."

49 John said: "Master, we saw a man who is not one of us driving
out demons using Your Name; so we tried to stop him."

50 "No, don't stop him," Jesus said, "for those who are not against
you are on the same side as you."

Jesus sets out for Jerusalem (9:51-56)

51 Jesus now set out for Jerusalem with a determined attitude, for the
time was approaching for Him to return to heaven. 52-53 He sent
messengers ahead of Him, who were to prepare for His arrival in a
Samaritan village; but the people there did not want to welcome
Him.

54 "Lord, shall we call down the fire of judgment from heaven
upon them to destroy them as Elijah did?" James and John, the sons
of thunder, asked. 55 But Jesus rebuked them for such a suggestion
and said: "You do not understand what spirit moves you to suggest
such a thing. The Son of Man has come to save men not destroy
them." 56 Then they continued their journey to another village
instead.

The cost of following Jesus (9:57-62)

57 On the way, a man approached Jesus and said: "I am ready to follow
You wherever You go."

58 Jesus said to him: "Foxes live in holes and birds have their nests;
but the Son of Man has no permanent dwelling place."

59 To another man Jesus said: "Follow Me." But the man answered:
"Lord, I must first go and bury my father."

60 Jesus told him: "Leave the dead to bury those who are dead. But
you are to go and preach about God's Kingdom."

61 Yet another man said: "I want to follow You, Lord; but allow me
first to go and say farewell to my family."

62 Jesus said: "Once a person has begun to plough, he must not
look back. Such a one is not fit for service in God's Kingdom."

Other disciples sent out (10:1-24)

10 Later the Lord appointed seventy-two other disciples whom
He sent out in pairs. They were to go ahead of Him to prepare
for His arrival in every town and place where He was to go. 2 Jesus
said to them: "There is an abundant harvest waiting to be reaped,
but only a few workers. So pray that the Lord of the harvest will
send out many more workers into the harvest fields. 3 And go yourselves! For I am sending you out, even though you feel like lambs
among wolves. 4 You will not need to take anything with you; neither
allow yourselves to be diverted from My purpose by anyone you
meet.

"On entering a house, speak these words, 'The blessing of God's
peace be upon this house.' 6 If you are welcomed, that peace will
come upon those who are there. But if you are rejected, that peace
will come upon you.

"Stay in the same house and eat and drink whatever they give
you; the worker deserves to receive. But do not move from one
house to another.

"So when you are welcomed in a particular town, eat what is
offered to you. 9 Then heal the sick in that place and tell them, 'God's
Kingdom is now within your reach.'

10-11 "However, when you come to a place that does not welcome
you, say publicly in the streets, 'We wipe the dust of your town off
our feet as a sign against you. Understand that you reject God's
offer of His Kingdom.' 12 I tell you clearly," continued Jesus, "on the
Day of Judgment the fate of that town will be worse than what
happened to Sodom.

13 "Korazin, you are cursed! Bethsaida, you too are cursed! For
Tyre and Sidon would have repented already if I had done there the
miracles that I have performed in you. Yes, they would have truly
turned away from their sins. 14 As it is, Tyre and Sidon will fare better
than you when the time for judgment comes!

15 "And you, Capernaum, will you be honoured and exalted
because of all the great things I have done there? Not at all, you will
be destroyed and your people condemned.
16 "The one who listens to you disciples listens to Me. And any
who reject you reject Me and also the Father who sent Me."
17 When the seventy-two returned they were filled with joy and
told Jesus: "Lord, even the demons obeyed us when we addressed
them in Your Name."
18 To this Jesus replied: "I witnessed Satan being thrown out of
heaven as swiftly as a flash of lightning! 19 I have given you authority
to trample on demonic spirits and to overcome every power the
enemy has. Nothing will be able to harm you as you exercise that
authority. 20 However, your real cause for joy is not that these spirits
submit to your authority, but that your names are written in heaven,
that you belong to God's Kingdom. That is why you are given such
authority."
21 Being full of the joy of the Spirit, Jesus then said: "Father, Lord
of heaven and earth, I give You praise for You have hidden these
things from those who consider themselves clever intellectuals and
have chosen to reveal them to Your humble children. Yes, Father,
this has been Your gracious will; this is what You wanted to do!
22 "The Father has entrusted everything into My hands," Jesus
then said. "Only the Father truly knows the Son, and only the Son
truly knows the Father, together with those to whom the Son chooses
to reveal Him."
23 Then Jesus said privately to His disciples: "You are blessed
because of what you have seen. 24 I tell you clearly that many
prophets and kings have wanted to see such things but never saw
them, to hear what you have heard but never heard them."

The parable of the Good Samaritan (10:25-37)

25 Once an expert in the religious law stood to test Jesus by asking:
"Teacher, what must I do to receive eternal life?"
26 Jesus replied: "What does the law say about this? What does
this teach you?"
27 The man answered: "'Love the Lord your God with all your
heart and with all your soul, and with all your strength and with all
your mind,' and 'Love your neighbour as you love yourself.'"
28 "You have answered your own question correctly," Jesus
replied. "If you put these words into action you will live."

10:27 Deuteronomy 6:5, Leviticus 19:18

29 Knowing he failed to do this fully, he then asked Jesus: "Who is
my neighbour?"

30 In reply Jesus used this illustration: "A man was going from
Jerusalem to Jericho when he was attacked by bandits who stripped
him of his clothes, beat him up and left him lying half dead on the
roadside. 31 When a priest came along and saw the man, he crossed
to the other side of the road. 32 A Levite reacted in the same way.
33-34 But a Samaritan traveller came to where the man was lying.
Seeing him there, he felt sorry for him, went to him and dressed his
wounds, pouring oil and wine on them. He then placed the man on
his own donkey and took him to an inn to care for him. 35 On the
following day he gave two silver coins to the innkeeper with the
instructions to look after him. 'When I return,' he said, 'I will cover
any other expense you have incurred.'

36 "Now which of these do you consider was the true neighbour
to the man who was robbed?"

37 The expert in the religious law replied: "The one who had compassion on him."

So Jesus told him: "Well, go and follow his example."

Mary and Martha (10:38-41)

38 On their journey, Jesus and His disciples came to a village where a
woman called Martha welcomed them into her home. 39-40 Her sister
Mary sat listening intently to all Jesus said while Martha was busy
preparing the meal. Indignant, she said to Jesus: "Lord, does it seem
right to you that my sister has left me to do all the work? Why don't
you tell her to help me?"

41 The Lord replied: "Martha, Martha, you get so easily anxious
and upset. 42 Only one thing is really important and this is what
Mary is doing. So I certainly won't deprive her of what is most
important: to listen to what I say!"

Jesus instructs the disciples how to pray (11:1-13)

11 On one occasion, when Jesus had been praying, one of His
disciples said to Him: "Lord, please teach us how to pray, in
the same way that John instructed his disciples." Jesus told them:
"You can pray like this:

2 "'Father in heaven, we worship Your Holy Name. May Your
Kingdom come. May Your will be done on earth as it is in heaven.
3 Give us whatever we need day by day. 4 Forgive all our sins, as we
forgive all those who sin against us. And do not lead us into temptation,
but deliver us from the evil one.'"

5-6 He then added: "Imagine that one of your friends goes to someone in the middle of the night and says, 'Friend, please lend me
three loaves of bread; one of my friends has just arrived after a long
journey and I have nothing to give him.'

7 "But he received the reply, 'Don't trouble me now! I have
already locked the door for the night and my family and I are all in
bed. I cannot disturb everyone and give you anything.' 8 I tell you
clearly, though the man will not get up and give him the bread on
the basis of their friendship, yet because of the man's bold persist-
ence he will stir himself and will give him whatever he needs.

9 "So I tell you: continue to ask and it will be given you; go on
seeking and you will find; keep knocking and the door will be
opened to you. 10 For everyone who asks in this way receives; he
who is determined when he seeks finds; and to him who persistently
knocks the door will be opened.

11 "Listen, you fathers: if your son asked you for bread, would you
give him a stone, or if he asked for a fish would you give him a
snake instead? 12 Or if he asked you for an egg, would you give him
a scorpion? 13 If you, who are far from perfect, know how to give
good gifts to your children, how much more will your Father in
heaven, who is perfect, give the Holy Spirit to those who ask Him?"

A divided kingdom will collapse (11:14-28)

14 After Jesus had driven out a demon that had made a man dumb,
he was able to speak, to the amazement of the crowd. 15 Yet some
said: "He drives out these demons through Beelzebub, the prince of
demons."

16 Others asked Him to give them some heavenly sign that would
prove who He was.

17 Jesus knew what they thought so He said to them: "If a kingdom
is at war within itself, it will collapse. In the same way, where there
is division in a family it is torn apart. 18 So if Satan fights against
himself, how could he continue to have any power? I tell you this
because you accuse Me of using Beelzebub to drive out demons. 19 If
it is true that I drive them out by Beelzebub, by whom do your own
people drive them out? So they are the judges of what you say.

20 "However, if I drive out demons by God's power then that
demonstrates that His Kingdom has come among you.

21 "If a strong man is well armed and guards his house, his property
is safe. 22 But if someone who is stronger attacks and overpowers
him, he can then rob him of both his protection and possessions.

23 "Anyone who is not on My side is against Me, and anyone who
does not gather people into My Kingdom with Me, scatters them
instead.

24 "When an unclean spirit leaves a man, it travels through dry
places looking for another home. When it is unable to find a suitable
place, it says, 'I will return to the place I left.' 25 When it returns it
finds the 'house' clean and ready. 26 So it enters again, together with
seven other evil spirits who are even worse. There they remain, so
the man's condition is now far worse than it was in the beginning."

27 While Jesus was speaking, a woman in the crowd called out:
"Blessed is the mother who gave You birth and nourished You."
28 But Jesus replied: "Those who hear God's Word and obey it are the
truly blessed ones."

An evil generation (11:29-32)

29 More and more people crowded around Jesus and He said to
them: "This is an evil generation because it looks for a miraculous
sign. It will only be given the sign similar to that of Jonah. 30 He was
a sign to the Ninevites, and the Son of Man will be a sign to this generation. 31 The Queen of the South will be raised up in the judgment
together with the men of this generation and will condemn them.
For she came from a great distance to hear Solomon's wisdom, and
now Someone greater than Solomon is here before you.

32 "The Ninevites will also rise up in their judgment of this generation and will condemn it, for they repented in response to Jonah's
message; and now Someone greater than Jonah is here before you.

Be filled with light (11:33-36)

33 "No-one turns a lamp on and then hides it where its light cannot
be seen. Instead, he puts it in a prominent place to give light to anyone who enters the room.

34 "Your eye is the lamp of your body. When your sight is good the
whole body is full of light. But when you look at what is evil your
body is full of darkness. 35 Be careful, therefore, and ensure that you
are filled with light, not darkness. 36 For if you are full of light there
is no room for spiritual darkness, and you then live in the full radiance
of the light that shines on you!"

Warnings to the spiritual legalists (11:37-54)

37-38 As soon as Jesus had finished speaking, a Pharisee asked Jesus to
eat with him. Jesus entered his house and reclined at the table, but
the Pharisee was surprised that Jesus had not washed before the

meal. 39 The Lord said to Him: "You Pharisees wash the outside of
the cup and you clean the dish, but inside you are full of selfishness
and evil. 40 What foolish men you are! Is it not true that the same
God created your soul as well as your body? 41 If you give yourself
to meet the needs of the poor, then you will be completely clean.

42 "You Pharisees are in danger of being cursed because you are
strict in the giving of the tithe, giving even a tenth of your mint and
other garden herbs, while neglecting justice and true love for God.
You should have been just in all your actions and devoted to God,
as well as being faithful in your tithing.

43 "You Pharisees are in danger of being cursed, because you have
loved the positions of prominence in the synagogues, and you like
to be greeted openly in the market places.

44 "You are in danger of being cursed because you are like hidden
tombs which people walk over without realising that they are doing
something that defiles them."

45 One of the religious legalists answered: "Teacher, You insult us
also by saying such things."

46 To this Jesus replied: "You legalists are also in danger of being
cursed because you lay burdens on people that are impossible to
carry, and you yourselves will do nothing to help them. 47 You are in
real danger because you build tombs for the prophets that your own
fathers killed. 48 This bears witness to the fact that you approve of
what they did. They killed the prophets and you build their tombs.
49 This proves that God was wise in saying, 'I will send prophets and
apostles to My people even though they will persecute and kill
them.' 50-51 So this generation will be held accountable for all the people
killed since the world began, from the murder of Abel to the killing
of Zechariah who was slain between the altar and the Holy Place.
Yes, I tell you, this generation will be held responsible for all of this.

52 "You are in danger of being cursed, you religious legalists,
because you have taken away the key to knowing the truth. You
refused to appropriate the truth yourselves and you prevent others
from doing so."

53 When Jesus left, the teachers of the religious law and the
Pharisees were furious. They drew up a list of their grievances and
looked for an opportunity to catch Him out through something He
said.

Avoid hypocrisy (12:1-3)

12 By now the crowd had grown to many thousands and was
so dense that people were treading on one another. Jesus

spoke first to His disciples: "Make sure you are not in any way influenced by the leaven of the Pharisees which is hypocrisy. 2 There is nothing concealed that will not be exposed, nothing hidden that will not be revealed. 3 Therefore, whatever you have said in the dark will be heard in broad daylight, and what you have whispered privately in the ear will be shouted openly from the rooftops.

Fear God not men (12:4-12)

4 "My friends, I assure you that you do not need to fear those who can kill the body but have no further power over you. 5 I warn you about the One you should fear: He who has the power to throw you into hell once the body is dead. Yes, I tell you clearly, fear Him!

6 "Five sparrows are sold for next to nothing, aren't they? And yet not one of them is forgotten before God. 7 He even knows the number of hairs you have on your head. So there is nothing to fear, for you are far more valuable than many sparrows.

8 "I tell you clearly that anyone who openly confesses faith in Me before others, I, the Son of Man, will openly acknowledge before God's angels, as one who belongs to Me. 9 But anyone who disowns Me before others will be disowned by Me before God's angels. 10 Everyone who speaks a word against the Son of Man will be forgiven. But anyone who blasphemes against the Holy Spirit will not be forgiven.

11-12 "And when you are hauled before the synagogue leaders or before other rulers and authorities, do not be fearful about what to say or how to answer the accusations they bring against you; for the Holy Spirit will show you what to say at that time."

Guard against covetousness (12:13-21)

13 Someone from the crowd called out: "Teacher, tell my brother to divide the inheritance with Me." 14 But Jesus replied: "Man, who appointed Me to be your judge or arbiter?"

15 Then He said to them all: "Be careful! Guard against any form of greed. You do not assess the value of a man's life by what he owns."

16 He then told them this parable: "A certain rich man's land was very productive. 17 So he thought to himself, 'What am I to do, for I don't have sufficient storage for such a harvest? 18 I know, I will pull down my present barns and will build larger ones. Then I will be able to store all the wheat, as well as the other crops. 19 Then I shall be able to say to myself, 'You have everything you need for many

years to come. So now you can ease up, eat and drink as much as
you want and be fully satisfied.'
20 "But God said to him, 'What a fool you are! For tonight you will
die; then what will you do with everything you stored up for yourself?'
21 "This is what it will be like for anyone who looks after himself,
but is not rich in his attitude towards God."

Seek first the Kingdom of God (12:22-34)

22 Then Jesus told His disciples: "So I tell you clearly, do not be concerned about yourself, what you will eat. Neither be concerned about
the clothes you wear. 23 Life is far more important than worrying
about what to eat or wear. 24 You only have to think about the ravens
to understand this. They neither sow nor reap; they have no storehouse or barn, and yet God feeds them. Think how much more
valuable you are than the birds! 25 And who among you can add to
his significance by being anxious? 26 If you are unable to do that,
why be worried about anything at all?
27 "Think of the lilies you see growing. Although they neither
weave nor spin, not even Solomon in his most splendid robes could
compare with one of these lilies. 28 If God causes the growth of natural
things that are here today and gone tomorrow, will He not care for
you? Your faith is so weak!
29 "So do not set your focus on what to eat or drink. Don't be worried
about such things. 30 You would expect pagan unbelievers to have
such concerns, but your heavenly Father knows your every need.
31 So put God's Kingdom first in your life, then everything else you
need will be given you as well.
32 "Don't be afraid, little flock, for it has already pleased the Father
to give you His Kingdom. 33 Sell the possessions you don't need and
give the money to the poor. Then make lasting 'purses' for yourselves, for you have an eternal treasure stored in heavenly places,
where no thief can come to rob you or moth destroy what is yours.
34 For your treasure is wherever you choose to set your heart – in this
world or the next!

Be ready for Christ's coming (12:35-40)

35-36 "Be dressed properly and ready, with your light shining brightly;
for you are to be like those waiting for their master to return from a
wedding feast. As soon as he arrives and knocks, they are ready to
open the door to him. 37 Such servants are blessed, because their

master finds them ready for his coming. I tell you truly, he will then
reverse the roles. He will dress himself ready to serve and will make
them recline at the table where he will then wait on them. 38 So such
servants will be truly blessed, for the master finds them ready, even
if he comes in the middle of the night or at the crack of dawn.

39 "However, be clear about this: If the owner of the house had
prior knowledge about when the thief was coming, he would not
have let him break into the house. 40 So you must be ready at all
times because you do not know when to expect the coming of the
Son of Man!"

Wise and wicked servants (12:41-48)

41 Peter asked: "Lord, are You addressing this parable to us disciples
or to everyone?"

42 The Lord answered: "Who is the wise and faithful servant, to
whom the master can entrust the management of his other servants,
ensuring they are fed and cared for properly? 43 The servant he finds
doing this when he returns will be truly blessed! 44 I tell you the
truth, he will place such a faithful servant in charge of all his possessions.

45 "But what if the servant says to himself, 'My master is delaying
his coming,' and so begins to mistreat the other servants and
indulges himself in eating and drinking to the point of drunkenness?
46 His master will return when he least expects him, at a time that
surprises him. He will then punish him severely and will place him
with the unbelievers.

47 "The servant who knows his master's will, but who neither
prepares nor puts his master's will into action, will be punished
with many blows. 48 The person who was ignorant of his purposes
will receive only a few blows, even though he is guilty and deserves
to be punished.

"Therefore much is expected of everyone to whom much has
been given. And those entrusted with much responsibility will find
that even more is expected of them.

Division on earth (12:49-53)

49 "I came to bring fire on the earth, and I wish that this fire had
already started to burn. 50 I have to suffer a baptism and I am under
pressure until it has taken place.

51 "Do you imagine that I came to bring peace on the earth? No, I
tell you clearly, I came to bring division. 52 From now on if there are

five in a house they will be divided three against two and two against
three. 53 A father will be against his son and the son against his father.
A mother will be against her daughter and the daughter against her
mother. A daughter-in-law will be against her mother-in-law."

Understand the times (12:54-56)

54 Jesus then said to the crowd: "When you see a cloud rising in the
west, you say immediately that a storm is brewing and it duly
arrives. 55 When the south wind blows, you say that it is going to be
hot and it accordingly becomes hot. 56 What hypocrites you are! You
know how to discern the weather on earth from the appearance of
the sky, but how is it that you cannot discern the spiritual significance
of what is happening now?

Settle disputes (12:57-59)

57 "Why are you not able to judge for yourselves what is right?
58 Before going to court about a dispute with your adversary, do all
you can to settle the matter with him first, or he may drag you
before the judge who in turn will deliver you to the official who will
then throw you into prison. 59 I tell you clearly, there is no way that
you will then be released until you have settled the debt in full."

Repent or die (13:1-5)

13 Some of those present told Jesus about the Galileans whose
blood Pilate had mixed with their pagan sacrifices. 2 Jesus
answered: "Do you imagine that these Galileans were worse sinners
than others because they suffered such things? 3 No, I tell you!
However, you will all perish unless you repent! 4 What about those
eighteen who were killed when the tower in Siloam fell and crushed
them? Do you think they were any more guilty than all those living
in other parts of Jerusalem? 5 Not at all, I tell you. But you will also
die eternally if you do not repent."

Parable of the fig tree (13:6-9)

6 Jesus told them this parable: "A man had a fig tree that had been
planted in his vineyard. When he went to see how much it would
produce he could not find any fruit at all. 7 So he told his vine-dresser,
'I have been looking for fruit from this tree for three years but have
found none. Cut it down. Why should it take up valuable space?'

8 "'Leave it alone for one more year, Sir,' the man replied. 'I will
care for it and feed it. 9 If there is still no fruit next year, then cut it
down.'"

Woman healed on the Sabbath (13:10-17)

10-11 One Sabbath Jesus was teaching in a synagogue when a woman
was present who had been the victim of a spirit of infirmity for
eighteen years. She was bent double and was unable to stand
straight. 12 When Jesus noticed her, He called her forward and said
to her: "Woman, you have been set free from your infirmity." 13 Then
He laid hands on her and immediately her back was straightened
and she praised God.

14 The leader of the synagogue was angry that Jesus had healed
her on the Sabbath and said to the people: "We are allowed to work
on six days of the week. Those are the days when you should come
to be healed, not on the Sabbath."

15 But the Lord responded: "What hypocrites you are! Isn't it true
that each of you unties his or her ass and leads him from the stable
to the drinking water on the Sabbath? 16 So this woman, one of
Abraham's descendants, who has been locked up by Satan for
eighteen years should surely be freed from her bondage on the
Sabbath!"

17 Such words stunned those who opposed Jesus, but the crowd
rejoiced over all the glorious things He did.

The Kingdom of God (13:18-21)

18 Then Jesus asked: "How can you describe God's Kingdom? To
what shall I compare it? 19 It is like a mustard seed which a man
planted in his garden. It grew into a tree large enough for the birds
to come and perch in its branches."

20 He added: "What is God's Kingdom like? 21 It is like yeast which
a woman added into a large amount of flour until it affected the
whole lump of dough, causing it to rise."

The narrow door (13:22-30)

22 Then Jesus travelled to Jerusalem, teaching in the towns and villages
on the way there. 23 Someone asked Him: "Lord, are only a few going
to be saved?"

24 Jesus replied: "Struggle to enter through the narrow door,
because I tell you clearly that many who will try to enter will be
unable to do so. 25 Once the owner of the house has risen and shut

the door, those on the outside will bang on it saying, 'Lord, open up
for us.' But He will answer you: 'I don't recognise you.' 26 Then you
will reply: 'We ate and drank with You, and You taught in our
streets.' 27 And He will answer you, 'I don't acknowledge you or
where you belong. Keep away from Me, you ungodly people.'

28 "There will be tears and grinding of teeth when you see
Abraham, Isaac and Jacob with all the prophets in God's Kingdom,
but you are excluded. 29 Others will come from the east, west, north
and south and will take their places at the feast in God's Kingdom.
30 And you will see that those considered to be the most humble now
will be honoured then, and those regarded as the most important
now will be the least significant then."

Jesus' heart for Jerusalem (13:31-35)

31 It was then that some Pharisees approached Jesus to warn Him:
"Leave here, for Herod is planning to kill You!" 32 He replied: "Go
and tell that fox: 'I cast out demons and heal people today and
tomorrow, and on the third day I will fulfil My purpose. 33 Of course
I must continue today, tomorrow and the third day, for no prophet
can die outside Jerusalem.

34 "Jerusalem, Jerusalem, you killed the prophets and stoned
those sent to you. Yet I have often wanted to gather your children to
Myself as a bird gathers her young ones under her wings; but you
would not allow Me to do so. 35 Now look! Your house is forsaken!
And I tell you, you will have no way of seeing Me again until you
say, 'Blessed is He who comes in the Lord's Name.'"

Man with dropsy healed on the Sabbath (14:1-6)

14 Jesus went to the house of a prominent Pharisee to eat on a
Sabbath day. Those present watched closely everything He
did. 2-3 A man with dropsy stood in front of Him; so Jesus asked the
religious lawyers and Pharisees: "Is it lawful to heal on the Sabbath
or not?" 4-5 But they remained silent. Then Jesus healed the man and
dismissed him, and then asked them: "If any of you have a son or
an ox that falls into a pit, would you not immediately pull him out,
even if it was the Sabbath?" 6 They had nothing to say in reply.

The one who humbles himself will be exalted (14:7-14)

7 He noted that those who had been invited chose the best seats for
themselves and so told them this parable: 8-9 "When you are invited
to a wedding feast don't take the best place for yourself in case

someone more important than you has also been invited by the
host, who will then come and say to you: ‘Make room for this other
guest.’ Then in embarrassment you will have to take an inferior
place.

10 “So when invited take the lowest place, for then your host will
come to you and say: ‘My friend, please take a more distinguished
place.’ Then you will feel honoured before all the other guests. 11 So
everyone who seeks honour for himself will be humbled, while the
one who humbles himself will be honoured.”

12 Then Jesus said to the host: “When you prepare a meal, don’t
invite your friends, relatives or your wealthy neighbours, for they
will only invite you back in return, so repaying you. 13 No, when you
have a party invite the poor, the crippled, those who are lame or
blind. 14 Then you will be blessed because they are unable to repay
you. Instead you will be rewarded when God’s children are raised
from the dead.”

Give up all to follow Jesus (14:15-24)

15 On hearing this, one of those at the table with Jesus said to Him:
“He who has a place at God’s Kingdom feast is truly blessed!”

16 Jesus replied: “A certain man prepared a great feast to which
he invited many people. 17 When everything was ready he sent his
servants to them all saying: ‘Come, everything has been prepared.’
18 But they each began to make their excuses. The first said, ‘I have
just bought a farm and I must go and see it. I ask you to excuse me.’
19 Another said, ‘I have just bought five yoke of oxen and I am going
to try them out. Please excuse me.’ 22 And another said, ‘I have just
been married, so I cannot come.’

21-22 “The servant came and reported these responses to his master,
which made him angry. So he ordered his servant, ‘Quickly, go out
into the streets and pathways of the city and bring the poor, the
crippled, the blind and the lame to the feast.’ Later the servant said,
‘Master, I have done what you ordered and there is still room for
more guests.’

23 “‘Well go into the country roads and make others come so that
my house is full. 24 For I tell you clearly that none of those who were
originally invited shall taste any of the feast!’ ”

The cost of following Jesus (14:25-35)

25-26 Turning to the crowds that followed Him, Jesus said: “If anyone
comes to Me but does not hate the very idea of placing his father

and mother, his wife and children, his brothers and sisters and even himself above His love for Me, he cannot be My disciple. 27 Whoever is not prepared to carry his own cross and follow Me cannot be My disciple. 28 Would any of you decide to build a tower without first considering what it would cost to do so, thus ensuring he can afford to complete the task? 29-30 Otherwise he might lay the foundation but be unable to finish the work. All those who saw this would laugh at him saying, 'What he began he couldn't finish!' 31 Or what king would go to war against another king without calculating if he was able with his ten thousand men to conquer the one with twenty thousand? 32 If he was unable to do so, he would send a delegation to make peace instead. 33 So, in the same way, anyone who holds onto what he has for himself cannot be My disciple.

34-35 "Salt is good unless it loses its taste, then it is useless, for how can you restore its taste? It is fit for nothing and may as well be thrown away.

"If you have any spiritual understanding, then listen carefully to what I am saying!"

Parable of the lost sheep (15:1-7)

15 A group of tax gatherers and sinners came close to Jesus to listen to Him. 2 But both the Pharisees and the teachers of the religious law murmured against Him. "This man receives sinners and even eats with them," they said.

3-4 So Jesus taught them this parable: "If anyone owned a hundred sheep but lost one of them, would he not leave the ninety-nine to fare for themselves while he went searching for the lost one until he found it? 5 Then he would return carrying it on his shoulders, full of joy. 6 And when he arrived home he would gather his friends and relatives and tell them, 'Rejoice with me, for I have found the sheep I had lost.'

7 "I tell you clearly, there is more joy in heaven over one sinner that repents than over ninety-nine godly men who do not need to repent.

Parable of the lost coin (15:8-10)

8 "Or what woman with ten valuable coins, if she lost one, would not take a lamp and search everywhere in the house until she found it? 9 Having done so, she would gather her friends and neighbours saying, 'Rejoice with me, because I have found the coin I lost.'

10 "So I tell you clearly, there is more joy before God's angels in
heaven over every sinner who repents."

Parable of the father with two sons (15:11-32)

11 Then Jesus said: "There was a father who had two sons. 12 The
younger one said to him, 'Father, please give me the share of the
inheritance that is due to me.' So he divided the property between
them.

13 "A few days later, the younger son gathered his possessions
together and left for a distant country, where he wasted his inheritance by indulging himself with an immoral life-style. 14 But a severe
famine struck that land when he was broke, leaving him destitute.
15 In desperation he found a job locally with a farmer, who sent him
into the fields to feed his pigs. 16 The son longed to eat the pig-swill,
but no-one gave him anything. 17 This brought him to his senses and
he thought, 'How many of my father's servants have more than
enough to eat, but I am starving with hunger. 18-19 I will return to my
father and will say to him, 'Father, I sinned before heaven and you;
I am no longer worthy to be called your son. Take me on as one of
your hired servants."

20 "So he set out for home. His father saw him in the distance and,
filled with compassion for him, ran to welcome him with a big hug
and a kiss.

21 "The son said, 'Father, I have sinned against God and you and
I am no longer worthy to be your son.' 22 But the father immediately
said to his servants, 'Go quickly and fetch the finest robe and put it
on him. 23-24 Bring a ring for his finger and shoes for his feet. Then kill
the fattened calf so we can celebrate because this son of mine was
dead and now he is alive again, he was lost but now he is found.' So
they began the celebration party.

25 "Meanwhile the older son returned home from the fields. As he
approached the house he heard the sound of the music and dancing.
26 So he called one of the servants and asked what was happening.
27 The servant replied, 'Your brother has returned home and your
father has killed the fattened calf in celebration because he has
received him back safely.'

28 "But the older son was angry and refused to join the feast. So
the father went to persuade him to join the celebration. 29 But he
answered his father, 'Look, for years I have served you faithfully
and have never disobeyed your orders. Yet you never gave me even
a goat for a feast with my friends. 30 But now this son of yours who

has wasted your money with prostitutes comes home and you kill
the fattened calf for him!'
31 "The father replied: 'My son, you are always with me and
everything that is mine is yours. 32 Come and rejoice because this is
your brother who was dead but has now come to life; he was lost
but now is found."

Parable of the unjust manager (16:1-12)

16 Jesus said to His disciples: "There was a certain rich man
who had a manager who was accused of wasting his master's
possessions. 2 So he called him and asked, 'What is this that I hear
about you? Give me an account for the way you have managed my
affairs, for I have decided to dismiss you.'
3 "The manager thought: 'What can I do if the master sacks me? I
am not used to manual labour and I would be ashamed to beg. 4 I
have an idea so that when I am no longer manager, others will readily
employ me.'
5 "So he called each of his master's debtors and said to the first,
'How much do you owe my master?' 6 'Eight hundred gallons of
oil,' he replied. So the manager told him, 'Pay me now and we will
settle for four hundred.'
7 "To another he said, 'How much do you owe?' 'A thousand
bushels of wheat,' he answered. Then the manager said, 'Pay me
now and we will settle for eight hundred.'
8 "The master congratulated the unrighteous manager for his
astuteness, because the worldly people of this generation act more
wisely than the sons of the light. 9 And I tell you clearly, make
friends for yourselves by the way you use the things of this world
so that when it ends, you will be welcomed into your eternal home.
10 For the one who proves faithful in small things will also prove
faithful when given greater responsibilities, and whoever proves he
cannot be trusted in small ways will not be trusted in more important matters. 11 So if you have not proved trustworthy in handling
worldly things, why should you be entrusted with true riches?
12 And if you do not handle other people's property with care, who
will give you property of your own?

More principles of the Kingdom (16:13-18)

13 "No one can serve two masters, for either he will hate the one and
love the other, or he will be faithful to one and despise the other.
You cannot serve both God and money!"

[14]Now when the Pharisees heard all these things they treated Jesus with disdain, for they loved money. [15]So Jesus told them: "You try to justify yourselves before men, but God knows your hearts. For what men value highly God hates. [16]The law and the prophets were needed until John began his ministry. But then it was preached that God's Kingdom was available and everyone is pushing to enter into it. [17]For it is easier for the earth to come to an end than for a tiniest part of the law to disappear.

[18]"Anyone who divorces his wife and marries someone else commits adultery. And if the woman who was divorced marries again she also is guilty of adultery.

Parable of the rich man and Lazarus (16:19-31)

[19]"There was a rich man who wore an expensive purple robe and the finest linen and who enjoyed a luxurious life-style. [20]And there was a poor man named Lazarus who was laid at his gate. [21]He was covered with sores and longed to receive the scraps remaining from the rich man's table. Even the dogs came and licked his sores.

[22-23]"Now the poor man died and was carried by the angels to be close to Abraham in paradise. The rich man also died, was buried and cast into hell where he was in torment. But he could see Abraham far away with Lazarus close to him. [24]So he called out, 'Father Abraham, have pity on me and send Lazarus that he might dip the tip of his finger in water to cool my tongue, for I am suffering terribly in this fire.'

[25]"But Abraham answered, 'Child, remember that in your lifetime you had everything you wanted and Lazarus had nothing. Now he is comforted here and it is your turn to suffer. [26]Besides all this, there is a great immovable gulf between us and you. It is impossible to cross that gulf, no matter how much you wish to do so; neither can any of us cross it to come to you.'

[27]"The man replied, 'If this is the case, father, please send Lazarus to my relations. [28]Let him warn my five brothers so they can avoid ending up in this place of torment.'

[29]"But Abraham said, 'They have Moses and the prophets; let them listen to what they say.'

[30]"He replied, 'No Abraham, they will repent if someone who has died appears to them.'

[31]"But Abraham answered, 'If they refuse to listen to Moses and the prophets, neither will they be persuaded if someone from the dead appears to them.'"

Dealing with sin (17:1-4)

17 Jesus said to His disciples: "It is inevitable that things will happen which will cause people to sin, but the one who causes others to sin is in danger of being cursed. 2 It would be better if a millstone were placed around his neck before being thrown into the sea than to be guilty of causing one of my little ones to sin. So be warned!

3 "If your brother sins, correct him; and if he repents then forgive him. 4 Even if he sins against you seven times in a single day and comes to you seven times saying, 'I am really sorry,' you must forgive him."

Faith the size of a mustard seed (17:5-10)

5 The apostles said to the Lord: "Please enable our faith to increase and be stronger."

6 Jesus answered: "You only need faith the size of a tiny mustard seed to be able to say to this sycamore tree, 'Be uprooted and planted in the sea,' and it will obey you.

7 "If one of you had a slave who had been busy ploughing or tending the sheep and who then returned home, would you say to him: 'Come and have a good rest'? 8 Would you not say instead, 'Now prepare my dinner and then serve me while I eat and drink; after that you can have something yourself.' 9 Would he even thank the slave for simply obeying his orders?

10 "This is how it should be with you. When you have done everything you are commanded to do, you should say, 'We are only unworthy slaves who have done what was expected of us!'"

Ten lepers cleansed (17:11-19)

11 On his way to Jerusalem, Jesus had to pass along the border between Samaria and Galilee. 12-13 When He entered a particular village ten lepers met Him. They remained a safe distance away but called out to Him: "Jesus, Master, have mercy on us."

14 When He noticed them, Jesus said to them: "Go and show yourselves to the priests (to have your healing verified)." On the way they were cleansed of their leprosy! 15 When he realised that he had been healed, one of them returned to Jesus shouting God's praises. 16 He fell on his face before Him and thanked Him. He was a Samaritan.

17 Jesus said: "Ten were healed; so where are the other nine? 18 Is this outsider the only one who has returned to give God the glory?"

19 Then He said to the Samaritan: "Stand up and go on your way; your faith has saved you."

The coming of the Kingdom (17:20-37)

20-21 Some Pharisees asked Jesus when God's Kingdom would come. He answered them: "God's Kingdom does not come by looking for it, neither will you be able to say, 'It is here' or 'It is over there.' For God's Kingdom is within you."

22 Then Jesus said to His disciples: "The time will come when you will long to see one of the days of the Son of Man, but you will not be able to do so. 23 Others will say to you, 'See, it is here' or 'See, it is there.' Do not follow such people. 24 For on His Day the Son of Man will come like lightning that flashes from one side of the skies to the other. 25 Before then He has to suffer many things and be rejected by this generation.

26 "As it was in Noah's time, so it will be when the Son of Man returns. 27 They were eating and drinking, getting married and carrying on as usual right up until the day when Noah entered the ark. But then the flood came and they were all destroyed. 28 It was the same in Lot's time. People were eating, drinking, buying, selling, planting and building as usual. 29 But on the day Lot left Sodom, fire and sulphur fell from heaven and they were all destroyed.

30 "It will be just like this on the Day when the Son of Man is revealed. 31 At that time, if someone is on the roof he should not go into his house to gather his belongings. Nor should anyone in the fields go home to retrieve his possessions. 32 Remember what happened to Lot's wife. 33 Whoever tries to save his life will lose it, but whoever loses his life for My sake will preserve it.

34 "I tell you clearly, on that night if two are in bed together one will be taken and the other left. Two men will be in the field; one will be taken and the other left. 35 If two women are grinding corn together, one will be taken but the other will be left behind."

37 They asked Him: "Lord, when and where will all this happen?"

He answered: "Wherever there is a dead body the vultures will gather!"

Parable of the persistent widow (18:1-8)

18 1-2 Jesus told them a parable to explain that they should pray with perseverance and not give up: "A judge in a certain city neither feared God nor had any concern for others. 3 A widow from that city came and said, 'Give me justice against my opponent.'

4-5 For some time the judge paid no attention to her, but after a while
he thought, 'Although I fear neither God nor man, I will give this
woman the justice for which she asks because she wearies me with
her constant demands.'"
6 Then the Lord said: "Listen carefully to what the unrighteous
judge says! 7 So will not God, who is right in all He does, be sure to
give justice to His chosen ones who cry out to Him in prayer day
and night? Will He keep refusing them? 8 I tell you clearly, He will
ensure that they receive justice, and quickly! However, when the
Son of Man returns, will He find such faith on the earth?"

Parable of the Pharisee and the tax collector (18:9-14)

9-10 Then Jesus used this parable to address the self-righteous, those
who placed their confidence in themselves and despised others:
"Two men went to the temple to pray. One was a Pharisee and the
other a tax-collector. 11-12 The Pharisee prayed about himself saying,
'God, I thank You that I am not like other men, extortionists, corrupt,
adulterers, or even like this tax collector. I fast twice a week. I give
the tithe of everything I receive.'
13 "The tax collector stood some way off and would not even lift
his eyes towards heaven when he prayed, but beat his breast and
said, 'God be merciful to me, a sinner.' 14 I tell you clearly, this man
went home acceptable before God rather than the other one. For
everyone with exalted ideas about himself will be humbled, but the
humble one will be exalted by his God!"

Become like children to inherit the Kingdom (18:15-17)

15 The people brought their babies to Jesus so He would touch them
and bless them; but the disciples tried to prevent them from doing
this. 16 Jesus told Him: "Let the children come to Me; don't stop them.
For God's Kingdom belongs to those who are like little children. 17 I
tell you truly that unless a person receives God's Kingdom like a
child, he or she will never be part of it!"

How to inherit eternal life (18:18-30)

18 A certain leader asked Jesus: "Good teacher, what must I do to
inherit eternal life?" 19 Jesus replied: "Why do you call Me 'good'?
Only God Himself is good! 20 You know the commandments: 'Do not
commit adultery; do not kill; do not steal; do not testify falsely; honour
your father and mother.'"
21 "I have kept all these things from my youth," the man said.

[22]On hearing his reply Jesus told him: "You still lack one thing.
Sell your possessions and give money to the poor; then you will
have riches in heaven and will be free to follow Me."

[23]The man appeared sad when he heard this because he was very
wealthy. [24]Seeing this, Jesus said: "How hard it is for the wealthy to
enter God's Kingdom. [25]It is easier for a camel to pass through the
eye of a needle than for a rich man to enter God's Kingdom."

[26]Those who heard Him say this asked: "Then who can be
saved?"

[27]He answered: "Whatever is impossible for men is possible for
God!"

[28]Peter said: "We have left everything behind to follow You."

[29-30]Jesus told them: "I tell you truly, that no one can leave his
home, wife, brothers, parents or children for the sake of My
Kingdom, without receiving much more in return while on earth,
and eternal life in the age that is to come."

Jesus predicts His death again (18:31-34)

[31]Taking the twelve aside, Jesus said to them: "Now we are going up
to Jerusalem and everything written in the prophets concerning the
Son of Man will be fulfilled. [32-33]He will be delivered to the Gentiles
and will be mocked, insulted and spat upon. After they have
flogged Him, they will then kill Him; but on the third day after His
death He will rise to life again." [34]But none of this made sense to
them, for the meaning of His words was hidden from them; so they
could not grasp the significance of what He said.

Jesus restores sight to a blind man (18:35-43)

[35]As He approached Jericho, there was a blind man begging by the
roadside. [36]Hearing a crowd passing he asked what was happening.
[37] "Jesus of Nazareth is passing by," he was told. [38]So the blind man
shouted: "Jesus, Son of David, have mercy on me." [39]Those in the
front of the crowd rebuked him and told him to be quiet. But he
shouted even more loudly: "Son of David, have mercy on me."

[40]Jesus paused and ordered that the man be brought to him.
When he was close enough Jesus asked him: "What do you want
Me to do for you?"

[41]He replied: "Lord, I want to see again."

[42]So Jesus said to him: "Receive your sight. You are healed because
of your faith." [43]Immediately he was able to see again and then he
followed Jesus, glorifying God. And all those who witnessed this
praised the Lord.

Zacchaeus the tax collector (19:1-10)

19 1-3As He was passing through Jericho, a man called Zacchaeus, who was chief tax collector and very wealthy, wanted to see Jesus; but being very short he was unable to do so because of the crowd of people. 4So he ran ahead and climbed a sycamore tree in order to catch sight of Jesus who was about to pass along that way. 5When He came to that place, Jesus looked up and said to him: "Zacchaeus, quickly come down from there. I must stay at your house today." 6So he climbed down immediately and welcomed Jesus with joy.

7When others saw this they complained: "He has gone to stay in the house of a sinner."

8Zacchaeus stood before the Lord and said: "Lord, I give half my possessions to the poor and if I have made false claims against anyone, I will restore four times the amount to him." 9Jesus said to him: "Today salvation has come to this house, because this man is a true son of Abraham. 10For the Son of Man came to seek and save those who are lost."

Parable of the diligent servants (19:11-27)

11He then told a parable to those listening to all He said, for He was nearing Jerusalem and there was speculation that God's Kingdom was about to appear. 12He said: "A nobleman was about to travel to a distant country to inherit a kingdom, before returning home. 13So he called ten of his servants and gave each of them a thousand, telling them, 'Use this money to trade while I am away.' 14But he was hated by the citizens who sent a delegation after him saying, 'We don't want this man to rule over us.'

15"In due course the nobleman returned, having received the kingdom, and summoned the servants to whom he had entrusted the money to discover how much profit they had made. 16The first came and said, 'Lord, I have increased the thousand to ten thousand.' The nobleman said to him, 'You have done well and are a good servant. Because you have proved faithful in this small matter I am giving you authority over ten cities.'

17-19"The second servant came and said, 'I have turned the one thousand into five.' So the nobleman said to him, 'I am giving you authority over five cities.'

20-21"A third servant came and said, 'Lord, here is the thousand you gave me. I have kept it hidden safely because, knowing how demanding you are, I feared you. I know you expect a return with-

out making a deposit and you reap where you have not sown any
seed.'
22 "The nobleman said, 'I will judge you by your own words, you
wicked servant! You were aware that I am a demanding man,
expecting a return when I have not made a deposit and reaping
where I have not sown. 23 Then why did you not at least put the
money in a bank to gain interest for my return?'
24 "He then said to the others standing nearby, 'Take the thousand
from him and give it to the one with ten thousand. 25 'But sir,' they
replied, 'he already has ten thousand!'
26 "The master replied, 'I tell you, to everyone who has, more will
be given, and from the one who has nothing, everything he has will
be taken away. 27 However, bring here to me my enemies who did
not want me to reign over them and execute them in front of me.'"

Triumphal entry (19:28-40)

28 After saying these things, Jesus set out for Jerusalem. 29-30 As He
drew near to Bethphage in Bethany near the mount of Olives, He
sent two of the disciples on ahead telling them: "Go to the village
ahead of you where you will find tethered a colt on which no one
has yet ridden. Untie it and bring it here. 31 If anyone asks you why
you are untying the colt, you are to answer, 'Because the Lord needs
it.' 32 So the two disciples went and found the colt exactly as Jesus
had said. 33 As they were untying the colt its owners asked: "Why are
you untying the colt?" 34 They replied: "Because the Lord needs it."
And they brought it to Jesus.
35 Then they threw their cloaks on the colt and put Jesus on it. 36 As
He went along, people threw their cloaks onto the road in front of
Him. 37 As He approached the Mount of Olives, the great crowd of
disciples were rejoicing and shouting to God for all the powerful
works they had seen, saying:

> 38 "Blessed is the King who comes in the Lord's name!
> Peace in heaven and glory in the highest!"

39 Some of the Pharisees in the crowd said to Jesus: "Teacher, tell
Your disciples to stop this." 40 But He answered: "I tell you clearly, if
all the people were to remain silent even the stones would cry out."

Jesus prophesies the destruction of Jerusalem (19:41-44)

41-42 When Jesus was near enough to see the city, He wept over it and
said: "If you only listened today to what would bring you peace,
but now it is hidden from you and you cannot see it. 43 The time will

come when your enemies will build a rampart and will surround
you on every side. 44 They will throw you to the ground, both you
and your children within you, and will not leave one stone upon
another, because you did not recognise the time of God's visitation."

Jesus dispels traders from the temple (19:45-48)

45-46 When He entered the temple courts, Jesus threw out the traders
telling them: "It is written: 'My house shall be a house of prayer, but
you have made it a robber's den!"'

47 Daily He taught in the temple courts, but the chief priests, the
teachers of the religious law and the leaders of the people planned
to kill Him. 48 However they could not find a suitable opportunity as
the people hung upon every word He spoke.

Jesus' authority questioned (20:1-8)

20 1-2 On one of those days, as He was teaching and preaching
the good news to the people in the temple courts, the chief
priests, together with the teachers of the religious law and the elders,
came and said to Him: "Tell us by whose authority You do these
things. Who gave You such authority?"

3 Jesus replied: "I will also ask you a question. 4 Tell me, John's
baptism, was this of God or man?" 5-6 They discussed among themselves how to answer. "If we say it is of God, He will ask us why we
did not believe what John said, and if we say it was of man the people
will stone us for they are convinced that John was a prophet." 7 So
they said: "We cannot tell."

8 Then Jesus told them: "Then neither will I tell you by what
authority I do these things."

Parable of the wicked tenants (20:9-18)

9 He then told the people this parable: "A man planted a vineyard
and leased it to tenants before going away for a considerable time.
10 At harvest, he sent a servant to the tenants to collect his portion of
the fruit. 11 But the tenants beat the servant and sent him away
empty-handed. So he sent another servant, but they also beat and
abused him, giving him nothing! 12 They also wounded a third servant
before throwing him out.

13 "So the owner of the vineyard said: 'What can I do? I will send
my own son whom I love dearly. Surely they will respect him!' But
when the tenants saw him they decided among themselves, 'This is

19:45-46 Jeremiah 7:11

the heir; let's kill him and then we can claim the inheritance.' So they threw him out of the vineyard and killed him.

14-15 "What will the owner of the vineyard do to these tenants? He will come and destroy them and will lease the vineyard to other tenants."

16 When the people heard this they said: "May it never be so!" 17 But Jesus looked at them and said: "What does this scripture mean then, 'The stone which the builders rejected has become the chief cornerstone?' 18 Everyone who falls on that stone will be smashed to pieces, but the one on whom it falls will be crushed to powder."

Paying taxes to Caesar (20:19-26)

19 Immediately the teachers of the religious law and the chief priests wanted to grab Him, but they were afraid of the people. 20 They knew He directed this parable against them. 21 So they sent spies who pretended to be honest people to watch Jesus carefully, hoping He would say something that would give them just cause to arrest Him and hand Him over to the authority of the governor. They put a trick question to Him: "Teacher, we know that You speak what is right and are impartial in the way You treat everyone, that You teach the true way of God. 22 So tell us, is it lawful for us to pay taxes to Caesar or not?"

23-24 Jesus immediately saw through their duplicity and said: "Show Me a coin. Whose image does it bear?"

25 "Caesar's," they said.

Then Jesus told them: "Give to Caesar what belongs to Caesar, and to God what belongs to God."

26 So they were unable to trap Him when He spoke publicly to the people. They were astonished at His answer, which reduced them to silence.

Sons of the resurrection (20:27-40)

27 Then some Sadducees, who do not believe there is any resurrection from the dead, approached Jesus. 28 They put this question to Him: "Teacher, Moses wrote that if a man dies leaving his wife childless, then his brother must marry the widow and have children on his behalf. 29 Now there were seven brothers. The first died leaving his wife childless. 30-31 The second and third brothers married her in turn but she remained without children. 32 In the end all seven married the woman but all died without producing any children. Then the

20:17 Psalm 118:22

woman also died. 33 In the resurrection, whose wife will she be, for all seven married her?"

34-35 Jesus answered them: "The people of this present age marry and are given in marriage, but those considered worthy of taking part in the age to come when the dead will be raised, neither marry nor are given in marriage. 36 They will be immortal like the angels. They are God's own children because they are sons of the resurrection.

37 "In the account of the burning bush, Moses made it clear that the dead are raised, for he called the Lord the God of Abraham, the God of Isaac and the God of Jacob. 38 And God is not the God of the dead but of the living! And He sees them all living!"

39 Some of the teachers of the religious law remarked: "Well said, Teacher!" 40 But no one dared to question Him further.

Be careful of the teachers of religion (20:41-47)

41 Jesus asked them: "Why do people say that the Christ is the Son of David? 42-43 For David himself said in the book of Psalms, 'The Lord said to my Lord: Sit at My right hand until I make Your enemies a footstool on which to place Your feet.' 44 Therefore if David calls Him 'Lord', how can he be His Son?"

45-46 Within earshot of all the people Jesus said to the disciples: "Be very careful of the teachers of the religious law. They love to walk about in their robes and to be greeted by everyone in the market-places. They want the important places in the synagogues and the best seats at banquets. 47 They devour widows' houses and pray long pretentious prayers. The judgment they shall receive will be severe."

The widow's offering (21:1-4)

21 Looking up, Jesus watched the wealthy people putting their gifts into the treasury. 2-4 Then He noticed a poor widow who gave two tiny coins and He said: "I tell you truly, this poor widow has given more than all the others; for they gave out of their abundant wealth, but this woman gave all that she had to live on."

Signs of the last days (21:5-38)

5-6 Some disciples were admiring the temple building, how beautifully the stones were dressed and how lovely the gifts that adorned it. Jesus said to them: "The days are coming when what you see now will be destroyed. Not one stone will be left on another."

20:43 Psalm 110:1

7 They asked Him: "Teacher, when will these things take place? And what will be the sign that will warn they are about to happen?"

8 Jesus replied: "Be very careful that you are not deceived, for many will come claiming to come in My Name, saying: 'I am he' and 'The time is now near.' Do not follow them.

9 "And when you hear of wars and revolutions do not be afraid. Such things must happen first, but they do not indicate that the end is imminent."

10 Then He added: "One nation will rise against another, and one kingdom will oppose another kingdom. There will be great earthquakes and some places will experience plagues and famines. 11 There will be cataclysmic events and great signs from heaven. 12-13 But before all these things take place, people will lay hold of you and will persecute you. They will hand you over to the synagogue authorities and have you thrown into prison. You will be brought before kings and governors because you believe in My Name, giving you the opportunity to testify to them.

14-15 "Decide now, that you will not have to worry beforehand how you will defend yourselves, for I will give you wisdom and the right words to speak, so that those who oppose you will not be able to stand against you or contradict what you say.

16 "You will also be betrayed by parents, brothers, other relatives and friends who will even be responsible for the death of some of you. 17-19 You will be hated by everyone because of your faith in Me, but not one hair of your head will perish eternally, for by enduring all this you will gain life for yourselves.

20 "But when you see Jerusalem being surrounded by the enemy's camps then you will know that the time of its destruction is near. 21-22 Then those who live in Judea should flee to the mountains, and the inhabitants of the city should leave at once. Those who live in the country districts should not enter the city because the time of retribution must take place, to fulfil what has been written.

23 "Pregnant women and those breast-feeding their little ones will feel cursed at that time, for there will be much distress everywhere in the land and all will consider themselves the victims of great anger and judgment. 24 They will be killed by the sword and taken as prisoners to other nations. Jerusalem will be trampled on by foreigners until the time of the Gentile nations is fulfilled.

25 "There will be signs in the sun, moon and stars. Fear will grip the earth and there will be great confusion like the raging of a tempestuous sea. 26 People will feel faint for fear of what will happen to them next, for it will be seen that even the heavens are being shaken.

27 "Only then will they see the Son of Man coming in a cloud with power and great glory! 28 When you see these things begin to happen, stand and lift up your hands, because the time of your redemption is drawing near."

29-30 Jesus then told them a parable: "When you see a fig tree, or some other tree, burst into leaf you know that summer is coming. 31 In the same way, when you see these things happen, know that God's sovereign reign is near. 32 I tell you truly that this generation will not end until all that God intends has taken place. 33 Heaven and earth as you know them will end, but My words will never end; they are eternal.

34-35 "Be careful that your hearts are not put into bondage because of excessive drinking or because you are full of anxiety. For this Day will come on you suddenly like a trap; yes it will come upon everyone who lives on the face of the earth.

36 "So always be on the alert, praying that you will be able to escape all that is going to happen, and that you will be able to stand accepted before the Son of Man."

37 Jesus taught in the temple courts every day, but He spent the nights on the Mount of Olives. 38 Crowds would gather to hear Him teach in the mornings.

Judas agrees to betray Jesus (22:1-6)

22 Now the Feast of Unleavened Bread, known as the Passover, was approaching. 2 The chief priests and the teachers of the religious law were trying to figure out how they could destroy Jesus, but they feared the reaction of the people. 3-4 Then Satan entered into Judas Iscariot, one of the twelve disciples, and he went to discuss with the chief priests and the officers of the temple guard how he could betray Jesus into their hands. 5 They were delighted and agreed to give him money in exchange for Jesus. 6 Accordingly, Judas looked for a suitable opportunity to betray Him, when crowds of people were not around.

The Last Supper (22:7-23)

7-8 On the day of Unleavened Bread, on which the Passover lamb had to be sacrificed, Jesus sent Peter and John telling them: "Go and prepare the Passover meal for us, that we may eat it together. 9 They asked Him: "Where do You want us to prepare it?" 10 Jesus replied: "When you enter the city, a man carrying a jar of water will meet you; follow him to the house to which he goes. 11 Then say to the owner of the house: 'The Teacher says, Where is the guest room that I and My disciples can eat the Passover meal together?' 12 He will show you to a large upper room already furnished and there you are to prepare for the meal."

13 When they went they found everything exactly as Jesus had said, and so prepared for the Passover.

14 At the appointed time Jesus and the apostles came and reclined around the table. 15-16 He told them: "I have longed to eat this Passover meal with you before I have to suffer, for I tell you clearly that I shall not eat it again until what it signifies is fulfilled in God's Kingdom."

17 Holding up a cup Jesus gave thanks to God and said: "Take this and share it among yourselves. 18 For I tell you that I shall not drink again from the fruit of the vine until God's Kingdom rule is established." 19 Then He held up a loaf of bread, spoke God's blessing over it and gave it to them saying: "This is My body given for you; do this to remember Me." 20 And after supper He took the cup in similar fashion and said: "This cup is the new covenant in My blood that is being shed for you. 21 However, the hand of the one who is about to betray Me is on this table with Me. 22 For the Son of Man goes as it has been determined He must. Nevertheless the man by whom He is betrayed is cursed." 23 They began to discuss who among them who would do such a thing.

The servant is the greatest (22:24-30)

24 They began to argue among themselves as to who was the most important. 25 So Jesus said to them: "Kings rule oppressively over their nations and those with authority claim to exercise it for the good of others. 26 But this is not how you are to behave. Among you, the most important will be the most humble, and the one with authority will behave as a true servant.

27 "Who do you think is greater, the one who reclines at the table or the one who serves him? Is it not the one who reclines at the table? But I am among you as one who serves.

28-30 "You have remained with Me through My testing times, and I give you the Kingdom that the Father gave Me, so that you may eat and drink at My table in My Kingdom. And you will sit on thrones to judge the twelve tribes of Israel.

Jesus predicts Peter will deny Him (22:31-38)

31-32 "Simon, Simon, Satan has longed to sift you as wheat, but I prayed for you all so that your faith will not fail. When you have turned back to Me, support your brothers."

33 Peter answered: "Lord, I am ready to go to prison or even die
for You."

34 But Jesus replied: "Peter, I tell you clearly today, before crock-
crow you will deny three times that you know Me!"

35 Then He said to them all: "When I sent you out without money
or footwear, did you have any needs?"

They replied: "None."

36 So He told them: "But now let he who has a purse or wallet take
it with him and let the one who has no sword sell his cloak and buy
one. 37 For I tell you clearly that what was written about Me must be
completed, 'And He was counted with the sinners.' Yes, this was
written about Me and must be fulfilled."

38 Then they said: "Lord, look we already have two swords." And
He replied: "That's enough!"

Jesus prays on the mount of Olives (22:39-44)

39 He then went to the Mount of Olives as usual, together with His
disciples. 40 When He arrived there He told them: "Pray that you
will not be tempted." 41-42 And He went apart by Himself, about a
stone's throw away from them, knelt down and began to pray, saying:
"Father, you are able to take this cup of suffering away from Me, but
only do so if it is Your will and not My own." 43 And an angel from
heaven appeared to Him to strengthen Him.

44 He grew even more distressed and prayed more earnestly, so
that His sweat fell to the ground as drops of blood.

Judas betrays Jesus (22:45-53)

45 After He had prayed, He returned to the disciples and found them
asleep, exhausted by their grief. 46 He said to them: "Why are you
sleeping? Get up and pray that you may not be tempted." 47-48 But
even as He was speaking, a crowd approached led by Judas who
was one of the twelve. He was about to kiss Him, when Jesus said:
"Judas, are you betraying the Son of Man with a kiss?"

49 When those around Him saw what was happening they said:
"Lord, shall we use our swords? 50 One of them did so and struck the
high priest's servant, cutting off his right ear. 51 Jesus answered:
"Stop that," and He touched the servant and healed his ear.

52 Then Jesus addressed the chief priests, officers of the temple
guard and elders who were among the crowd: "You have come with
swords and clubs as if you were coming to arrest a criminal. 53 I was

22:37 Isaiah 53:12

with you every day in the temple and you never raised so much as
a finger against Me. But this is your time, when darkness rules."

Peter denies Jesus (22:54-62)

54 They arrested Jesus and took Him to the high priest's house, and
Peter followed at a safe distance. 55 A fire had been lit in the courtyard and Peter went and sat with those gathered around it. 56 One of
the maids stared at him in the firelight and said: "This man was
with Him." 57 But Peter denied it saying: "I don't know Him,
woman." 58 Shortly afterwards another noticed him and said: "You
are one of them." But he said: "No, I am not!"

59 About an hour later another man said emphatically: "This man
was definitely with Him, and he is from Galilee."

60 But Peter said: "Man, I don't know what you are talking about."
As soon as he had said this the cock crowed. 61 The Lord turned and
looked at Peter and he remembered the Lord's word to him that he
would deny Him three times before the cock crowed. 62 And he went
outside and wept bitterly.

Jesus on trial before the Jewish Council (22:63-71)

63 Those in charge of Jesus mocked Him and hit Him. 64 They taunted
Him saying: "Prophesy. Tell us who hit You!" 65 And they said many
other blasphemous things to Him.

66 At daybreak the leaders of the people, both chief priests and the
teachers of the religious law, gathered together and brought Him
before the whole council.

67-68 They said to Him: "Tell us if You are the Christ."

He replied: "Even if I told you, you would still not believe Me,
and you will not answer anything I ask you. 69 However, from now
on the Son of Man will be seated at the right hand of God in power."

70 So they all said: "Then You are God's Son, are You?"

He answered them: "You say that I AM!"

71 They said: "What further evidence do we need? We have heard
it from His own mouth!"

Pilate finds no fault in Jesus (23:1-7)

23 Then the whole Council rose and led Him to Pilate. 2 They
began to accuse Him by saying: "We have found that this
man is perverting our nation, forbidding the payment of taxes to
Caesar and calling Himself Christ the King!"

3 Pilate questioned Him: "Are you the King of the Jews?"

And Jesus answered: "That is what you say."
[4]Then Pilate told the chief priests and those with them: "I do not find this man guilty of any crime."
[5]But they persisted, claiming: "Throughout Judea and all over the country from Galilee to here, He has stirred up the people with His teaching."
[6]On hearing this, Pilate asked if He was a Galilean. [7]Hearing that
He was, and was therefore under Herod's authority, he sent Him to Herod who happened to be in Jerusalem at that time.

Herod mocks Jesus (23:8-12)

[8]Herod was really pleased to see Jesus. For a long time he had wanted to meet Him because of all that he had heard about Him, and he
hoped to see Him perform a miracle. [9]Herod questioned Jesus at
length, but He said nothing in reply. [10-11]The chief priests and teachers
of the law accused Him aggressively, while Herod and His soldiers ridiculed and mocked Him. They dressed Him in a splendid robe
and sent Him back to Pilate. [12]That day Herod and Pilate became
friends, although before they had been enemies.

Jews urge Pilate to crucify Jesus (23:13-25)

[13-14]Pilate called together the chief priests and other leaders and told them: "You brought this man to me accusing Him of stirring rebellion among the people. I have questioned Him in your presence and have found no evidence to substantiate these accusations you have
brought against Him. [15]Nor could Herod find Him guilty, for He
returned Him to our jurisdiction, having found He has done nothing
deserving of the death penalty. [16]Therefore I will have Him flogged
and will then release Him."
[17-18]It was customary for Pilate to release one prisoner to the people at the feast so they all shouted: "Condemn this man and give us
Barabbas instead." [19]Barabbas had been thrown into prison for causing
an insurrection in the city and for murder.
[20-21]Again, Pilate made it clear to them that he wanted to release Jesus. But they shouted: "Crucify, crucify Him."
[22]For a third time Pilate said to them: "Why? What crime has He committed? I have found He has done nothing that deserves the death penalty. So I shall have him flogged and will then release Him."
[23-24]But the crowd persisted, shouting even more loudly and demanding that Jesus be crucified. Finally their voices prevailed

and Pilate decided to give in to their demands. [25]He released the
man who was in prison, guilty of rebellion and murder, and for
whom they had asked; Jesus he surrendered to their wishes.

Simon of Cyrene assists Jesus carry the cross (23:26-31)

[26]As they led Him away, they seized Simon of Cyrene who had come
from a country district and made him walk behind Jesus carrying
the cross. [27]A great crowd of people followed, including some
women who mourned and grieved for Jesus. [28-29]Turning to them He
said: "Daughters of Jerusalem, don't cry for Me. Weep for yourselves
and your children because the time is coming when they will say,
'Blessed are the barren and the breasts that never nursed.' [30-31]Then
people will say to the mountains, 'Fall on us,' and to the hills,
'Cover us', because if they do such things when the tree is full of sap
what will they do when it is dried wood?"

King of the Jews crucified (23:32-43)

[32]Two others, who were criminals, were also taken to be crucified
with Him. [33]When they came to the place called the Skull, they crucified
Him together with the two criminals, one on either side of Him.

[34]And Jesus said: "Father, forgive them, for they do not understand what they are doing."

They divided His clothes between them by casting lots for them.
[35]People stood by, staring and ridiculing Him. The leaders taunted:
"He saved others, now let Him save Himself! If this man really is
the Christ, God's Chosen One!"

[36-37]The soldiers also mocked Him. They came near and offered
Him vinegar, saying: "If You are the King of the Jews, save
Yourself." [38]And a sign was placed above Him on which was written:
THIS IS THE KING OF THE JEWS.

[39-40]One of the criminals cursed Him, but the other one rebuked
him and said: "Have you no fear of God; you are under the same
judgment. [41]We are being punished justly for we deserve the
sentence passed against us; but this Man has done nothing wrong!"

[42]Then he said: "Jesus, please think of me when You enter Your
Kingdom."

[43]And Jesus answered: "Truly I tell you, today you will be with
Me in paradise."

23:30 Hosea 10:8

Jesus' death (23:44-49)

44-45 By now it was about midday and darkness fell all over the land
and persisted until three o'clock; it was as if the sun had gone out.
And the curtain concealing the Holy of holies in the temple was
torn apart. 46 Jesus cried out in a loud voice: "Father, I commit My
Spirit into Your hands." And then He died.

47 Seeing what had happened, the centurion glorified God saying:
"This was truly a righteous man."

48 Those in the crowd that had been watching saw what happened
and returned to their homes, beating their breasts in anguish.

49 All those who knew Jesus, including the women who had followed Him from Galilee, stood at a distance watching these events.

Jesus buried in Joseph's tomb (23:50-56)

50-52 A member of the council called Joseph, from a Judean city named
Arimathea, came to Pilate to ask for Jesus' body. Joseph was a good
and godly man who had not agreed with the decision or actions
taken by the council. He was awaiting the coming of God's
Kingdom.

53 He took the body down from the cross, wrapped it in a linen
shroud, and placed Him in a new tomb that had been cut out of the
rock, where no-one had been laid to rest. 54 It was the day of preparation and the Sabbath was about to begin.

55 The women who had come from Galilee with Jesus, saw the
location of the tomb and watched His body being placed there. 56 So
they went to prepare spices and perfume, but rested on the Sabbath
in obedience to the commandment.

The Resurrection (24:1-12)

24 Very early on the Sunday morning, the women brought the
spices they had prepared to the tomb. 2 They discovered that
the stone that had covered the entrance to the tomb had been rolled
aside. 3 So they entered, but the body of the Lord Jesus was not
there. 4 While they were pondering where He could be, two men in
clothes that shone like lightning suddenly appeared and stood
beside them. 5 Frightened, the two women fell to the ground on their
faces. The man asked them: "Why look for the living among the
dead? 6-7 He is not here; He is risen! Remember what He told you
while He was still with you in Galilee: 'The Son of Man must be
handed over to sinful men to be crucified, but on the third day He
will be raised back to life.'" 8 Then the women remembered.

9 They told all this to the eleven and the others with them as soon as they returned from the tomb. 10 It was Mary Magdalene, Joanna, Mary the mother of James and the others with them that brought this news to the apostles. 11 But they did not believe what the women said; it seemed to make no sense to them.

12 However, Peter ran to the tomb to see for himself. He bent over, looked into the tomb and saw the strips of linen lying to one side. He left perplexed at what He had seen.

The road to Emmaus (24:13-32)

13 On that same day, two disciples were travelling to a village called Emmaus, about seven miles from Jerusalem. 14 They were discussing everything that had taken place. 15-16 While they were deep in conversation, Jesus Himself came and walked beside them; but they did not recognise Him.

17 He asked them: "What are you talking about?"

18 They stopped walking and appeared grief stricken. One of them, named Cleopas, asked Him: "Are you the only visitor to Jerusalem who has no idea about the events that have taken place here during the past few days?"

19 "What events?" He asked.

"About Jesus of Nazareth," they replied. "He was a prophet who spoke powerfully and performed mighty deeds in God's Name before all the people. 20 However, the chief priests and our rulers handed Him over to the Romans to be sentenced to death; so they crucified Him. 21 We had hoped that He was the One who would save Israel. And now it is the third day since this took place. 22-23 What is more, some of our women have amazed us by saying that when they went to the tomb early this morning, they could not find His body. And they came to tell us that angels had appeared to them, who said that He is alive. 24 When some of our friends went to the tomb themselves, they found it just as the woman had said, and there was no sign of Jesus."

25-26 He said to them: "You are so foolish and slow to believe in your hearts all that the prophets have said. The Christ had to suffer these things before entering into His glory, did He not?' 27 Then beginning with Moses and all the Prophets, He revealed to them all that was written in the scriptures about Himself.

28 As they neared their destination, Jesus appeared to be continuing further. 29 But they begged Him: "Stay with us here, for it is getting dark and the daylight has almost gone." So He agreed to stay with them.

30 While at table with them, Jesus took some bread and gave
thanks to God. Then He broke it and gave it to them. 31 Suddenly
their eyes were opened and they realised that this was Jesus: but
then He immediately disappeared from their sight. 32 They said to
each other: "While He talked with us on the journey and explained
the scriptures to us, did it not seem that our hearts were on fire?"

Jesus appears to the disciples (24:33-44)

33-34 At once they rose from the table and returned to Jerusalem. The
eleven disciples gathered together with the other believers and said:
"It is really true! The Lord has risen from the dead and has
appeared to Simon."

35 Then the two disciples explained what had happened to them
on the way to Emmaus, and how they had recognised Jesus when
He broke the bread.

36 While they were still explaining this, Jesus Himself suddenly
stood among them and said: "Peace be with you!"

37 They were amazed and frightened, thinking this must be a
ghost. 38 But He said to them: "What are you worried about and why
do you doubt in your minds? 39 Look at My hands and feet. It really
is Me! You can touch Me and see that I am real. A ghost does not
have flesh and bones as you can see I have."

40 Then He showed them His hands and feet. They could still
hardly believe what was happening, for they were so amazed and
full of joy.

41 Jesus asked them: "Do you have anything to eat here?" 42 They
gave Him a piece of broiled fish and He took it and ate it before
their eyes. 44 Then He said to them: "This is what I predicted while I
was still with you. Everything written about Me in the law of
Moses, the Prophets and the Psalms, must be fulfilled."

Jesus' departing instruction (23:45-53)

45 Then He explained the scriptures to them so that they could
understand. 46 He said: "This is what is clearly written: The Christ
will suffer and rise from the dead on the third day. 47 In His Name,
repentance and the forgiveness of sins will be preached to all
nations, beginning at Jerusalem. 48 You are witnesses of all this. 49 I
am going to send you the gift promised by My Father. But you are
to stay here in the city until you have received the power that will
be poured out on you from heaven."

50-51 Then Jesus led them out to a place near Bethany. There He
raised His hands and blessed them, and then He left them and was
taken up into heaven. 52 They worshipped Him and returned to
Jerusalem, overflowing with joy. 53 And they remained in the temple,
giving praise to God.

THE GOSPEL ACCORDING TO

JOHN

The Word and Light (1:1-5)

1 Jesus is the Word. He existed in the beginning, before time
began. This Word was with God and, indeed, the Word was
God. 2 He was the Word that God spoke in the beginning. 3 By this
spoken Word, through Jesus, everything was created. Nothing could
exist if it were not for Him. 4 In Jesus, in this Word, was the life that
brought God's light into people's lives. 5 This Light came and shone
into the spiritual darkness of the world; but the darkness did not
want the Light, and so did not receive Him.

John prepares the people (1:6-9)

6 Before Jesus came, God sent another man, called John, to His people.
7 God called him to be a witness, to prepare people for the coming
of the light, for He wanted everyone to believe in Jesus. 8 But John
was not the Light, only the one preparing for the coming of the
Light. 9 Jesus Himself was the true Light, able to give spiritual light
and understanding to all men; and He was coming into the world.

The Word became a man (1:10-18)

10 So Jesus came from heaven into this world, and although the
world was created through Him, people did not recognise who He
was when He came. 11 Even though He came among those who
rightly belonged to Him, they still did not accept Him.

12-13 However, some did welcome Him and they came to believe
that He was God's Son. To them He gave the right to become God's
children, those who were not only born naturally with a human
mother and father, but given a second birth by God.

14 The Word, then, became a Man and came to live among us.
Those of us who knew Him have seen His glory, the glory that could
only belong to the One and Only Son of God. He came from the
Father in heaven and was full of grace and truth. He was constantly
giving to people and always taught what was right.

15 John taught about Jesus. He openly proclaimed: "He is the One
of whom I spoke when I said, 'The One who comes after me is much
greater than I, because He existed long before I was born.'"

16 Jesus was full of grace and we all received from Him one act of
grace after another. He constantly blessed us in ways we could
never deserve. 17 God gave us the law through Moses, but grace and
truth came when He sent Jesus Christ.

18 No-one has ever seen God in His Majesty and glory, but Jesus,
the One and only Son who is Himself God and who is One with the
Father, came to make Him known to us.

A voice of one crying in the desert (1:19-28)

19 While John was testifying to the imminent coming of Jesus, the
Jewish leaders in Jerusalem sent a deputation of priests and Levites
to ask Him who He was. 20 John made it abundantly clear to them:
"I am not the Christ, the Messiah."

21 So they asked him: "Well, who are you? Are you Elijah?"

"No, I am not," said John.

"Are you the Prophet we have been expecting?"

"No," John answered.

22 Exasperated, they said: "Tell us who you are! Give us an answer
we can relay to the leaders who sent us. How do you describe yourself?"

23 John quoted some words of the prophet Isaiah in response: "I
am the voice of someone crying in the desert, 'Prepare for the coming
of the Lord!'"

24 Some of those sent to John belonged to the Pharisee party.
25 They questioned John: "If you are not the Christ, nor Elijah, nor
the Prophet, then why do you baptise people?"

26 John replied: "I only immerse them in water; but Someone is living
among us whom you do not recognise. 27 He is the One who comes
after me, and I am not worthy even to do the work of a slave for
Him."

28 All this took place at Bethany which is on the far side of the
Jordan, where John was baptising people.

God's Lamb (1:29-34)

29 On the following day, John saw Jesus approaching him and said:
"Look, this is God's Lamb who takes away the world's sin! 30 This is

1:23 Isaiah 40:3

He to whom I was referring when I said, 'The One who comes after
me is much greater than I, who existed long before I was born!'
31 Although I did not personally know of whom I spoke, He is the
reason I came baptising with water, to prepare the way for Him to
be revealed to Israel."

32 Then John proclaimed: "I saw God's Spirit descend from heaven
like a dove that came and rested upon Him! 33 I would not have
recognised Him but for the fact that the One who sent me to baptise
with water had told me, 'The man on whom you see My Spirit
descend and remain is He who will baptise in the Holy Spirit.'
34 Now I have seen Him and I can say assuredly that this is God's
Son."

The first disciples (1:35-42)

35 John was again in the same place on the following day, together
with two of his disciples. 36 When he saw Jesus walking by he said
to them: "Look, this is God's Lamb!"

37 On hearing this, the two disciples followed Jesus. 38 When He
saw them Jesus asked: "What do you want?"

"Teacher, where are You staying?" they replied.

39 Jesus said to them: "Come and you will see."

So they went with Jesus, saw where He was staying and spent the
rest of the day with Him, from four o'clock onwards.

40 Simon Peter's brother, Andrew, was one of the two disciples
who heard what John had said about Jesus and followed Him.
41 Andrew went and found His brother Simon and told him: "We
have found the Messiah," (that is the Christ, God's Anointed Son).
42 Then he took Simon to Jesus, who looked at him and said: "You
are Simon, son of John. From now on you will be called Peter, a
rock."

Philip and Nathaniel (1:43-51)

43 On the following day, Jesus decided to return to Galilee. He discovered Philip and said to him: "Follow Me." 44 Like Andrew and
Peter, Philip came from the town of Bethsaida. 45 Philip in turn found
Nathaniel and told him: "We have found the One we have been
waiting for, who Moses spoke about in the law, the One of whom
the prophets also wrote! He is Jesus of Nazareth, Joseph's son."

46 "Nazareth!" Nathaniel gasped, "How can anything good come
from there?"

"Come and see for yourself," said Philip.

47 When Jesus saw Nathaniel approaching, He said to him: "This
is a true Israelite and there is nothing false about him."
48 "How can You know anything about me?" Nathaniel asked.
"I noticed you before Philip called you. You were sitting under
the fig tree," Jesus answered.
49 Then Nathaniel exclaimed: "Teacher, You are God's Son, the
King of Israel."
50 "You believe in Me simply because I told you that I noticed you
under the fig tree! You shall see far greater things in the future,"
51 Jesus said. "I tell you the truth, you shall see the heavens open and
God's angels ascending and descending on the Son of Man."

Jesus turns water into wine (2:1-11)

2 1-2 Three days later, Jesus, together with His mother and disciples,
was invited to a wedding that took place at Cana in Galilee.
3 The wine ran out, which was a social disaster, and so Jesus' mother
said to Him: "They have no more wine."
4 "Dear woman, why involve Me in such a matter? It is not time
for Me yet," Jesus replied.
5 However His mother told the servants: "Do whatever He tells
you." 6 Six large water jars, each holding between twenty and thirty
gallons, were standing nearby. These were normally used for the
ceremonial washing that Jews performed. 7 "Fill the jars with water,"
Jesus told the servants. They did so, filling them to the brim.
8-10 "Now draw some out and give it to the master in charge of the
banquet to taste," Jesus told them. They did this and the master of
the banquet tasted the water that had now been turned into wine.
Although the servants knew its origin, the master had no idea
where it had come from. After tasting it, he took the bridegroom
aside and said to him: "People usually serve the choicest wine first
and then, when the guests have drunk well, they serve the cheaper
wine. But you have kept the best back until now!"
11 This miracle that Jesus performed at Cana in Galilee was the
first of the miraculous signs that revealed His glory, and His disciples
put their faith in Him as a result.

Jesus clears the temple (2:12-25)

12 Jesus, His mother, brothers and disciples went from there to
Capernaum, where they stayed for a few days. 13 When the Jewish
Passover drew near, Jesus went to Jerusalem for the feast. 14 When

He went to the temple He discovered men selling cattle, sheep and doves in the temple court. Others had set up stalls to exchange money.

15 Jesus made a whip of cords and drove all the cattle and sheep out of the temple precincts. Then He overturned the tables of the money changers, scattering their coins. 16 "Take these out of here," He said to those selling doves. "How dare you turn My Father's house into a market!"

17 This prompted the disciples to recall that it is written, 'Zeal for Your house will overwhelm Me.'

18 Then the Jewish leaders confronted Jesus and asked Him: "How can You prove to us that You have the authority to do these things? What miraculous sign will You perform?"

19 "Destroy this temple and in three days I will raise it again," replied Jesus.

20 "It took forty-six years to build this temple," the Jewish leaders replied. "How are You going to rebuild it in three days?"

21 Jesus had been speaking of His own body as the temple. 22 After He was raised from the dead, His disciples remembered that He had said this. They believed what the scriptures said about Him and the words Jesus Himself had spoken.

23 Many people witnessed the miraculous signs Jesus did in Jerusalem during the Passover Feast, and so believed in Him. 24-25 However, Jesus was wise in not trusting anyone, for He could perceive what was in each person's heart.

The need to be born again (3:1-15)

3 1-2 Nicodemus, one of the Pharisees and a member of the Jewish ruling council, came to Jesus secretly during the night and said to Him: "Master we know You are a teacher sent by God. You could not perform all these miraculous signs if God were not with You."

3 Jesus responded: "I tell you the truth, it is impossible for anyone to see God's Kingdom unless he is born again."

4 "How can it be possible for an old man to be born again?" asked Nicodemus. "Can he really enter his mother's womb for a second time and be born all over again?"

5 "I tell you the truth, nobody can enter God's Kingdom unless he is first born not only of water, but of the Spirit as well," Jesus explained. 6 "The natural flesh can only give birth to natural flesh; and God's Spirit alone can give birth to the human spirit. 7 So you do not need to be surprised when I say, 'You must be born again!'

2:17 Psalm 69:9

[8]The wind blows wherever it chooses. You can hear its sound, but you cannot see where it comes from, nor where it is going. It is just like that with everyone who is born of God's Spirit."

[9]"How can this happen?" asked Nicodemus.

[10]Jesus said in reply: "You are Israel's teacher and you do not understand these spiritual truths? [11]I tell you the truth, I know what I am speaking about and I can testify to what I have actually seen; but still you people will not believe what I say. [12]I have explained earthly things to you and you do not believe Me; so how will you react if I speak to you about heaven itself? [13]No-one has ever gone there; but I, the Son of Man, have come from there!

[14-15]"Moses lifted up the snake in the desert that the people might be healed; in the same way the Son of Man must be lifted up that everyone who believes in Him might be saved and receive eternal life as a gift."

John explains (3:16-21)

[16]In the same way, because God loved the people of the world, He gave His one and only Son so that whoever believes in Him shall not die eternally, but have God's gift of eternal life instead. [17]So God did not send His Son into the world to condemn everyone, but to save people from condemnation through faith in Him. [18]So whoever believes in Him is not condemned; but the one who refuses to believe that Jesus is God's one and only Son is already condemned by his own unbelief.

[19]This is the evidence: Light has come into the spiritual darkness of the world, but men loved the darkness instead of the Light because they loved the evil deeds of darkness. [20]Those who want to do what is evil hate the Light and will not come near the Light for fear that their evil deeds will become exposed. [21]However, the man who wants to live by the truth comes readily into the Light. He has nothing to be ashamed of, for the Light shows clearly that it is God who has inspired and enabled what he does.

John the Baptist exalts Jesus (3:22-4:2)

[22]Later, Jesus and His disciples left the city and went into the Judean countryside, preaching and baptising people. [23]John was continuing his ministry, baptising at a place called Aenon, near Salim, where the water was deep enough to immerse the people who constantly came to him. [24](This, of course, was before John was imprisoned).

[25]A Jew provoked an argument with some of John's disciples over a question of ceremonial washing. [26]So they came to John and com-

plained: "Teacher, the man you referred to when on the other side of the Jordan and spoke so well of, He is now baptising and everyone is turning to Him!"

27 "Any man can only receive what is gifted to him from heaven,"
replied John. 28 "You know that I made clear, 'I am not the Christ, but
have been sent to prepare the way for Him!' 29 The bride is for the
bridegroom. His friend only serves him, anticipates his coming and is full of joy on hearing the bridegroom's voice. This is the joy I now
have, and my mission is complete. 30 He must become greater; I
must become less important.

31-32 "He who has come from heaven is greater than all others. I am a mere man who belongs to the earth and can speak only as a man. The One from heaven is far greater than all others, for He can speak of what He has seen and heard in heaven itself. Even so, not everyone believes what He says. 33 Anyone who does accept what He
reveals can verify that God is the Truth! 34 For this One He has sent
speaks the very words of God, and to Him God has given the Holy Spirit in an unlimited way.

35 "The Father loves His Son and has now placed everything in
His hands. 36 Whoever believes that He is God's Son is given eternal
life; but whoever rejects Him as God's Son will never see heaven nor receive that life; for he remains under God's wrath."

4 The Pharisees were aware that more people were becoming disciples of Jesus than of John, for more were being baptised
through faith in Him. 2 Jesus Himself did not immerse them; He
gave that responsibility to His disciples.

Jesus talks to a Samaritan woman (4:3-30)

3 When the Lord heard about the unrest among the Pharisees, He left
Judea and returned to Galilee. 4 To do this He had to pass through
Samaria. 5 He came to a town there known as Sychar, which was
near to the area of land given by Jacob to his son Joseph. 6 Jesus was
tired from His journey and sat down by Jacob's well that was in that place. It was about noon.

7 A Samaritan woman came to draw water from the well, an
unusual thing to do at that time of day. Jesus spoke to her and
asked: "Please give Me a drink." 8 (Jesus was alone as His disciples
had gone into the town to buy food.)

9 The Samaritan woman was surprised and replied: "You are a
Jew and I am a Samaritan woman. How can You ask me to give You

a drink?" (For Jews will normally have nothing to do with Samaritans, and
it was most unusual for a man to address a strange woman in public.)
10 Jesus answered: "If you only understood who it is that is asking
you for a drink and the gift that God wants to give you, then you
would have asked Me and I would have given you living water."
11 "Sir, You have no jar with which to draw water from the well,
and it is deep," the woman said. "Where can You obtain this living
water? 12 Are You someone even greater than our father Jacob who
gave us this well? Jacob drank from this well himself as did his sons,
his flocks and herds."
13 "Anyone who drinks the water from this well will only become
thirsty again," Jesus answered. 14 "However, whoever drinks of the
water I will give him, will never thirst again, for the water will
become a spring of water within him, a fountain of eternal life."
15 "Sir, give me that kind of water," the woman said to Jesus, "then
I won't keep getting thirsty and have to return to this well every
day to draw water."
16 Jesus said to her: "Go and return with your husband."
17 "I have no husband," she replied.
"You are correct in saying you have no husband," Jesus said.
18 "The truth is that you have already had five husbands and the
man you are now living with is not your husband. Yes, what you
have said is right."
19-20 "Sir, it is obvious that You are a prophet," the woman replied.
Then she tried to change the subject: "Our fathers worshipped here
on this mountain, but you Jews say that we must go to Jerusalem to
worship."
21 Jesus told her: "Dear woman, believe what I say to you. There
will come a time when you will neither worship the Father here nor
in Jerusalem. 22 You Samaritans do not know the One you worship.
We do know Him; so salvation has to come from the Jews. 23 A time
is coming, in fact it has already come, when those who worship in
a true way will worship the Father in the power of His Spirit and in
the truth of His Word. These are the kind of worshippers that the
Father wants. 24 God is Spirit. This is why those who worship Him
must do so in Spirit and truth."
25 The woman replied: "I don't understand everything, but I do
know that the Messiah is coming and when He does, then He will
explain everything to us."
26 "He is speaking to you right now," Jesus told her.
27 At this point the disciples returned and were amazed to see
Jesus talking alone with a woman. None of them dared to ask Him:

"What do you want with her?" or "Why talk to a Samaritan
woman?"
28 The woman left her water jar, returned to the town and said to
everyone: 29 "Come with me. I want to show you a man who knew
all about me and told me all that I have done. I wonder, could this
be the Christ?" 30 So the people came from the town to the well, to
see the man for themselves.

The fields are ripe for harvest (4:31-38)

31 Meanwhile, Jesus' disciples encouraged Him: "Teacher, have something to eat."
32 "I have food to eat about which you know nothing," Jesus
replied.
33 The disciples questioned among themselves, "What does He
mean? Has someone already given Him some food?"
34 But Jesus explained: "My food is to do the will of My Father
who sent Me and to complete the work He has given Me to do. 35 It
is a common saying, 'The harvest will come in four months time,'
but I tell you clearly that you should open your eyes and look
around you! There are fields of people already ripe for harvest.
36-37 Already the reaper can draw his wages and gather a crop of people
for eternal life. Both the one who sows God's Word and the one who
reaps the results will then rejoice together. So this is a true saying,
'One sows, another reaps!'
38 "I send you to reap where you have not done the hard work of
sowing. Others have done that, and you are simply reaping the benefit
of their labour."

Jesus recognised as Saviour (4:39-42)

39 Because of the woman's testimony that Jesus knew all about her,
many of the Samaritans from that town believed in Him. 40 So they
encouraged Jesus to remain with them, and for two days He did so.
41 What He taught them caused many more to become believers.
42 Then they told the woman: "No longer is it because of your
testimony that we believe. Now we know that this Man is the
world's Saviour, because we have heard Him for ourselves."

Royal official's son healed (4:43-54)

43-44 After those two days, Jesus continued His journey to Galilee
(Jesus had warned the disciples that a prophet is not respected in

his own country.) [45]However, when He arrived in Galilee, He was
welcomed there. Those from that region had seen the mighty things
He had done in Jerusalem, when He had gone there for the Passover
Feast.

[46-47]Jesus visited Cana in Galilee again, the place where He had
turned the water into wine. There a royal official who had a sick son
in Capernaum came to Him as soon as he heard that Jesus had
arrived back in Galilee. He pleaded with Him to come and heal his
son, who was on the point of dying.

[48]"Unless you actually see Me performing miraculous signs and
wonders, you people will never believe in Me," Jesus told the royal
official. [49]But the man persisted: "Lord, come with me before my
child dies."

[50]"You can go in peace," Jesus replied. "Your son will live."

The man believed what Jesus had said and left. [51]While still on
his way to Capernaum, his servants met him with the news that his
son was alive and well. [52]When he asked the servants when his healing
had taken place, they replied: "The fever lifted yesterday at one
o'clock." [53]The father realised that was precisely the time at which
Jesus had said to him, "Your son will live." So he and all who
belonged to his household became believers.

[54]This was the second miraculous sign that Jesus performed
there, on His return to Galilee from Jerusalem.

Lame man healed at the Pool of Bethesda (5:1-9)

5 Some time later, Jesus went to Jerusalem for another Jewish
festival. [2-3]Near the Sheep Gate is a pool called Bethesda, which
is surrounded by five covered colonnades where a great many
blind, lame and paralysed people used to lie waiting for the water
to be moved. [4](It was believed that at times one of the Lord's angels
would come and stir the water. The first person to get into the pool
when this happened would be healed.)

[5]One man there had been lame for thirty-eight years. [6]Jesus
noticed him and on discovering that he had been an invalid for so
long, He asked the man: "Do you want to be healed?"

[7]The man replied: "Sir, there is no one here to help me get into the
pool when the water is moved. Someone else always gets there
before me, no matter how hard I try."

[8]"Stand up!" Jesus said to him, "Pick up your mat and walk."
[9]Immediately he was healed. He jumped to his feet, picked up his
mat and walked away.

Jewish leaders infuriated (5:10-18)

10 This took place on the Sabbath day. Some Jewish leaders challenged
the man who had been healed: "This is the Sabbath; according to the
law you are forbidden from working by carrying your mat." 11 He
replied: "The man who healed me told me, 'Pick up your mat and
walk.'"

12 The leaders asked him: "Who dared to tell you to do this?"
13 The man had no idea who had healed him, for Jesus had quietly
merged into the crowd around the pool.

14 Later, however, Jesus saw him in the temple and said to him:
"Look, you are now healed. Turn from your life of sin, or something
worse could happen to you." 15 The man went and told the Jewish
leaders that it was Jesus who had healed him.

16 Because Jesus did such things on the Sabbath, the Jewish leaders
were outraged and persecuted Him. 17 Jesus told them: "My Father
never stops working, even on Sabbath days; so I, too, work when
He does!"

18 This only infuriated these leaders still further and they became
even more determined to kill Jesus. It was bad enough that in their
understanding He was breaking the Sabbath rules. It was even
worse that He called God His Father, so making Himself equal with
God.

Jesus' submission to the Father (5:19-47)

19 Jesus continued: "I tell you the truth, the Son is incapable of doing
anything on His own; He can do only what He sees His Father
doing. Whatever the Father does, His Son also does. 20 Because the
Father loves the Son, He shows Him all He does. You will be
amazed when He shows Him even greater things than I am doing
at present. 21 The Father raises the dead and restores them to life. In
the same way, the Son is able to give life to those to whom He wants
to give it!

22-23 "What is more, it is not the Father who judges anyone, for He
has entrusted all judgment to His Son because He wants everyone
to honour the Son in the same way that they honour the Father.
Anyone who does not honour Me does not honour the Father who
sent Me.

24 "I tell you the truth, anyone who hears what I say and believes
that it is God who sent Me, has eternal life and will not be condemned
for ever. He has already crossed over from living in death to real
life. 25 I tell you most emphatically, the expected time has now

arrived when the dead will hear the voice of God's Son and will come to life. 26 This is because the Father, who is Himself eternal life, has granted that same life to His Son. 27 Accordingly, He has also given the Son the authority to judge because He has become the Son of Man.

28-29 "You should not be surprised at this, for a time will soon come when even those in their graves will hear the Son's voice and will rise. Those who have done what is good in God's sight will rise to enjoy His life eternally. But those who have done what is evil in God's eyes will rise only to be condemned eternally.

30 "I can do nothing on My own. When I judge, I do so correctly because I hear what My Father is saying; for I have no desire to please Myself, but only Him; for He sent Me.

31 "If I simply witnessed about Myself, My testimony would not be valid. 32 However, someone else bears witness in My favour and I know that what He says about Me is true.

33 "You questioned John the Baptist and he told you the truth. 34 I do not depend on human testimony for My authority; but I remind you of this so that you can receive salvation. 35 For John was like a lamp that shone brightly, and for a time you chose to think well of this light.

36 "But I bear witness in much greater ways than John. The work I am doing is what My Father is giving Me to do and I intend to finish His work. These things bear witness to the truth that the Father sent Me. 37 Even the Father Himself, therefore, bears witness as to who I am.

38 "You have never heard Him speak nor seen Him, nor does His Word have any place in your hearts. This is plain because you do not believe in Me, even though He sent Me. 39-40 You spend hour upon hour studying the scriptures that actually speak about Me, yet still refuse to come and receive from Me the life I have come to give.

41 "Praise from men means nothing to Me. That is not what I am looking for. 42 I know you have no love for God in your hearts. 43 This is why you do not accept Me even though I have come in My Father's Name and with His authority. You accept others readily enough, even if they come only on their own authority. 44 How can you believe the truth if you are only interested in accepting praise from one another, while making no attempt to obtain the only praise that really matters, that which comes from the only God?

45 "Do not imagine that it will be He who will accuse you before the Father. No, your accuser is Moses, the one you say you revere. 46 But if you truly believed what Moses said, you would believe in

Me, for He wrote about Me. 47 But if you do not really believe what He wrote, how will you ever believe what I say?"

Feeding the five thousand (6:1-15)

6 Some time later, Jesus crossed to the far side of the Sea of Galilee, otherwise known as the Sea of Tiberias. 2 Because of the miraculous signs He performed in healing the sick, a great crowd of people followed Him.

3-5 It was near the time for the Jewish Passover feast. Together with His disciples, Jesus went into the hills in order to teach the crowd that followed Him. Jesus asked Philip: "Where can we buy bread to feed all these people?" 6 This He said to test his faith, for Jesus had already decided what He needed to do.

7 Philip answered: "Even if we had a year's wages we still would not be able to buy enough to give each just a scrap!" 8-9 Andrew, another of His disciples, who was Simon Peter's brother, said: "A boy here has five small barley loaves and two small fish; but they won't go far amongst such a crowd."

10 Jesus said: "Tell the people to sit down." As there was plenty of grass there the crowd of about five thousand men sat. 11 Jesus took the five barley loaves and gave thanks to God for His provision and then oversaw the distribution to all who were seated. And each received as much as he wanted. Jesus then did the same with the two small fish.

12 When all of them were fully satisfied, Jesus told His disciples: "Gather up the remains of the meal. Nothing is to be wasted." 13 When they did so, they filled twelve baskets with remnants of the five barley loaves left by all who had eaten.

14 When the people saw this miraculous sign that Jesus performed, they responded by saying: "This must be the prophet who is expected to come to the world." 15 Jesus could tell that they intended to force Him to be crowned as their king; so He withdrew still further up the mountainside by Himself.

Jesus walks on water (6:16-21)

16-17 When evening came, His disciples returned to the lakeside, boarded their boat and set out across the lake for Capernaum. It was now dark and Jesus had not joined them. 18 It was a very windy night and the water was becoming rough. 19 They had already rowed nearly three and a half miles, when they saw Jesus coming towards them, walking on the water. They were scared. 20 So Jesus

called out to them: "Don't be afraid. It is I." 21 When they realised
that this was indeed Jesus Himself and not some ghost, they welcomed
Him into the boat. Immediately the boat reached their destination!

Jesus: The Bread of Life (6:22-59)

22 On the following day, the crowd that had remained on the far side
of the shore realised that Jesus had not boarded the only boat along
with His disciples; they had left Him behind. 23 Then some boats that
had crossed from Tiberias landed near the place where the people
had eaten the bread over which the Lord had given thanks. 24 As
soon as they realised that neither Jesus nor any of the other disciples
were still there, they boarded the boats and went to Capernaum,
looking for Jesus.

25 Having crossed the lake they found Him and asked Him:
"Teacher when did you arrive here?"

26 Jesus told them: "I tell you the truth, you are looking for Me not
because you saw a miracle, but because you had plenty of bread to
eat. 27 Don't work for food that rots, but for the kind of food that lasts
for eternity, which I, the Son of Man, will give you. For on Me God
the Father has set His seal of approval."

28 So they asked Him: "If we are to do the works that God wants
of us, tell us what to do."

29 "This is God's work," Jesus replied, "to believe in Me, the One
He has sent."

30 Then they asked Him: "Well, what miraculous sign will You
perform so that we may see it and believe in You? Show us what
You can do. 31 After all, our forefathers ate the manna in the desert
every day for years, not just once. It is written, 'He gave them bread
from heaven to eat.'"

32 Jesus replied: "I tell you the truth, Moses didn't give you the
bread from heaven; it is only my Father who gives you the true bread
from heaven. 33 I am this Bread of God, for I have come from heaven."

34 "Lord," they said, "give us this bread from now on."

35 "I, I AM the Bread of Life," proclaimed Jesus. "The one who
comes to Me will never be hungry; he who continues to believe in
Me will never be left thirsty. 36 Yet, as I have told you already, although
you have seen Me you still do not believe in Me. 37 Everyone who
the Father wants to belong to Me will come to Me, and I would
never drive away anyone who turns to Me. 38 The reason I have
come from heaven is not to do what I want, but to fulfil the purpose
My Father had in sending Me. 39 His purpose is this, that I should

not lose a single one of those He gives to belong to Me, but ensure
that they are all raised to glory on the last day. [40]Yes, this is My
Father's will, that all who turn to the Son and continue to believe in
Him shall receive the gift of eternal life; and I will surely raise them
up on the last day."

[41]The Jewish leaders grumbled and complained among themselves
when Jesus said, 'I, I AM the Bread that has come from heaven.'
[42]They said, "This Jesus, is He not merely Joseph's son? We know
well who His father and mother are! So how can He claim, 'I came
from heaven?'"

[43]Jesus said: "Stop complaining among yourselves. [44]It is impossible
for anyone to come to Me unless the Father who sent Me draws him
to Me. Yes, such a one I will raise up on the last day. [45]In the
prophetic scriptures it is written, 'They will all be taught by God
Himself!'. So everyone who listens to what the Father has said and
is ready to learn from Him, will come to Me. [46]No-one has ever seen
the Father except for Me, for I have come from Him. I am the only
One who has ever seen the Father.

[47]"I tell you the truth, he who believes in who I AM, already has
eternal life. [48]I, I AM the Bread of Life. [49]Even though your forefathers
ate the manna every day in the desert, they still died. [50]But here now
is the Bread that has come from heaven itself. If a man eats of this
Bread, he will never die.

[51]"I, I AM the living Bread that has come from heaven. If anyone
eats of this Bread, he will live forever. This Bread is My body, which
I will give for the salvation of all mankind."

[52]Then the Jewish teachers reacted angrily saying: "How can this
man give us His body to eat?"

[53]Jesus said to them: "I tell you the truth, if you do not eat of the
Son of Man's body and drink His blood, you do not have God's life
in you. [54]Whoever eats of My body and drinks My blood already
has eternal life, and I will surely raise him up on the last day. [55]My
body is the true food, and My blood the true drink.

[56]"Anyone who eats of My body and drinks of My blood remains
at one with Me and I with him. [57-58]The living Father sent Me; that is
why I am here on earth now. Anyone who feeds on Me because He
believes who I am, the Bread that has come from heaven, he will
have My life.

"I repeat, your forefathers ate manna and died: but anyone who
feeds on Me, the living Bread, he will live forever!"

6:45 Isaiah 54:13

Some disciples turn away from Jesus (6:59-71)

59 Jesus said all this while teaching in the synagogue at Capernaum.
60 But it was too much for some of the disciples who said: "This is
such hard teaching to accept. Who can believe it?"

61 Aware of their discontent, Jesus asked them: "Does this offend
you? 62 What would your response be if you could see the Son of
Man ascend back to heaven, where He was before? 63 It is the Spirit
who gives you life. Your natural life counts for nothing. The words
I have spoken to you contain the life of God's Spirit. 64 Yet there are
still some among you who do not believe what I say."

He said this because Jesus had known from the outset who
among them did not believe. He was even aware of which disciple
would betray Him! 65 This is why He told them that, "No-one can
come to Me unless the Father enables him to do so."

66 This was the point of departure for many of His disciples. They
turned away from Jesus and stopped following Him. 67 So Jesus
asked the twelve: "It is not your intention to leave Me as well, is it?"

68 Simon Peter answered: "Lord, to whom could we turn? You are
the One with the words of eternal life. 69 We believe and are certain
that You are God's Holy Son!"

70 Then Jesus declared: "I chose you, all twelve of you. Yet one of
you is a devil!" 71 (He referred to Judas, son of Simon Iscariot, who
was later to betray Him, even though he was one of the twelve.)

Jesus' brothers disbelieve in Him (7:1-14)

7 Then Jesus travelled around Galilee, deliberately avoiding
Judea where the Jewish leaders were longing to kill Him.
2-3 When it was nearly time for the Jewish Feast of Tabernacles, His
own brothers suggested to Him: "You should leave now and go to
Jerusalem; then Your disciples there will be able to see the miracles
You performed. 4 You cannot expect to become famous by hiding
away here. Let everyone everywhere see what wonderful things
You do." 5 They spoke sarcastically like this because, although they
were His brothers, they did not believe in Him.

6-7 But Jesus said to them: "This is not the right time for Me to do
what you say. You consider any time to be right because the world
doesn't hate you; but it does hate Me because I expose the evil in the
world. 8 So you go to the Feast yourselves. I will go at the appropriate
time, which is not immediately." 9 Having said this, Jesus stayed
longer in Galilee.

10 However, when His brothers had left to go to the Feast, Jesus
also made His way to Jerusalem, but secretly as He did not want

any public attention. 11 Of course the Jewish leaders were on the lookout for Him and were asking around: "Have you seen Him? Do you know where He is?"

12 Among the people generally there was wide-spread speculation about Jesus. Some said, "He is a good man." But others disagreed. "No," they said, "He deceives everyone." 13 However, everyone was careful not to say anything publicly about Him, for fear of getting into trouble with the Jewish authorities.

Jesus' teaching originates from the Father (7:14-24)

14 Midway through the Feast, Jesus went into the temple courts and began to teach publicly. 15 The Jewish leaders were amazed and questioned: "Where did this man obtain so much learning when He has never been to any of our schools?"

16 Jesus answered them: "This teaching is not My own. It originates from the Father who sent Me. 17 Anyone who wants to do God's will will discover for Himself whether My teaching comes from My Father or if I am merely speaking for Myself. 18 Anyone who speaks for himself does so because he wants honour for himself. But He who is concerned to honour the One who sent Him is a Man of truth and He has no false motives.

19 "Moses gave you the law, didn't he? You are proud of this and yet none of you keeps the law! So why judge Me and why do you want to kill Me?"

20 The crowd of leaders tried to cover up their intentions; so they responded by saying: "You must be possessed by a demon if You think anyone wants to kill You!"

21 Jesus said to them: "I performed one miracle and you are all astounded. 22 Yet because Moses said you must be circumcised you are prepared to do such 'work' on the Sabbath." (Circumcision did not originate with Moses but with the patriarch Abraham.) 23 Jesus continued: "If you can circumcise a child on the Sabbath to keep the law of Moses, why be angry with Me for healing people and making them whole in spirit, soul and body on the Sabbath? 24 Stop judging in such superficial ways. It is time for you to make right judgments according to God's will."

Jewish leaders disbelieve Jesus (7:25-36)

25 It was then that some of the general population of Jerusalem began questioning their leaders' motives: "Is this really the man they want to kill? 26 He is speaking openly and they cannot say any-

thing to refute what He says. Have they come to the conclusion that
He really is the Christ, the Messiah? 27 Yet it doesn't seem to make
sense. We know where this Man is from. But when the Messiah
comes He will suddenly appear and no one will know where He
has come from."

28-29 As He taught in the temple courts, Jesus shouted out: "Yes,
you know Me and you know where I have come from at one level.
But I am not here on My own authority, but the one true God has
sent Me. You do not know Him, but I do because I have come from
Him and it is He who sent Me."

30 This was too much for the leaders and they wanted to seize Him
immediately. Strangely, no-one was able even to lay hold of Him
because it was not yet the right time for Jesus to place Himself in
their hands.

31 At the same time, many in the crowd were persuaded by what
He said and put their faith in Him. They said, "Surely when the
Christ comes, He will not do any more miraculous signs than this
man!"

32 The Pharisees became aware that some of the crowd were quietly
saying such things about Jesus. So with the authority of the chief
priests, they sent temple guards to arrest Him.

33 Jesus continued with His teaching: "I am here with you for only
a brief period and then I shall return to the Father who sent Me.
34 You will search for Me then but will be unable to find Me, for
where I am going you are not able to come."

35 The Jewish leaders continued to question among themselves:
"Where does He intend to go so that we will not be able to find
Him? Will He go to the Jewish people that have been dispersed
among the nations? Will He go and teach in these other nations?
36 What on earth did He mean by saying, 'You will search for Me, but
you will not be able to find Me?' Why does He say, 'Where I am
going to be, you cannot come?'"

Rivers of living water (7:37-40)

37 The last day of the Feast was the greatest. It was then that Jesus
stood and shouted aloud: "Anyone who is thirsty, come to Me and
drink. 38 For from deep within anyone who believes in Me will flow
out rivers of living water, as the scripture says."

39 Jesus was referring to the Holy Spirit. Later those who believed
in Him would be filled with God's Spirit. Until then, His Spirit had
not been given to live within anyone. This would not happen until
Jesus had returned to heaven in glory!

40 Some who heard Jesus speak said: "This Man must be the
Prophet who is to come." Others actually said: "He is definitely the
Christ."

People divided about Jesus (7:41-53)

41 Yet there were still those who questioned: "How is it possible for
the Messiah to come from Galilee? 42 Surely the scripture says that
the Christ will come from David's family, from Bethlehem where
David lived!" 43 So the people were divided about Jesus. 44 But even
though some wanted to seize Him, no-one was able to touch Him!
45 When the temple guards returned to the chief priests and the
Pharisees who had sent them, they demanded: "Why haven't you
arrested Him?"
46 "No one has ever spoken the way this Man does," the guards
responded.
47 "Do you mean to say that you have allowed Him to deceive you
as well?" The Pharisees declared. 48 "Have any of our rulers or us
Pharisees believed in Him? 49 Of course not! This mob that accepts
Him knows nothing of the law in comparison with us. They are
under a curse."
50-51 Nicodemus was present, the one who had gone to Jesus earlier
by night. Because he was one of them he could ask: "Does our law
condemn someone before he has first been tried, to find out the
truth about him?"
52 The others retorted: "Are you also from Galilee? If you study
the matter you will find that no prophet comes from Galilee!"
53 Then they dispersed.

An adulterous woman brought before Jesus (8:1-11)

8 Jesus went to the Mount of Olives. 2 Early the next day He was
back in the temple courts. Again the people gathered around
Him and He sat to teach them. 3 However, He was interrupted when
some teachers of the law and Pharisees brought a woman and made
her stand in front of Jesus. She had been caught in the act of adultery.
4 They said to Jesus: "Teacher, this woman was caught committing
adultery. 5 Under the law Moses ordered that we should stone such
women to death. What do You say we should do?" 6 This, of course,
was a trap question. They hoped He would say something against
the law, and so have a reason for accusing Him.
Jesus bent over and with His finger began to write on the ground.
7 But they kept questioning Him, so He sat up and said to them: "Let

the one among you who has no sin be the first to throw a stone at
her." 8 Then He bent over again and continued to write on the
ground.
9 Those who heard what Jesus said drifted away one by one, the
older ones first. Only Jesus, the One without sin, was left with the
woman standing there in front of Him. 10 He sat up straight again
and asked her: "Dear woman, where have they all gone? Has no-one
remained to condemn you?"
11 "No-one, sir," she replied.
"Well, I do not condemn you either," Jesus said. "Now go, but
leave your life of sin."

Jesus and the Father are one (8:12-30)

12 Then Jesus addressed the crowd again and said: "I, I AM the Light
of the world. Anyone who follows me will never walk in spiritual
darkness because he has the life that gives him light."
13 Again the Pharisees challenged Him: "Your testimony about
Yourself is not valid because You claim to be Your own witness."
14 Jesus replied: "Even if I did bear witness to Myself, what I say
would be valid because I know where I have come from, the place
to which I shall also return. 15 You judge everything from a purely
human perspective. Yet I do not judge anyone. 16 If I were to do so,
My judgment would be correct because I would not judge on My
own, but together with My Father who sent Me.
17 "For a testimony to be valid under your law there have to be
two witnesses. 18 Well, I Myself am one witness and My Father, who
sent Me, is the other!"
19 So they asked Him: "Where is this Father of yours?"
Jesus replied: "None of you know Me or My Father. For if you
knew who I am, this would demonstrate that you know My Father
as well."
20 Jesus said this while teaching in the temple, near to the place
where people place their offerings. However, none of them could
lay a hand on Him because it was not the right time for Jesus to give
Himself over to them.
21 Jesus continued: "I am going to leave you; you will search for
Me, yet each of you who does not believe in Me will die in your sin.
This is why you cannot come where I am going!"
22 So the Jewish leaders asked among themselves: "Does He
intend to kill Himself? Is that why He says we cannot go where He
is going?"

23 Jesus explained: "You belong to the earth; I came from heaven.
You belong to the world but I belong to another Kingdom. 24 I have
warned you that you will die with your sins unforgiven if you
refuse to believe that I am who I have said I am. You will indeed die
in your sins."

25 "Who are You?" they demanded.

"I am who I have said I am," Jesus replied. 26 "I could say so much
in judgment against you. He who sent Me is faithful and true, and
I only tell the world what I hear from Him."

27-29 They still did not understand that Jesus was speaking of His
heavenly Father. So He said: "When you have lifted up the Son of
Man, then you will know that I really am who I claim to be and that
what I say does not originate with Me, but comes from My Father.
He tells Me what to say for He is always with Me. He never leaves
Me because I always do what pleases Him."

30 When He said this, many in the crowd put their faith in Him.

Freedom in the Son (8:31-36)

31 Jesus then addressed those among the Jewish leaders who had
believed what He said. "You will really be my disciples only if you
continue to believe the words I speak. 32 For then you will know the
truth, and knowing the truth about Me will set you free."

33 To this they said: "As Jews, we are descendants of Abraham. We
have never been in bondage to anyone. So how can You say that we
need to be set free?"

34 Jesus replied: "I tell you the truth, all those who sin are in
bondage; they are slaves of sin. 35 A slave does not belong to the family
he serves, but a son has a permanent position in the family. 36 So if
God's Son sets you free from your bondage to sin, you will be really
free.

Children of God or the devil? (8:37-59)

37 "I am well aware that you are descended from Abraham. And yet
you want to kill Me, which proves that in your hearts there is no
room for My Word. 38 I speak to you about what I have seen in My
Father's presence; but you act on what you hear from your father."

39 "Abraham is our father," they retorted.

"If you were true children of Abraham, then you would act in the
same way as Abraham did. 40 But you don't, for you want to kill Me,
even though I have told you the truth I have received directly from

God. Abraham never did such things. No, you do the things that
your father does," replied Jesus.
41 At this they protested: "We are not illegitimate children. We
only have one father and that is God Himself."
42 Jesus told them: "If God was truly your Father, you would love
Me because I have come from God. This is why I am here. I have not
come on My own initiative; it was the Father who sent Me. 43 Why
do you not hear what I tell you, even though I repeat these truths to
you again and again? 44 Because you are unable to hear what I say
because you belong to the devil. He is really your father and you
want to kill Me to carry out your real father's desires. The devil has
always been a murderer from the very beginning. He does not
believe in the truth because there is no truth in him. He is a liar and
the father of lies. So when he lies, he is speaking his own language.
45 "By contrast, I tell you the truth. Yet you do not believe Me!
46 Who among you can show that I am guilty of any sin? So if I tell
you the truth, why is it you do not believe in Me? 47 After all, anyone
who truly belongs to God will hear what God says. So it is clear
why you cannot hear: you do not belong to God."
48 In fury the Jewish leaders responded: "You are a Samaritan. You
are demon possessed. We are certainly right about that!"
49 "No demon possesses Me," answered Jesus. "I honour My
Father and you dishonour Me. 50 It is not as if I am seeking glory for
Myself. There is someone else who wants to see Me glorified, and
He is the true Judge. 51 I tell you the truth, anyone who believes My
Word and lives by it will never die eternally."
52 To this the Jews retorted: "This proves You are demon possessed!
Abraham died. The prophets died. And yet You claim that anyone
who lives by Your words will never die. 53 Are You saying that You
are greater than our father, Abraham? He died and so did the
prophets. So who do You think You are?"
54 Jesus replied: "If I was to seek glory for Myself, that glory would
mean nothing. It is My Father, who you claim is your God, who
wants to see Me glorified. 55 You do not know Him, but I certainly
do! If I were to deny that I knew Him, I would be a liar like you. I
not only know Him, but I obey every word of His. 56 In fact, your
father Abraham was happy at the thought of seeing My day. And
when he saw it, he rejoiced."
57 "How can You have seen Abraham?" the Jewish leaders
responded. "You are not even fifty years old!"
58 Jesus answered: "I tell you the truth, even before Abraham was
born, I AM!"

59 This statement of Jesus' divinity was too much for them. They picked up stones ready to kill Him. But Jesus merged into the crowd and slipped out of the temple area.

Jesus heals a blind man (9:1-12)

9 As He was walking along, Jesus saw a man who had been blind from birth. 2 "Teacher, why was this man born blind?" His disciples asked. "Was it the result of his own sins or those of his parents?"

3 Jesus answered: "This was not the direct consequence of sin in either this man or his parents. Although this has happened, God can work a miracle in his life. 4 For while we have the opportunity we must continue to do the work of My Father who sent Me. It is now the daytime, but night is coming spiritually and then no-one will be able to do such works. 5 Yet while I am here in the world, I am the Light of the world."

6 After saying this, Jesus spat on the ground and made some mud with His spittle before putting it on the man's eyes. 7 He told him: "Go and wash in the Pool of Siloam" (meaning 'Sent'). The man went and washed and then went home with his sight restored.

8 His neighbours and those who recognised him asked: "Is this really the blind man who used to sit and beg?" 9 Some said it was him, but others said: "No it cannot be, even though he does look something like him."

The man himself said: "Yes, I really am the man that once was blind."

10 "Then how is it that your sight has been restored and you can now see?" they asked.

11 He replied: "Jesus made some mud and placed it on my eyes. I then went and washed in Siloam because this is what He told me to do, and then I was able to see!"

12 "Where is this Jesus?" they asked.

"I don't know where He is now," the man replied.

Pharisees interrogate the healed man (9:13-23)

13 They then brought the man who had been blind to the Pharisees. 14 It was the Sabbath day on which Jesus had made the mud and healed the man's blindness. 15 So the Pharisees questioned him as to how his sight was restored. The man replied: "He put mud on my eyes, I washed and now I am able to see."

16 "This Jesus cannot be from God," some of the Pharisees said, "for He does not keep our Sabbath rules and regulations."

Others asked: "How can a sinner possibly do such wonderful things?" So the issue divided them. [17]In the end they again asked the man who had been blind: "What do you say about this Man, for it was your eyes He healed."

The man responded: "He must be a prophet."

[18]The Jewish leaders refused to believe that the man had really been blind and then received his sight. So they sent for his parents. [19]"Is this man your son?" they asked them. "Do you claim that he was born blind? If so, how do you account for the fact that he can now see?"

[20]The parents answered: "He is certainly our son and he was definitely born blind. [21]But we have no idea how he is able to see or who opened his eyes. You can ask him. He is old enough to speak for himself."

[22]The parents were defensive because they were afraid of the Jewish leaders, who had already decreed that anyone who said that Jesus was the Christ, the Messiah, would be excommunicated from the synagogue. [23]This is why the parents said that their son was old enough to answer for himself. The Pharisees should put this question directly to him.

Pharisees banish healed man (9:24-34)

[24]So they summoned the man for a second time and said to him: "Give glory to God. We know that this man who restored your sight is a sinner."

[25]He replied: "I don't know whether He is a sinner or not, but I am certain that once I was blind and now I can see."

[26]They asked him again: "What did He do to you? How was He able to open your eyes?"

[27]"I have already answered these questions," the man replied, "but you did not listen to what I said. Why do you want me to repeat it all over again? Is it because you also want to become His disciples?"

[28]They reacted angrily to this and started to insult the man. "You must be one of this Man's disciples! [29]We are disciples of Moses who gave us the law. As for this Jesus, we have no idea where He came from."

[30]The man replied: "That is truly astounding. He was able to open my eyes, yet you leaders cannot tell where He came from. [31]We know for sure that God will not listen to sinners, but He will listen to a godly person who does His will. [32]Nobody has ever heard

before of a man born blind having his eyes opened and his sight
restored. 33 If it was true that this Jesus was not from God, He could
do nothing like this!"
34 Angrily they replied: "You were born in sin and yet you dare to
lecture us. Get out!"

Jesus came to give sight to the spiritually blind (9:35-41)

35 Jesus heard that the Pharisees had thrown the man out and when
He next saw him He asked: "Do you believe in the Son of Man?"
36 "Tell me who He is, sir, so that I can believe in Him," the man
replied.
37 "You have already seen Him," Jesus said. "He is speaking to
You right now."
38 Then the man worshipped Him, saying: "Lord, I do believe in
You!"
39 Then Jesus explained: "I came into this world to establish judgment:
the blind will see and those who see will become blind!"
40 Some Pharisees heard Him say this and challenged Him:
"What! Are You saying we also are blind?"
41 Jesus replied: "If you were already blind, that would not make
you guilty of sin. But because you claim that you can see when you
cannot see the truth, this means that you remain guilty!"

The Gate for the sheep (10:1-10)

10 "I tell you the truth," Jesus continued, "anyone who climbs
into the sheep pen instead of entering by the gate is a thief
and a robber. 2 But the man who goes in through the gate is the shepherd
of the sheep. 3 The one guarding the sheep opens the gate for him
and the sheep know his voice. 4 He calls each of his own sheep by
name and leads them out of the pen. Because they recognise his
voice, all who are his sheep follow him when he goes ahead of
them. 5 They would never follow a stranger because they do not
know his voice; instead, they will run from him."
6 When Jesus used this illustration the people did not understand
what He meant. So He explained:
7 "I tell you the truth, I, I AM the Gate for the sheep. 8 All those
who came before Me were thieves and robbers; so the sheep did not
listen to them. 9 I, I AM the Gate. Whoever enters through Me will
be saved from a life of sin and become one of My sheep. He will be
able to go in and come out and will always find sufficient pasture.

10 "The purpose of the thief, the devil, is to steal, kill and destroy.
But I have come to give the fullness of God's life to those who
believe in Me.

The Good Shepherd (10:11-18)

11 "I, I AM the Good Shepherd, the One who gives His life for those
who are His sheep. 12 The one who is only hired to do a job is not like
the shepherd who owns the sheep. When the wolf comes to attack
the sheep, the hired hand flees and abandons the sheep. 13 He runs
because he is only a hired hand and does not really care for the
sheep.

14-15 "I, I AM the Good Shepherd; I know each of My sheep and
they know Me, in the same way that the Father knows Me and I
know the Father. What is more, I am ready to die for My sheep.

16 "I have other sheep that are not of this particular sheep pen. I
must gather them in as well, for they also will respond to My voice.
However, there shall only be one flock, belonging to one Shepherd.

17 "My Father loves Me because I am ready to die for the sheep,
only then to be restored to life. 18 No-one will be able to take My life
from Me; I will give it of My own free will. I have the authority to
surrender My life and the authority to be raised again. This is the
command given Me by My Father, and I obey Him."

Jewish leaders accuse Jesus of blasphemy (10:19-39)

19 Again the Jews were divided by Jesus' words. 20 Many said: "He
most certainly is possessed by a demon! He must be mad! There is
no point in listening to Him!"

21 However others said: "A man possessed by a demon does not
speak like this Man. And how can a demon open the eyes of the
blind?"

22-24 The Feast of Dedication takes place in Jerusalem during the
winter. When Jesus was walking in the area of the temple known as
Solomon's Colonnade, the Jewish leaders gathered around Him to
challenge Him again: "For how much longer do You intend to keep
us in suspense? Tell us clearly if You are the Christ, the Messiah."

25-26 Jesus replied: "I have already told you, but you did not believe
Me. The miracles I perform in My Father's Name confirm who I am,
but you do not believe in Me because you are not My sheep. 27 Those
who are My sheep listen to what I say. I know them personally and
they follow Me. 28 I give them eternal life and they shall not die eternally.
29 And no-one is able to snatch them away from Me because My

Father has given them to Me, and He is greater and more powerful
than any opposed to Me. Not one of those who belong to Me will be
taken away from My Father. 30 For I and the Father are one!"
31 Again the Jewish leaders were so infuriated that they picked up
stones and were ready to kill Him. 32 But Jesus said to them: "For
which of the many great miracles I have shown you do you want to
stone Me?"
33 The Jewish leaders replied: "We do not stone You for the miracles,
but for Your blasphemy. You are merely a man and yet You claim to
be God!"
34 "What about the place in your law where it is written, 'I have
called you gods,'" replied Jesus. 35-36 "If those to whom His word was
spoken were called 'gods', and the scripture is certainly trustworthy,
what about the One whom the Father has set apart as His own Son
and who He has sent into the world? So why accuse Me of blasphemy
because I told you, 'I am God's Son?'
37 "However, I would not expect you to believe Me if I did not do
what My Father does. 38 But if I do His works, even though you do
not believe what I say, you should at least believe the miracles. Then
you would know and would continue to understand that the Father
lives in Me and I live in the Father."
39 They were even more determined to seize Jesus, but yet again
He escaped from them.

Many across the Jordan believe (10:40-42)

40-41 Then Jesus went across the Jordan to the place where John was
baptising at the beginning of His ministry. He remained there and
many people came to Him because they said: "John never performed
such miracles, but what He said about this Jesus has certainly
proved to be true." 42 So many became believers in Jesus there.

Lazarus dies (11:1-24)

11 Lazarus, the brother of Mary and Martha, who lived in the
village of Bethany just outside Jerusalem, was sick. 2 It was
Mary who anointed the Lord's body with perfume and wiped His
feet with her hair.
3 Mary and Martha sent a message to Jesus, "Lord, Lazarus who
You love is sick." 4 Jesus' immediate response to this message was to
say: "This sickness will not end in death. Rather it is so that God's
glory can be revealed and so that His Son may be glorified through
what happens."

5Jesus loved this family of Martha, Mary and Lazarus. 6Despite this He did not rush immediately to Bethany, but stayed where He was for another two days. 7It was only then that He said to His disciples: "Let us now return to Judea." 8They reminded Him: "Master, not long ago the Jewish leaders there tried to stone You. Do You really intend to return there?"

9Jesus replied: "There are twelve hours of daylight, are there not? Anyone who walks in the light will not stumble. 10It is only when he walks at night he is likely to stumble, for then he has no light." 11He continued by explaining: "Our friend Lazarus has fallen asleep, but I am going to Bethany to awaken him!"

12The disciples said: "Lord, if he is only sleeping, he will wake up naturally." 13But Jesus had meant that Lazarus had already died, even though the disciples thought He meant natural sleep.

14-15So then Jesus told them explicitly: "Lazarus is dead, and I was glad not to have been there for your sake, so that when you see what happens you will believe. Come, let us go to him now."

16Thomas (called Didymus) said to the other disciples: "We may as well go and die with Him!"

17When Jesus arrived in the area of Bethany, He discovered that Lazarus had been buried four days earlier. 18-19Bethany was less than two miles from Jerusalem, and many had come from the city to comfort Martha and Mary because of their brother's death. 20However, when Martha heard that Jesus was nearby she went to meet Him while Mary stayed at home.

21When she saw Jesus, Martha said: "Lord, if only You had been here with us, my brother would not have died. 22But I know that, despite the situation, God will give You whatever You ask of Him."

23Jesus promised her: "Your brother will rise again."

24"I know he will rise again when the resurrection takes place on the last day," Martha replied.

The Resurrection and the Life (11:25-37)

25Jesus said to her: "I, I AM the Resurrection and the Life. Anyone who believes in Me will live eternally, even though he dies physically. 26Whoever lives in Me because He continues to believe in Me will never die eternally. Do you believe this?"

27"Oh yes, Lord," she said, "I do believe that You are the Christ, God's Son, the One God promised would come into the world."

28Having said this, Martha went back to her house and took Mary quietly aside: "The Teacher has arrived and wants to see you."

29 When Mary heard this, she left immediately to go to Him. 30 Jesus
had not yet entered the village but had remained at the place where
Martha had met Him. 31 Those who had come from the city to comfort
her followed Mary when they saw how quickly she left the house.
They assumed she was going to mourn at the tomb.
32 When Mary saw Jesus waiting for her, she fell at His feet and
said: "Lord, if only You had been here with us, my brother would
not have died."
33 Jesus was deeply moved and distressed at the sight of Mary and
those who had followed her weeping with grief.
34 "Where have you buried him?" He asked.
"Come and we will show You, Lord," they replied.
35 Jesus wept. 36 And the people said: "Look how deeply He loved
Lazarus!"
37 Yet there were some who questioned: "If He could open blind
eyes, could He not have prevented Lazarus from dying?"

Lazarus raised from the dead (11:38-45)

38 Jesus was still deeply moved when He arrived at the tomb, which
was in a cave with a stone placed across the entrance.
39 Jesus said: "Take away the stone."
"But Lord," Martha protested, "by now there will be a terrible
smell, for it is four days since he died and was buried."
40 But Jesus said to her: "Did I not tell you that if you believed, you
would see God's glory?"
41-42 So the stone was removed. Then Jesus looked up towards
heaven and prayed: "Father, I thank You that You have heard Me
and I know that You always hear Me. I say this for the sake of all
those standing here, that they might believe that You have sent Me."
43 Jesus then shouted: "Lazarus, come out!" 44 The man who had
died came out with his hands and feet still wrapped in the strips of
linen and with the burial cloth around his face.
Jesus ordered: "Remove his grave clothes and let him walk freely."

Jewish Council plots to kill Jesus (11:45-57)

45 Many of the Jews from the city who had come to visit Mary put
their faith in Jesus when they witnessed this. 46 But some went and
told the Pharisees what Jesus had done. So the chief priests and
Pharisees called a meeting of the Sanhedrin, the Jewish ruling Council.
47 "What are we accomplishing?" they asked. "This man is still
performing many miraculous signs. 48 If we allow Him to continue,

everyone will believe in Him. And where will that leave us? The
Romans will come and take our authority away. He will be the ruin
of our nation."
49 Then one of them, Caiaphas, who was the high priest at that
time, spoke: "You do not understand anything! 50 Do you not see
that it would be better for you if one man was to die for the sake of
the people, rather than to have the whole nation perish."
51-52 Because he was high priest for that year, he was not speaking
from his own understanding, but was prophesying that Jesus
would die for the whole Jewish nation and for all God's children
scattered everywhere in the world, that they may all be brought
together in unity through their faith in Jesus.
53 The outcome was that the Council now began to plot as to how
they could kill Jesus. 54 It was no longer safe for Jesus to move publicly
among the Jews in Jerusalem. So He went instead to Ephraim, a village
in the region near the desert. There He stayed with His disciples.
55 Near the time for the Jewish Passover, many pilgrims went
from the country areas to Jerusalem to take part in the ceremonial
cleansing before the Feast began. 56 They kept looking for Jesus in
the temple area where He normally taught. They questioned among
themselves: "Do you think He would dare to come to the feast at
all?" 57 For the chief priests and Pharisees had issued a decree, that
if anyone discovered where Jesus was, it was to be reported to them
immediately so they might arrest Him.

Mary anoints Jesus' feet (12:1-8)

12 Six days before the Passover, Jesus returned to Bethany
where Lazarus, who had been raised from the dead, lived.
2 A dinner was given in Jesus' honour and Martha served, while
Lazarus was among those reclining at the table with Jesus. 3 Mary
took a pint of very expensive perfume, pure nard, poured it on
Jesus' feet and wiped them with her hair. The whole house was
filled with the perfume's fragrance.
4-5 However, Judas Iscariot, the disciple who was to betray Jesus
later, objected: "This perfume is worth so much that it could have
been sold and the money distributed to the poor." 6 He did not say
this out of concern for the poor but because he was a thief. He had
the responsibility for keeping the money purse and used to help
himself from it.
7 Jesus replied: "Do not trouble her. She is doing what it was
intended that she should do by saving this perfume for the time of

My burial. [8]The poor will always be with you, but you will not
always have Me."

More Jews put their faith in Jesus (12:9-11)

[9]A large number of Jewish people discovered that Jesus was there at
Bethany and so came, not only to see Him but also to see Lazarus
who He had raised from the dead. [10]This caused the chief priests to
plan to kill Lazarus as well as Jesus. [11]Because of the way He was
raised from the dead, many Jews were turning to Jesus and putting
their faith in Him.

Entrance of the King (12:12-19)

[12]On the following day, the great crowd that had come to the city for
the feast heard that Jesus was making His way to Jerusalem.
[13]Taking palm branches they went to meet Him, shouting: "The
Lord our Saviour!"

"Blessed is He who comes in the Lord's Name!"

"Blessed be Israel's King!"

[14-15]Jesus was riding on a young donkey that had been provided
for Him, fulfilling what was written, "Daughter of Zion, do not fear.
Look, your King comes seated on a young donkey."

[16]His disciples did not understand what was happening at first. It
was only after Jesus had been glorified that they realised that these
things had been done to Jesus to fulfil what had been written
prophetically about Him.

[17]All those who had witnessed the way Jesus had called Lazarus
out of the tomb and raised him from the dead continued to tell about
what they had seen. [18]Many others, on hearing of such a wonderful
miraculous sign, went out to greet Jesus.

[19]The Pharisees were exasperated further. "We are getting
nowhere," they said. "Look at what is happening now. The whole
world is turning to Him!"

Jesus predicts His death (12:20-36)

[20]Some Greeks were among those who had come to worship at the
feast. [21]They came to Philip, who was a Galilean from Bethsaida,
with a request: "Sir, we want to see Jesus." [22]Philip told Andrew this
and then both went to tell Jesus. [23]He replied: "Now the time has come
for the Son of Man to be glorified. [24]I tell you most emphatically,

12:15 Zechariah 9:9

unless a seed of wheat falls into the ground and dies, it remains
only a single seed. But if it dies it reproduces itself many times over.
[25]Anyone who lives his life for himself will lose it, but anyone who
hates the idea of living in the world for himself, will inherit eternal
life. [26]So whoever chooses to serve Me must follow Me. Where I
choose to go, My servant will also go. And My Father will honour
all who serve Me.

[27]"Yet now I feel troubled. So what shall I say? 'Father save me
from this hour?' No, this was the very reason for which I came.
[28]Father, glorify your Name!"

Then a voice from heaven was heard saying: "I have glorified it
and will glorify it again." [29]The crowd said that it had thundered,
but others said an angel had spoken to Jesus.

[30]"This voice was for your benefit, not mine," Jesus said. "The
time of judgment on this world has come. [31]Now the prince of this
world, the devil, will be driven out. [32]But when I am lifted up from
the earth, I will draw all men to Myself." [33]This was a veiled reference
to the way in which He was going to die.

[34]Then the crowd responded: "In the law we are told that the
Christ will be eternal. How can you say, then, that the Son of Man
has to be lifted up? Who is this Son of Man to whom you refer?"

[35]Jesus answered: "The Light is going to be with you for only a
little longer. Walk in the Light while it is here with you, before the
darkness comes to overtake you. For anyone who walks in the dark
cannot see where he is going. [36]While the Light is here with you,
trust in that Light, and then you will become sons of that Light."

When He had said this, Jesus left them and went away secretly.

Unbelief in Jesus (12:37-50)

[37-39]Despite the fact that Jesus had performed so many miraculous
signs before their eyes, still they would not believe in Him, as was
predicted by the prophet Isaiah, "Lord, who has believed the message
you gave Me, and to whom has Your arm of power been revealed?"
Isaiah explains why the people could not believe: [40]"God has blinded
the eyes of their perception and their hearts are spiritually dead, so
they cannot see with their eyes nor can they understand with their
hearts and repent, for then they would be healed and set free."

[41]Prophetically Isaiah was shown God's glory and so could speak
about Him hundreds of years before He became man.

12:39 Isaiah 53:1
12:40 Isaiah 6:10

42 Although many did not believe in Jesus, some of their leaders
did. But because of the animosity of the Pharisees, they would not
express their faith publicly or they would have been excommunicated
from the synagogue. 43 Being accepted by others meant more to them
than doing what was acceptable to God.

44 Jesus shouted: "When anyone believes in Me, he not only
believes in Me, but also in the Father who sent Me. 45 To look at Me
is to look at the Father who sent Me. 46 I came to bring light into the
world, to deliver from darkness those who believe in Me.

47 "When someone hears what I say but does not act on My words,
I do not judge him for his disobedience. My purpose in coming was
not to judge people now, but to save them from the judgment they
deserve.

48 "However, anyone who rejects Me and the words I speak will
be judged. The Word I have spoken will be his judge and he will
finally be condemned because of his unbelief.

49 "I do not say this as My own opinion. The Father who sent Me
has told Me what to say and even how to say it. 50 I know that whatever He commands people to do will result in eternal life. So you
can be sure that I only say what the Father has commanded Me to say."

Jesus washes the disciples' feet (13:1-11)

13 Jesus knew the time for Him to return to the Father had
arrived. It was now just before the Passover feast. He had
loved all those who belonged to Him while in this world, and now
was about to demonstrate how great that love was.

2 Judas Iscariot, son of Simon, had already been swayed by the
devil to betray Jesus. Jesus and the disciples were together for the
evening meal. 3 He was well aware that the Father had given Him
complete control of the situation. He had come from heaven and
was now about to return there to be with God the Father.

4 During the meal Jesus rose from the table, removed His outer
garment and wrapped a towel around His waist. 5 He poured water
into a bowl and began to wash the feet of His disciples. He then
dried them with the towel.

6 When it was Simon Peter's turn, he objected: "Lord, surely You
are not going to wash my feet?"

7 Jesus told him: "You do not understand the significance of what
I am doing now, but later you will understand."

8 "Never," said Peter. "You shall never wash my feet."

"If I do not wash you, then you do not belong to Me," Jesus said.

[9]"In that case," Simon Peter replied, "Please wash my hands and
head as well as my feet." [10]Jesus told Him: "If someone has already
had a bath, he only has to wash his feet; the rest of his body is already
clean. And you disciples are spiritually clean, apart from one of
you." [11]For Jesus knew who was going to betray Him; so He could
not say they were all clean.

Jesus identifies His betrayer (13:12-30)

[12]After washing their feet, Jesus again put on His outer garment and
returned to His place at the table. He asked the disciples: "Do you
understand the significance of what I have just done for you? [13]You
call Me 'Teacher' and 'Lord' and it is right to do so, for this is what
I am.

[14]"Now if I, your Lord and Teacher, have humbly washed your
feet, you should also be ready to humble yourselves and wash each
other's feet! [15]This is an example I have given you, so that you
should do for one another what I have done for you. So humbly
serve one another. [16]For I tell you the truth, a servant is never
greater than his master, nor is the messenger more important than
the one who sent him.

[17]"You know what I have taught you. You will be blessed by
doing what I say!

[18]"Sadly I am not referring to every one of you. I know what is in
the heart of each person I have chosen. And there is a scripture that
has to be fulfilled: "Someone who eats My bread has turned against
Me."

[19]"I am warning you now before it happens, so that when it does
take place, you will still believe that I am the One sent by God. [20]I
tell you the truth, anyone who accepts someone I have sent, accepts
Me. And anyone who accepts Me, accepts also He who sent Me."

[21]Having said this, Jesus was clearly troubled and told them: "I
tell you truly, one of you is about to betray Me."

[22]This startled the disciples who looked at one another with no
idea as to whom He was referring. [23]John, the disciple who had a
special relationship of love with Jesus, was next to Him at the table.
[24]Simon Peter whispered to John: "Ask Him who He means."

[25]So being close to Jesus, John asked Him quietly: "Lord, who is
it?"

[26]Jesus answered: "When I have dipped this piece of bread in the
dish, I will give it to him." He dipped the piece of bread and gave it

13:18 Psalm 41:9

to Judas Iscariot, son of Simon. [27]When Judas took the bread, Satan
immediately entered into him.

Jesus said to Judas: "What you intend to do, do immediately."
[28]The others around the table did not understand why Jesus said
this to Judas. [29]Since he was responsible for the money purse, some
thought Jesus was telling him to go and buy what was needed to
celebrate the feast, or perhaps to give some money to the poor.

[30]Judas left immediately and outside it was already dark.

Jesus commands His disciples to love one another (13:31-38)

[31]When he had left, Jesus could now speak in a different way to the
other disciples. "The time has now come for the Son of Man to be
glorified and for God to be glorified in Him. [32]If God is glorified in
His Son, then He will in turn glorify the Son and will do so immediately.

[33]"My children, I am going to be with you for only a little while
longer. You will search for Me, and as I told the Jewish leaders, so
now I tell you: where I am about to go, you cannot come.

[34]"I am giving you a new command: love each other. In the same
way that I have loved each of you, so you must love each other.
[35]When you do this everyone will see that you are truly My disciples;
they will know this because of your love for each other.

[36]Simon Peter asked Him: "Lord, where are You going?"

Jesus answered: "You cannot come where I am going now, but
you will follow later."

[37]Peter asked: "Lord, why is it not possible for me to come now?
I would do anything for You, even give my life for You."

[38]Then Jesus said to him: "Are you really prepared to give your
life for Me? I tell you truly, before the cock crows at dawn, you will
have denied three times that you know Me!"

The Way, the Truth and the Life (14:1-11)

14 "Don't allow your hearts to be gripped by fear. Put your
trust in God and therefore also in Me. [2]There are many
places in My Father's house for those who believe in Me. If this was
not the case I would have warned you. [3]I am returning there now
and will prepare the place appointed for you. So you can see that if
I prepare your place for you, then I will return for you to ensure that
you will be with Me eternally in My heavenly glory. [4]You now
know the way to the place where I am going."

5 Thomas said to Jesus: "Lord how can we know the way, if we
don't know where you are going?"
6 Jesus replied: "I, I AM the way and I, I AM the Truth and I, I AM
the Life. Nobody can come to the Father in heaven except through
faith in Me. 7 To know Me personally is to know My Father as well.
So from this time you can say that you both know Him and have
seen Him."
8 "Lord, show us the Father and we shall be satisfied," Philip said.
9 Jesus answered: "I have been with you all this time, Philip, and
still you do not know Me? To see Me is to see the Father. So why ask
Me to show you the Father? 10 Simply believe that I am in the Father
and that the Father is in Me. Even the words I speak to you are not
My own; the Father who lives in Me is working through Me. 11 So
believe Me when I tell you that I am in the Father and the Father is
in Me. The miracles are the very evidence that what I say is true.

Prayer of faith (14:12-14)

12 "I tell you the truth, anyone who puts his faith in Me will do the
same things that I have been doing. He will be able to do even
greater things than these because of what will happen when I return
to be with the Father.
13 "And I give you this promise: I will give you whatever you ask
in My Name, and in this way the Son will bring further glory to the
Father. 14 Yes, you can ask Me for anything in My Name, that is in
My will, and I will surely do it.

Promise of the Holy Spirit (14:15-26)

15 "The evidence that you love Me will be seen in the way you obey
what I command you to do. 16 To enable this obedience, when I
return to heaven I will ask the Father to replace Me with another
Counsellor exactly like Me, who will remain with you forever. 17 He
is the Spirit of Truth.

"The world cannot receive Him, because those who belong to the world neither see the way He works nor do they know Him. But you know Him, for this Spirit of Truth lives with you and soon will be in you.

18 "I will not leave you alone; I will come to you. 19 Soon the world
will not be able to see Me any longer, but you will see Me. Because
I live, you will also live filled with My life. 20 Then you will know for
sure that I am at one with the Father, you are at one with Me and I
am living in you.

[21]"Who really loves Me? The one who not only has My commands but obeys them! Anyone who genuinely loves Me like that
will be loved by My Father. I will also love him and will continue to
reveal Myself to him."

[22]Then the other Judas (not Iscariot) asked: "Lord, why will You
reveal yourself to us, but not to everyone in the world?"

[23]Jesus answered: "If anyone genuinely loves Me, he will put My
teaching into practice. My Father will love him and both He and I
will come and live with him. Yes, we will make our home with him.
[24]But anyone who does not love Me will not obey what I have said.
What I tell you is not My own teaching; it comes from the Father
who sent Me!

[25]"I have told you all these things while I am still with you. [26]The
Father will send you the Counsellor, the Holy Spirit, in My Name.
When He comes He will teach you all you need to know and will
remind you of everything I have already taught you.

Jesus tells of His departure (14:27-31)

[27]"I leave you with the gift of peace. It is My peace that I give to you,
the kind of peace the world can never give you. Because you have
My peace, there is no need to allow your hearts to become fearful or
troubled.

[28]"You have heard Me tell you, 'I am about to leave you, but I am
going to return to you!' If you really love Me you should be glad
about this. You should rejoice that I am returning to be with My
Father in heaven, for He is greater in heaven than I am here in My
human body! [29]I have warned you of what is about to take place so
that when it does happen you will continue to believe.

[30]"There is not much more I can say to you now. The devil, the
prince of this world, is about to have his way. [31]Understand that he
has no control whatsoever over Me; but the world needs to see Me
demonstrate how I love the Father by doing exactly what He has
commanded Me.

"So let us be ready for what is about to happen.

The Vine and the branches (15:1-6)

15 "I, I AM the true Vine and my Father tends this Vine. [2]He
cuts out every branch in Me that does not produce fruit.
Even the fruitful branches He carefully prunes so that in future they
will bear even more fruit.

3 "You have already been pruned through the words I have spoken to you. 4 Stay living in Me and I will continue to live in you. It is impossible for any branch to be fruitful if it is separated from the Vine. It has to continue to live in the Vine. In the same way, it would be impossible for you to bear fruit if you were not to remain living in Me.

5 "I AM the Vine and you are the branches in the Vine. Anyone who continues to live in Me and I in him will be abundantly fruitful. But outside of Me you can do absolutely nothing. 6 For anyone who does not continue to live at one with Me is like a branch that is thrown away and so withers. All such branches are gathered, thrown into the fire and burned.

Remain in His love (15:7-11)

7 "By contrast, if you continue to live at one with Me and My words continue to live in you, you can ask for anything you want and it will be given you. 8 My Father will be glorified and honoured in your lives because you will bear much fruit and so demonstrate that you are truly My disciples.

9 "I have loved you in exactly the same way that My Father loves Me. So continue to live in My love. 10 You will remain in My love if you obey what I have commanded you, in the same way that I have remained in My Father's love by obeying what He commanded Me.

11 "I have told you this because I want you to have within you the same joy that is in Me. I want you to be absolutely full of My joy.

Friends of Jesus (15:12-17)

12 "The command I give you to obey is simply this: love one another in the same way that I have loved you. 13 No greater love than this exists, and it is expressed in your willingness to lay down your life for your friends. 14 If you obey what I command you, then you will be My friends. 15 I no longer refer to you only as servants, because it is not a servant's place to know about his master's business. No, I have called you My friends because I have relayed to you whatever the Father has revealed to Me.

16 "You did not choose Me. No, it was I who chose you. But I not only choose you to belong to Me; I also commission you to go and bear fruit that will be of eternal significance. As you go to do that, the Father will give you whatever you ask in My Name, those things that you know to be consistent with My will.

17 "So this is My command: love each other!

Rejection is inevitable (15:18-16:6)

18 "If you experience hatred from worldly people, remember that
they hated Me first. If you belonged to the world and lived by its
standards, then they would love you as their own. 19 The truth is that
you do not belong to the world, but I have chosen to take you out
of worldliness to belong to My Kingdom. That is why the world
hates you and is opposed to you.

20 "Remember what I have already taught you: 'No servant is
greater than the master he serves!' So if they persecute Me, it is certain
that they will also persecute you. On the other hand, those who
have obeyed what I have taught them will also obey what you teach
them. 21 In other words, you will be treated by people in the same
way that they have treated Me, simply because you speak and act
in My Name, on My behalf. What is more, those who oppose you
do not know the Father who sent Me.

22 "They would not be guilty in the same way if they were simply
ignorant. But the fact that I have come and told them the truth com-
pounds their guilt. They have no excuse for their sin of rejecting Me
and what I have said. 23 Anyone who hates Me hates My Father as
well. 24 In rejecting Me and My teaching, they have clearly rejected
what I did among them, the miraculous signs that verified My
message. So their guilt is even greater. They have shown their
hatred of both Me and My Father despite the miracles.

25 "This only shows that what is written in their law is correct and
has now been fulfilled, 'They hated Me without cause.'

26 "However, when I send you the Counsellor from the Father, the
Spirit of Truth who comes from the Father, He will bear witness to
all I have said and done. 27 And you also will be My witnesses, for
you have been with Me from the beginning of My ministry here.

16 "I have told you all these things to prevent you from wandering away from the truth. 2 They will excommunicate you
from the synagogue. They will even think that they are serving
God's purposes by killing you. 3 And they will do such things
because they know neither the Father nor Me.

4-5 "I have warned you so that when these things happen you will
remember what I said. There was no need for Me to tell you these
things while I was still with you; but now I am returning to the Father
who sent Me. Yet none of you asks Me, 'Where are you going?' 6 You
are merely filled with grief because of what I have said.

15:25 Psalm 35:19

The role of the Holy Spirit (16:7-15)

7 "But I tell you the truth, it is for your own good that I am now
going away. For unless I leave you, the Counsellor cannot come to
you. But when I return to the Father, I will send Him to you.
8 "When the Holy Spirit comes He will reveal to the world what
is sinful and what is right in God's eyes. He will warn people of the
judgment that is to come. 9 People will see they remain bound in sin
and guilt because they do not believe in Me. 10 They will see that I
have revealed what is true and right by the way I return to the
Father, even though this means people will no longer see Me in the
flesh. 11 They will be faced with the reality of judgment because the
prince of this world now stands judged and condemned.
12 "There is so much more I have to say to you, but you would not
be able to take it now. 13 But when the Spirit of Truth comes He will
give you the complete revelation of the truth. He will not speak on
His own initiative, but only what He hears from the Father and the
Son; and He will prepare you for what lies ahead.
14 "The Holy Spirit will glorify Me because He will take hold of all
I have said and done, and will reveal it to you. 15 Everything that the
Father has, I also have. And everything I have, the Spirit will take
and reveal to you in your experience. So I tell you clearly that everything the Father, the Son and the Holy Spirit have is yours!

Authority in the Name of Jesus (16:16-24)

16 "Soon you will no longer see Me but then, shortly afterwards, you
will see Me again."
17-18 Some of the disciples questioned among themselves: "What
do you think He means by saying, 'Soon you will no longer see Me,
then, shortly afterwards, you will see Me again?' We don't understand what He means."
19 Jesus perceived that they wanted Him to explain further, so He
said to them: "Are you discussing what I meant when I said, 'Soon
you will see Me no longer but, shortly afterwards, you will see Me
again?' 20 I tell you the truth, you will cry with grief while the world
rejoices. But then your grief will be replaced by great joy.
21 "Immediately prior to the birth of her child a woman experiences
pain; but as soon as her baby is born she forgets all her pain and
concern; she is so delighted that her child is now safely born. 22 So
shall it be with you. Now you are full of grief and concern; but
when I see you again all that will be forgotten. You will be overcome
with a joy that no one will be able to take away from you.

23 "At that time you will no longer question Me about anything. I tell you the truth, you will speak directly to the Father and He will give you whatever you ask in My Name. 24 Until now you have not asked for anything using the authority of My Name, the authority I have given you. But now when you ask in this way you will receive and this will give you great joy.

25 "In the past I have spoken to you using parables and illustrations, but the time is about to begin when I will no longer speak with you figuratively, but will tell you about My Father in clear, precise language. 26 Then you will pray in My Name. I am not promising to ask the Father on your behalf for what you need. 27 This will not be necessary, for the Father Himself loves you because you have loved Me and have believed who I am, the One who has been sent by God. 28 I came from the Father in heaven into this world. Now I am leaving the world and returning to My Father in heaven."

Disciples have confidence in Jesus (16:29-33)

29 At this, Jesus' disciples said: "Now You are speaking in plain language we can understand. 30 Now we realise that You know everything, that You do not need anyone to question You. This encourages our faith, that truly You have come from God."

31 "At last you believe!" Jesus replied. 32 "A time is coming and has already come when you will be scattered, each of you to his own home. Yes, you will leave Me all by Myself. Yet I will not be alone, for My Father is always with Me.

33 "All these things I have told you now so that by trusting in Me you will be able to maintain your peace. In this world you are bound to experience trouble. But you do not need to be down-hearted about this, for I have already defeated the world."

Jesus prays for Himself (17:1-5)

17 After Jesus had said all these things, He looked up towards heaven as He prayed: "Father, now the time has come for You to glorify Your Son so that Your Son might glorify You. 2 You gave Him authority over everyone so that He could give eternal life to all those You gave Him. 3 And eternal life is to know You personally as the only true God, and to know Jesus Christ whom You sent into the world.

4 "I have brought You glory while I have been here on earth because I have completed the task You appointed Me to accomplish. 5 So now, Father, restore Me to the glory of Your presence in heaven with the glory I had with You before the world was created.

Jesus prays for His disciples (17:6-19)

6 "I have made You known to those You set apart and gave to Me.
They were Yours and You chose to give them to Me; and now they
have obeyed Your Word. 7 Now they are sure that You are the source
of everything You have given Me.

8 "I spoke to them the words You gave Me to speak and they
received them as the truth. They became certain that I came from
You; they believed that You sent Me to be the Saviour of the world.

9 "So I pray for them, Father. I am not praying for everyone in the
world, but for those you have given Me out of the world, for they
belong to You. 10 All those who belong to You belong to Me, and I
have received glory and honour through them.

11 "I will not remain in the world any longer, but they have to
remain here, even though I am returning to be with You. So, Holy
Father, keep them under the protection of Your powerful Name, the
Name You gave Me, so that they may remain united in the same
way that we are always one.

12 "I could protect them while I was with them and keep them safe
by the power and authority of the Name You gave Me. Not one of
them has been lost along the way, except the one who had to be lost
and destroyed so that the prediction of scripture would be fulfilled.

13 "Now I am returning to You. I say these things while I am still
with them in the world, so that they will have the complete measure
of My joy in them. 14 I have given them Your Word and the whole
world has hated them because they believed what I said. This
demonstrated that they do not belong to the world any more than I
do. 15 I do not pray for You to take them out of the world, but to protect
them from the power of the evil one. 16 They do not belong to the
world any more than I do.

17 "Let their lives be consecrated and made holy by the truth, for
the words You have given Me are the truth. 18 In the same way that
You sent Me into the world, I have commissioned and sent them
into the world as witnesses of the truth.

19 "It is for their sakes that I now consecrate Myself completely to
Your will, so that through the shedding of My blood they, too, may
be truly consecrated to Your purposes.

Jesus prays for future believers (17:20-26)

20 "I do not pray only for them, but for all those who in the future
will believe in Me through the truth they shall proclaim. 21 I pray
that they will be one in faith and love, Father, in the same way that

You and I are always in complete harmony and agreement: You in Me and I in You. May they continue to live in Us so that the world will believe who I AM, the One You sent to be their Saviour and Lord.

22 "The glory You gave Me I have given to all who believe in Me that they may be united in faith and love, reflecting the unity that is between Us as Father and Son. 23 I will live in them as You live in Me. Yes, I want them to come to a place of being completely united in faith and love to demonstrate to the world that You sent Me, and that You have loved them in the same way that You have loved Me while I have been here on the earth.

24 "Father, My desire is that all those You have given Me, now and in the future, will be with Me where I am going to be, so that they can see My glory for themselves, the glory You have given Me because You loved Me even before We created the world.

25 "Righteous Father, even though those who belong to the world do not know You, I know You, and those who believe know that You sent Me. 26 I have revealed the truth about You to them and I will continue to make You known to them, so that the same love You have for Me will be in them, and that I Myself will be expressed in their lives."

Jesus arrested (18:1-14)

18 After He had prayed, Jesus and His disciples crossed the Kidron Valley to an olive grove where they had often spent time together. 2 Judas, who betrayed Him, knew the place. 3 He came there now, followed by a group of soldiers and officials sent by the chief priests and Pharisees, carrying both torches and weapons.

4 Jesus was well aware of everything that was going to happen to Him and went to meet them. "Who do you want?" He asked them.

5 "Jesus of Nazareth," they replied.

"I am He," said Jesus. (Judas was there with the group.) 6 When He said this, they all fell to the ground.

7 Jesus repeated the question: "Who do you want?"

They said: "Jesus of Nazareth."

8 Jesus said: "I have already told you that I am He. If it is Me you want, then you can allow these men to go." 9 The words that Jesus had spoken had to be fulfilled, 'I have lost none of those You gave Me.'

10 Simon Peter had a sword which he then drew and used to strike the high priest's servant, cutting off his right ear (the man's name was Malchus).

[11] Jesus ordered Peter: "Put away your sword! I have to drink the cup the Father has given Me. Do you think you can prevent that?"

[12-13] Then the officers, soldiers and Jewish officials arrested Jesus. They bound Him and led Him first to Annas. Caiaphas was the high priest at that time and Annas was his father-in-law. [14] It was Caiaphas who had told the Jewish leaders that it was beneficial for one man to die on behalf of the people.

Peter denies he is Jesus' disciple (18:15-18)

[15-16] Simon Peter and another of the disciples followed at a safe distance. This other disciple knew the high priest and so gained access to the courtyard where Jesus was taken; but Peter had to remain outside until the other disciple who knew the high priest had spoken to the servant girl on duty at the door. Then Peter was also allowed to come into the courtyard.

[17] She said to Peter: "Are you not one of this man's disciples?"

"No, I am not," Peter replied.

[18] The servants and officials stood round a fire to keep warm, for it was a cold night. Peter stood with them warming himself.

The High Priest questions Jesus (18:19-24)

[19] Meanwhile, the high priest had begun to question Jesus about His disciples and what He taught.

[20] Jesus replied: "I have spoken publicly so everyone could hear. I always went to the synagogues and the temple to teach, places where Jews meet openly. I have not spoken in secret. [21] So why do you need to question Me about what I have said? You can ask those who have listened to Me: they know well what I have been teaching."

[22] When Jesus replied in this manner, one of the nearby officials hit Jesus in the face saying: "Is that the right way to answer the high priest?"

[23] Jesus replied: "Tell Me what I said that was wrong. But if what I said was true, then why hit Me?" [24] While still bound, Annas then sent Jesus to Caiaphas the high priest.

Peter denies Jesus again (18:25-27)

[25] As Simon Peter was warming himself, he was again asked: "Are you not one of this man's disciples?"

He repeated his denial saying: "No, I am not."

[26] Another of the high priest's servants, who was a relative of the man whose ear Peter had cut off, challenged him: "I saw you with

Him in the olive garden, didn't I?" [27]For the third time Peter denied Jesus, and then the cock crowed!

Jesus before Pilate (18:28-37)

[28]Jesus was taken from Caiaphas to the Roman governor's palace. By now it was the early hours of the morning and the Jewish leaders did not want to make themselves ceremonially unclean by entering the palace, or they would not have been able to eat the Passover meal. [29]So Pilate came out of the palace to ask them: "What accusations do you bring against this man?"

[30]They replied: "We would not hand Him over to you unless we were sure of His guilt. He is a criminal."

[31]"Well take Him and judge Him according to your own law then," said Pilate.

[32]The Jews responded: "But we do not have Roman authority to execute anyone." What Jesus had said about the way He would die had to be fulfilled.

[33]Pilate went into the palace and had Jesus brought before him. "Are You really the king of the Jews?" he asked him.

[34]Jesus replied: "Is that what you think, or is this what others have told you about Me?"

[35]Pilate answered: "Am I a Jew? This is what Your own people and the chief priests who have handed You over to me, say You claim. What have You done?

[36]"My Kingdom is not a worldly kingdom," Jesus replied. "If that was the case, My followers would have fought to prevent the Jews arresting Me. No, I have an altogether different kind of Kingdom."

[37]"So You are a king in that case!" Pilate said.

"Yes, it is correct to say that I am King. I came into this world to reveal the truth; that is why I was born. So I cannot deny that I am King," said Jesus. "Everyone who really wants to know the truth listens to what I say."

Pilate finds no fault in Jesus (18:38-40)

[38]"But what is truth?" asked Pilate. He then went outside again to speak to the Jewish leaders: "I do not find Him guilty of any charge.
[39]But as it is customary for Me to release one prisoner to you at Passover time, do you want me to release this 'King of the Jews?'"

[40]"No, no! Not Him!" they shouted in response. "Release Barabbas!" Now Barabbas was a terrorist!

Jesus mocked and flogged (19:1-3)

19 So Pilate had Jesus flogged. 2-3 The soldiers made a crown out of thorn branches and put it on His head. They placed a purple robe on Him, the colour of royalty, and bowed before Him again and again in a mocking fashion saying: "Hail, King of the Jews!" And they hit Him about the face.

Pilate's dilemma (19:4-16)

4 Pilate went outside to the Jewish leaders again and said: "Listen, I am bringing this man out to you again because I want to make it clear that I do not find Him guilty of any charge brought against Him." 5 Then Jesus came out still wearing the crown of thorns and the purple robe. Pilate said: "Here He is!"

6 But as soon as the chief priests and their officers saw Him, they shouted out, "Crucify! Crucify Him!"

Pilate responded: "Take Him yourselves and crucify Him. I have made it clear that I have not found Him guilty of anything."

7 But the Jewish leaders were insistent: "According to our law He must die because He claimed to be God's Son."

8-9 This made Pilate even more fearful and He went back into the palace to question Jesus further. "Where do You come from?" he asked. Jesus stood silent, refusing to answer.

10 "Why do You not speak to me?" Pilate asked Him. "Surely You understand that I have the power to free You or to crucify You!"

11 Then Jesus said: "You could have no power over Me unless this was given you from heaven. Those who have handed Me over to you are far more guilty."

12 That settled it. Pilate now wanted to free Jesus, but the Jews kept up their opposition by shouting: "You are no friend to Caesar if you release this man. It is treason against Caesar for anyone to claim to be king."

13 This hypocrisy put Pilate in a dilemma. So he sat down on the Seat of Judgment and had Jesus brought before him again at the place known as the Stone Pavement. 14 It was now about noon on the Day of Preparation for the Passover.

Pilate said to the assembled Jews: "Here is your King."

15 They shouted back: "Take Him away. Take Him away! Crucify Him!"

"You want Me to crucify your King?" asked Pilate.

"We have no king apart from Caesar," answered the chief priests.

16 So Pilate finally relented and handed Jesus over to them to be crucified!

King of the Jews crucified (19:17-24)

17-18 Then the soldiers took charge of Him, leading Him to Golgotha, the Place of the Skull, where they were to crucify Him. He had to carry His own cross there. They crucified two others at the same time, one on either side of Jesus.

19 Pilate had ordered that a sign be nailed to the cross reading: 'JESUS OF NAZARETH THE KING OF THE JEWS.' 20 Many people read this sign which was written in Aramaic, Latin and Greek, for the place where Jesus was crucified was just outside the city. 21 The Jewish chief priests were incensed by this and protested to Pilate: "Do not write 'King of the Jews', but that this man *claimed* to be the king of the Jews."

22 Pilate answered them: "What I have written, I have written."

23 The soldiers who crucified Jesus divided His clothes among the four of them. But His undergarment was seamless, woven in one piece from top to bottom. "We will not tear this," they agreed, "it is too valuable. Let's cast lots to decide who shall have it."

24 This fulfilled the scripture that reads: 'They divided My apparel among them and cast lots for My clothing.' So the soldiers fulfilled what had been predicted.

John to care for Mary (19:25-27)

25 Jesus' mother, her sister, Mary the wife of Clopas and Mary Magdalene stood near the cross where Jesus hung. 26-27 When He noticed His mother and also John, the disciple He loved deeply, standing there, He said to His mother: "Dear woman, here is your son," and then to John, "Here is your mother." From that day John took Mary into his home.

It is finished (19:28-37)

28 Jesus now knew that His mission on earth was completed and the scriptures that had prophesied His crucifixion were being fulfilled. So later He said: "I am thirsty." 29 A jar of wine vinegar, used to dull the pain, was nearby. So a sponge was soaked in it, placed on a hyssop stalk and lifted to Jesus' lips.

30 When He had received the drink, Jesus said: "It is finished." Now that everything had been accomplished, He bowed His head and died, giving up His Spirit.

31 This was the preparation day before the special Sabbath. The Jewish leaders did not want the bodies left on the crosses on the

19:24 Psalm 22:18

Sabbath. So they came to Pilate and asked for the legs to be broken
to hasten their deaths, and then their bodies could be taken down.
32-33 They broke the legs of those crucified alongside Jesus, but found
that He had already died. So they did not break His legs. 34 Instead
one of the soldiers thrust His spear into Jesus' side and out flowed
both blood and water.

35 I, John, personally bear witness to the truth of this, for I saw it
myself. I know this is the truth and I testify to this to encourage you
to believe.

36-37 And so in this way other scriptures were fulfilled: 'Not one of
His bones will be broken,' and, 'They will gaze on the One they
have pierced.'

The burial of Jesus (19:38-42)

38-39 Joseph of Arimathea came to Pilate later and asked him to release
Jesus' body. Joseph had become a disciple of Jesus, but secretly
because he had been fearful of the Jewish leaders. Pilate gave permission and together with Nicodemus, who had earlier visited
Jesus at night, Joseph came and took the body. Nicodemus had
brought about a hundred pounds of a mixture of myrrh and aloes
to prepare the body for burial. 40 So the two of them wrapped the
body in strips of linen together with the spices, according to the
Jewish burial customs.

41 Near the place where Jesus was crucified was a garden in which
was a new unused tomb. 42 As it was the Jewish Day of Preparation
and time before the Sabbath was short, they laid Jesus in that tomb
which was conveniently nearby.

The empty tomb (20:1-9)

20 Very early on the Sunday morning, while it was still dark,
Mary Magdalene went to the tomb and discovered that the
stone that had covered the entrance had been removed. 2 She ran to
find Peter and the disciple who Jesus loved and told them: "They
have taken the Lord's body from the tomb and we don't know
where He is now!"

3-5 So Peter and John ran to the tomb, John arriving first. He
stooped down and looked into the tomb and saw the strips of linen
lying there, but no body. However he didn't enter the tomb. 6-7 When
Peter arrived he went in and saw the strips of linen lying there

19:36-37 Psalm 34:20
19:36-37 Zechariah 12:10

along with the burial cloth that had been wrapped around Jesus' head. This was folded neatly by itself, separate from the strips of linen. [8-9] Then John also entered the tomb. He saw and believed for himself that Jesus had risen, (although at that time the disciples did not know that the scriptures predicted that Jesus had to arise from the dead).

Jesus' Resurrection (20:10-18)

[10] Then the two disciples returned home, but Mary remained at the tomb. [11-12] She was weeping as she looked into the tomb. There she saw two angels clothed in white sitting where Jesus' body had been laid, one at the head, the other at the feet.

[13] They asked Mary: "Woman, why are you weeping?"

"They have taken the Lord's body away and I don't know where they have placed Him." [14] She then turned round and saw Jesus standing there, although she did not recognise that it was Him.

[15] He asked Mary: "Woman, why are you weeping? Who are you looking for?"

She thought that this must be the gardener and so said: "Sir, if You have moved Him, please tell me where You have placed His body and I will come and collect it."

[16] "Mary," Jesus said.

She turned back towards Him and cried out: "Teacher!"

[17] Jesus said: "Do not cling to Me, for I have not yet returned to be with My Father. Go now to My brothers and give them this message, 'I am about to return to My Father and your Father, to My God and your God.'"

[18] So Mary Magdalene went to the disciples and told them: "I have seen the Lord!" And she gave them the message from Him.

Jesus appears to the disciples (20:19-23)

[19-20] On the Sunday evening, when the disciples were meeting behind closed doors for fear of the Jewish leaders, Jesus was suddenly there in the room, standing among them. "Peace be with you," He said, and showed them the wounds in His hands and side. The disciples were overjoyed at seeing the Lord.

[21] Jesus repeated: "God's peace be upon you. I am now sending you, just as the Father has sent Me." [22] He then breathed on them and said: "Receive the Holy Spirit. [23] If you forgive a person his sins, they are forgiven. Those you do not forgive remain unforgiven."

Thomas believes when he sees Jesus (20:24-31)

24 One of the twelve, Thomas (known as Didymus), was not present
when Jesus appeared to the other disciples. 25 They told him: "We
have seen the Lord!"

But Thomas told them: "Unless I see for myself the wounds made
by the nails in His hands and put my finger into the holes and into
His side, I will not believe it."

26 A week later, the disciples were again meeting together in the
house, and this time Thomas was with them. Jesus came and stood
among them as before, even though the doors were locked. "Peace
be with you," He said.

27 He then addressed Thomas: "Place your finger here in the
wounds you see in My hands. You can put your hand in My side.
Stop doubting and believe!"

28 Thomas said to Jesus: "My Lord and My God!"

29 Jesus said to him: "You have believed because you have seen
Me. Those who have not seen for themselves and yet believe are
truly blessed."

30 Jesus performed many other miraculous signs when His disciples
were present which are not recorded in this book. 31 But what is
recorded here is to encourage you to believe that Jesus is the Christ,
the Messiah, God's Son, and so enable you to receive the life He
came to give to those who believe in His Name.

Miraculous catch of fish (21:1-14)

21 Jesus later appeared again to His disciples, this time by the
Sea of Tiberius. This is what happened. 2-3 Simon Peter,
Thomas (called Didymus), Nathanael who was from Cana in
Galilee, the two sons of Zebedee, together agreed to go fishing
when Peter took the lead by saying: "I am going fishing." So they
boarded the boat together, fished all night, but caught nothing.

4 Early in the morning they saw Jesus standing on the shore, but
did not recognise that it was Him. 5 He called to them: "Friends,
haven't you caught anything?"

"Nothing," they answered.

6 "Cast your net on the right side of the boat and you will find fish
there," He said. They did so and were unable to haul the net on
board because of the large number of fish that had been caught.

7 Then John, the beloved disciple, said to Peter: "It's the Lord!"
When Peter heard this, he took his outer garment, put it on and
jumped into the water. 8 The rest of the disciples followed in the boat

dragging the net laden with fish, for they were only about a hundred
metres from the shore. 9 When they landed, they saw a fire of burning
coals with fish being grilled over it, together with a supply of bread.
10 Jesus said to them: "Bring some of those fish you have just caught."
11 Simon Peter climbed aboard and dragged the net to dry land. It
was full of 153 large fish and yet, despite their weight, the net was
not torn.
12 "Come and have some breakfast," Jesus invited them. None of
them dared to ask, "Who are You?" for they knew it was the Lord.
13 Jesus gave each of them some bread together with the freshly-
cooked fish.
14 This was the third occasion on which Jesus appeared to His
disciples in His risen body after His resurrection from the dead.

Jesus commissions Peter (21:15-19)

15 When they had all eaten, Jesus addressed Simon Peter: "Simon,
son of John, do you truly love Me with God's love? Do you love Me
more than all these fish you have just caught?"
"Lord, You know that I love You with my human love," he
answered.
"Then feed My lambs," Jesus told him.
16 Then Jesus asked him again: "Simon, son of John, do you truly
love Me with God's love?"
Peter answered: "Lord, You know that I love You with my human
love."
"Look after My sheep," Jesus said to Him.
17 Then Jesus asked a third time: "Simon, son of John, do you love
Me with your human love?"
It hurt Peter that Jesus would question his love three times; so he
replied: "Lord, You know everything; You must know that I do really
love You with my human love."
Jesus said to him: "Then feed My sheep. 18 When you were
younger you dressed yourself and went wherever you chose to go;
but I tell you truly, when you are old you will stretch out your
hands, someone else will dress you and then take you where you
would never choose to go." 19 By saying this, Jesus was indicating
the kind of death Peter would have to endure for God's glory. Then
Jesus said to Peter: "Follow Me!"

Validity of John's testimony (21:20-25)

20 As Peter followed he noticed John also following. (John, the disciple
who Jesus loved in a special way, was the one who leaned his head

on Jesus' chest at the Last Supper to ask Him who was about to
betray Him). 21 So Peter said to Jesus: "What about John? He is coming
too."

22 Jesus answered: "If I want him to remain alive with Me until I
come again, of what concern is that to you? You obey Me by following Me yourself."

23 Because of what Jesus said about John, a rumour spread among
the believers that he would not die. But Jesus never said that he
would not die. He said: "If I want him to remain alive with Me until
I return, of what concern is that to you?"

24 I am that disciple, John, and I testify to the truth of all I have
written here, as someone who was an eyewitness and who therefore
can account for the accuracy of this testimony.

25 Jesus did so many other wonderful things that are not recorded
here. If they were all to be written down, would the world be able
to contain so many books?

THE

ACTS

OF THE APOSTLES

Promise of the Holy Spirit (1:1-11)

1 1-2 Theophilus, I have already written an account for you of
Jesus' teaching and the works He performed before His return
to heaven. Before His departure, He gave the apostles He had chosen
the commission they were to fulfil through the Holy Spirit. 3 After
His death on the cross, He appeared in His risen body to these men,
demonstrating that He was very much alive. During a period of
forty days He appeared to them on a number of occasions and
spoke further to them about God's Kingdom.

4 While eating with them on one occasion He commanded them:
"Stay in Jerusalem until you have received the gift of the Holy Spirit
that My Father promised, and of which I spoke to you. 5 For John
only baptised people in water for the forgiveness of their sins, but
within a few days you will be immersed in the Holy Spirit, baptised
in His life and power."

6 When the apostles saw Him in His risen body, they asked Him:
"Lord, is this the time when You will restore Israel as Your Kingdom
people?"

7 Jesus told them: "The Father alone has the authority to determine
when such things will happen. That is not your business. 8 However,
you will receive God's power when you are baptised in the Holy
Spirit. Then you will be My witnesses in Jerusalem, the whole of
Judea and Samaria and in every part of the earth."

9 After saying this, they watched as Jesus ascended until a cloud
hid Him from their sight. 10 They kept staring up at the sky until two
men robed in white garments stood beside them. 11 "You Galileans,
why stand here looking into the sky? Jesus, who has now been taken
from you, will Himself come back in a similar manner to the way
He has just departed into heaven."

Matthias replaces Judas (1:12-26)

12 This took place at the Mount of Olives just outside Jerusalem.

13 When the apostles returned to the city, they went to the upstairs room in the house where they were staying. Those present were Peter, John, James and Andrew, Philip, Thomas, Bartholomew, Matthew, James son of Alphaeus, Simon the Zealot and Judas son of James. 14 They met and prayed constantly together, along with the women including Jesus' mother Mary and His brothers.

15-16 During this period, Peter addressed the group of one hundred and twenty believers, saying: "My brothers, it was necessary for the scripture referring to Judas to be fulfilled. This scripture was given by the Holy Spirit through David's words. 17 Even though He was one of us and shared this ministry with us, Judas guided those who arrested Jesus."

18 (This Judas bought a field with the money he was paid for his betrayal; and it was there that he fell, and his intestines burst out of his body. 19 This was common knowledge in Jerusalem and the field was named in Aramaic as the Field of Blood).

20 Peter continued: "It is written in the Psalms, 'Let his place be desolate so that no-one can live there,' and 'let another take his position.'

21-22 "Therefore we must choose someone to replace him; one of the men who has been among us throughout the time the Lord Jesus was with us, from the time of John's baptism to the time when He was taken from us by ascending to heaven. The one we elect must, like us, be a witness of His resurrection."

23 Two men were put forward: Joseph called Barsabbas (also known as Justus) and Matthias. 24-25 Then they all prayed: "Lord, you know every person's heart. Make clear to us which of these two is your choice to share in this apostolic ministry in the place of Judas, who has gone where he belongs."

26 Matthias was chosen by casting lots and was added to the eleven apostles.

Outpouring of the Holy Spirit (2:1-13)

2 1-2 It was on the day of Pentecost, when they were all gathered together, that suddenly there came a sound from heaven like the blowing of a gale force wind, filling the place where they were meeting. 3 They saw, coming upon each of them, what appeared to be flames of fire. 4 All of them were filled with the Holy Spirit and began to speak in other languages that the Spirit gave them.

1:20 Psalm 69:25, Psalm 109:8

[5]At this season, many God-fearing Jews from different nations
were staying in Jerusalem. [6]The sound of the believers speaking in
all these languages caused a crowd to gather. They were bewildered
because each of them heard the believers speaking in their own
native languages. [7]This so astounded them that they asked: "Surely
all these men are Galileans, aren't they? [8]How is it possible, then, that
we can hear them speaking in our own languages? [9-11]For among us
are Parthians, Medes and Elamites; those who live in Mesopotamia,
Judea and Cappadocia, Pontus and Asia, Phrygia and Pamphylia,
Egypt and the area of Libya near Cyrene. There are visitors from
Rome (both Jews and those converted to Judaism) and also Cretans
and Arabs. Yet we hear these men speaking of God's wonders in our
own languages!" [12]They were so amazed and perplexed that they
questioned among themselves: "What could this mean?"

[13]However, there were some who ridiculed the believers suggesting:
"They are merely drunk!"

Peter explains to the crowd (2:14-36)

[14]Then Peter stepped forward, together with the other Eleven apostles,
and shouted to the crowd: "Fellow Jews and residents of Jerusalem,
listen carefully to me. [15]These men are not drunk as some of you
suggest. After all, it is only nine o'clock in the morning! [16]No, what
you see here is the fulfilment of the prophecy spoken by Joel. God
says:

> [17]'In the last days I will pour out My Spirit on all people.
> Then your sons and daughters will prophesy, your young
> men will be given visions and your old men dreams. [18]In
> those days I will pour out My Spirit on My servants, both
> men and women, and they will prophesy. [19]I will demon-
> strate wonders in heaven above and signs on the earth
> below, blood, fire and clouds of smoke. [20]The light of the
> sun will disappear and the moon will look like the colour
> of blood before the great and glorious day when the Lord
> comes. [21]All who call on the Lord's Name will be saved!'

[22]"Listen to this, people of Israel: God demonstrated who Jesus of
Nazareth was by the miracles, wonders and signs He performed
through Him. You are well aware of these things. [23]Yet God allowed
this Man to be handed over to you because this was His pre-ordained

2:21 Joel 2:28-32

purpose. And you, with the help of sinful men, had Him put to
death by crucifixion. [24]But God freed Him from the barrier of death
and raised Him back to life. It was impossible for death to keep Him
in its grip! [25]Referring to Him, David said:

> 'I saw the Lord always before me. Because He is by my
> side I shall never be shaken. [26-27]So my heart is full of joy
> and I praise God with my tongue. And my body can live
> in hope because You will not leave me among the dead,
> nor will You allow the body of Your Holy One to decay.
> [28]Instead, You have shown me the path of life and will fill
> me with joy in Your eternal presence.'

[29]"My brothers, I tell you with authority that our forefather David
died and was buried; his tomb is now here in Jerusalem. [30]But he
spoke as a prophet, knowing that God had solemnly promised to
place one of his descendants on his throne. [31]With foresight he
spoke of Christ's resurrection, that His soul was not left in Hades,
nor was His body left in the grave to decay. [32]Rather, God has raised
this Jesus back to life; and we can all bear witness that this is
absolutely true. [33]Now He has been exalted to heaven to be at God's
right hand. As promised, the Father has given Him the authority to
pour out the Holy Spirit in the way you can now both see and hear.

[34-35]"It was not David who ascended into heaven and yet God said
through him, 'Sit in the place of honour at my right hand until I
cause your enemies to be a footstool beneath your feet.'

[36]"So all the people of Israel need to be sure of this: God has made
this Jesus, who you put to death on the cross, both Lord and Christ,
your Messiah!"

3,000 repent and are baptised (2:37-41)

[37]These words were like an arrow to the heart of the people and they
said to Peter and the apostles: "Brothers, what can we do?"

[38]Peter answered: "All of you need to repent and be baptised. You
need to turn to God and be immersed to show you have been purified
from all your sins, made new and made one with Jesus Christ. Then
you will receive the gift of the Holy Spirit who will come to live in
you. [39]For God's promise of His Spirit is for you, your children and
even for other nations who have lived far from God, for all who the
Lord our God chooses and calls to belong to Him."

2:28 *Psalm 16:8-11*
2:34-35 *Psalm 110:1*

40 Peter warned them at length of the consequences if they refused
to repent and pleaded with them: "Save yourselves from the corruption
of the world that is so evident now."
41 Those who responded to this message were baptised, about
three thousand people on a single day!

Devotion of the believers (2:42-47)

42 They then devoted themselves to being taught God's Word by the
apostles and to sharing their lives with one another in love. They
were also committed to the breaking of bread, recalling all that
Christ had done for them, and to praying together. 43 There was a
sense of awe among them because of the miracles and wonderful
works that God performed through the apostles.
44 All the believers lived as members of one Body and shared
whatever they had with one another. 45 They sold possessions and
gave to everyone who was in need.
46 They continued to come together in the temple courts every
day. They also met in one another's homes, sharing the Lord's Supper
and eating their meals with glad and thankful hearts. 47 They praised
God and were shown favour by everyone. And every day the Lord
added to their numbers those who were being saved.

Crippled beggar healed (3:1-10)

3 One day Peter and John went to the temple for the afternoon
time of prayer at three o'clock. 2 At the entrance to the temple
called the Beautiful Gate, was a man who had been crippled from
birth. He was carried there every day to beg for money from those
entering the temple courts. 3 So when he saw Peter and John about
to enter, he asked them for some money. 4 Both looked directly at
him and Peter said: "Look us in the eye!" 5 The man did so, expecting
to receive something from them.
6 Peter said to him: "I don't have any silver or gold to give you,
but what I do have I give you now. Walk, in the Name of Jesus
Christ of Nazareth." 7 He took the man by the right hand and began
to pull him to his feet. Immediately his ankles were healed and were
made strong. 8 He jumped up and began to walk. Then he went with
Peter and John into the temple courts, walking freely and jumping
about, praising God as he did so. 9-10 When all the people saw the
way he walked and heard his shouts of praise, they recognised him
as the one who used to beg for money at the Beautiful Gate. They were
amazed and filled with awe because of what had happened to him.

Peter preaches to the crowd (3:11-26)

11 The man clung to Peter and John in gratitude and soon a crowd of astonished people came running to them and surrounded them in Solomon's Colonnade. 12 Peter used the opportunity to address them:

"People of Israel, why does this amaze you? Why look at us as if we have caused this man to walk by some power of our own or by our godliness? 13 Your God, the God of Abraham, Isaac and Jacob, has glorified His servant Jesus through this miracle. You handed Him over to the Roman authorities to be crucified and you rejected Him before Pilate, even though he wanted to release Him. 14 You denied the Holy and Righteous One and demanded that a terrorist murderer be released instead. 15 You were responsible for putting to death the One who gave you life. Yet God raised Him from the dead and we are witnesses of His resurrection.

16 "So by faith in the person of Jesus this man has been healed and he is someone you clearly recognise. It is by the Name of Jesus and the faith that comes from knowing Him that this complete healing has been given to this man, as you can all see clearly for yourselves.

17 "Brothers, I acknowledge that you and your leaders only acted in ignorance. 18 But realise that God has fulfilled what He promised through all the prophets. He foretold that the Christ would suffer. 19-20 So repent now; turn to God so that you can be forgiven and freed from all your sins, that you can enjoy times of refreshing that only the Lord Himself can give, that the living Christ will come to you now and that Jesus will return at God's appointed time. 21 He has to remain in heaven until the time comes that has been promised through the holy prophets, when God will restore everything to His purposes.

22 "It was Moses who said: 'The Lord your God will raise up a prophet from among your own people, a prophet for you who will be like Me. You must listen to all that He says to you. 23 For anyone who does not listen to this Prophet will be cut off completely from God's people.'

24 "In fact, all the prophets from the time of Samuel onwards have spoken these things. 25 Because of the covenant God made with your forefathers, you are heirs of all the prophets foretold. He said to Abraham, 'All the peoples of the earth will be blessed through your offspring.' 26 So when God raised up His Servant, Jesus, He sent Him to you first in order to bless you by turning you away from your sinful ways."

3:23 Deuteronomy 18:15, 18, 19
3:25 Genesis 22:18

Peter and John face opposition (4:1-12)

4 While Peter and John were addressing the people, some priests
and Sadducees, together with the captain of the temple guard,
approached them. 2 They were extremely disturbed because the
apostles were teaching that through Jesus the dead are definitely
resurrected. 3 They arrested Peter and John and, because it was late
in the day, had them thrown into prison overnight. 4 Despite this,
many who had heard their message became believers; and their
number grew to about five thousand men.

5 On the following day, the rulers, elders and teachers of the law
met in Jerusalem. 6 Annas the high priest was present, as were Caiaphas,
John, Alexander and others of the high priest's family. 7 They
ordered Peter and John to be brought before them and demanded to
know: "By what power and in whose name did you heal that man?"

8 Peter, filled with the Holy Spirit, replied: "Rulers and elders of
the people! 9-10 If we are being charged because of an act of mercy
shown to a cripple and you want to know how he was healed, then
you and all the people of Israel need to understand this: It is by the
Name of Jesus Christ of Nazareth, whom you crucified but whom
God raised from the dead, that this man can stand before you completely healed. 11 He is the One referred to in the scripture that says,
'The stone rejected by you builders has become the corner-stone on
which the whole building depends.'

12 "No one else can provide salvation! Through His Name alone is
it possible for people to be saved."

Peter and John before the council (4:13-22)

13 When they saw the boldness and authority with which Peter and
John spoke, although they knew them to be ordinary men who had
received no theological training, they realised that they were followers
of Jesus. 14 But there was nothing they could say because the man
was standing before them clearly healed. 15 So they ordered them
out of the council chamber while they conferred together.

16 They discussed together: "What are we going to do with these
men? Everyone in Jerusalem is well aware that they have performed
an outstanding miracle. We cannot deny this. 17 However, we must
stop them spreading their teaching any further by warning them
not to speak to anyone in this Name."

18 So they called Peter and John before them and ordered them not
to speak or teach again in the Name of Jesus. 19 But Peter and John

4:11 Psalm 118:22

responded: "You can judge for yourselves whether it is right in
God's eyes for us to obey you rather than to obey Him. 20 We cannot
remain silent but must speak about what we have seen and heard."

21 The council threatened them further before releasing them.
They could not agree on any suitable form of punishment because
all the people were praising God for the wonderful miracle that had
happened. 22 For the man who had been a cripple was over forty
years old!

A fresh infilling of the Holy Spirit (4:23-31)

23 Once released, Peter and John returned to the other believers to
report on all that was said to them by the chief priests and elders.
24 In response, the believers all prayed aloud together, thanking God
by saying: "Sovereign Lord, You created the heaven, the earth, the
sea and everything in them. 25 You spoke by the Holy Spirit through
Your servant, our father David, 'Why do the nations rage? Why do
the people make their own useless plans? 26 The kings of the earth
and rulers together stand against the Lord and His Anointed One.'
This is what happened here in this city. 27 Herod and Pontius Pilate,
Gentiles and the people of Israel together, plotted against Your holy
Servant Jesus, Your Anointed One. 28 But they were only doing what
You had decided by Your power and will should happen. This was
Your plan.

29 "But now, Lord, because You are aware of their threats, enable
us as Your servants to speak Your words of truth with great boldness.
30 We need to see You stretch out Your hand to heal the sick and to
perform more signs and wonders through the Name of Your holy
Servant Jesus."

31 After they had prayed in this way, the meeting place shook.
They were all filled with the Holy Spirit again and spoke God's
Word boldly.

Unity among the believers (4:32-37)

32 There was great unity among the believers. They were one in what
they believed and in the ways they thought and acted. No-one
thought of his possessions as belonging to himself, but they shared
everything they had with others.

33-35 The apostles continued to witness to the resurrection of Jesus,
speaking and acting with great power. So great was God's grace on
the whole body of believers that nobody among them was left in

4:26 Psalm 2:1-2

need. Some who owned land or houses sold them and brought the
proceeds from the sales to the apostles, and they ensured that it was
distributed to those in need.
36 Joseph, a Levite from Cyprus called by the apostles Barnabas,
meaning son of encouragement, was one such. He sold a field he
owned and brought the money to the apostles.

Ananias and Sapphira lie to the Holy Spirit (5:1-11)

5 Another man called Ananias, together with his wife Sapphira,
sold some property. 2 But he kept back part of the money for
himself, with his wife's full knowledge. The rest he brought to the
apostles.
3 However, Peter said to him: "Ananias, what has Satan done to
your heart that you have lied to the Holy Spirit and have kept some
of the money from the sale for yourself? 4 It was your property
before it was sold, was it not? So after the sale the money was yours
to use as you wished. How could you make it appear that you had
given the full amount? You have lied to God, not only to men!"
5 On hearing this, Ananias fell to the ground and died. Those who
heard of this were shocked and were filled with fear. 6 The young
men took Ananias' body, wrapped it in a sheet and carried it out for
burial.
7 About three hours later, his wife arrived, unaware of what had
happened. 8 Peter asked her: "Tell me truthfully, was this the whole
price that you and Ananias received for the land?"
"Yes," she replied, "that was the full amount."
9 Peter asked her: "How could the two of you agree to test the
Spirit of the Lord? Look! The men who are now entering have just
buried your husband and they will do the same to you."
10 Immediately she fell to the ground at Peter's feet and died.
Then the young men came forward, confirmed that she was dead
and carried her body out for burial next to her husband. 11 Great fear
took hold of the whole church and others who heard of what had
happened.

The apostles perform many signs and miracles (5:12-16)

12 The apostles performed many signs and wonders among the people.
All the believers used to congregate in the area of the temple known
as Solomon's Colonnade. 13 Although people thought highly of
them, they were reluctant to join them. 14 Even so, more and more
men and women became believers in the Lord and were added to
the church.

15 Because of the apostles' reputation, people brought the sick and laid them on mattresses and beds in the streets, hoping that even Peter's shadow might fall on some of them as he walked along. 16 Crowds came from the towns and villages surrounding Jerusalem, bringing their sick and those in bondage to evil spirits; and all of them were healed!

Apostles continue despite opposition (5:17-39)

17 By now, the high priest and the fellow members of the council who were Sadducees, were filled with jealousy. 18 They arrested the apostles and had them thrown into prison. 19 However, during the night one of the Lord's angels came and opened the prison doors and led them out. 20 He told them: "Go into the temple courts and give the people the message of the new life." 21 They obeyed and entered the temple courts at daybreak and began to teach openly.

When the chief priests and their officials arrived, they called the Council together, the full assembly of the elders of Israel, and sent word to the prison for the apostles to be brought before them. 22 But the officers found that they were not in the prison. So they returned to the Council to report this. 23 "We found the prison locked securely with the guards in place at the doors. But when we looked inside no one was there!"

24 This report puzzled the captain of the guard and the high priests, who were concerned about what would happen next. 25 Then someone arrived with the news: "The men you put in prison are now standing in the temple courts teaching the people." 26 On hearing this, the captain of the guard took some officers to arrest the apostles again but without using any force, for they feared that the people might turn on them if they did.

27 They brought the apostles before the Council to be questioned by the high priest. 28 "We ordered you specifically never to teach again in this Name," he said. "Yet you have filled the whole city of Jerusalem with your teaching and you are determined to place the guilt of His death on us."

29 Peter and the other apostles replied: "We must obey God, for His authority is higher than that of men! 30 The God of our fathers raised Jesus from the dead, He whom you killed by having Him nailed to a cross. 31 Yet God exalted Him to the place of honour at His right hand where He is both Prince and Saviour. Now He gives the whole nation of Israel the opportunity to repent and receive forgiveness for their sins. 32 We are personal witnesses of these things, as is the Holy Spirit who God has given to those who obey Him."

33 The Council was furious when they heard this and wanted to kill them. 34-35 But a Pharisee called Gamaliel, a teacher of the law greatly respected by the people, stood and ordered the apostles to be put outside the chamber while he addressed the Council: "Men of Israel, be careful about what you decide to do with these men! 36 Remember that some time ago Theudas claimed to be someone great and about four hundred men supported him. However, he was killed and his supporters dispersed; the whole thing came to nothing. 37 Then there was Judas the Galilean who, at the time of the census, led a group of rebels to revolt. But he, too, was killed; then all his followers scattered. 38 Therefore, I advise you to leave these men alone. Release them. For if what they are saying and doing is merely from themselves, it also will fail. 39 But if their purpose has been initiated by God, you can do nothing to stop these men. To attempt to do so will mean you will find yourselves fighting against God."

Apostles flogged for the name of Jesus (5:40-42)

40 This persuaded the Council. They called the apostles before the Council again and had them flogged. They ordered them not to speak in the Name of Jesus again and then released them.

41 The apostles left the Council, rejoicing that they had been given the privilege of suffering disgrace for the Name of Jesus. 42 Undeterred, they went daily into the temple courts, as well as from house to house, and continued to teach and proclaim the good news that Jesus is the Christ, the Messiah.

Seven men chosen to serve (6:8-15)

6 As the number of disciples increased, the Greek-speaking Jews complained about the Hebrew-speaking Jews, because their widows were not receiving a fair amount in the daily distribution of food. 2 So the twelve apostles called a meeting of all the disciples and said: "We should not be involved in these administrative details but should be able to concentrate on preaching and teaching God's Word. 3-4 So, brothers, select some men from among you who have the reputation of being wise and men of the Spirit. We will hand this responsibility over to them, while we devote ourselves to prayer and the ministry of the Word."

5 Everyone responded well to this proposal. They selected Stephen, who was full of faith and the Holy Spirit, Philip, Procorus, Nicanor, Timon, Parmenas and Nicolas who came from Antioch and was a convert to Judaism. 6 These seven men were presented to the apostles, who laid their hands on them and prayed for them.

7 As a result of these changes, God's Word spread further and the
number of disciples increased rapidly in Jerusalem. Even a large
number of priests became obedient believers.

Stephen falsely accused (6:8-15)

8 Stephen, full of God's grace and power, performed extraordinary
wonders and miraculous signs among the people. 9 However, opposition also arose, especially from those who belonged to the so-called
Synagogue of the Freed Slaves. These were Jews from Cyrene and
Alexandria and the provinces of Cilicia and Asia. 10 But when they
argued with Stephen they had no answers to his wisdom, nor to the
anointed words he spoke by the Spirit.

11 So they quietly spread false rumours about Stephen. Some
claimed they had heard him speak blasphemous words against
Moses and God. 12 In this way they stirred up opposition among the
people generally, but especially among the elders and teachers of
the law. They had Stephen arrested and brought before the Council.
13 There they produced false witnesses who claimed: "This man
speaks continually against the Temple and against the Law of
Moses. 14 We have heard him say that this Jesus of Nazareth will
destroy the Temple and set aside the customs Moses handed down
to us."

15 As the members of the Council stared at Stephen, his face shone
like the face of an angel.

Stephen recounts Israel's history: Abraham's call (7:1-7)

7 1-2 "Are these charges true?" the High priest asked Stephen,
who replied: "Brothers and fathers, hear what I have to say!
The God of glory appeared to our forefather Abraham while he
lived in Mesopotamia before leaving for Haran. 3 God told him, 'Leave
your country and your people and I will show you the land to
which you are to go.'

4 "So Abraham left the land of the Chaldeans and went to live in
Haran, where he stayed until his father's death. Then God led him
to the land where you now live. 5 But God did not give him any
inheritance here, not even a tiny piece of land. However, He did
promise him that he and his descendants would possess the whole
land, even though, at the time, Abraham was childless. 6 This is
what God promised him, 'Your descendants will live as strangers in

7:1-2 Genesis 12:1

a foreign land where they will be mistreated and live as slaves for four hundred years. [7]But I will punish the nation that enslaves them.' Then God added that after those four hundred years they would leave that country and come to worship Him in this place.

[8]"It was to Abraham that God gave circumcision to be a sign of the covenant between them. As his father, Abraham had Isaac circumcised eight days after he was born. In due course Isaac became the father of Jacob, who was the father of the twelve patriarchs of our nation.

[9-10]"But because they were jealous of Joseph, his brothers sold him and he became a slave in Egypt. However, God was with him and delivered him from all his troubles. He gave Joseph wisdom that enabled him to gain the favour of Pharaoh, Egypt's king, who made him governor of the whole of Egypt and placed him over the affairs of the palace.

[11]"When the whole of Egypt and Canaan was struck by a famine that brought great suffering, our ancestors were facing starvation. [12]So on hearing there was grain in Egypt, Jacob sent his sons, our forefathers, on their first visit there. [13]Joseph revealed his true identity to his brothers on their return visit and Pharaoh was made aware of Joseph's family and their plight. [14-15]So Joseph then sent for his father Jacob and all seventy-five members of his family came to live in Egypt, where in time they all died. [16]Their bodies were duly brought back to Shechem and buried, along with Abraham, in the tomb he had bought from Hamor's sons.

[17]"The number of our people in Egypt had grown considerably by the time God fulfilled the promise He gave to Abraham. [18]By then there was a new Pharaoh ruling Egypt, who knew nothing about Joseph. [19]He dealt harshly with our people and oppressed them by forcing them to abandon their newborn babies so that they would die.

God delivers Israel out of captivity (7:20-38)

[20-21]It was during this period that Moses was born; but he was no ordinary child. He was cared for in his own home for the first three months, but when his parents had to conceal him he was found by Pharaoh's daughter who brought him up as her own son. [22]So Moses was taught all the wisdom of the Egyptians and grew to become powerful in speech and action.

7:7 Genesis 15:13-14

23 "When forty years old, Moses decided to visit his natural relatives.
24 He witnessed a Hebrew being mistreated by an Egyptian and
went to his rescue, but ended up killing the Egyptian. 25 Moses
expected that his own people would realise that God had sent him
to be their saviour; but they didn't! 26 When Moses saw two Israelites
fighting on the next day, he again intervened wanting to bring
reconciliation. 'Men, you are brothers,' he said, 'Why fight each other?'

27 "But the one mistreating the other pushed Moses aside saying,
'Who made you our ruler and judge? 28 Do you intend to kill me as
you killed the Egyptian yesterday?' 29 On hearing this Moses fled to
Midian, where he lived as a foreigner and where two sons were
born to him.

30 "When he had been there for forty years, an angel of the Lord
appeared to Moses in the flames of a burning bush while he was in
the desert near Mt. Sinai. 31-32 This was an amazing sight and when
he approached, he heard the Lord speak to him from the bush saying,
'I am the God of your fathers, the God of Abraham, Isaac and Jacob.'
Moses shook with fear and had to look away from the bush.

33 "Then the Lord told him, 'Take off your sandals; you are standing
on holy ground. 34 I have seen the way My people in Egypt are being
afflicted. I have heard their cries to be delivered from their oppression
and I have now come to rescue them. So go now, for I am sending
you back to Egypt.'

35 "So, through the angel who appeared to him in the bush, God
sent back as their ruler and deliverer the same Moses whom the
Israelites had rejected with the words, 'Who made you our ruler
and judge?' 36 It was Moses who led them out of Egypt after performing
miraculous signs at the Red Sea and during the forty years they
wandered around in the wilderness.

37 "Moses himself told the Israelites, 'God will send you another
prophet like me, someone from among your own people.' 38 It was
while Moses was leading the people in the wilderness that the angel
spoke to him on Mount Sinai. He could receive God's living words
on behalf of the people, words that are passed on to us today.

Israelites worship the golden calf (7:39-43)

39 "But our forefathers refused to obey what God said through
Moses. They rejected him and wanted to return to Egypt. 40 They
told Aaron to make them an idol that they could follow as their god.
'As for Moses,' they said, 'we don't know what has become of him!'

41 "This was the occasion when they made an idol in the form of
a calf. They offered sacrifices to it and treated with honour something

they had made with their own hands. [42]So God turned away from
them and left them to worship the heavenly planets like pagans. No
wonder the prophet wrote, 'O house of Israel, did you bring Me
sacrifices and offerings in the desert for forty years? [43]No, you
venerated the shrine of Molech and Rephan's star. For this I will
send you into exile in Babylon.'

God's temple (7:44-50)

[44]"Our forefathers carried the tabernacle with them in the wilderness,
made to the instructions God gave Moses. [45]Our fathers brought
this tabernacle with them when, under Joshua, they took the land
from the nations they had to drive out. It remained here until
David's time. [46]Because he enjoyed favour with God, he wanted to
provide a permanent temple as God's dwelling place among them.
[47]But it was his son, Solomon, who actually built the temple.

[48-49]"However, the Most High God does not live in houses built
with human hands. As the prophet writes, 'The Lord says, 'Heaven
is My throne and earth My footstool. So what kind of house can you
build for Me? How can you determine where I dwell? [50]Am I not the
Creator of all things everywhere?'

Israel resists the Holy Spirit (7:51-53)

[51]"You leaders are so stubborn! Your hearts are hardened and your
ears deaf to the truth. You are exactly like your forefathers. You
always resist the Holy Spirit! [52]Your fathers persecuted all the
prophets; they even killed those who predicted the coming of the
Righteous One. Now you have betrayed and murdered the One of
whom they spoke. [53]Yes, you who are so proud that you received
the law through angels, have disobeyed His words."

The stoning of Stephen (7:54-60)

[54]The leaders were furious when they heard what Stephen said and
shouted abuse at him. [55]But Stephen was full of the Holy Spirit and
as he looked up to heaven he saw God's glory, with Jesus standing
at God's right hand in the place of honour. [56]He said: "Look, I see
heaven open and Jesus, the Son of Man, standing at God's right
hand."

[57]The Jewish leaders covered their ears when they heard this and
rushed at Stephen, yelling abuse at him. [58]They dragged him out of

7:43 Amos 5:25-27
7:50 Isaiah 66:1-2

the city and began to stone him. The officials took their coats off and laid them at the feet of a young man called Saul.

59 As they stoned him, Stephen prayed: "Lord Jesus, receive my spirit." 60 He fell on his knees and shouted: "Lord do not condemn them for this sin." When he had said this he died peacefully.

The believers scatter (8:1-8)

8 Saul witnessed Stephen's death with approval. This event triggered a great persecution against the church in Jerusalem. All the believers, except the apostles, fled to places of safety in Judea and Samaria. 2 But godly men buried Stephen's body and mourned deeply for him.

3 Saul tried to destroy the church wherever he could. He went from house to house dragging off both men and women to be thrown into prison.

4 But those who were scattered as a result of the persecution preached the gospel of Jesus wherever they went. 5 For example, Philip went and proclaimed the Christ to a city in Samaria. 6 When the crowds heard Philip's preaching and saw the miraculous signs he performed, they listened attentively to his message. 7 Evil spirits came out of people with shrieks, and many paralysed and crippled people were healed, 8 causing great joy in that place.

Believers receive the Holy Spirit (8:9-25)

9 For some time in that city, a man named Simon had practised sorcery and claimed to be someone great because he did things that amazed the Samaritans. 10 He drew everyone's attention, from the most important to the least. It was even said of him that he had divine power, 'the Great Power!' 11 He had a large following because he amazed people with his magical deeds.

12 However, those who believed Philip's preaching about the good news of God's Kingdom and the Name of Jesus Christ, were baptised, both men and women. 13 This magician Simon also professed to believe and was baptised. He then followed Philip everywhere, and was amazed at the great signs and wonders he saw Philip perform.

14 When the apostles in Jerusalem heard that Samaria had accepted the gospel, they sent Peter and John there. 15-16 On their arrival they discovered that the believers had not yet received the Holy Spirit; they had only been baptised in the Name of the Lord Jesus. 17 So Peter and John laid hands on them and prayed for them to receive the Holy Spirit.

18-19 When Simon saw that God's Spirit was given to people when
the apostles laid their hands on them, he offered them money saying:
"Give me this power so that everyone on whom I lay my hands will
receive the Holy Spirit."

20 Peter answered him: "Let your money perish with you for
imagining that God's gift could be purchased. 21 You cannot share in
this ministry because your heart is not right before God. 22 Repent of
your wickedness and pray to the Lord. Perhaps then He will forgive
you for thinking such a thing. 23 I see that you are still full of bitterness
and are a prisoner of sin."

24 So Simon said: "Pray to the Lord for me so that nothing awful
will happen to me."

25 When Peter and John had testified and preached God's Word,
they returned to Jerusalem, stopping to proclaim the gospel in
many villages on the way.

Philip and the Ethiopian eunuch (8:26-40)

26 An angel of the Lord told Philip: "Go south to the desert road that
goes from Jerusalem to Gaza." 27 He obeyed and on the way met an
Ethiopian eunuch, an important official from the court of Candace,
queen of the Ethiopians. He was in charge of her treasury and had
been in Jerusalem to worship. 28 Now he was returning home and
sitting in his chariot, reading the book of the prophet Isaiah. 29 The
Holy Spirit said to Philip: "Go and walk alongside that chariot."

30 As Philip ran to be close to the chariot, he heard the man reading
from the prophecy of Isaiah and so asked him: "Do you understand
what you are reading?"

31 "How can I understand unless someone explains it to me?" the
eunuch replied. He then invited Philip to enter the chariot and sit
with him. 32 He was reading the passage that says, 'He was led to the
slaughter like a sheep and did not open His mouth, just as a lamb is
silent before the shearer. 33 He was humiliated and deprived of justice.
Who can speak of His descendants? For His life was taken from the
earth.'

34 The official asked Philip: "Please tell me who is the prophet
speaking of, himself or someone else?" 35 Using that passage of scripture
as a starting point, Philip told him the good news about Jesus.

36 As they continued along the road they came to a pool of water.
So the eunuch said: "Look! Here is some water, surely I can be baptised
now!"

8:35 Isaiah 53:7-8

37 Philip replied: "You can be baptised if you believe with all your
heart."
"I believe that Jesus Christ is God's Son", the eunuch answered.
38 He gave orders for the chariot to stop. Then both of them went
down to the water and Philip baptised the eunuch.
39 When they came up out of the water, suddenly the Lord's Spirit
took Philip away. Although the eunuch did not see him again, he
continued on his journey rejoicing. 40 Meanwhile, Philip suddenly
found himself at Azotus, a city further to the north. From there he
set out for Caesarea, preaching the gospel in every place on the way.

Saul's conversion (9:1-16)

9 Meanwhile, Saul was still making dire threats against the
Lord's disciples. 2 He asked the high priest for letters to the
synagogues in Damascus, giving him authority to take as prisoners
anyone he found there who belonged to the 'Way of Jesus', whether
men or women. He would then bring them to Jerusalem. 3 As he
neared Damascus, suddenly a brilliant light shone from heaven and
seemed to envelop him. 4 He fell to the ground and heard a voice
saying to him: "Saul, Saul! Why are you persecuting Me?"
5 "Who are You, Lord?" Saul asked.
"I am Jesus, whom you are persecuting," came the reply. 6 "Now
get up and go into the city and you will be told what you must do."
7 Those travelling with Saul stood speechless; they heard the
voice yet saw no-one. 8 Saul rose from the ground, but discovered
that he had gone blind; he had to be led by the hand into Damascus.
9 He remained blind for three days and did not eat or drink anything
during that time.
10 There was a disciple in Damascus called Ananias. The Lord
spoke to him in a vision: "Ananias!"
"Yes, Lord." he answered. 11 The Lord told him: "You are to go to
the house of Judas on Straight Street and ask for Saul of Tarsus, who
is praying there. 12 In a vision he has seen a man called Ananias coming
to lay hands on him to restore his sight."
13 Ananias answered: "Lord, I have heard many reports of this
man, how he has done much harm to your saints in Jerusalem.
14 And now he has come here with authority from the chief priests to
arrest all those who call on Your Name."
15 But the Lord said to Ananias: "Go! I have chosen this man to be
My instrument in bringing the truth about Me to the non-Jewish
people and their rulers, as well as to the people of Israel. 16 And I will
show him how much he must suffer for the sake of My Name."

Saul filled with the Holy Spirit (9:17-25)

17 So Ananias went to the house. On entering, he placed his hands on Saul saying: "Brother Saul, the Lord Jesus, who appeared to you on the road as you were coming here, has sent me to restore your sight and so that you may be filled with the Holy Spirit." 18-20 Immediately it was as if scales fell from Saul's eyes and he could see again. He was then baptised and soon regained his strength once he had eaten.

Saul spent several days with the disciples in Damascus, preaching in the synagogues that Jesus is God's Son. 21 Everyone who heard him was amazed and queried, "Isn't this the man who has caused such destruction among the believers in Jesus in Jerusalem? Did he not come here to take His followers to the chief priests as prisoners?" 22 Yet Saul's preaching increased in power and to the Jews of Damascus he proved, to their consternation, that Jesus is the Christ.

23-24 After some time, the Jewish leaders decided to kill Saul, but he learned of their plans. They kept a close watch on the city gates both day and night in order to murder him. 25 So one night some fellow believers lowered him in a basket through an opening in the city wall.

Saul meets the apostles (9:26-30)

26 Saul tried to join the disciples when he arrived back in Jerusalem; but they were all suspicious of him. They did not believe that he had become a true disciple. 27 However, Barnabas brought him to the apostles. He related to them how, on the journey to Damascus, Saul had encountered the Lord, who had spoken to him personally. He told them of how he had preached fearlessly there in the Name of Jesus.

28 So Saul remained with the apostles and moved about freely in Jerusalem, speaking boldly in the Name of the Lord. 29 When he debated with the Grecian Jews, they plotted to kill him. 30 When the other believers heard of this, they took Saul to Caesarea from where they sent him home to Tarsus.

The gospel spreads as Peter performs miracles (9:31-43)

31 Then the church throughout Judea, Galilee and Samaria had a time of peace when it could gather strength and increase in numbers. The believers were encouraged by all the Holy Spirit was doing among them and they lived in the fear of the Lord.

32 While travelling around the country, Peter went to visit the saints in Lydda. 33 He found there a man called Aeneas, who was

paralysed and had been bed-ridden for eight years. 34 Peter said to
him: "Aeneas, Jesus Christ heals you. Get up and make your bed!"
Immediately Aeneas was healed. 35 Everyone living in Lydda and
Sharon turned to the Lord when they saw Aeneas walking around
completely healed.

36 There was a disciple in Joppa named Tabitha, otherwise known
as Dorcas. She was continually doing good by serving others,
especially helping the poor. 37 But she became sick and died. Her
body was washed and laid upstairs. 38 The disciples in Joppa heard
that Peter was in Lydda, which was nearby. So they sent two brothers
to him to beg him to come immediately to Joppa.

39 Peter went with them and on his arrival at the house was taken
immediately to the upstairs room. All the widows had gathered to
mourn and showed Peter the clothes Dorcas had made for the poor.

40 Peter asked them all to leave the room. He sank to his knees and
prayed. Then he turned to the dead woman and said: "Tabitha, get
up." She opened her eyes, saw Peter and sat up. 41 Peter took her by
the hand and helped her to stand. Then he called in the other believers
and widows and presented her to them, alive and well!

42 News of this spread throughout Joppa and many became
believers in the Lord. 43 So Peter prolonged his stay there, living with
Simon, a leather-worker.

Cornelius sends for Peter (10:1-8)

10 Cornelius, a Roman centurion of the Italian Regiment, lived
in Caesarea. 2 He and his household were God-fearing people.
Cornelius gave generously to those in need and was a man of
prayer. 3 At around three in the afternoon one day, he had a vision of
an angel coming from God and calling his name: "Cornelius."

4 Cornelius was afraid but couldn't help staring intently at the
angel: "What is it, Lord?" He asked.

The angel replied: "God has heard your prayers and is aware of
your gifts to the poor. 5 Send some men to Joppa to fetch a man
called Simon Peter, 6 who is staying with Simon the leather-worker
who lives by the sea."

7 When the angel had disappeared, Cornelius called two of his
servants and also a devout soldier who was one of his personal
staff. 8 He told them of the vision and sent them to Joppa.

Peter's vision (10:9-16)

9 Around noon on the following day, while they were making their
way to Caesarea, Peter was praying on the roof of the house where

he was staying. 10 He was hungry and wanted something to eat but
fell into a trance while his meal was being prepared. 11 In a vision he
saw that the heavens were opened and what appeared to be like a
large sheet was being let down to the ground by its four corners. 12 In
the sheet were a variety of animals, reptiles and birds. 13 Then Peter
heard a voice telling him: "Rise, Peter, kill and eat."

14 Shocked, Peter replied: "No way, Lord! Never have I eaten anything forbidden or considered ritually unclean."

15 The voice addressed him again: "Do not say that anything is
unclean if I have made it clean."

16 This happened three times before the sheet was taken up into
heaven.

The Lord sends Peter to Cornelius' household (10:17-26)

17 While Peter was wondering what this vision meant, those sent by
Cornelius had found their way to the house and were at the gate.
18 They called out, enquiring if Simon Peter was staying there.

19 While Peter was still thinking about the vision, the Holy Spirit
said to him: "Simon, three men are calling for you. 20 Get up and go
down to meet them. Do not hesitate to go with them, for I have sent
them."

21 So Peter went downstairs and told the men: "I am the one you
want. Why have you come?"

22 The men replied: "The centurion Cornelius sent us. He is a good
and God-fearing man, greatly respected by all the Jewish people. A
holy angel told him to invite you to come to his house so he can hear
whatever you have to say." 23 So Peter invited them in to stay as his
guests.

On the next day Peter, together with some of the brothers from
Joppa, set out with the messengers for Caesarea, where they arrived
on the following day. 24 In anticipation of their arrival, Cornelius had
gathered together his relatives and close friends. 25 When Peter
entered the house Cornelius met him and fell before him in worship.
26 But Peter pulled him to his feet, saying: "I am only a man like
yourself."

Peter preaches the truth to the Gentiles (10:27-48)

27 After talking briefly to Cornelius, Peter went into the room where
he found a large gathering of people. 28 He addressed them: "You
know it is against our religious law for a Jew to have anything to do
with a Gentile or to set foot inside his house. However, God has

made it clear to me that I should not consider as forbidden what He has stated to be acceptable. 29 So when I was sent for I responded, without raising any objections. I want to know why you sent for me."

30 Cornelius replied: "Four days ago, while I was praying here in my house at about three in the afternoon, suddenly a man in shining clothes stood in front of me. 31 He told me, 'Cornelius, God has heard your prayers and has taken note of your gifts to the poor. 32 Send to Joppa for one known as Simon Peter, who is staying in the house of Simon the leather-worker who lives by the sea.' 33 So immediately I sent for you and I am grateful you have come. Now we have come together in God's presence to hear all that the Lord has told you to say to us."

34-35 Then Peter replied: "It is clear to me now that God certainly does not show favouritism but accepts men of all nations who fear Him and do what pleases Him. 36 You must have heard of the revelation that God gave to His people Israel, the good news of how peace with God has been made possible through Jesus Christ, who is Lord of all. 37 You have heard of the events that took place in Judea, the series of events that began in Galilee following the baptism that John preached. 38 God anointed Jesus of Nazareth with the Holy Spirit and power. Because God was with Him, He then went from place to place doing good things and healing all who had been oppressed by the devil.

39-40 "We apostles saw everything He did among the Jews and what happened in Jerusalem. There they killed Him by crucifying Him, but on the third day after His death God raised Him back to life and caused Him to be seen by certain witnesses whom God had specially chosen. 41 He was not seen by everyone, but we actually ate and drank with Him after He rose from the dead. 42 He ordered us to preach to everyone and to testify that He is the One appointed by God to be the Judge of the living and the dead. 43 He is the same One of whom all the prophets spoke, saying that everyone who believes in Him receives forgiveness of sins in His Name."

44 The Holy Spirit fell on the whole gathering while Peter was still speaking. 45 The Jewish believers who had accompanied Peter were amazed that the gift of the Holy Spirit should be poured out on those who were not Jewish. 46 This undoubtedly had happened, for they heard them speaking in tongues and praising God.

47 Then Peter said: "Is there any reason why these people should not be baptised in water? For they have already received the Holy Spirit in just the same way that we did." 48 So he commanded that

they should be baptised in the Name of Jesus Christ. And they asked Peter to remain with them for a few days.

Peter criticised by Jewish believers (11:1-18)

11 The apostles and other believers in Judea received news that the non-Jewish nations had accepted God's Word. [2]So when
Peter returned to Jerusalem, he was criticised by the Jewish believers.
[3]They challenged him by saying: "You visited the house of Gentiles and ate with them."

[4-5]So Peter explained the whole situation to them exactly as it happened: "While praying in the city of Joppa I fell into a trance and saw a vision. What appeared like a large sheet was being let down from heaven by its four corners, right there in front of me. [6-7]I
saw that it contained a variety of animals and wild beasts, reptiles, and birds, and I heard a voice commanding me, 'Get up Peter, kill and eat.'

[8]"Amazed I replied, 'No way, Lord! I have never eaten anything that is forbidden or that is considered ritually unclean.' [9]But this
heavenly voice spoke again, 'You are not to call anything unclean that God has made clean!' [10]Three times this happened before the
sheet was pulled up heavenwards again.

[11]"At that very moment, three men arrived at the house where I was staying. They had been sent from Caesarea to find me. [12]The
Holy Spirit told me not to hesitate in agreeing to go with them. These six brothers here accompanied me.

[13]"When we entered the man's house, he told us that an angel had appeared to him in his house and said, 'Send to Joppa for Simon Peter. [14]He will tell you how you and all your household will
be saved.'

[15]"I had not been speaking long before the Holy Spirit fell on them in the same way that we received Him right at the beginning.
[16]I recalled what the Lord had told us: 'John baptised with water, but you will be baptised with the Holy Spirit.' [17]So if God saw fit to
give them the same gift that He gave us, who was I to imagine that I could oppose Him?"

[18]Those present raised no further objections when they heard this but praised God saying: "So God has also given to the Gentiles the opportunity to repent and receive eternal life."

The gospel spreads to Gentile regions (11:19-23)

[19]Meanwhile, those who had dispersed during the persecution that followed Stephen's death travelled as far as Phoenicia, Cyprus and

Antioch, proclaiming the gospel wherever they went, but only to Jews. [20]However, some from Cyprus and Cyrene went to Antioch and began to witness to Greeks as well, telling them the good news about the Lord Jesus. [21]The Lord anointed them and worked through them so that a great number of people turned to the Lord and became believers.

[22]When news of this reached the church in Jerusalem they sent Barnabas to Antioch. [23]On his arrival there he saw for himself the evidence of God's grace at work among them. So he rejoiced and encouraged them to remain faithful to the Lord, and to serve Him with all their hearts.

Saul and Barnabas go to Antioch (11:24-30)

[24]Barnabas had a good reputation and was a man full of the Holy Spirit and with strong faith. Through his ministry a great number of people came to know the Lord personally.

[25-26]Then Barnabas went to Tarsus, found Saul and brought him back to Antioch. Both Barnabas and Saul remained there for a whole year, meeting with the church and teaching God's Word to larger numbers of people. It is at Antioch that the believers were first called 'Christians'.

[27]A number of prophets from Jerusalem visited Antioch during this period. [28]One of them was called Agabus and he predicted, under the inspiration of God's Spirit, that the whole Roman world was about to experience a severe famine, an event that took place during the reign of Claudius. [29]The disciples there decided to provide help for their fellow believers in Judea. [30]Each gave as generously as he could, and the elders entrusted their gift to Barnabas and Saul to take to Jerusalem.

An angel frees Peter from jail (12:1-11)

12 About this time a persecution began, when King Herod arrested some believers in the church. [2]He had the apostle James, John's brother, killed with a sword. [3]Seeing that this pleased the Jewish leaders, Herod then had Peter arrested during the Passover Feast. [4]He had him thrown into prison where he was guarded around the clock by four squads, each of four soldiers. Herod's intention was to try Peter publicly after the Passover.

[5]But while he was in prison the church prayed earnestly for Peter. [6]On the eve of the day set by Herod for his trial, Peter was asleep between two soldiers, bound by two chains with sentries also standing guard at the entrance to his prison.

[7]Suddenly a bright light shone into the cell and one of the Lord's angels appeared. He shook Peter to awaken him and said: "Get up quickly!" Immediately the chains on Peter's wrists fell off!

[8]The angel said to him: "Get dressed and put your sandals on." Peter did so. "Wrap your cloak around you and follow me," the angel instructed him. [9]So Peter followed him out of the prison. But the whole event seemed so unreal, he didn't realise that this was actually happening; he thought he must be seeing a vision.

[10]They passed both the first and the second guards and when they came to the prison gate it opened for them by itself. They passed out into the city and when they had walked down one street together, the angel disappeared suddenly!

[11]Peter then realised that this was not his imagination and thought, 'Now I know for sure that it is true! The Lord really did send his angel to rescue me from Herod and from all that the Jewish people intended to do to me.'

Peter returns to the believers (12:12-17)

[12]When he realised this, Peter went to the house of Mary, John Mark's mother, where many had gathered to pray for him. [13]He knocked on the outer gate and a servant girl called Rhoda came to see who was there. [14]When she recognised Peter's voice she ran back into the house without opening the door and told everyone: "Peter is at the door!"

[15]"You must be imagining things," they replied. But she kept insisting that it was true. So they said: "Well, it must be his angel."

[16]Meanwhile Peter continued to bang on the door. When finally they opened it and saw that it was indeed Peter they were amazed. [17]Peter indicated with his hand that they should be quiet and then explained how the Lord had freed him from the prison. "Tell James and the other brothers what has happened," he said before leaving for another place.

Herod struck dead (12:18-25)

[18]There was great consternation among the soldiers on the following morning; they had no idea what had become of Peter. [19]Herod ordered a thorough search to be made for him. This proved fruitless, so he then interrogated the guards before ordering their execution.

[20]Then Herod left Judea for Caesarea where he stayed for a time. He was very angry with the people of Tyre and Sidon; so they sent a delegation to settle the dispute. With the support of Blastus, one

of the king's close personal assistants, they made peace with Herod,
as they were dependent on his country for their food supply.
21 On the appointed day of the audience Herod sat on his throne
in his royal robes and made a speech. 22 The people shouted: "This is
not a man speaking, but the voice of a god!"
23 Immediately one of the Lord's angels struck him with a terrible
disease, because he received the acclaim for himself and did not
give praise to God. Herod was eaten by worms and died.
24 However, God's Word continued to spread and the number of
believers increased.
25 When Barnabas and Saul had completed their mission in
Jerusalem, they returned to Antioch, taking John Mark with them.

13 There were a number of prophets and teachers in the church
at Antioch: Simon known as the black man, Lucius from
Cyrene, Manaen (who had been brought up with Herod Antipas)
and Saul. 2 On one occasion, while they were worshipping together
during a time of fasting, the Holy Spirit told them: "You are to consecrate Barnabas and Saul for the work to which I have called
them." 3 So after a further time of fasting and prayer, they laid hands
on them and sent them on their way.
4 Knowing they were commissioned by the Holy Spirit, Barnabas
and Saul went to Seleucia from where they sailed to Cyprus. 5 They
preached God's Word in the synagogues when they arrived at
Seleucia. (John Mark had accompanied them as their assistant).

Governor of Paphos believes (13:6-12)

6 They then travelled throughout the island until they reached
Paphos. There they encountered a Jewish sorcerer and false prophet
called Bar-Jesus. 7 He was an associate of the governor, Sergius
Paulus, who was an intelligent man. He sent for Barnabas and Saul
because he wanted to hear God's Word for himself. 8 But Elymas the
sorcerer (for this is what his name means in Greek) opposed what
they said and tried to dissuade the governor from believing. 9-10 Then
Saul, who was becoming known as Paul, filled with the Holy Spirit,
looked directly at Elymas and said: "You child of the devil, you are
an enemy of the truth and all that is right. You are full of deceit and
falsehood. Will you never stop perverting the Lord's revelation of
the truth? 11 Now the Lord's hand is against you and you will be
struck blind and unable to see anything for a time."
Immediately mist and darkness fell on him. He stumbled around
pleading for someone to take his hand and guide him. 12 When the

governor saw what had happened, he became a believer and was
amazed at what he was taught about the Lord.

Paul preaches in Pisidian Antioch (13:13-43)

13 Paul and his companions sailed from Paphos to Perga in
Pamphylia, where John Mark left them to return to Jerusalem. 14 From
Perga they travelled to Pisidian Antioch and attended the synagogue
service there on the Sabbath. 15 After the readings from the Law and
the Prophets, the leaders sent them word saying: "Brothers, please
speak to us if you have a message of encouragement for the people."

16 So Paul stood and motioned with his hand for the people to be
quiet: "People of Israel and those of you from other nations who
worship God, listen to me," he began. 17 "Israel's God chose our forefathers and caused them to prosper during their time in Egypt.
Then He led them out of that country with a display of His mighty
power. 18 Then He endured their rebellious conduct in the wilderness
for about forty years. 19 He conquered seven nations in Canaan and
gave His own people their land as their inheritance. All this activity
covered a period of about four hundred and fifty years.

20 "Then God gave them leaders known as judges until the time of
the prophet, Samuel. 21 It was then that the people demanded to
have a king to rule over them, and He gave them Saul, the son of
Kish, of the tribe of Benjamin, and he reigned for forty years. 22 After
his death, he made David their king, saying of him: 'I have made
David, son of Jesse, a man after My own heart. He will accomplish
all I want him to do.'

23 "From David's descendants God has given Israel the Saviour
He promised, Jesus. 24 But before His ministry began, John preached
that all the people of Israel needed to repent of their sins and be
baptised. 25 While John was fulfilling his mandate he asked, 'Who do
you believe I am? I am not the Christ, the Messiah. No, He is coming
after me and I am not worthy even to do the work of a slave for Him!'

26 "Brothers, you children of Abraham and those of other nations
who fear God, we have been given this message of salvation; the
Saviour was sent to us. 27 But the people of Jerusalem and their
rulers failed to recognise Jesus as their Saviour, as the Christ, and in
condemning Him fulfilled the prophetic words that are read every
Sabbath. 28 Despite the fact that they could not find Him guilty of
any crime worthy of death, they asked Pilate to have Him crucified.

29 "When they had fulfilled the words written about Him in the
scriptures, they took Him down from the cross and laid His body in

a tomb. 30-31 Yet God raised Him from the dead and, over a period of
many days, He was seen in His risen body by those who had come
with Him to Jerusalem from Galilee. They are now witnesses of His
resurrection to our people.

32-33 "We proclaim to you this good news: What God promised our
forefathers, He has fulfilled for us, their children, by raising Jesus.
God says of Him in the second Psalm, 'You are My Son; today I have
become your Father.' 34-35 The truth that God raised Him from the
dead so that His body would never decay, is expressed in these
words: 'I will give you the holy and certain blessings I promised to
David,' and elsewhere, 'You will not allow Your Holy One to decay.'

36 "When David had fulfilled God's purpose for him in his generation he died, was buried with his ancestors and his body decayed.
37 But He whom God raised from the dead has not suffered any decay!

38 "Therefore I want you to know, brothers, that through Jesus you
can receive forgiveness of all your sins. This is what we proclaim to
you. 39 Through faith in Jesus everyone who believes is made acceptable
to God, and is brought into a right relationship with Him. No one
could achieve such acceptance through the law given to Moses.
40-41 So make certain that what the prophets said does not apply to
you, 'Understand, those of you who scoff at the truth; you will perish, for I am going to do something in your day that is so wonderful you would never believe it, even if someone revealed it to you.'"

42 Paul and Barnabas were about to leave the synagogue when the
people asked them to explain these things further on the following
Sabbath. 43 After the service many Jews and devout converts to
Judaism followed Paul and Barnabas, who talked further with them
and urged them to continue to live in God's grace, in the good of all
He gives.

The gospel spreads despite opposition (13:44-52)

44 It seemed that the whole city had come together on the following
Sabbath to hear the Word of the Lord. 45 But when the Jewish leaders
saw the crowds had gathered around Paul and Barnabas they were
filled with jealousy and spoke aggressively against Paul's teaching.

46-47 Then Paul and Barnabas answered their allegations boldly:
"We had to speak God's Word to you first. As you choose to reject it
then, clearly, you do not consider yourselves worthy of receiving

13:32-33 Psalm 2:7
13:34-35 Isaiah 55:3
13:34-35 Psalm 16:10
13:40-41 Habakkuk 1:5

eternal life. So now we will turn to the other nations, for the Lord has commanded through the prophet Isaiah: 'I have made You a light to the Gentile nations, that You might take the message of salvation to every part of the earth.' "

48 When the Gentiles present heard this, they were really pleased and decided to obey the Word of the Lord. And all those chosen by God for eternal life believed!

49 So the gospel then spread throughout the whole region.
50 However, the Jewish leaders initiated a persecution against Paul and Barnabas by stirring up women of influence who were faithful to their religion, and also the leading men in the city. They expelled
Paul and Barnabas from that region. 51 So they shook the dust of that place from their feet as a sign against their rejection of the truth and
then travelled to Iconium. 52 Yet all who became disciples were filled with joy and the Holy Spirit.

Paul and Barnabas speak boldly in Iconium (14:1-17)

14 At Iconium Paul and Barnabas went together to the Jewish synagogue, where they spoke so powerfully that a great
number believed, both Jews and Gentiles. 2 But those Jews who rejected their message and refused to believe stirred up opposition
among the Gentiles by slandering Paul and Barnabas. 3 Even so, they spent some time there and continued to preach boldly for the Lord, who endorsed their message of His grace by empowering
them to perform miraculous signs and wonders. 4 The city population was divided; some supported the apostles, others sided with the Jewish opposition.

5 However, a group of Gentiles and Jews including some of the leaders plotted violence against Paul and Barnabas, wanting to
stone them. 6-7 But they heard of the plot and fled to Lycaonia, to the cities of Lystra and Derbe and the surrounding country, where they continued to proclaim the good news.

8 In Lystra they encountered a man who from birth had crippled
feet and had never been able to walk. 9-10 He listened intently to Paul's preaching. When Paul looked at the man, he perceived that he had faith to be healed and so called to him: "Stand up on your feet." Immediately the man jumped up and started to walk.

11 The crowd that witnessed this shouted out in their own language:
"These are gods come to visit us in human form." 12 They called
Barnabas 'Zeus' and Paul they called 'Hermes', as he was the main

13:46-47 Isaiah 49:6

spokesman. [13] The priest from the temple of Zeus that was just outside the city brought bulls and wreaths of flowers to the city gate
because both he and the crowd wanted to offer sacrifices to
Barnabas and Paul. [14-15] When the two apostles realised this they tore
their robes in disgust and ran among the crowd shouting: "Why are
you doing this? We are merely human like you. We bring you the
good news that you can turn away from such worthless things and
know the only living God, who created heaven and earth, the sun
and every living creature. [16-17] In the past, He allowed nations to go
their own ways, although He never was without witnesses to the
truth about who He is. Even though you did not know Him, He
showed you His generosity by giving you rain and enabling you to
grow seasonal crops, thus providing you with plenty of food and
cause to be grateful."

Paul stoned for the truth (14:18-22)

[18] Despite what they said, the two apostles had the utmost difficulty
in preventing the crowd from offering sacrifices to them. [19] But when
some Jews from Antioch and Iconium arrived, they turned the crowd
against them. They stoned Paul and dumped his body outside the
city, thinking he was dead. [20] But when the believers gathered around
him in prayer, he stood up and then went back into the city. Both
Paul and Barnabas left for Derbe on the following day.

[21-22] There a large number became disciples in response to their
preaching. Then they returned to Lystra, Iconium and Antioch
where they strengthened the believers, encouraging them to remain
true to the faith. "We must persevere through many trials and hardships to inherit God's Kingdom," they told them.

Apostles appointed elders (14:23-28)

[23] Paul and Barnabas appointed elders for each church. They prayed
for them after a time of fasting, entrusting them to the Lord in whom
they believed.

[24] Then, passing through Pisidia, they arrived in Pamphylia.
[25-26] They preached God's Word in Perga before moving on to Attalia,
from where they sailed back to Antioch, the city where they had
been entrusted to God's grace for the work they had now completed.
[27] So when they arrived there they called the church together, reporting
all that God had accomplished through them and how He had
opened the door of faith to the Gentiles. [28] Then they stayed with the
disciples in Antioch for a prolonged time.

Paul and Barnabas contest wrong teaching (15:1-21)

15 While there some men arrived from Judea. They taught the
believers, "You cannot be saved unless you are circumcised
according to the custom taught by Moses." 2 Paul and Barnabas
argued strongly against such teaching and so confronted these men.
Paul and Barnabas, together with a delegation from the church,
were appointed to go to Jerusalem to discuss the matter with the
apostles and elders. 3 As they travelled through Phoenicia and
Samaria, they told of how Gentiles had now been converted; and
that brought joy to the believers there.

4 When they arrived in Jerusalem, they were given a warm
welcome by the apostles, elders and the whole church. They then
reported all that God had done through them.

5 Some believers who were Pharisees declared: "The Gentiles
must be circumcised and told that they have to obey the Law of
Moses." 6 The apostles and elders met to consider this matter. 7 There
was much debate before Peter stood to address them: "Brothers,
you remember that some time ago God made it clear to you that He
had chosen me to take the message of the gospel to the Gentiles so
that they could believe. 8 God, who knows the heart of every man,
showed that He had accepted them by imparting the Holy Spirit to
them in the same way that He had to us. 9 He made no distinction
between Jew and Gentile, for He purified the hearts of both groups
of believers through their faith in Him.

10 "Now why do you question what God has done by putting a
yoke on the necks of these Gentile disciples that neither we nor our
fathers were able to bear? 11 This cannot be right! We believe that we
are saved through the grace of our Lord Jesus Christ, just as these
Gentiles have been."

12 The whole gathering listened attentively as Barnabas and Paul
told of the miraculous signs and wonders God had performed
through them among the Gentiles. 13 In conclusion, James summed
up: "Listen to me, my brothers. 14 Simon has reminded you of how
God first showed that it is His purpose to take a people for Himself
from among the Gentiles. 15 This agrees with the written prophecies
that have been handed down to us:

> 16-18 'Then I will return and restore David's fallen kingdom.
> I will rebuild its ruins and restore it, that the faithful remnant
> may seek the Lord, together with all the Gentiles who

15:16-18 Amos 9:11-12

believe in My Name. This is what the Lord says, for this
is the purpose He determined long ago.'

19 "Therefore, in my judgment we should not add unnecessary
difficulties for the Gentiles who are turning to God. 20 It would be
better for us to write to them, informing them that they should not
eat meat offered to idols, nor indulge in sexual immorality. They
should not drink blood nor eat the meat of strangled animals. 21 For
the Law of Moses has been read and preached on every Sabbath in
the synagogues in every city from the earliest times."

Apostles' message to church at Antioch (15:22-35)

22 Then the apostles and elders, together with the whole church,
decided to select representatives to send with Paul and Barnabas to
Antioch. They chose two of their leaders, Judas Barsabbas and Silas.
23 With them they sent this letter:

From the apostles and elders, your brothers,
To the Gentile believers in Antioch, Syria and Cilicia:
Greetings.

24 We have had reports about the way you have been disturbed by those from the church here who came to you
without our authorisation; how you were troubled by
their teaching. 25-27 So we have all agreed to send our official
representatives to you, Judas and Silas, along with our
dear friends Barnabas and Paul, two men who have
endangered their lives for the sake of our Lord Jesus
Christ. They will confirm by word of mouth what we
write in this letter.

28-29 It seemed good to the Holy Spirit and to us not to
burden you with anything further than these requirements:
You are not to eat food offered to idols, nor are you to
drink blood or eat the meat of strangled animals. And
you must not indulge in any form of sexual immorality.
You will do well if you obey what we say. Farewell.

30 Then the four men left Jerusalem for Antioch, where they gathered
the church members and delivered the letter to them. 31 They were
greatly encouraged by its contents. 32 Judas and Silas, both of whom
were prophets, also said many encouraging things that strengthened
the faith of the believers. 33 After spending time in Antioch, the
brethren there sent them back to Jerusalem with the blessing of God's
peace. 34 But Silas believed it to be right that he should remain there.

35 Paul and Barnabas remained in Antioch where they taught the Word of the Lord, along with many other preachers.

Paul and Barnabas part company (15:36-41)

36 After some time, Paul suggested to Barnabas: "We should make a return visit to the believers in all the towns where we have already preached the Lord's Word, and monitor their progress." 37-38 Barnabas wanted John Mark to accompany them, but Paul thought otherwise because he had left them in Pamphylia and had not persevered with them in the work.

39-41 They disagreed so deeply about this that they decided to go their separate ways. Barnabas and Mark sailed for Cyprus, while Paul took Silas with him, going through Syria and Cilicia, where they strengthened the churches. They were all entrusted to the Lord's grace by the believers in Antioch.

Paul and Timothy (16:1-5)

16 Paul and Silas went to Derbe and then to Lystra, where they met Timothy, a disciple whose mother was a Jewish believer and whose father was Greek. 2 Timothy had a good reputation with the believers in Lystra and Iconium. 3 Because Paul wanted him to accompany him on their onward journey in an area where there were many Jews, Timothy was circumcised, as it was widely known that his father was a Greek.

4 In every town they spoke of the decision made by the apostles and elders in Jerusalem, so that the local believers could comply. 5 As a result, the churches in that area were strengthened in faith and continued to grow daily in numbers.

Paul's vision leads them to Macedonia (16:6-12)

6 Paul, Silas and Timothy then travelled through the area of Phrygia and Galatia, as the Holy Spirit had made it clear they were not to go to the province of Asia at that time. 7 However, when they arrived at the border of Mysia they wanted to go into Bithynia; but again the Spirit of Jesus would not permit this. 8 So they bypassed Mysia and went to Troas. 9 That night Paul saw a Macedonian man in a vision. He stood pleading with him, "Come and help us in Macedonia." 10 Having received such a vision, Paul concluded that God was leading them to preach the gospel in Macedonia; so we prepared to go there immediately. (It was at this point that Luke, the author of this book, joined Paul and his companions).

[11]From Troas we sailed to Samothrace, and then the next day on to Neapolis. [12]From there we journeyed to Philippi, a Roman colony that was the leading city of Macedonia, where we stayed for several days.

Lydia baptised at Philippi (16:13-15)

[13-14]We went outside the city gate to the riverside on the Sabbath, expecting to find others gathered there for prayer. We sat down and began to speak to some women, among whom was Lydia, who came from the city of Thyatira and traded in exclusive purple cloth. As she was a worshipper, the Lord opened her heart to respond to Paul's preaching. [15]After she and the members of her household were baptised, Lydia invited us to her home. "If you accept that I am a true believer in the Lord, please come and stay at my house," she said. So, at her insistence, we agreed to this.

Deliverance of possessed girl (16:16-28)

[16]On another occasion, when we were going to the place of prayer we encountered a demon-possessed slave girl. She was used by her owners to earn much money by telling fortunes and predicting the future. [17]The girl followed us shouting: "These men are servants of the most high God and they are letting you know how you can be saved." [18]She did this continually for several days until Paul became so exasperated that he turned towards the girl and addressed the spirit operating through her. "In the Name of Jesus Christ I command you to come out of her!" he said. Immediately the spirit obeyed and left her.

[19-20]However, when the girl's owners realised that they could no longer use her to make money, they seized Paul and Silas and hauled them before the magistrates in the market place. They claimed: "These Jews are fermenting uproar in the city. [21]They are encouraging people to do things that are contrary to our Roman customs."

[22]As the crowd joined in the attack against Paul and Silas, the magistrates ordered that they be stripped and beaten. [23]They were severely flogged and then thrown into prison, where the jailer had strict orders to guard them carefully. [24]So he put them in a cell and secured their feet in the stocks.

[25]Around midnight, Paul and Silas were praying and singing praises to God while the other prisoners listened. [26]Suddenly a violent earthquake shook the foundations of the prison; all the prison doors flew open and everyone's chains were unfastened. [27]The jailer

awoke and seeing the prison doors open was about to kill himself, because he assumed all the prisoners had escaped. 28 But Paul shouted: "Stop! Don't kill yourself. We are all here!"

The jailer and his household are baptised (16:29-34)

29 The jailer called for lights, rushed into their cell and fell to the ground before Paul and Silas, trembling with fear. 30 He then led them out of the cell and asked them: "Sirs, how can I be saved?" 31 They told him: "Believe in the Lord Jesus and you and your whole household will be saved."

32 Then they revealed the Word of the Lord to the jailer and his whole household. 33 Even though it was the middle of the night, they were all baptised, once the jailer had washed Paul and Silas' wounds. 34 He welcomed them into his house and set a meal before them and was filled with such joy because he and his whole family had now become believers.

Paul and Silas pardoned (16:35-40)

35 At daylight, the magistrates sent officials to order the jailer to release Paul and Silas. The jailer told Paul: "You are free to go. 36 The magistrates have ordered that you are to be released. So go in peace."

37 But Paul told the officials: "The magistrate had us beaten publicly without trial, even though we are Roman citizens, and then had us thrown into prison. And now they want to be rid of us secretly? Never! Let them come here themselves and release us."

38 The officials went and reported this to the magistrates, who were alarmed when they realised that Paul and Silas were Roman citizens. 39 They came apologetically and escorted them out of the prison and asked them to leave the city. 40 But first, as soon as they were released from the prison, Paul and Silas went to Lydia's house where they met with the believers and encouraged them before leaving.

Paul preaches Christ in Thessalonica (17:1-4)

17 Passing through Amphipolis and Apollonia, they arrived in Thessalonica. 2-3 As was his custom, Paul went to the Jewish synagogue and on three successive Sabbaths explained and proved from the scriptures that the Christ, their Messiah, had to suffer and then to rise from the dead. He told the people: "This Jesus of whom I speak is the Christ, your Messiah." 4 Some of the Jews were convinced

and joined Paul and Silas, together with a large number of God-
fearing Greeks and several prominent women.

Jewish leaders turn on Jason's household (17:5-9)

5 This only made the Jewish leaders jealous. So they gathered a mob
of undesirable characters from the market place and began a riot in
the city. They made for Jason's house looking for Paul and Silas,
intending to deliver them into the hands of the mob. 6 Failing to find
them there, they dragged Jason and some believers before the city
officials shouting: "These men have caused trouble everywhere they
have been and now they have come here. 7 This Jason has welcomed
them into his home. They all speak against Caesar's laws, claiming
there is another king who they call Jesus."

8 This claim threw both the crowd and the city officials into confusion. 9 They forced Jason and the others to post bail and then
released them.

The Bereans receive the gospel (17:10-15)

10 When night fell, the believers sent Paul and Silas to Berea. As soon
as they arrived there they went to the Jewish synagogue. 11 The
Bereans were more open to the gospel than the Thessalonians and
received their message readily. Every day they examined the scriptures
to verify what Paul said. 12 Many Jews became believers, together
with prominent women and many Greek men.

13 When the Thessalonian Jews heard that Paul was preaching
God's Word in Berea, they came and stirred up trouble there. 14 The
believers immediately sent Paul to the coast with an escort, while
Silas and Timothy remained in Berea. Paul and those with him
moved on to Athens. 15 There the others left him and returned to
Berea with instructions for Silas and Timothy to join them as soon
as possible.

Paul preaches to Athenian philosophers (17:16-34)

16 While Paul was waiting for them in Athens he was deeply distressed
to see that the city was full of pagan idols. 17 In the synagogue he
debated with the Jews and God-fearing Greeks and preached openly
to all in the market place. 18 A number of Epicurean and Stoic
philosophers started to argue with him. "What strange notion has
this babbler picked up?" some asked, while others said, "He seems
to be promoting some foreign gods." They only said such things
because Paul was preaching the good news about Jesus and His
resurrection.

19 They brought him to a meeting of philosophers at the Areopagus
and asked him: "Tell us about this new teaching you are giving.
20 What you say seems very strange to us and we cannot understand
what you mean. 21 (The Athenians and the foreign population in
the city loved to spend time doing nothing but debating the latest
fashionable ideas.)

22-23 Paul stood to address the meeting and said: "Men of Athens!
It is obvious that you are very religious, for as I have walked around
I have observed carefully how many objects of worship you have. I
even found an altar that bears the inscription: 'To an unknown god.'
I am now going to tell you about this God whom you do not know.

24 "He is the God who created the world and everything in it. He
is Lord of both heaven and earth, but He does not live in a temple
built by human hands. 25 There is nothing men can do to meet His
needs, for He does not have any! It is He who gives life to all men
and breath to every living creature.

26 "He created the first man, from whom every nation of men has
descended, so that now they inhabit the whole earth. It is He who
has determined when and where they should all live. 27 His purpose
in doing this was to encourage men to seek to know Him, to reach
out to Him, although He is not difficult to find as He is not far from
each one of us. 28 Because we live in the presence of this God, every
move we make is known to Him and we are dependent upon Him
for our very being. Even some of your own poets have said that 'we
are His offspring.'

29 "Therefore, if we are His offspring we should not think of God
as one fashioned in gold, silver, stone or any other image devised by
a craftsman. 30 For centuries God permitted such ignorance, but now
He commands everyone to turn away from such ignorance and
embrace the truth. 31 And He has set a day when the entire world
will be judged with justice by the Man He has appointed, the same
Man He has raised from the dead as proof of His intentions."

32 Some treated this talk of resurrection from the dead with derision,
but others told Paul: "We want to hear more about this." 33 Then
Paul left the meeting. 34 A number became believers on hearing more
from Paul, among whom was Dionysius who was a member of the
council, and a woman called Damaris.

Paul in Corinth (18:1-13)

18 Then Paul left Athens and went to Corinth where he met a
Jew called Aquila. 2 He had been born in Pontus and had
recently arrived from Italy with his wife Priscilla, because the

Emperor Claudius had decreed that all Jews must leave Rome. 3 Like them, Paul was a tent maker by trade; so he stayed and worked with them.

4 Every Sabbath Paul spoke in the synagogue, trying to convince both Jews and Greeks of the truth of the gospel.

5 When Silas and Timothy arrived from Macedonia, Paul spent all this time preaching, proclaiming to the Jews that Jesus was their Messiah. 6 However, when they opposed and insulted him, Paul shook his cloak before them in protest and said: "Your blood be on your own hands. I have discharged my responsibility by telling you the truth. Now I will go to the Gentiles."

7 When he left the synagogue, Paul went next door to the house of a true worshipper, Titius Justus. 8 The synagogue ruler, Crispus, and his whole household believed in the Lord, and many Corinthians became believers and were baptised as a result of his testimony.

9 One night the Lord gave Paul a vision in which He said: "Don't be afraid. Keep speaking boldly and do not be silent. 10 For I am with you, to protect you from attack or injury, for I have many loyal people in this city." 11 So Paul remained there for eighteen months teaching God's Word.

12 But the Jews made a concerted attack on Paul while Gallio was the proconsul of Achaia. 13 They brought this charge against him in court, "This man is persuading people to worship God in ways that are against the law."

Paul challenges the Jewish leaders (18:14-23)

14 As Paul was about to speak in his defence, Gallio told the Jews: "I would listen to you Jews if you made a justifiable accusation of some serious crime. 15 But as you are only concerned about questions concerning words and names of your own religious law you can settle the matter among yourselves. I refuse to act as the judge in such matters." 16 So he dismissed them from the court. 17 In anger the Jewish leaders rounded on Sosthenes, the leader of the synagogue, and beat him there in the courtroom. But Gallio ignored them.

18 Paul continued his stay in Corinth for some time. He then left the believers there and sailed for Syria, accompanied only by Priscilla and Aquila. However, before he sailed he had his head shaved at Cenchrea as a sign that he had made a vow. 19 They arrived at Ephesus where Paul left Priscilla and Aquila. However, before leaving he went into the synagogue and debated with the Jews there. 20-21 Although they asked him to prolong his visit he declined, but promised to return when it was God's will for him to

do so. 22 He then sailed from Ephesus to Caesarea where he met with the church before travelling on to Antioch.

23 Having spent some time there, Paul then travelled throughout Galatia and Phrygia, strengthening and encouraging the disciples in that region.

Priscilla and Aquila teach Apollos (18:24-28)

24-25 At the same time a Jew called Apollos came to Ephesus from Alexandria. He was a scholar with a thorough knowledge of the scriptures, who had been taught about the way of the Lord and spoke with great zeal. What he taught about Jesus was accurate, but he had only experienced John's baptism.

26 Priscilla and Aquila heard him speak boldly in the synagogue and invited him to their home, where they gave him further revelation of God's way in Christ.

27 When Apollos decided to visit Achaia, the believers in Ephesus encouraged him and wrote a letter of commendation to their brethren there. Apollos proved to be a great help to those in Achaia who had become believers through God's grace. 28 He argued strongly with the Jews at public meetings, proving from the scriptures that Jesus is the Christ.

Corinthians baptised in the Spirit (19:1-10)

19 While Apollos was in Corinth, Paul took the inland route to Ephesus. 2 There he found a group of disciples to whom he put the question: "When you believed, did you receive the Holy Spirit?"

"No," they replied, "We have not heard anything about the Holy Spirit."

3 So Paul then asked them: "Then what baptism have you received?"

"John's baptism," they replied.

4 Paul explained: "John's baptism was for repentance. But he made it clear to people that they were to believe in the One who was to come after him, Jesus."

5 On realising this, they were baptised into the Name of the Lord Jesus. 6-7 Then Paul laid his hands on them, praying for the Holy Spirit to come upon them. When he did so, all twelve spoke in tongues and prophesied.

8 Paul spoke boldly in the synagogue for three months, arguing persuasively about God's Kingdom. 9 But some of the Jews obstinately refused to believe and openly insulted the Way. So, together

with those who had become disciples, Paul left the synagogue and
began daily meetings in the lecture hall of Tyrannus. [10]They continued
to meet there for two years, enabling both Jews and Greeks who
lived in the province of Asia to hear the Lord's Word.

God works miracles through Paul (19:11-16)

[11]God worked amazing miracles through Paul. [12]When handkerchiefs
or cloths that he had touched were laid on the sick they were healed
of their diseases and set free from demonic oppression.

[13]Some Jewish teachers who travelled from place to place tried to
use the Name of the Lord Jesus to drive out evil spirits. They said
such things as, "In the Name of Jesus whom Paul preaches, I command
you to come out." [14]The seven sons of Sceva, the Jewish chief priest,
tried this. [15]One day an evil spirit answered back, "Jesus I know and
Paul I know about, but who are you to command me?" [16]Then the
man with the evil spirit leaped on them and overpowered all seven.
They were attacked so violently that they fled naked from the house
with their wounds bleeding.

Fear of God grips people of Ephesus (19:17-22)

[17]When both the Jews and Greeks who lived in Ephesus heard of
this, the fear of God came on them and they highly honoured the
Name of the Lord Jesus. [18]As a result, many of the believers were
moved to confess their sins openly. [19]Those who had been involved
with occult practices brought their books of so-called magic and
burned them publicly. The scrolls that were destroyed were reckoned
to be worth a fortune.

[20]So God's Word was spread more and more widely and became
increasingly influential and powerful in its effect.

[21]Later, Paul decided to go to Jerusalem, taking the route through
Macedonia and Asia. "After I have been to Jerusalem, I must visit
Rome," he said. [22]He sent two of his assistants, Timothy and
Erastus, to Macedonia while he spent a further short period in Asia.

Idol maker stirs riot against Paul (19:23-41)

[23]It was around this time that a great controversy arose concerning
the Way. [24]Demetrius was a silversmith who made silver shrines of
the goddess Artemis, a business that involved several craftsmen.
[25]He called them and workers in other related trades together and
said: "Fellow workers, you know we prosper financially from this
business. [26]But you have both seen for yourselves and have heard

how this man Paul has persuaded large numbers of people here in
Ephesus and in nearly the whole province of Asia to depart from
the worship of the gods. He says that man-made gods are not gods
at all. 27 Our trade is in great danger and will lose its good reputation.
Even the temple of the great goddess Artemis will become discredited
and the goddess herself, who is worshipped not only in Asia but
throughout the world, will be robbed of her divine honour."

28 These words so angered them that they began shouting:
"Artemis of the Ephesians is great!" 29 It was not long before the
whole city was in an uproar. The people seized Gaius and Aristarchus,
who had travelled with Paul from Macedonia, and dragged them to
the theatre. 30 Paul wanted to address the crowd but the other disciples
wouldn't allow him to do so. 31 Even some of their provincial officials,
as well as their friends, sent Paul a message imploring him not to go
near the theatre.

32 The crowd there was in complete confusion, shouting contradictory things. Most did not even know why they were there. 33 The
Jews pushed Alexander forward to be their spokesman, wanting
him to explain their position. He called for silence so that he could
defend their cause. 34 But when the crowd realised he was a Jew,
they shouted for two hours: "Great is Artemis of the Ephesians!"

35 Finally the city clerk managed to quieten the crowd and said:
"People of Ephesus, the whole world knows that the city of Ephesus
is the guardian of the temple of the great Artemis, whose image fell
from heaven. 36 This fact is undeniable; so you ought to be quiet and
not take matters into your own hands. 37 These men who have been
brought here have neither robbed our temples nor have they blasphemed our goddess.

38 "So if Demetrius and his fellow craftsmen have some charge to
bring against anyone, the courts are available and there are proconsuls
to judge such matters. That is the right way to press charges. 39 If
there are any other matters of dispute they must be settled according
to our legal system. 40 As it is, we are in danger of being charged ourselves. Because of what has happened today we could be charged
with causing a riot. If that was the case we could give no adequate
explanation for all this commotion, for there is no reason for it."
41 He then dismissed the crowd.

Paul continues to travel (20:1-6)

20 When the uproar was over, Paul sent for the disciples
and encouraged them before leaving for Macedonia. 2 He
encouraged the believers wherever he went, arriving finally in

Greece where he stayed for three months. 3-4As he was about to set
sail for Syria he became aware of a Jewish plot against him, and so
decided to return to Macedonia accompanied by Sopater the son of
Pyrrhus from Berea, Aristarchus and Secundus from Thessalonica,
Gaius from Derbe, Timothy, Tychicus and Trophimus from the
province of Asia. 5These men went ahead and waited for us at Troas.
6After Passover we sailed from Philippi and joined them five
days later in Troas, where we stayed for one week.

Young man brought to life (20:7-12)

7We met together to break bread on the Sunday and because he
intended to leave on the following day, Paul spoke to the people
until midnight. 8The upstairs room where we met was lit by many
lamps. 9Seated on the windowsill was a young man called Eutychus,
who fell asleep while Paul was speaking at such length. While
asleep he fell to his death from the third story. 10Paul went down to
him, bent down to him and embraced him. "There is nothing to be
alarmed about," he said, "he is alive!" 11Then he returned upstairs
where we broke bread and ate together. 12The young man was taken
home alive and well, much to everyone's relief.

Paul continues to travel (20:13-16)

13We went by ship to Assos, while Paul travelled on foot. 14There he
joined us on board and we sailed to Mitylene. 15On the following
day we sailed past Kios, crossed over to Samos and then on the
following day arrived at Miletus. 16To avoid spending time in the
province of Asia, Paul had decided to bypass Ephesus. He wanted
to reach Jerusalem quickly, by the feast of Pentecost if possible.

Paul exhorts Ephesian elders (20:17-38)

17Paul summoned the elders of the church at Ephesus to meet with
him at Miletus. 18When they arrived he said to them: "From the time
I arrived in the province of Asia you have seen the example I set by
the way I lived among you. 19I served the Lord humbly and often
with tears. I was sorely tried by the way the Jews plotted against
me. 20Yet, as you know, I never hesitated to preach whatever would
be helpful to you. I taught you at the public meetings and face to
face. 21I proclaimed to both Jews and Greeks alike that they had to
turn to God in true repentance and put their faith in our Lord Jesus.
22"But now I am going to Jerusalem, believing that the Holy Spirit
is urging me to do so even though I have no idea what will happen

to me once I am there. 23 However, I do know that in every city I
visit, the Holy Spirit warns me that prison and suffering await me.
24 But the only thing that matters to me is that I complete the work
the Lord Jesus has given me to bear witness to the gospel of God's
grace. Nothing else matters by comparison!

25 "I know in my heart that none of you to whom I have preached
the Kingdom of God will ever see me again. 26 So I affirm to you now
that I have faithfully fulfilled God's purpose. 27 I have never hesitated
to make His will clear to you. Yes, I have preached every aspect of
God's Word. 28 So I charge you to watch diligently over both yourselves and all those the Holy Spirit has given you to oversee. Be
good shepherds of God's church, all those he purchased for Himself
with His own blood.

29 "I am well aware that after I have gone, savage wolves will seek
to come into the church and they will care nothing for the sheep.
30 Some will even emerge from your own number who will distort
the truth because their motive will be to create their own followers.
31 Watch out for such people. And remember that I watched over you
diligently myself for three years by both day and night, often with
tears.

32 "Now it is time for me to entrust you to God, to the Word of His
grace that has the power to build you up and enable you to share in
the inheritance that He gives to all those He has called and set apart
for Himself.

33 "I have never been jealous of those with money and fine possessions. 34 As you well know, I worked to meet the needs both of
myself and my assistants. 35 In every way I showed by my example
that we must work hard so that we are able to help those in need,
never forgetting the words of the Lord Jesus, 'It is more blessed to
give than to receive.'"

36 When Paul had finished speaking, he and the elders knelt and
prayed together. 37-38 As they parted they embraced Paul and wept,
for they were touched deeply by his statement that they would
never see him again. Then they accompanied him to the ship.

Paul sets sail again (21:1-9)

21 After this emotional farewell, we set sail first to Cos, then on
the following day to Rhodes and from there to Patara.
2 When we found a ship bound for Phoenicia, we boarded and set
sail. 3 We passed to the south of Cyprus and sailed to Syria, landing
at Tyre where our ship was to unload its cargo. 4 We met with the
disciples there and stayed for a week with them. Through prophesies

from God's Spirit they told Paul not to go to Jerusalem. [5]Despite this
we returned to the ship when it was time to set sail. All the disciples,
together with their families, escorted us out of the city and knelt
with us on the beach to pray. [6]After greeting each other we boarded
the ship and they returned home.

[7]From Tyre we continued our journey to Ptolemais, where we
landed and were greeted by the believers. [8]We spent the day with
them before leaving for Caesarea, where we stayed with Philip the
evangelist, one of the seven set apart by the apostles. [9]He had four
unmarried daughters, all of whom prophesied.

Agabus prophesies Paul's fate (21:10-14)

[10]When we had been there a few days, a prophet from Judea named
Agabus arrived. [11]He came over to us, took hold of Paul's belt and
tied his own hands and feet with it, declaring: "The Holy Spirit says,
'This is how the Jewish leaders in Jerusalem will bind the owner of
this belt and deliver him to the Gentile authorities!'"

[12]On hearing this, both we and the local people begged Paul not
to go to Jerusalem. [13]But Paul was adamant. "Why weep like this?"
he asked. "Are you trying to break my heart? I am prepared not
only to be bound but to die in Jerusalem for the sake of the Lord
Jesus." [14]Because he would not be swayed by anything we said, we
surrendered to the inevitable saying: "May the Lord's will be done."

Paul returns to Jerusalem (21:15-26)

[15]Then we prepared ourselves for the journey to Jerusalem. [16]Some
of the Caesarean believers accompanied us and took us to the home
of Mnason, one of the early disciples from Cyprus, and we stayed
there with him.

[17]When we arrived in Jerusalem the believers there welcomed us
with joy. [18]On the following day we went with Paul to visit James
and all the elders of the church. [19]Having greeted them, Paul gave a
detailed report of all that God had done among the Gentiles through
his ministry.

[20]They gave God the glory for what they heard and then told of
the many thousands of Jews who had become believers. "And all of
them are truly obedient to the law of God," they said. [21]"But they
have been told that you teach the Jews who live in Gentile lands
that they do not have to keep the law of Moses, that they should not
circumcise their children nor live by our customs. [22]What shall we
do? Your coming faces us with a dilemma.

23 "This is what we suggest: Four men in the church here have
taken a vow. 24 Go with these men to the temple, join with them in
the purification ceremony and pay for them to have their heads shaved.
This will prove to everyone that there is no truth in the rumours
about you, and that you yourself live in obedience to the law.

25 "We have already written about our decision as far as Gentile
believers are concerned, that they should not eat food that has been
sacrificed to idols nor the meat of strangled animals. They should
not drink blood and must refrain from sexual immorality."

26 So on the following day Paul went with the men and took part
in the purification ceremony. At the temple he announced publicly
that when the time of their vows expired, the appropriate offering
would be made for each of them.

27 When the seven days of purification were nearly completed,
some Jews from the province of Asia saw Paul in the temple and
stirred up a large crowd by shouting: 28 "Men of Israel, help us! Here
is the man who teaches against our law and this temple everywhere
he goes. Not only that, but he has defiled this sacred place by bringing
Gentiles into the temple." 29 Earlier they had seen the Ephesian,
Trophimus, with Paul in the city and had assumed that he had
brought him into the temple.

Paul arrested at the temple (21:30-36)

30 The discontent spread rapidly and people came running from
every direction. They seized hold of Paul and dragged him out of
the temple. The gates were then shut. 31 However, while they were
trying to kill him, news of the disturbance that had now spread to
the whole city reached the Roman commander. 32 Immediately he
led a troop of officers and soldiers to where the crowd had gathered.
When those involved in the riots saw the commander and his soldiers,
they stopped beating Paul.

33 When he arrived at the scene the commander arrested Paul and
ordered him to be bound with two chains. He then asked about his
identity and crime; but some in the crowd shouted one thing and
some another. 34 Because of the confusion the commander could not
find out the truth and ordered Paul to be taken to the barracks. 35 But
when they reached the steps, the crowd became so violent that Paul
had to be lifted clear by the soldiers. 36 Still the crowd followed
shouting: "Take him and kill him!"

Paul addresses the crowd (21:37-22:21)

37 As they neared the barracks, Paul asked the commander: "May I

speak with you?" The commander was surprised that Paul spoke
Greek. 38 "I thought you were the Egyptian who started the revolt of
four thousand terrorists in the desert some time ago!"

39 Paul replied: "No, I am a Jew from Tarsus in Cilicia, a city of
note. Please allow me to speak to the people." 40 The commander
consented and Paul stood on the steps and motioned to the crowd
to be quiet. When they were all silent he addressed them in Aramaic:

22 "Brothers and fathers, hear what I have to say in my
defence." 2 When they heard him speaking in Aramaic they
paid close attention.

3 Then Paul continued: "I am a Jew by birth, from Tarsus in Cilicia,
although I was brought up here in Jerusalem. I was trained in the
precise practice of the law of our fathers under Gamaliel. I was zealous
about God, as you are today. 4 I persecuted the followers of the Way,
arresting both men and women, having them thrown into prison. I
wanted them dead. 5 The high priest and the whole council can verify
this for I received letters of authorisation from them to the Jewish
leaders in Damascus, giving me authority to take these people prisoner
and bring them to Jerusalem for punishment.

6 "It was around noon and I was approaching Damascus when
suddenly a great light from heaven shone all around me. 7 I fell to
the ground and heard a voice saying to me, 'Saul! Saul! Why are you
persecuting Me?'

8 "'Who are You Lord?' I asked.

"'I am Jesus of Nazareth whom you are persecuting!' He replied.

9 "Those with me saw the light but could not understand what the
voice was saying to me.

10 "I asked: 'What shall I do, Lord?' And the Lord said, 'Get up
and go into Damascus, and there you will be told everything you
have been appointed to do.'

11 "As the brilliance of the light had blinded me, my companions
had to lead me by the hand into Damascus.

12 "There Ananias, a devout observer of the law, highly respected
by all the Jews, came to see me. 13 He stood by my side and said:
'Brother Saul, receive your sight!' Immediately I could see him!

14 "Then he told me: 'The God of our fathers has chosen you to
know His will, to see the Righteous One for yourself and to hear His
voice. 15 You will testify about Him to everyone, telling them what
you have both seen and heard. 16 Now why delay? Be baptised
immediately for the cleansing of all your sins, as you call on His
Name.'

17 "While praying in the temple on my return to Jerusalem, I fell
into a trance and saw the Lord Jesus in a vision. 18 He said to me, 'Be
quick. Leave Jerusalem immediately, because they will not believe
what you say about Me here.'
19 "I replied, 'Lord, everyone knows I went from one synagogue
to another to imprison and beat anyone who believes in You. 20 When
Your martyr Stephen's blood was shed, I was there approving of
what was happening and guarding the clothes of those who actually
killed him.'
21 "Then the Lord commanded me, 'Go! I will send you to the
Gentiles in distant places.'"

Paul's Roman citizenship (22:22-29)

22 Up to this point, the crowd had listened attentively to Paul; but
then they started shouting at the top of their voices: "Take him
away. Such a man does not deserve to live!" 23 They tore their clothes
in disgust and threw dirt into the air. 24 So the commander ordered
Paul to be taken into the barracks to be flogged and questioned as
to why the people shouted such things at him. 25 As they were binding
Paul ready to lash him, he said to the centurion: "Is it lawful for you
to flog a Roman citizen before he has been found guilty?"
26 The centurion went and reported what Paul had said to the
commander. "What are you going to do, for this man is a Roman
citizen?" he asked.
27 The commander went personally to Paul and asked: "Is it true
that you are a Roman citizen?"
"Yes, I am," Paul replied.
28 The commander told him: "I had to pay a high price to buy my
citizenship."
"But I was born a citizen of Rome," Paul said.
29 Those who were about to interrogate Paul withdrew quickly.
The commander himself was alarmed when he realised that he had
placed a Roman citizen in chains.

Paul on trial before Jewish council (22:30-23:11)

30 On the following day, the commander ordered the chief priests
and the Jewish Council to meet and brought Paul, now released
from his chains, before them.

23 Paul looked at the council members boldly and said: "My
brothers, I stand before you with a clear conscience that to
this day I have lived to fulfil God's will." 2 Ananias ordered those

near Paul to strike him on the mouth. 3 Then Paul retorted: "God
will strike you. You are like a whitewashed wall! You sit there to
judge me according to the law, yet you yourself break the law by
commanding me to be struck."

4 Those standing near Paul said: "How dare you insult God's high
priest!"

5 Paul replied: "Brothers, I did not know that he was the high
priest, for it is written, 'You are not to speak badly about the ruler
of your people.'"

6 Then Paul, realising that some of those present were Sadducees
while others were Pharisees, said to the whole Council: "My brothers,
I am a Pharisee and the son of a Pharisee. I am on trial here because
I hope in the resurrection of the dead." 7 Immediately an argument
broke out between the Pharisees and Sadducees and the gathering
was divided. 8 (The Sadducees do not believe there is resurrection;
neither do they believe in angels or spirits, while the Pharisees
believe in all of these).

9 The assembly was in chaos. Some teachers of the law who were
Pharisees stood and argued strongly. "We can see nothing wrong
with this man," they concluded. "Perhaps a spirit or an angel has
spoken to him."

10 There was such sharp division the commander feared for Paul's
safety. So he ordered the guards to go and rescue him and take him
to the barracks.

11 On the following day Paul saw the Lord standing by him. He
said: "Take courage! As you have testified faithfully about Me in
Jerusalem, it will be necessary for you to testify also in Rome."

Jewish leaders conspire to kill Paul (23:12-22)

12-13 Early on the following morning the Jewish leaders conspired
against Paul. More than forty of them took an oath saying they
would neither eat nor drink until they had killed him. 14 They went
and told the chief priests and elders: "We have taken a solemn oath
not to eat until we have killed Paul. 15 We want you and the whole
Council to ask the commander to bring him before you so you can
examine his case further. We will be ready to kill him before he arrives."

16 However Paul's nephew heard of this intended ambush and
went to the barracks to inform Paul. 17 He in turn called one of the
centurions and said: "Take this young man to the commander; he
has a message for him." 18 The centurion did so, saying: "The prisoner

23:5 Exodus 22:28

Paul sent for me and asked me to bring this young man to you as he
has a message for you."
19 Taking him by the hand, the commander took the young man
aside and asked: "What have you to tell me?"
20 He replied: "The Jewish leaders have agreed to ask you to bring
Paul before the Council tomorrow on the basis that they want more
accurate information about him. 21 Don't do as they ask, because
over forty of them have planned to ambush him. They have taken
an oath not to eat or drink anything until they have killed him. They
are already prepared and await your consent."
22 The commander dismissed the young man telling him: "Don't
tell anyone that you have warned me of these plans."

Paul escorted to governor Felix (23:23-35)

23 Then he ordered two centurions: "Prepare an escort of two hundred
soldiers, seventy cavalry and two hundred spear men to leave for
Caesarea at nine this evening. 24 Provide mounts for Paul and take
him to the governor Felix. 25 He wrote the following letter:

> 26 Claudius Lysias
> To the Most Excellent, Governor Felix:
> Greetings,
>
> 27 This man was arrested by the Jews who were about to
> kill him, when I came with a detachment of my soldiers
> and rescued him. I have learned that he is a Roman citizen.
> 28 I wanted to discover the basis of the accusations against
> him and so brought him before the Jewish Council.
> 29 However it seems that the charges involved questions
> about their own religious law but certainly did not warrant
> the death penalty or even imprisonment.
> 30 I was then informed that some Jews were plotting to
> kill him and so immediately sent him to you. I have also
> commanded those who accuse him to present their case
> against him to you personally.

31 The soldiers obeyed their orders and that night took Paul as far as
Antipatris. 32 On the following day the cavalry continued their journey
with Paul, while the rest of the detachment returned to barracks.
33 On arriving at Caesarea, they delivered the letter to the governor
and put Paul into his custody.
34-35 The governor read the letter and asked Paul what province he
came from. On hearing that he came from Cilicia he said: "I will

hear your case when your accusers arrive." Then he gave orders for Paul to be put under guard in Herod's palace.

Paul on trial before Felix (24:1-27)

24 Four days later, Ananias the high priest arrived in Caesarea, together with some of the elders and a lawyer called Tertullus, to bring their accusations against Paul. 2 When Paul was summoned, Tertullus presented their case to Felix the governor: "Under your authority we have enjoyed a long period of peace and through your wisdom you have been responsible for bringing about reforms for our benefit.

3 "Most excellent Felix, we are aware of all this and are deeply thankful to you. 4 We do not want to weary you but ask you to be gracious enough to hear our charges against this man. 5-6 We have found him to be a trouble maker who causes unrest among the Jews wherever he goes. He is the leader of a sect called the Nazarenes and we arrested him because he attempted to desecrate the temple in Jerusalem. So we seized him, wanting to judge him according to their own law. 7 But Lysias, the commander, came and took him from us with considerable force. He ordered our accusations to be made before you. 8 If you question him yourself you will be able to verify that these charges we bring against him are true."

9 The other Jews in the delegation supported his allegations.

10 When the governor invited Paul to respond, he said: "I am aware that you have ruled this nation for several years and are able to judge such matters; so I gladly make my defence before you. 11 It can be proved that I went up to Jerusalem to worship no more than twelve days ago. 12 My accusers here did not see me causing any arguments in the temple, nor inciting crowds in the synagogues or anywhere else in the city. 13 So they are unable to prove any of these charges they are bringing against me.

14-15 "However, I openly admit that I worship the God of our fathers and am a follower of the Way which they refer to as a sect. I consent to everything written in the Law and the Prophets and like these men my hope in God leads me to believe that there will be a resurrection from the dead of both the righteous and the ungodly. 16 Believing this, I always endeavour to keep a clear conscience before both God and man.

17 "I came to Jerusalem after being away for several years, bearing gifts for the poor among my people and to worship the Lord. 18 When my accusers saw me in the temple courts I was completing

a time of ritual purification and was therefore ceremonially clean.
No crowd surrounded me, neither was I involved in starting a riot.
19 But some Jews from the province of Asia were there, and they
should be here now to bring before you any charges they have
against me. 20 Or else those who are here should state clearly what
crime they found me guilty of when I appeared before the Jewish
Council. 21 As I stood before them I only shouted: 'I am on trial before
you today because of my faith in the resurrection of the dead.'"

22 Then Felix, who knew about the Way, adjourned the hearing,
saying: "I will judge your case when the commander, Lysias,
arrives." 23 He ordered the centurion to keep Paul under guard while
allowing him some freedom. Also his friends were permitted to
visit him and take care of his needs.

24 Some days later Felix, with his Jewish wife Drusilla, sent again
for Paul and listened as he spoke of faith in Christ Jesus. 25 When
Paul spoke on righteousness, self-control and future judgment,
Felix became afraid and said: "Enough for now; you can go. I will
send for you again when it is convenient." 26 He hoped Paul would
offer him a bribe and therefore sent for him frequently that they
might talk further.

27 After two years Felix was succeeded by Porcius Festus, but he
kept Paul in prison as a favour to the Jews.

Paul appeals to Caesar (25:1-27)

25 1-2 Three days after Festus had arrived in Caesarea he went
up to Jerusalem where the chief priests and Jewish leaders
came before him to present their charges against Paul. 3 As a favour
to them they asked Festus to have Paul transferred to Jerusalem,
intending to ambush and kill him on the way there.

4 Festus answered that Paul was being held in Caesarea, where he
himself was going soon. 5 "Let some of your leaders come with me
and press charges as to anything wrong the man may have done,"
he said.

6 After spending eight to ten days in Jerusalem, Festus left for
Caesarea where he arranged for the trial to take place on the day
following his arrival. 7 When Paul was brought before him, the Jews
from Jerusalem brought many serious accusations against him,
none of which they could prove.

8 Paul then denied the charges: "I have not broken any laws, neither
those of the Jewish people, nor of the temple, nor of the Roman
authorities."

9 Wanting to ingratiate himself with the Jewish leaders, Festus
asked Paul: "Are you prepared to go and stand trial in Jerusalem on
these charges?"

10 Paul replied: "I am already standing before a Roman court. I
have not wronged the Jews in any way, as you well know.
11 However, if I was guilty of a crime deserving death, I would not
be afraid to die. But as these are serious charges that the Jewish
leaders are bringing against me, nobody has the authority to hand
me over to them. I appeal to Caesar!"

12 Festus then conferred with his advisors before declaring: "You
have appealed to Caesar, so to Caesar you shall go!"

13 A few days later King Agrippa and his sister Bernice arrived at
Caesarea to pay their respects to Festus. 14-15 As they were spending
several days there, Festus discussed Paul's case with Agrippa.
"Felix left a prisoner here, against whom the chief priests and elders
brought serious charges when I met with them in Jerusalem. They
want him to be condemned to death.

16 "I made it clear that Rome does not condemn anyone until he
has had the opportunity to defend himself against his accusers.
17 Their leaders came here with me and I heard the case on the day
following my return. 18 When Paul came before the court his accusers
did not bring any of the charges against him that I was expecting.
19 Instead, they argued with him over some details of their own religion,
and in particular about a dead man called Jesus, whom Paul claimed
was still alive.

20 "I had no idea how to proceed in such a case; so I asked him if
he would be prepared to go Jerusalem where these charges could be
properly assessed. 21 It was then that this Paul appealed to the
emperor, and so I ordered him to remain in detention until I could
send him to Caesar."

22 "I would like to speak with this man myself," Agrippa told
Festus. "You will hear him tomorrow," Festus replied.

23-24 With great pomp, Agrippa and Bernice entered the audience
room on the following day, together with the high officials and leading
men of the city. Festus ordered Paul to be brought before them and
said: "King Agrippa and all of you present, this man you see before
you is the subject of a petition I have received from the entire Jewish
community from Jerusalem and Caesarea. They demand he be put
to death. 25 But as far as I can see he has done nothing that deserves
such a punishment. However, because he has appealed to the
emperor, I have decided to send him to Rome. 26 But I am at a loss as
to what to write to the emperor about him. So I have brought him

before this assembly, and especially before you, King Agrippa, so
that as a result of this examination I shall know what to write. 27 For
I can hardly send a prisoner to the emperor without detailing the
specific charges against him!"

Paul tells Agrippa of his conversion (26:1-32)

26 Then Agrippa told Paul: "You have freedom to speak in
your defence." So Paul raised his hand and began to speak:
2-3 "King Agrippa, I am truly fortunate to stand before you today
to make my defence concerning all the accusations brought against
me by the Jews, especially as you are so knowledgeable about Jewish
customs and controversies. So I ask you to listen to me patiently.
4 "The Jews are well aware of how I have lived since childhood,
both in my own country and in Jerusalem. 5 Not only have they
known me for a long time, but they can also acknowledge, if they
are prepared to, that I lived as a Pharisee, the strictest party in our
religion. 6 And now I stand on trial here today because I expect God
to fulfil what He promised to our forefathers. 7 This is the same
promise that all the twelve tribes of Israel expect to see fulfilled as
they faithfully serve God by day and night. Majesty, it is because of
this hope we all have, that these Jewish leaders are accusing me!
8 Why should it seem incredible to any of you that God is able to
raise the dead?
9 "There was a time when I was convinced that I should do everything possible to oppose the Name of Jesus of Nazareth and all He
stood for. 10 And I did just that in Jerusalem, receiving authority from
the chief priests to imprison many believers, and I cast my vote
against them when they were condemned to death. 11 On many occasions I went from one synagogue to another to have them flogged
in an attempt to force them to blaspheme. I was so obsessed with
opposing these saints that I even went to foreign cities to persecute
them.
12-13 "Majesty, on such a journey I was travelling on the road to
Damascus with the authority and commission of the chief priests,
when at about noon I saw a bright heavenly light, brighter even
than the sun. It shone around me and my companions. 14 We all fell
to the ground and I heard a voice speaking to me in Aramaic, 'Saul,
Saul! Why are you persecuting me? It is hard for you to keep kicking
against a rock!'
15 "'Who are You, Lord?' I asked.

"'I am Jesus, the One you persecute continually,' the Lord
replied. 16 'Now stand to your feet. I have appeared to you to
appoint you as My servant. You are to tell others what you have
seen of Me and what I shall reveal to you in the future. 17-18 I will protect
you from both your own people and the Gentiles. I am sending you
to open their eyes and to turn them from their spiritual darkness to
the light of the truth, from the devil's power to God, so they can
receive forgiveness of their sins and be numbered among those who
are made holy through their faith in Me!'

19 "So you see, King Agrippa, I have not been disobedient to the
heavenly vision I received. 20 First in Damascus, then in Jerusalem
and throughout Judea and then among the Gentiles also, I have
preached to people, telling them that they must repent. They must
turn to God and prove that they have submitted themselves to Him
by the evidence of the things they do.

21 "This is the reason why the Jews seized me in the temple courts
with the intention of killing me. 22-23 But God has continued to help
me right up to this present time, enabling me to stand here and testify
to great and small alike. I teach nothing beyond what was predicted
by Moses and the prophets, that the Messiah would suffer and
would be the first to rise from the dead; that through Him the light
might be made known to both His own people, the Jews, and to
Gentiles alike."

24 Festus then interrupted: "You must be mad, Paul!" he shouted.
"Your great learning has driven you crazy!"

25 "Most excellent Festus, I am not crazy," Paul replied. "What I
am saying is both true and reasonable. 26 These things are well
known by King Agrippa and so I can speak freely before him. I am
sure that none of these things has escaped his attention, for nothing
has happened in secret. 27 King Agrippa, do you believe the prophets?
I am sure that you do!"

28 Then Agrippa answered Paul: "Do you imagine you can persuade
me to become a Christian so easily, in such a short time?"

29 Paul replied: "Whether it takes a short or a long time, I pray to
God that not only you but all those within the sound of my voice
today will become what I am, apart from these chains I wear!"

30 At this the King, the governor, Bernice and those with them
stood to close the meeting. 31 They left the room and conferred
together concluding, "This man is not guilty of anything that
deserves death or even imprisonment." 32 Agrippa told Festus: "If it
had not been for the fact that he has appealed to Caesar, he could
have been set free."

Journey to Rome begins (27:1-8)

27 When it was time for us to set sail for Italy, Paul and some
other prisoners were put under the charge of a centurion
named Julius of the Imperial Regiment. 2 We boarded a ship from
Adramyttium that was due to sail to ports along the coast of the
province of Asia. When we sailed, Aristarchus, a Macedonian from
Thessalonica, was also with us.
3 We landed at Sidon on the following day and Julius kindly
allowed Paul to visit his friends there who could provide for his
needs. 4 From Sidon we sailed to the north of Cyprus because of the
strong headwinds. 5 After sailing across the open sea off the coast
of Cilicia and Pamphylia, we landed at Myra in Lycia. 6 There the
centurion put us aboard an Alexandrian ship sailing for Italy. 7 But
for many days we made only slow progress and neared Cnidus
with great difficulty. The wind was so strong we could not maintain
our course and so sailed on the protected side of Crete around the
Cape of Salmone. 8 We could only follow the coastline with difficulty
before finally arriving at a place known as Fair Havens, near the
town of Lasea.

Paul warns of the ship's disaster (27:9-12)

9-10 We had lost much time and sailing had already become dangerous
because it was late in the year. So Paul warned all on board: "Men,
I can tell that our voyage will end in disaster, with the loss of both
the ship and its cargo. Even our lives will be in danger."
11 Instead of heeding Paul's words, the centurion followed the
advice of the pilot and ship's owner. 12 Because this harbour did not
provide sufficient protection for the winter, the majority voted to
continue the voyage, hoping to spend the winter at Phoenix, a harbour
in Crete that faced both southwest and northwest.

A storm arises (27:13-20)

13 When a gentle southerly wind arose, it seemed they had the ideal
conditions they wanted. So they weighed anchor and sailed along
the coast of Crete. 14 But before long a tempestuous wind known as
the 'north-easter' arose. 15 It took hold of the ship and drove it out to
sea away from the land. It was impossible to battle against such a
wind, so we had to allow ourselves to be driven along by it. 16 As we
passed a small island called Cauda, it was almost impossible to
keep the lifeboat secure. 17 The crew had to hoist it aboard and even
had to pass ropes under the ship itself to strengthen the hull.

The crew feared we would run aground on the sand bars of Syrtis off the African coast, so they lowered the anchor and allowed the ship to be driven by the wind. 18 The gale-force winds continued to batter the ship to such an extent that on the following day the crew began to jettison the cargo. 19 On the third day of the storm they even threw overboard the ships tackle and other equipment. 20 We saw neither the sun nor the moon for several days as the storm continued to rage. It seemed that there was no hope of being spared ourselves.

Paul encourages those on board the ship (27:21-44)

21 Everyone had gone for days without food before Paul addressed them: "Men, you should have heeded my advice and not set sail from Crete; then you would not have suffered this damage and loss, and your own lives would not have been in danger. 22 But now I urge you not to lose heart. Maintain your courage, for I assure you that no-one's life will be lost; only the ship shall be destroyed. 23-24 Last night the God to whom I belong and whom I serve sent an angel to me. He stood by my side and said, 'Paul do not fear. You have to stand trial before Caesar, and God has graciously granted you the safety of all who sail with you.' 25 So, men, maintain your courage. I believe that everything will happen exactly as God has told me. 26 But we must run this ship aground on an island."

27 We were still being driven across the Adriatic Sea on the fourteenth day of the storm when the crew sensed at about midnight that we were nearing land. 28 When they took soundings they found the water was about a hundred and twenty feet deep. When they took another sounding shortly afterwards, they found it was ninety feet deep. 29 To prevent being dashed against the rocks, they dropped four anchors from the stern and prayed for daylight. 30 The sailors let down the lifeboat into the sea, in an attempt to escape from the ship. They made it appear that they were letting down further anchors from the bow. 31 But Paul told the centurion and the soldiers: "Unless these men stay aboard the ship, they cannot be saved." 32 So the soldiers cut the ropes that held the lifeboat and allowed it to fall away.

33 Just before daybreak Paul urged everyone to eat, saying: "For the past fourteen days you have been in constant danger and have eaten nothing. 34 Now I urge you to eat, for you will need strength to survive. Not a hair of your heads will be lost." 35 Having said this Paul took some bread and thanked God for it before them all; then he broke it and began to eat. 36-37 This encouraged everyone else and

they all did likewise, all 276 who were on board. 38 When everyone
had eaten, the crew lightened the ship by throwing the grain overboard.

39 At first light they were unable to recognise the coastline, but
they saw a sandy bay that appeared suitable for beaching the boat
if they could. 40-41 So they cut the anchors adrift, leaving them in the
sea, and untied the ropes that had secured the rudder, then they
hoisted the foresail and headed for the beach, but the ship ran
aground on a sand bar. The bow stuck fast and would not move,
while the stern was smashed to pieces by the pounding of the
waves.

42 The soldiers intended to kill the prisoners to ensure that they
did not escape by swimming ashore. 43 But because the centurion
wanted to spare Paul's life, he did not allow them to do so. Instead
he ordered that those able to swim were to jump overboard first and
make for the beach. 44 The rest were to cling to planks of wood from
the ship, and in this way everyone reached land safely.

Shipwrecked on Malta (28:1-6)

28 Once safely ashore we discovered that the island was called
Malta. 2 The local people treated us with great kindness.
They welcomed us warmly and, because it was both wet and cold,
they built a fire. 3 Paul gathered an armful of wood but as he put it
on the fire a poisonous viper, driven out by the heat, fastened onto
his hand. 4 When the local people saw the snake hanging from his
hand, they said to each other: "This man must be guilty of murder.
He may have escaped from the sea but justice has been served on
him and he cannot live." 5 However, Paul merely shook the snake off
into the fire, totally unharmed. 6 Those watching expected him to
swell up with the poison or suddenly fall dead; yet after waiting
some time it became obvious that he had come to no harm. So then
they had a change of mind and decided he must be a god.

Paul heals an island official (28:7-10)

7 The chief official of the island, Publius, owned a nearby estate and
he welcomed us to his home, where he extended hospitality to us
for three days. 8 His father was sick with fever and dysentery. So
Paul went to pray for him; he laid his hands on him and healed him.
9 Other sick people on the island then came, and they also were
healed. 10 They truly honoured us and gave us all the supplies we
needed when we were ready to sail.

Paul encouraged by believers en route (28:11-16)

[11] For three months we wintered on the island before sailing in an
Alexandrian ship with the twin gods Castor and Pollux as its figure-
head. [12] We called at Syracuse where we stayed for three days before
setting sail for Rhegium. [13] Then, after arriving there, a southerly
wind arose enabling us to reach Puteoli on the following day.
[14] There we found some believers with whom we stayed for a week
before travelling on to Rome. [15] The believers there were expecting
us and came as far as the Forum of Appius and the Three Taverns
to meet us. When Paul saw them he was encouraged and thanked
God.

[16] When we arrived at Rome itself, Paul was placed under house
arrest, with only a single soldier to guard him.

Paul shares the truth with Jewish leaders in Rome (28:17-31)

[17] Three days later, Paul called the Jewish leaders together and said
to them: "My brothers, I was arrested in Jerusalem and handed over
to the Romans, even though I was not guilty of any offence against
our people or the customs of our forefathers. [18] After examining me
they wanted to release me as I did not deserve the death penalty.
[19] When the Jewish leaders objected, I was forced to appeal to Caesar,
although I had no intention of pressing charges against my own
people. [20] This is why I wanted to see you and talk with you. I am
bound with this chain because of my faith in the hope of Israel, the
Messiah."

[21] They replied: "We have not received any letters about you from
Judea and none of the brothers who come from there has reported
anything bad about you. [22] But we want to hear for ourselves what
you believe, for we are aware that everywhere people are denouncing
these Christians."

[23] They arranged a meeting with Paul when an even greater number
of Jews came to the place where he was staying. He explained the
Kingdom of God to them from morning until evening, trying to
persuade them from the law of Moses and from the prophets that
Jesus is the Messiah. [24] He convinced some, but others refused to
believe. [25-26] So they disagreed among themselves and left after
Paul's final statement: "The Holy Spirit spoke the truth to our forefathers when He spoke through the prophet Isaiah, 'Go to these
people and tell them, 'You will forever hear but never understand.
You will always be looking but never perceiving.' [27] For the hearts of
these people have become hardened; they cannot hear with their

ears, and they have closed their eyes to the truth. If this was not the case they would be able to see with their eyes, hear with their ears and understand with their hearts; then they would turn to me in repentance and I would heal them.'

[28] "Therefore I want you to understand that salvation has been
sent to those who will listen – the Gentiles!" [29] At this the Jews
departed, arguing and disputing among themselves.

[30] Paul lived in his own rented house for two years, welcoming all
who came to him. [31] He preached about the Kingdom of God and
taught about the Lord Jesus Christ boldly and without any hindrance!

28:26-27 Isaiah 6:9-10

ROMANS

Introduction: Jesus, God and Man (1:1-4)

1 From Paul, a servant of Christ Jesus, who called me to be an
apostle, setting my life apart for the cause of God's gospel, 2 the
good news He promised long ago through His prophets, as recorded
in the Holy Scriptures. 3-4 This gospel is about His Son, who was both
God and Man. As far as His human nature is concerned, He was a
descendant of the royal line of David. As for His divinity, His God
nature, God's own Spirit of holiness declared with power that He
was the long-expected Christ or Messiah, God's own Son, and this
was demonstrated by His resurrection from the dead. So Jesus
Christ is our Lord!

God's grace on those who believe (1:5-15)

5 It was through Him and for the outworking of His purposes that I
received the grace, the spiritual enabling, to be an apostle, calling
people from the nations to be obedient to God, an obedience only
made possible through faith in Jesus Christ. 6 And you also are
included among those who have been called by God to belong to
Jesus Christ.

7 I am writing this to all of you in Rome and to all who are loved
by God and are called to be saints, those whom He has set apart for
Himself and His purposes.

May God our Father and the Lord Jesus Christ impart grace and peace to you, everything you could ever need to be at one with Him and to serve Him faithfully.

8 First of all, I thank my God through my Lord Jesus Christ for all
of you and for all you mean to me. I am so thankful because the
quality of your faith and trust in Jesus is now known everywhere;
yes, all over the world!

9-10 God knows how faithful I am in praying for you. I serve Him
with all my heart and strength by preaching the good news about
Jesus and I pray that it may be God's will that I should come and
visit you. 11 I am eager to see you in order to impart to you some gift

from God's Spirit to enable you to be strong in your faith and witness. 12 But I am sure that I will also receive from you as well, that we will be able to encourage one another as we share our faith together.

13 I want you to know that on many occasions I have planned to come to you but until now it has not proved possible. I want to see a harvest of souls for God's Kingdom being reaped among you in the same way that I have been privileged to witness in other nations.

14 I feel an obligation towards every nation, to both those who are wise in accepting the gospel and the foolish who live in a way that is deeply offensive to God. 15 This is why I am so keen to preach in Rome, to encourage you and to challenge those who do not believe in Jesus!

The power of the gospel (1:16-17)

16 I could never be ashamed of believing and proclaiming the gospel. I know that it is God's powerful way of making salvation available to everyone who believes in Jesus, first the Jews to whom He came as Man, then also for people of other nations. 17 All who believe the good news of Jesus are saved because they are placed in a right relationship with God, regardless of who they are or of what they have done in the past. This relationship with God can only be received as a gift from Him, and is given to those who place their faith in who Jesus is and what He has done for them. It is a matter of faith from beginning to end. Nothing we could ever do by our own efforts could ever make us pleasing to God or place us in a relationship of righteousness with Him; of being made fully acceptable to Him. This is borne out by the fact that the scriptures declare that those who are acceptable to God will live by faith.

God's judgment on sin (1:18-32)

18 To appreciate this good news, you also have to understand the bad news, that God's anger towards all the sin, ungodliness and wickedness in which people indulge is revealed from heaven. Yes, this anger is as real as His love.

19 We know the truth about God through our faith in the gospel. Yet God has also made plain to those who do not believe that He is real. 20 People only have to look at the creation around them to know that an invisible hand has brought into being all they can see. The visible creation is the work of the One who is invisible! So no man has any excuse for believing that God does not exist, simply because he does not want to be accountable to a higher authority.

21 Some have known that God is real, but they have had no desire
to honour Him or to be thankful for all He has given them. The way
they think is futile; they are truly foolish people with no understanding of how important it is to know God personally.

22-23 Many consider themselves wise; they exalt their reason about
the revelation of truth God has given us. They think they are so
clever, yet the reality is this: instead of knowing God's glory and
being part of His Kingdom, they worship their intellectual prowess,
or other people that they idolise. They even make images of people
or animals of various kinds and worship them!

24 It seems unbelievable that they should do such things. But God
has allowed them to do exactly what they want. They fulfil the
desires of their sinful hearts by indulging in perverse acts of sexual
impurity with one another. Their bodies were created for God's glory
and honour, not for such depravity.

25 Instead of believing the truth about God as the Creator they are
content to be deceived, considering it fine to do whatever they
want, without any reference to their Creator. It does not occur to
them that they were made to fulfil His purposes! However, you
know that God is to be praised forever. Amen! It shall be so!

26 You see, God will not interfere with our free will or it would not
be possible for us to choose to love Him. So He has allowed the
ungodly to indulge their lusts, even though He hates such behaviour.
Women have unnatural relations with other women, something He
never intended. 27 Likewise, some men are inflamed with lust for
one another instead of enjoying natural relations with women. The
acts they indulge in are unmentionable, but sadly each will receive
the penalty which is inevitable for such perversion, unless of course
they repent and turn to Christ.

28 Is this likely when they have already thrown away the opportunity to know God and to please Him? God has allowed their
minds to become more and more depraved as they seek further
ways to please themselves. 29 Their lives are already filled with every
kind of sin, greed and depravity, all of it evil in God's eyes.

Just think of all the other ways people have no regard for God's
order. Some are full of envy, their lives eaten away by discontent.
There is murder and conflict wherever you look. People are corrupt,
deceiving others, often motivated by such greed that they do not
care about anybody else. Gossip is rife. 30 Some think nothing of
slandering others. They are God-haters, and proud of the fact. People
are insolent, arrogant, full of boasting. They think up new ways of
doing what is evil. Children disobey their parents without any

respect for authority. 31 There are so many whose lives have no meaning. They are people without faith, with no compassion for others, absolutely ruthless in the way they use others for their own ends.

32 If they know anything about God's commands they certainly do not take any notice of them! However they fail to realise that He is the only One who will ultimately judge them. He has already made clear that those who live in such ways deserve death, a spiritual separation from Him eternally. Even though they are warned of this, they continue to do the very things that will lead to their own condemnation, and they even applaud others who live in the same way.

Beware of judging others (2:1-4)

2 Beware of judging others, for in judging them you may be condemning yourself if you are guilty of doing the same things. There is no excuse for these judgmental attitudes. 2 God alone is the true Judge, as we all know well! He is the Truth and so always judges the immoral and ungodly with true justice.

3 When you, in your human frailty, judge them, even though you also sin in similar ways, do you think this diverts attention away from yourself so that you will avoid God's judgment on your own life? 4 Such an attitude would be to treat with contempt the wonderful kindness, tolerance and patience He has shown you. Surely you realise that God is so merciful that He can lead people to repentance, to turn away from a life of sin!

Do what is right in God's eyes (2:5-11)

5 If you have a stubborn and unrepentant heart it is only a matter of time before God catches up with you and you experience His wrath yourself. Listen, when He comes to judge, people will see that His wrath is as real as His love. 6 He has promised that 'each person will be rewarded for what he or she has done.' 7 If you are going to be judged for your actions, how important it is to do what is good and right in God's eyes, for this demonstrates that you are serious about desiring to experience His glory and honour and to receive the immortality that comes with His gift of eternal life.

8 On the other hand, if you only live for yourself, rejecting the truth of God's Word that reveals what is right and wrong in His eyes, there will inevitably be a price to pay. You show that you care nothing

2:6 Psalm 62:12

about God's anger and judgments. 9 There will be condemnation for every person whose life has been full of evil, whether he be Jewish or not. 10 But there will be glory, honour and peace for everyone who does what is good, for the Jew first and then also for the Gentile. 11 God will not show favouritism; He will judge with justice and in truth.

Live in obedience to His Word (2:12-16)

12 It is not a matter of being legalistic; for God will judge each according to his knowledge of what is right. He expects a higher standard from those who claim to know what is right. 13 You see, knowing what God commands does not make you righteous in His sight; it is obedience to His Word that He considers to be the right way to live.

14 Even in nations where there is ignorance of God's law, some people have an inward awareness of what is right and so act accordingly. 15 It is as if God's purpose is somehow written on their hearts, even though they have never been taught God's commandments. Their consciences tell them what is right or wrong; they feel uncomfortable when they do wrong, but at peace when they do what is right.

16 On the Day of Judgment, God will judge each person according to the nature of his or her heart. No secrets will be hidden from Him. How wonderful that we can be spared from the judgment we deserve through faith in Jesus Christ, as my gospel declares.

The Jews are also to live in obedience (2:17-29)

17 If you are a Jew you may boast that God has given your people the law so that you can relate to Him as your God. 18 You may claim to have clear knowledge of His will and that you live on a higher level of revelation from the ungodly nations. 19 You may even be convinced that you are able to guide the spiritually blind and give light to those who live in darkness. 20 You may consider yourself wise and others foolish by comparison, because they lack your knowledge. You probably think that you are able to teach young people about God's ways. You have these attitudes because you consider the law embodies the knowledge of God's true will.

21 Then let me ask you: those of you who teach others, do you need teaching yourselves? Those who preach against sin such as stealing, are you guilty of stealing yourselves? Do you withhold from God what is rightfully His? 22 You who speak against committing

adultery, are you guilty of adultery yourself, at least in your hearts?
You who say that you hate idols, do you idolise yourself or others?
[23]You who are proud about the law, do you keep every command God
has given, or do you dishonour God through your own disobedience?
[24]God has said that His Name is blasphemed and dishonoured
among the nations because a proper example has not been set by
those to whom He has given revelation of His will!

[25]To you Jews, circumcision is an outward sign that you belong to
God's covenant people. So it is a meaningful sign of your relationship
to God if your aim is to obey His laws. However, if you live in disobedience to God your circumcision means nothing. [26]In fact, an
uncircumcised person who obeys God is living as if he is circumcised.
[27]Such a one may not have the outward sign of belonging to God's
Jewish people, yet his obedience shows you up and is a challenge to
you. His obedience condemns your disobedience, even though you
have been given the written commandments and the outward sign
of circumcision. You are the lawbreaker, not the obedient person!

[28]I would go as far as to say that the one who only has the outward
mark of circumcision but not an obedient heart, is not really a true
Jew. [29]The circumcision God wants is a circumcision of the heart,
something only the Holy Spirit can do. This is what makes a real
Jew and this is someone in whom the Lord Himself delights!

God is Righteous and Just (3:1-8)

3 When you consider this, what advantages do you have as a
Jew because of your circumcision? [2]A great many. For a start,
God entrusted His words to you; He spoke to you as a nation through
the prophets and then by His own Son. [3]Although not all believe
God's words, this did not affect His faithfulness towards those He
had chosen. It is unthinkable that He would ever be unfaithful; He
is true and trustworthy in every way, even though no man can
make such a claim about himself. [4]If every man was a liar, God
would still remain true!

It has been written that 'God is proved right when He speaks and
His judgments are always sound.'

[5]You see, no matter how unrighteous we may be, this only serves
to show the wonder of God's righteousness by comparison. So we
can never accuse God of being unjust in His judgments, can we? If
we are objects of His anger, that is no more than we deserve, looking
at it from a purely human perspective. [6]We could never accuse Him

3:4 Psalm 51:4

of wrongdoing! For He would be in no position to judge the world if He were like us.

[7] There are always some who want to twist the truth. I have heard it suggested that if our sin reveals God's truthfulness and glory by comparison, then we should not be condemned as sinners! [8] What a crazy argument! You may as well say straight out that we are free to do whatever evil we desire, so that good will come out of our sin. It might be difficult to believe, but some slander us by suggesting that this is what we teach. Such slanderers are certainly under condemnation themselves.

Salvation attained by faith (3:9-31)

[9] What is the conclusion of my argument? Am I suggesting that we Jews are better than others? No, that is to miss the point altogether. I have already stated clearly that all are under the power of sin, whether Jew or non-Jew. [10] It is written:

> "There is not even one person who is righteous, not one.
> [11] No-one understands God, nobody who truly seeks Him.
> [12] For all have turned away from Him and have chosen to walk in their own corrupt ways, and so have become worthless in His sight. Nobody is good in all he or she does. Nobody!
>
> [13] "People speak so many things at odds with God's truth that their throats are open graves; it is common practice to speak deceitfully. Their words are often filled with venomous poison. [14] They curse God and are bitter in their attitudes towards Him. [15] Mankind is renowned for violence, destroying lives that God counts precious. [16-17] No wonder the course of their lives contains so much misery that they have no hope and no peace. [18] In short, they have no fear of God; they have no desire to honour Him although He is their Lord."

[19] This seems a desperate situation. And it is, for those who live under religious law; for when you look at the demands that God makes of His people, everyone is silenced. Nobody in the world can claim to have obeyed His laws perfectly. [20] For this reason, there is not one person that could be judged as right in God's eyes because of his or her perfect obedience to His will. All the religious law does

3:12 Psalm 14:1-3
3:13 Psalm 5:9, 140:3
3:14 Psalm 10:7
3:15-17 Isaiah 59:7-8
3:8 Psalm 36:1

is to point out our inability to please God in our own strength, proving
that we are all sinners.

21 But God has His answer for this seemingly hopeless situation.
He has made it possible for us to be right and acceptable in His eyes,
but this has nothing to do with religious law. The writings of the
Prophets and even the law itself pointed to the way that God would
solve this dilemma. 22 He provided the gift of righteousness! Yes, we
can be made right in His eyes, free from the guilt of sin and all condemnation, but only through faith in Jesus Christ. This righteousness,
this total acceptance by God, is His gift to all who believe in Jesus
as their Saviour and Lord.

23 Listen, I have made it clear that every living person, Jew or non-
Jew, has sinned and has therefore fallen short of the glory God
intended for mankind. 24 The good news is this: that anyone, Jew or
non-Jew, can now be made completely acceptable to God. This
acceptance is a free gift from God, the work of His grace, because
Jesus gave His life for us on the cross, making it possible for all our
sin and failure to be forgiven.

25 God even made His own Son the perfect sacrifice that would
restore us to unity with God. Only faith in the power of His blood
is needed to cleanse us and make us right with God.

Why should it be necessary for God to make His own Son a sacrifice?
Because He had to demonstrate that He is just. He could not say
that our sin did not matter, even though until the cross He had not
shown the full judgment our sins deserved. 26 Sin had to be judged
because it separates us from God. So His just and righteous judgment
on sin had to be executed. But instead of punishing us sinners, His
Son bore the punishment we deserve. As you believe that Jesus did
this for you personally, so you are made totally righteous and
acceptable in God's sight!

27 What have you to boast about? You did absolutely nothing to
make your salvation possible. You cannot claim that you are right
with God because of your perfect obedience to His commands. Your
salvation is possible only by your personal faith in Jesus and what
He has done for you.

28 We teach clearly that there is no other way for a person to be
saved from his or her sins and the eternal condemnation he or she
deserves. Faith in Jesus is the only way of salvation, and this has
nothing to do with God's law. 29 It is clear, then, that He is God not
only of the Jews but of anyone of any nation who puts his faith in
Jesus. 30 There is only one God and He alone can make people
acceptable in His sight, regardless of their nationality, whether they

have been ritually circumcised or not. It is a matter of faith in Jesus, and faith alone!

[31] Does this mean that the religious law is of no account? No, for those who are made acceptable to God are then able to fulfil His will!

Abraham considered righteous (4:1-25)

4 Those of you who are Jews know that Abraham was our forefather. So what did he understand about all this? [2] If the basis
of Abraham's relationship with God had been the works he did, then he would have had cause to boast, although not before God. No one has cause to boast before Him!

[3] God's Word helps us to understand that 'Abraham was considered to be righteous because he believed God' – by faith, not by works.

[4] A man's wages are not a gift but his right because of the work he
has done to earn those wages. [5] However, the person who knows
that no amount of work can make him pleasing to God understands that he must put his faith in God's mercy, for only He is able to forgive sinners and make them acceptable and righteous in His eyes.

[6] David also understood this principle. He speaks of the way God has blessed those He accepts as righteous, quite apart from any works of their own:

> [7] "Blessed are those whose sins are forgiven because they
> have been covered by God's mercy. [8] Blessed is the person
> whose sins God will never hold against him."

[9-10] Are these blessings only for the Jews, or have they been extended to people of other nations? Well, we have already seen that it was Abraham's faith that put him into right relationship with God, and this had nothing to do with the fact that he was circumcised, for he was counted as righteous by God before his circumcision. In fact, the act of circumcision was a sign of the righteous relationship he could now enjoy with God. It was a seal of that relationship, a demonstration of God's approval of Abraham because of the faith he placed in the Lord.

[11] This means that Abraham is the father of all who are put right with God through their faith, no matter whether they are Jews or not. God regards as righteous and acceptable any who have put
their faith in Jesus Christ. [12] Of course, Abraham is the father of all

4:3 *Genesis 15:6*
4:8 *Psalm 32:1-2*

true Jews, those who have not only received the rite of circumcision,
but also walk as Abraham did, in the kind of faith he had before he
was circumcised.
13 Therefore, it was not through the law that was given much later
that Abraham and his sons received the amazing promise from
God, that he would inherit the nations of the world. No, it was
because he was brought into right relationship with God by his faith.
14 If those who lived by law could inherit the nations, there would
be no need of faith and God's promises would be worthless. 15 We
have seen that, because of disobedience, religious law can only lead
to failure and condemnation and God's subsequent judgment of
wrath. But at least the law points out where we go wrong!
16 So we can see clearly that God's promises are given to a people
of faith; and they will only be fulfilled by His grace, what He does
in and through us. These promises are guaranteed to *all* the children
of Abraham, not only those brought up under the Jewish law, but
also to all who live by faith in God, trusting in Him and not themselves.
So, then, Abraham is the father of all of us who believe. 17 This fulfils
God's Word to Abraham: "I have made you a father of many
nations." In God's eyes, Abraham is a father to all who believe. He
believed that God gives life to those who are spiritually dead and is
able to speak of things that have not happened as if they had
already taken place, so sure is His Word.
18 If you had looked at Abraham's situation when God spoke to
him, you would have thought it beyond any possible hope or
expectation that he could become the father of many nations. But
God had spoken and said this would be the case; he would have
children in many nations!
19-20 When he was about a hundred years old and his wife Sarah
way beyond the time when she could bear a child naturally, Abraham
still believed God's promise without wavering in his faith. Sexually
his body must have seemed as good as dead, yet he was not guilty
of unbelief about God's promise that he would have a son.
21 Instead, he was strengthened in his faith and gave glory to God for
the outcome. He was utterly convinced that God had the power to
make possible what He had promised, even if, humanly, it looked
impossible.
22 So you can see why God considered Abraham righteous. It was
because of his faith. 23-24 Yet this principle is not only for him, but for

4:17 Genesis 17:5

all of who believe in the One who raised Jesus from the dead; they are all considered righteous by God. 25 This is only possible because Jesus was deliberately made the sacrifice for our sins. Yes, He died and was raised back to life because this was the only way we could be made acceptable to God.

Forgiveness, eternal life and grace (5:1-11)

5 We come, then, to this wonderful conclusion. We have been brought back into right relationship with God, and made completely acceptable to Him, through our faith in Jesus Christ. 2 Through Him we now have peace with God, and all the blessings of His grace are made available to us by means of our faith. We stand daily in the flow of God's free gifts to us and we can rejoice that a greater revelation of His glory awaits us. This is our sure and certain hope.

3-4 At the same time, we can also rejoice in whatever cost, or even suffering, that is involved in being faithful to the Lord. Affliction teaches us perseverance and perseverance builds character. And it is part of our character to be people of hope, looking to the future positively. 5 Such hope does not end in disappointment because God has already filled our hearts with His love through His Holy Spirit, whom He has given to live within us.

6 You understand that at God's appointed time Christ died for all the ungodly. He did this while we were still powerless to please Him because of all our sins. 7 It is a rare event for anyone to die for another, even for someone who seems a good person, living a righteous kind of life. 8 How great the love that God has demonstrated in sending His Son to die for us, while we were still sinners and unacceptable to Him!

9 We can be sure of our acceptance because of the power of that sinless blood that Christ shed for us. We should be equally confident, then, that the process of salvation will continue in the future, that at the judgment that is to come we will be saved from God's anger, because of Jesus' great love for us.

10 We used to be God's enemies but now we have been reconciled to Him through the death of His own Son. His death has brought about our reconciliation; so we can be confident that the life He has given us will continue the work of salvation within our lives. 11 Such wonderful truth causes us to rejoice in God because of this reconciliation we have with Him through our Lord Jesus Christ. Now we are one with God!

Adam and Jesus Christ (5:12-21)

12 Understand, then, that sin entered the world through one man,
and the consequence of that sin is death; all will die because all have
sinned! 13 Sin existed long before God gave the law to His people. If
there had been no law, then men would not be aware of what God
regarded as sinful.

14 From Adam to the time of Moses, death reigned because people were living in sin through ignorance, not because they were deliberately disobeying God's commands. Adam was guilty of doing this, and everyone else followed him in doing what they wanted. Yet God was awaiting the time when He would undo Adam's sin by sending His own Son.

15 Many died because of one man, Adam. Now through the grace of one Man, Jesus Christ, God's grace flows to many and we can receive His gift of eternal life. One man brought sin and death. Another Man brought forgiveness and eternal life – for all who believe in Jesus Christ!

16 One man's sin brought judgment and condemnation. God's gift is entirely different in its consequences. Despite all our sin, His gift has restored us to a relationship of righteousness and total acceptance with Him!

17 Through the sin of one man, death reigned for all through that man. Now consider the contrast! Those who receive this wonderful grace that God has supplied and the gift of righteousness He imparts to those who believe in Him, are able to share in His Kingdom now, here on earth. They can share in the reign of the one Man, Jesus Christ; yes, even in this present life!

18 One man's sin led to condemnation for all mankind. Yet one act of righteousness, the sacrifice of God's perfect Son, has brought about more than acceptance; He has made His own life available to everyone who believes.

19 Through one man's disobedience many became sinners. Through one Man's obedience many are made righteous and totally acceptable in God's sight.

20 So why was the law given? In order that men would know
clearly what was sinful and their sense of guilt would increase.
Only then would they see their need of the grace that God made
available to deliver them from the consequences of their guilt. And
God's grace is so much greater than our sin. 21 Because of that grace,
sin no longer reigns in our lives, resulting in spiritual death. Now
grace reigns in us instead, because of God's gift of acceptance that

makes us able to receive the gift of eternal life, made possible through Jesus Christ our Lord.

Baptised into Christ (6:1-11)

6 What can we say in the face of such wonderful love and grace? Shall we continue to sin so that God will be even more gracious to us? [2] Certainly not! What a suggestion! We have died to sin; so can we continue to live in ways that displease God? [3] Surely you understand that all of us who have been baptised live now in Christ Jesus. Through our baptism we were made one with His death. [4] Our old sinful lives were even buried with Him. You were made one with His death and burial so that, as Christ was raised from the dead through the power of God's glory, you are now one with Him in His risen life.

[5] It is simple; if we have been united with Him in His death, we shall also certainly share in His resurrection. [6] You can be sure that your old self, lived outside of Christ, was crucified with Him, freeing you from the control of sin. [7] Now you are no longer a slave to sin, for your death on the cross freed you from your sinful nature!

[8] Now, because we died with Christ we believe that we will continue to live with Him. [9] Listen, it is clear that because Christ was raised from the dead, it is not possible for Him ever to die. Death can have absolutely no influence or control over Him. [10] He only needed to die once, and when He did so He dealt with the power of sin once and for all. Now He lives to reveal the truth of God and His amazing grace.

[11] In a similar way, realise that you can consider yourself to have died to sin, but that you are now raised to an entirely new life that you can enjoy through your unity with Christ as you live for God's glory!

Freed from the power of sin (6:12-23)

[12] So do not allow sin to reign in you now, no matter how much your body may sometimes crave for self-indulgence. Do not obey such evil desires. [13] Do not use the parts of your body for sinful purposes. Do not let them be instruments of sin. No, offer yourselves wholeheartedly to God, as those who have been carried through death into a new life. Then you will offer the parts of your body to God for His purposes. They will be instruments for doing what is right.

[14] Sin is not your master any longer. Neither do you live under religious laws, but in the grace that God has supplied for you.

15 Do you really think, as some suggest, that this means we can sin as much as we want because we are not under law? What a ridiculous suggestion! That would be a complete distortion of the truth.

16 Surely you can see that you are a slave to whatever controls your life! If you offer yourself to sin, you are a slave of sin and will obey your sinful instincts. Such a lifestyle leads to spiritual death. On the other hand, offering yourself to live in obedience to God leads to a life of righteousness.

17 I thank God that although you used to be slaves of sin, this is no longer the case. For you have obeyed wholeheartedly the teaching of God's truth that was revealed to you, and you are to be guardians of that truth. 18 For you have been liberated from sin and can now think of yourselves as slaves of doing what is right because you belong to God!

19 I am trying to put this in practical terms. You see, I know how weak you are naturally. That is true of all of us. Yes, you used to be slaves of impurity because of what you did with your bodies. Sin was on the increase in your lives. But now you use your bodies in the right way, you will do what is right, living holy lives that please our holy God.

20 When you were living as slaves of sin, righteousness certainly did not control your actions. 21 What reward did you gain from all that sin? Why, you are now ashamed of those things you once did! You wish you had never done them, and now you understand that all sin leads to spiritual death!

22 However, now that you are liberated from that past life of sin, you can live as God's slave. That is not bondage, for it leads to holiness and eternal life as your inheritance. 23 You have seen for yourself that sin pays wages: eternal death and separation from God. But God's gift to you is eternal life that is yours in Christ Jesus, your Lord.

Free from religious law (7:1-13)

7 I speak to you as my brothers and as those who know the religious law. You are aware that the law only has authority over a person while he is alive. When he has died it is of absolutely no relevance to him. 2 For example, a woman remains married to her husband as long as he lives; but if he dies her marriage also ends according to the law. She is free to marry again, if she so desires, without being guilty of adultery. 3 Whereas if she were to enter into another relationship while her husband was alive then she would be an adulteress.

4 So, my brothers, understand that it was only possible for you to become a living member of Christ's body because you had died to

the law first. You cannot be 'married' to both the law and Christ. It is clear that you live in Christ Jesus, He who was raised from the dead, so that now you might live a life that fulfils God's purpose for you, not simply obeying a set of religious laws. When you died with Christ you died to the religious law; now you are united with Him in His risen life.

5 In the past, when you were under the control of your flesh, your natural inclination was to sin and to break God's law. In fact, whatever the law says you are not to do aroused in you a perverse desire to do those very things. Consequently, you used your body in sinful ways that only led to spiritual death.

6 Yet the situation is now completely different. Because you have died with Christ, you are free from the sinful passions that once put you into bondage. You have been liberated from the very idea that you can please God by trying to obey a set of religious rules and regulations. You understand now that the only way you can serve God and please Him is by walking in the new way, led by the Holy Spirit. This is such a better way of life that it is pointless to return to your former way of trying to please God in ways that you failed to keep anyway!

7 There is no need to suggest that the law itself is sinful. That is out of the question. The law actually taught you what pleased God and what was sinful. How did I know it was wrong to covet other people's possessions? Only because under the law God said, 'Do not covet.' 8 Despite knowing that this is His command, I was still filled with longing for what others had. Knowing this was wrong caused an even greater desire for what I wanted for myself. I would not have been so guilty if I was ignorant that it was wrong to covet.

9 You see, when you know that a particular action is wrong and you still do it, then you sin knowingly and deliberately. The law made me even more guilty because I knew I was going against God's will when I sinned. 10 All these commands brought death, not life, because I could not obey them all! God intended the law for my good, but instead of bringing me life it produced death in me because I sinned by failing to obey all that He had commanded.

11 In those days I was so deceived, for although I failed again and again to obey God's laws, I thought I was still serving Him, and did not appreciate that really I was spiritually dead because of all my disobedience.

12 The law in itself is good, for it was given us by a holy God. All His commands are holy, right and good. 13 Did those commands create

7:7 Exodus 20:17

this death in me? Certainly not, for God has no desire to do such a thing. He had to show me that I had no power in myself to please Him. Even though what He commanded me to do was good, my sinful nature caused me to make wrong, sinful choices, which only goes to show how completely sinful I was, despite all my religious fervour.

Paul's former sinful life (7:14-25)

14 The law was not the problem; the fault was entirely mine. The law itself is spiritual because it is given by God. I came to realise that in my natural state I am unspiritual, a slave to sin and disobedience. 15 In fact, I often did not understand myself or why I made these wrong decisions. I wanted to please God, but ended up doing the very opposite, even though I hated the idea of being a sinner in His sight. 16 Even though I disobeyed the law, I have to admit that it is good and was given by God for my welfare.

17-18 The problem is this principle of sin that lived in me. I felt under its control and knew that nothing good lived in me, that is in my natural being. 19 For even though I wanted to do what is right, I was powerless to obey. I ended up doing the very thing I was determined not to do. I kept on sinning and doing what was evil in God's eyes. 20 To sin persistently in this way demonstrated that I was motivated by the sinful disposition that lived in me. It seemed I was out of control!

21 So this is the law that was at work in me: whenever I wanted to do what is good and right, evil was ready to work in me. 22-23 I could have God's law in my heart, but another law was seemingly in charge, urging me to sinful action. I felt there was a kind of war going on within me, a battle that I was constantly losing because I was a prisoner of the law of sin that urged me to use my body in sinful ways. 24 What a dilemma! What a mess! Can you see how wretched I felt about myself? Was there anyone who could save me from this terrible predicament? 25 Yes, thank God! And His name is Jesus Christ our Lord!

25 So in my heart and mind I considered myself a slave of God's law because I wanted to please Him, yet this principle of sin made me a slave of sin.

Saved from condemnation (8:1-4)

8 How wonderful to be liberated now from all the condemnation this continual failure brought. For those who live in Christ Jesus have been set free from all condemnation. 2 Through Christ Jesus a different principle now lives in me, a new law: the Spirit of

Life. He has set me free from the law of sin and death. 3 Under the
law I could not do what God wanted because of my weak, sinful
nature. God dealt with that by sending His own Son to become man,
to live among sinners and then to make His life a sinless offering to
God on their behalf.

Through His action God dealt with the condemnation under
which all sinners live. 4 In Christ, all the demands God expressed in
the laws He gave were fulfilled. So we now live in the good of what
He accomplished. 4 He succeeded where we had all failed miserably,
so that now we can live as if we had succeeded. His success has
become our success, so long as we no longer live in the weakness of
our old sinful nature but now live led by and filled by God's Spirit.

Led by the Spirit (8:5-14)

5 Those who live according to their own natural desires are always
intent on getting what they want for themselves. That is their focus.
But those who truly want to please God by being led by His Spirit
make Him their focus. 6 Sinful thinking leads to spiritual death; but
to allow your life to be under the control of the Holy Spirit will
result in sharing in God's life and knowing His peace.

7-8 Sinful thinking is totally against God's will. Such attitudes
show there is no submission to Him and His purposes, for you cannot
serve God while your mind is full of sinful, selfish thoughts. That
would suggest you were being controlled by your desires, not His!

9 However, this is not the case with you. You are not under the
control of selfish, sinful desires because you have surrendered your
life to God to be under the power and influence of His Spirit, who
actually lives in you. You would not be a Christian at all if you did
not possess the Holy Spirit. 10 But because His Spirit is in you, Christ
is in you. Your body may still crave for self-indulgence, yet your
spirit has now been brought to life by His Spirit, so that in your
heart you want to do what is right before God.

11 This Spirit who lives in you is the same Spirit who raised Jesus
from the dead. If He could do that, then He is certainly able to give
God's life to your natural bodies, because His Spirit lives in you.

12 This means that you no longer are obliged to obey your sinful
desires, my brothers. 13 To do that would lead to spiritual death. Now
you have God's Spirit in you, enabling you to rule over any lingering
sinful desires to indulge your fleshly instincts. So the Spirit enables
you to enjoy real life, not death. 14 You see, those who live as God's
sons are happy to be led by God's Spirit.

We are God's children (8:15-25)

15 When He came to live in you, He did not lead you back to your
past life, making you a slave of fear again. No, you received the
Spirit that enables you to live as a son of God. You can call Him,
'Father, my Father.' 16 The Holy Spirit urges us to remember that we
are God's children; to know this deep in our hearts. 17 For if we
know we are His children, then we know also that we are His heirs.
Yes, we are heirs of God and inherit all His blessings along with
Christ. We may have to face cost in being obedient to Him, but this
is only so that we will also share eternally in His glory!

18 Now you can see why I consider my current predicament as a
minor inconvenience compared with the wonderful glory that will
be revealed in us. 19 Why, even creation itself is in suspense, longing
for God's sons to reveal who they are. 20-21 You see, it was His will
that His purposes for His creation would be frustrated until this
happens. People did not choose this frustration for themselves; it
was imposed on them by God, because creation can only be liberated
from bondage, from that death principle we see at work all around
us, by being brought into the liberty that God's children enjoy
because they know and reflect His glory.

22 Everywhere around us it seems that creation is groaning just
like a woman about to give birth. 23 There is even a sense in which
we believers are also groaning inwardly. Although we know the
Spirit is already at work within us, we long for the time when we
will go to be with the Lord as His sons, when we experience the
resurrection of our bodies. 24 This is the hope we have because of the
salvation we have received.

You cannot see now that for which you hope, because hope refers
to what lies in the future. If we could experience what we hope for,
that would not be true hope. How can anyone say he already has
what he hopes for? 25 No, we have to wait patiently for what God
has promised us in the future.

Depend on the Spirit (8:26-34)

26 Similarly, we depend on the help the Holy Spirit gives us because
of our weakness. We are so weak in ourselves that we do not even
know how to pray. Yet the Holy Spirit Himself prays in us and for
us, sometimes with such intensity that we find ourselves groaning;
no words can express the depth of what He is working in us.

27 God searches our hearts and He certainly knows what He causes
His Spirit to pray for us as His saints, the people He has set apart

for Himself. His Spirit will always pray in and through us according
to God's will.

28 We can be sure, then, that in everything God is working for the
welfare of those who love Him, those He has called according to His
purpose. 29 He knew who would be His, because He decided before
He created us that He would have a people who would be like His
Son, those who would live as His brothers and sisters.

30 This is why He called you as part of His eternal purpose. This
is why, having called you, He made you totally acceptable to Him.
This is why you are destined for the glory that is already yours in
Christ!

31 How can we respond to such wonderful truths? If we are part
of God's divine will, how can any opposition prevent His purposes
for us? 32-34 So intent is He on seeing His plans fulfilled, He did not
protect His Son from the necessary cost of giving His life for us all,
because through His grace He wanted to give us everything that
belongs to Christ. Yes, what He has, we are to have. He died, was
raised back to life and is now seated in glory at God's right hand,
all for our benefit. His blood liberates us. His Spirit enables us and
speaks on our behalf.

God's love for us (8:35-39)

35 So who could ever separate us from God's love for us, a love He
has so clearly demonstrated already? Do you really think God has
forgotten all about you because you experience trouble or find the
going tough, or because you have to suffer persecution of some
kind? Do you really think God has stopped loving and caring for
you because there is famine, or you are in great need, or you are in
danger even of losing your life? 36 It was written: 'It was for your
sake that we faced death and are as sheep that are being led away
to be slaughtered.'

37 No, in all these things we are more than victorious through
Him, for He has already won the victory for us and demonstrated
such love for us. 38-39 I am totally convinced that death cannot separate
us from Him or His love. Neither can anything that could ever happen
to us in this life! No angels can stand in the way of God's personal
love for us, nor can any demons prevent that love. Nothing in the
present, nor anything that could happen in the future, would be
able to destroy God's love for us. There is no spiritual power, nor
any created power, that will ever be able to separate us from God's

8:36 Psalm 44:22

love for us that has already been so clearly expressed in Christ Jesus
our Lord!

The Jews rejected Jesus (9:1-5)

9 My only desire is to speak the truth in Christ. I do not want to
lie or exaggerate. My conscience is clear about this and the
Holy Spirit, who works in and through me, bears witness to this.
2 He knows how heavy my heart is, and He understands the great
sorrow and anxiety I feel about my fellow Jews. 3 There are times
when I feel that I would be prepared to be cursed and separated
from Christ if only this would cause people of my own race, the
people of Israel, to turn to Him.

4 Because they are His chosen people, they are the very ones who
should know the wonder of being adopted as His sons. They should
be able to experience God's glory. They should be part of the new
covenant and the new relationship with God, as they were His people
under the old covenant. They received the law; so God longs for
them to accept His grace. He gave them the temple as a place of
worship, but they rejected Jesus Christ when He came as God's
living Temple. God gave them wonderful promises, but they are
only fulfilled by faith in Christ, a faith they do not have.

5 The Lord is the God of Abraham, Isaac and Jacob, their forefathers,
and when Jesus came as a man He came as a Jew. All this was the
purpose of God, who is to be praised forever. Amen! This shall be
so!

God's Sovereign will (9:6-24)

6 All this does not mean that God's Word is faulty or that His purposes
have failed. The failure is not with God, but with His people. It is
clear that not all who are the descendants of Israel are true Israelites.
7 Because they can trace their ancestry back to Abraham, does not
make them His true children. Far from it! God's true children would
be like Isaac, children born as a result of His actions in fulfilment of
His promise. 8 To be born naturally does not make anyone a child of
God!

It is those who believe His promises who are really Abraham's
offspring. 9 God told Abraham that at His appointed time He would
ensure that Sarah would give birth to a son, even though that
seemed physically impossible.

10 Besides this, we can see that God's purpose was worked out
through Isaac's sons. Rebekah gave Isaac two sons, born as twins.

11-13 But even before their birth, when neither had done anything good or bad, God decreed that the older one would serve the younger. This was His purpose, His calling on Jacob's life, not the result of anything he had done. It was simply God's purpose to use Jacob rather than Esau, who counted his birthright and blessings of such little value.

14 Shall we charge God with being unjust? Never! His judgment was proved to be correct! 15 What did He say to Moses?

> "I will have mercy on the one on whom I have chosen to have mercy, and I will show compassion to the one to whom I have chosen to show compassion."

16 Whatever God does depends on the ways in which He has chosen to reveal His mercy. No desire or striving on man's part can ever bring His will about. 17 Look at what the scriptures say about Pharaoh: "I raised you up for My purposes so that I could display My awesome power, and do such mighty things that My Name would be known throughout the world!"

18 He can show His mercy to anyone to whom He chooses to show His mercy; and He can harden the heart of anyone who opposes Him.

19 Now someone may want to argue that if God is able to harden hearts, why does He blame us for disobedience to His will? 20 Who do you think you are, to judge God for the way in which He has chosen to work? Is it right for a created one to even question His Creator? Can you ask God why He made you as you are, as if your failings are His fault? 21 A potter can make whatever he wants out of a lump of clay, some beautiful articles and others for mundane, everyday purposes.

22 So consider this. How is God to reveal everything about Himself? How can He show people that His anger is real unless there are those who deserve to be judged and condemned? Yet at the same time he showed such great patience with the one who opposed Him, even though He knew what the final outcome would be!

23 By contrast, God is also able to reveal the richness of His glory that He shows to those who receive His mercy, those like us who He has determined in His pre-ordained purposes should know His glory. 24 For whether we are Jewish or not, He has called us believers to know His mercy and His glory!

9:15 Exodus 33:19

Christ: a stumbling block to the Jews (9:25-33)

25 He said through His prophet Hosea: "I will call 'My people' those
who formerly were not My people; I will declare My personal love
for those who had not known My love." 26 He also says that it will
come about that people who were told that they were not His chosen
ones shall become sons of the living God.

27 God spoke about Israel through Isaiah, saying that their number
would be as grains of sand on the seashore, but that only a select
number would know His salvation. 28 With great speed the Lord will
in due time judge those living on earth; and His judgment will
prove to be final!

29 Isaiah also said that if it were not for His mercy, the Lord
Almighty would have no descendants at all. For if He treated all of
us as we deserved, we would be wiped out like Sodom and Gomorrah!

30 So what conclusion can we reach? Even non-Jewish people, who
never even sought to live in ways that are right and pleasing to
God, have been put right with God and made acceptable to Him as
a result of their faith. 31 Yet Jews, who sought to be right with God
through trying to obey the law, never obtained their objective.
32 Why was this? Because instead of living by faith, they tried to
make themselves acceptable to God through their own accomplishments. They stumbled over Jesus, the 'stumbling stone', by rejecting
Him. 33 God had warned that He would lay among His chosen people
a Stone that would cause people to stumble and a Rock that would
be their downfall. And He was proved correct. But He also said that
anyone who put their trust in that Rock would never be put to
shame!

Paul's desire for the Jews to know Jesus (10:1-21)

10 Dear brothers, I have a longing in my heart that I express in
prayer to God, that those of my own race will come to know
the salvation that has been made possible through their Messiah,
Jesus. 2 I can tell you from first hand experience that the Jewish people
are serious about God, but the religious fervour they show does not
come from the revelation that God has given in His Son. 3 As a result,
they do not understand that we can only be put right with God and
made acceptable to Him through faith in Jesus Christ. Instead they

9:25 *Hosea 2:23*
9:26 *Hosea 1:10*
9:28 *Isaiah 10:22-23*
9:29 *Isaiah 1:9*
9:33 *Isaiah 8:14, 28:16*

persist in trying to establish their own righteousness through their own actions; they refuse to accept that God has now provided a far better way, the only way to true righteousness and acceptance.

[4] With the coming of Christ and the establishing of the new way, the religious law that God gave has now been superseded. Everyone who accepts that Jesus is the Way can now receive God's gift of righteousness, regardless of his or her race.

[5] Moses summed up the kind of righteousness that was possible under the law by saying that the person who lives by the law will
do what the law says. [6] However, there is now a different approach
because of the total acceptance that He has been given by faith in Jesus.

A believer does not need to have the heart attitude that he has to
break through to heaven to bring Christ down into this life. [7] Neither
does he have to think that he must wait until death before he can know the Lord personally!

The word of truth and faith (10:8-21)

[8] What should He believe then? "The Word of truth is near you now; if it is in your heart it will be expressed in what you say." It is this
word of faith that I am explaining to you. [9] If you openly declare that
Jesus is the Lord and have heart conviction that God raised Him
from the dead, you will certainly be saved. [10] You see, your faith
must come from your heart, for then you are made one with God; but you must also openly declare your faith to receive the full salvation
that is His gift to you. [11] For it is written: "God will never put to
shame anyone who trusts in Him." [12-13] In the matter of faith there is
no difference between Jew and non-Jew. The same Lord Jesus is Lord of all and willingly gives His rich blessings to all who turn to Him, for it is also written: "Everyone who calls on the Lord's name shall receive salvation."

[14] But how is it possible for people to turn to Jesus if they do not believe who He is? How can they believe if they have never received revelation of the truth? And how will they ever hear unless
someone tells them about Him? [15] And who will the Lord send to
open their eyes and hearts to the truth?

It is written: "Those who bring the good news to others have
beautiful feet." [16] Sadly, not all Jews were prepared to accept the

10:5 Leviticus 18:5
10:8 Deuteronomy 30:14
10:11 Isaiah 28:16
10:13 Joel 2:32
10:15 Isaiah 52:7

good news. No wonder Isaiah said: "Lord, who has believed the message you gave us?" [17]Faith in the truth can only come when you have heard the truth, and that truth is contained in the words of Christ.

[18]I ask myself whether they truly heard. Then I realised that they certainly did because God's Word is now being proclaimed everywhere around the world. [19]I cannot help wondering whether the Jewish people understand the truth they heard. After all, God spoke through Moses by saying: "I will make my chosen nation jealous because of those who do not form a nation. I will make you angry because revelation is given to people who have no understanding of Me!"

[20]He says through Isaiah: "I was found by those who were not searching for Me; I made Myself known to those who did not even enquire about Me." [21]Yet Isaiah also tells us that God said: "I have continually held out My hands to My people, but they have been disobedient and obstinate."

A faithful remnant (11:1-12)

11 So I ask, has God rejected the Jews? Not at all! I am a Jew myself. I am descended from Abraham by birth, from the tribe of Benjamin. [2]God did not reject His chosen people; He came to them. Surely you know what the scriptures say about the way Elijah complained about Israel. [3]He said: "Lord, they have killed those you sent to them as prophets. They have desecrated your places of worship. It seems I am the only one who remains faithful to you, and they are trying to kill me too!" [4]How did God answer him? "I have seven thousand that I have kept faithful, who have refused to worship the false gods."

[5]The same is true today. There is a remnant, a small number of Jewish people whom God has chosen to know and receive His grace. [6]They understand that it is only by His free gift of grace, and not by their own works, that they have been made one with the Lord. They know that if they could achieve what they have received by their own efforts, God would not be the God of grace!

[7]So what conclusion do we reach? What the Jewish people longed for they did not receive. But those God has chosen to know His grace did receive what had been promised. Those who refused

10:16 Isaiah 53:1
10:19 Deuteronomy 32:21
10:20 Isaiah 65:1
10:21 Isaiah 65:2
11:3 1 Kings 19:10, 14
11:4 1 Kings 19:18

to accept Jesus as God's Son did so because of the hardness of their hearts. [8]This is why it is written that God caused them to be spiritually blind. They did not have eyes that could see or ears that could truly hear. And it is the same to this very day!

[9]David prayed prophetically by suggesting that their religious ways would become a trap for them. Their self-righteousness would be a stumbling block that would result in punishment. [10]They deserved to be spiritually blind and to remain so. They deserved to remain overburdened forever!

[11]There is another question we need to consider. Did the Jewish people fail to such an extent that they could never recover their place in God? Definitely not! It was because of their sin and rejection of the gospel that so many non-Jewish people are now being saved, and this should make the Jews jealous of what they have received. [12]But think of this: if their failure has brought God's great riches to others throughout the world and their emptiness has resulted in non-Jewish people receiving the great riches of God's grace, how much more wonderful will it be when they do enter into their inheritance and receive the fullness of God's life in Christ!

Gentile believers grafted in (11:13-24)

[13]Yes, I am now addressing those among you who are not Jewish. God has made me an apostle to the non-Jewish nations; He has sent me and given me this ministry among all these peoples. [14]I want to make the most of this calling, trusting that in doing so I will cause my own people to think again because they see how others are being blessed by God. Instead of being jealous, I want at least some of them to receive the salvation God wants for them.

[15]I have to admit that their present rejection of the gospel has enabled many throughout the world to be reconciled to God; yet I am excited about the prospect of what will happen when they accept Christ. Instead of the death of trying to please God by their own efforts, they will receive the free gift of His life!

[16]If one part of the lump of dough is considered holy, then the whole lump is holy! If the root of the tree is holy, then so are its branches!

[17]Israel can be likened to an olive tree; some of the original branches have been broken off. You non-Jewish believers were once wild olive shoots that have now been grafted into this tree. You are

11:8 Deuteronomy 29:4, Isaiah 29:10
11:10 Psalm 69:22-23

nourished by the sap that flows through your lives from the roots.
18 So you have no cause to boast or think that you have nothing to
do with Israel. It is obvious that you do not give life to the root; the
root gives life to you! 19 You could say that the unbelieving branches
were cut off so that you could be grafted into this olive tree. 20 That
is true. But you are only where you are by faith, not by your own
accomplishments. So you have nothing to boast about. Rather, you
should be in awe of what God has done. 21 If He dealt so strongly
with the unbelieving branches, He will deal just as strongly with you.

22 You see, God is both kind and strict. He enforces His judgments
strictly on those who reject His grace, but is kind to those who
believe, on the understanding that they will continue in faith and so
continue to be objects of His mercy. You do not want to fall into
unbelief and be cut out of this tree, do you?

23 If the Jewish people do not continue in their unbelief, they will
be grafted back into the tree. God is surely able to do such a thing!
24 If He could cut you out of a wild olive tree and graft you into the
tree He Himself has cultivated, how much easier it must be for the
branches that rightly belong to His tree to be grafted back into it!
After all, it was originally their tree!

God wants Israel to be saved also (11:25-36)

25 Brothers, I do not want you to be ignorant about this subject,
which to some is a mystery. You must not become conceited. The
reason why the Jewish people have been subjected to a hardening
of their hearts is so that God can gather into His Kingdom all the
non-Jewish people that He is calling. 26 But then He wants all Israel
to be saved also. It is written:

> "He who God sends as the deliverer of His people will
> come from among His chosen people, the Jews, and He
> will be the One to save them from their godless ways.
> 27 For they are still a covenant people; a people of promise
> and He will save them from all their sins."

28 At present they are enemies of the gospel, but only for your benefit.
Yet they still retain God's calling; they are still the objects of God's
love. He will still fulfil the promises given them through their forefathers. 29 For once God has called a people and set them apart for
Himself, He will not change His mind, just as He will not take away
the gifts He has already given us.

11:27 Isaiah 59:20-21

30-31 You were once disobedient towards God; yet now you have
received His mercy and forgiveness. This is only because the gospel
came to you through their disobedience. Just as you were disobedient
and have now been saved, cannot they also turn from their disobedience and also receive the same mercy and forgiveness from
God that you have already received? 32 God considered that all were
disobedient to Him, whether Jewish or non-Jewish; so all are in
need of His mercy. And He wants everyone to experience His mercy
and forgiveness.

33 I am overwhelmed by the extent of the great riches that come
from knowing and understanding God's wisdom. His judgments
cannot be questioned, and no one can do what only He can do in
leading people to salvation.

34 "Who can claim to understand everything about the way the
Lord thinks? Who could dare to give Him advice? 35 What could any
of us give to God that would obligate Him to give to us in return?"

36 Everything that we receive comes from God and is given through
Christ, all for the outworking of His purposes. Yes, it is true: all the
glory belongs to Him. He alone deserves to be honoured! Amen! It
shall be so.

Living sacrifices (12:1-3)

12 In the light of this wonderful mercy God has shown us, I
strongly encourage you, as my brothers, to give your bodies
to God in living sacrifice; do what is holy and pleasing to Him. This
is the kind of worship He really wants and that is the outworking
of the life of His Spirit who lives within us.

2 In order to live like this you cannot also live according to the
standards of the world around you. You need a completely different
mindset so that you are certain of God's will for your life and are
prepared to put His will into action, for His will is good; it pleases
Him because it is perfect!

3 God has given me apostolic grace and so I can tell all of you not
to think too highly of yourselves. No, have a realistic estimate of
yourselves, according to the faith God has graciously given you.

All members of the same body (12:4-15)

4 Every one of us has a body with several different parts, each with
its distinctive function. 5 In the same way, all those who belong to

11:34 Isaiah 40:13
11:35 Job 41:11

Christ form His one Body. So we all belong to Him and also to one another. [6]As with the parts of a human body, we do not all have the same functions. No, we have different gifts according to the way God has appointed that His grace is to operate in our lives. Some are particularly gifted to speak prophetically, bringing a word from God to others. The way they are able to do this effectively depends to what extent they live by faith in God. [7]Others have servant hearts and are therefore content to serve God by serving others. Still others are gifted to teach God's Word and they should use this gift for the benefit of others. [8]Some are really great at encouraging their fellow believers, and this should be recognised as a gift from God for the good of the whole Body. Others are called to give financially to help others and they should give generously.

The church needs leaders who realise the importance of their calling and so devote themselves to the welfare of those they lead. Others are people with great compassion and mercy, and so need to be joyful about the way they show God's love to others.

[9]For we must be sincere about the way in which we love others: from the heart, not simply as a duty. We should hate anything that God regards as evil, but love what He considers good.

[10-11]As members of the same Body, we are to be devoted to one another, loving each other as members of the same family. This involves honouring others above ourselves and always being eager to serve the Lord by doing whatever He asks of us, and doing it with all our hearts.

[12]We are also to radiate joy because we are a people of hope. Whenever we have to suffer affliction we are to bear it patiently. And we will be faithful in prayer. [13]We will be a people who love to give, sharing our resources with God's people who are in need and welcoming others into our homes.

[14]As members of Christ's Body you are to bless those who oppose you because of your faith. Yes, bless them, do not resent or curse them! [15]There will be times when you need to rejoice along with those who are happy and blessed, but other times when you will share in the grief of those who are mourning.

Godly instruction (12:16-21)

[16]It is an essential witness that we are seen to live in harmony with one another. Such unity is destroyed by pride. So we will not be proud, but willing to show God's love to anyone, regardless of who or what they are. And we will not be conceited!

[17]Do not retaliate when anyone offends or hurts you. Make sure
that others can see clearly that you do what is right. [18]And always
live at peace with others, as far as this is possible. [19]There is no point
in taking revenge; you are to forgive, my friends, not judge others.
That is God's prerogative. He is the only one who can judge, punish
or demonstrate anger, as He Himself has told us. [20]He also tells us
to "feed our enemies if they are hungry, to give them something to
drink when they are thirsty. For in giving to them when they least
deserve it, you will bring them under conviction of their sin."
[21]Never let evil have the upper hand in your life. Rather, let your
goodness defeat evil!

Submit to authority (13:1-7)

13 It is necessary for you to have a right and submissive attitude
to those in authority, including those in civic government.
For all authority originates from the Lord, who is the ultimate
authority. God Himself has put these governing authorities in place.
[2]So anyone who rebels against authority rebels against God who
set that authority in place. All those who rebel will only bring judgment on themselves. [3]If you do what is right you do not need to fear
the authorities. It is another matter for those who do wrong! There
is no need to be afraid of those in authority, for if you are a good citizen
who obeys the law you will be well thought of. [4]Those in authority
are there for your good so that there will be order in society. In fact,
they are serving God's purposes, even in punishing those who do
wrong. [5]However, you should submit to those in authority, not out
of fear of punishment, but because your conscience tells you this is
the right thing to do!

[6]For you can see that it is right that you should pay taxes, for
those who govern are serving God's purposes and they need the
necessary resources to do what, after all, is their full-time job! [7]It is
a good principle to pay everyone what you owe so that you are not
in debt. Pay your taxes and bills on time, for in this way you show
respect and honour others.

Live a life of love (13:8-14)

[8]There is one debt that you should always have: to love each other.
The one who loves fulfils God's purpose for His life. For love is really
the fulfilment of what God has commanded us to do. [9]You know the

12:19 Deuteronomy 32:35
12:20 Proverbs 25:21-22

commandments, 'Do not commit adultery,' 'Do not murder,' 'Do not steal,' 'Do not covet other people's possessions.' There is a principle that underlies all such commands and is summed up in the one command to love your neighbour as yourself. [10]Because those who love will not want to harm their neighbours, they will obey all these other commands; for the way to fulfil God's law is through love.

[11]No matter what the situation, love is always to be the guiding principle by which you live. It is time to stir yourself and ensure that you do this in practice, demonstrating that you are living in the good of the salvation God is giving you. The time of having to give account of yourself to God is nearer now than when you first became a believer. [12]It may seem that there is so much darkness around you, but a new dawn is about to break. So be sure that you are free from any activity that belongs to the darkness and that you are walking in the light. [13]If this is the case, you will have nothing to be ashamed of in the way you behave. You will never engage in orgies or drunkenness like those who belong to the darkness. You will not be party to any form of sexual immorality or depravity. Neither will you be a person with an independent mindset or one whose life is ruined by jealousy.

[14]Instead you will radiate the life of the Lord Jesus Christ, living as His witness. How much better to have that as your aim than to live to gratify your fleshly, self-indulgent desires.

Do not judge others (14:1-13)

14 Do not judge those whose faith is weak; encourage them. There are bound to be issues about which you disagree, over diet for example. [2]One person believes he or she can eat anything, but another with a different level of faith believes it is right only to eat vegetables.

[3]The one who feels free to eat anything should not have a condescending attitude towards others, just as the vegetarian should not judge the one who eats meat. God has accepted all those who are His servants. [4]So do not judge those He has called to serve Him. Each will be responsible to Him for what he or she does, for He is the Master of us all. And the Lord enables us all to stand confidently before Him.

[5]There is another issue of contention. One believer regards some days as being more holy than others. Another regards every day as of similar importance. Who is right? Well, each person must do

13:9 Exodus 20:13-15, 17

what he or she firmly believes to be right. [6]Those who believe that certain days have special significance are convinced they are honouring the Lord. The meat eater thanks God for His food; similarly the vegetarian is also thankful.

[7-8]This is the principle, then. That in whatever we do, we are convinced that we are serving the Lord in ways that please Him. We are not living for ourselves, but for Him! Because we belong to Him, we should even be prepared to die for the Lord. What significance are petty differences when compared with that?

[9]Christ died and rose again and so is Lord of both those who have died and all who are alive now. [10]On what authority, then, do you judge your brother? What gives you the right to think He is in any way inferior to you? Every one of us will have to stand before God on Judgment Day. [11]He has said:

> "I declare that as surely as I live, every person will have to bend his knee in homage to me and every tongue will declare that I alone am God."

[12]At that time, each of us will be held responsible for what we have believed and done. [13]In light of this, we had all better stop judging each other. We must be determined not to cause any of our fellow believers to stumble; nor do we want to make things difficult for them.

Attitude towards food (14:14-23)

[14]You know I live in close relationship with the Lord Jesus and I am personally certain that no food is forbidden by God. However, if someone believes that it is not right to eat certain foods, then He should obey His conscience in this matter.

[15]If you eat anything when you are with other believers who are genuinely upset to see people eating meat, then you are not acting in love towards them. You do not want to cause your brother to have any unnecessary distress, for Christ died to free them as He died to free you.

[16]I do not suggest that you should allow others to speak negatively of what you consider to be good and right. [17]God's Kingdom has nothing to do with what we eat or drink. No, this Kingdom to which we belong is expressed in righteousness, peace and joy through the Holy Spirit living in us. [18]This is where our focus needs to be, for then we are truly serving Christ, pleasing God and will be well thought of by others.

14:11 Isaiah 45:23

19 How important it is, then, to attempt to live in ways that encourage unity among us, seeking to edify one another. 20 We do not want to damage the cause of God's Kingdom for the sake of differences over what we should eat!

Even if you believe, as I do, that it is permissible to eat anything, it would be wrong to eat in a way that would cause a problem for others. 21 So when you are with those who think it is wrong to eat meat or drink wine, refrain from doing so. Then you will not offend their tender consciences!

22 Your personal beliefs about such matters are between yourself and God; you are responsible to Him! So you are blessed if you can eat or drink without any qualms of conscience. 23 But it would be wrong for another to be forced to eat anything he considers it wrong to eat, for then he would feel condemned for not doing what he believed to be right for him. For whenever we fail to act out of what we believe to be right, we sin!

Help the weak in faith (15:1-13)

15 Those who are strong in faith should be sensitive towards those weaker in faith, and should not behave in ways that simply please themselves. 2 You want to bless your neighbour and do him good, to build him up and encourage him. 3 Even Christ did not live to please Himself, as the scripture makes clear. "He is insulted in the same way that God is insulted." 4 And we are to learn from what the scriptures say, even those things written long ago. God's truth will encourage us to persevere through the testing times and will help us to maintain our hope that we shall see the fulfilment of God's purposes.

5-6 God Himself enables this perseverance and gives us encouragement. So may He cause the Spirit of unity to be imparted to you so that you may give glory and honour to God the Father and the Lord Jesus Christ with both your hearts and mouths.

7 Simply accept one another in the same way that Christ has accepted you; this will give true praise to God. 8 Let me remind you that Christ came to the Jewish people as a servant, to reveal the truth about God and to ensure that the promises given to their forefathers would be fulfilled. 9 For this would enable those who are not Jews to live for God's glory and honour, being thankful that they, too, have known His mercy first hand. It is written "I will be praised among

15:3 Psalm 69:9
15:9 2 Samuel 22:50

the other nations; they too will lift their voices to worship Me." 10 He
tells these other nations to rejoice along with His chosen people.
11 Yes, He commands all nations to praise the Lord, along with the
Jewish people.

12 Isaiah prophesied that from among the Jews God would raise
up the One who would rule over the nations; and He would be the
hope of all people everywhere. 13 So I pray that this God of hope,
who keeps us looking expectantly to the future, will fill you with
His joy and peace as you continue to live by faith in Him. May the
power of the Holy Spirit work in you in such a way that you will
always overflow with hope, expecting God's best!

Paul's responsibility to proclaim the gospel (15:14-33)

14 My dear brothers, I am sure that you want to live good lives, to
know and understand God's purposes. And you want to be able to
teach one another the way of truth. 15 This is why I have felt free to
be outspoken about certain matters in the way I have written. I am
only reminding you of what you already know to be right. 16 I
always depended on the grace God has given me to be Christ Jesus'
faithful minister to the nations. I have a responsibility as His representative to proclaim His gospel so that among all nations there will
be those who offer their lives in service of God's Kingdom, people
who are made holy by God's Spirit and set apart for His purposes.

17 I am so thankful to Christ Jesus for this ministry God has given
me. 18-19 I would not dare to take any glory to myself, for truly it is
only what Christ has done through me that has led to many from
different nations being brought to obedience to God. Yes, He has
used what I have said and done, even enabling me to perform
supernatural signs and miracles. But these are all the result of the
power of His Spirit.

From Jerusalem to the farthest reaches I have proclaimed Christ's
gospel fully in word and deed. 20 My aim is always to preach the
gospel where people have never even heard of Christ. I want to
begin new works rather than build on foundations laid by others.
21 For we have God's word that says, "Those who were not told
about Him will see, and those who have never heard of him will
come to understand who He is." 22 It is for this reason that I have
been prevented from coming to you personally.

23 However, I feel my calling in these areas is now fulfilled and so
I am planning to visit you, something I have longed to do for many

15:12 Isaiah 11:10
15:21 Isaiah 52:15

years. 24 It is my intention to do this on my way to Spain, and then you will be able to speed me on my onward journey there, after I have enjoyed sharing fellowship with you for a time.

25 First, though, I have to go to Jerusalem to serve the saints, our fellow believers, there. 26 It is good that the believers in Macedonia and Achaia have wanted to support financially their brothers in Jerusalem who are fighting poverty. 27 They were really pleased with the opportunity to help them in this way. You could say that they owe such a debt to their Jewish brethren. After all, even though they are not Jewish themselves, they now share in the spiritual blessings that are the inheritance of the Jews. How fitting to give their material blessings in return!

28 After I have fulfilled this responsibility, making sure these financial gifts arrive safely, I will then be free to go to Spain, visiting you on the way. 29 And I am confident that when I arrive I will be able to impart great blessing to you through Christ, for we enjoy the full measure of His life.

30 Let me encourage you strongly as my brothers to pray to God for me, for this will help me in all my difficulties. I am sure that the Lord Jesus wants you to support me in this way, and so express the love you have for me through the Holy Spirit. 31 The difficulties to which I refer are caused by the opposition of unbelievers in Judea. And I really desire that my ministry in Jerusalem will be well received by God's people there. 32 Then I can become confident that it will be God's timing for me to come to you with joy, that together we may be refreshed by the Lord. 33 May the God of peace be with you all! Amen! It shall be so!

Final greetings (16:1-27)

16 Phoebe is about to visit you and I want you to receive her in a way that will bless the Lord. She is our sister in faith and a servant of the church in Cenchrea. 2 So I am sure you will treat her in a worthy manner, as befits the saints of God, and that you will help her in any way necessary. She is herself a wonderful servant, and has helped many others, including me.

3 Give my greetings to Priscilla and Aquila. They have been fellow workers with me in Christ Jesus. 4 They even risked their lives for me. All the churches among the nations are thankful to God for them, as I am myself. 5 And greet all those who belong to the church that meets in their home.

I send my love to my dear friend Epenetus. He was the first person
I led to Christ in the province of Asia. 6 And greet Mary, for she has
given herself tirelessly for your sakes.
7 Give my kindest regards to my relatives Andronicus and Junias.
We were in prison together and they have proved to be outstanding
apostles. In fact they were believers in Christ before I was myself.
8 I love Ampliatus with the Lord's love. 9 Give him my greetings,
along with Urbanus, another fellow-worker in Christ, and my dear
friend Stachys.
10 Apelles has been through times of testing, but has surely proved
himself to be approved in Christ. So greet him along with all those
who are part of Aristobulus' household. 11 And greet another relative
of mine, Herodion. And greet all those in the household of
Narcissus who belong to the Lord. 12 Also I want you to remember
me to Tryphena and Tryphosa. These two women work so hard in
the Lord's purposes. And also another hard-working woman, Persis.
13 Give my love to Rufus, clearly one chosen by the Lord; and to
his mother who has also been like a mother to me. 14 And also greet
Asyncritus, Phlegon, Hermes, Patrobas, Hermas and all the brothers
that belong to that group of believers. 15 Also greet Philologus, Julia,
Nereus and his sister, Olympus, and all the saints in their group.
16 Show your love for one another with a holy kiss. All the churches
of Christ that I represent join me in sending their greetings.
17 I love you so much, brothers, that I am concerned that you
beware of any who would cause divisions to arise among you, or
who in any way would hinder you in your faith and witness, by
teaching things that are not in agreement with the gospel you have
already received. Avoid such people. 18 They do not serve the Lord
Christ but only their own ambitions. They have their own agendas
which they promote through deceptive talk and flattery, easily
influencing the minds of naïve people.
19 Your obedience to the Lord is well known everywhere and this
causes me to rejoice over you. However, you still need to be wise
and focus on what is good, so that you do not allow any form of evil
among you.
20 Satan will soon be crushed beneath the feet of the God of peace.
Meanwhile the grace of our Lord Jesus Christ will be with you.
21 Timothy is working faithfully with me and sends his greetings
to you all, along with Lucius, Jason and Sosispater, more of my
relatives.
22 (Paul dictated this letter to me, Tertius, and I also greet you in
the Lord).

23 The whole church where I am now enjoys the hospitality of
Gaius, who is also caring for me. They all send their greetings, as do
Erastus, the city's director of public works, and another brother,
Quartus.

24 May the grace of our Lord Jesus Christ be imparted to you all.

25 Above all else I want to give glory and honour to Him who has
the power to keep you well grounded in my gospel and the revelation
of who Jesus Christ is, that mystery that was formerly hidden for
such a long time. 26 All that was prophesied about Him is now made
known because this has been the will of the eternal God. He has
commanded this so that all nations may now believe and obey Him.
27 He is the only God and is wise in all the ways He works. To Him
belongs all the glory forever through Jesus Christ. Amen! It shall be
so!

1 CORINTHIANS

God's holy people (1:1-3)

1 From Paul, who by God's will was called to be an apostle of
Christ Jesus, and from our brother Sosthenes.
2 To God's church in Corinth; to those who have been made holy
in Christ Jesus, set apart by Him for God and consecrated to His
purposes. Since He has made you holy you are called to be holy,
together with all the other believers in every place, those who call on
the name of our Lord Jesus Christ; for He is their Lord and ours also.
3 May God our Father and the Lord Jesus Christ impart both His
grace and peace to you.

Living in Christ (1:4-9)

4 I am always thankful to God for you because He has shown you so
much grace through your union with Christ Jesus. 5 Because you
live in Christ you have been blessed with all His riches. He has
blessed you in every conceivable way. You know that all His riches
are yours and you are able to speak His many blessings over your
lives. 6 This is possible because all we taught you about Christ was
imparted to you when you believed in Him. 7 For this reason, you
do not lack any of His spiritual gifts. They are yours to enable you
to persevere in faith as you look with eager expectation for our Lord
Jesus Christ to be revealed in His full majesty and glory.
8 He will keep you strong to the very end so that on that glorious
day, when you come before our Lord Jesus Christ, you will be without
any blame or guilt. 9 God is faithful and He is able to do this because
He has called you to live at one with His Son Jesus Christ our Lord.

Live in unity with one another (1:10-17)

10 I urge you strongly in His name to be in agreement with one
another. There should not be any divisions among you. You should
be united perfectly, even agreeing together in the way you think.
11 Yet, my brothers, I have heard from some who belong to Chloe's
household that there are disputes among you. 12 One person says, "I

am one of Paul's followers," while another says, "I follow Apollos." Still others claim, "I follow Cephas," and others say, "I am a follower of Christ." Such claims cause divisions among you.

13 Is Christ divided into such party factions? Was Paul crucified on your behalf? Or were you baptised in Paul's name? 14-15 If such things are being said, I am only thankful that I baptised none of you except for Crispus and Gaius, so that none can claim to be baptised in my name. 16-17 Yes, I did baptise the household of Stephanas also, but I cannot remember baptising anyone else, for Christ did not send me to baptise you but to preach the gospel. And I did not do this in words that come from my own human wisdom, or you would not have seen the power of the cross of Christ.

Christ is God's power and wisdom (1:18-29)

18 The revelation of what Jesus accomplished on the cross seems foolish nonsense to those who will perish, but it is God's power at work in all of us who are being saved. 19 This is why God has written, 'I will destroy the wisdom of those who consider themselves wise; and I will frustrate the intelligence of those who think themselves clever.'

20 Where is the man who has been saved by his own wisdom? Where is the scholar who has received God's life through studying? Where is the philosopher who understands what God is doing at this time? Is it not true that God has made all such worldly wisdom appear utterly foolish?

21 It was wise of God to ensure that nobody could come to know Him through his or her worldly wisdom. Rather, it pleased Him to save those who believe what was preached to them, even though it appeared foolish to their natural thinking.

22-23 Jews are always looking for miraculous signs and Greeks trust in their own wisdom; but we preach that salvation is only possible because of Christ's crucifixion. This is a stumbling block to those Jews who cannot understand why the Messiah had to be crucified; and it seems utterly foolish to those others who trust in their own intellectual understanding.

24 To those who God has called to belong to Him, whether they are Jews or not, Christ is both God's power and God's wisdom. 25 People may regard God's purpose as being foolish, but His so-called foolishness is wiser than all man's wisdom put together. Those who consider God to be weak should realise He is more powerful than all the strength that men could muster between them!

1:19 Isaiah 29:14

[26]My brothers, pause and think for a moment of the condition you were in when God first called you to belong to Christ. Not many of you were renowned for what the world regards as intellectual prowess; and few of you could claim to be of noble birth. [27]So you can see that God chose those whom worldly people call foolish to have a wisdom greater than they possess. He chose those whom others call weak to have a greater power than any human power. [28-29]He chose those whom the world regards as worthless and useless, of absolutely no account, to show the futility of human wisdom, so that no-one would be able to boast before God because of his intellectual ability or human strength.

Boast only in the Lord (1:30-2:10)

[30]It is only through God's own work of grace that you now live in Christ Jesus, at one with Him. Jesus Himself has become for us who believe the true wisdom that God has supplied. He is our righteousness. He is our holiness. He is our redemption, the one who has made it possible for us to be God's children. [31]This is why it is written that if anyone wants to boast, let him boast about what the Lord has done!

2 My brothers, when I first came to you it was not with eloquent language, neither did I claim to have superior wisdom. My purpose was to tell you clearly the truth about God. [2]I was determined to focus only on Jesus Christ and the meaning of His crucifixion. [3]In myself I felt very weak and even fearful when I came to you; I was actually trembling with apprehension. [4]The way I preached and presented my message was not by using wise or persuasive words; rather I wanted to give you a demonstration of the Spirit's power. [5]Then your faith would not be based on any man's wisdom, but on God's power.

[6]However, it is true to say that our message is one of wisdom, as the mature among you realise. But I do not mean the wisdom of contemporary natural thinkers, nor what passes as wisdom by those who rule over us, a wisdom that is futile before God. [7]No, we speak the wisdom that comes from God, a secret wisdom that has been hidden since before time began, but has now been revealed by God to enable us to know His glory and even be partakers of that glory ourselves.

[8]None of the present political rulers understand this wisdom. If they had they certainly would not have crucified Christ, the Lord of

1:31 Jeremiah 9:24

glory. [9]However, it has been written, “Nobody has seen, nor heard, nor understood what God has prepared for those who love Him.” [10]Yet God has now revealed this to us by His Spirit.

Spiritual wisdom and understanding (2:11-16)

Only the Spirit is able to understand all things, including the deep things about God. [11]Nobody can know the thoughts of another person, but each knows his or her own thoughts. Similarly, nobody knows God’s thoughts except His own Spirit. [12]And we who believe in Jesus have not been given the spirit of this world but God’s own Spirit, whom He sent to us so that we can understand all that He has given us.

[13]So we do not speak in words of worldly wisdom, but the Spirit gives us the words to speak, and He enables us to express spiritual truths in spiritual words. [14]Someone who does not have the Spirit does not believe the truths that come from God’s Spirit. They seem foolish to him and he does not understand, because these truths only make sense to those who possess God’s Spirit.

[15]The man who has been blessed by receiving the Spirit is able to make correct judgments about everything; he can discern what is right or wrong. And no-one can judge him for the wisdom given him by God. [16]”For who can out-think God and instruct Him?”

However, we have been given the mind of Christ, so we know how He views things!

Warning against divisions (3:1-15)

3 My brothers, I want to speak to you as spiritual people, but you are still so worldly in your thinking, like little babes in Christ. [2]This is why I had to feed you with milk rather than the solid food for which you were not ready. And this is still the case. [3]You are still worldly in your attitudes. This is proved by the fact that you are jealous of one another and quarrel among yourselves. This is to act as mere men, isn’t it? [4]For when you say such things as, “I follow Paul,” or “I follow Apollos,” you act as worldly people.

[5]Who is Apollos really, or Paul come to that? We are only servants used by God to bring you to faith in the gospel. The Lord Himself assigned us our tasks, as He does with everyone. [6]He used me to plant the seed of the gospel in your hearts and Apollos watered that seed; but it was God who made it grow. [7]Neither the one who plants

2:9 Isaiah 64:4
2:16 Isaiah 40:13

nor the one who waters is of any significance, but only God who
caused that seed of truth to grow in you. [8]Both he who plants and
the one who waters have a common purpose and each will be
rewarded by God for faithfulness to his calling. [9]We simply work
together with God. And you are God's field, God's building.

[10]It was only through the grace given me by God that I was able
to lay a foundation among you as a skilful builder; but it was left to
someone else to build on that foundation of truth. However, everyone must be careful how he builds.

[11]No-one can change the foundation that has already been laid,
for that is the truth of Jesus Christ. He personally is the foundation.
[12]So if someone builds on this foundation using spiritual gold, silver
or precious stones, his work will survive. But if someone uses only
wood, hay or stubble, his work will be burned up on the Day of
Judgment. [13]For then the value of each man's work will be seen
clearly because the testing of God's fire will prove the quality of
what each person has produced. [14-15]For those whose work survives
there will be a reward; but for the one whose work is burned up
there will be loss. He will be saved, but only like someone who has
escaped from the flames.

You are God's temple (3:16-23)

[16]Surely you understand that you are God's temple, His dwelling
place, because His Spirit lives in you? [17]God will destroy anyone
who destroys His temple, because He regards His temple as sacred;
and you are that temple!

[18]There is no point in deceiving yourselves. If any of you regards
himself as wise because of his powers of reason, he had better
realise that he is no better than a fool, for then he will seek to
become truly wise. [19]Worldly wisdom is utter foolishness to God. It
has been said, "God catches out the wise through their own craftiness."
[20]It was also written that, "The Lord knows that the thoughts of
those who consider themselves wise are, in reality, futile."

[21-23]So then, stop boasting about men! You inherit all that God
gives, whether you receive revelation from Paul, Apollos or Peter.
Yes, everything is yours, the things of this present world, that which
you receive through the life of Christ and that which will be yours
beyond death. Everything God has for you in the present or the
future is yours because you belong to Christ, and He is God's Son!

3:19 Job 5:13
3:20 Psalm 94:11

Never go beyond what is written (4:1-7)

4 In view of all this, others should realise that we are Christ's servants, entrusted by God with those things that were formerly hidden. 2-3 It is necessary for those given such trust to prove faithful; so it does not concern me if I am judged by you or any human court; I do not even judge myself. 4 Although my conscience is clear, this does not mean I am innocent. I know that the Lord judges me; that is what matters!

5 So do not rush to any hasty judgments; when the Lord comes you will see the truth about everything. He will bring into the light those things that were hidden in darkness and then the motives of all our hearts will be exposed, and each will receive whatever praise is right!

6 My dear brothers, I have used Apollos and myself as examples only for your instruction, so that you may gain understanding from us as to the meaning of the saying, "Never go beyond what is written." Apply that and you will not follow one man as opposed to another. 7 After all, what is unique about you? And what do you have apart from that which you received through God's grace? If you received it as a gift, why boast as if you achieved it by your own efforts or goodness?

Christ's apostles (4:8-13)

8 You boast that you have already all you want, that you have become rich! You make it sound as if you were kings, and all of your own making without any reference to us. I wish you really were kings for then we would also be kings with you! 9 That is far from the case, for it appears to me that God has appointed us apostles to be at the very end of the procession, the position given to those who have been condemned to die in the arena. It seems we are a spectacle to everyone, to angels as well as men. 10 Yes, we appear to be fools, but for the sake of Christ. Yet you make it appear that you are so wise in Christ! We appear weak, you claim to be strong! While you are honoured, we are dishonoured!

11 Even now we hunger and thirst, we are dressed in rags, are brutally treated and homeless. 12 We work hard with our hands to support ourselves. But when we are cursed we do not retaliate; we bless instead. We endure the persecution we have to face. 13 When people slander us we answer with kind words. Yes, until now we have been treated like the scum of the earth, the very lowest form of human being in the world.

Spiritual fathers (4:14-17)

[14]My purpose in writing like this is not to put you to shame, but to warn you because you are my dear children. [15]You may think that you have ten thousand to protect you because you are in Christ, but you do not have many spiritual fathers. And this is what I became, your spiritual father in Christ Jesus through the gospel. [16]So instead of standing on your pride, I beg you to follow my example. [17]This is why I am sending Timothy to you. He is both like a son whom I love and someone who is faithful to the Lord. He will remind you of the way I live in Christ Jesus, a way of life that reflects what I teach in all the churches.

Kingdom of power (4:18-21)

[18]Some of you have become so arrogant, acting as if I will never return to you. [19]But I will be arriving shortly, if the Lord so allows, and then I will see for myself not only what the proud people say, but whether they demonstrate any power of the Spirit! [20]For God's Kingdom is not about empty talk, but revealing God's power.

[21]Which would you prefer, for me to come and scold you, or to come in love with a spirit of gentleness?

Don't allow immoral behaviour (5:1-8)

5 I have heard that there are some among you guilty of sexual immorality, and of a particularly evil kind that even the ungodly would condemn. A man is actually living with his father's wife! [2]How can you be proud when you allow such things? Don't you think that such outrageous behaviour should cause you so much grief that you would expel this man from the fellowship? [3]I may not be with you physically, but I certainly am present in spirit, and I have already decided as if I was there with you, that this is definitely the right decision for this man.

[4]This is what you are to do when assembled together in the name of our Lord Jesus Christ. Not only will I be with you in spirit, but the Lord Jesus will also be present in power. [5]You are to hand this man over to Satan. It is better for his flesh life to be destroyed so that his spirit will be saved when Jesus comes on that great and terrible Day of the Lord.

[6]You can see that your boasting is not good! You should know by now that a little yeast can work through the whole lump of dough! [7]So be rid of this old corrupt yeast so that you may become a new lump without any such corruption in your midst. It was to make

you pure and holy that Christ became our sacrificial Passover Lamb; and this is what God has called you to be.

[8]So when you keep this Feast, do so without the old yeast of malice and wickedness. Instead be the bread of sincerity and truth, without any such yeast.

Expel the rebellious (5:9-13)

[9]I have written to you previously not to have fellowship with those who are sexually immoral. [10]I refer to those who claim to be your brothers, not those who still belong to this world. For the world is full of immoral or greedy people, as well as confidence tricksters and those who worship idols, whether these idols be people, possessions or false gods. You would have to depart from this world altogether to avoid all such people.

[11]What I write now should make it clear that you are not to have fellowship with anyone who claims to be in Christ, but is sexually immoral or greedy, someone who has his own idols or slanders others, a drunkard or someone who manipulates and swindles others. You should not think of eating with such a person.

[12]What concern do I have in judging those outside the church? But are you not to weigh the actions of those who belong to the church? [13]Leave God to judge those outside. Remember this principle: "Expel from among you the wicked man who refuses to repent."

Settle disputes with propriety (6:1-8)

6 So if you have some kind of disagreement with another brother, surely you would not think of taking the matter before ungodly people, would you? Instead, bring it before the saints, your fellow believers in Christ. [2]Do you not realise that ultimately the saints will judge the world? If you are among those who will do that, surely you are now able to settle cases that are trivial by comparison! [3]Why, we will even judge angels! Do you know that? That being the case, surely we are competent to judge the things of this present life!

[4]So if there are disputes among you, appoint your own judges in the church, men who are fair even though they may have no leadership status. [5]It is shameful that I should even have to suggest such a thing. Do you really think that there is no-one among you wise enough to judge differences between your church members? [6]For what happens now? One brother takes another to court, and wants the matter settled by unbelievers. What kind of a witness is that?

5:13 Deuteronomy 17:7

7 By even having lawsuits against one another, you appear as
those already defeated. Would it not be better to let the matter go,
even if you have been wronged in some way? Would you not rather
be cheated than to be a poor witness to unbelievers? 8 Yet instead of
having such attitudes, you are cheating one another, doing wrong
even to your own brothers!

No inheritance for the wicked (6:9-11)

9 You know that the wicked have no inheritance in God's Kingdom,
don't you? Don't be deceived about this. The sexually immoral,
those who love their idols and those guilty of adultery will not inherit
God's Kingdom. 10 Neither will male prostitutes, nor homosexuals
who live in sin, nor others who sin sexually. Neither will thieves,
nor greedy people, nor drunkards, nor those who slander others or
swindle them. None of these people will inherit God's Kingdom
unless they repent.

11 In your former way of life you yourselves would have been
numbered among such people. But look what Christ has done for
you! Now you have been washed of your sins and have been made
holy before God, fully accepted by Him because you belong to the
Lord Jesus Christ and have received God's Spirit.

Don't indulge the flesh (6:12-18)

12 You hear some people say, "Everything is possible for me." However not everything is beneficial for you. You may say, "Everything
is permissible for me;" but I will not allow any fleshly desire to be
my master.

13 Others say, "Food is for the stomach and the stomach is for
food." Yes, but both food and stomach will be destroyed by God. He
has given you your body to be used for His purposes, not for sexual
immorality. That is why the Lord has come to live in your body.

14 God used His power to raise the Lord Jesus from the dead and
by that same power He will raise us as well. 15 Do you not realise that
your bodies are members of Christ Himself because you belong to His
Body? Would you expect me to take members of Christ and make
them one with prostitutes? Of course not! 16 You know that anyone
who unites himself with a prostitute has made himself of one body
with her, don't you? God has said, "The two become one flesh,"
when they have sexual relations. 17 How much better for the believer
to unite himself with the Lord, so He will be one with Him in Spirit!

6:16 Genesis 2:24

18 Turn your back completely on sexual immorality. All the other sins a man can be guilty of do not involve his body in the same way. But the man who sins sexually actually commits sin against his own body!

Temples of the Holy Spirit (6:19-20)

19 Surely you realise that God has made your body a temple of the Holy Spirit, who now lives in you? This is God's doing; and so you do not belong to yourself, to do as you please. 20 God has purchased you for Himself; He has paid the price for you with His Son's blood. So honour Him in the way you use your body!

Marriage principles (7:1-16)

7 Now I have to address the matters you raised when you wrote to me. Yes, it is good if a man decides not to marry. However, this is not the norm. 2 Because there is so much immorality about, it is advisable for each man to have his own wife and every woman her own husband. 3 The husband should fulfil his marital responsibilities towards his wife, and the wife likewise towards her husband. 4 The wife is no longer sole owner of her body, for now she is united with her husband. In the same way, the husband is no longer the sole owner of his body because he has given himself to his wife.

5 Do not deprive each other of sexual pleasure, unless you do so for a period of time by mutual consent so that together you may devote yourselves to prayer. Then be joined together again so that you are not tempted by Satan to have any sexual relationships outside of your marriage because you lack self-control.

6 All this I say as a concession because of the circumstances in which we find ourselves. I am not ordering anyone to be married. 7 Actually, I would prefer all men to be as I am, 'married' to the work of the gospel. But God gives different forms of grace to each one; one has the gift of celibacy, others have different gifts.

8 So to those not yet married or who have been widowed I give this advice: It is good for you to remain unmarried as I am myself. 9 However, if you feel you must marry, for you cannot control your feelings, then you should do so; for it is better to marry than to burn with unfulfilled passion for someone you love.

10 To those who are married, I can speak with the Lord's authority, not my own. His command is clear: a wife must not divorce her husband. 11 If she does, she must remain unmarried or be reconciled to her husband. Likewise a man is not to divorce his wife.

[12]This is my advice to others, not a word from the Lord: if a brother has a wife who does not believe, yet she still wants to live with him, he must not divorce her. [13]Likewise if a woman has an unbelieving husband and he still wants to live with her, she must not divorce him. [14]You see, the unbelieving husband has been sanctified by his wife, so he too is regarded as holy. And the unbelieving wife has been made holy through her husband who is a believer. If this was not the case, then your children would be unclean in God's sight; yet God regards them as holy, set apart for Him.

[15]However, if the one who is not a believer decides to leave, you should not prevent him or her from doing so. The believing man or woman should not feel condemned in such circumstances. God wants us to live in peace and harmony.

[16]Wife, do not give up on your husband, but believe for his salvation. Husband, do not abandon your wife, but believe that you will see her saved.

Contentment in life (7:17-28)

[17]The principle is this: everyone should be content to remain in the circumstances to which God has assigned him and to which He has called him. And this is the guiding principle I teach in all the churches.

[18]If a man was circumcised when called to belong to Christ, he should remain circumcised. If he was not circumcised when he became a believer, he must not seek to be circumcised. [19]It is of no significance whether you are circumcised or not. Obedience to God's command is what matters. [20]Every believer should remain as he was when God called him.

[21]Were you a slave when you became a believer? Do not be concerned about that, although if you are able to gain your freedom, do so. [22]Even if you were a slave when you were called, you are free in Christ. In like manner, the one who was free when called is now Christ's slave. [23]It cost His blood to purchase you for God; so don't put yourselves in slavery to men. [24]Everyone should be content to serve God in the position he was when called.

[25]I do not have any word from the Lord for virgins; but by the Lord's mercy I can speak as one who is considered trustworthy. [26]I think the present circumstances indicate that it is best for you to remain as you are!

[27]If you are married, do not contemplate divorce. If you are not married this is not the time to think about finding a wife. [28]How-

ever, you would not sin by getting married; neither would it be sinful
for a virgin to marry. You must realise that to be married brings you
added responsibilities and I want to spare you from any unnecessary
pressure.

Maintain focus on God (7:29-40)

[29]I speak in this way because in this present climate life could be
very short. In view of this, those who have wives must keep their
focus on the truth as an unmarried person would. [30]Those who
would naturally mourn are to live as if they had no grief. When you
buy things, understand that you might not have them for long. [31]Do
not become infatuated with the things of this world even though
you have to use them, for this present world as we know it is passing
away.

[32]I want you to be free of unnecessary concerns. A person who is
unmarried can be totally devoted to the Lord's business and focus
on living to please Him alone. [33]However, a married man has to be
concerned about practical issues of this world and naturally wants
to please his wife also. So he has divided interests.

[34]An unmarried woman or virgin is concerned solely with the
Lord's business. Her desire is to be devoted to the Lord completely,
both in body and spirit. However, a married woman has to be involved
with worldly affairs and she also wants to please her husband.

[35]I am trying to be helpful, not restrictive; it would be for your
own good to live completely devoted to the Lord.

[36]If someone thinks he is not doing the right thing by his fiancée
and he feels he should marry her, he should do as he thinks best,
especially if she is getting older. He does not sin by marrying her;
they should be married.

[37]Another man may not feel under this pressure and is at peace
about the present situation. He does not feel compelled to be married,
for he has the will-power to keep his emotions under control. So he
makes the right decision in choosing not to marry immediately.
[38]My conclusion is this then: the man who decides to marry his
fiancée does the right thing, but the man who decides not to marry
does even better.

[39]In marriage, a wife is committed to her husband as long as he
lives. But if her husband dies, she is free to marry whoever she
wishes, so long as he also belongs to the Lord. [40]My judgment is that
she will be happier to remain a widow, and I think this is the leading
of God's Spirit in the present circumstances.

Proper use of freedom (8:1-13)

8 You raise the matter of what to do about food that has been sacrificed to idols. Although we all have knowledge, we must beware of being puffed up with pride, for we are called to love in ways that build others up. [2]Even the person who is convinced of what he knows, does not yet know everything. [3]Remember, God knows all about every person who loves Him.

[4]Bearing this in mind, what should our attitude be towards eating food offered to idols? We are certain that any worldly idol is absolutely nothing, and there is only one God. [5-6]Even if so-called gods existed, either in the heavens or on the earth, for us there is only one God, the Father who created all things. We live for Him and for Jesus Christ who is our only Lord, even though in the world there are many so called 'gods' and 'lords'. It is through Christ alone that all creation came into being and we have life through Him alone.

[7]Not everyone knows or believes this. Some people are still so conscious of the idols they once worshipped that their weak consciences are troubled if they are asked to eat food that was once sacrificed to idols. [8]However, food has no ability to influence our relationship with God; so it does not matter whether we choose to eat such food or not. If we eat, we are neither the worse nor the better for doing so!

[9]However, you should be careful that in exercising your freedom to eat such food, you do not cause problems for those with weak consciences. [10]Perhaps you think that if someone with a weak conscience saw you eating temple food, he would be encouraged to eat what has been offered to idols. [11]But if this weaker brother, for whom Christ died, follows you against the dictates of his conscience, he might then feel devastated as a result of your exhibition of freedom. [12]In this case you would be guilty of sin against such brothers because you have wounded their consciences; and so you have sinned also against Christ. [13]If eating meat caused my brother to sin, I would never eat it again, for I do not want to be the means of causing anyone to fall into sin.

Paul's apostolic validity (9:1-27)

9 Am I not free? Am I not an apostle? Have I not had the wonderful privilege of seeing Jesus our Lord? And are you not the fruit of my work in the Lord? [2]Not everyone wants to regard me as their apostle, but surely you recognise me as your apostle! For you are the very evidence of my apostolic calling from the Lord.

3 I say this to defend myself from those who sit in judgment on me. 4 Don't we apostles have the right to receive food and drink? 5 Surely those of us with wives can bring them with us? After all, other apostles, the Lord's brothers and Peter also do this. 6 Or should Barnabas and I be the only apostles who have to work to support ourselves?

7 Does a soldier serve in the army at his own expense? The one who plants a vineyard is allowed to eat some of the grapes, isn't he? And the one who shepherds a flock is allowed to drink some of the milk, surely? 8 Am I speaking from a purely human perspective? 9 What does the Law of Moses say about this? It is written, "Do not put a muzzle on the ox while it is treading out the grain." Is God only concerned about oxen? 10 Surely this is a principle from which we are to learn! Yes, this applies also to us because both the ploughman and the one who threshes the crop expect to share in the profits from the harvest.

11 So if we have sown good spiritual seed among you, should we not expect to reap a material harvest from you? Surely that is not too much to expect! 12 If others claim the right to your support, is not our claim even greater?

We have not used this right in the past. In fact, we were so concerned not to hinder people from receiving the gospel of Christ that we were prepared to suffer any necessary sacrifice. 13 Yet surely you are aware that those who work in the temple are provided for by the temple, and those who serve at the altar share in the offerings made at the altar? 14 Well, in the same way, the Lord has commanded that those who preach the gospel should be supported by those who receive the gospel!

15 So far I have not claimed any of these rights. I am not writing about these things in the hope that you will now decide to support me. I would rather die than be deprived of my boast that I preach the gospel free of charge. 16 Not that I can really boast about this, for I feel compelled to preach. I would feel condemned if I was not to preach the gospel. 17 If I preach free of charge, I still have a reward. If I preach under compulsion, I would only be discharging the trust I have been given. 18 What is my reward? Simply this: that when I preach I offer the gospel free of charge and therefore do not use my right to be supported by those to whom I preach.

19 I am free and am not indebted to anyone. Yet I make myself a slave to everyone so that I can win as many as possible for the Lord.

9:9 Deuteronomy 25:4

20 When with Jewish people, I act as one of them to win them over to
the gospel. Even though I am no longer under the law I act as one
who is when I am with those who still live under the law, to win as
many as possible to the truth that sets them free from the religious
law.

21 When with those who do not live by the law, I live as one who
is no longer governed by religious rules and regulations, although I
continue to live willingly under the law of Christ. My purpose is to
win those who have no such legalistic framework to their lives.

22 To weak people I share my own weakness, so I can also win the
weak for Christ. I am ready to be adaptable and to use every possible
means to influence people so that at least some will be saved. 23 I act
like this for the sake of the gospel, for it blesses me to see others
receive Christ.

24 In a race, everyone competes but only one wins the trophy for
coming first. You know this well. Run as if you are determined to
win that trophy. 25 Every competitor has to go into strict training if
he expects to win the crown, even though such an honour has no
lasting value. But we run to receive a crown of eternal significance.
26 So I do not run in an aimless fashion; I am not like a boxer beating
the air. 27 No, I discipline my body so that it stays under my control;
for when I have preached to others, I do not want to be disqualified
myself from winning the prize.

Lessons from Israel's history (10:1-33)

10 My brothers, I don't want you to be uninformed about our
forefathers; they were under the cloud of God's glory and
all passed miraculously through the Red Sea. 2 They were made one
with Moses in both the cloud and the sea. 3-4 They all ate the same
spiritual food that God provided in the wilderness, and they all
drank the same spiritual drink from the spiritual rock that accompanied
them on their journey. That Rock was Christ Himself!

5 Despite this, most of them displeased God and their dead bodies
lay scattered in the desert. 6 These things are an example and a
warning for us, so that we will not set our hearts on doing what is
evil in God's sight, as they did. 7 Do not fall into idolatry as some of
them did, for we read: "The people sat to eat and drink and then
rose up to indulge themselves in pagan activities." 8 We should not
follow their example by committing sexual immorality; in judgment
twenty-three thousand of them died in one day. 9 Neither should we

10:7 Exodus 32:6

follow the example of those who put the Lord to the test and were
killed by snakes. [10]And do not murmur and grumble against the
Lord like some of them did; God sent an angel to destroy them.

[11]These awesome events are examples for us of what happens
when you turn away from the Lord, and they have been written
down to warn us not to behave in similar fashion. We have the
important task of fulfilling God's purposes in this present age.

[12]You may think you are standing firm in your faith; but be careful
that you don't become complacent and fall from God's grace!
[13]Temptation is always around, although you have not suffered any
greater temptation than others experience. In His faithfulness to
you, God will not allow you to be tempted in ways impossible for
you to resist. When you are tempted, He provides the escape route
so that you are able to overcome the temptation.

Do what benefits others (10:14-32)

[14]So, my dear friends, shun all forms of idolatry. [15]I am sure you will
be sensible about this, and you can then judge for yourselves the
wisdom with which I speak.

[16]Think of the cup of thanksgiving we share and over which we
give thanks together. Is this not a way of participating in the blood
of Christ? And when we break bread together, are we not sharing in
the body of Christ? [17]Although we are many, we all share in the one
loaf, showing that we are all part of the one body of Christ.

[18-20]Think for a moment about the people of Israel; those who offer
the sacrifices at the altar also eat of those sacrifices, don't they? [19-20]A
sacrifice offered to a pagan idol means nothing at all, for such sacrifices
are offered to demons. [21]It makes no sense to think that you can
share in the cup of the Lord one moment and then the cup of
demons at another time. You cannot share in both the Lord's table
and the table of demons.

[22]Should we do anything to make the Lord jealous? Do we claim
to be stronger than He is? [23]"I can do whatever I choose," you say.
Yes, but is everything you do beneficial? "I am free to do what I
want," you say; but is everything you do serving God's purposes?
[24]You are not to live to please yourself, but to do what would benefit
others!

[25-26]Yes, you can eat any meat sold in the market without having
any qualms of conscience because the earth belongs to the Lord,
together with everything in it. [27-30]If you want to accept an invitation
to a meal with an unbeliever, you are free to eat whatever he places
before you without wondering whether you are doing the right

thing. Why should I be condemned by another for the freedom I
have? So long as I partake of the meal with thanksgiving to God, I
should not be criticised for eating it! However, if someone tells you
that the food has been dedicated to an idol, then do not eat it. This
will be a witness to the one who has provided the meal and will also
enable him to have a clear conscience.

31 The guiding principle in this matter is simple: In everything
you do, including what you decide to eat or drink, be sure to do it
for God's glory. 32 And do nothing to cause others to stumble,
whether they are Jewish or not, or fellow members of God's church.
33 I endeavour to do whatever is right no matter who I am with, for
I do not focus on my own good, but on the welfare of others so that
they may be saved.

Submission to authority (11:1-19)

11 Just as I follow Christ's example, I suggest you follow mine.
2 I congratulate you for taking note of whatever I have said
to you and for remaining true to the teaching that I passed onto you.
3 Now I want you to know that Christ is the authority over every
man, and man is the authority over the woman, just as Christ during
His humanity submitted to the authority of God.

4 It is dishonouring to God whenever a man prays or prophesies
with his head covered. 5 But it is dishonouring for a woman to pray
or prophesy with her head uncovered; it is as bad as having her
head shaved, for you know what kind of women are treated in that
way! 6 For a woman to go about with her head uncovered is a disgrace;
she may as well have her hair cut off! Because it is a disgrace for a
woman to have her hair short or her head shaved, she should cover
her head.

7-9 However, it is considered different for a man; there is no need
for him to cover his head. Man has been made in the image and
glory of God and the woman is considered the glory of man,
because God first created man, and then the woman for the man.
10 So you can see that the fact that a woman should have her head
covered as social convention can also have a spiritual significance,
that she submits to the authority she is under. Even the angels
would agree with this.

11 Because we belong to the Lord, we see that it is not right for
women to be independent of men, nor men independent of women.
12 Yes, the woman was created for man, but man is also born of
woman. Both need each other and both are created by God.

13-15 You can ask yourself: Is it really right for a woman to pray to God with her head uncovered, as if she were an immoral woman? Such women flaunt their long hair, but this should not be the case for men. It is equally a disgrace for a man to have long hair as if he were a woman. This should be obvious to you. Yes, a woman's long hair can be her glory. It is her covering, but only to be shown off at the proper time. 16 If anybody wants to argue the point, this is the practice we encourage, and it is the same in God's other churches.

The Lord's Supper (11:17-34)

17 Now I need to speak words of stern correction. Your meetings are doing more harm than good and do you no credit. 18 First, I have been told that when you meet together as a church you are divided among yourselves, and I am prepared to believe at least some of what I have heard. 19 There may well be differences among you, but those who hold to the truth have God's approval.

20 When you meet, it is not the Lord's supper you share. 21 Each of you simply looks after himself without any regard for others. One of you could be hungry, another drunk. 22 Surely you have homes to eat and drink in? Do you despise God's church and humiliate those with nothing? What can I possibly say about such behaviour? Shall I praise you? Definitely not!

23-24 I am going to relate to you what I received personally from the Lord. On the night that He was betrayed the Lord Jesus took bread, gave thanks to God, then broke it and said, "This is my Body which is given for you: do this to remember Me." 25 After supper He took the cup in like manner and said, "This cup indicates the new covenant that is ratified by the shedding of My blood; whenever you drink of this cup remember My sacrifice for you." 26 So whenever you eat this bread and drink of this cup, you are proclaiming all that the Lord's death signifies until He comes again.

27 Therefore, anyone eating this bread or drinking the Lord's cup in an unworthy manner will be considered guilty of committing sin against the Lord's body and blood. 28 He should instead examine himself before eating the bread and drinking from the cup. 29 For anyone who eats and drinks without recognising that he shares in the Lord's body only brings judgment on himself. 30 No wonder many among you are weak and sick, and some have even died, if that is how you behave. 31 But if we judge ourselves and first repent of our sins, then we would not place ourselves under such judgment.

32 To be judged by the Lord is to be disciplined by Him, so that we will not be condemned along with the world. 33 So, brothers, when

you come together for your fellowship meal, wait for one another.
34 If you are hungry you should eat at home first, so that when you
come together there is no cause for you to be judged for selfish or
unruly behaviour. When I next visit you I will teach you further on
this subject.

The working of God's Spirit (12:1-11)

12 My brothers, I want you to be well informed about spiritual
things. 2 You are well aware that you used to be influenced
by dumb idols when you were pagans. You were certainly deceived
in those days. 3 I can tell you for certain that anyone who says "Jesus
be cursed", is definitely not speaking under the influence of God's
Spirit. On the other hand, no one can say that he believes "Jesus is
Lord" unless he has been influenced by the Holy Spirit.

4-5 There is only one Holy Spirit of God but He manifests Himself
in different ways, just as there are different ministries in the church,
but all inspired by the same Lord. 6 Although God works in different
ways, it is still the same God who is doing His work in every believer.

7 Every manifestation of the Spirit is given for the good of all who
meet together. 8 The Spirit can give to one a word of wisdom, to
another a word of knowledge that could only be revealed by the
same Holy Spirit. 9 God inspires a gift of faith in another, and He
does this by the same Spirit. Others receive gifts of healings, but it
is the same Holy Spirit at work. 10 Another can be used to perform
miracles, another be given prophetic words, another the ability to
distinguish between true and false spirits, another the ability to
speak in a language he has never learned, and to yet another the
ability to explain what God was saying through that language. 11 Very
different gifts, but all the work of the same Spirit, the Holy Spirit of
God. And He uses different people in the way that He decides.

The Body of Christ (12:12-31)

12 The human body consists of many different parts but they all work
together as a single unit; many parts, but one body! It is similar with
the Body of Christ.

13 When we were all baptised, the Spirit of God was at work to
make us parts of the one Body of Christ, whether we were Jews or
not, slaves or free men. And we have all drunk the same Living
Water, the one Spirit of God.

14 We have seen that the body has not one part, but many.
15 Imagine the foot saying, "I am not a hand, so I do not belong to the
body." To say such a thing would not mean that the foot was not

part of the body. 16 Or suppose the ear said, "I am not an eye so I don't belong to the body." Would that mean that the ear ceased to be part of the body? 17 If the body consisted only of an eye, it would not be able to hear. And if the whole body was an ear, how would it be able to smell anything? 18 But in His wisdom, God has arranged every part of the body precisely according to His plan.

19 If everyone was alike, there could be no body. 20 Yet, the facts are clear – we are made of many parts, but have only one body.

21 So the eye cannot say to the hand, "I have no need of you!" Nor can the head say to the feet, "I don't need you!" 22 Quite the opposite, for even what appear to be the weaker parts of the body are indispensable. 23-24 We take care even of those parts we think to be less important. Those parts we do not wish to display publicly we treat with modesty, while other parts need no special consideration.

In the Body of Christ God has drawn together diverse members and has given greater honour to those who have never in the past been honoured. 25 He wants no division in the Body, but for all to be regarded as important and to have concern for one another. 26 When one suffers, every other part shares in that suffering. When one member is honoured, all can rejoice together with him or her.

27 Now you are Christ's Body and every one of you a member of it. 28 God has appointed certain people in the church to be apostles. They should be regarded as first and essential for they oversee the welfare of the whole Body. Then there are prophets who speak words from God's heart to the hearts of the people. Third in line are those who teach God's Word. Then come those who work miracles, and those through whom others receive gifts of healings. There are those with the ability to help others and those who can organise and handle administrative matters. And there are all those able to speak in different languages given by God.

29 Are all apostles? Certainly not! Are all prophets? No! Do all have the ability to explain God's Word to others? No! Do all work miracles? No! 30 Do all manifest gifts of healings? No! Do all speak in tongues or interpret their meaning? 31 What you should do is to desire the greater gifts that will enable you to serve others; and I will now show you the most excellent way in which to live.

Be motivated by love (13:1-3)

13 Even if I speak in many languages, naturally or spiritually, I am only a noisy gong or a crashing cymbal unless I speak in love. 2 If God has given me a prophetic gift so that I am able to

understand what are mysteries to others, and even though I have deep spiritual knowledge, I am nothing if the gift is used without love. The same would be true if I used the gift of faith without love; yes, even faith that can move mountains is worthless without love.

3 If I give everything I have to the poor and even sacrifice my body for the sake of the gospel, I gain nothing if I am not motivated by love.

Characteristics of love (13:4-13)

4 These are the qualities of the love God gives us: His love in us enables us to be patient and kind. When motivated by this love we do not envy others, neither do we boast. Nor are we proud!

5 God's love in us is not rude, nor self seeking. We are not roused to anger quickly, and we certainly do not keep a mental record of the wrongs others have committed. 6 When God's love works through us, we take no delight in what He regards as evil. Rather, we rejoice in the truth that sets people free from evil. 7 Those who truly love always protect others, they always trust and are always full of hope. They always persevere, regardless of the circumstances.

8 So God's love never fails us.

The time to share prophetic words will come to an end. Then there will be no further use for tongues. Even human knowledge will be redundant. 9 At best, our knowledge is only partial and our prophecies imperfect. 10 When we are made perfect, we will have no need of the imperfect things; they will all disappear.

11 All this contrasts with my actions when I was a child. Then I could only think, reason and speak like a child. When I became an adult, I grew out of my childish ways. 12 Yet still I can see myself only as a poor reflection in a mirror compared with what God intends me to be. But when I see Him face to face I shall be like Him. Now I can only partially understand myself, but then I shall know God fully, and will see how complete is His knowledge of me.

13 Everything will then pass away, apart from these three things that will remain eternally: faith, hope and love. And I consider that love is the most important of these.

Prophecy and tongues (14:1-25)

14 So walk in the way of love, but at the same time eagerly desire that you will manifest spiritual gifts, especially that of prophecy, so you can tell others what is on God's heart. 2 When someone speaks in a language given by the Spirit he speaks to God, not man, and so nobody is able to understand what he says. He is

speaking with his spirit of things that remain a mystery to his
understanding and to those who hear him.

3-5 I want all of you to use this gift of tongues, but I urge you to
prophesy when with others, for then you will strengthen them by
the words you speak; you will encourage and comfort them. But the
one who speaks in an unknown language only benefits himself,
while the whole church can benefit from words of true prophecy.

In the public context, then, it is more important to prophesy than
to speak in tongues, unless someone interprets what is said for the
edification of the whole church.

6 So, my brothers, suppose I come to you and speak only in
tongues, how could I possibly be of any use to you? But if I bring
you revelation or impart some knowledge of the truth, bringing you
a prophetic word from God's heart or a word that shows you how
to live your life as a Christian, then I would certainly be of great
benefit to you.

7 Consider musical instruments such as the flute or harp. In themselves they are lifeless yet they make meaningful sounds when
someone plays a tune on them, one note following another. 8 In the
same way, if the trumpet does not make a clear sound, how will the
soldiers know they must prepare for battle? 9 This applies to you,
doesn't it? Unless you use words others can understand when you
speak, how will they know what you want to communicate?
Otherwise you may as well talk to yourself!

10 Even though there are many languages in the world, they all
have meaning to those who understand them. 11 But if I am unable
to understand what someone means when he speaks to me, I am a
foreigner to him and he to me. 12 Apply all this to yourselves. It is
good to desire eagerly to manifest spiritual gifts, but when together
concentrate on those gifts that build up everyone in the church.

13 So, if someone speaks publicly in a language given by the Spirit,
he should pray that God will enable him to interpret what he says.
14 You see, when I pray in such a tongue, my spirit is being strengthened
but my mind does not benefit. 15 As this is the case, what should I
do? I will certainly pray with my spirit, but I will also pray with my
mind, using words I and others can understand. I will sing with my
spirit, but I will also sing with words that are intelligible.

16 If you only praise God with your spirit, how can those among
you who do not understand say "Amen" to your thanksgiving,
since they have no idea what you are saying? 17 You may well be
thanking God, but the others cannot meaningfully join in with you;
so they are not encouraged.

[18] I thank God that I use the gift of speaking in tongues more than
any of you. [19] However, in the church meeting I would prefer to
speak five intelligible words to communicate the truth to others
than ten thousand words they could not understand.

[20] So, my brothers, stop thinking like little children. You can be
like babies who are ignorant of evil, but you now need to be adult
in the way you think. [21] It is written in God's law, "I will speak to these
people through men of strange tongues and by the lips of foreigners;
even so they will not heed what I say, says the Lord."

[22] Tongues can be a sign of the Spirit's presence and power to
unbelievers as well as believers. But prophecy is for the benefit of
those who believe, not for unbelievers.

[23] However, when the whole church comes together, if anyone
speaks in tongues without any interpretation, will not unbelievers
who come in among you think you are all out of your minds? [24-25] If,
on the other hand, an unbeliever or someone who does not understand the workings of the Spirit, comes in among you while people
are prophesying, he may well hear words that will convict him that
he is a sinner in danger of judgment because the secrets of his heart
are being exposed. If this is the case he will fall on his knees before
God and worship Him saying, 'God is real and He is here among
you!'

Order in church meetings (14:26-40)

[26] How then can we sum up, brothers? When you meet together,
everyone can have something to contribute, a hymn, a word of
instruction, a revelation from God, a word in a language given by
the Spirit, or interpretation of that word. But it is important that you
use all these in ways that strengthen the whole church. [27] You need
only two or three to bring a message in tongues, speaking one at a
time, but then someone must interpret what has been said. [28] If no
one present is able to interpret, it would be better that the one who
speaks in tongues talks to God and himself, and not to everyone
else.

[29] Likewise, only two or three prophetic utterances are needed,
and others present should consider carefully what has been said, to
discern if this is truly a word from God and what actions need to be
taken in response. [30] If another receives a revelation from God while
someone is already speaking, the speaker should give way so that
the revelation can be heard by all. [31] You do not need to speak at the

14:21 Isaiah 28:11-12

same time; you can all prophesy in turn. Then everyone will hear
what is said and receive both instruction and encouragement. 32No-
one should ever be out of control when he prophesies, and he is
subject to those with the responsibility to weigh what is being said.

33There should never be disorder in the meeting, for God is a God
of order, not chaos.

34It is the usual practice among the congregation of saints that the
women should remain silent. They are not permitted to speak, but
must demonstrate their submission as indicated in the law. 35If they
have questions they should ask their husbands at home; for in our
present society it would be considered a disgrace for a woman to
speak publicly in a church meeting.

36Did you decide what should be written in God's Word? Are you
the only people who know the truth? 37Let anyone among you who
regards himself as a prophet or one spiritually gifted, acknowledge
that I write only what the Lord has commanded. 38To ignore this
would be a sign of ignorance.

39So, my brothers, it is right to be ready to prophesy and certainly you are not to forbid the speaking in tongues. 40But ensure that
everything is done in an orderly way which benefits God's saints.

The gospel of Christ (15:1-11)

15 Now, brothers, there are certain aspects of the gospel about
which I want to remind you. This is the truth I preached to
you and on which you stand firm. 2It is by the gospel that you are
saved, so long as you continue to hold on firmly to the Word I
preached to you. To give up would be to have believed for nothing!

3What I passed onto you as of primary importance I had first
received: that Christ died for our sins to fulfil the scriptures. 4He
was buried and was raised back to life on the third day, again to fulfil
what was promised in scripture. 5He appeared to Peter and then to
the twelve disciples. 6Then He appeared to over five hundred of the
brethren at the same time, most of whom are still living, although
some have fallen asleep in the Lord. 7He next appeared to James
and then to all the apostles. 8Last of all, He even appeared to me as
well, despite my total unworthiness because of my former opposition.

9You see, I consider myself to be the least of the apostles because
I persecuted God's church. I do not even deserve to be called an
apostle. 10Yet by God's grace alone I am what I am, and that grace
has proved effective. I worked harder than all the other apostles,
although not in my own strength but through God's grace working
with me.

11 No matter who preaches, the other apostles or myself, we agree in what we preach and this is the gospel that you have believed.

Resurrection of the dead (15:12-24)

12 Now if it is preached that Christ has been raised from the dead, how is it possible for some of you to say that there is no resurrection of the dead? 13 If there is no resurrection of the dead, then even Christ Himself would not have been raised. 14 If that was the case, our preaching is of no value, nor is your faith! 15 Not only that, but we could be accused of being false witnesses in what we say about God, for we have openly and clearly testified that God raised Christ from the dead. If God did not do that, then it would be true to say the dead are not raised. 16 If the dead cannot be raised, then clearly Christ could not have been raised. 17 And if this is the case, your faith is useless and you are still in the bondage of sin. 18 Then we would also conclude that those who were in Christ but have already died, are lost eternally. 19 But if we only have hope in Christ for our time on earth in this life, we are to be pitied more than anyone.

20 The truth is, Christ has certainly been raised from the dead, the first to be resurrected of all who have died. 21 Death entered man's experience through Adam's sin; but the resurrection of the dead has also come through a man – the Lord Jesus Christ. 22 All share in Adam's death, but all those in Christ will be made alive with Him.

23 God has His order in this: Christ was the first to be raised; then when He comes again those who belong to Him will be raised with him. 24 Then it will be the end of this age as we know it. Christ Jesus will destroy all the dominion, authority and power of this present order; then He will hand over to God the Father all who belong to His Kingdom.

Christ's authority (15:25-34)

25-26 He must reign until all His enemies are placed beneath His feet, including death itself, the last enemy to be destroyed. 27 This fulfils the scripture that states, "He has placed everything under His feet."

Although it says that 'everything' is placed under Him, clearly this does not include God Himself, for He is the one who placed everything under Christ's authority. 28 When all this has taken place, the Son will remain subject to God who placed everything under His authority, so that God is Lord over all.

15:27 Psalm 8:6

29 Of course, if resurrection does not ever take place, there would
be no point in some people thinking they can be baptised on behalf
of the dead. If the dead are never raised, this would be a ridiculous
thing to do!

30 As for ourselves, in what ways can we be in danger? 31 There is
a sense in which I die every day, die to myself I mean. It is worth it
so I can give God glory for you, because you are in Christ Jesus and
so belong to Him.

32 It is not for my own human reasons that I fight against those in
Ephesus who oppose me as if they were wild beasts; for I would
gain nothing if that were the case.

Do not be misled by those who think there is no resurrection and
so adopt the attitude, "Let us eat and drink as much as we want, for
tomorrow we die anyway." 33 If you associate with such bad company,
your good character will be affected, for 'bad company corrupts
good character.' 34 You know it is right to be sensible and to stop every
sinful practice. Not to do so shows ignorance of God, and it is really
to your shame that I need to say such things to you.

The resurrection (15:35-58)

35 You may wonder, "How are the dead raised? What will the resurrection body be like in those who return with Christ?" 36 Such speculation is foolish!

What is sown cannot reproduce life unless it first dies. 37 You sow
only a seed, not the plant that will result, perhaps of wheat or some
other crop. 38 God gives the 'body' of the plant according to the
nature of the seed, just as He has determined in creation.

39 All creatures are not the same. Men have one kind of body,
animals another and fish are different again. 40 There are heavenly
creatures as well as earthly ones. The glory of those with heavenly
bodies is of another order compared with the glory of those with
earthly bodies. 41 The sun has its particular radiance, the moon and
the stars a different radiance altogether. Even one star can differ
from another in brightness.

42 So in the resurrection of the dead, the risen body will be different
from the natural body. The earthly body will perish; but in its risen
state it is imperishable. 43 It has no particular honour in its natural
state, but is raised in glory. The natural body is weak but it is raised
in power. 44 On earth it is natural; it is raised as a spiritual body and
so is supernatural.

15:32 Isaiah 22:13

So if you have a natural body now, you will have a spiritual body then. 45 It is written, "The first man Adam was created as a living being." But the last 'Adam', Jesus Christ our Lord, is a life-giving Spirit. 46 The natural came before the spiritual. 47 The first man was created from the dust of the earth; but the second Man came from heaven.

48 All on earth follow after the earthly man, Adam; but those who were born from above are as the One who now reigns in heaven. 49 We have been like the earthly man, Adam; we shall be like the man who came from heaven, Jesus Christ!

50 I tell you clearly, my brothers, our natural bodies of flesh and blood cannot inherit the eternal Kingdom of God, nor can that which is perishable inherit the imperishable.

51-52 Listen to me carefully, for I am unfolding a mystery to you: All of us will not simply die, but we will be transformed in a moment of time, in the twinkling of an eye, when the last trumpet sounds. Then those of us who have died in Christ will be raised with imperishable bodies, and we will be transformed. 53 The time will come when that which was perishable must be clothed with the imperishable, what was mortal will become immortal.

54 When the perishable body has been clothed with the imperishable and the mortal has put on immortality, then it will be seen that the saying that it is written is true and has been fulfilled: "Victory has swallowed up death."

55 "So, death, where is your victory? Where is your sting?" 56 Sin is death's sting and the power of sin is seen through our inability to keep God's law. 57 Yet now God gives us the victory over sin and death through our Lord Jesus Christ.

58 In light of this, stand firm in your faith, my brothers. Let nothing shake you. Give yourselves totally and continually to the Lord's work, because you know that whatever you do in the Lord is not futile, but will bear lasting fruit.

Offerings for God's people (16:1-4)

16 Now I want to speak to you about the gift you have been collecting for God's people. You are to follow the same instructions I gave to the churches in Galatia. 2 Every one of you should set aside a sum of money on the first day of the week, one

15:45 Genesis 2:7
15:54 Isaiah 25:8
15:55 Hosea 13:14

that reflects your personal income. Save these offerings until I come,
so that I do not need to raise a special collection then. [3]I will write
letters of introduction when I arrive for those men you have chosen
to take your combined offering to Jerusalem, those worthy of such
trust. [4]If it seems right that I should go there myself, then they will
accompany me.

Paul's plans (16:5-12)

[5-6]I intend to pass through Macedonia on my way to Corinth. I must
go to Macedonia first, but when I come to you I hope it will be possible
for me to stay in Corinth for a time. I may even be able to spend a
winter with you, so you can help me prepare for my onward journey,
wherever that may be. [7]This would be much better than trying to
see you now for what could only be a brief visit. If the Lord allows,
I really want to spend some time with you. [8-9]However, I will remain
at Ephesus until Pentecost, because a wonderful opportunity has
been given me for the effective work of the gospel, even though
many oppose me.

[10]If Timothy visits you, make him feel at home; he should have
nothing to fear while he is with you for, like me, he is doing the
Lord's work. [11]Be sure that no one refuses to accept him. Then send
him back to me in peace, for I am expecting him along with the
other brethren.

[12]Let me explain about Apollos. I really wanted him to come to
you with the other brothers, but he was very reluctant to do so now;
but he will certainly come as soon as he has a suitable opportunity.

Closing farewell (16:13-23)

[13]Always be on your guard and stand firm in your faith. Be men full
of courage and be strong. [14]At the same time, let everything you do
be done in love.

[15-16]You are aware that Stephanas and his household were the first
to be converted in Asia. Ever since, they have been devoted in the
way they have served the saints. I strongly encourage you, my
brothers, to have a right heart of submission to such believers and
to all others who work hard for the cause of the gospel.

[17]I was pleased when Stephanas, Fortunatus and Achaicus
arrived, for they brought me the encouragement which I could not
receive from you personally. [18]I felt refreshed in my spirit by these
men, and they will refresh you as well. Such men deserve to be
recognised and honoured.

19 Greetings from the churches in the province of Asia. Aquila and
Prescilla also send their warmest greetings in the Lord, together
with all those who belong to the church that meets in their home.
20 All the other brethren here send their greetings, as well.

Share the love of Christ among you in a holy way.

21 I, Paul, close with this greeting written in my own hand.

22 A curse is on anyone who does not love the Lord. Come, O Lord,
come!

23 May the Lord Jesus impart His grace to you. 24 My love to all of
you who are in Christ Jesus. Amen! It shall be so!

2 CORINTHIANS

Hope in the midst of suffering (1:1-11)

1 From Paul, an apostle of Christ Jesus by God's will, and our
brother Timothy.

To God's church in Corinth and all the saints, the born-again
believers throughout Greece.

2 May God our Father and the Lord Jesus Christ impart grace and
peace to you.

3-4 We praise the God and Father of our Lord Jesus Christ, for He
is the Father of compassion and is full of mercy. He is the God of all
comfort, who daily gives us strength. Yes, He sees us through all our
difficulties, so that we are able to strengthen others in their troubles
with the same strength we have received from Him ourselves.

5 The sufferings that Christ endured spill over into our lives; but,
in the same way, His strength overflows through us into the lives of
others. 6 So if we have to suffer any distress it will have a positive
affect on you, for you will receive strength and God's saving grace.
If we are strengthened by God it is so that you in turn will be
enabled to endure patiently whatever suffering you have to face.
7 This encourages us to believe that your future hope is secure, for it
is sure that if you have to suffer for the gospel as we do, then you
will also be strengthened as we are!

8-9 Brothers, we do not want you to be ignorant about the troubles
we faced in the province of Asia. We felt so completely overwhelmed
by the pressure we were under that it seemed impossible for us to
be able to survive; it was as if we were living under a death sentence.
Now we understand that this was allowed to happen to us so that
we would not rely on ourselves at all, but only on God who has the
power to raise the dead. 10 And that is what it was like, as if we had
been delivered from death itself. Now we can be confident that He
will always deliver us, no matter what we have to face in the future.

11 So we have set our hope on God; we are sure our future is in His
hands and that He will continue to free us, helped as we are by your
prayers for us. This being the case, many will join with us in giving

thanks for the way we experienced God's grace and His favour, a definite answer to all your prayers for our safety and well being.

God's enabling grace (1:12-24)

12 Now we have great confidence and our consciences bear witness that we have behaved righteously in this world, and especially in the ways we have related to you in the holiness and sincere love that we received from God. This is not the outworking of any worldly wisdom but the result of God's grace, of all He has given
us. 13-14 This grace enables me to write to you in a way you can readily understand. I really trust that you will not be satisfied with partial understanding, but will come to a full appreciation of what we say, so that you can have confidence in us, just as we will have confidence about you when the Lord Jesus Christ returns.

15 Because of this confidence I have about you, I planned to visit
you to impart a double blessing. 16 I wanted to visit you on my way
to Macedonia and then again on my return journey. Then you could have sent me on my way to Judea.

17 This was not some frivolous wish, because I do not make decisions in a worldly way. I do not say 'Yes' and 'No' in the same breath!

18 God is faithful in what He says. So our message to you is not,
'Yes' and 'No.' 19 Jesus Christ, God's Son, about whom Silas, Timothy
and I preached to you, was not 'Yes' and 'No.' In Him the truth is
revealed as always being 'Yes.' 20 No matter how many promises
God gives us, they are all affirmed in Christ with a mighty 'Yes.' We can say 'Amen,' 'It shall be so', to all that is said through Him, and such faithful affirmation gives glory to God.

21-22 So it is God Himself who enables both you and us to stand firm in Christ. For He Himself anointed each of us personally, thus setting His seal of ownership upon us by placing His own Spirit in our hearts. This wonderful deposit that we have received from Him is a guarantee of what is to come, our full inheritance.

23 God is my witness when I tell you that the true reason why I did
not return to Corinth was because I had your own interests at heart.
I did not want to have to rebuke you further. 24 I did not want you to
think that I was always putting you down, telling you what to do; we need to work together for the gospel with joy, as you stand firm in your faith!

Paul's love for the Corinthians (2:1-4)

2 This is why I decided not to make another painful visit to you.
2 What purpose would it serve to grieve you? If I only did that,

how could you ever cause me to rejoice in you. 3 This is why I wrote as I did, so that by the time I visited you these distressing matters would have been resolved. Then instead of causing you further grief, those same brethren would give me joy! Yes, I had such confidence that all of you would share my joy, not my grief. 4 For when I wrote before I was so deeply upset, so heart-broken, that I was in tears, not tears of grief but tears that flowed from the depth of love I want you to know that I have for you.

Forgive the troublemaker (2:5-11)

5 The troublemaker who has grieved me has actually done more to grieve all of you than to hurt me. And that is putting it mildly. 6 The judgment passed on him by the majority of the church is sufficient punishment for him. 7 Now it is time for him to know that you have forgiven him and want to restore him, so that he does not believe he is past redemption, that there is no hope for him.

8 So I encourage you now to let him know that you really love him and are concerned for him. 9 What I wrote before was a real test for you, to see if you would obey what I told you to do and take the necessary action. 10-11 If you forgive him, be sure I also forgive him. And whatever I forgive, and whenever I forgive, it is always before Christ and for your benefit, so that Satan may not have any advantage over us. For we know well his evil intentions.

Paul continues to spread the truth (2:12-17)

12-13 When I went to preach the gospel of Christ in Troas and found that the Lord had opened a door of great opportunity for me, I still was not at peace because my brother Titus was not there as I had expected. So I left there and made for Macedonia.

14 But thanks be to God, for He always leads us in His triumphant procession because we are in Christ. And He uses us everywhere we go to spread the truth about Him. 15-16 For we are to God like the perfume of Christ among those who are being saved; the sweet fragrance of His life. But it is different among those who are perishing because of their rejection of the gospel. To them we have the smell of death about us.

17 However, we are not like those who preach God's Word simply for their own financial gain; quite the opposite. We speak before God as those who live in Christ. So we preach with sincerity, as men sent by God with His commission.

Ministers of a new covenant (3:1-18)

3 Does it sound as if we are commending ourselves again? Do
we need letters of recommendation, as some do? Are we asking
you to recommend us to others? 2 No, you are the only letter we
need, for you are written on our hearts and everybody can see clearly
what is written there. 3 You demonstrate that as a result of our ministry,
you are a letter from Christ, not written on paper with ink, not
chiselled out on tablets of stone, but written with the Spirit of the
living God on human hearts.

4 This is the confidence we have before God through our faith in
Christ. 5 We are not able because of our natural abilities to claim any
credit for ourselves. Our ability comes from God. 6 He has made us
able to be ministers of the new covenant, which is based not on the
letter of the law, but on the Spirit of God. For religious legalism kills,
but God's Spirit gives life!

7 The ministry based on letters engraved on stone resulted in failure
and death. Even so, that ministry expressed something of God's
glory, for the Israelites were not able to stare at Moses' face because
it shone with that glory, even though it was a glory that faded. 8 But
how much more of God's glory will be revealed through the
ministry of His Spirit? 9 If the ministry that condemns men for failing
to keep the law is glorious, how much more of God's glory is
revealed through the ministry that makes men righteous and
acceptable to God! 10 For the glory of the old covenant is as nothing
compared with the glory of the new. 11 The glory of the old faded; so
how much greater is the glory of the new, the glory that lasts forever!

12 Having this as our hope makes us very bold. 13 For we are not
like Moses who had to cover His face so the Israelites would not see
the radiance fading as they stared at him. 14 Even to this day a veil
covers the minds of those who hear the old covenant being read,
causing them to be incapable of spiritual understanding. Only
through faith in Christ can that veil be removed. 15 Yes, that veil still
covers their hearts when the books of Moses are read. 16 Yet as soon
as someone turns to the Lord, that veil is removed and he can
understand the truth!

17 Now the Spirit is the Spirit of the Lord God and where His
Spirit is present, people have been set free. 18 So our faces are not
covered or veiled, but we are all able to reflect the Lord's glory. The
more that glory is revealed in us, the more like Him we become! So
this glory that comes from the Lord is continually increasing in our
lives because the Spirit of glory lives in us.

Suffering for the gospel (4:1-18)

4 Therefore we have no cause to be downhearted because, by
God's mercy, we have been given this ministry of glory. 2 For this
reason we have put all shameful ways behind us and have nothing to
hide. We do not deceive people, nor do we try to make God's Word
say what we want it to say. Quite the opposite; we proclaim the truth
simply and clearly so that everyone can see our integrity before God.

3 If the gospel we preach is not understood, this is only because
those who are perishing are blind to the truth. 4 The god of this age
has blinded their minds and understanding so they are incapable of
receiving the glorious light of Christ, who is exactly like God the
Father and is revealed through the gospel. 5 So we do not preach for
our own glory or adulation but as your servants, to reveal Jesus to you.

6 For God has declared, "Light is to shine where before there was
darkness," and so He has caused His light to shine in our hearts. He
has given us the light that comes from knowing God's glory in our
experience, as revealed through the person of Christ.

7 We already have this treasure of Christ's glory in our bodies,
which are but clay jars by comparison. It is evident that this power
is greater than any other power and is already within us, a gift from
God, not something we could produce ourselves.

8 There are times when we seem to be surrounded by insur-
mountable problems, but we are never crushed or defeated by them.
At times we are thoroughly perplexed about why certain things
happen to us, but we never despair. 9 We are persecuted for our
faith, but God never abandons us. Even if we are sometimes struck
down by some adversity, we are not destroyed. 10 For when we suffer
in our bodies, we share in Jesus' own passion and death, so that His
risen life may also be revealed through our bodies.

11 While we are in the world it seems that we have to die continually
to self for Jesus' sake, so the life of His Spirit can be revealed
through our natural bodies. 12 This process of death is at work in us,
to enable God's life to be at work in you!

13-14 It is written in the Psalms, "I have spoken what I have
believed." By the same Spirit of Faith we also believe the truth and
speak it openly and boldly because we know that the Father who
raised the Lord Jesus from the dead will also raise us up with Him.
Yes, Jesus will present all believers to the Father so we can live
eternally in His Presence.

4:6 *Genesis 1:3*
4:14 *Psalm 116:10*

15 Whatever we suffer is for your benefit and enables many more
people to receive God's grace, causing them to be profoundly
thankful that God is glorified in them.
16 Therefore we are not discouraged. Even if outwardly we seem
to grow weaker, yet inwardly we are daily becoming stronger. 17 For
the difficulties we face now are only temporary and trivial, compared
with the eternal glory we inherit. 18 For this reason we keep our
focus, not on what we see or experience now, for such things are
only temporary. No, we focus on what we do not yet see, but which
is ours eternally.

Looking forward to heaven (5:1-10)

5 Now we are assured that when this earthly tent we live in is
destroyed, when we die physically and have finished with
these present bodies, we have a new home to look forward to in
heaven, a house that has not been constructed with human hands,
but an eternal body! 2 We grow tired of our present bodies, longing
for the time when we will be clothed with our new heavenly bodies.
3 We will not feel exposed then as we do now. 4 In this present body
we struggle and feel burdened by our sufferings; but our spirits will
have new spiritual bodies in heaven. Our mortal lives will give way
to the immortal, to eternal life.
5 God has made us His children for this very reason. This is
proved by the fact that He has already given us His eternal Spirit,
the guarantee of our future destiny. 6 Therefore we have good cause
to be confident, no matter what the situation; for we know that
while we live in these present bodies we are not yet at one with the
Lord in our heavenly bodies. 7 But we live by faith in what He has
promised, not in what we see happening at present. 8 I repeat, we
can have absolute confidence that it will be much better when we
have finished with these present bodies and have been taken home
to be with the Lord eternally.
9 This being the case, we have made it our aim to please Him in
every way possible, both now in this life and in the life that is to
come. 10 For we all have to come before the judgment seat of Christ,
so that each of us will receive the right reward for what he or she
has done in this present body. And He will determine what has been
good and what has been bad in His eyes.

No longer live for ourselves (5:11-17)

11 Because we know what it means to live in fear of the Lord, not
wanting to displease Him in any way, we do all we can to persuade

others to believe the truth of the gospel. God knows this is our intention and I trust you also realise this. 12 We are not trying to promote ourselves again, but we do want you to be proud about what we are doing. Then you will have a ready answer for those who are interested in what the world offers, instead of being concerned about the condition of their hearts before God. 13 We are only being faithful to God in what we do, even if it appears to some that we are out of our minds. We are actually in our right minds, and so you are able to benefit. 14 It is our love for Christ that compels us to action.

We are convinced that He died for all and therefore all have died with Him. 15 But if He died for all it means that those of us who have received His risen life should no longer live for ourselves, but for the One who died and was raised again for us!

16 So from this point onwards we will not assess anyone by worldly standards. We used to have a very worldly view of Christ, but that is no longer the case. 17 Now we are sure that if anyone is in Christ, made one with Him by their faith in Him, then that person is a new creation. The old person he was has died, is buried and finished with – gone forever. Now he has become a new person.

Message of reconciliation (5:18-6:2)

18 All this is entirely the work of God Himself. He alone could reconcile us with Himself, and He has done this through Christ. This is why He has now given us the ministry of reconciliation, to see others made one with Him in His love.

19 In Christ, God was doing all that was necessary to reconcile the whole world to Himself, a reconciliation that can only take place when men's sins are forgiven and God no longer regards them as guilty.

Yes, He has given us this message, this gospel of reconciliation. 20 This means we are Christ's ambassadors; He reaches out to others through us. This is why we beg on Christ's behalf that all of you be reconciled to God, so that you live at one with Him.

21 Look at what it cost God to make this possible! He caused His perfect Son, who was sinless, to take all our sin upon Himself. He suffered the punishment for sin that we deserve, so that now we might become those who live in right standing with God!

6 Because we work with God in the cause of the gospel, we implore you not to reject the grace He has offered you. 2 He says, "Because this is the time of My favour I have heard you. Because

this is the day of salvation I have helped you." Listen to me! This is now the time of His favour. This is the day of His salvation when you can be reconciled and made one with Him.

The cost of living for the gospel (6:3-13)

3 So we have no desire to hinder anyone from receiving what God
wants to give. If we were to do that, our ministry would be discredited. 4 No, we are able to commend ourselves in every way
because of the cost we have been prepared to embrace for the cause
of the gospel. We have needed great endurance in the face of many
difficulties and hardships and in circumstances that have caused
much distress. 5 We have suffered floggings, imprisonment and
even riots. We certainly have worked hard and have known what it
is to be without sleep and food. 6 We have had to live in purity. We
have needed understanding, patience and kindness. We have followed
the leading of the Holy Spirit and have acted with love. 7 We have
spoken the truth and have been instruments of God's power. We
have needed to use the spiritual weapons of righteousness to be on
the offensive, and also in self-defence.

8 We have known times of glory and yet have been treated with
dishonour. Sometimes we have been praised, at other times we have
been slandered. Although we are genuine we have been regarded
by some as impostors. 9 Sometimes we are well known, in other
places nobody knows who we are. We have been close to death, but
we are still here! We have been beaten, but not killed. 10 Even in times
of sorrow we have continued to rejoice. Even when poor ourselves,
we have been able to make many rich through what they have
received from God. We have nothing ourselves, yet truly we have
everything in Christ!

11 My beloved friends at Corinth, we have spoken freely to you
from hearts that are wide open to you. 12 We do not hold back from
showing our love for you. So do not withhold your love and affection
from us. 13 Treat us as we treat you and open your hearts to us as my
dear children.

A people set apart (6:14-7:1)

14 Do not be joined together with unbelievers. How can you, who are
made righteous and acceptable to God, be one with those who are
still numbered among the ungodly? What could you have in common
with them? 15 What unity could ever exist between Christ and the

6:2 Isaiah 49:8

devil? What unity can ever exist between a believer and a non-
believer? [16]You are a living temple of God, so how can you be one
with those who make idols of other people or the things that they
do?

Remember what God has said, "I will live in them and will walk
with them; and I will be their God and they will be My own special
people." [17]And so He has also commanded, "Therefore, be a people
set apart from the ungodly. Have nothing to do with anything that
is unclean in My sight, and you will draw close to Me. [18]I will be
your Father and you My sons and daughters, says the Lord God
Almighty."

7 What wonderful promises God gives us, dear friends! So let us
cleanse ourselves from everything that causes our spirits or
bodies to be defiled and unclean in His sight. Instead let us seek to
be completely holy in all we do, because we take God's purposes
seriously.

Godly sorrow leads to repentance (7:2-16)

[2]So I repeat: open your hearts to us. Look at our record. We have
never wronged anyone, nor corrupted or exploited them. [3]I am not
condemning you, for I assure you that we love you from the heart
and are ready to live or die for you. [4]Actually, I have great confidence
that you will do what is right, and I take great pride in you, for you
have encouraged me in all my troubles, giving me great joy.

[5]When we entered Macedonia we had no rest but were opposed
in whatever we did. We had to contend with the external conflicts
and the internal fears caused by being so hounded. [6-7]However, God
strengthens the downhearted, and we were encouraged when Titus
arrived with the news that you had given him encouragement. He
told us that you were longing to see me, that you were deeply sorry
about the issues that had to be resolved and now had a heartfelt
concern for my welfare. And this news gave me even greater joy!

[8]Although I did regret it at the time, I no longer regret causing
you the sorrow and pain that resulted from the letter I sent you.
[9]Now I am content, not at having to cause you any distress, but
because your sorrow has led to real repentance, a change of heart
and mind on your part. God knew this sorrow was necessary, and
so you were not harmed by it in any way. [10]When God causes sorrow

6:16 Leviticus 26:12
6:18 2 Samuel 7:14, 7:8

it leads to repentance, which in turn leads to salvation. We do not
regret that kind of sorrow; but the sorrow the world causes is totally
different and leads to death, not life!
11 Consider, then, what changes have taken place in you as a result
of this godly sorrow. You are now more earnest about the things of
God. You are keen to clear yourselves of any guilt. You now feel
indignant about the sin you once allowed. You were even alarmed
about the situation and longed to see good order restored. Now you
are concerned that those involved are dealt with justly. So you have
proved ready to do everything in a righteous manner.
12 When I wrote, I was not taking sides either with the guilty party
or with those who were wronged. Before God you needed to
demonstrate that you are devoted to us by taking note of what we
wrote. 13 And we are truly encouraged by your response.
Not only are we encouraged, but we are especially pleased to see
how happy you made Titus by the way you received him. He was
refreshed spiritually as a result. 14 I had told him great things about
you, and you did not let me down. We spoke the truth to you, but
we also spoke the truth about you to Titus. 15 Now he remembers
your obedience with great affection because you listened to him
with both respect and concern to do what was right. So it pleases
me to be able to have such confidence in you.

Generosity encouraged (8:1-15)

8 Brothers, we want to tell you about the grace the Macedonian
churches have received from God. 2 Despite the fact that they
had to face extreme difficulties themselves, they still overflowed
with great joy and gave with such wonderful generosity, regardless
of their own dire poverty. 3-4 I can assure you that they gave as much
as they were able to give, and more besides. On their own initiative,
they begged us to allow them to share in the privilege of giving to
their fellow saints. 5 So they went far beyond our expectations,
devoting themselves first to the Lord and then to us, being prepared
to accept the direction God would give them through us.
6 So we have encouraged Titus, who had originally inspired you
to give, to return and help you complete this generous action. 7 You
have shown that you excel in everything, in your faith, in the things
you say, in your knowledge of God's will and in truly longing to see
His will for you fulfilled. Yes, you also excel in your love for us. So
now also prove that you excel in this grace of giving. 8 I am not
ordering you to give, but I am testing the genuine nature of your

love by comparing it with the way others have been so enthusiastic in the way they have given.

[9]You are well aware of the nature of the grace our Lord Jesus Christ has demonstrated. In heaven He was rich beyond measure, yet for your sakes He came to share the poverty of our humanity, so that now through that poverty you are able to share in His heavenly riches.

[10]I believe this to be the best course of action for you. Last year you were the first to express the desire to give to the saints in need, and you gave accordingly. [11]Now complete what you began, to show that you are just as eager to complete the task as you were to begin it, using whatever means you have. [12]The amount is acceptable if given willingly. You can only give what you have, not what you do not have.

[13]Our intention is not that you put yourselves in a difficult financial position in order to relieve the needs of others, but that there shall be sharing among the brethren. [14-15]At this time you can supply for their needs out of your surplus, so that at another time they can supply for your needs out of their surplus. So in time there is equality among you all, for it is written, "The one who gathered much did not have more than he needed, and the one who gathered little did not have too little."

Titus returns to Corinth (8:16-24)

[16]I thank God that He gave Titus the same heart for you as I have. [17]He not only welcomed my request to make a return visit, but was genuinely eager to see you all again. [18]We are sending with him a brother who has been praised by all the churches for the way he has served the cause of the gospel. [19]In addition, this brother was selected by the churches to accompany us when we take the gift to Jerusalem. Administering this gift honours the Lord and shows how eager we are to help the brethren there. [20]But we are going to be careful to avoid any criticism for the way in which we handle this generous gift. [21]We will go out of our way to show that everything is seen to be done righteously before the Lord and in the eyes of men.

[22]We are also sending with Titus another brother, who has proved himself in many ways to be truly zealous in serving others. This is even more the case now, because he has such confidence in you.

[23]I regard Titus as my partner who works with me for your good. And all these brothers represent the churches and honour Christ by

8:15 Exodus 16:18

the way they conduct themselves. [24]Therefore, show these men how genuine is your love for them and that our pride in you is fully justified, for this will be a good witness to all the churches.

Sowing and reaping (9:1-15)

9 I do not need to write further to you about serving your fellow saints in Jerusalem through this gift. [2]I know you are so keen to help them that I have been boasting about you to the brethren in Macedonia, telling them that for a whole year you brethren in Greece have been ready to give. In fact, your enthusiasm has been catching and has inspired others to action. [3]And I am sending these brothers to you now so that what we have said about you might prove true and not be empty words, that you will give generously as I told others would be the case.

[4]If any Macedonians who accompany me when I come to visit you find that your gift is not ready I will feel ashamed of you and humiliated before them, having spoken so well of you. [5]So I thought it wise to send these brothers ahead of me to ensure that everything is in place and that the generous gift you promised is already collected willingly and not given begrudgingly.

[6]Remember this spiritual principle: he who sows a little will only reap a little, and he who sows to bless generously will reap generous blessings. [7]But each person has to decide in his own heart what he will give, not reluctantly or because he feels under pressure to give; for God loves those who give willingly and joyfully. [8]He is able to cause all His grace to overflow in your lives, so that in all things at all times, you will have all you need and much more besides, so that you will overflow in the way you bless others. [9]As it is written, 'He has given generous gifts to the poor and his righteous actions will never be forgotten.'

[10]The Lord supplies seed for the sower so we can have bread to eat; and He will also supply you with many opportunities to give so that you will reap a great harvest through your righteous deeds. [11]As a result, you will be made rich in every way so that you will have even more to give when the opportunity arises. And many will be thankful to God for what they have received through your generosity.

[12]So you can see that this present situation will not only serve to meet the needs of God's people, but will also cause them to overflow with praise and thankfulness to God for His provision. [13]At the same time, you will have demonstrated the reality of your love and

9:9 Psalm 112:9

so they will praise God for your loving obedience, the outworking of the faith you claim in the gospel of Christ. They will thank God for you because of your willingness to share what you have with them and with others.

14 So they will hold you before God in prayer because of this wonderful grace that He has given you – the grace to give generously, willingly and joyfully. 15 So thanks be to God for the greatest and most wonderful gift of His grace to us all, His Son Jesus Christ.

Demolishing enemy strongholds (10:1-6)

10 You regard me as a timid person when I am with you, and think that I am bold when I write to you from a distance. 2 Well I, Paul, appeal to you now in the humility and gentleness of Christ to take note of all I am saying to you, so that when I visit you I will not have to be bold as I have to be with those who think that we Christians can live by worldly standards. 3 True, we live in this world; but we do not fight our battles as people who belong to the world. 4 We have other weapons to fight with, not those of the world. By contrast, our weapons have God's power that shatters the enemy's strongholds that oppose us. 5 With the weapon of truth we demolish rational arguments that oppose the walk of faith. We have the answer to every false way of thinking that seeks to undermine the truth about God. We exercise authority in the way we think, denying negative or rebellious thoughts, and accepting only those that glorify Jesus so that we might obey Him. 6 But we must be prepared to punish those who refuse to obey so that, as a church, we might be united in obedience.

Paul's God-given authority (10:7-18)

7 You look at things superficially. If you are assured that you belong to Christ, you must remember that we also belong to Him in just the same way. 8 I do not hide the truth; the Lord gave us His authority to encourage you and build up the church, not to discourage or destroy you. I refuse to be ashamed of the authority He has given me. 9 At the same time, I have no desire to intimidate you by what I write. 10 For some say, "his letters are full of authority and power, but he does not appear to be an impressive character when you see him; and he is not a great speaker."

11 Those with such attitudes should understand that I am the same person when I write from a distance as I am when with you in person, as my actions prove.

12 I would not dare to think of myself as highly as those who
commend themselves, nor would I want to compare myself with
them. They are not wise to measure themselves by their own standards,
or to compare themselves with others around them. 13-14 I will not
make any claims beyond those it is right to make, but will restrict
the use of my authority to the areas God has assigned to me. So I am
not going too far in the authority I claim to have over you, for I
brought the gospel of Christ to you. I would not expect to have the
same authority if I had nothing to do with you.

15-16 Neither do I claim the credit for the work done among you by
others. My hope is that I will have even greater influence among
you as your faith continues to develop, so that I can then move on
to preach the gospel in other places further away that have not yet
been reached with the gospel! I never want to be satisfied with
working where others are also working. 17 The scripture declares,
"Anyone who boasts should boast only in what the Lord does."

18 So the person who commends himself is not necessarily
approved, but only he whom the Lord commends!

Paul jealous about the church (11:1-9)

11 I trust that you will continue to bear with me if I go on talking
foolishly for a moment. 2 I feel jealous about you, but with
jealousy that comes from God. I promised you to Christ as your
only Husband; a pure virgin given to Him as His bride. 3 However,
I fear that you might wander away from your heartfelt and pure
devotion to Christ, in the same way as Eve was deceived by the
devil's cunning. 4 For you are influenced in the ways you think by
those who come and preach a different Jesus than the Jesus who was
preached to you. You even allow yourselves to come under the
influence of a different spirit from the Spirit given you when you
believed the truth. You end up believing a different gospel from the one
you accepted at the beginning. And you do all these things so readily!

5 I know I am not at all inferior to those 'super-apostles.' 6 I may
not be a great orator, but I do know the truth, as I have made
abundantly clear to you.

7 Do you think I sinned in humbling myself before you when my
purpose was to see you raised up by preaching the good news from
God to you, without asking anything from you? 8 Did I 'rob' the
other churches because they gave me financial support so that I
could serve you with the gospel?

10:17 Jeremiah 9:24

9 And when I needed anything while I was with you in Corinth, I
never became a burden to you, for the Macedonian brothers who
visited met all my needs. I was determined not to be a financial burden
to you and this is still the case.

Paul warns of deceivers (11:10-23)

10 Because I have the truth of Christ living in me, nobody anywhere
in Greece will prevent me from boasting about these things. 11 Does
this mean that I do not love you? God knows well that I do love
you! 12 Yet I will persist in acting in the way I do to remove the
ground from under those who want to be considered as having
equal status with us, believing their works are just as significant as
ours. 13 Such men are not truly apostles, even if they call themselves
such. They are false, deceitful workmen who want others to regard
them as apostles.

14 We should not be surprised that there are such people, for even
Satan appears to be what he isn't, an angel of light. 15 Those who
honour him will follow him in deceiving others by appearing as
servants of righteousness, when all they are really concerned about
is their own prestige and self-importance. They will be judged in
the way their actions deserve!

16 I say again, do not think of me as a fool. If that is your attitude,
I will indulge you with a little foolish boasting. 17 Such self-confident
talk does not come from the Lord, but I speak as a fool. 18 These false
people boast about their exploits, so I also will indulge in some
boasting. 19 You think that you are wise even though you willingly
indulge these false foolish people. 20 You even receive those who
enslave you by their false teaching and those who exploit you for
their own ends. They take advantage of you and promote themselves, while at the same time hitting you in the face. 21 Do you think
I should feel ashamed for not acting as they do? Is this a sign of my
weakness?

If you want me to boast as they do, I am certainly capable of
doing so. 22 Are they true Hebrews? Well, so am I. Are they Israelites?
So am I. Are they descended directly from Abraham? I am also
descended from him. 23 Are they Christ's servants? It is really crazy
to talk in this way, but I am even more a servant than they are!

Paul's suffering for the gospel (11:23-33)

I have worked much harder for the cause of the gospel than these people; I have been in prison more frequently for my faith than any

of them. 24 I have been flogged more severely and have been in danger
of my life on numerous occasions. I have received the Jewish
punishment of thirty-nine lashes no less than five times. 25 On three
occasions I was beaten with rods. Once I was stoned and I have
been shipwrecked three times. I spent a whole night and day drifting
in the sea.

26 I have travelled constantly, often in danger from rivers, bandits
and even from my fellow Jews as well as from Gentiles. I have
known danger in the city, in the country and at sea. Even those who
claimed to be brothers, but who were really false, put my life in danger.

27 I have known what it is to feel continually tired and have often
had to forgo getting any sleep. I have known what it is to be hungry
and thirsty, starving even! I have been freezing cold with insufficient
clothing to keep me warm.

28 On top of all these things, I carry daily the pressure I feel
because of my concern for all the churches. 29 Do you not realise that
I empathise with the weak and seethe inwardly with anger towards
the devil when he leads people into sin?

30 If I boast at all, it is only to show how weak I am humanly. 31 I
praise forever the God and Father of the Lord Jesus Christ who
knows that I do not lie. 32 There was even an occasion in Damascus
when king Aretas had the whole city on alert in order to arrest me.
33 But I was lowered in a basket from a window in the city wall and
slipped through their hands.

Dependence on God's strength (12:1-13)

12 Although there is nothing to be gained from it, I will show
you that I have good cause to boast. I will tell of visions and
revelations I have received from the Lord.

2 Fourteen years ago I was caught up in a vision to the third heaven,
into paradise itself. I could not tell whether my spirit was still in my
body or had momentarily left it. I really do not know, but God
knows. 3-4 But I am sure that I was lifted up into paradise and heard
things I cannot express, that should not be told to anyone.

5 A person who has had such an experience has something to
boast about! But I do not claim any credit for this myself. I will only
boast about my personal weaknesses. 6 I could not be accused of
speaking foolishly if I did boast about such experiences, for I only
speak the truth about what happened. But I will not go into detail
for I do not want to promote myself. I want people to judge me by
what I say and do, not by the revelations I have received.

[7]And the Lord ensured I would not be puffed up with pride, for
I was given a thorn in my flesh to stop me from being proud
because of these great encounters. This thorn was a messenger from
Satan, someone he sent to torment me.

[8]I pleaded with the Lord on three occasions for this 'thorn' to be
taken away. [9]"My grace is always sufficient to meet your need," He
told me; "My power is revealed more perfectly through your weakness!" This is why I am happy to boast about my weaknesses, for
then Christ's power will work through me. [10]Yes, for Christ's sake,
I even delight in being so weak, in suffering rejection and hardships, in being persecuted and having to face so many difficulties.
For the more I am aware of my own weakness, the more I can depend
on His strength.

[11]See what you have driven me to! If you had commended me in
the way you should have done, I would not have had to speak so
foolishly! Even though I regard myself as nothing, I am not in the
least inferior to those 'super-apostles'. [12]What is the evidence that a
person is an apostle? He continually performs signs, wonders and
miracles among you!

[13]Were you inferior to any other churches? Only in that I was
never a financial burden to you. If that makes you inferior, please
forgive me for being the cause of this!

Working for the welfare of the church (12:14-21)

[14]Well, I am ready to make my third visit to Corinth, and I will not
be a personal burden to you then, because I do not want your possessions but your hearts. It is clear that the young children do not
have to provide for their parents, but the parents for their young
children. [15]This being the case, I will give myself and all I have with
joy for your sake. But if I show you even greater love, will you love
me less in return? [16]No matter what you choose to do in the future,
I certainly have not been a burden to you in the past, even though
some accuse me of being crafty and trying to manipulate you. [17]Be
honest; did I ever try to exploit you through any of the brothers I
sent to visit you? [18]For example, when I persuaded Titus to visit
you, along with another brother, did he do anything to exploit you?
No, for we always act in the same Spirit, with the same intention of
working for your welfare.

[19]Do you think that all we are doing is trying to justify ourselves
in your eyes? Not at all, for we speak as those who live in Christ and
before God. So everything we say and do is aimed at strengthening
you in your faith.

20 However, I fear that when I come to Corinth I may be disappointed in what I find, and then you might be disappointed in what
I have to do. Will you be what I want you to be? I am afraid there
may be quarrelling, jealousy, anger with one another and factions
among you. I might find that you slander one another, gossip about
each other, that you are proud and disorderly.
21 I fear that when I next meet you I shall be humbled before God
because of what I find. And I will be truly grieved if I find that there
has not been genuine repentance of the earlier sins of which you
were guilty; the impurity, the sexual immorality and even the
debauchery in which you used to indulge.

Warnings to the church (13:1-14)

13 So this will be my third visit to you. The scripture declares
that, "Every case must be settled on the testimony of two or
three witnesses." 2 Well, I gave you clear warnings on my second
visit and I now repeat these warnings from a distance. When I
arrive I will not spare the guilty or any who have not repented and
changed their ways. 3 I will give you ample proof that Christ speaks
through me. He certainly does not deal with you in a weak and feeble
manner, but He acts in power. 4 It is true He was crucified in the
weakness of His humanity, but He lives now in God's power. In the
same way, we are weak in ourselves even though we live in Him;
yet by God's power we are able to serve you because of our unity
with Him.
5 So examine yourselves to test whether you are living in genuine
faith. Surely it is evident that Christ Jesus is in you, unless of course
you fail the test! 6 I trust it will be apparent to you that we have not
failed the test!
7 I pray to God that you will not do anything wrong, not simply
to demonstrate that our ministry among you has not been a failure,
but because you are intent on doing what is right. 8 We must not be
seen doing anything that denies the truth we preach, but only that
which demonstrates and promotes the truth. 9 We are not worried
about appearing weak so long as you are really strong, and we pray
that you will fulfil God's purpose as mature believers should.
10 This is why I write from a distance in the way I do, so that when
I arrive I will not have to be harsh in any way. I exercise my apostolic
authority which the Lord gave me to encourage and build you up,
not to destroy you!

13:1 Deuteronomy 19:15

11 Beloved ones, my final word to you is this: Aim for perfection,
to fulfil completely God's purpose for your lives. Take notice of all
I have said and live in unity and peace with one another. Then the
God of love and peace will be with you.
12 Greet one another in God's holy love. 13 All the saints here send
their greetings!
14 May the Lord Jesus impart His grace to you, and may God keep
you in love. And may you all share in the life and fellowship of the
Holy Spirit.

GALATIANS

Paul greets churches in Galatia (1:1-5)

1 From Paul, an apostle, one raised up and sent, not by men or
through men but through Jesus Christ and God the Father, who
raised Him from the dead. 2 I write, together with the brothers who
are with me.

To all the churches in Galatia:

> 3-5 May grace and peace be imparted to you from God our
> Father and the Lord Jesus Christ, who sacrificed Himself
> for our sins to free us from this present evil age, according
> to the will of our God and Father, to whom be glory for
> all eternity. Amen. It shall be so!

One true gospel (1:6-9)

6-7 I am amazed that you have fallen away so quickly from God, who
called you through the grace He showed you in Christ; to follow
another gospel, which is really not good news at all. There are some
who are causing trouble among you because they want to distort
the true gospel of Christ. 8 But if any of us, or even an angel from
heaven, should preach any other gospel other than that which we
have already taught you, let him be cursed. 9 As I have already said
and repeat again: if anyone preaches a gospel that is any different
from the one received through our teaching, let him be cursed.

Paul: set apart for God's purposes (1:10-24)

10 Does that sound as if I want your approval or God's approval? Am
I trying to please men? If I still wanted to please men, I certainly
would not be a servant of Christ! 11 For, my brothers, the gospel I
continue to make known to you does not originate with any man.
12 No, I did not receive it from man, nor was I taught it by anybody.
Rather I received it by direct revelation from Jesus Christ Himself!

13 For you have heard how I conducted myself as a devout Jew,
that I persecuted the church of God aggressively and did all I could

to destroy it. 14 I also advanced in Judaism beyond many of my contemporaries, being such an ardent zealot to maintain the traditions passed down from our fathers.

15-17 But I now realise that from the time of my birth it pleased God to set me apart for His purposes. He called me by His grace to reveal His Son in me, so that I might preach the gospel among the nations. When He did this, I did not confer with others, nor did I go up to Jerusalem to see those who were already apostles, but I went to Arabia before returning to Damascus. 18 Then three years later I went up to Jerusalem to meet Peter, and I stayed with him for fifteen days. 19 Of the other apostles I saw only James, the Lord's brother.

20 I assure you before God that what I am telling you is no lie. 21 Later I went to the regions of Syria and Cilicia. 22 I was personally unknown to other churches in Judea, comprised of all those who are in Christ. 23 They only heard that the one who had persecuted them was now preaching the faith he had tried to destroy. 24 And they gave glory to God because of me.

An apostle to the nations (2:1-10)

2 Fourteen years later I went up to Jerusalem with Barnabas, taking Titus with me as my companion. 2 I went in obedience to revelation I received from God and I described privately to the leaders there the nature of the gospel which I proclaim among the nations, for I wanted to be sure that I was teaching what was right. 3 Although he is a Greek, it was not deemed necessary for my companion Titus to be circumcised. 4 But some false brothers came among us in a covert way to spy on us because of the freedom we have in Christ, wanting to return us to slavery. 5 But we would not submit to their wishes even for a moment, so that you might continue to walk in the truth of the gospel – that we are saved by faith in Christ, not through trying to obey religious laws.

6 I am not concerned about anybody's reputation, for God does not judge by appearances. However, those who were regarded as important leaders added nothing to what I was preaching. 7 Quite the opposite; they saw that I had been entrusted with proclaiming the gospel to the uncircumcised Gentiles, as Peter was commissioned to take the gospel to the circumcised Jews.

8 For God's Spirit anointed Peter to be an apostle to the Jews and that same Spirit anointed me for the nations. 9 James, Peter and John, who were regarded as the pillars of the church, gave the right hand of fellowship to Barnabas and myself, recognising that God had

given me grace for the Gentile nations, as they had for the Jewish people. 10 They only asked that we should remember the poor, something I was very keen to do.

Paul opposes Peter (2:11-21)

11 But when Peter visited Antioch, I had to oppose him to his face because of the shameful way he acted. 12 He ate with the Gentiles until some men arrived who had been sent by James. He then sat apart from the Gentiles out of fear of the Jewish believers who belonged to the circumcision party. 13 The Jewish believers also acted wrongly and they even persuaded Barnabas to join them.

14 When I saw that they were not behaving according to the truth of the gospel, I said to Peter in front of everybody else: "If as a Jew you do not live as a Gentile, why should you make the Gentiles live as if they were Jews?" 15-16 We are Jews by birth and not Gentile sinners, but we know that no man is made acceptable before God by doing the works of the law, but only through faith in Christ Jesus. We Jews were saved through that same faith in Christ Jesus, for it is only by faith in Christ and not by the works of the law that we were saved; for by such works no one is made acceptable to God.

17 But if in seeking to be found acceptable to God because we are in Christ we find that we still act as sinners, does this mean that Christ encourages sin? Don't even suggest such a thing! 18 For if I build again things that were once destroyed, I demonstrate that I myself am a law breaker. 19 For through the law I died to living in religious legalism that I might now live for God.

20 I have been crucified together with Christ; the person I was no longer lives, but Christ now lives in me. The life I live in my body I live by faith in God's Son, who has loved me by giving Himself on my behalf. 21 I do not set aside God's grace. For if I could have gained acceptance through the religious law, then Christ died for nothing!

Saved only by faith in God (3:1-12)

3 How foolish you Galatians are! Who has cast a spell on you to prevent you from obeying the truth? It was clearly shown to you that Jesus Christ has won complete acceptance for us when He was crucified. 2 So I want you to tell me this: Did you receive the Spirit through obeying the religious law, or by responding with faith when you heard the truth about Jesus Christ? 3 Are you really so foolish? Having begun in the Spirit, are you now trying to be

made perfect through your self effort? 4 Have you suffered so much
for nothing – if all that has been accomplished is more self-effort!
5 So did the One who gave you the Spirit and who worked miracles
among you do so because of your obedience to religious rules and
regulations, or because you responded with faith when you heard
the truth?
6-7 In the same way that Abraham was considered right and
acceptable because he believed God, know that those who believe
now are the true sons of Abraham.
8 The Scripture foresaw that God would make the nations acceptable
to Him by faith, and so the gospel was preached to Abraham long
ago by saying that "All the nations will be blessed by you."
9 Therefore those who have faith are blessed together with Abraham,
who also had faith.
10 Those who depend on obeying the religious law are under a curse,
for it is written, "Everyone who does not obey everything written in
the book of the religious law is cursed." 11 So clearly no one can be
made acceptable before God by the religious law for "those who are
right before God shall live by faith." 12 But the law is not based on
faith. It depends on what a man does, not what he believes.

Access to the blessings of Abraham through Christ (3:13-25)

13 Christ has saved us from the curse of not being able to obey the
law perfectly by becoming a curse for us, for it is written: "Everyone
who is hung on a tree is cursed." 14 In this way, He brought us back
to God so that the Gentile nations might receive the blessings of
Abraham through Christ Jesus, and that we might receive by faith
the promise of receiving God's Spirit.
15 Brethren, I put it to you in human terms. Nobody can cancel or
add to a legal agreement made between people. 16 Now God gave
His promises to Abraham and to his seed. He did not use the plural
'seeds' referring to many, but to 'Seed' meaning to One, even Christ
Himself.
17 Let me explain: The law that was given 430 years later did not
cancel out the agreement previously made by God, so that His
promises would be of no account. 18 If it were possible to receive the
inheritance by your own actions, no promises would have been
needed. But God made definite promises to Abraham.

3:8 Genesis 12:3
3:10 Deuteronomy 27:26
3:11 Habakkuk 2:4
3:13 Deuteronomy 21:23

19 If this is the case, why was the law given in the first place? It was given because of people's sins, and was to last until the coming of the Seed referred to in the promise. It was delivered through angels by the hand of a go-between. 20 Such a mediator does not represent one party only; but God is one.

21 Does this mean that the law contradicts God's promises? Certainly not! For if it were possible for the law to give men God's life, then they could be made acceptable before Him by the law. 22 But the scripture declares that everyone is in bondage to sin, so that what was promised by faith in Jesus Christ might be given to those who believe in Him.

23 Before this faith was possible we were guarded by the law, restricted until the time came for faith to be revealed. 24 Therefore the law was a guide to point us to Christ, so that we might be made acceptable to God by faith in Him. 25 Now that this faith has arrived, we have no further need for such a guide.

Adoption as God's sons (3:26-4:7)

26 For all of you are made sons of God through faith in Christ Jesus. 27 All those who have been baptised into Christ have been clothed with Christ. 28 In Him there is neither Jew nor Gentile, neither slave nor free man, neither male nor female, for all of you in Christ Jesus are made one with God. 29 And if you belong to Christ then you are Abraham's seed and heirs of all that is promised.

4 I will explain it like this: While the heir is a minor he differs little from a servant, even though he inherits everything. 2 He is put under the authority of guardians and trustees until the time appointed by his father.

3 Similarly, while we were minors we were in bondage to worldly powers. 4-5 But at His appointed time God sent His Son, born of a woman and born under the law, so that He might save those who live under the law, that they might be adopted as His sons.

6 And once you became His sons, God sent the Spirit of His Son into your hearts, enabling you to call Him, 'Abba, Father!' 7 So you are no longer a slave but now a son! And because you are a son, you are one of God's heirs.

Paul's concern for the Galatians (4:8-20)

8-9 Before you knew God personally, you were in bondage to false gods; but now that you know Him, or, rather, since God knows you

personally, how can you turn back to those weak and useless
things? Do you want to be in bondage to them again? 10 You are again
observing special days, months, seasons and years like unbelievers!
11 I fear that all my hard work among you has been in vain.
12-13 Brothers, I urge you to identify with me in my freedom, as I came
and identified with you. I am not accusing you of doing anything
wrong against me personally, for you are aware that it was in a time
of physical weakness that I preached the gospel to you. 14 Even
though my condition was a trial, you neither despised nor rejected
me, but you received me as an angel of God, as you would have
treated Christ Jesus Himself!

15 What, then, has happened to your life of blessing? For I can testify
that if it were possible, you would have torn out your eyes and
given them to me. 16 So have I now become your enemy because I
speak the truth to you?

17 There are people who show great concern for your welfare, but
in completely the wrong way. They want you to break fellowship
with me, so that you might follow them. 18 But it is good for you to
remain zealous for the truth at all times, not only when I am present
with you. 19 You are my little children, for whom I continue in labour
until Christ has been fully formed in you! 20 I wanted to be with you
at this time and to be able to speak in a different tone; but I am worried
about you.

Children of the free woman - not the slave (4:21-31)

21 Tell me, those of you who want to return to living under the law,
do you not take seriously what the law says? 22 For it is written that
Abraham had two sons, one by a slave girl and the other by a free
woman.

23 The son born to the slave girl was born of the flesh, by the natural
course of events, while the one born to the free woman was the
result of God's promise. 24 Now this is symbolic of two different
covenants. One was established on Mount Sinai, which gives birth
to children who live in slavery, like Hagar the slave girl. 25 So Hagar
stands for Mount Sinai that is in Arabia, and this corresponds to the
present city of Jerusalem that is in bondage with her children. 26 But
the heavenly Jerusalem is free and is the mother of all of us that are
free. 27 For it is written:

> "Rejoice, barren one who does not give birth. Break out
> with shouts you who are not in labour, for the children of

the desolate woman are more than the one who has a
husband."

28 Now, brothers, like Isaac we are children of promise. 29 But just as
the one born according to the flesh persecuted the one born according
to the Spirit, so it is still the same now. 30 So what does the scripture
say? "Be rid of the slave girl and her son, for surely the slave girl's
son will not share the inheritance of the free woman's son."
31 So then, my brothers, we are not children of the slave girl but of
the free woman!

Freedom in Christ (5:1-15)

5 Christ has set us free to live in freedom. So stand fast in that
freedom and do not allow yourselves to be yoked again in slavery.
2 Listen carefully: I, Paul, tell you clearly that if you allow yourselves to become legalistically religious again, Christ will be of no
value to you. 3 I say it again to everyone, if you have become legalistic you are obligated to obey every aspect of the religious law. 4 For
those of you who are trying to make yourselves acceptable through
obeying the religious code have become separated from Christ; you
have deserted the life of grace. 5 For it is by the Spirit that we eagerly
await the hope of our eternal acceptance by faith. 6 For in Christ
Jesus neither being a Jew nor a Gentile is of any significance; all that
matters is that you live a life of faith that is expressed in a life of love
for God and others.
7 You were making such good progress. So who is now preventing
you from obeying the truth? 8 This certainly is not the influence of
the One who has called you. 9 A little yeast soon affects the whole
lump of dough!
10 In the Lord I have confidence in you, that you will not be side-
tracked. Anyone who tries to influence you in that way will certainly
be judged, no matter who he may be. 11 Brothers, if I am still preaching
conformity to the religious law, why am I still being persecuted? For
in that case the offence caused by the cross would have been abolished.
12 I wish that those who cause all this trouble, persuading you Gentile
believers that you must be circumcised and so become subject to the
religious law, would apply the knife to themselves.
13 Brothers, you were called to live in freedom, but do not use
your freedom from legalism as an opportunity to do whatever you
like. No, instead serve one another as the outworking of your love

4:27 Isaiah 54:1
4:30 Genesis 21:10

for one another. [14]For the whole of the law can be fulfilled through obedience to the one command that says, "You are to love your neighbour as yourself." [15]However, if you fight and snap at one another you had better watch out or you will destroy each other.

Life in the Spirit (5:16-26)

[16]So I say, walk in the ways the Spirit leads you, and you will not gratify what your self-life desires! [17]For that self-life desires what opposes the Spirit and the Spirit leads you in ways that involve denying that self-life. These are two contradictory ways. This means that you are not free to do whatever you wish. [18]But if you choose to be led by the Spirit you will not live under the bondage of the religious law.

[19-21]This self-life will manifest itself in such works as these: adultery, sex outside of marriage, other forms of immorality and lust, idolatry, witchcraft, hatred, divisions, jealousy and outbursts of anger, selfish ambition, dissentions to authority, party factions, envy, murder, drunkenness, orgies and other such things. As I have warned you before, those who live in such ways will not inherit God's Kingdom. [22-23]However, the fruit the Spirit produces in you is love, joy, peace, patience, kindness, goodness, faithfulness, gentleness and self-control. There is no law against such things! [24]Those who belong to Christ Jesus have nailed to the cross their passions and desires that contradict the Spirit!

[25]So if we live by the Spirit, let us keep ourselves in line with what the Spirit desires. [26]Let us not become conceited, neither provoking nor envying one another.

Continue to do good (6:1-18)

6 Brothers, if someone yields to sin, you who are spiritual should restore him in a spirit of gentleness. Be careful in case you also are tempted. [2]Carry each others burdens, for by doing so you will fulfil Christ's law. [3]For if anyone considers himself important when he is really nothing, he only deceives himself. [4]Let each one test the things he does to see if he has anything to boast about, without worrying about what others do. [5]In this sense each one has to look out for himself.

[6]Let the one who is taught the Word share all that is good with his teacher. [7]Do not be fooled; God is not to be mocked! For anyone will reap according to what he has sown. [8]So the one who sows to

5:14 Leviticus 19:18

please himself will reap the destruction that comes from such a
lifestyle. But he who sows obedience to the Spirit will reap what the
Spirit gives: eternal life.

9 So let us never be discouraged from doing what is good, for in
due course we shall reap abundantly if we persevere. 10 Therefore,
let us do good to everyone whenever we have the opportunity to do
so, but especially in regard to our fellow members in the family of
faith.

11 Look at these large letters; I am now writing in my own hand
(instead of dictating). 12 Those who are concerned about appearances
want you to obey the external requirements of the religious law;
they would like to force you to be circumcised. But the real motive
is so that they will not be persecuted for trusting in the cross of
Christ Jesus. 13 For even though they were circumcised, they do not
keep the law themselves; they only want to boast that they have
exercised control over you.

14 As far as I am concerned, I will boast in nothing except the cross
of our Lord Jesus Christ, through whom the world has been crucified
to me and I to the world. 15 For neither circumcision nor uncircum-
cision means anything; all that matters is that you are a new creation.
16 May peace and mercy be on those who follow this rule, for they
belong to God's true Israel.

17 Last of all, let no one cause me any further trouble for I bear in
my body the wounds of Jesus.

18 The grace of our Lord Jesus Christ be with your spirit, my
brothers. Amen! It shall be so!

EPHESIANS

Greetings (1:1-2)

1 From Paul, an apostle of Christ Jesus by God's will.
To all in Ephesus who are saints, set apart by God for His purposes; those who live out their lives in Christ Jesus in a faithful way.
2 May God our Father and the Lord Jesus Christ impart grace and
peace to you.

Blessed with every spiritual blessing (1:3-6)

3 Give praise to Him, the God and Father of our Lord Jesus Christ.
For He has blessed us through our life in Christ with every spiritual
blessing that belongs to His heavenly Kingdom. 4-5 This is because
He chose us before He created the world to belong to Christ, to be
made holy and blameless in His sight. Because of this amazing love,
He decided that we should be adopted as His sons when we place
our faith in Jesus Christ. Yes, this was His purpose and even His joy!
6 Why should He do such a thing? Because this causes His people
to praise Him for His glorious grace, that which He gives freely to
those who deserve nothing from Him. All this grace He has given
us in Jesus, the Son whom He loves.

Chosen to belong to Christ (1:7-19)

7-8 In Christ we have been redeemed. With His own blood He has
made it possible for all our sins to be forgiven and so has purchased
us with the price of His blood, so that now we belong to Him. All
this is the result of the immense riches of God's grace that He has
lavished on us. Yes, He has given us wisdom to receive His grace
and to understand the wonderful ways in which He has blessed us.
9 He has even made His will known to us. Although this remains
a mystery to others, it has been His good pleasure to reveal His
purposes to those who now live in Christ. 10 His purposes will only
be fully realised when time as we now know it will have reached its
climax. Then we shall see that God has brought everything in heaven
and on earth together under the headship and authority of Christ.

11 We were chosen to belong to Him. This was God's plan from the
beginning, and He works out everything so His will and His purposes
are completely fulfilled. 12 All this is so that we who first put our
hope in Christ might live for His praise and glory. 13 But you also,
like us, were placed in Christ when you heard the truth of the
gospel of salvation and believed. Then He marked you in a very
special way by placing His personal seal upon you: He gave you
His own promised Holy Spirit to live within you. 14 The gift of His
Spirit is a deposit from God that guarantees our inheritance and
keeps us as those who are His possession, living in the power of His
redeeming love. Yes, that we might live for His praise and glory!

15-16 Ever since I heard of your faith in the Lord Jesus and the way
you love your fellow saints, those who also belong to Him, I have
been continually thankful that you also share in His life. So I keep
remembering you when I pray. 17 I ask that the glorious Father of our
Lord Jesus Christ may impart to you the Spirit of wisdom and
revelation of who He is and what He has done for you, so that you
will come to know Him better. 18-19 I also pray for your heart to be
filled with light, that you will see for yourself, and know in your
experience, the hope to which He has called you, the purpose He
wants to see fulfilled in your life. What is this hope? That His saints,
all those who belong to Him, will enjoy the riches of a glorious
inheritance; and that they may also know His power working in
them because they believe in Him, a power so great that it cannot
be compared with any other power!

Jesus reigns over all (1:20-23)

You have an example of this power, of exactly how mighty it is, in
the resurrection of Christ. 20 Yes, the power that raised Him from the
dead and caused Him to be seated in heaven at His Father's right
hand is that same power which is within you now. 21 As a result of
this power, Jesus is now reigning far above every other ruler,
authority, power and dominion. He is greater than anyone else could
ever be, not only in this present age but also in the future age that He
will inaugurate.

22-23 God has placed everything under Jesus' feet. He has appointed
Him to have authority over everything for the sake of the church,
which is His Body on earth. And He intends the fullness of Christ's
life to fill everything in every way, first in the church, and then in
the new creation.

Alive in Christ (2:1-5)

2 What you are now is in direct contrast to what you used to be. Once you were spiritually dead because your lives were full of sin and disobedience to God's Word. [2]That is how you used to live, when you lived according to the world's standards, because you were subject to God's enemy, belonged to his negative kingdom of darkness and were controlled by the spirit who still works in the disobedient.

[3]All of us at one time shared in that ungodly lifestyle, longing to satisfy our flesh. We all sought to gratify our fleshly desires and sin filled much of our thinking. Just like everybody else, we were subjects of God's anger because of our sinful disposition.

[4-5]Despite all this, because of His great love for us, God who is so rich in mercy and because He loves us so much, actually brought us to life with Christ, even when we were spiritually dead because of our sins. What a wonderful work of His grace to save us out of the death and darkness of sin, out of the hands of the evil one we once served!

Seated with Christ (2:6-7)

[6]Now He has actually raised us up with Christ and sees us seated with Him in heavenly places because He has placed us in Christ Jesus. [7]He has done this so that in the future we might demonstrate that the riches of His grace are so immense that nothing can be compared to such riches. And this grace has been shown to us because of His kindness towards us, expressed in all Christ Jesus has done for us.

Saved by His grace (2:8-10)

[8]You see, it is only because of His grace that you have been saved. All you did was to put your faith in His willingness to be merciful and gracious towards you. So your salvation is not anything you could possibly have worked out for yourselves; it is completely God's gift to you. [9]You can never boast that you achieved acceptance by God through the works you have performed.

[10]The truth is that we are the work of God's own hands. Now we live in Christ Jesus, we are able to do the good works that are the evidence of our salvation. It is good to know that these are the very works that God planned and prepared for us to accomplish!

Reconciliation to God and one another (2:11-22)

[11]So never forget that you used to be foreigners, outside of God's Kingdom, because you had only natural birth and were not among

those whom God had set aside for Himself by entering into covenant
with them. The relationship you have with Him now has nothing to
do with outward actions such as circumcision, works done by men.
12 You used to be separated from Christ because of your sin. You
were excluded from having citizenship in Israel, God's chosen people.
You were outside the covenant relationship with God based on His
promises. You were without hope for the future and had to live
your life in the world without God.
13 Look at the difference now that you are in Christ Jesus and
belong to Him. Instead of living far away from God, you have been
united with Him through what Jesus did by shedding His blood for
you.
14 So He is our peace. Because we have been forgiven and accepted
by God, we are at peace with Him. Those who were outside the
covenant, the relationship God has made possible for His people,
are now made one with those who belong to the covenant. He has
made these two one, Jew and non-Jew, by destroying the barrier
that once divided them, that was like a dividing wall of hostility
that existed between them.
15-16 Through what He accomplished when He became man, He
abolished the whole idea of serving God through a legalistic
approach of obeying a series of religious rules and regulations. His
intention was to create a new people out of the two opposing
groups that existed before. The only way was to make it possible for
anyone, no matter what His race, to be at peace with God, and to
draw them together into one Body, to reconcile them to one another. He accomplished all this through the cross which dealt a death
blow to their former hostility.
17 Jesus came and preached peace with God to those outside His
covenant with Israel, as well as those who were part of that relationship. 18 Now through Him we all have direct and personal access to
the Father through the same Holy Spirit who lives in every believer
in Jesus Christ.
19 So as a result, you are no longer foreigners outside of God's purpose; you are not aliens but children of God, fellow citizens with all
who belong to Christ. Together you are God's people and members
of His household. 20 Your life together is built on the foundation of
truth that has come to us through the apostles and prophets, Jesus
Himself being the chief Cornerstone, the pivotal truth of the revelation
God has given us through them. 21 In Christ Jesus the whole building
of living stones, whether believing Jews or non-Jews, is built to be a
holy temple housing the Lord's presence. 22 Yes, in Him you are

being built together to be those in whom God Himself lives by His
Spirit.

A servant of the gospel (3:1-13)

3 This is the reason why I, Paul, am happy to be a prisoner of
Jesus Christ; it is for your sake. 2-3 You have heard about the
way God has given me such grace for your benefit, so that I could
tell you of the hidden things that have been revealed to me. 4 Now
that I am writing in this way you will be able to understand the insight
I have been given into these truths about Christ that remained hidden
to those of other generations.

5 These things have now been revealed by the Spirit to those
whom God has raised up as apostles and prophets. 6 It seems strange
that because of the gospel those who are not Jews are heirs together
with Israel, of all that God has promised. Both Jewish and non-
Jewish believers in Christ form one Body and they share together in
the promises given by God through Him.

7 God called me to be a servant of this gospel and gave me His
grace so He would work powerfully through me. 8 I consider myself
less than the very lowest of God's people; yet, He gave me such
grace. He enabled me to preach the gospel to the Gentile nations,
telling them of the immense riches of Christ. 9 I have been able to
explain to everyone those things that formerly remained hidden in
the purposes of God, who created everything. 10 His plan has always
been that now His great wisdom should be revealed through the
church, His people; that the church should declare these truths even
to the heavenly rulers and authorities.

11 It has always been His purpose from the very beginning that all
this should be made possible in Christ Jesus our Lord. 12 Because
you live in Him and have faith in Him, you are able to approach
God freely and with confidence. 13 So I ask you not to be put off
because I have had to suffer for your sake. Rather regard these sufferings as a means by which you have come to know God's glory!

Prayer for the saints on earth (3:14-21)

14-15 You can see from all this why I kneel before the Father, the One
who is responsible for His entire family, those already in heaven
and those on the earth. 16 I pray that out of His glorious riches you
will be strengthened with power by the working of His Spirit in
your inmost being. 17-19 This is so that you will know the presence of
Christ in your hearts because of your faith in Him.

I also pray that your lives will be deeply rooted in His love; that you will be so steadfast in this love that, like all those who believe in Jesus and who are set apart for His purposes as His saints, you will be able to comprehend something of the amazing extent of Christ's love. This love seems boundless and unlimited and through that love you can be filled to the fullest extent with God Himself.

20 He is able to do so much more than all you would ever dare to ask Him or even imagine that He would give you, through His power that He has already placed within you. 21 So let His glory be revealed in the church. And let those who belong to Him live to give Him glory; yes, believers of every successive generation, for ever. Amen! It shall be so!

Maintain unity with the believers (4:1-6)

4 I am a prisoner for the Lord's sake and I encourage you to live in a way that is worthy of this great calling you have received from Him. 2 This involves remaining humble and gentle, being patient and sensitive to the needs of others out of your love for them. 3 Do everything you can to maintain the unity you have with other believers in the power of the Spirit by remaining at peace with them. 4 For there is one Body of Christ and only one Holy Spirit, and we all share in the one hope to which we were called in Christ. 5-6 There is only one Lord, and we all share in the same faith in Him. There is only one baptism into Christ, only one God and Father of us all. He is over all of us, He works through all of us and His life is in all of us!

Grace given to fulfil the call (4:7-10)

7 Yet, at the same time, each one of us is given the particular grace we need to fulfil our calling, and it is Christ Himself who imparts this grace to us. 8 This is why we can understand, from what was written years ago, that when He ascended back to heaven He led a procession of those who had formerly been captives and gave gifts to those who were to continue the work of His Kingdom here on earth.

9 We need to understand that before He ascended to heaven, Christ first descended to where the souls were kept waiting for the release He alone could give. 10 Yes, He who descended there to free them is the same Lord who ascended to the highest place in heaven, so that the whole universe could be filled with His glory!

4:8 Psalm 68:18

God's order in His body (4:11-16)

11 This same Lord Jesus appointed some of those who belonged to
Him to be apostles, responsible for the ordering of His church, others
to be those through whom He would speak prophetically to His
people. Some were anointed to be evangelists who would reap a
harvest of souls for God's Kingdom, others He made pastors with
hearts of love and compassion to care for His people. Still others He
made teachers, those who live His Word and can enable others to do
likewise.

12-13 All these various ministries have a common purpose. They are
to prepare God's people to serve Him, happily doing the works
God prepared for them. This is what will enable the Body of Christ
to be built up in the way He desires, and will bring people into
unity in their faith, sharing in a common knowledge and experience
of God's Son. Having servant hearts shows that people are mature
in their life in Christ and that they are able to enjoy everything God
has made available to us in Him, the fullness of His life that He
came to impart.

14 Those who are mature in this way will no longer be like immature
toddlers easily swayed and pulled this way and that. They will not
be like corks bobbing about on the sea, or like falling leaves that are
at the mercy of any wind that blows them around. Immature people
are like that because they do not have a grasp of the truth of God's
Word. So they are easily swayed by the latest fashion in 'spiritual'
teaching. They are deceived by those who want to manipulate and
use them and their money for their own ends.

15 The mature are not like that. They speak the truth to others out
of love for them and, therefore, in a loving way. They are believers
who keep growing in their faith, becoming more and more like
Christ who is the Head of the Body to which they belong. 16 From
Him, the Head, the whole Body is to draw together in unity. Every
part is to fulfil its function in love, for the health of the whole Body.
And this is accomplished by each fulfilling the work Christ has
appointed for him or her.

Keep walking in God's ways (4:17-32)

17 Now I will tell you something so important that I insist in the
Lord's Name that you respond to what I say. You must no longer
live in the way that those who belong to the world live. Worldly
thinking is futile. 18 Worldly people live in spiritual darkness, without

understanding God's purposes. They do not possess His life and
they remain in ignorance. Because their hearts are hardened they
resist the truth of the gospel. [19]They have no spiritual sensitivity
because of the way they indulge their sensual appetites. So they
indulge themselves in pleasing their flesh, their natural desires, in
all kinds of impurity. They are never satisfied, but continually lust
after ways that are even more ungodly.

[20]You never came to know Christ by living in such ways. [21]No,
you heard about Him when you were taught the truth of the gospel,
for the truth is only to be found in Jesus. [22]As far as your former way
of life is concerned, you were taught from the very beginning to put
off your old sinful nature, that old self that was corrupted by its
deceitful desires.

[23]Instead you were made new with a totally different mindset.
[24]And you made the decision to put on the new life which enables
you to become what God wants you to be, living in ways that are
right in His eyes, being His holy people, set apart from the world to
live the life of His Kingdom here on earth.

[25]So it is essential for each of you to rid yourselves completely of
everything that is false and instead speak truthfully to others; for
we are all members of the one Body of Christ, a Body of truth! [26-27]It
is said, "even if you are angry do not sin". Do not hold onto your
anger; be rid of it before the end of the day, otherwise you could
give the devil a foothold to take advantage of you. [28]Anyone who
used to steal in his old life must, of course, no longer steal. Instead
he must have a proper job, working for his living by doing something useful with his hands. Then, instead of taking he will have
something to give to needy people.

[29]Do not speak in an impure or critical way. Instead of mouthing
unclean or negative things, speak in a way that will encourage and
benefit others because you are addressing their needs. [30]And do not
grieve God's Holy Spirit in any way. Remember you have had the
seal of the Spirit placed on you to keep you walking in God's ways
until the day when He takes you to be with Himself.

[31]Rid yourselves of every negative thing, being bitter in your
attitudes, being angry and resentful. Do not get into disputes with
others, especially physical ones! Do not slander others or have
any malicious attitudes towards them. [32]Instead be kind and compassionate to one another, always ready to forgive in the same way
that, through Christ, God has always been willing to forgive you!

4:26 Psalm 4:4

Live in love (5:1-7)

5 Therefore, because you are His dearly loved children, seek to be like God your Father. [2]Live a life full of love. Christ has commanded us to love others as He has loved us by giving His life in sacrifice for us, an offering to God that was totally pleasing to Him.

[3]To live in such love means that there must not be any sexual immorality among you, nor any kind of impurity in your hearts. There is to be no greed. You see, all these things are totally out of order for people who belong to God, His holy people. [4]You should be careful how you use your mouths, so you do not speak in any obscene or foolish way and you avoid all jokes with improper innuendos. All these things are so out of place that you should not even want to be involved in any of them. How much better to use your mouth to thank God for His amazing love and blessings!

[5]You see, it is absolutely certain that there is no inheritance in the Kingdom of God and of Christ for any immoral, impure or greedy person! [6]So do not be deceived by the empty platitudes of those who say that everyone will go to heaven. Such deception hides the truth that God's anger will come on the disobedient. [7]This is why you are not to align yourself with those who live in such ways.

Walk in the light of truth (5:8-10)

[8]Yes, you lived in darkness in your old life, but now you are the children of light, living in the One who is the Light. So live as children who walk in the light of God's truth. [9-10]What is the evidence of such a walk? That you express God's goodness, righteousness and truth; that you know what to do to please Him.

No compromise (5:11-14)

[11]You cannot compromise. Have absolutely nothing to do with the things God regards as darkness. These things are sinful and produce nothing good in your lives. You should expose sin, not walk in it. [12]It would be shameful for you even to talk about the things disobedient people do, often in secret. [13]The time will come when everything will be exposed by the light, even the things people have tried to hide. [14]By its very nature, light exposes things and there should be nothing in your lives that you would be ashamed of when everything is exposed. Such a time will come which is why we are told:

> "It is time to wake up if you are asleep spiritually; rise up from a life of dead works and Christ will shine on you with His Light."

Be wise about the way you live (5:15-20)

15 This causes you to realise that you will have to be very careful
about the way you live; to be wise, not foolish. 16 Make use of every
opportunity to please God by the way you live, especially as there
is so much evil in the world around you. 17 How much better to
understand what God wants of you than to live in a sinful, foolish
manner.

18 For example, if you think there is nothing wrong in getting
drunk you have an ungodly mindset and a depraved lifestyle. How
much better to be filled with God's Spirit. 19 He will inspire you to
rejoice together using psalms, hymns and spiritual songs. Sing because
there is a song of praise for God in your hearts. That is infinitely better
than drunkenness or bawdy revelling. 20 In fact, if you rejoice in the
Lord you will always be thanking your heavenly Father for the way
He orders your life, because you are so grateful that you live in
Christ Jesus, your Lord.

Marriage between Christ and His church (5:21-33)

21 What you are to do, then, is this: because you want to honour
Christ in your life, submit to one another.

22-23 Wives, be submissive to your husbands in the same way that
you would be towards the Lord. Christ is Head of the church which
is His Body, those whom He has saved. God's order is that your
husband is responsible for you in the same way that Christ is
responsible for His Church. 24 So as the members of the church submit
to Christ, it is only right that wives should submit to their husbands
in everything.

25-26 However, this does not mean that husbands are to dominate
their wives. No, they are to love them in the same way that Christ
has shown His love for His church. He did this by serving and then
giving His life for His Body. This sacrifice has made the church a
holy Body, a people set apart for His purposes; a people made pure
because they have been cleansed by the purifying power of God's
Word. 27 His intention is that all who belong to His Body will become
a radiant people, revealing His glory; a church set free from the
imperfections that so clearly exist at present. In fact, He is preparing
for Himself a church without any blemishes, holy and blameless in
His sight.

28 When you consider these truths, you can see how husbands need to love their wives. Christ loves His church as His own Body; so husbands love your wives as you would your own bodies. You see, the husband who loves his wife also loves himself. 29-30 So treat your wife in the same way that you would treat your own body. You do not hate your body by willingly inflicting any harm on it; instead you feed and care for it, even as Christ feeds and cares for us because we are members of His Body, the church.

31 In order to love your wives in the way God intends, it is written clearly that a man will leave his father and mother and become one with his wife. Husband and wife become one flesh.

32 This is a profound truth about Christ and His church that not everyone understands. 33 Yet in the same way, every one of you must love his wife as he loves himself; and a wife should always show respect for her husband because he cares for her.

Children and parents (6:1-4)

6 What about children? They are to obey their parents in the same way that they would obey the Lord, for this is right in His eyes. 2-3 He has commanded, "Give honour to your father and mother." This is the first of the commandments that has a promise attached to it, "then you will prosper in the long life that God will grant you on the earth."

4 Fathers, you are not to cause your children to be frustrated; you are not to suppress them or their giftings, but rather you are to train them, instructing them in the Lord's ways.

Demonstrate a right attitude in the workplace (6:5-9)

5 And what should your attitude be in the workplace? Show a good, obedient attitude towards those in authority over you. Respect them and the position they hold and do this sincerely from your heart, even in the same way that you would obey Christ your heavenly Master.

6 It is not a matter of simply wanting to find favour with your bosses, especially when they are watching what you are doing. No, you need to have a submissive heart and attitude, doing what is right because you want to please Christ who also sees what you are doing. 7 If you regard what you do at work as serving the Lord rather than men, then you will do it wholeheartedly with a good

6:3 Deuteronomy 5:16

heart attitude. [8]What is more, the Lord is the one who will reward
us for the way we have worked, whether we are bosses or workers.
[9]So a word for those of you who have responsibility over others
at work: treat them as Christ treats you. Do not threaten them because
your Lord does not threaten you; and He is Master over everyone,
reigning as He does in heaven. He does not show favouritism to
anyone, but deals fairly and justly with all; so that is what you are
to do.

Your spiritual armour (6:10-18)

[10]Above all, be strong in your faith and dependence on the Lord, on
His might and power. [11]He has provided His protection for you in
several ways. Clothed with His gifts and resources, you will be able
to stand against all the devil's disruptive tactics. [12]Your battle is not
against people but against the negative spiritual forces that influence
and control them; against the spiritual rulers, authorities and powers
that are at work in this world that is in bondage to the darkness of
sin. They are in league with those evil spiritual forces that exist outside the world.
[13]So accept everything God has made available to you, to enable
you to stand steadfast when evil attacks. Yes, no matter what happens
you are able to stand firm and to remain standing. [14]You stand firm
with His truth like a belt you keep around your waist for support.
His righteousness is like a breastplate that protects you. [15]You wear
the shoes of the gospel so that you are always ready for any even-
tuality and can walk in peace. [16]Your faith is like a shield that you
have to take hold of and that enables you to overcome anything
the devil throws at you. [17]The assurance of your salvation is like a
protective helmet, enabling you to counter all the devil's lies and
efforts to deceive you in your thinking.
[18]You have, not only a defensive shield, but an offensive weapon,
the sword of the Spirit which is God's Word. Whenever you pray,
depend on the Spirit to lead you and fill your prayer with His life
and power, no matter what you are asking of God. How important
to pray in the Spirit continually for all your fellow believers.

Final greetings (6:19-24)

[19]And pray for me also. Whenever I speak in the Lord's Name I need
Him to supply what I say, so that I will be able to reveal the truth of
the gospel to those with no spiritual understanding. [20]I am still an
ambassador of the truth, even though I am in chains at present. So

I pray that, despite everything, I will be bold in declaring the truth without any fear.

21 Tychicus is a dear brother and the Lord's faithful servant. He can tell you far more about my circumstances than I can write now.
22 This is why I am sending him to you. However he will also be a great encouragement to you.

23-24 I bless all the brothers with God's peace. May God the Father and the Lord Jesus Christ impart both love and faith to you, together with the grace that He delights to pour out freely on all who love our Lord Jesus Christ with a never-ending love!

PHILIPPIANS

The saints in Philippi (1:1-2)

1 From Paul and Timothy, servants of Christ Jesus.
To all our fellow saints in Christ Jesus at Philippi, to all who
have been called by Him and are set apart to live for Him; and to all
those in leadership and ministry among you, those whom God has
placed in authority to oversee your lives and to serve you in His
Name.
[2]May God our Father and the Lord Jesus Christ impart grace and
peace to you all.

Paul's love for the Philippian church (1:3-11)

[3]I am so thankful to God whenever I think of you. [4-5]I pray regularly
for you all with great joy because I know you partner with me in
spreading the gospel. You have done this from the very beginning
of our relationship and you continue to do so. [6]This causes me to be
confident that, because the Lord has begun such a good work in you,
He will enable you to complete the purpose He has for you as you
await the Lord Jesus Christ's return.
[7]My attitude towards you all is justified because I have such love
for you in my heart. You share God's grace with me no matter what
my situation, whether I am in chains for the gospel or speaking out
boldly and defending the truth of God's Word. [8]God Himself knows
how deep my affection is for you all, not a carnal affection but that
which comes from Christ Jesus. I simply long to be with you.
[9]This is what I pray for you: that your love for God and for one
another will become stronger and stronger, that you grow to know
Him better and will have great depth of insight into the truth. [10]For
then you will be able to discern God's best purposes, and you will
walk in pure and blameless love until Christ calls you home. [11]You
will bear much fruit because of the right relationship you have with
God that is only possible through Jesus Christ. And you will live for
God's praise and glory.

Making Jesus known to others (1:12-18)

12 My dear brothers, I want you to understand that God has allowed
what has happened to me so that it can be used to further the work
of the gospel. 13 The whole palace guard and all others here know
clearly that I am in these chains because I serve Christ. 14 These
chains of mine have even encouraged most of our brothers in the Lord
to be more courageous and fearless in the way they proclaim God's
Word!

15 It is a sad fact that some preach Christ out of wrong motives of
envy and rivalry; but others preach out of right motives, seeking the
good of those to whom they witness. 16 They share the truth with
others in love, and they are well aware that I am in this present
situation only because I have defended the truth of the gospel.

17 Those who preach Christ out of selfish ambition are not sincere,
and they take the opportunity to speak against me because I am
confined in these chains. 18 Does this really matter? Well, even if their
motives are false, at least Christ is being preached! But how much
better it is when people's motives are right and true. Yet I rejoice in
every way in which Jesus is made known to others.

Live for Christ (1:19-30)

19 No situation will stop me continuing to rejoice, for I know that I
am strengthened by your prayers for me, and the Spirit of Jesus
Christ continues to help me. So what has happened to me will end
in my freedom. 20 My expectation and hope is that I will not act in
any way of which I would be ashamed, but will be given the
courage I need so that Christ will continue to be exalted in my body,
whether I live or die.

21 The way I see things is clear; if I live it will be for Christ, and if
I die it will gain my heavenly inheritance in Him. 22 If I continue to
live in this present body I can continue to work fruitfully for God's
Kingdom. What choice would I make if it was left to me? I am not sure!
23 I feel drawn in both directions: One part of me longs to depart this
present world and be with Christ in His glory; that would surely be
the better option. 24 But another part of me is willing to remain in
this present body if, by doing so, I can continue to serve you.

25 That being the case, I know that I will make the decision to
remain with you and will continue to help you in any way I can, so
that you will progress in your faith with true joy. 26 I want your joy
in Christ Jesus to overflow because I have been restored to you
again.

27-28 However, no matter what happens, it is important that you
behave in ways that are worthy of Christ's gospel. For then whether
I come and visit you again or can only hear about you because I am
separated from you, I will be confident that you are united together
for the faith of the gospel and do not allow any opposition to cause
you to hold back through fear.

Your faith will be a warning to those who oppose the truth, that
they will be destroyed but that you will be saved by God Himself.
29 Through Christ it has been given you, not only to believe in Him
but also to suffer for Him. 30 This is why you experience the same
struggle that I continue to suffer, as you have heard.

Humility (2:1-11)

2 See what great encouragement you have because you are united
with Christ. Look at how you are strengthened by His love for
you. And because you live at one with the Spirit, you are tender-
hearted and compassionate. 2 So you will complete my joy if you are
united in the way you think, in the love you have for each other and
in the way you live in the Spirit to fulfil God's purpose.

3 To fulfil these aims, be sure never to act out of selfish ambition.
And do not be conceited, for that is only empty vanity. Rather, live
humbly, thinking that others are better than yourselves. 4 Yes, you
will have to be responsible about your own affairs, but you should
be equally concerned about the interests of others around you. 5 In
fact your attitude should reflect that of Christ Jesus Himself:

> 6 By nature He is God, but He did not hold onto His
> divine status of being equal in heaven with the Father.
> 7 He was prepared to make Himself nothing, taking the
> nature of a servant and becoming thoroughly human.
> 8 He was a man in every respect, even though He retained
> His divinity. Even so, He humbled Himself to such an
> extent that He obeyed the Father's will, that He should
> die the death of a criminal on the cross. 9 Because of His
> obedience, God the Father has now exalted Him to the
> highest place in heaven, and has given Him the Name
> that is far superior to any other name. 10 Every knee in
> heaven, on earth and even in the underworld, will bow at
> the Name of Jesus. 11 Every tongue will have to acknowl-
> edge that Jesus Christ is Lord, for this is the Father's
> glorious will.

Faithful witnesses (2:12-18)

12 My dear friends, you see why it has been so important for you to obey the Lord, not only when I am with you but even more when we are apart. Continue to live as those who are saved, who fear the Lord, dreading the idea of ever denying Him. 13 For God Himself is at work within you so that you want to do what is good in His eyes.

14-16 Therefore, there is to be no complaining or arguing among you, no matter what you are asked to do, for this will enable you to become blameless and pure, living as God's children in an unrighteous and depraved generation. You are to shine like the stars in the universe as you share the Word of life with others. Then on the great Day of the Lord I will be able to boast that all my work among you was not for nothing.

17 Even if my life was poured out in sacrifice, even if it is costly to serve you so that you live as people of faith, I am content and rejoice with you all. 18 That being the case, it is only right that you should also be content and rejoicing with me.

Paul commends his colleagues (2:19-30)

19 I hope that it will be the Lord's will to send Timothy to you in the near future, for then he will be able to bring me news about you, and that will encourage me. 20 He is unique in the way he is genuinely concerned about your welfare. 21 Everyone seems more concerned about their own interests than those of Jesus Christ! 22 But Timothy has already proved himself, as you know. He regards me as his spiritual father and, like a good son, he has served with me in working for the gospel. 23 This is why I hope to send him to you just as soon as I can spare him. 24 And I trust the Lord that my circumstances will change so that I will soon be able to visit you myself.

25 Meanwhile, I think it expedient to send my brother Epaphroditus back to you. He is my fellow worker and soldiers along with me. And he is your messenger, whom you sent to care for me. 26 But he misses you all and was really upset that you heard about his illness. 27 He was very sick and almost died; but God showed His mercy and healed him. That was God showing mercy to me as well as him, to save me from any further sorrow on top of what I was already experiencing.

28 This is why I am so keen to send him back to you, for you will be reassured when you see him, instead of being anxious about his welfare. 29 Welcome him back, joyfully thanking God for him. Always honour men like him. 30 It was because of his faithfulness to the

work of Christ that he almost died. He was prepared to risk his life to help me in ways you are unable to fulfil.

Righteousness through faith in Christ (3:1-11)

3 My brothers, rejoice in the Lord! I do not consider it a burden to remind you of this again and again for your own good. Keep rejoicing in the Lord!

2-3 Be on your guard for those who want to draw you away from the truth. They are no better than dogs. All they want to do is mutilate the flesh, whereas we are those who are truly circumcised by the Spirit working in our hearts. It is by the Spirit that we worship and our glory is in Christ Jesus, not in what is done to the flesh. We put absolutely no confidence in the flesh.

4 If it would be justifiable for anyone to put confidence in these outward physical things, I would certainly be the first to qualify! 5-6 Yes, as a Jew I was circumcised on the eighth day; I certainly belong to the people of Israel. I belong to the tribe of Benjamin, a true Hebrew of the Hebrews. I kept the law like a good Pharisee and was full of zeal in the way I persecuted the church. And I was perfect in my legalistic righteousness!

7 I used to think all these things were to my credit, and yet now I have Christ I realise I gained nothing from them. 8-9 So I now regard those things as worthless compared to the greatest privilege of all, of knowing Christ Jesus as my Lord. For His sake I left everything of the past behind and considered those things rubbish, so that I could have Christ and live in Him. Seeking my own righteousness through obeying the law was futile when compared to the righteousness I have now through faith in Christ. This is the true righteousness that comes as a gift from God and can only be received through faith in Christ.

10-11 I want to know Christ and His resurrection power. I am prepared to be at one with Him by sharing in His sufferings. Like Him, I am ready to die for the truth and then somehow by His power be raised from the dead.

Aim for the prize (3:12-16)

12 I do not claim to have received all that God has for me, neither have I yet been made perfect. But I am always moving forward to take hold of everything that Christ Jesus had planned to give me when He laid hold of my life.

13 My brothers, I know I have not yet appropriated everything; but I maintain my focus. So I forget what lies behind me in the past and I reach out with longing for what lies ahead. 14 Yes, I press on towards my goal, which is to gain the prize that God has for me when He calls me home to heaven in unity with Christ Jesus.

15 If you are mature in the way you view spiritual things, then you will think in the same way. If you believe differently, God will bring the correction you need and make everything clear to you. 16 At least continue to live in the good of what you have already received and do not slip back.

Citizens of God's heavenly Kingdom (3:17-4:3)

17 So, brothers, join with those who follow my example and learn from those who adopt the pattern of life we showed you.

18 I repeat now with tears in my eyes what I have already told you in the past. Many face destruction because they live as enemies of the cross of Christ. 19 They make their stomachs their God and are even proud of the shameful ways in which they live. They are obsessed with earthly things.

20 By contrast, we know that we are citizens of God's heavenly Kingdom. This is why we await eagerly the time when the Lord Jesus Christ, our Saviour, will return to earth from heaven. 21 Then He will transform these earthly bodies of ours by the power by which He is able to bring everything under His control. Then our bodies will be like His glorious body!

4 In view of all this, my brothers, you should stand strong in the Lord. I love you and long to be with you, for I regard you as my joy and my crown, my dear friends!

2 I beg both Euodia and Syntyche to let the Lord bring them to agreement with one another. 3 Yes, I ask you as those who are bound in loyalty to me, to help these women who have worked with me in the cause of the gospel, together with Clement and all my other fellow workers, whose names are written in the Book of Life.

Rejoice, pray and give thanks (4:4-9)

4 Always rejoice in the Lord! I repeat: Rejoice! 5-6 Let your gentle spirit be obvious to others. The Lord is near; so there is no need to be anxious about anything. Instead pray about everything, following your petitions with thanksgiving whenever you ask anything of God!

[7]God's peace is beyond understanding and will keep your hearts
and minds at one with Christ Jesus. [8]What, then, should fill your
thoughts? Whatever is true and noble and right in God's eyes; what
is pure and lovely to Him; what He admires, which is everything
that is excellent and worthy of praise.
[9]Put into practice all you have learned from me; whatever you
have received or heard from me. The Lord's peace will continue to
be with you.

Contentment in all circumstances (4:10-13)

[10]Your renewed concern for me has caused me to rejoice greatly in
the Lord. I appreciate that in the past you had no opportunity to
show such concern. [11]I am not suggesting that I am in need, for I
have learned to be content regardless of the circumstances in which
I find myself. [12]I certainly have known what it is to be in need and I
have also known times of abundance. I learned how important it is
to be content no matter what the situation, whether I am well fed or
hungry, whether I am living in abundance or am lacking what I
need. [13]I discovered that I am able to do everything through trusting
in the One who always gives me strength.

Thankfulness for Philippians' generosity (4:14-20)

[14]Yet I do appreciate your willingness to share in my troubles. [15]You
Philippians are also fully aware that when you were first introduced
to the gospel, you were the only church that undertook to share in
the cost involved when I moved on from Macedonia. As a result,
you also shared in the benefit of receiving. [16]Even when I was in
Thessalonica, again and again you sent me the support I needed. [17]It
is not that I am seeking a gift, only that more may be credited to
your heavenly account! [18]I have received all I need and more besides.
Now that I have received the gifts you sent by Epaphroditus I have
plenty. Your gifts are a sweet offering, an acceptable sacrifice that
pleases God.
[19]And my God will surely supply for all your needs, drawing on
the glorious riches He has given us through our unity with Christ
Jesus.
[20]Glory belongs to God our Father for all eternity. Amen! It shall
be so!

Final greetings (4:21-23)

[21]Please give my personal greetings to all the saints, those who live

at one with Christ Jesus. The brothers here with me send you their
greetings. 22 And all the saints here in Rome, especially those in
Caesar's household, send their greetings also.

23 The grace of the Lord Jesus Christ be imparted to your spirit.
Amen! It shall be so!

COLOSSIANS

Greetings (1:1-2)

1 From Paul, by God's will an apostle of Christ Jesus, and from Timothy, my brother in the faith.

[2]To the brothers in Colosse who are also in Christ, called to be holy and faithful to the Lord.

May God our Father impart His grace and peace to you all.

A rich inheritance (1:3-6a)

[3-4]We are always thankful to God, the Father of our Lord Jesus Christ, when we pray for you, because we know about your faith in Him and the love you have for all the saints, those whom God has called and set apart for Himself and His purposes. [5-6]This faith and love are the result of the hope that you have; for you are sure He has a rich reward for you in heaven, the inheritance about which you have heard already through the Word of truth, the good news you have received of who Jesus Christ is and all He has done for you.

The gospel spreads (1:6b-8)

[6]This gospel is now being spread effectively all over the world; the good news of God's Kingdom. The power of this gospel has been growing among you since you first heard about and understood the wonder of God's grace, the wonderful truth that has come to all of us who believe. [7-8]You first learned about this great truth through Epaphras, our beloved brother and fellow servant of Christ, who visited you faithfully on our behalf and has now told us of the love that fills your lives, through all the Holy Spirit has imparted to you.

Paul's continuous prayer (1:9-14)

[9]This is why, since we heard of what God is doing among you, we have never stopped praying for you, asking God to make you aware of His will; that He will give you all the spiritual wisdom and understanding you need. [10]The reason why we pray like this is simple.

We want you to live lives worthy of the Lord, so that you please Him
in every way possible. For then you will produce much fruit for His
glory, through all the good works you do as you continue to know
Him better. 11-12 He strengthens you with all the power of His glorious
might, and it is this power at work in you that gives you patience,
enables you to persist in doing His will and causes you to maintain
your joy, thanking God the Father for all He has done in you.

Yes, it is His work in you that means you are now qualified to
share in the inheritance He has prepared for all those He has called
and set apart to belong to the Kingdom of light. 13 For He has already
rescued us from the devil's dominion of darkness and has brought
us into His own Kingdom, the Kingdom that belongs to the Son He
loves. 14 It is through Him that we have been made worthy in God's
sight through the forgiveness of all our sins, so that now we belong
to Him.

Christ supreme over all (1:15-18)

15-16 Jesus Christ is exactly like His Father, who remains invisible to
us. He is God's firstborn, with authority to rule over all creation
because everything was created by Him, whether in heaven or on
earth, both the visible and invisible, every ruling power and authority.
Yes, everything was created by Him and for His purposes.

17 So the Son has pre-eminence above all that has been created, for
He existed before creation began and only in Him is everything
sustained.

18 He is the Head of His Body, the church, for He was the first to
rise from the dead, so that having conquered everything that opposed
God's purposes He should now have supremacy over all things.

Reconciled to God through Christ (1:19-23)

19-20 You see, it was God's good purpose to place the fullness of His
life in His Son so that through His life, death and resurrection,
everything on earth could be brought back to His will and made
one with all that is in heaven. And all this has been made possible
through the cross, for through the shedding of His blood the Son
has made peace between God and man.

21 You used to be separated from God. You were His enemies
because of the ways you thought and believed, which were evil in
His sight. 22 But now, through what Christ endured in His physical
body, you have been reconciled to God so that you are now one
with Him. It is through His death that He has made you holy before

God, and it is Christ who will one day present you to His Father
perfect, free from any accusation the devil could bring against you.
23 However, for Him to complete this purpose you have to persist in
your faith, allowing nothing to shake your trust in Him, so that you
attain the hope you have received through the gospel, your rich
inheritance in heaven.

This is the good news you heard at the beginning of your Christian walk, the hope that is held out to the whole of creation. And I, Paul, have become a servant of this wonderful gospel!

Paul's service to the church (1:24-29)

24 I rejoice in what I had to suffer for your sake. It was only suffering
to my flesh, my natural man, and a continuation of the affliction that
Christ Himself suffered for the sake of His Body, the church. 25 I have
become your servant in this because of the commission God gave
me, to bring you God's Word in all the fullness of its truth and
power. 26 He is now revealing the secrets that have been hidden during
previous times and generations; but these truths are revealed only
to His saints, to those who belong to Him. 27 He has chosen to reveal
to all who are His among the nations, the glorious riches that are
centred in this mystery that Christ has now come to live in you, and
in Him alone is your hope of glory, now and for all eternity.

28 This is why we speak only of Christ, encouraging, correcting
and teaching everyone with the wisdom He has given us, so that we
can present everyone perfect in Christ because they believe the
gospel we proclaim. What a wonderful prospect! 29 And it is this that
inspires me to work so hard, depending on His power to work in
and through me, and enabling me to prevail through all the strug-
gles.

Understanding truth guards against deception (2:1-5)

2 And I want you to know that I do have to struggle for you, for
those at Laodicea and for others, even though I do not know
them personally. 2 My intention is that I might be able to encourage
their hearts and urge them to be united in love. I want them to come
to a complete understanding of all the riches that are available to
them as the mystery of the fullness of Christ is unfolded to them.
3 For in Him all the riches of wisdom and true knowledge are to be
found!

4 I speak in this way to warn you against those who want to
deceive you with teaching that sounds right but is not grounded in

the truth of Christ. 5 Even though I am not with you physically, I am with you in spirit and it gives me great joy to know that you maintain good order in the church and that you remain strong in your faith in Christ.

Be built up in Christ (2:6-8)

6 So this is my message to you: because you have already received Christ Jesus as your Lord, continue to live in Him. 7 You have been rooted in Him, so now grow up in Him. Let your trust in Him continue to grow stronger as you live in the good of what you have been taught. And let your hearts overflow with thankfulness to God.

8 Be sure that no one puts you into bondage through clever sounding but empty talk that is the result of worldly thinking and dependence on the traditional way of looking at things, instead of being revelation of the truth in Christ.

Sinful nature buried with Christ (2:9-15)

9 For in Him the complete revelation of who God is has come to us in human form. 10 In Christ you have been given the fullness of His life. And He is supreme above every power and authority. 11 Because you live in Him, you have received a spiritual circumcision, not one done by men but by Christ Himself. 12 This circumcision involved cutting away your old sinful nature, which was buried once and for all with Christ when you were baptised. Now you have been raised to new life with Him through believing in God's power; that as He raised Christ from the dead, so He has also raised you from the death of sin to a new life with Him.

13-14 You were spiritually dead because of your unforgiven sins, because that old sinful nature had not been cut away. But then God brought you to life with Christ, He forgave all your sins and cancelled the written code of rules and regulations that were impossible for you to keep, and only consigned you to failure and defeat. Jesus removed this code by nailing it to the cross. 15 There He also disarmed the demonic powers and authorities that oppose us. His triumph over them on the cross was a public defeat for them!

Don't be bound by legalism (2:16-23)

16 So now you do not have to allow anyone to judge you according to the old rules and regulations about what you should eat or drink, for example. Neither do you have to observe the religious festivals,

the New Moon celebration or the Sabbath day. [17]Such things were a shadow of what God would reveal in the future. But now we have the reality itself that is only to be found in Christ.

[18-19]There will be those who want to influence you by drawing you away from the truth so that you are not able to lay hold of your inheritance. Such people put on a display of false humility and they hold to strange doctrines about angels.

Beware of anyone who goes into great detail about what he has claimed to see in spiritual visions; his unspiritual mind is full of pride and useless thoughts and he is no longer submitted to Christ, the Head of the Body. For it is only Christ who is able to keep all the various parts of the Body working together in unity, enabling it to grow in the way He desires.

[20]When you died with Christ, you died to those worldly principles that stand opposed to the principles of God's Kingdom. So it makes no sense to live as if you still belong to the world rather than to Christ. [21]Neither do you have to submit to those religious rules, 'Do not handle this!' 'Do not taste that!' 'Do not touch'. [22]These religious regulations contain no life because they are really human commands and teachings. [23]They can appear to be wise because they promote a discipline of worship and seem to encourage humility, although really this is a false kind of humility. They even encourage strict discipline of the body, but are totally incapable of dealing with the real problem – the need to deal with the sensual indulgence of the flesh.

A new life in Christ (3:1-4)

3 You have been raised with Christ to share in His risen life. So set your hearts on heavenly things, for that is where Christ is now seated at God's right hand. [2]You need to have heavenly thinking and not be restricted by mere worldly thoughts.

[3]Because you died with Christ, your life is now hidden with Christ – in God! [4]Because He is your life, you will appear with Him in glory when He comes again.

Made into the likeness of Christ (3:5-10)

[5]So put to death anything that belongs to the old earthly nature, such things as sexual immorality, any kind of impurity or lust, all evil desires and greed, for that is idolatry. [6]In His wrath God has condemned all such things and those guilty of such sin. [7]In your old life you were bound by such things. [8]But now you are to have a

completely different walk, in which you can free yourself of all such
things, together with anger, rage, malice, slander and speaking in a
foul or unclean way. 9 Neither are you to lie to each other because
you have left that old self behind with all the things you used to do
then. 10 Now you have a new self that receives fresh revelation of
God your Creator and makes you more and more like Him.

Living in unity with others (3:11-17)

11 In Christ there is no difference between Greek and Jew. It doesn't
matter whether you are circumcised or uncircumcised, what your
nationality or background is, whether you were born in slavery or
freedom. Christ is everything to all who believe in Him, and He
lives in them all!

12 So I speak to you as God's chosen people. You are holy, set apart
by God to belong to Him as His own children. You are dearly loved
by Him and can clothe yourselves with compassion, kindness,
humility, gentleness and patience. 13 Yes, be patient with one another and forgive any differences that arise between you. Forgive as the
Lord forgave you, no matter how deeply hurt you feel.

14 The highest virtue is love, for this keeps all these other qualities
in their right place and enables you to live in unity with others.

15 As members of the one Body of Christ, you have been called to
live at peace with all the other members. So let the peace of Christ
be a guiding principle of your life. And always be thankful to God.

16 Let the truth, the Word of Christ, live in you in all its richness.
Then you will be able to teach, encourage and correct one another
with godly wisdom. Keep praising God by singing psalms, hymns
and spiritual songs with hearts full of thankfulness to God.

17 Be sure that no matter what you say or do, you are able to do
everything in the Name of Jesus, because you do what pleases Him,
and you do it with thankfulness to God the Father because of all
you received in His Son.

Instructions to Christian families (3:18-21)

18 It is right before God that you wives submit to your husbands.
19 And husbands, you are to love your wives and not treat them
harshly.

20 Children, you are to obey your parents at all times for this pleases
the Lord. 21 And fathers, be careful not to frustrate your children or
cause them to feel bitter, for they will then be discouraged from
following the Lord.

Instructions for workers and employers (3:22-4:1)

22 When you are at work, be good examples through your obedient attitude towards those who are over you. Do your best at all times, not only when you are being watched by your boss or because you want to be in his good books. No, always serve with a good heart and because you are intent on honouring God. 23 Do everything wholeheartedly as if you were doing it directly for the Lord, not for men. 24 Your reward will come from Him, the rich inheritance He has promised you. At all times you are serving the Lord Christ!

25 On the other hand, those who do what is wrong store up for themselves a different kind of return, for God does not act with favouritism but treats everybody justly.

4 Those of you in positions of responsibility in the workplace, be sure to treat your employees in ways that are right and honourable, because you know that you will be held accountable by your Master in heaven.

Be devoted in prayer (4:2-4)

2 Be sure that you are devoted in prayer, that you have a disciplined prayer life so that you are alert spiritually, living in dependence on the Lord and thankful to Him in all things. 3-4 Pray for us as well, that He will provide ready-made opportunities for us to proclaim the message of Christ, in order to give people revelation of the truth. I am held captive for doing this; yet even so I want to proclaim the message of the Kingdom clearly in the way that I should.

Be wise with unbelievers (4:5-18)

5 You have to be wise in the way you behave towards unbelievers and to make the most of every opportunity you have to share the gospel with them. 6 You will need to be gracious in the way you speak, and able to answer the questions asked of you. Your words can come as salt to bring seasoning into tasteless lives.

7-8 I am sending Tychicus to you so he can bring you further news about my circumstances. He is a dear and faithful brother, a fellow minister and the Lord's true servant. What he tells you will encourage your hearts.

9 Onesimus, another faithful and dear brother, will come with him. He is one with you and will tell you all about what is taking place here.

10 Aristarchus is held prisoner with me and sends you his greetings,
as does Mark, Barnabas' cousin. If he comes to visit you, welcome
him in the way you have already been instructed. 11 Jesus Justus also
greets you. These are the only Jewish brethren who work with me
for God's Kingdom and they have each been used to bless and
encourage me.

12 Epaphras, one of your own servants of Christ Jesus, greets you.
He continues to wrestle in prayer for you so that you will be strong
in doing God's will, showing your maturity in the faith and how
confident you are in the Lord. 13 I can assure you that he works so
hard for you and your fellow believers at Laodicea and Hierapolis.

14 Our dear brothers Dr. Luke and Demas also greet you. 15 Please
pass my own greetings onto the brothers at Laodicea, and the
church that meets at Nympha's house.

16 When you have read this letter and taken note of what I have
said, pass it on to the church at Laodicea. Be sure that in return you
receive the letter I wrote to the Laodiceans.

17 I have a message for Archippus: "Make certain that you finish
the work the Lord gave as His commission to you."

18 I, Paul, write this final greeting in my own hand. Remember me
in my chains. The Lord's grace be with you always.

1 THESSALONIANS

Greetings (1:1-3)

1 From Paul, Silas and Timothy.

To the church in Thessalonica, those who live in God the Father and the Lord Jesus Christ:

May grace and peace be imparted to you.

[2] We continually thank God for all of you when we pray for you. [3] We are always mindful before our God and Father of the work that is the result of your faith, your deeds that have been the outworking of your love, and your perseverance that is inspired by your hope in our Lord Jesus Christ.

Lead by example (1:4-10)

[4-6] Brothers, you are loved by God who has chosen you through the preaching of our gospel, not simply through words but also with demonstrations of His power. We ministered in the power of the Holy Spirit and with great assurance. It was for your sake that we lived among you and you are well aware that our lifestyle was an example to you; and so you were able to imitate us and the Lord, doing what pleases Him.

Even though there was much suffering, you received the message with the joy that the Holy Spirit gave you. [7] You in turn became a model for all the believers in Macedonia and Achaia. [8-9] It was not only in these regions that the Lord's message was proclaimed through you; your faith in God is known everywhere. So we do not need to speak further about your reputation, for it is well known what a great reception you gave us. People speak about the way you turned from idol worship and now serve the true and living God. [10] They know that you long for the return of God's Son from heaven, Jesus who was raised from the dead and who rescues us from the wrath that will come at the time of judgment.

Time in Thessalonica (2:1-20)

2 So, my brothers, you know that our time among you was not a
failure. 2 Before our arrival, you knew we had suffered greatly
in Philippi, but despite this, with God's help we boldly proclaimed
this gospel to you, regardless of strong opposition.

3 We have not appealed to you out of any wrong motives; we have
no desire to deceive you in any way. 4 Quite the opposite! We speak
to you as those commissioned by God Himself. He has entrusted us
with the task of spreading the gospel as those He has approved. So
we are certainly not attempting to please man, but God who tests
our hearts.

5-6 You know that we have never flattered you, nor have we used
the gospel as a front to cover up any desire for personal gain. God
Himself is our witness that this is the case. We are not expecting
praise from you, nor from anyone else.

Because Christ has made us His apostles, we would have every
right to expect you to support us, but we never allowed ourselves
to be a burden to you. 7 Instead we dealt with you as a mother deals
gently with her small children. 8 Our love for you was so great that
it was sheer joy for us not only to share the gospel with you but also
to make our own lives available to you. This is the very evidence of
how precious you are to us.

9 Dear brothers, surely you have not forgotten the way we
worked so hard among you! We worked day and night to support
ourselves while we preached the gospel of God to you.

10 Not only is God our witness but you yourselves know well that
we lived holy, righteous and blameless lives among you believers.
11 You can vouch for the fact that we treated you as a father would
deal with his own children. 12 We encouraged you, strengthened you
and urged you to live in ways that are worthy of God, who calls us
to reveal His Kingdom and His glory.

13 Because you received what we preached to you as God's Word,
rather than our own words, we thank God continually for you. So
now His Word is at work in you because you believed. 14 As a result,
my brothers, you reflect the same life as God's churches in Judea,
for you too are in Christ Jesus.

You have suffered persecution from your own countrymen as the
Judean churches suffered from the Jews. 15-16 As a people they not
only killed Jesus but also the prophets who preceded Him; and they
also disassociated themselves from us. This displeased God for they
do everything in their power to prevent us from taking the truth to

the Gentile nations, so that they may be saved. It seems that there is
no limit to the sins they compile, placing themselves under God's
wrath and judgment.

17 Never did we leave you in our hearts, even though, my brothers, we had to leave you physically for a time. We made every effort
to return to you as soon as possible. 18 Again and again this was my
purpose personally, but the devil prevented this from happening.
19 For is it not true that when the Lord Jesus comes it will be seen that
you are our hope, our joy, the crown in which we will glory in His
presence? 20 Yes, you are our glory and joy.

Timothy sent to encourage the believers (3:1-5)

3 When I could stand my separation from you no longer, 2 I sent
Timothy to you while I remained in Athens. He is a faithful
brother and God's fellow worker in spreading Christ's gospel in
order to strengthen and encourage your faith, 3 so that you would not
be disturbed by the trials you have to face. You know clearly that we
were destined to face such things. 4 In fact, when we were with you
we kept warning you that we will all be persecuted. It was
inevitable and so it turned out.

5 When I could no longer stand being without news of how you
were coping, I sent Timothy so I could hear about your faith. I was
fearful that the enemy might have tempted you to deny your faith,
for then all our work among you would have come to nothing.

Timothy's good report (3:6-13)

6 However, Timothy has just arrived back here bringing good news
about your faith and love. He has reported that you continue to
think well of us and long to see us again, just as we are longing to
be reunited with you. 7 Therefore, my brothers, despite all the distress
and persecution, your steadfast faith has greatly encouraged us.
8 Because you continue to stand strong in the Lord, we have received
a new lease of life! 9 So how can we thank God enough for you
because of all the joy we have in our Lord's presence because of
you? 10 We pray earnestly night and day that we may return to you
and strengthen your faith still further.

11 I pray that our God, the Father Himself, and our Lord Jesus will
provide an opportunity for us to visit you. 12 May the Lord cause
your love to increase and overflow for one another and for others,
in just the same way that our love overflows to you. 13 May He keep
your hearts strong so that you will be blameless and holy in the

presence of God our Father when our Lord Jesus comes together
with all His holy ones.

Devote yourselves to please God (4:1-8)

4 Finally, my brothers, we taught you how to live in ways that
please God; and this you are indeed doing. Now we plead with
you in the name of the Lord Jesus to devote yourselves more fully
to pleasing Him. [2]For you are aware of the instructions we gave you
by the authority the Lord Jesus Christ gave us.

[3-4]It is God's will that you should lead a holy life; that you should
avoid sexual immorality and that each of you should learn to control
his or her body in the way that is holy and honourable in God's
eyes. [5]Avoid the passionate lust typical of the heathen, the unbelievers
that do not know God. [6]No one should wrong his brother or sister
or take advantage of another believer in this matter of sexual relationships. The Lord will surely punish those who are guilty of such sins,
as we have already warned you. [7]For God did not call us to live
impure lives, but to walk in holiness. [8]So anyone who ignores these
instructions rejects not man but God, who gives you His Holy Spirit
to enable you to live a holy life.

Love one another (4:9-12)

[9]Now we do not need to write to you about brotherly love, for God
has Himself taught you to love one another. [10]In fact, you have
shown your love for all the believers throughout Macedonia. Yet we
encourage you, dear brothers, to continue to do this even more
fully.

[11-12]Aim to live a quiet life; this should be your ambition. And
mind your own business! Obey our instructions to work diligently
so that you will win the respect of outsiders by the way you live day
by day. At the same time you will not need to be dependent upon
anyone.

The Lord's return (4:13-18)

[13]My brothers, we want you to be informed about those believers
who have died, for you should not grieve like those who have no
hope. [14]Because we believe that Jesus died and rose again, we also
are confident that God will ensure that those who have died in
Christ Jesus will accompany Him when He returns.

[15]Based on what the Lord has said Himself, we can assure you
that we who are still alive on earth when the Lord comes again will

certainly not rise to meet Him ahead of those who have already
died.

16 For the Lord Himself will descend from heaven shouting His
command. The voice of the archangel will be heard, together with
God's call, sounding like a trumpet. Those who have died in Christ
will be the first to rise. 17 Then those believers who are still alive on
earth will rise together with them in the cloud of glory to meet with
the Lord. Thus we shall be with the Lord for all eternity.

18 So encourage one another with these truths.

Remain spiritually alert (5:1-10)

5 Now, my brothers, I have no need to write to you about when
these events will take place, 2 for you can be sure that the Day of
the Lord will come unexpectedly, as a thief who comes in the night.
3 While some are saying: "Everything is peaceful and we are safe,"
sudden destruction will come upon them, in the same way that a
pregnant woman suddenly has labour pains. They shall not escape!

4 However, my brothers, you do not live in ignorance, so that this
Day will surprise you like a thief. 5 For you are all sons of the light
and of the day. No, we do not belong to the spiritual night where all
is darkness. 6 So let us be alert and ready, and not like those who are
asleep spiritually. 7 People sleep at night and get drunk at night. 8 But
because we belong to the day, let us be self-controlled in the way we
live. Wear your faith and love like a breastplate and your hope of
salvation like a helmet. 9 For God has not condemned us to suffer
His wrath, but to receive salvation through our Lord Jesus Christ.
10 He died for us so that whether we are alive or have died at that
time, we will live together with Him.

Closing instructions (5:11-28)

11 So continue to encourage one another and build each other up, as
you are already doing.

12 Now, my brothers, I ask you to have true honour for those who
work hard on your behalf, whom the Lord has placed over you and
who warn and correct you as necessary. 13 Maintain the highest
regard for them and love them wholeheartedly because of their
work. And live in peace and harmony with one another.

14 My brothers, I also urge you to warn any who are lazy, to
encourage the fearful, to help the weak and to be patient with everyone. 15 Be certain that none of you retaliates with wrong for wrong.
Instead always aim to be kind to one another and to anyone else.

16 Always be full of joy. 17 Keep praying all the time. 18 Give thanks
to God, regardless of your circumstances. All this is God's will for
you in Christ Jesus.

19 Do nothing to dampen the fire of God's Spirit within you. 20 Do
not treat genuine prophetic words from the Lord with contempt by
ignoring them. 21 Test whatever is said and hold onto what is good
because it is clearly from God. 22 Shun evil in all its forms.

23 And may God Himself, the God of peace, cause you to be holy
in every aspect of your lives, so that everything about you in spirit,
soul and body will be kept blameless in God's eyes at the coming of
our Lord Jesus Christ. 24 He who has called you is the Faithful One
and He will work this in you.

25 Pray for us, brothers. 26 Greet all the brethren with genuine love.
27 In the Lord's Name I insist you ensure this letter is read to the
whole church.

28 May the grace of the Lord Jesus Christ be with you all.

2 THESSALONIANS

Thessalonians commended on their faith (1:1-12)

1 From Paul, Silas and Timothy:
To the church of the Thessalonians who are in God our
Father and the Lord Jesus Christ:
2 May grace and peace be imparted to you from God the Father
and the Lord Jesus Christ.
3 We ought always to thank God for you, brothers. This is fitting for
your faith is growing stronger and your love for each other continues
to increase. 4 We are able to boast about you in God's churches
because of your faith and the perseverance you show in the face of
the persecutions and afflictions you have to endure. 5 This shows
that God is just in His judgment of you, considering you worthy of
His Kingdom for which you suffer.
6-7 God is right to repay with affliction those who afflict you; but He
gives relief to all who are afflicted, both to you and ourselves. This will
take place when the Lord Jesus is revealed from heaven in flames of
fire, together with His powerful angels. 8 Then full vengeance will be
given to those who do not know God and do not obey the gospel of
our Lord Jesus. 9-10 They will pay the penalty of eternal destruction,
being excluded from the Lord's presence and from the glory of His
might when He comes to be glorified in His saints, His holy people.
All who have believed will be filled with awe and wonder of Him,
because they believed our testimony of what will happen on that Day.
11 We always pray for you along these lines, that our God will
consider you worthy of His calling; that by His power He may fulfil
every one of your good intentions and the actions you undertake in
faith. 12 Then the Name of our Lord Jesus will be glorified in you and
you in Him, because of the grace of God and the Lord Jesus Christ
that is at work among you.

The coming of the lawless one (2:1-12)

2 We ask you, brothers, not to be disturbed or upset about what
will happen when our Lord Jesus Christ comes again, or how

we will be gathered up to meet Him. 2 Reject any spirit, teaching or
letter that is supposed to come from us suggesting that the Day of
the Lord has come already. 3 Let no one deceive you in any way. First
the rebellion has to take place, when the man of lawlessness is
revealed, the one who is destined for destruction. 4 He opposes the
truth and exalts himself above everything associated with God. He
presumes to sit in God's holy sanctuary, wants to be worshipped
and even declares himself to be God.

5 Surely you remember that I told you about this while I was still
with you! 6 And now you know what is restraining him so that he
will not be revealed until the right time. 7 This lawlessness is already
working secretly and the power that restrains it will continue to do
so until it is time for that restraint to be removed. 8 Then the lawless
one will be revealed, whom the Lord Jesus will destroy with the
breath of His mouth, bringing him to nothing by the glory of His
coming.

9 The coming of the lawless one will be the work of Satan and will
be accompanied by all kinds of false miracles, signs and wonders.
10 His wickedness will deceive those who are perishing because they
have refused to love the truth and so have not received salvation.

11-12 So God sends on them a powerful delusion causing them to
believe a lie, so that all may be condemned who have not believed
the truth but have taken pleasure in what is evil.

Stand firm and hold onto the truth (2:13-17)

13 We ought always to thank God for you, brothers loved by the
Lord, because God chose you from the beginning to be saved, by the
work of the Spirit who makes you holy and through faith in the
truth. 14 To this salvation He called you through our gospel, so that
you might share in the glory of our Lord Jesus Christ.

15 So then, brothers, stand firm and hold onto what we taught
you, either by word of mouth or by letter.

16-17 May the Lord Jesus Christ Himself and God our Father, who
loved us and gave us through His grace eternal strength and good
hope, now strengthen your hearts and establish you in every good
deed and word.

Warning against idleness (3:1-18)

3 Finally, brothers, pray for us, that the Lord's Word may spread
rapidly and be honoured by others, as it has been with you, 2 so
that we may be delivered from perverse and evil men. For not all are

people of faith. 3However, the Lord is faithful and He will strengthen
you and keep you from evil.

4The Lord causes us to feel confident about you, because you
obey and continue to do what we tell you. 5May the Lord direct
your hearts into God's love and Christ's patience.

6Now, brothers, we charge you in the Name of the Lord Jesus
Christ to have nothing to do with any brother who lives in idleness,
and does not live according to the teaching you received from us.
7For you yourselves know how you need to follow our example,
because we were never idle while among you. 8Nor did we eat anyone's bread without paying! Rather, we worked hard by day and
night so as not to be a burden to you. 9We did this to give you a
good example, not because we had no right to such help. 10For even
when we were with you we gave you this order: "If anyone does
not want to work, do not let him eat!" 11We hear that some of you are
living in idleness. Instead of being busy, they are busybodies! 12We
command such people and urge them in the Lord Jesus Christ to
start earning their own living, so that they will have bread to eat.

13And you, brothers, do not grow tired of doing good. 14If anyone
refuses to obey what we say in this letter, note that person and do
not associate with him, so that he may feel ashamed. 15Do not
regard him as your enemy, but correct him as a brother.

16Now may the Lord of peace Himself give you peace at all times
and in every way. The Lord be with you all.

17I, Paul, am writing this greeting in my own hand, as you can tell
from my handwriting.

18May the Lord Jesus Christ impart His grace to you all.

1 TIMOTHY

Personal greeting (1:1-2)

1 From Paul, made an apostle of Christ Jesus by the command of
God our Saviour and Christ Jesus who is our hope for the
future.
2 To Timothy, my true son in the faith.
May grace, mercy and peace be imparted to you from God the
Father and Christ Jesus our Lord.

Prevent men from teaching false doctrine (1:3-7)

3-4 When I entered Macedonia I urged you to stay in Ephesus so that
you could command certain men not to teach false doctrines any
longer, nor indulge themselves in controversies concerning myths
and traditions from the past. Such things never enable people to do
God's work, which can only be accomplished by faith in Him.
5 Love is the motive behind this command, the kind of love that
comes from a pure heart, is inspired by faith and results from having
a clear conscience. 6 By their senseless talk it is clear that some have
strayed from these virtues. 7 They want to be teachers of the law yet
they have no idea what they are talking about, even though they
sound so confident.

The necessity of the law (1:8-11)

8 We know that the law has good influence when used properly. 9 But
we are also aware that the law cannot make us acceptable to God. It
exists to restrain the actions of disobedient and rebellious people, of
ungodly sinners, of those who have no regard for what is holy or
sacred to God. The law is needed for those guilty of killing their
mothers or fathers. 10 The law is necessary because of murderers,
adulterers and perverts, those who trade in human misery, those
who lie, cheat and perjure themselves. 11 It exists for those who teach
whatever contradicts the truths of the glorious gospel of our great
God, the truth He has entrusted me to proclaim.

Jesus came to save sinners (1:12-20)

12 He has given me strength to do this, and I thank Christ Jesus our
Lord that He regarded me as being faithful and so appointed me to
serve Him in this way.

13 I used to blaspheme Jesus, persecute the church and was a violent
man. Despite this I was shown mercy by God because I had acted in
ignorance and unbelief. 14 God lavished His grace on me so abundantly,
together with the faith and love that are only found in Christ Jesus!

15 This is a truth that everyone needs to believe: Christ Jesus came
to this world to save sinners, of whom I regard myself as the worst.
16 That is why I was shown such great mercy, so that in me, the worst
of sinners, Christ Jesus might demonstrate the full extent of His
patience, as an example that would encourage others to believe in
Him and so receive eternal life.

17 Now to Him, the One who is the eternal King, the immortal,
invisible and only true God, be honour and glory for ever and ever.
Amen. It shall be so!

18-20 Timothy, my son, in line with the prophecies that have been
spoken over your life, I give you these instructions so that by obeying
them you may fight the good fight of faith that comes from having
a clear conscience. By rejecting these instructions, some have shipwrecked their faith, including Hymenaeus and Alexander. I have
handed them over to Satan so they will learn not to blaspheme
against God.

Pray for all people (2:1-4)

2 1-2 First of all, I urge you to pray for all people. Ask for God's
mercy to be upon them and pray with thanksgiving, even for
kings and those in positions of authority, that we will be able to live
in peace, stability and in godliness as His holy people. 3 Such prayer
is good and pleases God our Saviour. 4 He desires all men to be
saved by coming to know the truth.

Jesus the mediator between God and man (2:5-8)

5-6 For there is only one God and One who mediates between God
and man, Jesus Christ, who was born as a man and gave Himself as
a sacrifice on behalf of all men, to pay the necessary price to restore
them to God. This is the message that He gave to the world at the
appointed time. 7 And I tell you truly that I was appointed an apostle
to proclaim this truth, to teach the true faith to the Gentiles. This is
no exaggeration!

8 So I want everyone everywhere to lift up their hands to the Holy One in prayer, without any anger or disagreements in their hearts.

Appropriate behaviour for women (2:9-15)

9 Women should dress modestly; their whole appearance should be decent and proper. There is no need for them to have elaborate hair styles, nor to adorn themselves with gold or pearls. Neither do they need to wear expensive clothes. 10 It is far better that attention is on their behaviour, to ensure this is appropriate so they are seen to be women of God who honour Him.

11 Women should learn with quiet and fully submissive hearts. 12 I personally do not allow a woman to teach men or exercise authority over them; she should remain silent in the public meeting. 13-14 God created Adam first and then Eve, and it was the woman who was first deceived by the devil and so became a sinner. 15 However, women are to accept that they are called to be mothers who continue to walk in faith, love and holiness, being modest in their appearance and behaviour.

Standards for church leaders (3:1-15)

3 It is certainly true that anyone who sets his heart on being a leader desires what is honourable. 2-3 However, he must realise that a church leader has to be above reproach. He is to be faithful to his only wife and have a temperate lifestyle. This means that he will be self-controlled, respectable and certainly not an excessive drinker. He will be gentle, not violent nor argumentative. He will also be hospitable and needs to be a gifted teacher of God's Word.

4 He will not desire financial riches but will manage his family well, ensuring that his children obey him and show proper respect to others. 5 How can anyone care properly for God's church if he cannot even manage his own family well?

6 A recent convert should not be placed in leadership or he might become proud and abuse his position, as the devil did, and fall under judgment as a result.

7 It is essential for a leader to have a good reputation with those outside the church, so it is clear that he does not yield to the devil's temptations and fall into disgrace.

8 Those called to serve as deacons are to be men held in high regard by others. They, too, must be people whose word can be trusted, not heavy drinkers nor those who resort to questionable practices for financial gain. 9 They must be men of genuine faith in the truth who can serve with clear consciences.

[10]They should prove themselves faithful in lesser responsibilities first and when they have demonstrated a godly character, they can be appointed as deacons. [11]Also their wives must be women who are respected by others; not malicious gossips but temperate and trustworthy in everything they do.

[12]A deacon must also be faithful to his only wife and must manage his children and household well. [13]Those who have served well in this office will gain great respect from others and will demonstrate considerable confidence because of their great faith in Christ Jesus.

[14-15]I hope to visit you soon, but I put these instructions in writing in case I am delayed; so you will know how people should behave as members of God's household, the church of the living God, the pillar and foundation of the truth.

Jesus' nature (3:16)

[16]The mystery of Christ's godly nature is undoubtedly great:

> He appeared in a human body and was shown to be totally acceptable to God when the Spirit came upon Him. He was in the company of angels and has been preached to the nations. People in the world believed Him to be God's Son before He returned to the glory of heaven.

Beware of deceiving spirits (4:1-7)

4 The Spirit has clearly revealed that in due course some will abandon their faith in Christ and will follow deceiving spirits, believing demonic teaching that opposes the truth. [2]People who give such teaching are hypocritical liars whose consciences no longer respond to the truth. [3]They appear to be religious by forbidding people to marry and by ordering them to refuse to eat certain foods, which God intended us to enjoy with thankful hearts, because we believe the liberating power of the truth.

[4-5]For everything God created is good and so does not need to be rejected. By giving thanks to God for His provision, whatever we eat becomes consecrated through faith in God's Word and by prayer.

[6]You will be Christ Jesus' faithful minister if you teach these things to the believers. This will demonstrate that you have been brought up to believe the truth and have followed the teaching of God's Word. [7]So refuse to have anything to do with whatever disagrees with His Word or with any old wives tales. Instead, you are to train yourself to be godly.

Godly character (4:8-16)

[8]Physical exercise is of some value, but a godly character influences
everything you do, and has great value in the present life and in the
life that is to come.

[9-10]Here is another truth that you can depend upon and is true for
every believer: That we have placed our hope in the living God,
who is the Saviour of all mankind, but especially of those who
believe in Him.

[11]Teach these things with authority. [12]Do not allow anyone to put
you down because you are so young. Set the other believers an
example by the way you speak and live, in your love for people,
your faith in God and the purity of your heart. [13]Continue to be
faithful in reading the scriptures publicly and in preaching and
teaching the Word of truth until I arrive. [14]Use fully the gift that was
imparted to you when the whole body of elders laid their hands on
you and prophesied over you.

[15]Be wholehearted in doing all these things so that everyone will
see how you have progressed spiritually. [16]Keep a close watch on
the way you live and on what you teach. If you persevere in the
truth, God will save both you and those who listen to you.

Respect other church members (5:1-16)

5 [1-2]Never speak harshly of an older man; rather appeal to him as
if he were your father. Regard younger men as your brothers;
treat older women as you would your mother and younger women
as your sisters, with complete purity of heart.

[3]Ensure that widows who are in real need are cared for properly.
[4]However, a widow who has children and grandchildren should be
cared for by them. They should put their religion into practice by
caring for their own family members and in this way they will
return the love their parents and grandparents have given them;
this pleases the Lord.

[5]However, the widow who is in genuine need with no one to care
for her has to put her trust in God and prays continually to Him for
help. [6]But the widow who lives only for her own pleasure is spiritually
dead, even if she is physically alive.

[7]Give these instructions to the people so that everyone understands his or her responsibilities. [8]Those who do not provide for
their relatives, especially those of their immediate family, have
denied their faith and are behaving in ways worse than you would
expect from an unbeliever.

[9] No widow should be put on the official list for aid unless she is over sixty and is known to have been faithful to her husband. [10] She should have a reputation for her good deeds, that she has brought up her children well and has served her fellow believers by helping those in trouble; she is someone devoted to the welfare of others.

[11] So younger widows should not be named on such a list because their sensual desires will grow stronger than their devotion to Christ and they will want to remarry. [12] Then they could prove unfaithful to promises made to the Lord. [13] In any case, if you were to support them you would encourage them to be lazy and they would only go from house to house sharing gossip and proving to be busybodies, interfering where they have no right to do so.

[14-15] So I advise younger widows to remarry, have children and manage their households well. Then they will not give the enemy any opportunities to slander them; for some have already turned away from following the Lord and follow sin instead.

[16] Therefore, a woman who is a believer with widows in her family should help them rather than allow them to become a burden on the church. Then the church can help those who are truly in need.

Honour the elders in the church (5:17-20)

[17] The elders who order the affairs of the church well are worthy of receiving double honour from the rest of the believers. This is true especially of those who preach and are responsible for teaching the brethren. [18] After all, the scripture says, "Do not prevent the ox from eating while it treads out the grain." And it also says, "The worker deserves his wages."

[19] Do not listen to any accusation against an elder unless it is substantiated by at least two or three witnesses. [20] But elders who are proved to be guilty are to be publicly rebuked as a warning to others.

Further instructions (5:21-25)

[21] Now in the sight of God, of Christ Jesus and of His chosen angels, I give you this charge: obey these instructions without showing any partiality or favouritism. [22] Do not be in a rush to lay hands on people and do not compromise your own standards of purity because others sin.

[23] Instead of drinking only water, drink a little wine for the sake of your stomach and because you are often physically weak.

5:18 Deuteronomy 25:4, Luke 10:7

24 The sins of some men are all too obvious. Even though they are plainly destined for judgment, others follow their evil examples. 25 But in the same way, good deeds are also obvious and cannot be hidden!

Be good employees (6:1-2)

6 All believers should consider their bosses in the workplace worthy of full honour, so that they have no grounds to speak against God's Name or what we teach about Him. 2 Those with Christian bosses should not take advantage of them, but must show them the respect they deserve because they are fellow believers. In fact, they should work even harder for them because those who benefit are fellow Christians and so are precious to them. Teach these things and urge people to put them into practice.

Effects of false doctrine (6:3-5)

3-4 Anyone teaching false doctrine that does not agree with the words of truth given by our Lord Jesus Christ and other godly teachers is clearly conceited without any real understanding of the truth. 5 He loves to be involved in controversial discussions and will quarrel about the interpretation of words. This only leads to jealousy and division. People even speak blasphemously and undermine confidence in others. Because of their continual wranglings, their minds become corrupted and they allow themselves to be robbed of the truth. They are more concerned with financial rewards than with godliness.

True godliness brings real rewards (6:6-16)

6 However, true godliness brings real rewards. 7 For we were born with nothing and we can take nothing with us when we die. 8-9 We should be content with having enough to eat and wear, for people who aim to become wealthy fall into temptation and a trap laid by the devil. Their many foolish and harmful desires will plunge them into spiritual ruin and destruction. 10 Having a love for money is the root of many forms of evil. Some are so desperate to be rich they have strayed away from the faith and have only caused themselves many problems.

11 But you are a man of God and are to run from all such fleshly desires so that you can pursue a righteous way of life, full of godliness, faith, love, perseverance and gentleness. 12 So fight the good fight of the faith, living in the good of the eternal life given you

when you were called, when you made your public confession of faith in Christ Jesus.

[13-14]I charge you before God, who is the source of all life, and before Christ Jesus, who made His good confession while testifying to Pontius Pilate, keep this command with a pure heart. [15]At His appointed time, God will cause the return of our Lord Jesus Christ. And God is the Blessed One, the only Ruler, the King of kings and Lord of lords. [16]He alone is immortal and He lives in unapproachable light, so brilliant that no-one has seen or could see Him as He is. To Him belongs all honour and power forever. Amen! It shall be so!

Don't put confidence in earthly wealth (6:17-19)

[17]Tell those who have great wealth in this present world that they are not to be proud, nor should they put their future hope in the fact that they are rich. All wealth is only temporary and uncertain. However, those who hope in God find that He provides abundantly for them. He provides for all our needs and our pleasure as well.

[18]So tell the wealthy to be generous in the way they handle their riches, doing good and sharing with others. [19]Then they will store up heavenly riches for themselves, a necessary foundation for the future! In this way they will be able to take hold of the only life that is real and eternal.

Put your faith in the truth (6:20-21)

[20-21]Timothy, guard the deposit of truth that has been entrusted to you. Have nothing to do with empty talk and with the ideas that oppose the truth but are promoted under the banner of 'reason.' In believing such false so-called 'knowledge', some have strayed from putting their faith in the truth.

God's grace be with you.

2 TIMOTHY

Paul encourages Timothy (1:1-14)

1 From Paul, whom God has made an apostle because this was
His will, and because I live in the promise of life that is in Christ
Jesus.
2 To Timothy, my dear son in the faith.
May grace, mercy and peace be imparted to you from God our
Father and our Lord Jesus Christ.
3 I thank God for, like my forefathers, I serve Him with a clear
conscience and pray for you unceasingly by day and night. 4 I
remember your tears and long to see you so that I might be filled
with joy. 5 I recall your strong faith. It is like the faith that was obvious
in your grandmother Lois and your mother Eunice, and that I now
realise is in you also.
6 So I remind you to fan the flame of God's gift that is in you, that
was imparted to you when I laid my hands on you. 7 For God has
not given us a Spirit of cowardice but a Spirit of power and love that
enables us to exercise self-discipline and right thinking.
8-9 Therefore do not be ashamed to testify about the Lord nor of
me his prisoner; rather be prepared to suffer for the gospel. For by
God's power He has saved us and has given us a holy calling that
cannot be outworked through our own works, but only by being
one with His purpose, through His grace and divine enabling that
He chose before the beginning of time to give us in Christ Jesus.
10-11 That purpose and grace have been revealed when our Lord Jesus
Christ came. He abolished death and brought life and immortality
to light through the gospel, this same gospel for which I was
appointed by God to be a herald, an apostle and a teacher. 12 This is
why I suffer as I do!
But I am not ashamed, for I know the One in whom I have
believed, and I am convinced that He is able to guard what He has
entrusted to me until that great Day when He comes again.
13 Follow the pattern of sound teaching which you received from
me, in the faith and love you have in Christ Jesus. 14 Through the

Holy Spirit who lives in us, guard the deposit of truth entrusted to
you.

Paul rejected in Asia (1:15-18)

15 You know that in the province of Asia everyone has rejected me,
including Phygelus and Hermogenes. 16 May the Lord give mercy to
the household of Onesiphorus because he has often encouraged me
and is not ashamed of my chains. 17 When he arrived in Rome he
searched for me with great determination until he found me, and
you know well the way he served me in Ephesus. 18 May the Lord
grant that we will receive His mercy on that Day when He comes
again.

Further exhortations (2:1-26)

2 Therefore, my dear son, be strong in the grace that is in Christ
Jesus. 2 And the things you have heard me say before many
witnesses, entrust to faithful men who will be able to teach others.
3 Be prepared to suffer adversity as a good soldier of Christ Jesus.
4 No soldier is involved in civilian life, so he can be free to please the
one who enlisted him. 5 And no athlete will win the gold medal
unless he competes according to the rules. 6 The first to receive his
share of the crop should be the hard working farmer.

7 Think about what I am saying, for the Lord will give you all the
understanding you need. 8-9 Remember Jesus Christ was raised from
the dead and was descended from David, according to the gospel I
preach, the same gospel for which I suffer and am imprisoned as if
I was a criminal. 10 But all these things I endure for the benefit of
God's chosen ones, so they can obtain the salvation that is in Christ
Jesus and that leads to eternal glory.

11-12 God's Word is true and is to be trusted: "If we died with Him,
we shall also live with Him; if we persevere we shall also reign with
Him; but if we deny Him He will also deny us. 13 If we are without
faith He will still remain faithful, for He cannot deny Himself."

14 Keep reminding the believers of these things, warning them
before God not to fight over words. Such disputes achieve nothing
and only have a negative affect on those who hear them. 15 Do your
very best to present yourself before God as one who is approved of,
a workman who has nothing of which to be ashamed and who handles
the Word of truth with care.

16 Avoid ungodly conversation; it only produces more ungodliness.
17 Those who indulge in it spread disease like gangrene. Hymenaeus

and Philetus are prime examples of this. 18 They have departed from the truth by saying that the resurrection of all believers has taken place already. As a result they have destroyed the faith of some people.

19 However, the firm foundation God has laid still stands, for He has placed His seal on it. "The Lord knows those who belong to Him," and "Let everyone who calls on the Lord's Name turn away from sin."

20 Now in a house there are not only gold and silver objects but also utensils made of wood and pottery. Some things are for special purposes, others are for common use. 21 If anyone cleanses himself of whatever produces evil he will be fit for special use that will honour the master, for he is devoted to him and is prepared to do anything good his master asks of him.

22 Timothy, run from the evil desires of youth and run after righteousness, faith, love and peace, together with all the other believers who pray to the Lord with clean hearts. 23 Refuse to have anything to do with foolish and ignorant disputes, knowing they only promote quarrels. 24 And the Lord's servant should not be involved in such quarrels, but should be gentle in his dealings with everyone. 25 He shall be able to teach others, to be patient with them, to bring correction sensitively to those who oppose him, trusting that the Lord will work in them, causing them to repent and come to a full acceptance of the truth. 26 Then they will escape the devil's trap that captures people, causing them to do his will.

The last days (3:1-13)

3 1-4 Understand that in the last days there will be terrible times, for men will fall in love with themselves and with money. They will be boastful and arrogant. They will blaspheme against God, be disobedient to their parents, be ungrateful, unholy and without proper love. They will be impossible to please and will slander others. They will not exercise any self-control themselves, nor will it be possible for others to control them. They will hate what is good, betray the trust others place in them and will act in reckless and conceited ways. In short, they will live for their own pleasure rather than to please God.

5 Some may put on an appearance of being godly, but they will lack the power that goes with true godliness. Have nothing to do with such people. 6-7 Some of them work their way into the homes of weak-willed women who are weighed down with many sins and who readily yield to their fleshly desires; the kind of people who listen but never seem able to grasp hold of the truth.

8 These men oppose the truth in the same way as Jannes and Jambres opposed Moses. They are men with depraved minds and false faith. 9 They will not get very far for their foolish sinfulness is obvious to everyone, as was also the case with those two.

10 However, you are aware of my teaching, the way I believe, the purpose for which I live, my faith, patience, love and endurance. 11 You know of the persecutions and sufferings I have experienced in Antioch, Iconium and Lystra; persecutions I endured but from all of which the Lord delivered me. 12 Indeed, all those who wish to live holy lives in Christ Jesus are bound to be persecuted. 13 At the same time, evil men and impostors will go from bad to worse, deceiving many while being themselves deceived.

Importance of scripture (3:14-4:4)

14 But you are to continue in what you have learned and have believed, knowing from whom you learned these things. 15 From early childhood you have been familiar with the holy scriptures which give you revelation about the salvation that comes through faith in Christ Jesus.

16-17 God has breathed His life and truth into all scripture which is therefore beneficial for teaching what is right, rebuking what is wrong, bringing correction and instruction and equipping people for righteousness so that the man of God may be ready for every good work.

Closing words (4:1-22)

4 1-2 I command you before God and Christ Jesus, the One who will judge the living and the dead when He appears in the full majesty of His Kingly rule: Be prepared to preach His Word at all times, regardless of the circumstances. Correct, rebuke and encourage others, exercising much patience as you teach. 3 For a time is coming when people will not put up with teaching of the truth, choosing instead to listen to those who will teach what they want to hear. 4 They will turn away from listening to the truth and will turn instead to myths.

5 As for you personally, be consistent in everything, even when there is adversity. Do the work of the evangelist who brings people to Christ, and so fulfil your calling from God.

6 I am already at the point of being poured out like a sacrifice, and it is now time for my departure. 7 I have fought the good fight, I have finished the course God had for me and I have been faithful.

[8]Now the crown of righteousness awaits me, which the Lord, the
righteous Judge, will award to me on that Day; and not only to me,
but also to all who have longed for His appearing.
[9]Do all you can to visit me soon. [10-11]Demas has deserted me, for
he loves this present life and has gone to Thessalonica. Crescens has
gone to Galatia and Titus to Dalmatia; Only Luke is with me. Bring
Mark with you, for he is useful to me in the ministry. [12]And I have
sent Tychicus to Ephesus. [13]Bring with you the cloak I left with
Carpas in Troas, together with my scrolls, especially the parchments.
[14]Alexander the coppersmith did much to harm me; the Lord will
deal with him as he deserves. [15]Be careful of him yourself, for he has
strongly opposed our words of truth.
[16-17]When I had to make my first defence there was no one to
stand with me; they had all left me alone. But may it not be counted
against them, for the Lord stood with me and enabled me to proclaim
fully the message that all the nations need to hear. And I was saved
from the lion's mouth! [18]The Lord will keep me from all evil and
will save me for His heavenly Kingdom. To Him be glory forever
and ever. Amen! It shall be so!
[19]Give Priscilla and Aquila my greetings, together with the
household of Onesiphorus. [20]Erastus remained at Corinth, but I had
to leave Trophimus in Miletus as he was sick. [21]Make every effort to
come before winter sets in. Give my love to Eubulus and Pudens, to
Linus and Claudia, and to all the brethren.
[22]May the Lord be with your spirit, and may He impart His grace
to you.

TITUS

Paul writes to Titus (1:1-4)

1 From Paul, God's servant, called to be an apostle of Jesus Christ
to encourage faith in God's chosen ones and to bring them
knowledge of the truth that leads to godliness. [2]This is the result of
the hope of eternal life that was promised by God from the beginning
of time; and He never lies! [3]At the appointed time, this life was
revealed through the preaching entrusted to me by the command of
God our Saviour.
[4]To Titus, my true child in the faith we share. May God the Father
and Christ Jesus our Saviour impart grace and peace to you.

Elders and overseers (1:5-9)

[5]I left you in Crete so that you could set in place the things that were
lacking in the church there and so that you could appoint elders in
every town, as I directed you. [6]Elders should be men who live
blameless lives, have only one wife, with children who are believers
and not open to charges of being wild or unruly.
[7]It is essential that an overseer of God's people also leads a
blameless life, for he is called to please God by doing His works
rather than living for himself. So he is not to have a liberal sexual
lifestyle, nor be a drunkard, nor one who is violent or out for his own
gain. [8]No, he should be hospitable, one who loves what is good, and
is upright, holy and self-controlled. [9]He must be a firm believer in
God's revealed Word, so that he may be able to teach others correctly
and stand against those who oppose the truth.

Rebuke the rebellious (1:10-16)

[10]There are many rebellious people who speak empty words to
deceive others. I refer especially to the Jewish legalistic party. [11]They
must be silenced, for they upset whole households by teaching what
they have no right to teach, only to fulfil their own base objectives.
[12]One of their own prophets actually said, "All Cretans are liars, evil
beasts, who are greedy and lazy." [13-14]Truly this is what was said.

Therefore be strong in the way you rebuke such so-called prophets so that the people may believe the truth, instead of listening to Jewish myths or to the commands of men who pervert the truth.

15 To those who are pure, everything is pure; but to the corrupt and unfaithful, nothing is pure; both their minds and consciences have been defiled. 16 They claim to know God, but their actions deny this, for they do what is abominable in God's sight. They are disobedient and incapable of doing anything good!

Orderly living (2:1-15)

2 But you are to be very different because you teach what is right. 2 Encourage the older men to live sober lives, being serious, sensible and sound in what they believe, in the way they love and in persevering in obedience. 3-5 In like manner, older women should have a godly disposition. They should not slander others nor be slaves to drink. Instead, they should teach what is good and right so that they can train the younger women correctly: to love their husbands and children, to be sensible and pure, to be good homemakers who are kind and submissive to their husbands, so that God's Word is not in any way discredited.

6 In the same way, you are to encourage the younger men to be self-controlled. 7-8 Show them by your example how to live a good life. Teach with integrity, with depth and with the soundness that cannot be refuted; so that any who oppose the truth may be shamed, having nothing bad to say about us.

9 Teach workers to obey their employers in every way, seeking to please them and not argue with them. 10 They are not to steal anything, but are to prove themselves trustworthy, so that they are good examples of the teaching of God our Saviour.

11 For the saving grace of God has appeared for all men. 12-14 He teaches us to deny our fleshly desires and lusts so that we might live sober, upright and godly lives in this present time, as we await the fulfilling of the great blessing for which we long, when the glory of our great God and Saviour Jesus Christ is revealed, He who sacrificed Himself on our behalf. In doing this, He paid with His own blood to rescue us from all that is sinful, and to make us a people God could possess for Himself, who long to please Him by doing good.

15 Titus, proclaim these things clearly. Both encourage and correct, using fully the authority given you. And do not allow anyone to despise you!

Devotion to that which is good (3:1-15)

3 Remind the people to submit themselves to the secular rulers and authorities by being obedient to the law and ready to do good in any way possible. 2 Tell them not to speak badly of anyone, nor be argumentative. Instead, they are to be patient, giving an example of humility to everyone.

3 There was a time when we ourselves were foolish, disobedient, easily led astray and more than ready to satisfy our lusts and fleshly desires. We did what was evil, envying others; we were hated by others and hated them in return!

4-6 But when our God and Saviour's kindness and love were revealed He saved us, not by any works of our self-righteousness, but through His own mercy. He saved us by washing away our past and giving us a new birth, by making us new through the Holy Spirit that He poured out on us abundantly through Jesus Christ our Saviour. 7 So we are made completely acceptable to God by His grace and have become heirs with the expectation of eternal life. This is the Word of truth on which you can depend.

8 I want you to affirm these truths with great confidence, so that those who trust in God may be careful to devote themselves to doing what is good and pleasing to Him. This is the right and profitable way for everyone to live.

9 Avoid foolish arguments, interest in family trees, quarrels and fighting over legal niceties. All such things are vain and useless.

10-11 If anyone causes unrest and division, warn him once or twice, knowing that such a person has departed from the truth, is sinful and self-condemned.

12 When I send Artemas and Tychicus to you, come as soon as possible to Nicopolis where I have decided to spend the winter. 13 Do all you can to help Zenas the lawyer and Apollos, so they lack nothing. 14 Let all our people learn to persist in doing good deeds, so that those with pressing needs can be helped, and so that they will not themselves prove to be unfruitful.

15 All with me send you their love. Give my best to those who love us in the faith. May God's grace be with you all.

PHILEMON

Greetings (1-3)

1-2 From Paul, a prisoner of Christ Jesus, and Timothy, my brother.

To Philemon, my dear friend and our fellow worker, and to
Apphia our sister and Archipus our fellow soldier and to all who
belong to the church that meets in your home.

3 May God the Father and the Lord Jesus Christ impart grace and
peace to you all.

Paul gives thanks for Philemon's love and faith (4-7)

4-5 I always thank my God when I remember you in my prayers,
because I have heard of your love for all your fellow believers and
the faith that you place in the Lord Jesus. 6 I pray that, as you share
your faith with others, so you may become fully aware of everything
good that we have in Christ. 7 For I have received much joy and
strength through your love, my brother, because you have refreshed
the hearts of the saints, your fellow believers.

Paul's appeal on behalf of Onesimus (8-20)

8-10 So, although I am bold enough to tell you to do what is right, yet
I want to appeal to your love. I, Paul, who am now advancing in
years as a prisoner of Jesus Christ, appeal to you on behalf of my
spiritual child, Onesimus, whom I brought to the Lord while I was in
chains. 11 In the past he was of no use to you, but now he has become
useful both to you and to me. 12-13 As I send him back to you it is like
sending my own heart, for I would love to keep him here with me
so that, on your behalf, he could serve me while I am in chains for
the gospel. 14 But I decided to do nothing without your consent, so
that I was not forcing you to express such kindness to me, leaving it
to your own free choice instead.

15-16 Perhaps this is the reason why he left you for a while, so that
you might have him back permanently, no longer as a slave but now
more than a slave – a dearly loved brother in the Lord. He is already
precious to me; and how much more precious he should be to you,
both as a man and as a brother in the Lord.

[17] So if you think of me as your partner in the faith, receive him as
you would me. [18] And if he has wronged you in any way or owes
you anything, charge it to my account. [19] I, Paul, write this with my
own hands and tell you that I will repay his debt, without saying
anything of the debt you owe me – your very self! [20] Yes, my brother,
I need some help from you in the Lord; so refresh my heart in
Christ.

Final greetings (21-25)

[21] I write to you confident of your obedience, knowing you will do
even more than I ask of you. [22] And I take this opportunity to ask you
also to prepare a room for me as I hope to visit you in response to
your prayers.

[23-24] Epaphras, my fellow prisoner in Christ, sends you greetings,
together with Mark, Aristarchus, Demas and Luke, my fellow workers.

[25] May the grace of the Lord Jesus Christ be with your spirit.

HEBREWS

Jesus sustains creation (1:1-4)

1 In the past God spoke to our forefathers through the prophets,
on many occasions and in a variety of ways. 2 Now, however,
He has spoken to us through His Son, whom He has made the heir of
everything that has been created. For through Jesus, God created the
entire universe, and He is the One who shines with God's own glory.
3 When He became man He expressed God's nature perfectly. Not
only is He the Word through whom everything was brought into
being, but the whole of creation is sustained through Him.

The reason He became man was to provide the means by which
we can be purified from all our sins. This He accomplished, and so
He now sits in triumph at God's right hand, reigning in Majesty in
heaven. 4 When He returned to heaven He took His rightful place,
far superior to that of the angels; for the name of Jesus is so much
greater than the name of any created being in heaven or on earth.

Christ superior to the angels (1:5-14)

5 Did God ever say to any of the angels: "You are My Son and I have
now become Your Father"? Did He say to any of them: "I will be
Your Father and You will be My Son"?

6 However, when God sent His firstborn Son into the world He
said: "Let all the angels of God worship Him." 7 How does He
regard the angels then? "He makes His angels as winds, servants
who are as flames of fire." 8 What He says about His Son is entirely
different. He addresses Him as God and says:

> "O God, Your throne will last for all eternity; and You will
> rule with authority in Your Kingdom because of Your
> righteousness. 9 For You have loved what is right and
> hated what is evil. For this reason I, Your God, have set
> You above all others by anointing You with the oil of joy."

1:5 Psalm 2:7, 2 Samuel 7:14
1:7 Psalm 104:4
1:9 Psalm 45:6-7

[10] God also says of Him:

> "O Lord, You created the earth at the very beginning, and even the heavens were made by You. [11] The earth and the heavens will come to an end, but You will outlive them. [12] In due course of time they will cease; they will be as worn out clothes that need to be replaced. But You will not change and You will never die."

[13] Did God ever say to an angel: "Sit at My right side until all Your enemies are crushed beneath Your feet"? [14] Angels are spiritual beings sent by God to serve those who are chosen to inherit salvation!

Take seriously the message of salvation (2:1-4)

2 How important it is that we take seriously what we have heard, so we do not drift away from the truth. [2] The messages God gave people through angels were considered to be binding on those who received them; any disobedience to the commands given would result in just punishment. Now that we have received a greater revelation of the great salvation made possible through faith in Jesus, it is surely even more important to realise that to ignore such truth will lead to even greater punishment!

[3] This salvation, by which we are made totally acceptable to God, was first revealed by the Lord Himself as has been confirmed by those who heard Him speak personally. [4] God also verified this message of salvation through the signs, wonders and different miracles that Jesus performed. And it is proved beyond doubt by the gifts of the Holy Spirit He has given to His people, according to His purposes.

All authority given to Christ (2:5-9)

[5] We are not speaking only of this present world but of one that is to come. [6] God has not put angels in charge of this, for it is written:

> "How can man be so important to You that You think so highly of him? How can it be that You care for him as You do? [7] You made him slightly inferior to the angels and yet have crowned him with glory and honour, and have put everything under his authority!"

1:12 Psalm 102:25-27
1:13 Psalm 110:1
2:7 Psalm 8:4-6

8 Because God placed everything under his authority, all things are
subject to man. This does not seem obvious at present, but we
already see this in Jesus. 9 When He became man He was in a slightly
inferior position to the angels; but now He is crowned with glory
and honour because He suffered death on behalf of all humanity.
This is the measure of the grace and favour God has shown us.

He shared in our humanity (2:10-18)

10 In this way, many sons are now able to inherit God's glory. Everything and everyone was created for His sake. Yet it was necessary
that He should make Jesus the author of our salvation, the perfect
sacrifice that would bring us back to God. 11 So we are now made
holy in God's sight and this has been accomplished through Jesus,
the only One who could make us holy. He is like our elder Brother,
and we share in the same family and have the same inheritance. It
is amazing that Jesus is not ashamed to call us His brothers. 12 Long
ago He said: "I will proclaim Your Name to My brothers; in the
company of Your people I will sing Your praises."

13 He also said: "I will put My trust in Him." And then He adds:
"Here I am, together with the children God has given Me."

14 Jesus shared in our humanity, having flesh and blood like us, so
that through His death on the cross, He could utterly destroy the devil,
the one who holds the power of death. 15 Now all those who have spent
their lives in bondage because of their fear of death and what lay
beyond, are set free. 16 These are the people of faith, the true descendants of Abraham. It is these He has raised to His glory, not angels.

17 To accomplish this, Jesus had to be made like His brothers in
every respect. He became our High Priest, the One who offered the
perfect sacrifice of Himself to God; the merciful and faithful High
Priest who was obedient in His service to God. In this way, He made
the act of atonement, the act by which we are again made one with
God because all our sins are forgiven. 18 However, to be the One who
would act on our behalf He had to be subjected to temptation, just
as we are. And so now He is able to help us when we need to overcome temptation.

Moses the servant, Christ the Son (3:1-6)

3 1-2 So we are holy brothers who share together in a heavenly
calling; brothers of Christ set apart for God's glory. Fix your

2:12 Psalm 22:22
2:13 Isaiah 8:17,18

thoughts on Jesus, the One in whom you believe. He is your Apostle,
who faithfully fulfilled the commission given Him by God. He is
your High Priest, who offered the perfect sacrifice on your behalf.
3-6 Moses was faithful in fulfilling what God asked of Him as a
member of His household. Jesus has proved worthy of much
greater honour than Moses, for He is over the entire household. The
one who builds the house has greater honour than the house itself.
Someone may build a house, but God has created everything.
Moses was a faithful servant in God's household, but He could only
point the way forward to what God would do in the future. Christ
is the faithful Son over the entire household, and we form that
household as we continue to live as the people of courageous faith,
who have a wonderful future of which we can rightly boast!

Do not harden your hearts towards God (3:7-19)

7-8 So listen to what the Holy Spirit says:

> "If you hear God speaking to you today, do not harden
> your heart against what He says. This is what you did in
> your days of rebellion against His authority, when you
> were subjected to a time of testing in the desert. 9 Your
> forefathers continually tested Me and tried My patience,
> even though they saw the miracles I performed for them
> over forty years. 10 You can understand My anger towards
> that generation and why I said, 'They have not walked in
> My ways because their hearts are turned against Me!'
> 11 This is why in My righteous anger I promised they shall
> never enter the place of eternal peace with Me!"

12 For this reason, my brothers, make sure that none of you has a
sinful and unbelieving heart that opposes the living God. 13 Instead,
encourage one another all the time, every day in fact; the deceitfulness
of sin will only make your hearts hardened against God and His
purposes.
14 We already live in Christ and will continue to do so if we remain
confident in the faith we had at the beginning of our relationship
with Him, until we have reached the conclusion of His purposes.
15 So let me remind you again: "If you hear God speaking to you
today, do not harden your heart against what He says; this is what
you used to do when you lived in rebellion against His authority."

3:11 Psalm 95:7-11
3:15 Psalm 95:7-8

[16]Who heard Him speak and rebelled? All those whom Moses led
out of Egypt in that mighty act of deliverance. [17]And with whom
was God angry for forty years? Was it not with those who sinned
and rebelled against Him in the desert where they died? [18]To whom
did He swear that they would never enter into their promised
inheritance? It was to those who disobeyed Him, wasn't it? [19]Their
unbelief prevented them from entering into God's rest, as we can
see clearly!

Enter God's rest (4:1-11)

4 However, the promise of entering into His inheritance still
stands. So make sure that none of you fails to enter into what
is promised. [2]We have received the gospel through those who
brought it to us; but our forefathers also received God's message.
Yet it was of no value to them, for although they heard what was
said, they did not respond with faith.

[3]We have believed what God said and so are able to enter into
that inheritance and have peace with Him. Yet His Word still
applies: "So I promised in My anger, 'They will never enter into my
inheritance.'"

[4]God's work was finished when the creation of the world was
complete. Then He spoke about the seventh day in these words:
"And God rested from all His work on the seventh day." [5]This is the
same God who promised that the disobedient shall never enter into
that inheritance, eternal rest with Him.

[6]It is true, therefore, that some will enter the rich inheritance of
His rest, and some will not. Those who had God's words of deliverance
preached to them did not enter because of their disbelief. [7]When-
ever you hear God's voice it is always 'today' that He wants you to
respond. So, centuries after Moses, God spoke through David in
these words I have quoted already: "If you hear God speaking to
you today, do not harden your hearts against what He says."

[8]If they had entered into this rich inheritance of His rest under
Joshua, God would not have needed to speak about another 'today'
in David's time. [9-10]There remains a kind of Sabbath rest for God's
people today; for those who enter into the inheritance He has promised,
have ceased to try and impress God with their own works. Just as
God rested from His work, so they have rested from their works.

4:3 Psalm 95:11
4:4 Genesis 2:2
4:7 Psalm 95:7-8

11 All our effort is now channelled into entering that inheritance that God has given us, so that no one will fail by following their example of disobedience.

Nothing is hidden from God (4:12-13)

12 God's Word is always alive and will work actively in all who believe. His Word is sharper than any blade. It separates spirit and soul, showing us what is of God and what is of self. It demonstrates what is merely external and what is of the heart. It even shows us whether our thoughts and heart attitudes are right or not! 13 There is nothing in the whole of creation that is hidden from God. He sees and knows everything that takes place. Yes, everything is exposed before His eyes; we are naked before Him and it is to Him that we will have to give account for what we have done with our lives.

Our High Priest (4:14-5:10)

14 However, we can hold on firmly to the faith we have already. For Jesus, the Son of God, is our great High Priest who has ascended through the heavens. 15 He is able to sympathise with our weaknesses because He was tempted in every way that we have experienced. Yet He was different from us in this respect: He never yielded to temptation, so He never sinned.

16 Because of what He has done in going ahead of us, we are now able to come close to God's throne of grace with confidence. And when we do so, we are able to receive mercy and discover God's abundant grace that will help us, no matter what the nature of our needs.

5 When the high priest is normally selected, he is but a man chosen to represent all men before God, to offer gifts and sacrifices for their sins. 2 He can deal sensitively with the ignorant and those who have departed from God's will because he, too, is subject to human weakness and failure. 3 So when he offers the sacrifices, they are for his own sins as well as those of the people.

4 No-one would dare to claim this privilege for himself. Just like Aaron, he must be called by God. 5 In the same way, Christ did not claim this honour of being High Priest for Himself. God said to Him: "You are My Son and I have become Your Father." 6 He also spoke of Jesus when He said: "You are an eternal priest in the line of Melchizedek."

5:5 Psalm 2:7
5:6 Psalm 110:4

7During His life on earth, Jesus prayed to His Father with loud
cries and tears, for only He could save Him from death. And the
Father heard Him because He prayed with such submission to His
Father's will. 8Even though He was God's Son, He had to obey
through everything He suffered. 9In this way He was perfect, not
only in nature but also in action, and could be the One through
whom all who are obedient to God could receive eternal salvation
and be made one with Him forever. 10So it was God Himself that
made Jesus High Priest in the line of Melchizedek.

Importance of spiritual maturity (5:11-14)

11There is much we could write about all this, but it is difficult to
explain these truths to those who are not ready to learn. 12Really by
now you should be teachers of the truth, yet still you need someone
to teach you these basic truths of God's Word again and again. You
are still like infants feeding on milk and not yet ready for solid food!
13Spiritual infants are not familiar with God's teaching about living
in righteousness. 14No, it is only the spiritually mature who can take
solid food, those who have learned for themselves to distinguish
between what is good and what is evil in God's sight.

Remain steadfast in your faith (6:1-20)

6 It is time to move on from the basic teaching about Christ to a
more mature understanding of God's purposes. We should not
need to lay again for you the foundational truth that you need to
turn away permanently from acts that lead to spiritual death. Nor
should we have to keep reminding you to put your faith in God.
2And you should not need continual instruction about baptisms and
the laying on of hands. By now you know about resurrection from
the dead and the eternal judgment of all men that is to come. 3So
by God's grace we will move you on in your understanding of His
purposes.

4-6You must realise this: it is not possible for those who have
received revelation of the truth, who have tasted the joy of heavenly
salvation and have shared in the life of the Holy Spirit, who know
that God's Word is good and true, who are aware of the power God
will release in the age that is to come, to be brought back to unity
with God if they deny all they have known and experienced. To
deny what they know to be true is to be guilty of the equivalent of
nailing God's Son to the cross again, subjecting Him to public disgrace
and ridicule.

7 The land that receives frequent rainfall and produces a good
harvest for the farmer is truly blessed by God. 8 On the other hand,
the land that produces only thorns and thistles is useless and
appears to be cursed. The only thing to do is to burn it!

9 Dear friends, these are uncomfortable truths of which we speak.
However, we are confident that you will not deny what you know
to be the truth, but will remain steadfast in your faith and live in the
good of your salvation.

10 You cannot accuse God of being unjust. He will never forget
your faithful work, nor the love for Him that you have shown by
continuing to help His people. 11 We urge every one of you to continue
in this faithfulness to the very end. Then you will not need to fear
the outcome, but will be certain about your hope of eternal life with
God. 12 This is why we do not want you to become spiritually lazy,
but rather to be like those who inherit what He has promised
because they persevere patiently in their faith!

13 God gave Abraham His solemn promise on His own honour, for
there was no one greater by whom He could swear, that He would
be faithful. 14 He said: "Without doubt I will bless you and give you
many descendants." 15 After waiting patiently, Abraham saw the
promise fulfilled.

16 When men make solemn promises they swear by someone
greater than themselves. By taking an oath they confirm that what
they say is true and beyond any argument.

17 Why should God make His promises on oath? Because He
wanted to make absolutely clear that His purposes never change. It
is clear to all His children that He is faithful in keeping His Word,
because He confirmed His promises by taking an oath. 18 He chose
to do this for our sakes, so that we would know for certain that God
would never lie and that His promises are utterly dependable. It is
simply not possible for God to lie, because He is the Truth!

19-20 We have left behind the deceptiveness of the world and have
taken hold of the sure and certain hope of what lies ahead; and this
should cause us to be greatly encouraged. This hope of what awaits
us in the future is a firm anchor for our souls. This truth keeps us
secure and means that we have access directly into the Holy of
holies, God's very presence. We can pass through the curtain that
was torn apart when Jesus went before us through death and into
the glory of resurrection. He did all this on our behalf as our High
Priest, an eternal High Priest in the line of Melchizedek.

6:14 Genesis 22:17

A priests in the order of Melchizedek (7:1-17)

7 [1-2]So who was this Melchizedek? He was both king of Salem and priest of God Most High. He met Abraham after he had defeated the kings and blessed him: in response Abraham gave Melchizedek a tenth of everything.

The name Melchizedek means first of all, 'King of Righteousness.' His title, 'King of Salem' means he is 'King of Peace.' [3]He had no parents, no forbears; there was no point at which he began life, or a moment in time when his life ended. In other words, like God's Son, he remains an eternal priest.

[4]Abraham recognised his greatness by giving him a tenth of all the plunder he had taken. [5]Under the law that was given later, Levi's descendants, the priestly tribe, were to collect a tenth from the people, their brethren from the other tribes, all of whom were descendants of Abraham. [6]However, Melchizedek predated the tribe of Levi; he was not of natural priestly descent. And yet he was given a tenth by Abraham and then blessed Abraham as the one who had received God's promises.

[7]It is obvious the lesser person is blessed by the one who is greater. [8]The descendants of Levi are men who will die, yet they receive the tenth allotted to them. Melchizedek is declared to be eternal and was the first to be given the tenth. [9-10]You could even say that when Melchizedek met Abraham, Levi was still in his loins; and so in a sense even Levi honoured Melchizedek through Abraham, by giving him the tenth.

What do we learn from this? That the priesthood of Melchizedek was far superior to that of Levi. [11]If it was possible for the levitical priesthood to be perfect (and remember that the law given to the people recognised this priesthood had descended from Aaron), why was it necessary for another Priest to come, One not like Aaron, but in the lineage of Melchizedek? [12]A change of priesthood implies there is to be a change of law.

[13]Melchizedek is of an altogether different priestly tribe from which no-one has ever served at the altar of the temple, as the Levites do. [14]Jesus Christ, our Lord, was descended from the tribe of Judah, and Moses makes no mention of there being any priests from that tribe.

[15-16]It is clear, then, that if another priest appears, One that is like Melchizedek, His Priesthood is not based on the regulations of the law, but on the fact that He ministers in the power of an eternal, indestructible life! [17]This is why it is said: "You are an eternal Priest in the lineage of Melchizedek."

7:17 Psalm 110:4

The new and better way (7:18-28)

18 So the previous regulations of the law are put to one side because, by comparison, they are weak and useless. 19 It is certain that nothing was ever made perfect by the law! Now something far better has replaced it, by which we have a much better hope for the future, and by which it has now been made possible for us to draw really close to God Himself.

20 And this new and better way was established by the promises He gave under solemn oath. No oath was sworn by God in establishing the levitical priesthood under the law. 21 When God swears a promise on His own honour, His Word cannot be changed, and God said of His Son: "The Lord has taken an oath and will never change His mind; 'You are an eternal Priest!'" 22 He refers, of course, to the Priesthood of Jesus, who guarantees that we are part of a better covenant. We are able to enjoy a closer relationship with God than was possible under the law, the old covenant with its former human priesthood.

23 Over the centuries there were numerous priests because, of course, they had a natural life-span and could not continue to officiate once they had died! 24-25 By contrast, because Jesus lives eternally, He has a permanent Priesthood by which He is able to save completely all those who come to God through faith in Him. He lives continually to intercede on their behalf through His blood shed for them.

26 Such a wonderful and eternal High Priest is able, therefore, to meet every need we could ever have. For He is holy, blameless, pure, totally different in nature from sinners, and is now exalted and reigning in heaven.

27 He does not have to keep offering sacrifices day after day for His own sins and those of the people, like those other priests. He was without sin and offered the one perfect sacrifice of Himself for the sins of all mankind; a sacrifice that needs never to be repeated.

28 The law could only appoint weak men as high priests; but by His solemn promise God appointed His own Son as High Priest, and He is eternally perfect. So the weakness of the law is now superseded by the perfection of Christ!

A new covenant and a new High Priest (8:1-13)

8 The reason we speak these things to you is simply this: We do have an eternal High Priest who has sat down at the right hand of the Majesty of God in heaven. 2 He is the One who serves eternally

7:21 Psalm 110:4

in the true sanctuary, the Holy of holies in heaven, created by God,
not man.
3 Every high priest has to be appointed before he has the right to
offer both gifts and sacrifices on behalf of others. For Jesus to be our
High Priest He also had to offer a gift, to provide a sacrifice. 4 He
could not be part of the earthly priesthood that was authorised to
offer gifts according to the law. 5 They serve in a sanctuary that is
only an imitation or shadow of the one in heaven. It was for this
reason that God warned Moses when He ordered him to build the
tabernacle: "Be sure that you make everything according to the
plans I showed you on the mountain."
6 Yet the priestly ministry Jesus has received is so far superior to
that of this earthly priesthood, just as the new covenant He has
established is far superior to the old covenant, for it has been founded
on better promises given by God.
7 If the first agreement God had made with His people had been
perfect or complete, there would have been no need for a further
agreement. 8 However, God was well aware of the people's failure to
keep the old agreement with all its laws and said:

> "A time is coming, proclaims the Lord, when I will establish
> a new covenant with the people of Israel and Judah. 9 This
> will be different from the covenant I made with their fore-
> fathers when I led them by the hand out of the bondage of
> Egypt. For they did not remain faithful to that covenant,
> and so I turned away from them, says the Lord. 10 This is
> the new agreement that I will make with my people Israel
> at the appointed time, proclaims the Lord. I will place My
> laws in their minds and write them on their hearts, rather
> than on tablets of stone. I will be their personal God and
> they shall be My own people. 11 A man will no longer need
> to teach his neighbour or his brother to know Me,
> because they will all know Me personally, from the least
> of them to the greatest. 12 This will be possible because I
> will have forgiven them for their wickedness and decided
> that their sins will be blotted out, never to be remembered."

13 It is God who has called this His new covenant, and by doing so
He has made the former covenant obsolete. So what is already obsolete
will in due course disappear altogether.

8:5 Exodus 25:40
8:12 Jeremiah 31:31-34

Worship in the earthy sanctuary (9:1-10)

9 Under the former system, regulations were given for the ordering
of worship and of the earthly sanctuary. 2 A meeting place was
set up. The first room was called the Holy Place, and the lampstand,
table and consecrated bread were placed there. 3 There was a second
curtain behind which was the Holy of holies. 4 There the golden
incense altar was placed, together with the Ark of the Covenant that
was covered with gold. In this Ark was the gold jar containing some
of the manna God provided to feed His people in the desert,
Aaron's staff that had budded and the stone tablets containing the
law of the old covenant. 5 The cherubim, glorious heavenly beings,
were above the ark. However this is not the time to describe these
things in detail.
6 When everything had been arranged in the right way, the priests
entered the outer room regularly to perform their duties. 7 Only the
High Priest was allowed to enter the inner room, the Holy of holies,
and then only once a year on the Day of Atonement. He had to carry
an offering of blood to plead for forgiveness for himself and for the
sins of the people, even those committed in ignorance of God's will.
8 This was the Holy Spirit's way of showing that entrance into the
Holy of holies for everyone had not yet been established, neither
could it be while the former tabernacle was in operation. 9 We can see
now that the old system was not effective, for the gifts and sacrifices
offered there were not able to cleanse the guilt out of the consciences
of those who worshipped. 10 The regulations concerning food and
drink, the various ceremonial washings and the other external rules
would only apply until God established the new order.

The blood of Christ (9:11-28)

11 This He did when Christ came as High Priest, initiating the good
things that we believers are able to enjoy already. He passed
through to the Holy of holies in a more perfect tabernacle, to the
heavenly throne itself. This is not a man-made tent or building; it is
not even part of this earthly creation. 12 And when He entered into
the eternal Holy of holies He did not carry with Him an offering of
the blood of goats and calves. No, He entered into the Holy of holies
only once, with the offering of His own blood. And by that blood He
made it possible for us to be one with God eternally. He literally
bought us with the price of His own blood!
13 The only thing that could be accomplished by the continual
offering of the blood of goats and bulls and by sprinkling the ashes

of a heifer on those considered to be ceremonially unclean, was to give them an external cleansing. People only had an outward holiness.

14 The offering of Christ's blood accomplished so much more. In the power of God's eternal Spirit, He offered Himself as a perfect sacrifice to God, making it possible for us to have an inner cleansing from all the sinful acts that lead to spiritual death. We can now have consciences clear of all guilt and we are able to serve God as a truly holy people!

15 In this way, Christ established a new covenant. Those who were called to be part of this new relationship with God received the promise of an eternal inheritance. He literally gave His life as a ransom to set people free from all the sins committed under the former system.

16 A will only comes into effect when the death of the one who made it has been proved. 17 Until his death that will has no meaning, for it cannot be enforced while he is alive. 18 In the same way, the original agreement could not come into effect without the shedding of blood, even though in that case it was only the death of animals that took place. 19-20 When Moses proclaimed to the people all the commandments of the law that God have given him, he took calf's blood, scarlet wool and hyssop branches and sprinkled the scroll and all the people with the blood saying: "This is the blood of the covenant that God has commanded you to keep." 21 In similar fashion, he sprinkled with blood the tabernacle and all the articles used in the ceremonies that took place there. 22 Under the law nearly everything was cleansed and made holy with the use of blood. There could be no forgiveness without the shedding of blood.

23 Now if it was necessary for these copies of the heavenly things to be made holy with the sacrifices of animals, the heavenly things themselves would be established with much greater sacrifices. 24 You see, Christ did not enter a man-made sanctuary that was only a copy of the true one; He entered heaven itself and now stands in God's presence on our behalf. 25 In heaven He does not need to keep offering Himself again and again in sacrifice. The earthly high priest has to enter the Holy of holies every year and repeat the offering of the blood of animals. He never offers his own blood. 26 If Christ was like those high priests he would have to repeat the sacrifice of Himself over and over again. Instead, He has already entered heaven itself, victorious over sin through the one sacrifice of Himself that need never be repeated. The effects of this one sacrifice will last until the end of time.

9:20 Exodus 24:8

27 Listen, you will only die once and then have to face the Judgment. 28 So Christ only had to die once, but His sacrifice has taken away our sins so we do not have to fear the Judgment. When He comes again, it will not be to sacrifice Himself again. No, He will bring eternal salvation to all those who eagerly await His return.

Accepted in Christ (10:1-10)

10 Under the law it is only possible to experience a shadow of the really good things that are to come. The endless repetition of the sacrifices of animals year after year could never make perfect those who draw near to God in worship. 2 If such a sacrifice could have that effect, there would have been no need for it to be repeated! Those of every generation who worship would have been cleansed forever and would no longer experience any guilt for their sins. 3-4 The fact that those animal sacrifices had to be repeated only served as a reminder of people's sins, for the blood of bulls and goats is powerless to take those sins away.

5 So when Christ came into the world He said: "You did not want continual sacrifice and offerings, but You gave me a body to offer. 6 You were not satisfied with burnt offerings and sin offerings. 7 So then I said: 'I am here and have come to do Your will O God, as has been written about Me.'"

8 First Christ said that God did not really want sacrifices and offerings, neither burnt offerings nor sin offerings, even though these were required under the law. 9 Then He declared: "I am here and have come to do Your will." He thus sets aside the former things in order to establish something entirely new. 10 So by God's divine will, we have already been made holy through the one sacrifice of Jesus Christ's own body. Now we are set apart for God, made totally acceptable and pleasing to Him.

Jesus sacrificed once and for all (10:11-18)

11 This was never achieved by the priests performing their religious duties day after day. They could only keep offering the same sacrifices which could never take away our sins. 12 But when this Priest, Jesus Christ, had offered the one sacrifice of Himself for our sins, a sacrifice that would never need to be repeated, He could sit down in triumph at God's right hand, for He had accomplished His purpose. 13 Now He awaits the time when all His enemies are under His feet and are

10:7 Psalm 40:6-8

made subject to Him. [14]But understand what this one sacrifice has
achieved: those who are being made holy, set apart for God, He has
made perfect already!
[15-16]The Holy Spirit explains this to us, for He says: "This is the
covenant I will make with them in due course, says the Lord. I will
place My commands in their hearts and will write them on their
minds." [17]He says also: "I will never remember their sins and their
acts of rebellion against Me."
[18]Once sins are forgiven, there is no need for any further sacrifice
to take away our sins!

Access into the Holy of holies (10:19-23)

[19]Therefore, my dear brothers, since we believe in what He has
accomplished for us through the shedding of His blood, we have
confidence to enter boldly into the Holy of holies, the inner sanctuary
of His heavenly presence. [20]He is the new living Way that enables us
to pass through the curtain that prevented people from entering the
Holy of holies. [21]So He has become the great Priest over all who
belong to God's household.
[22]Therefore, let us come near to God with true hearts and with
great faith, because our hearts have been sprinkled with His blood
to cleanse us from all guilt. We can now have clear consciences and
be at peace with God. Our bodies are even made clean by receiving
the pure living water of the Holy Spirit. [23]So let us not allow anything
to distract us from the hope of what lies ahead of us in fulfilment of
all He has promised us, for He is faithful in keeping His Word.

Don't sin deliberately (10:24-31)

[24]What is more, we can encourage one another to walk in love,
blessing one another in practical ways. [25]We certainly must not give
up meeting together, as some have mistakenly done. No, we need
the encouragement of being together as one Body, and even more so
as we eagerly await the Day when the Lord will return.
[26-27]But of what value is this great sacrifice that Christ has made
for us, if we deliberately continue to sin against Him, even though
we have received the knowledge of the truth? It is as if we do not
care about that sacrifice. There is no further sacrifice for sins, only a
terrible expectation of judgment and being condemned to the fire
that will burn up God's enemies.

10:16 Jeremiah 31:33
10:17 Jeremiah 31:34

[28]After all, anyone who rejected the law God gave through Moses, died without being shown any mercy. Only two or three were needed to testify against him. [29]If that was the punishment under the old order, how much greater the punishment that a person will deserve if he has trampled underfoot God's own Son, treating the sacrifice of His blood as of no account, even though it was this that had made him holy before God! Such a person has insulted the Holy Spirit and thrown God's grace back in His face!

[30]We know that God has said: "It is in My power to avenge; I will repay." He also said: "The Lord will judge His people." [31]What a dreadful thing it would be to fall into God's hands when He judges the ungodly!

Persevere in faith (10:32-39)

[32]When you first believed, because you received the light of God's truth into the spiritual darkness of your life you stood firm in your faith no matter what the opposition or what you had to suffer. [33]Sometimes you were insulted publicly and were persecuted. At other times you supported those who were treated in this way, standing shoulder to shoulder with them. [34]You could identify with those in prison for their faith and even accepted the confiscation of your property with joy, because you knew that you now had acquired greater possessions that would last eternally.

[35]So do not throw away now the confidence you had then. Your continuing faith will be richly rewarded! [36-37]You must persevere in faith so that, having done God's will, you will receive the promised inheritance. You will not have to wait long for, "The One who is coming will not delay His coming. [38]But he who is at one with God will live by faith. If he shrinks away from the truth because of fear, I will not be pleased with him."

[39]However, we do not belong to those who shrink away and are destroyed. We are counted among those who believe and are saved!

People of faith (11:1-7)

11 True faith is being sure of the hope we have and being certain that we shall see what has been promised, even though we do not see these things at present. [2]This is the kind of faith for which God commended former believers.

10:30 Deuteronomy 32:35, Deuteronomy 32:36
10:38 Habakkuk 2:3-4

3 We can only understand that the entire universe was created by God's command as a matter of faith. For it is by faith that what is naturally invisible becomes visible!

4 Abel demonstrated true faith in God by giving his best to Him, unlike his brother Cain. Because of his faith, God regarded him as righteous and spoke well of his offerings. And faith has an ageless dimension, for even though Abel died centuries ago, we still speak of his faith today.

5 This eternal dimension of faith is seen in Enoch, for he did not experience death. He was nowhere to be found, for God had simply taken him to Himself because he was someone who pleased the Lord.

6 By now you can see that it is impossible to please God without faith. In our relationship with Him, we have to believe that He not only exists, but actually wants to answer us when we pray. He longs to give us what we need when we seek Him with sincere and earnest faith.

7 Noah was another man of faith. He showed that he lived in holy awe and reverence for God by building the ark to save his family, because he believed the warning God had given him. His faith made him an heir of those in right standing with God; he could inherit all that God had prepared for them. But such faith also condemned the world for its unbelief, for those who laughed at Noah perished in the flood.

The faith of Abraham (11:8-19)

8 Abraham was another man of great faith. When God told him to go
to a place that would later become his inheritance, he believed what
was said, obeyed and went, even though he had no idea of his
destination. He simply trusted God to lead him to the fulfilment of
what He had promised. 9 So it was by faith that he entered into the
promised land to make his home, even though he was a stranger
entering a foreign country. He lived as a nomad, as did his descendants
Isaac and Jacob, who inherited the same promise that God had given
Abraham.

10 He was happy to live in tents because his future hope was set on a heavenly city with no natural foundations, the city only God Himself could design and build!

11 Abraham also demonstrated his faith by becoming a father when a hundred years old and his wife, Sarah, was long past the age of child-bearing. And she had never been able to have children

naturally anyway! Abraham became a father because he believed
that God always proved faithful to whatever He promised.

12 What was the result? From this one very old man was descended
a people as numerous as the stars in the sky. Like the grains of sand
on the seashore, you could never count them all!

13 All these heroes of faith continued to trust God right up to the
time of their deaths. This does not mean that they saw in their own
lifetime the fulfilment of everything promised them. Some things
would only be accomplished fully a long time in the future; yet by
faith they saw them as fulfilled. They were certain that what God
had said would surely happen, even though they may not live to
see it all, for they regarded themselves as only temporary residents
here on earth. 14 They knew their true home lay with God. 15 They
were not holding onto territory they had left behind, longing to
return to a place they could call their own. 16 No, they were longing
for something better than this world could offer, a heavenly home.
God was delighted to tell them He was their God, personal to them,
and that He had prepared a heavenly city for them.

17-18 Abraham also had to go through another severe test of his faith
in God when the Lord told him to offer his son Isaac in sacrifice.
Imagine, this was his one and only son that God had promised him
and through whom God's promise would be fulfilled, "Through Isaac
all your descendants will be numbered." You can see Abraham's
faith in the way he thought. He reckoned that God must raise Isaac
from the dead in order to fulfil His promises. 19 In a manner of speaking
this is really what happened, for Abraham was fully prepared to kill
Isaac in obedience. So he received Isaac back from being as good as
dead!

Walk in faith not fear (11:20-29)

20 Isaac showed his faith in the way he blessed Jacob and Esau,
speaking of what would happen to them in the future. 21 Likewise,
Jacob was a man of faith and, when dying, he blessed each of Joseph's
sons, worshipping God for His faithfulness.

22 By faith, when near death, Joseph prophesied about the deliverance of the Israelites from Egypt and even gave instructions about
what was to happen to his bones.

23 Moses' parents showed their faith by hiding him for three
months after his birth. They knew that he was no ordinary child and

11:18 Genesis 21:12

they were not afraid of Pharaoh's edict that all male Hebrew children
were to be killed at birth.

24 Even though he enjoyed the privileges of Pharaoh's court,
Moses refused as an adult to become known as the son of Pharaoh's
daughter. 25 He identified with his own people instead, choosing to
be mistreated along with them rather than enjoy the transitory
pleasures of the sinful flesh. 26 Disgrace for Christ's sake meant more
to him than the wealth of Egypt, for he was looking ahead to the
reward faith brings. 27 So he left Egypt by faith, unafraid of Pharaoh's
anger. Like a man of true faith he persevered, reaching out for what
was not yet visible.

28 Later, by faith he observed the Passover. The destroyer of the
first-born could not touch any of the first-born of Israel because the
doorposts and lintels of their homes were sprinkled with blood!

29 The people passed through the Red Sea as if it was dry land
because of the miracle God did in response to Moses' obedient faith.
When the Egyptians tried to follow them, they were drowned.

Faith overcomes (11:30-40)

30 This obedient faith was also exhibited at Jericho when the walls
came crashing down, after the people had obeyed God by marching
around the city for seven days.

31 Even Rahab, a prostitute, is commended for her faith. She was
bold enough to welcome those sent to spy out the land and so was
not killed along with those who were disobedient to God's purposes.

32 I could go on and on, but there is no time now to tell you the
exploits of faith of Gideon, Barak, Samson, Jephthah, David, Samuel
and the prophets. 33 Through faith they conquered kingdoms, admin-
istered justice and were able to receive what God had promised
them. 34 Such heroes of faith shut the mouths of lions, overcame the
scorching heat of fire, escaped when others wanted to kill them. Their
weaknesses became their strength because they trusted in God. So
they were powerful in battle, overcoming foreign armies. 35 Women
even received back their dead who had been raised to life again.

Others chose torture rather than deny the Lord. They did not
choose the easier option of being released because their hearts were
set on the resurrection that lay ahead of them. 36 Yes, some faced
ridicule and were flogged; others were put in chains and in prison.
37 Others were stoned to death or beheaded.

They suffered all manner of deprivation; they were sometimes
destitute, often persecuted and mistreated. 38 They rose above the

standards of this world, which was not worthy of such people. They
were exiled, fleeing to desert or mountainous areas. Some had to
live in caves and to hide in secret places.
39 Yet all these people were commended by God for their faith,
even though none of them was able to receive what He had promised,
those things that we are now able to enjoy. 40 However, now that
Christ has died and risen again, they are able to share with us in the
rich inheritance that is the result of being made perfect in God's
sight.

Fix your eyes on Jesus (12:1-3)

12 All these heroes of faith are like a great crowd of witnesses
that surround us and encourage us to keep faith with God.
So let us shrug off everything that comes against us and refuse
every temptation to sin, with which the devil wants to entangle us.
Let us persevere in running the race in which God has entered us,
with our eyes fixed on Jesus who is always ahead of us. Without
Him we could not have faith, nor could we grow in faith. He gave
us faith and He will perfect our faith.
2 Look at the way He ran the race. He always aimed for the eternal
joy that lay ahead of Him, even though along the way He had to
suffer to the point of death on the cross, regardless of the shame that
was attached to such a death. He finished the race and is now seated
in heaven at God's right hand.
3 Yes, think of Him who put up with continual opposition from
sinful people. Then you will not grow tired of the opposition you
have to face and become discouraged.

He disciplines those He loves (12:4-13)

4 You struggle against sin. Yet you have not had to resist the temptation
to deny Christ by dying for Him! Do not forget the encouraging
words that God spoke when addressing you as His sons: "My son,
do not think lightly about the way the Lord disciplines you. 5 Do not
be discouraged when He corrects you. 6 For He disciplines those He
loves and punishes when necessary everyone who He has accepted
as His son."
7 So you can regard the various hardships you have to face in a
positive way, as discipline. God is dealing with you as His true
sons! After all, every good father disciplines his children. 8 If God

12:6 Proverbs 3:11-12

did not discipline you, then you would not be His true son or
daughter; you would be spiritually illegitimate instead.
9 We all know what it is like to have human fathers who disciplined
us, and we respected them as a result. How much more important
it must be that we should gladly submit to whatever discipline we
need to receive from our spiritual Father, and so live to please Him!
10 Our human fathers disciplined us in our early years in ways they
thought were right. But God knows how to discipline us for our
eternal good, so that we might share in His holy life.
11 None of us likes to be disciplined; it can sometimes be painful.
Later we are grateful, though, because it has had positive results,
enabling us to live righteous lives that please God and to be at peace
with Him. In fact, without discipline we could not become trained
disciples!
12 So be encouraged when you feel weak and feeble, even if sometimes you feel like giving up because the way before you seems so
difficult. 13 God wants to make level paths for you to walk on, so that
instead of limping through life you walk steadily with Him, as
those healed and set free from whatever would hinder their walk.

Holiness (12:14-17)

14 So do all you can to ensure that you live at peace with others. And
be holy; live as one whom God has set apart for Himself. For without
holiness no-one will see the Lord and belong to Him eternally.
15 Be sure also that you never lose sight of God's grace which is
always available to you. Let no bitterness be allowed to tarnish your
relationships with others, for that only causes trouble and has ruined
many lives.
16 Certainly no believer should be involved in sexual immorality
of any kind. Nor should he be like Esau, who valued his rights of
inheritance as the oldest son so little that he sold them. Such behaviour
is ungodly. 17 Later he was rejected when he wanted his inheritance
back. There was no way in which he could change God's mind on
the matter, even though he sought the blessing with tears.

Approach God with confidence (12:18-29)

18 Things are different now from the old order, for you do not
approach a mountain you are forbidden to touch that erupts with
fire. You do not belong to the darkness, to despair or to God's anger.
19 You are not dependent on someone blowing a trumpet to tell you
He is about to speak to you. Neither do you hear words of such

terrible judgment from God that you beg Him to stop speaking to you. 20 You do not have to worry about such commands: "If even an animal touches this mountain, it must be stoned to death." 21 Nor is the presence of God so terrifying to you as it was to Moses when he said: "I tremble with fear."

22 No, you are able to approach Mount Zion, the heavenly Jerusalem, the city where God has His throne. You can join with thousands upon thousands of joyful angels as they worship the Lord. 23 You belong to the church of the first-born of the Son of God, whose names are written in His Book in heaven. You are able to approach God Himself, even though He is the Judge of all men. And you can do so with confidence because you have been made righteous in His sight and in your spirit you are made perfect. 24 You belong to Jesus, who has made you part of the new covenant He has established. You have been 'sprinkled' with His blood, which is far more powerful than Abel's blood.

25 Be sure, then, that you do not reject anything the Lord says to you. Under the old order, those who did that could not escape the disasters about which God warned them. They simply did not listen to Him. If this was the case for them, how shall we escape if we turn away from God's words when He warns us directly from heaven?

26 In the past His voice shook the earth, but listen to what He has promised now, "Once more I will shake not only the earth but the heavens as well." 27 In saying 'once more', God is implying that whatever can be shaken will be removed so that whatever remains cannot be shaken. Earthly things will pass away, but we belong to what is eternal and unshakable.

28 So we have received His unshakable Kingdom, as a gift from God. We can be thankful, therefore, and worship Him as He deserves, with reverence and in awe of who He is. For our God is a fire that consumes His enemies.

Final exhortations (13:1-25)

13 Continue to love one another as true brothers in Christ. 2 Always be ready to entertain strangers, for some have unknowingly entertained angels by doing this. 3 Remember those of the faith who are in prison as if you are there with them, and those who are being persecuted as if we are suffering along with them.

12:20 Exodus 19:12-13
12:21 Deuteronomy 9:19
12:26 Haggai 2:6

4 Let every one of you honour marriage, for this is God's purpose.
Keep the marriage bed pure, for God will judge those guilty of adultery
and sexual immorality. 5 Be content with what you have materially,
for you want to live free from the love of money. God will care for
you, for He has promised: "I will never leave you, nor will I ever
forsake you."

6 We can respond to this with confidence by quoting another
scripture: "The Lord is my Helper; so I will not be afraid. What can
man do to me, if God is for me?"

7 Remember to honour your leaders and to pray for them. They
have spoken God's Word to you. You can see from their example
that they live their message and that they demonstrate how to walk
by faith. 8 Jesus Christ is the same today as He has been in the past,
and He will always remain the same for all eternity.

9 Do not be seduced by the different forms of strange teachings
that circulate at times. Your hearts will be strengthened by depending
on God's grace, and this is good! Eating ceremonial foods is of no
account at all. 10 We have consecrated food to eat that those who
keep to the old order have no right to share.

11 Under that order the high priest enters the Holy of holies with
the blood of animals as an offering for the sins of the people.
However, the bodies of the animals are burned outside the camp.
12 So Jesus was crucified outside the city gate, sacrificing His blood
to make the people holy.

13 We do not want to stay within the safe confines of our own
walls, then, but are ready to be His witnesses, even if this means
bearing the same kind of disgrace He suffered. 14 For we do not have
an eternal city here on earth, but we are looking forward to the
heavenly city that is to come.

15 We, too, have a sacrifice to make, a continual offering of praise
to God for all He has done for us through Jesus. We have lips that
keep expressing faith in His Name, in all that He is.

16 Do not neglect giving to others and seeking to do them good,
for God is also pleased with such sacrifices of love.

17 It is important to obey your leaders and to submit to the authority
God has given them over you, for they are to care for you as those
who will be held accountable to the Lord. By being obedient to
them, they will enjoy fulfilling this responsibility; it will not be a
tiresome burden to them. Certainly you will gain no advantage
from making life difficult for them.

13:5 Deuteronomy 31:6
13:6 Psalm 118:6-7

18 Pray for them and for us. Our consciences are clear and we want
to live in ways that always honour God. 19 Please pray especially
that I may be able to return to you soon.

20 May the God of peace equip you in every way necessary to
enable you to do His will. He raised our Lord Jesus from the dead
once He had established the new covenant and ratified it with His
blood. He is our great Shepherd and we His sheep.
21 May He equip you through Jesus Christ with everything you
need so that you can please Him in the way you live. Let Him be
glorified for ever and ever. Amen! It shall be so!
22 My brothers, I ask you to take seriously my words of exhortation,
even though I cannot say much in a short letter. I am happy to tell
you that our brother 23 Timothy has now been released. If he joins
me soon, we will come together to see you.
24 Give my greetings to all your leaders and all God's people. The
believers here in Italy send you their greetings.
25 May God impart His grace to you all!

JAMES

Perseverance (1:1-21)

1 From James, servant of God and of the Lord Jesus Christ.
To all the Jewish believers that are dispersed among the nations:
Greetings!
2-3 My dear brothers and sisters, react with real joy when you have
to face many kinds of opposition and difficulty, for you know that we
only learn to persevere when our faith is tested. 4 This perseverance
is essential if we are to become mature, being the people God wants
us to be, lacking nothing.
5 You should ask God to supply the wisdom you need, for He
gives generously and unreservedly to all who ask. 6 However, you
must believe when you ask and not doubt His willingness to give,
for anyone who doubts is like a wave of the sea that is driven and
tossed by the wind. 7-8 Such a person is double minded and unreliable
in everything he does and should not expect to receive anything
from the Lord.
9 The believer who comes from a humble background ought to
be thankful for the noble status God has given him. 10 The wealthy
one should be thankful that God has humbled him, for despite his
possessions he will suffer the same fate as the wild flower. 11 For
when the sun shines with scorching heat, the plant withers, its
bloom fades and its beauty is destroyed. In like manner, the wealthy
one will fade even though he prospers in his worldly affairs.
12 The man who perseveres in his faith, when tested, is blessed.
Having passed the test, he will be rewarded with the crown of life
that God has promised to those who love Him.
13 When facing temptation, no one should ever say "God is tempting
me." It is impossible for God to be tempted by evil, nor will He ever
tempt anyone. 14 A person is tempted by his own evil desire. This is
what entices him. 15 If he dwells on the desire it will lead to sin, and
fully-developed sin ends in spiritual death.
16 So, my dear brothers, do not be deceived. 17 Everything that is
good and perfect is a gift from God. It comes from the Father who

created the universe, who never changes as moving shadows do.
[18]Through the Word of truth, He chose to give us new birth so that
out of His whole creation we are those who come first, as His own
children.

[19]My dear brothers, be sure to take notice of this: Everyone
should be quick to listen but slow to speak or become angry. [20]Man's
anger can never bring about the good life that God desires. [21]So rid
yourselves of everything that is morally corrupt and the evil that is
so prevalent today. Instead, accept humbly the seed of God's Word
that has been planted in your heart, for this can save you.

Do what the Word says (1:22-27)

[22-24]You deceive yourselves if you only listen to God's Word. You
need to do what He says, for the person who listens to the Word but
fails to act on it is like someone who sees his face in a mirror and
then immediately forgets what he looks like. [25]By contrast, the person
who takes seriously what God commands us to do enjoys freedom.
He continues to obey because he does not forget what he has heard,
and so is blessed in what he does.

[26]Anyone who considers himself to be a good religious person,
and yet does not keep tight control of his tongue, simply deceives
himself. His religion is useless. [27]The kind of religious life that is
accepted by God, because it is pure and genuine, is typified by those
who care for orphans and widows who are in need and who refuse
to allow the world to corrupt them.

Love others as you love yourself (2:1-13)

2 My brothers, because you are believers in our glorious Lord
Jesus Christ, be sure not to favour some above others.

[2]For example, suppose someone was to come to one of your
meetings expensively dressed and with gold jewellery, while another
came in shabby clothes. [3-4]If you were to give special attention to the
wealthy one by giving him a good seat, while telling the poor man
to stand or sit on the floor, have you not made a false distinction
between them? Have you not dealt with them out of wrong motives?

[5]Listen to what I say, my dear brothers: Has not God chosen those
the world regards as poor to be rich in faith and to inherit the
Kingdom He promised to those who love Him? [6]But if you were to
act in such a way, you would insult the poor and allow the rich to
exploit you! [7]And they are the ones who drag you before the courts
and slander the Name of the One to whom you belong!

[8] You do well to obey the royal law revealed in scripture, "Love
others as you love yourself." [9] However, you sin if you are guilty of
favouritism. For God's law not only tells you what to do, but also
convicts you as a lawbreaker when you disobey His Word. [10] For
even if you do all He says and yet fail in only one thing, you are still
guilty of breaking the law.

[11] So God said, "Do not commit adultery," and He also said, "Do
not murder." If you resisted committing adultery but murdered
someone, you have still broken the law.

[12] You will be judged by the law that gives freedom; so you need
to speak and act accordingly. [13] For those who have not been merciful
will be judged without mercy. But mercy triumphs over judgment!

Faith is proved genuine by what you do (2:14-26)

[14] My brothers, of what value is the faith a man claims to have if that
faith is not reflected in his actions? Does he really possess the faith
that can save him?

[15] For example, suppose a brother or sister needs clothing and
food. [16] If any one of you was to say, "God bless you; keep warm and
well fed," but did nothing to relieve his physical needs, what good
would your faith be? [17] So you can see that unless faith gives birth to
action, it is dead!

[18] Someone may say, "You have faith; I do practical things." Well,
show your faith without positive actions and I will show you that
my faith is genuine because of what I do!

[19] You believe there is only one true God. Good! But even demons
believe that, and they tremble with fear before Him. [20] How foolish
you are if you need any further evidence to see that faith that does
not lead to positive actions is useless.

[21] Surely our forefather Abraham was considered acceptable to
God because of what he did when he offered his son Isaac on the
altar of sacrifice! [22] You can tell from his example that his faith led to
positive action. Faith and action were working together. His faith
was only complete because of what he did.

[23] This is how he fulfilled the scripture that says, "Abraham
believed God and so was considered to be righteous." And God called
him His friend because of his obedience. [24] You see, a person can only
please God and be right in His eyes through what he does, as well
as through what he believes.

2:8 Leviticus 19:18
2:11 Exodus 20:13-14
2:23 Genesis 15:6

25 God even considered the prostitute Rahab to be acceptable in
His eyes because of her actions in hiding the spies and then sending
them away by a safe route. Is that not so? 26 Therefore, just as a body
without a spirit is dead, so faith that is not expressed in positive
action is also dead.

Proper use of your tongue (3:1-12)

3 My dear brothers and sisters, not many of you will aspire to be
teachers of God's Word if you realise that we who have been
given the responsibility to teach will be judged more strictly than
other believers. 2 All of us fail in many ways. For if anyone claims he
is never wrong in what he says, then he must be perfect, with complete
control over every aspect of his body, especially his tongue.

3 We place bits in the mouths of horses so we can control them,
making them obey us by turning in any direction we choose. 4 Or
think of how a ship is guided. It can be very large and driven by
strong winds; yet the pilot uses only a tiny rudder to steer the ship
in whatever direction he chooses.

5 In the same way, the tongue is only a tiny part of your body, but
it can do great harm. A forest fire can be started by a small spark!
6 And the tongue is like fire, for it can give rise to such evil that it is
able to corrupt your whole life. It can ruin the whole course of your
life when it is set on fire by the fire of hell.

7-8 Man has tamed a variety of animals, birds, reptiles and sea
mammals; but no one has ever succeeded in taming the tongue. It
can be an uncontrollable evil, full of deadly poison.

9 We use the tongue to praise our Lord and Father and yet we can
also use it to speak curses over people whom God has made in His
image. 10 So out of the same mouth comes both praise and curse. My
brothers, obviously this should not be the case. 11 How can fresh
water and salt water flow out of the same spring? 12 My friends, is it
possible for a fig tree to produce olives, or a vine produce figs? Well,
it is impossible for a salt spring to produce fresh water.

Wrong motives lead to disorder (3:13-16)

13 So who among you has wisdom and understands these things?
Let him demonstrate that this is the case by the good life he leads,
the positive actions he performs while maintaining the humility
that is an expression of true wisdom.

14 But if your heart is bitter, full of envy and selfish ambition, do
not boast about being wise, neither deny the truth. 15 For that kind of

so-called 'wisdom' has certainly not been given to anyone by heaven.
No, it is earthly, unspiritual, a work of the devil. 16 For there is disorder
and all kinds of evil whenever people are motivated by wrong and
selfish ambition.

Heavenly wisdom (3:17-18)

17-18 The true wisdom that comes from heaven is totally different. First of all it is pure. Then it promotes a life of peace. It makes people considerate towards others and submissive to those in authority. Wisdom inspires people to be merciful at all times and produces good fruit in their lives, causing them to be impartial and sincere; so they become peacemakers, sowing seeds of peace that produce a harvest of doing what is right.

God opposes the proud, but gives grace to the humble (4:1-10)

4 Why are there fights and disputes among you? Are they not the
results of the evil desires that rage within you? 2 You want
something you don't have, so you plan and are even ready to kill to
get what you want. You quarrel and fight, yet you do not have
because you do not ask God for what you want. 3 Even if you do ask,
you do not receive because your motives are wrong when you ask;
you want only what will please the natural desires of your self-life.

4 You are an adulterous people! Surely you know that to be
friends with the values of this world is tantamount to hatred
towards God! Yes, anyone who decides to be the world's friend
makes himself God's enemy. 5 Do you imagine that the scripture is
meaningless that says the Spirit that God causes to live in us longs
for us to be true to Him? 6 And He gives us all the grace we need to
please Him. This is why the scripture says: "God opposes the proud,
but gives grace to the humble."

7 So submit yourselves wholeheartedly to God, stand against the
devil and he will run from you. 8 Draw near to God and He will
draw near to you. You sinners, wash your hands from the stain of
sin and purify your hearts, for you are double-minded. 9 You need
to grieve, mourn and wail until you are free from your sin. Until
then it is time to mourn, not laugh, to be sad instead of joyful. 10 So
in repentance humble yourselves before the Lord and He will raise
you up so you can truly rejoice.

4:5 Proverbs 3:34

Do not judge (4:11-17)

11 My brothers, do not speak against each other, for to do so is to
judge your brother and to treat God's Word as being of no account.
When you have such an attitude you do not obey the law but sit in
judgment on it. 12 God is the only One who gives us the law and then
the only Judge who determines whether we have obeyed Him. He
is the same One who has the power to either save or destroy. After
all, who gave you the right to judge your neighbour?

13 Now listen carefully. Some of you say, "Today or tomorrow we
will decide to go to this or that place for a year. And our business
will then make a good profit." 14 Yet you have no idea what will happen
tomorrow. Your life is like a mist that appears in the early morning
but soon vanishes when the sun rises.

15 It would be much better if you were to say, "If it is the Lord's
will, we live to do this or that." 16 Without such an attitude you are
proud and will boast, and all such boasting is evil. 17 If you know
what you should do but fail to do it, then you are guilty of sin.

Honour God with your wealth (5:1-6)

5 Listen, those of you who are rich: if you realised the misery you
face you would grieve with anguish. 2 By then your wealth will
have come to nothing and your fine clothes will be in tatters. 3 Your
gold and silver will be useless to you. The wealth you have hoarded
will testify against you, and your flesh life that you have indulged
will simply rot away. You have held onto your wealth when it could
have been used for God's purposes.

4 Consider this, you rich oppressors: you paid only a pittance to
those who worked for you and their lack is now crying out against
you, and these cries have reached the ears of the Lord Almighty. 5 You
have a life of luxury and self-indulgence, but have only fattened yourself for the slaughter. 6 You have condemned and ridden rough-shod
over innocent people who have nothing against you.

Wait patiently for the Lord (5:7-12)

7 Faithful believers, wait patiently for the Lord's coming. Notice
how the farmer waits patiently for the autumn and spring rains to
water the land so the crops can grow and develop. 8 In the same way,
you have to be patient and remain steadfast in your expectation that
the Lord could come at any moment.

9 So do not complain about each other, my brothers; for to do so
is to invite judgment on yourself. Realise that the Judge of all is
always at hand!

[10]My brothers, those who have suffered patiently, such as the
prophets who spoke in the Lord's Name, are an example for you.
[11]You know we believe that those who have persevered in their faith
are blessed. You have heard how Job was finally rewarded by the
Lord, who is full of compassion and mercy.

[12]It is really important, my brothers, that you never take an oath,
swearing by heaven, by earth or by anything else. It is enough for
everyone to know that your 'Yes' means yes, and your 'No' means
no! Do not bring any condemnation on yourself by going beyond
that.

Encouragement to pray (5:13-20)

[13]If anyone among you has a problem, he should pray. If anyone is
happy, he should thankfully sing praises to God. [14]If anyone is sick,
he should call the church leaders to visit him so they can pray for
him and anoint him with oil in the Lord's name. [15]The prayer of
faith will cause the sick person to be healed and the Lord will raise him
from his bed of sickness. If he has sinned, he will need to be forgiven.
[16]So openly confess your sins before one another and pray for one
another to be healed. The prayer of anyone made acceptable in
God's sight is powerful and effective.

[17]Elijah was only human as we are. He prayed earnestly that it
would not rain and for three and a half years there was no rain.
[18]When he prayed again, the heavens were opened and it poured
with rain. When the drought ended the crops grew!

[19-20]My brothers, seek to bring back anyone who wanders from
the truth, remembering this: Whoever turns a sinner from his evil
ways will save him from death, because he is freed from his many
sins!

1 PETER

Greeting from Peter (1:1-2)

1 From Peter, apostle of Jesus Christ:
To those who have been chosen by God and who are therefore strangers in the world, wherever they may be throughout the
regions of Pontus, Galatia, Cappadocia, Asia and Bithynia. 2 You
have been chosen deliberately by God the Father for the sanctifying
work of the Holy Spirit. It is He who enables your obedience to
Jesus Christ, as those set apart for His purposes. And you have also
been chosen to know the cleansing power of His blood that covers
all sin and failure.

May He impart grace and peace to you abundantly!

Our inheritance in Christ (1:3-4)

3 The God and Father of our Lord Jesus Christ is to be praised for all
He has done for us. He has given us a new birth through the great
mercy He has shown us. He has given us a living hope so we can
look to the future with great expectation because Jesus Christ has been
raised triumphantly from the dead. 4 He has given us an inheritance
that can never be ruined, taken from us or even reduced in any way,
the inheritance kept for you in heaven.

Faith tried and tested (1:5-7)

5 Meanwhile, because of your faith in Him, God shields you by His
power until the full realisation of the salvation that shall be revealed
at the end of time. 6 So you have much that causes you to rejoice,
even though at present there are many different trials and setbacks
that have caused you grief. 7 But these have only been allowed so
that your faith can be demonstrated as genuine and well-founded.
This proves that your faith is of much greater value than gold,
which also has to be refined by fire. Yes, your faith will enable you
to be one with Jesus Christ when He is revealed in His full praise,
glory and honour.

The era of grace (1:8-13)

8 You have never seen Him in the flesh, yet still you love Him. Even
though you cannot see Him physically now, you still believe in Him
and are filled with a tremendous sense of glorious joy! 9 For even
now you are in the process of receiving the objective of your faith,
the salvation of your souls.

10 The prophets spoke about this salvation, but they could only
look forward to the grace you already experience. 11 They did all
they could to try and discover the time and situation in which the
work of salvation would be accomplished. The Spirit of Christ
working in them enabled them to predict the sufferings of Christ
and the glory that would follow His victory on the cross.

12 These prophets understood that their words would benefit
those to whom these things would be revealed in due course, and
this includes you. They could only look forward to what has now
been revealed to you by those who have preached the gospel to you
in the power of the Holy Spirit, sent from heaven by God to those
who believe. Not only prophets but even angels long to look into
these things that are now common knowledge to you.

13 Because you have now received this revelation, you need to
have mindsets of those who are ready for action and will be self-
controlled in their way of life. You have already received grace from
God, so your hope for the future is that this grace will be given to
you fully when Jesus Christ returns.

Be holy in all you do (1:14-17)

14 You are called to be God's obedient children and not to give way
to the evil desires that marked your lives when you lived in ignorance
of His purposes. 15 He who called you is Holy; so to please Him you
are to be holy in all you do, living as one who knows his or her life
is set apart for God's purposes and glory. 16 To live such a life fulfils
God's written command: "Be holy, because I am Holy."

17 You pray to God as your Father and He judges impartially what
each person does. So live in fear, in reverent awe of Him, as if you
are living as a stranger here on earth because you belong to His
heavenly Kingdom.

You were bought with a price (1:18-21)

18 How did God redeem you? In what way did He pay the price for
you, so that you could belong to Him eternally? It was not with the

1:16 Leviticus 11:44-45

perishable things of this world, such as silver or gold. Something
much greater was needed to save you from the empty way of life
that many in the past have lived.

19 No, He redeemed you with the precious blood of Christ, God's
sacrificial Lamb that was without any blemish or defect. 20 Even
before the world was created, God in His foreknowledge knew that
such a sacrifice would be needed to bring His people back into
unity with Him; and this is what has now been accomplished, and
all for your benefit. 21 It is because of Jesus Christ that you have put
your trust in God, who raised Him from the dead and glorified Him
in His heavenly presence. So now you look to the future with both
faith and hope, secure in your personal knowledge of God.

Obey the truth of the Word (1:22-2:3)

22 You have already purified yourselves by obeying the truth of
God's Word, fulfilling the command to love your brothers sincerely,
deeply, from the heart. 23 Yes, you have been born again. But this second
birth was not like the first. The seed of the natural birth perishes,
but the seed planted in you at your new birth is imperishable; it is
eternal. And it was planted in you because you believed the living,
eternal Word of God.

24-25 It is written: "All people are like grass. Their glory is like the
wild flowers. Grass withers, flowers die, but the Lord's Word
endures forever." And it is this eternal Word that was preached to
you!

2 Because this is the case, get rid of all hatred of others, of all
desires to see them hurt or wronged. Be rid of all deceit and
hypocrisy or jealousy. And never speak evil of others in any way.

2-3 Because you have received your second birth, you are to be as
new born babies who long for pure spiritual milk that will nourish
you and enable you to grow in the process of salvation, which
began in you when you first tasted the Lord's goodness.

Christ, the Living Stone (2:4-8)

4 You have turned to Him, the Living Stone that was rejected by men
but chosen by God and is precious to Him. 5 So now you are to be
living stones yourselves that God can build into a spiritual dwelling
place for Himself. You have become a holy priesthood because of all

1:25 Isaiah 40:6-8

you offer to God through your faith in Jesus Christ, spiritual sacrifices that please Him. For it is written in scripture:

> [6]"Look and see, I lay in Zion a chosen and precious Corner-stone. Anyone who trusts in Him will never be ashamed."

[7-8]This Stone is so precious to you, but not to those who do not believe in Jesus. This Stone that the builders rejected became the Keystone; so to those who do not believe, "He is a Stone that causes men to stumble and a Rock that makes them fall." It is because they disobey the message given them that they stumble, and so are destined for the condemnation that is inevitable for those who reject their means of salvation.

A chosen people (2:9-12)

[9]By contrast, see what you have become, people chosen by God Himself. You are a royal priesthood because you offer your lives in sacrifice as those who live in the King. You are a holy nation, not a nation with geographical boundaries but a people set apart for God, a people who truly belong to Him.

Why has God done all this for you? So that you can declare with your mouths and by the way you live, the praises of this wonderful God who called you out of darkness and has brought you into His wonderful light.

[10]There was a time when you did not belong to these people who form God's Kingdom on earth; but now each of you is one of God's people. Before you did not experience His mercy; but now you are who you are because of that mercy.

[11]So I implore you, my dear friends, because you are strangers and do not belong to this world, refuse to yield to any sinful desires that will only fight against the well-being of your souls. [12]Give such an example to the ungodly among whom you live, that they will see God's goodness in your lives, even when they bring all manner of false accusations against you. For your example will help them to embrace the glory of God that is to be revealed when Christ returns.

Set a good example (2:13-25)

[13-14]Set a good example by having a submissive attitude to all those in authority over you. You are to do this for the Lord's sake, whether you have to submit to the king or the president as the supreme

2:6 Isaiah 28:16
2:8 Isaiah 8:14

authority, or to those who govern you. For God creates order so that those who do wrong are punished and those who do right are commended.

15 God's purpose is that you silence those who speak as fools in ignorance of the truth; that you silence them by the example of goodness that you set. 16 This is true freedom, to live obediently in ways that please the Lord. But do not use the freedom He has given you as a front for evil. Live as true servants of God, who show proper respect to everyone.

17 Of course, you are to love all your fellow believers. But you also are to live in fear of God, in reverent awe of Him and submission to His will. And you are to honour the secular authorities.

18 In the workplace, then, have a good, humble and submissive attitude towards those to whom you are accountable. Treat your bosses with respect, not only those who are considerate and treat you well, but even those who are hard task masters. 19 You will be commended for maintaining a positive witness in the face of those who deal unjustly with you, because you want to glorify God who is present with you in every situation.

20 There is no credit in being punished for doing what is wrong. But if you suffer unjustly and even endure that for a time, God will commend you for this. 21 In fact, this is the life to which you have been called, that reflects the way Christ suffered for you. He has set you an example that you are to follow, for you are to walk in His steps!

22 "He never sinned. Neither did He ever deceive by what He said." 23 So when Christ was insulted, instead of retaliating He remained silent. When He suffered He issued no threats; instead He placed Himself in God's hands, knowing that He always deals justly with everyone. 24 This is He who took all our sins upon Himself when He hung on the cross, so that now we might die to a life of sin and live in ways that are right and pleasing to God. It is through His wounds that we are healed and set free completely.

25 You used to wander around like lost sheep, but now you have turned to the one who is your Shepherd, who oversees your souls because of His concern for your welfare.

Instruction to wives (3:1-6)

3 Wives, let Christ's example show you how you are to have a right submissive attitude to your husbands. Those who do not believe will not be convinced by their wives' words, but by their

2:22 Isaiah 53:9

change in behaviour. [2]They will need to see the purity of their
hearts and lives and the respect they have for their husbands.
[3]Your true beauty, wives, will not come from wearing expensive
clothes, nor the way you braid your hair, nor from the cost of the
jewellery you wear. [4]From deep within your spirit, your inner self,
should come the beauty that can never fade with time, that of a gentle
and quiet spirit that is so precious in God's sight.
[5]In the past this is how holy women showed that they placed
their hope in God. To them this was real beauty, to have a beautiful
spirit before God. As part of this, they were submissive to their
husbands. [6]For example, Sarah obeyed Abraham and even called
him her master. You will be as Sarah's daughters if you live in right
ways that please the Lord and walk by faith, not fear.

Instruction to husbands (3:7)

[7]Husbands, in the same way you are to show proper consideration
for your wives by the way you behave. You are to treat them with
proper respect as the weaker partner for whom you truly care.
Together you have inherited the great gift of life, and you do not want
any wrong attitudes towards your wives to hinder the effectiveness
of your prayers.

Instruction to all believers (3:8-12)

[8]Finally, a word to all of you: Live together in the church in true
harmony with one another. Be sympathetic towards those who are
troubled. Love each other as brothers in the same family. Always be
merciful and compassionate. And be humble! [9]Never retaliate in a
wrong way when others wrong you. Do not insult others, even if
they insult you. Instead of reacting negatively to others, bless them,
because this is what God has called you to do. And if you bless others,
you will yourselves be blessed. [10]For it is written:

> "Anyone who desires a life full of love and goodness
> should refrain from speaking evil of others or in ways
> that will deceive them.
> [11-12]Instead, he must turn away from all that is evil and
> devote himself to doing what is good and right. He must
> always endeavour to live at peace with others, for the
> Lord watches over those who live in right ways and He
> listens attentively to their prayers; but He turns away
> from evil doers."

3:12 Psalm 34:12-16

Suffering for doing right (3:13-22)

13 If your aim is always to do good, how are you going to come to
any harm? 14 Even if you have to suffer for doing what is right, you
will be blessed. You know the saying: "Do not fear what others fear,
neither be frightened." 15 Instead, Christ is to be Lord in your hearts!

Of course, you must always be ready to answer those who question why you have this hope that is expressed in these positive attitudes. But do not answer in an aggressive manner, but with gentleness and
respect. 16 If your conscience is clear you will not be troubled by
those who speak critically of your behaviour when you reveal Christ's will. Instead, they will be put to shame for the ways they have slandered you.

17 If this is God's will, it is better to suffer for doing what is right
rather than for what is wrong. This is the way Christ suffered. He
did not deserve to die, but He has died for the sin of others. 18-20 He
only needed to make the sacrifice once, for all time and on behalf of all sinners. He was the Righteous One giving His life for the unrighteous in order to bring you into right relationship with God. His body was put to death but God's Spirit brought Him back to life, enabling Him to go and preach to the spirits of those in prison through their disobedience. God had waited patiently for their repentance at the time Noah was building the ark; but only eight
people were saved from the flood. 21-22 This water is a symbol of
baptism by which you are now also saved.

Your water baptism did not signify that your body was being washed, but that you were promising to live in ways pleasing to God. You were saved because in His resurrection Jesus Christ overcame death and has now ascended into heaven where He reigns at God's right hand, together with the angels, authorities and powers that are in submission to Him.

Live for God (4:1-19)

4 Because Christ suffered in His body, you must be prepared to
do likewise, demonstrating that you have turned away from a
life of sin. 2 Such a person demonstrates that he does not live the rest
of his earthly life to please himself, but to fulfil God's will.

3 In your past life you spent enough time doing what unbelievers
do, living in debauchery, lust and drunkenness, taking part in
orgies, living in ungodliness and worshipping idols. 4 Those who
belong to the world find it strange that you do not want to share in

3:14 Isaiah 8:12

their immoral behaviour and they even abuse you as a result.
5 However, they will be called to account by He who will judge the
living and the dead.

6 This was why Jesus went to preach the gospel to those who had
already died. They were under judgment for the way they had lived
in their bodies, but were given opportunity to turn to God in the
spirit realm.

7 The end of all things is drawing near. Therefore, you need to
think clearly and be self-controlled in the way you live, for then you
can pray effectively. 8 It is most important for you to love one another
deeply because that love covers a multitude of sins.

9 Have open house for one another without complaining about
the way this can inconvenience you. 10 And every person should use
the gifts God has given him to serve others, faithfully showing them
His grace in a whole variety of ways.

11 When you are called upon to speak, do so with God's enabling,
desiring Him to be present in all you do through Jesus Christ who
lives in you. To Him belongs the glory and the power for all eternity.
Amen! It shall be so!

12 My dear friends, it is not surprising that you have to suffer
painful trials at times; it is not that something strange or unexpected
is happening to you when you do so. 13 Rather rejoice that you are
participating in suffering for Christ, so that you will participate in
the great joy there will be when He is revealed in glory!

14 You are blessed if you are insulted for the Name of Christ.
Remember, God's Spirit and His glory remain upon you. 15 Of
course, you should not suffer for the wrong reasons, because you
are a murderer, a thief, some kind of criminal or just a busybody.
16 But there is nothing of which to be ashamed if you suffer because
you are a Christian. You should praise God for the privilege, even if
sometimes it is costly!

17 You see, this is a time of judgment and it has begun among
God's own people, His family. But what we experience is as nothing
compared with the judgment that will come on those who do not
obey God's gospel. 18 For it is written: "If it is difficult for godly people
to be saved, what will the outcome be for the ungodly and the
sinner?"

19 Therefore, those who suffer through obeying God's will should
place themselves in the hands of this faithful Creator and continue
to walk in ways that please Him.

4:18 Proverbs 11:31

Instruction to leaders (5:1-4)

5 1-2 I appeal to my fellow elders among you, as one who witnessed
Christ's sufferings and will also share in His glory that is to be
revealed: Be good shepherds of God's sheep, those He places under
your care. Serve them as those called to oversee their lives. Do this
not as a duty but because you really want to fulfil God's purpose for
you. Be eager to serve the people and do not be concerned about the
financial rewards. You serve out of love for the people, not love of
money!
3 You are not to be authoritarian in your attitudes, suppressing
those God has entrusted to you. Rather, you are to be examples to
the flock as to how to please God. 4 And when the Chief Shepherd
returns you will receive your reward, the eternal crown of His glory.

Instruction to younger men (5:5-11)

5 The young men among you must be submissive to those who are
older. All of you are to clothe yourselves with humility towards
each other because, "God opposes proud people, but gives His grace
freely to the humble."
6 All of you are to humble yourselves under God's mighty hand of
authority, so that in His time He will lift you up to be with Him.
7 Because He is so concerned about you, He wants you to lay all
your problems, troubles and anxieties on Him.
8 Keep firm control of yourselves so that you do not live to please
your natural, sinful desires. And be constantly aware that your
enemy the devil is always prowling around like a roaring lion, looking
for those he can devour. 9 Resist him firmly because your faith gives
you the power to do so. Your brothers in other parts of the world are
experiencing the same kinds of trials that you have to face.
10 However, God pours all His grace upon you because He has
called you to know His glory eternally through your unity with
Christ. Yes, you will have to suffer and face the cost of obedience to
Him first; but He Himself will restore and keep you strong, firm in
your faith and steadfast in your obedience. 11 To Him alone belongs
power for all eternity. Amen! It shall be so!

Final Greeting (5:12)

12 I have only written to you briefly with the help of my dear and
faithful brother, Silas. My purpose has been to encourage you and

5:5 Proverbs 3:34

to remind you of the grace that God has truly given you to enable
you to stand firm in the face of all adversity and opposition.
13 The sister who lives in Rome, this 'Babylon', who like you has
been chosen to belong to Christ, sends her greetings, as does my
son, Mark. Greet one another in the love of Christ. And may His
peace be imparted to all of you who are one with Him.

2 PETER

Escape from corruption (1:1-11)

1 From Simon Peter, a servant and apostle of Jesus Christ.

To those who have obtained a faith as precious as ours in believing the full acceptance we have in our God and Saviour Jesus Christ. 2 May grace and peace be given you abundantly through your knowledge of God and Jesus our Lord.

3 Through His divine power He has given us all we need for life and godliness, because we know Him personally. He has called us to live for His glory and in His goodness, by which He has given us such great and precious promises.

4 So we have become those who share in His divine nature and escape from the corruption caused by desiring what the world desires. 5-7 For this reason, make every effort to add goodness to your faith and to add knowledge to your goodness, self-control to your knowledge, perseverance to your self-control and holiness to your perseverance. Add friendship for the brethren to your holiness and to that friendship add God's love. 8 If all these qualities abound in you, they will prevent you from being ineffective and unproductive in your relationship with our Lord Jesus Christ. 9 For whoever lacks these things is blind and has forgotten that his past sins have been forgiven.

10-11 Therefore, my brothers, be more eager to stand firm in the reality of your calling and election, for by doing so you will never fail and you will receive a wonderful welcome into the eternal Kingdom of our Lord and Saviour Jesus Christ.

Beware of false teachers (1:12-2:3)

12 Therefore I intend to keep reminding you of these things, even though you already know them and are now well established in the truth. 13-14 I consider it right, while I remain in this body, to stir you by reminding you of these truths; for I know that it will not be long before I will put this body aside, as our Lord Jesus Christ has made clear to me. 15 I wanted to be sure that after my departure you will always be able to remember these things.

16 For we did not tell you cleverly devised stories when we revealed the power and presence of our Lord Jesus Christ, for we were eye-witnesses of His Majesty. 17 For when He received honour and glory from God the Father, a voice came to Him from the majestic glory, "This is My beloved Son, with whom I am well pleased." 18 And we heard this voice from heaven when we were with Him on the holy mountain (where He was transfigured before our eyes).

19 And we can verify the words the prophets spoke about Him, and you will do well to take careful note of such words. They are like a light shining in a murky place, anticipating the dawning of a new day when the morning-star rises in your hearts. 20-21 You must understand that no prophecy in scripture is fulfilled by self-interpretation, because no genuine prophecy came from man's will but because men were inspired by the Spirit, and so spoke from God.

2 But there were also false prophets among the people, just as there will be false teachers among you. They will use deceptive means to introduce heresies that are destructive because they deny the sovereignty of the Lord who purchased their salvation with His blood. They are bringing hasty destruction upon themselves. 2 Many will be influenced by them, following their shameful ways and bringing the way of truth into disrepute. 3 These teachers are motivated by greed and will exploit you by their false testimonies. Their condemnation has only been a matter of time and their destruction is inevitable!

Consequences of sinfulness (2:4-22)

4 God did not have mercy on the angels that sinned but consigned them to hell where they are confined to dark dungeons as they await the final judgment. 5 He did not save the ancient world when He caused the flood to destroy sinful people. He only saved Noah, who preached the necessity of living in right relationship with God, and some others who were with him. 6 God condemned the cities of Sodom and Gomorrah, burning them to the ground as an example of the judgment awaiting the ungodly. 7-8 He rescued Lot, another righteous man, who was greatly upset by the immoral lives of rebellious men. Lot lived among those men daily and, because of their lawless deeds that he witnessed, felt tormented in his soul.

9 If God could do all these things, then He certainly knows how to spare godly men from trials and to keep the ungodly in turmoil

1:17 Matthew 17:5

until the Day of Judgment. This applies particularly to those who give
in to the evil desires of their self-life and despise those in authority.
[10-11] Such men are so bold in their arrogance that they are not afraid
to speak evil of heavenly beings. But not even the angels slander
these evil men before the Lord, even though they are stronger and
more powerful. [12] Those men blaspheme about things they do not
understand. They are brutal, living only to satisfy their basic
instincts and will inevitably be trapped in their own sins. They
should be destroyed like beasts.

[13] This will be the consequence of the harm they have caused.
They have sunk to such depravity that they take pleasure in parading
their licentious behaviour before others. They are marked by their
sins and stand out like blemishes when they share in your feasts.
[14] They look with adulterous lust on others and sin continually. They
seduce the weak-willed, are well practised in satisfying their greed
and spread curse all around them. [15] They have departed from the
straight way and follow the example of Balaam, son of Beor, who
loved the rewards of wickedness. [16] He was rebuked for his evil
works by a donkey, an animal normally incapable of speech, who
spoke in a human voice to restrain the prophet in his madness.

[17-18] Such men are like waterless springs and mists driven along by
stormy winds. The deepest darkness awaits them, for they speak in
empty and boastful ways, appealing to the lustful desires of the corrupt
nature, enticing those who are in the process of being freed from
those who live in error. [19] They give promises of freedom while they
are slaves of corruption themselves. [20] For if, having escaped being
defiled by the world through a full knowledge of our Lord and Saviour
Jesus Christ, they again become entangled in worldly corruption,
they are far worse off than they were before. [21] It would have been
better for them not to have known the way of righteousness than,
having known it, only to turn away from the command given to
them to be holy. [22] They truly fulfilled the proverbs, "A dog always
returns to its vomit," and, "A washed sow wallows again in the mud."

The Day of the Lord (3:23-18)

3 My beloved friends, this is the second letter I have written to
you. Both are intended to stir you to sound thinking by
reminding you of the truth. [2] Remember the words spoken by the
prophets of old and the commandment our Lord and Saviour gave
through the apostles.

2:22 Proverbs 26:11

3 First, understand that in the last days those who ridicule the
truth will follow their own evil desires instead. 4 They will say such
things as, "What has happened to His promised second coming?
For since the time of our forefathers everything has continued as it
was before, since creation began." 5 They deliberately ignore the fact
that the heavens existed long ago by God's Word and the earth was
formed out of water and through water. 6 It was also by water that
the world was flooded and destroyed. 7 But by the same Word, fire
awaits the present heavens and the earth, for the Day of Judgment
will see the destruction of ungodly people.

8 So do not ignore the truth, my friends, that with the Lord one
day is as a thousand years and a thousand years as one day. 9 The
Lord is not slow in fulfilling His promise, as some understand slowness.
He is patient with you, not wanting anyone to be destroyed but
desiring that all men turn to Him in repentance.

10 For the Day of the Lord will steal up on people like a thief and
then the heavens will vanish with a roar and the elements will be
dissolved by fire. The earth and all its works will be exposed.

11-12 Because everything will be destroyed in this way, what holy
and godly lives you should live as you await God's Day and hasten
its coming, when the heavens will be destroyed and the elements
will melt in the fire. 13 But according to His promise we await the
new heaven and the new earth where only righteousness will exist.
14 Therefore, my dear friends, as you long for these things to be fulfilled,
do all you can so that He will find you spotless and without blemish
when He comes, for then you will be at peace. 15-16 And consider our
Lord's patience with us as the consequence of the salvation He has
given us. Our brother Paul wrote to you in the wisdom God gave
him, speaking of these things in all his letters, even though some of
what he says is difficult to understand. Ignorant and unreliable people
twist what he says, as they do other scriptures, but only to their own
destruction.

17 Therefore, dear friends, because you have been forewarned,
make sure that none of you are deceived by the errors of unsubmitted
men and so lose your security. 18 Rather, grow in the grace and
knowledge of our Lord and Saviour Jesus Christ. To Him all the
glory belongs, both now and forever. Amen. It shall be so!

1 JOHN

The living One (1:1-4)

1 I want to tell you about the Word of Life. He existed before time began. I and the other apostles heard Him, saw Him with our eyes; yes, we looked at Him and even touched Him with our hands when He became a man and lived among us. 2 The One who is Life itself appeared; we saw this Life and I can testify to what He did. We tell you clearly that He is eternal life; He was with the Father in heaven and He came and revealed Himself to us.

3-4 So we speak to you of what we have seen and heard, for we are first-hand witnesses. We tell you these things so that you may share in His life with us. Yes, we share in the life of the Father and His Son Jesus Christ and it gives us great joy to tell you about these things.

Walk in the light (1:5-7)

5 This is the message, the revelation that we heard from Him and now reveal to you: God is Light; in Him there is no darkness at all. 6 If we claim to share in His Light and yet walk in spiritual darkness, we only lie and do not live according to the truth. 7 But if we walk in the Light, just as He is in the Light, we share in His Life together and the blood of Jesus, His Son, purifies us from all sin, from everything we have done against His will.

Confess sin (1:8-2:2)

8 This does not mean that we never sin. If we claim such a thing we only deceive ourselves and the truth does not live in us. 9 Yet if we are honest with Him and confess our sins, He then forgives our sins and purifies us from everything that is not right in His eyes. He is always Faithful and Just to do this. 10 But if we claim we have no sin, and therefore have no need of forgiveness, that is tantamount to calling God a liar and is evidence that the truth of His Word has no place in our lives!

2 I am writing this to you as my dear children so that you will
not deliberately sin against Him. However, if anyone does sin,
we have Someone who speaks to the Father in our defence, Jesus
Christ – the One who is always right. 2 He is the sacrifice that was
offered to cleanse us from sin and restore us to unity with God. He
offered Himself, not only as the punishment for our sins but also for
the sins of everyone in the world.

Obey His Word (2:3-2:8)

3 We are sure that we have really come to know Him if we obey His
commands. 4 The man who says, "Yes, I know Him", but does not
do what He commands is a liar and the truth does not live in Him.
5-6 But if anyone obeys His Word, God's love is truly expressed and
fulfilled in Him. This demonstrates that we truly live in Him.
Whoever claims to live in Him has to demonstrate this by walking
as Jesus did.

7 Dear friends, I am not telling you anything new. This is not a new
command that you have never heard before. It is the same message,
with the same command, that you have heard already. 8 At the same
time I am giving you a new command. The truth of this command
is to be seen in Him and also in you, because the spiritual darkness
of sin and disobedience to God is passing away and the true Light
is already shining into our hearts and lives.

Love your brother (2:9-14)

9 Anyone who claims to be living in that Light but has no love for his
brother is still in spiritual darkness. 10 On the contrary, whoever
loves his brother is living in the light of God's truth and there is
nothing in him that will cause him to stumble in his walk with the
Lord.

11 However, whoever has no love for his brother is truly in spiritual
darkness and even walks around in that darkness. He has no idea
where he is going, for that darkness has caused him to be spiritually
blind.

12 I am writing these things to you, dear children, because your
sins have been forgiven because of Jesus, whose Name means
Saviour.

13 I am writing to the fathers among you because you have come
to know the One who existed before time began.

I am writing to the young men among you because you have
overcome the evil one who tempts and accuses you.

Dear children, I can write like this to you because you are in relationship with your heavenly Father.

14 I repeat to you fathers, you know the Eternal One who lived before the beginning of creation.

One further thing I say to you, young men. Through your faith in Christ you are strong and God's Word lives in you. This is what has enabled you to overcome the evil one.

Do not love the world (2:15-17)

15 Now I say to you all: Do not love worldliness or anything that the
world offers you. If anyone loves and longs for the things of this
world, he does not have love for the heavenly Father in him. 16 For
everything that the world offers, the sinful cravings of the flesh,
lusting after the things you see, whether this be people or things,
and boasting about what you have and do – all these things do not
come from your heavenly Father but from the world. 17 The world
and all the desires it inspires are passing away; but the man who obeys
God's will by putting His words of love into action lives forever.

Beware of opposition to the truth of Jesus Christ (2:18-29)

18 My children, we are living in the end times. You have heard that
the antichrist is coming, but I am telling you that many antichrists
have already come. This is how we can tell that these are the end
times! 19 These people who oppose Christ actually left us because
they were not truly saved and did not, therefore, belong to us. If
they were really part of us they would have remained at one with
us. The fact that they left shows that none of them truly belong to
us.

20 By contrast, you have an anointing from the Holy One, God
Himself. So all of you know and experience the truth for yourselves.
21 So I do not write to you because you are ignorant of the truth, but
because you know well what is true and right. You know that the
truth contains no lies or deception.

22 Who is truly a liar? Whoever denies that Jesus is the Christ,
God's anointed Son. Such a man is the antichrist, one opposed to
the truth of who Christ is. He denies not only the Son but the Father
as well. 23 And anyone who denies who Jesus is does not love Him
or His Father. However, whoever believes and trusts in the Son has
God for his Father also.

24 So ensure that the truth that you heard at the beginning of your
Christian life continues to live in you. If it does, you will continue

to live in the Son and in the Father. 25 And He has promised His gift
of eternal life to all who truly believe.

26 The reason why I remind you of these things is to warn you
against any who try to lead you astray from the truth. 27 Remember,
the anointing you have already received from Him continues to live
in you. So you do not need anyone to teach you where the truth lies,
for the anointing of the Spirit of truth teaches you about all these
things. The anointing of truth is real; it is not like the counterfeit
work of the enemy. So, just as the Spirit of truth has already taught
you, continue to live in Him who is the Truth, Christ Jesus your Lord.

28 Therefore, dear children, continue to live in Him so that when
He comes again you may stand with confidence before Him,
unashamed of anything in your life that His penetrating light will
then reveal. 29 Because you know that He is right in all He is and
does, you can be sure that all of you who do what is right have
received the new birth that He alone can give.

God's children (3:1-10)

3 The love the father has lavished on us is so great it cannot be
put into words adequately. What a wonder it is that we should
be called God's children! And this is precisely what He has made
us. The world does not understand this, because those who belong
to the world do not know Him. Therefore they cannot recognise us
for what we are by His grace.

2 Dear friends, He has already made us His children and it is still
to be revealed what we will become when Jesus comes again.
However, we do know this, that at that time we shall be like Him.
Yes, when we see Him in the fullness of who He is, we shall be
transformed into His likeness. 3 Everyone who believes this wonderful truth keeps himself pure in the way he lives, for Christ Jesus
is pure; we are one with Him and our destiny is to be united with
Him forever. This is our hope.

4 What a contrast with those who live lawless, sinful lives, who
have no heart for God's purposes. 5 How thankful you can be that
when Jesus came for the first time it was to free us from our sins.
You see, in Him there is no sin.

6 Now you live in Him and those who continue to live in Him do
not continue in a life of sin. Anyone who persists in a life of sin has
clearly no personal knowledge of Him and does not see Him for
who He truly is!

7 Dear children, do not allow anyone to lead you away from the
truth. You are to live in ways that please the Lord. This means that

you will do what is right, just as Jesus your Lord always does what
is right. 8 The person who walks in sin serves the devil, because it
has always been the devil's nature to sin. The Son of God came to
destroy the devil's work on the cross. 9 So no-one who has received
the new birth that God alone can give will continue to live in sin.
No, he has the seed of God planted within him and that seed
remains in him. So it is not possible for him to continue in a life of
sin because he has received a second birth from God.

10 This is how we know who have received that second birth and
are God's children and who remain as the devil's children. Anyone
who does not do what is right is not a child of God; nor is anyone
who fails to love his brother.

Love for your brothers (3:11-20)

11 This is the same message that you heard at the very beginning of
your life as a Christian: You are called to love your fellow believers
and allow them to love you. 12 So do not be like Cain. Because he
belonged to the evil one, he murdered his brother. Why did he do
such a thing? He was jealous because what he did was wrong in
God's eyes, but what his brother did was right. 13 So do not be surprised,
my brothers, if the world is against you, hates you even.

14 We know that we have passed through death with Jesus on the
cross to the new life we have in Him, and the evidence of this is that
we now love our brothers.

You see, anyone who does not love in this way remains spiritually
dead. 15 So anyone who has no love for his brother is a murderer like
Cain. And you know full well that no murderer has God's eternal
life in him.

16 We have a way of knowing what true love is: Jesus Christ laid
down His life for us. That is true love. And we ought, therefore, to
lay down our lives for our brothers in true love.

17 I will give you an example of what this means in practice. If
someone has financial resources and sees one of his brothers in
need, yet he has no compassion on him and does nothing to help
him, how can you imagine that he has God's love in him?

18 Dear children, it means nothing to say you love others; it is only
your actions that show whether you truly love them or not. 19-20 This
is how you can be sure that you or anyone else belongs to the truth,
and how you can be at peace with God when in His presence, without any condemnation in your heart. For God is far greater than our
hearts and He knows and understands everything that is going on
in our lives.

Anything we ask (3:21-24)

21-22 My dear friends, if there is nothing in our hearts to make us feel
condemned, we can have confidence before God when we pray and
so are able to receive from Him anything we ask. This is because we
are living in obedience to His commands and are doing what pleases
Him. 23 And this is His command, as you know well: first to believe
that Jesus Christ is God's Son, your Saviour and Lord, and then to
love others and allow them to love you, as He has commanded us.
24 Those who obey His commands show they continue to live in Him
and He lives in them. We can be sure that He does live in us because
He has given us His Spirit.

Test the spirits (4:1-6)

4 Dear friends, do not trust in every spiritual power. Test the
various spiritual forces that want to influence your life so that
you can determine what is truly from God and what is not. Realise
that there are many false prophets in the world, inspired by false
spirits. 2-3 There is a sure way to recognise those inspired by God's
Spirit: they acknowledge that Jesus Christ is God come in human
flesh. Every person who does not acknowledge Jesus in this way is
not under the influence of God's Spirit but is under the spirit of
antichrist. You have heard that this spirit was coming and I tell you
that it is already present in the world.

4 However, dear children, because you belong to God you have
overcome these false spirits and those influenced by them. The
Spirit of God lives in you and He is far greater than this spirit of
antichrist that is at work in the world.

5 These other spirits that are at work in the world speak from the
ungodly viewpoint of the world and those who belong to the world
listen to them. 6 But we belong to God, and so others who also
belong to God listen to what we say. Those who do not belong to
God do not listen to us. So this is how you can recognise who is
motivated by the Spirit of truth and those under the influence of
what is false: whether they listen to you when you speak God's
truth, or whether they refuse to listen.

Living a life of love (4:7-21)

7 Dear friends, it is essential that we love our fellow believers and
receive love from them, for this love comes from God. Yes, this love
is in every person who has received the second birth that God alone
can give. Putting this love into action demonstrates to the world
that you know God in your experience.

8 Whoever does not put such love into practice does not have
personal knowledge of God, for He is love. How did He reveal His
love among us? 9 By sending His one and only Son into the world
that we might have God's eternal life through Him.

10 You see, this is true love: not that we have loved God, but that
He has demonstrated His love for us by sending His Son to be the
sacrifice offered on the cross, to bring us back to unity with God
through the forgiveness of all our sins. 11 Dear friends, I repeat, if this
is the extent of God's love for us, then surely we ought to love one
another! 12 No-one has ever seen God as He is. Yet if we truly put our
love for one another into action, His love is revealed and fulfilled in
us and the world can see that love.

13 We can be certain that we continue to live in Him and that He
continues to live in us, because we have His own Spirit living in us.
14 We have seen this clearly and tell others that God the Father sent
His Son to be the Saviour of the entire world. 15 So if anyone truly
believes that Jesus is God's Son, God truly lives in him and he lives
in God. 16 In fact we can be sure of this, that we are able to depend
completely on the love that God has for us.

God is love. So if love is your way of life, it is clear that you live
in God and that He lives in you. 17 This is how God's love is revealed
among us, and it is this obedience to Him that will give us confidence
on the Day of Judgment. Such love shows the world that we are like
the One in whom we believe.

18 There is no fear in this kind of love that comes from God. His
love is perfect and it drives fear out of our lives. The one who is
afraid fears that he will be punished by God. Such a one does not
have this perfect love operating fully in his life.

19 We love because we are responding to His great love for us.
20 Listen, if someone says, "I love God", but you see that he does not
love his fellow believer, it is obvious that he lies. For anyone who
does not love his brother, who is right in front of him, cannot possibly
love God, whom he has never seen with the naked eye. 21 And, anyway, this is the command that God has given us: whoever truly lives
in love for God must also live to love his fellow believer. This is a
simple matter of obedience.

Believe in the Son (5:1-15)

5 Everyone who truly believes that God is the Christ, God's Son,
has received the birth that comes from God. He is your Father.
So if you love Him, you will love His children as well.

2 How can you tell for sure that you love God's children? Because
you love God, you obey His command to love others. 3 The only
way to express true love for God is to be obedient to what He has
told you to do. If you really love Him, those commands are not a
burden to you.

4 Everyone who has received the new birth that God gives overcomes the spirit that influences the world around him. It is our faith
in Jesus and what He has done that gives us victory over worldliness.
5 I ask you, "Who has really overcome this worldliness?" Obviously
only he who believes and trusts in Jesus as God's victorious Son.

6 He is the One who came as a man into the world, completely
identified with our need in the water of baptism and shed His blood
for us; Jesus Christ, God's sacrifice! He not only shared our humanity;
He shed His blood for us. God's own Spirit testifies to this and He
is certainly the Spirit of truth.

7-8 There is common agreement between the Spirit, the water and
the blood. All three are in agreement and bear witness to the truth.

9 We readily accept what others tell us. Should we not all the more
readily accept what God says, for His testimony is far greater than
that of any man. And God has given us this revelation about His
Son. 10 So the one who believes in Jesus as God's Son believes in his
heart what God Himself has revealed. But anyone who does not
believe what God says calls Him a liar. Such a person only does this
because he or she has refused to believe what God has revealed
about His Son.

11 What is this testimony that God has given us? Simply this: that
God has given us eternal life and this life can only be received
through Jesus, His Son. 12 So he who belongs to Jesus has this life;
but he who does not belong to Jesus does not have this life.

13 I write these things to you because you do believe who Jesus is
and what He has done for you; and so I give you this assurance, that
you possess His eternal life. 14 So you can have great confidence
when you come before God in prayer. You can be sure that if you
ask anything according to His revealed will, He certainly hears you.
15 And if you are confident that He hears what you say, no matter
what you ask, you can be sure that you have whatever you have
asked of Him!

Look out for one another (5:16-17)

16 If you should ever see a fellow believer commit a sin that does not
lead to spiritual death, you should pray for him, asking God to forgive

him and restore him to His way. I am speaking of those sins that do
not lead to spiritual death. Yes, there is a sin that leads to death and
I am not saying you should pray about that.
17 Whatever is not God's will is sinful, and there are plenty of
other sins that do not lead to such dire consequences.

Worship only Him (5:18-21)

18 We can be sure that anyone who has received the birth that God
gives does not continue to sin and so grieve God. He lives in God's
Son who keeps him safe from the power of the evil one so that he
cannot be harmed.
19 We are certain that we are God's children, even though the rest
of the world is under the control of the evil one. 20 We are also sure
that God's Son has come and has revealed Himself to us so that we
can know and understand Him, the One who is the truth. Yes, we
continue to live in Him who is the truth: Jesus Christ, God's Son. He
is both true God and eternal life.
21 So, dear children, keep yourself from the worship of anyone or
anything else. Worship only Him!

2 JOHN

1-2 From the elder, John.
To the lady chosen by God, and to her children whom I love in
the truth; and not only I, but all who know the truth. That truth lives
in us and will always be with us.
3 May God the Father and Jesus Christ, the Father's Son, impart
grace, mercy and peace to us in truth and love.
4 I have been filled with joy to discover that some of your children
are walking in the truth, as the Father commanded us. 5 And now,
dear lady, I ask that we should all love one another. I am not writing
a new commandment, but one we were given from the beginning.
6 And this is love for God, that we walk in obedience to His commands.
And this is the commandment that you heard from the beginning;
this is how we are to walk, in love!
7 Many deceivers, who do not believe that Jesus is the Messiah
who came in the flesh, have gone out into the world. Every such
person is a deceiver, the antichrist. 8 Therefore be careful, ensuring
that you do not lose what we have worked for, so that you may
receive the full reward of your faith.
9 Everyone who does not remain in the teaching of Christ in his
daily walk does not have relationship with God. But the one who
remains in His teaching is in relationship with both the Father and
the Son.
10-11 If anyone who visits you does not bring this teaching, you are
not to receive him into your house or even welcome him; for to
acknowledge him is to share in his wicked work.
12 There is much I want to write to you about that cannot be
adequately expressed with paper and ink. Still, I am hoping to visit
you when we can speak face to face, so that our joy can be complete.
13 The children of your sister, who is also chosen, send you their
love.

3 JOHN

1 From the elder, John.
To Gaius, dearly loved by God and whom I love in the truth.
2 My dear friend, I pray that you might prosper in every way and
enjoy good health, for all is well with your soul.
3 It gave me great joy when some brothers came and testified that
you live in the truth and told of how you continue to walk in the
truth. 4 There can be no greater joy for me than to hear of my spiritual
children walking in the truth.
5 My dear friend, you prove yourself faithful whenever you serve
your fellow believers, even though some are strangers to you. 6 They
have told the church of your love. You will do well to send them on
their way in a manner that is worthy of God. 7 For they have gone
out for the sake of His Name, taking nothing from those to whom
they witness. 8 We ought to support such men, for by so doing we
work with them in promoting the truth.
9 I wrote to the church, but Diotrephes does not want to receive us
for he loves to be first, the most important one. 10 So if I do come I
will confront what he is doing in speaking against us in such evil
ways. Even that does not satisfy him, for he refuses to receive other
believers and prevents anyone else from doing so, putting them out
of the church instead.
11 My dear friend, never imitate what is evil, only what is good.
He who does good is of God; he who does evil has not seen God.
12 Everyone speaks well of Demetrius, for he lives according to the
truth. And I also speak well of him and I know that what I say is
true.
13 I want to write to you about many things, but cannot adequately
express them with pen and ink. 14 But I hope to see you soon and
then we can speak face to face.
May God's peace be with you. Give my love to all my friends,
greeting them by name.

JUDE

Greetings (1-2)
1 From Jude, brother of James and a servant of Jesus Christ.
To those who have been called, who are loved by God the Father
and kept for the purposes of Jesus Christ.
2 May God's mercy, peace and love be imparted to you abundantly.

Fight for the faith (3-4)
3 My dear friends, because I have been so keen to write to you about
the salvation we share, it has been necessary for me to urge you to
fight for the faith which has been revealed to the saints, the revelation
received once for all time. 4 Certain men have infiltrated your ranks,
men whose condemnation was written about long ago. They are
ungodly men who use God's grace as a pretext for their immorality,
and so deny our only Lord and Master, Jesus Christ.

The rebellious will perish (5-19)
5 My intention is to remind you of what you already know, that the
Lord, after delivering His people from their bondage in Egypt, then
destroyed those who did not believe. 6 Also the angels who did not
keep to their appointed positions of authority in heaven, but left the
place where they belonged, are now kept in darkness, bound eternally
in chains awaiting final judgment on the great Day of the Lord.
7 Likewise, Sodom and Gomorrah and the surrounding cities, which
indulged in immorality and sexual perversion, serve as a warning,
for they experienced the punishment of eternal fire.
8 In the same way, these dreamers on the one hand defile their
own bodies and on the other despise God's authority and mock
those who belong to His glory. 9 But the archangel Michael stood
against the devil when he disputed with him about Moses' body,
saying, "The Lord rebuke you."
10 But these men mock what they do not understand and they are
destroyed because they give in to their natural instincts as if they
were animals. 11 They are cursed because they follow the way of

Cain and have given themselves to the same error as Balaam. They
will perish as Korah did when he rebelled against God's authority.
12 Yet these men participate in your love feasts. They stand out as
blemishes and are not even embarrassed, even though they serve
only their own interests. They are like waterless clouds driven along
by the wind, trees that bear no fruit in the autumn, uprooted and
totally worthless. 13 They are wild sea waves whose foam is their
own shame; wandering stars reserved for eternal darkness.
14-15 Enoch, of the seventh generation after Adam, prophesied
about such men, saying, "See, the Lord came with tens of thousands
of His holy ones to judge all men and to condemn all the ungodly
for the immoral deeds of which they are clearly guilty, and condemn
all the ungodly sinners for the harsh words they spoke against Him."
16 They grumble and are never satisfied. They want only to gratify
their own lusts. They display their arrogance through what they say
about themselves and they flatter others in order to take advantage
of them.
17-18 But you, my beloved friends, must remember the warnings of
the apostles of our Lord Jesus Christ when they told you, "In the last
days there will be those who mock the truth, interested only in fulfilling their own ungodly lusts." 19 These men have caused division;
they are worldly people who do not possess God's Spirit.

Remain in God's love (20-25)

20 However, my dear friends, you are to build yourselves up in your
most holy faith, praying in the Holy Spirit. 21 Keep yourselves in
God's love as you await your inheritance of eternal life through the
mercy of our Lord Jesus Christ.
22-23 And be merciful towards those who doubt, seeking to snatch
them from the fires of judgment. Show others mercy, together with the
kind of fear that hates having to do with anything that is corrupt.
24 Now to Him who is able to prevent you from stumbling and
who can, with joy, present you perfect in His glorious Presence, to
the only God our Saviour be glory, majesty, might and authority
through Jesus Christ our Lord throughout all ages, now and forever.
Amen! It shall be so!

REVELATION

John's revelation (1:1-11)

1 1-2 Revelation of Jesus Christ which God gave to show His servants
what must soon take place. He revealed it by sending His angel
to His servant, John, who bears witness to all that he saw through
God's Word and personal revelation of Jesus Christ. 3 Anyone who
reads the words of this prophecy, hearing what God says and
believing what is written, is blessed because the time is near.
4-5 From John,
To the seven churches in the province of Asia:
May grace and peace be imparted to you from He who is and was
and is to come, and from the seven spirits that are before the throne,
and from Jesus Christ the Faithful Witness, the first to be raised to
heaven from the dead and the Ruler of the kings of the earth.
Eternal glory and might be to Him, for He continues to love us
and has freed us from our sins by His blood. 6 He has made us to be
a Kingdom and priests for God His Father. Amen! It shall be so.
7 Look, He is coming with the clouds and every eye will see Him,
including those who nailed Him to the cross. And all people everywhere will grieve because of Him. Amen! It shall be so!
8 "I am the Alpha and Omega," says the Lord, "the First and the
last, the One who is and was and is coming again, the Almighty."
9 I, John, your brother who shares with you in the suffering, the
Kingdom and the patient endurance that are ours in Jesus, was
detained on the island of Patmos because of God's Word and for
bearing witness to Jesus. 10-11 I was in the Spirit on the Lord's Day,
when I heard a loud voice behind me that sounded like a trumpet,
saying: "Write on a scroll what you see and distribute it to the
seven churches in Ephesus, Smyrna, Pergamum, Thyatira, Sardis,
Philadelphia and Laodicea."

An encounter with Jesus (1:12-20)

12-13 I turned to see who had spoken to me and saw seven golden
lampstands and among them was Someone 'who looked like a son

of man'. He was clothed in a robe that went down to His feet, with a golden sash around His chest. 14-16 The hair on His head was as white as wool, as white as snow. His eyes were like a flame of fire and His feet were as bronze that glowed in a furnace. His voice sounded like the rushing of many waters and in His right hand He held seven stars. From His mouth came a sharp, double-edged sword and His face shone like the sun at its brightest.

17 When I saw Him I fell at His feet as though dead. But He placed His right hand on me and said: "Do not be afraid. I am the First and the Last, the Living One. 18 I was dead and, see, I am alive for all eternity; and I have the keys of Death and Hades. 19 Therefore write down what you see, both what is now and that which is to take place in the future.

20 "The mystery of the seven stars which you saw in My right hand and of the seven golden lampstands is easily explained: The seven stars are the angels, who are My messengers to the seven churches and the lampstands are the seven churches themselves.

To the church at Ephesus (2:1-8)

2 "To the angel of the church at Ephesus write: 'These are the words of the One who holds the seven stars in His right hand, who walks among the seven golden lampstands. 2 I know what you have done, your hard work and your endurance: that you cannot stand evil men and have dismissed the teaching of those who call themselves apostles but are not, because you discovered them to be false deceivers. 3 You have persevered through all you have suffered because of My Name and you have not grown tired in the process.

4 'But I have this against you: you have departed from the love you had in the beginning. 5 Remember, then, that place from which you have fallen. Turn back to Me and to the works you did at first. If you fail to do this, I will come among you and will remove your lampstand from its appointed place.

6 'However, you have this in your favour that, like Me, you hate what the Nicolaitans do, teaching and practising what is immoral.

7 'Let anyone with spiritual understanding hear what the Spirit says to the churches. I will allow anyone who is victorious to eat from the tree of life that is in the paradise of God.'

To the church at Smyrna (2:8-11)

8-9 "To the angel of the church at Smyrna write this message: 'These are the words of the First and the Last, who died and was raised to

life again: I know of your suffering and your poverty, yet you are
rich. I know how you are slandered by those who call themselves
Jews but are not, for they belong to Satan's synagogue.

10 'Do not be afraid of what you are about to suffer. Be warned, the
devil is about to have some of you thrown into prison. This will be
a severe test that will last for ten days. Remain faithful, even to the
point of dying for what you believe, and I will give you the crown
of life.

11 'Let anyone with spiritual understanding hear what the Spirit
says to the churches. No-one who is victorious will be harmed by
the second death, the lake of fire.'

To the church at Pergamum (2:12-17)

12-13 "To the angel of the church at Pergamum write this message:
'These are the words of He who has the double-edged sword: I
know where you live, where Satan has established his throne. You
remained true to My Name, and did not deny your faith in Me, even
when Antipas was martyred for faithfully bearing witness to Me in
that place where Satan lives.

14 'Nevertheless, I have a few things that I hold against you. Some
of you follow the teachings of Balaam, who taught Balak to put a
stumbling block in the way of the sons of Israel by encouraging
them to eat sacrifices made to idols and to commit sexual immorality.
15 As a result, some of you followed the teaching of the Nicolaitans
who promote such immorality.

16 'Repent of this. Turn away from all such evil, or I will come
among you speedily and will deal with those concerned by the sword
of My mouth.

17 'Let anyone who has spiritual understanding hear what the
Spirit says to the churches.

'To he who is victorious I will give the hidden manna and a white
stone of complete forgiveness. On this stone a new name will have
been written, which no one will know except the one who receives
it, signifying that he has a completely new inheritance.'

To the church at Thyatira (2:18-29)

18 "To the angel of the church at Thyatira write this message: 'These
are the words of God's Son, who has eyes that flame with fire and
feet that glow like brass in the furnace. 19 I know all you have
accomplished; I know of your love, your faith, your acts of service
and the way you have persevered. I know that what you do now
exceeds what you did at first.

[20]'Yet I hold this against you, that you have given room to that woman, Jezebel, who calls herself a prophetess although she deceives many, teaching my servants to commit sexual sins and to eat food dedicated to false gods. [21]I gave her time to repent but she has no desire to turn away from her immorality. [22]See, I am now putting her on a bed of suffering and those who commit adultery with her share in the great affliction, unless they repent by turning away completely from her false ways. [23]And I will strike her children dead and then all the churches will know that I am He who searches minds and hearts and deals with each one according to his deeds.

[24-25]'But to the rest of you at Thyatira, those who reject such teaching and so do not know of Satan's so-called deep things, I say this: I am not laying on you another burden, but keep hold of what you have until I return.

[26-27]'To him who is victorious, who keeps My ways until the end, I will give authority over the nations, just as I received authority from My Father. 'He will shepherd them with an iron rod that breaks clay pots into pieces.' [28]I will also give the morning star Myself to everyone who is victorious.

[29]'Let he who has spiritual understanding hear what the Spirit says to the churches.'

To the church at Sardis (3:1-6)

3 "To the angel of the church at Sardis write this message: 'The words of He who has the seven spirits of God and the seven stars. I know all you do, that you have a reputation for being lively while in reality you are dead. [2]Wake up and strengthen what remains but which also is about to die; for I have not found your deeds complete in the sight of My God. [3]So remember what you have received and put into practice what you have heard. Repent, turn away from anything that conflicts with that.

'If you fail to wake up I shall come like a thief and you will not know at what time I shall come upon you. [4]But you do have a few among you in Sardis who have not soiled their clothes. They will walk with Me in white robes because they are worthy. [5]He who is victorious will be clothed in a white robe and I will not remove his name from the Book of Life. Instead I will acknowledge him before My Father and His angels.

[6]'Let he who has spiritual understanding hear what the Spirit says to the churches.'

2:27 Psalm 2:9

To the church at Philadelphia (3:7-13)

7 "To the angel of the church at Philadelphia write this message: 'These are the words of the one who is Holy and True, who possesses the key of David, the authority of kingship. What He opens no-one can shut and what He shuts no-one can open.

8 'I know what you have done. Look, I have set before you an open door which no one can shut. You have little power but you have kept my Word and have not denied My Name.

9 'There are some who belong to Satan's synagogue, who call themselves Jews but who lie because they are not true Jews. See, I will cause them to come and humble themselves before you and they shall know that I have loved you. 10 Because you have obeyed My Word with patient endurance, I will keep you from the time of trial that is coming on the whole world to test everyone who lives on the earth.

11 'I am coming soon. So keep hold of what you have so that no-one steals your crown. 12 I will make the one who is victorious a pillar in the temple of My God. He shall never leave that temple and I will write on him the Name of My God and the name of the city of My God, the new Jerusalem, that will descend from heaven from My God. And I will write on him My own new Name!

13 'Let he who has spiritual understanding hear what the Spirit says to the churches.'

To the church at Laodicea (3:14-22)

14 "To the angel of the church at Laodicea write this message: 'These are the words of the Amen, the faithful and true Witness, the Ruler of God's creation. 15 I know what you have done, that you are neither cold nor hot. I wish you were either cold or hot. 16 But because you are only lukewarm and neither hot nor cold, I am about to vomit you out of My mouth. 17 You say, 'I am wealthy: I have acquired riches and need nothing.' Yet you do not realise that you are wretched, pitiful, poor, blind and naked.

18 'I advise you to buy from Me gold that has been refined by fire so that you may be truly rich, and white robes to wear that will prevent your nakedness from being exposed, and a salve for your eyes to enable you to see clearly.

19 'I correct and discipline all those I love. So repent and become hot! 20 Look, I am standing at the door and am knocking. If anyone hears My voice and opens the door, I will come in and eat with him and he with Me.

21 'To the one who is victorious, I will give the privilege of sitting
with Me on My throne, in the same way that I was victorious and
sat with My Father on His throne.
22 'Let the one who has spiritual understanding hear what the
Spirit says to the churches.'"

Before the throne (4:1-11)

4 After this I looked and clearly before me a heavenly door stood
open. And I heard the voice that had spoken before, and that
sounded like a trumpet, speaking to me saying: "Come up here and
I will show you what must happen after this." 2 Immediately I was
in the Spirit and I saw a heavenly throne with Someone sitting on
the throne. 3 His appearance was like jasper and carnelian. And an
emerald coloured rainbow surrounded the throne.
4 Around the central throne there were twenty-four thrones upon
which twenty-four elders sat, all clothed in white robes with gold-
en crowns on their heads. 5 From out of the throne came flashes of
lightning, voices and peals of thunder.
Seven lamps of fire, which are the seven spirits of God, were
burning before the throne.
6 In front of the throne was a sea of glass that gleamed like crystal.
Around the throne on each side were four living creatures that were
full of eyes, both in front and behind. 7 The first of these living creatures
was like a lion, the second like a calf, the third had a face like that
of a man and the fourth was like a flying eagle. 8 Each of the four
living creatures had six wings and were full of eyes around and
within. Day and night they say repeatedly: "Holy, holy, holy is the
Lord God Almighty, who was and is and is coming."
9-11 Whenever the living creatures give glory, honour and thanks to
the One who sits on the throne, who lives forever and ever, the
twenty-four elders fall before Him and place their crowns before the
throne saying:

> "You are worthy, our Lord and God, to receive glory, honour and power, because You created all things and it is by Your will that they came into existence and were created."

The victorious Lamb (5:1-14)

5 To the right of the One sitting on the throne I then saw a scroll
with words written on both sides and sealed with seven seals.
2 And I saw a strong angel proclaiming with a loud voice: "Who is

worthy to open the scroll and break its seals?" 3 But there was no-
one in heaven or on earth or under the earth that was able to open
the scroll, or to see what was written on it. 4 I cried because no-one
was found worthy to open the scroll or to see what was written.
5 One of the elders said to me: "Do not cry. Look, the Lion of the
tribe of Judah, the Root of David, has been victorious. So He is able
to open the scroll and break its seven seals."
6 Then I saw in the centre of the throne, surrounded by the four
living creatures and the twenty four elders, a Lamb standing and
yet looking as if He had been slain. He had seven horns and seven
eyes which are the seven spirits of God released over the whole
earth. 7 The Lamb took the scroll from the right hand of the One
sitting on the throne. 8 When He took it, the four living creatures and
the twenty four elders fell before the Lamb. Each was holding a
lamp and a golden bowl full of incense which are the prayers of the
saints. 9 They sang a new song:

> "You are worthy to take the scroll and to break open its
> seals because You were slain, and by Your blood You
> purchased for God men of every tribe and language, from
> all people groups and every nation. 10 And You made
> them to be a Kingdom and priests to serve our God; and
> they will rejoice on the earth."

11-12 Then I looked and heard the voice of many angels that were
around the throne, the living creatures and the elders. There were
thousands and even millions of them, saying loudly again and again:

> "Worthy is the lamb who was slain to continue to receive power, riches, wisdom, strength, honour, glory and blessing."

13 And I heard every creature in heaven, on the earth, under the
earth, on the sea and all that is in this creation saying:

> "To Him who sits on the throne and to the Lamb be blessing, honour, glory and might for ever and ever."

14 And the four living creatures said: "Amen! It shall be so." And the
elders fell before Him in worship.

The seals are opened (6:1-17)

6 When I saw the Lamb open one of the seven seals, I heard one
of the four living creatures saying with a voice that sounded
like thunder: "Come." 2 As I looked I saw a white horse. Its rider had

a bow; a crown was given him and he went forth as a conqueror to
be victorious.
3 When He opened the second seal I heard the second living creature
say: "Come." 4 Another horse, red in colour, came out and its rider
was commissioned to take peace from the earth, causing men to kill
each other. A great sword was given him.
5 When the Lamb opened the third seal I heard the third living
creature say: "Come." As I looked I saw a black horse whose rider
held a pair of scales. 6 And I heard what sounded like a voice coming
from among the four living creatures, saying: "A quart of wheat, or
three quarts of barley for a day's pay; but do not damage the oil or
wine."
7 When He opened the fourth seal I heard the fourth living creature
say: "Come." 8 As I watched I saw a pale green horse, whose rider was
called 'Death', and Hades followed him. They were given authority
to kill a quarter of the earth's inhabitants with the sword, through
famine and disease or by the earth's wild beasts.
9 When the Lamb opened the fifth seal I saw the souls of those
who had been martyred because of God's Word and for bearing
witness to Him. 10 They were under the altar and cried out with loud
voices: "Holy and true Master, when are you going to avenge our
blood and judge those who live on the earth?"
11 To each of them was given a white robe and they were told to
wait a little longer, until the number was complete of their fellow
servants and their brothers who, like them, were to be martyred.
12 When the Lamb opened the sixth seal there was a great earthquake and the sun became as black as sackcloth and the moon
looked the colour of blood. 13 The stars in the sky fell to earth like a
fig tree shedding its unripe figs when shaken by a strong wind.
14 The sky vanished like a scroll being rolled up and every mountain
and island was moved from their places.
15 Then the kings of the earth, the great men, the generals, the rich,
the strong and every slave and freeman, hid themselves in caves
and among the rocks of the mountains. 16-17 They called to the mountains
and rocks: "Fall on us and hide us from the face of He who sits on
the throne and from the wrath of the Lamb, because the great day
of their anger has come, and who is able to withstand it?"

Many to be saved (7:1-17)

7 Then I saw four angels standing at the four corners of the earth
holding back the four winds of the earth so that no wind
should blow on the earth, at sea nor on any tree. 2-3 And I saw another

angel coming from the east, having a seal of the living God. In a
loud voice he said to the four angels, to whom was given the power
to harm the earth and sea: "Do not damage the earth, the sea nor the
trees until the servants of our God have received His seal on their
foreheads."

4 Then I heard a number of those who were to be sealed, one
hundred and forty-four thousand from all the tribes of Israel.
5-8 From the tribe of Judah twelve thousand received the seal, another
twelve thousand from the tribe of Reuben. Each of the following
tribes had twelve thousand who were sealed: Gad, Asher, Naphtali,
Manasseh, Simeon, Levi, Issachar, Zebulun, Joseph and Benjamin.

9 Then, as I watched, I saw a crowd so great it was impossible to
count, from every nation, tribe, people group and language. They
stood before the throne and in front of the Lamb, clothed in white
robes with palm branches in their hands. 10 And they cried out with
loud voices:

> "Salvation belongs to our God who sits on the throne and
> to the Lamb."

11-12 All the angels standing around the throne, the elders and their four
living creatures fell on their faces before the throne and worshipped
God, saying:

> "Amen! Blessing, glory, wisdom, thanks and honour,
> power and strength be to our God forever and ever.
> Amen. It shall be so."

13 One of the elders asked me: "Where have they come from, all these
who are clothed in white robes?" 14 I answered him: "Sir, you know."
Then he told me: "They are those who have come out of the great
tribulation, who have washed their robes in the Lamb's blood and
made them white. 15 So they are before God's throne and serve Him
day and night in the holy sanctuary, and He who sits on the throne
will spread His canopy over them. 16-17 No longer will they hunger or
be thirsty, neither will they be burned by the sun nor any scorching
heat, because the Lamb in the centre of the throne will be their
Shepherd. He will guide them to springs of living water and God
will wipe away every tear from their eyes."

Prayers of the saints (8:1-13)

8 When the Lamb opened the seventh seal there was silence in
heaven for about half an hour. 2 And I saw seven angels who
stood before God and to whom seven trumpets were given.

3Another angel with a golden censer came and stood at the altar. He
was given much incense to offer with the prayers of the saints on
the golden altar before the throne. 4The smoke from the incense in
the angel's hand descended before God with the prayers of the
saints. 5Then the angel took the censer, filled it with fire from the
altar and threw it on the earth. There were peals of thunder, flashes
of lightning and an earthquake took place.
6Then the seven angels with the seven trumpets prepared to blow
their trumpets. 7When the first blew his trumpet, hail and fire mixed
with blood fell on the earth. A third of the earth was burnt up. A
third of the trees and of all green grass was burned.
8The second angel blew his trumpet and a great mountain of
burning fire was thrown into the sea. 9A third of the sea turned to
blood and a third of the living creatures in the sea died and a third
of all ships were destroyed.
10When the third angel sounded his trumpet, a great burning star,
blazing like a torch, fell from the sky onto a third of the rivers and
springs of water. 11The star was called 'Wormwood', 'Bitterness'! A
third of the waters became bitter and many men died from drinking
this bitter water.
12The fourth angel blew his trumpet and a third of the sun was
struck, together with a third of the moon and a third of the stars, so
that a third of their light was extinguished. A third part of the day
had no light and likewise a third part of the night.
13As I watched I saw a flying eagle crying aloud in mid-air: "Cursed,
cursed, cursed, are those who live on the earth at the sound of the
trumpets of the remaining three angels."

The opening of the bottomless pit (9:1-21)

9 When the fifth angel blew his trumpet, I saw a star that had
fallen to the earth from the sky. The star was given the key to
the shaft of the bottomless pit. 2He opened the shaft of the bottomless pit and smoke billowed out of it like smoke from a great furnace,
causing the sun and the whole atmosphere to be darkened by this
smoke. 3Out of the smoke locusts came upon the earth. They had
been given power like that of earthly scorpions. 4They were told not
to damage the grass nor the green vegetation nor the trees of the
earth, but they had authority to harm those people who did not
have God's seal on their foreheads. 5They were not to kill those they
harmed, but only torture them for a period of five months. Their
sting was like the agony of a scorpion sting.

6 During that time people will want to die but will be unable to do so. Even though they long for death, it will elude them.

7 These locusts looked like horses ready for battle with what appeared like golden crowns on their heads, but their faces appeared human. 8 Their hair was long like women's hair and their teeth were like lion's teeth. 9 They had breastplates that appeared to be made of iron and the sound of their wings was like the roar of many horse-drawn chariots charging into battle. 10 They had tails and stings like scorpions and in these tails they possessed the power to torture people for five months.

11 The angel of the bottomless pit ruled as king over them. His name in Hebrew is 'Abaddan', in Greek 'Apollyon'; meaning 'Destruction.'

12 After the first curse had ended, two further curses were to follow.

13-14 When the sixth angel blew his trumpet I heard a voice speak from the four horns of the golden altar that stood before God, saying to this sixth angel with the trumpet: "Release the four angels who are bound at the great river Euphrates." 15 So the four angels were released. They had been held ready for the appointed hour, day, month and year when they should kill a third of mankind. 16 I heard the number of their mounted troops: two hundred million!

17 I saw in the vision the horses and their riders, who wore breastplates the colour of fire, of sapphires and of sulphur. The heads of the horses looked like lions' heads and from their mouths streamed fire, smoke and sulphur. 18 By these three plagues of fire, smoke and sulphur that streamed from their mouths, a third of mankind was killed. 19 The horses' power was in their mouths and their tails, which were like snakes with heads that could wound.

20 The rest of mankind, who were not killed by these plagues, still refused to repent of their sinful deeds. Nor did they stop worshipping demons and idols made of gold, silver, bronze, stone or wood, idols that cannot see, nor hear nor walk. 21 Neither did they repent of their murders, witchcraft, their sexual immorality or their thefts.

A mighty angel and the scroll (10:1-11)

10 Then I saw another mighty angel descend from heaven enfolded in a cloud with a rainbow over his head. His face shone like the sun and his legs were like pillars of fire. 2-3 In his hand he held an open scroll. He placed his right foot on the sea and his left on the land and shouted in a loud voice that sounded like a roaring lion. When he spoke, the voices of the seven thunders were

heard. 4 When the seven thunders had spoken, I was about to write
but I heard a voice from heaven saying: "Seal up what the seven
thunders have said and do not write that down."

5-6 The angel whom I saw standing on the sea and the land lifted
his right hand towards heaven and swore by He who lives for ever
and ever, who created heaven and all in it, the earth and all on it, the
sea and everything in it, that there should be no further delay. 7 In
the days when the seventh angel is about to sound his trumpet, the
mystery of God will be fulfilled, as He announced to His servants
the prophets.

8 Then the voice I heard from heaven spoke again to me saying:
"Go and take the scroll from the hand of the angel who stands on
the sea and on the land." 9 So I went towards the angel, telling him
to give me the little scroll. And he told me: "Take it and eat it, and
although in your mouth it will be as sweet as honey, it will be bitter
in your stomach."

10 So I took the little scroll out of the angel's hand and ate it. It was
as sweet as honey in my mouth, but when I had eaten it, my stomach
turned sour. 11 I was told: "You must prophesy again before different
peoples and nations, those of other languages and before many
kings."

Two witnesses (11:1-19)

11 And I was given a reed for a staff with the instructions:
"Stand up and measure God's holy sanctuary, the altar and
those worshipping there. 2 But do not measure the court outside the
temple for it was given to the nations and they will trample over the
holy city for forty-two months. 3 And I will give authority to My two
witnesses to prophesy for one thousand two hundred and sixty
days, clothed in sackcloth."

4 These are the two olive trees and the two lampstands that stand
before the Lord of the earth. 5 Anyone who wishes to harm them will
be consumed by the fire that comes from their mouths to devour
their enemies. So anyone wanting to harm them must be killed.

6 They have the authority to shut up the sky so that no rain may
fall during the period that they prophesy. They also have authority
over the waters, with the power to turn them to blood, and to strike
the earth with every kind of plague as often as they wish.

7 When they have finished their testimony, the beast that will
come out of the abyss will go to war against them, will conquer and
kill them. 8 Their bodies will lie openly in the street of the great city

which is called, figuratively, Sodom and Egypt, where the Lord was
crucified.
9 People from different tribes, languages and nations will see
them lying there for three and a half days and they will not allow
them to be buried. 10 Those who live on the earth will rejoice over
them and will be glad. They will exchange gifts, because these two
prophets had tormented them.
11 But after three and a half days, a breath of life from God entered
them and they stood to their feet, causing great fear to fall on those
who had seen them. 12 The two heard a great voice from heaven tell
them, "Come up here." And they ascended to heaven in a cloud in
front of their enemies.
13 At that time a great earthquake occurred, destroying a tenth of
the city, killing seven thousand men and causing the rest to be so
terrified that they gave glory to the God of heaven.
14 The second curse has now taken place and the third will follow
soon afterwards.
15 The seventh angel blew his trumpet and there were loud voices
in heaven saying: "The kingdom of this world has become the
Kingdom of our Lord and of His Christ; and He shall reign for ever
and ever."
16-17 The twenty-four elders who were sitting on the thrones fell on
their faces and worshipped Him, saying: "Lord God, the Almighty,
who is and was, we thank You because You have taken Your great
power in order to reign. 18 The nations were angry but Your wrath
has come and it is time for the dead to be judged. It is time for Your
servants the prophets and the saints, all who fear Your Name both
small and great, to receive their reward. It is time also to destroy
those who destroy the earth."
19 Then God's heavenly sanctuary was opened and the ark of the
covenant could be seen in His sanctuary. And then there were flashes
of lightning, voices, peals of thunder, an earthquake and a great
hailstorm.

The woman and the dragon (12:1-17)

12 And a great sign was seen in heaven: a woman clothed with
the sun and with the moon beneath her feet. On her head
was a crown with twelve stars and she was pregnant. 2 She cried out
with her labour pains, longing to give birth.
3 And another sign was seen in heaven: a great red dragon with
seven heads, ten horns and seven diadems on its heads. 4 Its tail

dragged down a third of the stars of the sky and threw them to the
earth.
The dragon stood before the woman who was about to give birth
so that it might devour her child as soon as it was born. 5-6 She gave
birth to a male child who would rule all the nations with a rod of
iron. Her child was seized and taken up to God's throne and the
woman fled into the desert, to a place prepared for her by God,
where she would be nourished for one thousand two hundred and
sixty days.
7-8 And there was war in heaven as Michael and his angels fought
with the dragon. And the dragon and his angels retaliated but were
defeated. There was no longer any place for them in heaven. 9 That
great dragon was thrown down to the earth – that ancient serpent
called the devil and Satan, who had deceived the whole world. And
his angels were thrown out of heaven and cast down to the earth
with him.
10 Then I heard a loud voice saying in heaven: "Now the time of
salvation power, of God's Kingdom and Christ's authority, has
come because the accuser of our brethren has been thrown down, he
who accused them before God day and night. 11 But they overcame
him through the Lamb's blood, because of the word of their testimony
and because they loved not their own lives, even to the point of
death.
12 Rejoice then, heaven and all who live there! But cursed is the
earth and sea because the devil has come down to you in his great
anger, knowing that he has but a short time.
13 When the dragon saw that it had been thrown down onto the
earth, it pursued the woman who had borne the male child. 14 And
the woman was given the two wings of a great eagle so that she
might fly to her place in the desert, where she was protected from
the serpent for a time and times and half a time.
15 Then a serpent spewed a river of water out of its mouth to
sweep her away in the flood. 16 But the woman was helped by the
earth that opened up and swallowed the river that the dragon had
spewed out of its mouth. 17 Then the dragon was furious with the
woman and went to make war against her other children, those
who kept God's commandments and were faithful to Jesus.

The two beasts (13:1-18)

13 As the dragon stood on the seashore, I saw a beast emerge
from the sea. It had ten horns and seven heads, with a diadem

on each horn and blasphemous names on its head. [2]This beast that
I saw was like a leopard with the feet of a bear and a mouth like that
of a lion. The dragon gave its power, its throne and great authority
to the beast. [3]One of its heads seemed to have a mortal wound, but
this fatal wound had been healed. The whole earth was astonished
by the beast and followed it. [4]People worshipped the dragon because
he had given his authority to the beast, and they also worshipped
the beast saying: "Who is like the beast and who can fight against
it?"

[5]The beast was given a mouth that it used to speak proud and
blasphemous things. And it was given authority to act for forty-two
months.

[6]It opened its mouth and spoke blasphemies against God, cursing
His Name, His holy sanctuary and those living in heaven. [7]It was
allowed to fight against the saints and to defeat them. And it was
given authority over every tribe, people group of different languages
and over the nations. [8]All who live on the earth will worship the
beast, everyone whose name had not been written in the Book of
Life that belonged to the Lamb, who was slain before the beginning
of the world. [9-10]Let anyone with understanding hear what is said:
"If anyone is destined for captivity, into captivity he goes. If anyone
is destined to be killed by the sword, he must be killed by the
sword." This calls for endurance and faithfulness from the saints.

[11]Then I saw another beast emerge from the earth. It had two
horns like those of a lamb but spoke like a dragon. [12]It exercised the
authority of the first beast on its behalf and forced the earth and all
those living in it to worship the first beast, whose mortal wound
had been healed. [13]It performed great signs, even causing fire to
descend to earth from heaven in the sight of men. [14]Through the
signs it was allowed to perform in the presence of the first beast, it
deceived all those living on the earth, commanding them to make
an image to honour the beast, which had been fatally wounded by
the sword and yet lived.

[15]This second beast was then allowed to breathe life into the
image of the first beast, so that this image could speak, causing all
those who would not worship the image of the beast to be killed.
[16]And it caused all, both small and great, both rich and poor, both
freemen and slaves, to receive a mark on their right hands or on
their foreheads. [17]No one could buy or sell anything unless they had
this mark which bore the name of the beast or its number. This
needs wisdom. Let everyone with ability calculate the beast's number. Its human number is six hundred and sixty-six.

The mark of God (14:1-8)

14 As I watched, I saw the Lamb standing on Mount Zion
together with one hundred and forty-four thousand who
had His Name and His Father's Name written on their foreheads.
[2]And I heard a sound coming from heaven like that of cascading
water and as the sound of loud claps of thunder. And I heard what
sounded like many harpists playing their harps. [3]And they sang a
new song before the throne, the four living creatures and the elders.
Nobody except for the one hundred and forty-four thousand could
learn this song.

[4]These are the ones who had been saved from all those on the
earth. They had not defiled themselves with women, but had
remained pure. They follow the Lamb wherever He goes. These are
those redeemed as the first fruits among men for God and the
Lamb. [5]They never lied and remain spotless.

[6]Then I saw another angel flying in mid-air, with an eternal
gospel to preach to those who live on the earth, people of every
nation, tribe and language. [7]He was saying in a very loud voice:
"Fear God and give Him glory, for the time has come for Him to
judge. Worship Him who created heaven and earth, the sea and the
springs of water."

[8]A second angel followed saying: "Fallen, Babylon the great has
fallen! She made all the nations drink of the wine of her anger and
immorality."

The mark of the beast (14:9-13)

[9-10]A third angel followed them saying in a loud voice: "If anyone
worships the beast and its image and receives its mark on his forehead
or hand, he shall drink the wine of God's anger, poured undiluted
into the cup of His wrath. He will be tortured by fire and sulphur
before the holy angels and the Lamb. [11]The smoke of their torment
ascends eternally, and they have no rest by day or night because
they worship the beast and its image, and received the mark containing its name."

[12]This means the saints need to endure, persevering in keeping
God's commandments and maintaining their faith in Jesus.

[13]Then I heard a voice from heaven saying: "Write this: 'Blessed
are the dead who from this time die in the Lord.'"

"Yes," says the Spirit, "So they can rest from their hard work, for
their good deeds follow them!"

The earth's harvest (14:14-20)

14 Then as I watched I saw a white cloud. Sitting on the cloud was
Someone who looked like Jesus, the Son of Man. He had a golden
crown on His head and held a sharp sickle in His hand. 15 Another
angel emerged from the holy sanctuary, calling out with a loud
voice to the One sitting on the cloud: "Wield your sickle and reap;
the earth's harvest is ripe." 16 And the One sitting on the cloud wielded
His sickle over the earth and the earth was harvested.

17 Then another angel emerged from the heavenly sanctuary. He
also had a sharp sickle. 18 Another angel, who had authority over the
fire, emerged from the altar. He spoke with a loud voice to the angel
with the sharp sickle saying: "Wield your sharp sickle and gather
the bunches of grapes on the earth, for they are now ripe."

19 So the angel wielded his sickle over the earth and gathered the
bunches of grapes from the earth and threw them into the winepress
of God's great anger. 20 The winepress was outside the city. As the
fruit was crushed, blood flowed from the winepress as deep as horses'
bridles, for almost one hundred and eighty miles.

Seven angels with seven plagues (15:1-8)

15 Then I saw another great and awesome sign in heaven:
Seven angels with the seven last plagues, for with them
God's anger has ended. 2 And I saw what looked like a sea of glass
mingled with fire. Those who had conquered the beast, its image
and the number of its name, stood beside the sea of glass with harps
given them by God. 3 They sang the song of God's servant Moses,
and the Lamb's song, saying:

> "Great and wonderful are Your works, Lord God Almighty.
> Righteous and true are Your ways, King of the nations.
> 4 Who will not fear You, Lord, and glorify Your Name? For
> You alone are Holy and all the nations will come and
> worship before You because Your judgments have been
> revealed."

5 After this I saw the heavenly sanctuary open. This is the tent of the
testimony in heaven. 6 Seven angels emerged out of the holy sanctuary,
carrying the seven plagues. They wore clean, bright linen clothes
with golden sashes around their chests. 7 One of the four living
creatures gave the seven angels seven golden bowls filled with the
anger of God, who lives for ever and ever.

[8]And the holy sanctuary was filled with the smoke of God's glory
and with His power. No-one could enter the holy sanctuary until
the seven plagues of the seven angels were ended.

The seven bowls of anger (16:1-21)

16 Then I heard a loud voice coming from the holy sanctuary
saying to the seven angels: "Go and pour out the seven
bowls of God's anger on the earth."

[2]The first went and poured out his bowl on the earth, and foul
malignant sores came upon those who had the mark of the beast
and who worshipped its image.

[3]The second poured out his bowl on the sea, and it became like
the blood of a dead man and every living creature in the sea died.

[4]The third angel poured out his bowl on the rivers and springs of
water, and they were turned to blood. [5]And I heard the angel of the
waters saying: "You are right in these judgments, for You are the
Lord who is and who was, the Holy One. [6]For those who shed the
blood of Your saints and prophets are now given by You blood to
drink. It is what they deserve." [7]And I heard the altar reply: "Yes,
Lord God Almighty, Your judgments are just and true."

[8]The fourth angel poured out his bowl onto the sun and it was
given power to scorch men with fire. [9]They were burnt by its great
heat and blasphemed God's Name, who had control over the
plagues; for they refused to repent or give Him glory.

[10-11]The fifth angel poured out his bowl on the beast's throne and
its kingdom was plunged into darkness. Men chewed their tongues
in agony and blasphemed the God of heaven because of their pain
and their sores; but they still did not repent of their evil deeds.

[12]The sixth angel poured out his bowl onto the river Euphrates
and its water dried up to prepare the way for the coming of the
kings from the east. [13]And I saw three foul spirits looking like frogs
coming from the dragon's mouth, the beast's mouth and from the
mouth of the false prophet. [14]They are demonic spirits performing
signs and they go to all the kings of the earth to assemble them for
battle on the great Day of God, the Almighty. [15]He says: "Look, I am
coming like a thief. Blessed is he who is on the watch with his
clothes ready, so that he will not go about naked, his shame exposed
to others."

[16]These evil spirits gathered the kings together at the place called
in Hebrew, Armageddon.

[17-18]The seventh angel poured out his bowl into the air and a loud
voice came from the throne out of the holy sanctuary, saying: "It is

done!" and there were flashes of lightning, voices, claps of thunder
and a great earthquake took place, such as there has never been
since men inhabited the earth, so great was that earthquake.
19 The great city was split into three parts and the cities in the
nations were destroyed. And God remembered the greatness of
Babylon and made her drink the cup filled with the wine of His
anger. 20 Every island disappeared and the mountains could not be
found. 21 Great hailstones, each weighing a hundred pounds, fell
from heaven on men. And they cursed God because of the plague of
hailstones, so terrible was that plague.

The woman on the beast (17:1-18)

17 1-2 Then one of the seven angels who had the seven bowls
came and spoke to me: "Come, I will show you the judgment
that befalls the great prostitute who sits on many waters, with
whom the kings of the earth have indulged in sexual immorality.
The earth's inhabitants have become drunk from the wine of her
adulteries."
3 The angel carried me away in the Spirit into a desert. There I saw
a woman sitting on a scarlet beast covered with blasphemous
names. It had seven heads and ten horns. 4 The woman was clothed
in purple and scarlet and was glittering with gold, precious stones
and pearls. She had a golden cup in her hand that was filled with
abominations and the filth of her sexual exploits. 5 On her forehead
was written the name of a mystery: 'BABYLON THE GREAT. THE
MOTHER OF PROSTITUTES AND OF EARTHLY ABOMINATIONS.'
6 I saw that the woman was drunk with the blood of the saints
and from the blood of those martyred for Jesus.
7 I was greatly surprised to see her. And the angel said to me:
"Why are you so surprised? I will tell you the secret of this woman
and of the beast on which she sits, the beast with seven heads and
ten horns. 8 The beast that you saw, that was, and is no more, is
about to emerge from the abyss and go to its destruction.
"The earth's inhabitants, whose names were not written in the
Book of Life at the beginning of creation, will be astonished to see
the beast that was, is not and is to come. 9 This needs a wise mind.
10 "The seven heads are seven hills on which the woman sits and
seven kings. Five of them have already fallen, one exists now and
the other has not yet come. When he does come, he will not remain
for long.

11 “The beast that was and is not now is an eighth king. He
belongs to the seven and goes to his destruction.
12 “The ten horns which you saw are ten kings who have not yet
received a kingdom, but they will receive authority to be kings
together with the beast, but only for one hour. 13 They agreed together
to give their power and authority to the beast.
14 “They will fight against the Lamb and the Lamb will defeat
them because He is Lord of lords and King of kings, and those with
Him are called chosen and faithful.”
15 Then the angel said to me: “The waters you saw in the place
where the prostitute sits are people, crowds, nations of many tongues.
16 The ten horns and the beast that you saw will hate the prostitute.
They will ruin her and strip her naked. They will eat her flesh and
burn her with fire. 17 For God has put it into their hearts to carry out
His purpose by making them agree to give the beast their kingly
power, until God’s words are fulfilled. 18 The woman you saw is the
great city that rules over the kings of the earth.

The fall of Babylon (18:1-24)

18 After this I saw another angel come down from heaven,
having great authority. His glory brought light to the earth.
2 He cried out in a loud voice: “Fallen, Babylon the great has fallen!
It has become a dwelling place of demons and a prison for every
evil spirit and of every unclean and hateful bird. 3 For all the nations
have drunk the detestable wine of her immorality, and the kings of
the earth have committed adultery with her. The earth’s businessmen
have become rich through her power and luxurious lifestyle.”
4 Then I heard another voice from heaven saying: “Come out of
her, my people, come out of her, lest you share in her sins and so
receive a share in her plagues. 5 For the pile of her sins reaches up to
heaven and God has remembered her iniquity. 6 Give back to her
what she deserves; repay her double for her evil deeds. Mix for her
a double portion of what she has mixed for herself in her cup. 7 She
glorified herself and spoilt herself with every luxury; so give her as
much in torture and grief, for she says in her heart: ‘I sit as a queen;
I am not a widow nor shall I ever know grief.’
8 “Therefore plagues will come upon her in a single day; death,
grief and famine. And she will be consumed by fire, for the Lord
God who judges her is mighty.
9 “The kings of the earth, those who committed adultery with her
and shared in her luxury, will weep and wail with grief over her

when they see the smoke from her burning. 10 They will stand at a
distance in fear of her torture saying, 'Cursed, cursed, is the great
city, Babylon the mighty city, because your hour of judgment has
come.'

11-12 "And the businessmen of the earth weep and grieve over her
because no one trades with them anymore; there is no trade in gold,
silver, precious stones, pearls, fine linen, expensive silks of rare
colours, scented wood and articles made of ivory, costly wood,
bronze, iron or marble. 13 There is no trade in cinnamon, spices,
incenses, ointment, frankincense, wine, oil, flour and wheat. There
is no trade in cattle, sheep and horses; in carriages, slaves and
human lives.

14 "The fruit for which your soul longed has disappeared from
you. All the luxuries and attractive things have vanished, never to
be seen again. Those who trade in these things have vanished, never
to be seen again. 15-18 Those who trade in these things, who gained
their wealth from her, will also stand at a distance for fear of sharing
in her torture. They will weep with grief, saying, 'Great city; you are
cursed, you are cursed. Once you were clothed in fine linen of purple
and scarlet, adorned with gold, precious stones and pearls; but in
one hour your great wealth disappeared and you became desolate.'

"Every sea captain, sea-farer and sailor, all who work at sea,
stood at a distance and cried out when they saw the smoke of her
burning, saying, 'What can compare with this great city?' 19 They
threw dust on their heads, wept with sorrow and cried out saying,
'You are cursed, great city, you are cursed, for all who had ships at
sea were made rich from her wealth. Yet in one hour you have been
made desolate.'

20 "Heaven, rejoice over her. Saints, apostles and prophets rejoice,
because God has passed judgment on her on your behalf."

21 Then a mighty angel lifted up a great millstone and threw it into
the sea saying: "Babylon, the great city, will be destroyed with such
violence and shall no longer exist. 22 No longer shall the sound of
harpists, musicians, flautists or trumpeters, be heard in you. No
craftsmen will ever be found in you again, and the sound of the
millstone at work shall never be heard in you again. 23 No light shall
ever shine in you again and the voice of the bride and bridegroom
shall never be heard in you again. Your traders were great men of
the world because all the nations were deceived by your witchcraft,
24 and in her the blood of martyred prophets and saints is found,
together with all who have been killed on the earth."

A great multitude celebrate (19:1-10)

19 Then I heard the mighty sound of a great multitude in heaven shouting:

"Hallelujah! Salvation, glory and power belong to our
God because [2]His judgments are true and just. He has
judged the great prostitute who defiled the earth with her sexual immorality and He has avenged on her the blood of His servants."

[3]Again they shouted: "Hallelujah! Her smoke ascends for ever and
ever." [4]And the twenty-four elders and the four living creatures fell down and worshipped God who is seated on His throne, saying:
"Amen! Hallelujah!" [5]And a voice came from the throne saying:

"Praise our God all His servants, those who fear Him, both small and great."

[6]And I heard the sound of a great multitude that sounded like cascading water and like a sound of great claps of thunder, saying:

"Hallelujah, because the Lord our God, the Almighty,
reigns. [7]Let us rejoice and exalt Him, giving Him glory, because it is time for the Lamb's wedding and His Bride
has prepared herself. [8]She has been given fine, clean linen to wear, signifying the righteous deeds of the saints."

[9]And the angel said to me: "Write this: 'Blessed are those who are invited to the Lamb's wedding banquet.'" And he said to me:
"These are the true words of God." [10]And I fell at his feet to worship him. But he said to me: "Don't do that, for I am a fellow servant and one of your brothers who continues to maintain witness about Jesus. Worship God. For the witness of Jesus is the spirit of prophecy."

Rider on a white horse (19:11-21)

[11]Then I saw heaven opened and look, a white horse! He who sat on it is called Faithful and True. He judges justly and makes war.
[12-13]His eyes are as a flame of fire and on His head are many crowns. He has a name written on Him that He alone knows and He wears a robe that has been dipped in blood. He is called by the name, 'The Word of God.'

[14]The heavenly armies followed Him on white horses, all dressed
in fine, clean linen. [15]Out of His mouth came a sharp sword with which to smite the nations and He will rule them with an iron sceptre. He will tread the winepress that produces the wine of His anger, the wrath of God, the Almighty.

[16]On His robe and on His thigh a name was written: "KING OF
KINGS AND LORD OF LORDS.'
[17-18]Then I saw a single angel standing in the sun who cried out in
a loud voice to all the birds that were flying in mid-air: "Come,
gather together for God's great banquet so that you might eat the
flesh of the kings and their armies, the flesh of strong men, of horses
and their riders, of the flesh of both freemen and slaves, both small
and great."
[19]Then I saw the beast, the kings of the earth and their armies,
gathered to fight against He who sits on the horse and His army.
[20]The beast was captured together with the false prophet who had
done great signs in his presence, by which he deceived those who
had received the mark of the beast and those who worshipped his
image. Both were thrown alive into the lake of fire and burning
sulphur. [21]The rest were killed with the sword that proceeded from
the mouth of the One mounted on the horse. And all the birds ate
their fill of their flesh.

The lake of fire (20:1-15)

20 Then I saw an angel coming down from heaven who held in
his hand the key of the abyss, the bottomless pit, and a great
chain. [2-3]He seized the dragon, that ancient serpent, the devil or
Satan, and bound him for a thousand years and threw him into the
abyss. He then shut up the entrance to it and sealed it so he could
no longer deceive the nations until the thousand years had elapsed.
Then he had to be released for a short time.
[4]Then I saw thrones. Those who sat on them had been given
authority to judge. I also saw the souls of those who had been
beheaded because of their faith in Jesus and God's Word and who
had not worshipped the beast or its image, nor had they received
his mark either on their forehead or hand.

They came to life and reigned with Christ for a thousand years.
[5]The remainder of the dead did not come to life again until the
thousand years had elapsed. This is the first resurrection. [6]He who
shares in this first resurrection is blessed and holy! The second
death has no power over them, but they shall be priests of God and
of Christ and will reign with Him for the thousand years.
[7-8]When the thousand years have elapsed, Satan will be released
from his prison and will go to every part of the earth to deceive the
nations, like Gog and Magog, to assemble them for battle; numberless
like the grains of the sand on the seashore. [9]And they marched

across the whole earth and encircled the camp of the saints and the
beloved city. But fire fell from heaven and consumed them. 10 And
the devil, who had deceived them, was thrown into the lake of fire
and sulphur, where the beast and the false prophet had also been
thrown, and they were tortured day and night for ever and ever.

11 Then I saw a great white throne and the One who sat on it. From
His presence the earth and sky fled; there was no place for them.
12-13 And I saw the dead, both great and small, standing before the
throne; and the books were opened. There was another book
opened, the Book of Life. The dead were judged according to what
was written in the books, according to what they had done.

14 Then Death and Hades were thrown into the lake of fire. This
lake of fire is the second death. 15 If anyone's name was not found
written in the Book of Life, he was thrown into the lake of fire.

The new Jerusalem (21:1-27)

21 Then I saw a new heaven and a new earth, for the first heaven
and the first earth had passed away and the sea no longer
existed. 2 And I saw the holy city, the new Jerusalem, descending
from heaven, from God, prepared as a Bride beautifully dressed for
her husband.

3 And I heard a loud voice coming from the throne, saying: "Look,
the holy dwelling place of God is with men and He will remain
among them. They will be His people and God Himself will be with
them. 4 He will wipe away every tear from their eyes and there will
be no more death, no more grief nor crying nor pain, for the old
order has passed away."

5 He who sat on the throne said: "Look, I make everything new."
He added: "Write this down, because these words are trustworthy
and true." 6 Then He said to me: "It is accomplished. I am the Alpha
and the Omega, the Beginning and the End. To those who are
thirsty I will give freely from the spring of the water of life. 7 The victorious shall inherit these things, and I will be his God and he shall
be My son. 8 But as for the cowardly, the unbelieving, the morally
filthy, murderers, the sexually immoral and those who practice
witchcraft, those who worship idols and all deceivers, their destiny
will be in the lake that burns with fire and sulphur, the second
death."

9 Then one of the seven angels who had the seven bowls filled
with the seven last plagues came and spoke to me saying: "Come
and I will show you the bride, the Lamb's wife." 10 And he carried

me away in the spirit to a great high mountain and showed me the
holy city Jerusalem coming down out of heaven from God, radiant
with His glory. 11 It shone like a precious stone, like jasper, clear as
crystal. 12 It had a great high wall with twelve gates attended by
twelve angels. The names of the twelve tribes of the sons of Israel
were written on the gates. 13 There were three gates on the eastern
side, three on the north, three on the south and three gates on the
west. 14 The city wall had twelve foundation stones, on which were
written the twelve names of the Lamb's twelve apostles.

15 The angel who was speaking to me had a measuring rod of gold
with which to measure the city, its gates and wall. 16 The city was in
the form of a square, the length being the same as the breadth.

He measured the city with the rod and the length, breadth and
height were each fifteen hundred miles long. 17 When he measured
the wall it was two hundred feet thick by human measurement that
the angel was using. 18 The wall was built of jasper and the city of
pure gold that was as clear as glass. 19-20 The foundations of the city
wall were decorated with every kind of precious stone: on the first
foundation jasper, on the second, sapphire, the third agate, the
fourth emerald, the fifth onyx, the sixth carnelian, the seventh
chrysolite, the eighth beryl, the ninth topaz, the tenth chrysoprase,
the eleventh jacinth and the twelfth amethyst.

21 The twelve gates were made from twelve pearls, each being
made of a single pearl. The city street was of pure gold, as transparent
as glass.

22 I saw no sanctuary in the city, for the Lord God Almighty and
the Lamb were its holy sanctuary.

23 The city had no need of the sun or moon to give it light for it
shone with God's glory and the Lamb is its light. 24 The nations will
walk by its light and the kings of the earth shall bring their glory
into it. 25 The gates shall never be shut by day and no night shall
exist there. 26-27 The glory and honour of the nations shall be brought
into the city; but nothing unclean will be permitted to enter, nor
anyone who does what is abominable or false. Only those whose
names are written in the Lamb's Book of Life may enter.

Christ to return (22:1-21)

22 1-2 Then the angel showed me the river of the water of life,
sparkling like crystal, flowing from the throne of God and
of the Lamb through the middle of the city's street. On either side of
the river was the tree of life, bearing twelve kinds of fruit every
month; and the leaves of the tree were for the healing of the nations.

3 No longer will any curse exist. For the throne of God and of the
Lamb will be in the city and His servants will serve Him. 4 They will
look upon His face and His Name will be written on their foreheads.
5 The night shall no longer exist and they will have no need of the
light from lamps or the sun because the Lord God will shed His
light on them and they shall reign for ever and ever.

6 Then the angel said to me: "These words are reliable and true.
The Lord, the God of the spirits of the prophets, sent His angel to
show His servants what must happen soon."

7 "Look, I am coming soon! He who keeps the words of the
prophecy in this book is blessed."

8 I, John, heard and saw these things. When I did so, I fell down
to worship at the feet of the angel who showed me all this. 9 But he
told me: "Do not do that! I am your fellow servant, together with
your brothers the prophets and all who keep the words of this book.
Worship God."

10 Then He told me: "Do not seal up the words of the prophecy in
this book, for the time is near. 11 Let him who is evil continue to do
what is evil; let the filthy continue to do what is filthy. But let the
righteous continue to do what is right and the holy one what is holy."

12 "Look, I am coming soon! My reward is with Me, to give to each
person what his deeds deserve. 13 I am the Alpha and the Omega, the
First and the Last, the Beginning and the End. 14 Blessed are those
who wash their robes, that they may have the right of access to the
tree of life, who may enter the city through the gates.

15 "Outside the city are the dogs; those who practise the occult, the
sexually immoral, murderers, those who worship idols and everyone who loves and does what is false.

16 "I, Jesus, sent My angel to reveal these things to you for the benefit
of the churches. I am the Root and the Offspring of David, the bright
Morning Star."

17 The Spirit and the bride say: "Come." Let he who hears say:
"Come." And let the thirsty come, he who wants to receive the free
gift of the water of life.

18 I warn all who hear the words of this prophecy in this book: If
anyone adds to them, God will add to him the plagues described in
this book. 19 And if anyone takes away from the words of the prophecy
in this book, God will take away his share in the tree of life and in
the holy city, which are described in this book.

20 He who testifies to these things says: "Yes, I am coming soon."
Amen! It shall be so! Come Lord Jesus!

21 The grace of our Lord Jesus be with you all. Amen.